CANARIES, HYBRIDS AND BRITISH BIRDS

IN CAGE AND AVIARY

BY

JOHN ROBSON

AND OTHER LEADING SPECIALISTS

EDITED BY

S. H. LEWER

OF "THE FEATHERED WORLD," AND "CANARY AND CAGE-BIRD LIFE"

British Library Cataloguing-in-Publication Data
A catalogue record for this book is available from the
British Library

Aviculture

'Aviculture' is the practice of keeping and breeding birds, as well as the culture that forms around it, and there are various reasons why people get involved in Aviculture. Some people breed birds to preserve a specific species, usually due to habitat destruction, and some people breed birds (especially parrots) as companions, and yet others do this to make a profit. Aviculture encourages conservation, provides education about avian species, provides companion birds for the public, and includes research on avian behaviour. It is thus a highly important and enjoyable past time. There are avicultural societies throughout the world, but generally in Europe, Australia and the United States, where people tend to be more prosperous, having more leisure time to invest. The first avicultural society in Australia was The Avicultural Society of South Australia, founded in 1928. It is now promoted with the name Bird Keeping in Australia. The two major national avicultural societies in the United States are the American Federation of Aviculture and the Avicultural Society of America, founded in 1927. In the UK, the Avicultural Society was formed in 1894 and the Foreign Bird League in 1932. The Budgerigar Society was formed in 1925.

Some of the most popular domestically kept birds are finches and canaries. 'Finches' are actually a broader category, encompassing canaries, and make fantastic domestic birds, capable of living long and healthy lives if given the requisite care. Most species are very easy to breed, and usefully do not grow too large (unlike their larger compatriot the budgerigar), and so do not need a massive living space. 'Canary' (associated with the *Serinus canaria*), is a song bird is native to the Canary Islands, Madeira, and the Azores – and has long been kept as a cage bird in Europe, beginning in the 1470s. It now enjoys an international following, and the terms *canariculture* and *canaricultura* have been used in French, Spanish and Italian respectively, to describe the keeping and breeding of canaries. It is only gradually however (a testament to its growing popularity) that English breeders are beginning to use such terms. Canaries are now the most popular form of finch kept in Britain and are often found still fulfilling their historic role of protecting underground miners. Canaries like budgies, are seed eaters, which need to dehusk the seed before feeding on the kernel. However, unlike budgerigars, canaries are perchers. The average life span of a canary is five years, although they have been known to live twice as long.

Parakeets or 'Budgies' (a type of parrot) are another incredibly popular breed of domestic bird, and are originally from Australia, first brought to Europe in the 1840s. Whilst they are naturally green with yellow heads and black bars on the wings in the wild, domesticated budgies come in a massive variety of colours. They have the toes and beak typical of parrot like birds, as in nature they are climbers; budgies are hardy seed eaters and their strong beak is utilised for dehusking seeds as well as a climbing aid. When kept indoors however, it is important to supplement their diet of seeds with fresh fruit and vegetables, which would be found in the wild. Budgies are social birds, so it is most important to make sure they have company, preferably of their own kind. They do enjoy human companionship though, and may be persuaded, if gently stroked on the chest feathers to perch on one's finger. If not kept in an aviary, they need a daily period of free flight, but great care must be taken not to let them escape.

Last, but most definitely not least, perhaps the most popular breed of domestic bird, is the 'companion parrot' – a general term used for *any* parrot kept as a pet that interacts with its human counterpart. Generally, most species of parrot can make good companions. Common domestic parrots include large birds such as Amazons, African Greys, Cockatoos, Eclectus, Hawk-headed Parrots and Macaws; mid-sized birds such as Caiques, Conures, Quakers, Pionus, Poicephalus, Rose-Ringed parakeets and Rosellas, and many of the smaller types including Budgies, Cockatiels, Parakeets, lovebirds, Parrotlets and Lineolated Parakeets. The *Convention on International Trade in Endangered Species of Wild Fauna and Flora* (also known as CITES) has made the trapping and trade of all wild parrots illegal, because taking parrots from the wild has endangered or reduced some of the rarer or more valuable species. However, many parrot species are still common; and some abundant parrot species may still be legally killed as crop pests in their native countries. Endangered parrot species are better suited to conservation breeding programs than as companions.

Parrots can be very rewarding pets to the right owners, due to their intelligence and desire to interact with people. Many parrots are very affectionate, even cuddly with trusted people, and require a lot of attention from their owners. Some species have a tendency to bond to one or two people, and dislike strangers, unless they are regularly and consistently handled by different people. Properly socialized parrots can be friendly, outgoing and confident companions. Most pet parrots take readily to trick training as well, which can help deflect their energy and correct many behavioural problems. Some owners successfully use well behaved parrots as therapy animals. In fact, many have even trained their parrots to wear parrot harnesses (most easily accomplished with young birds) so that they can be taken to enjoy themselves outdoors in a relatively safe manner without the risk of flying away. Parrots are prey animals and even the tamest pet may fly off if spooked. Given the right care and attention, keeping birds is usually problem free. It is hoped that the reader enjoys this book.

A CINNAMON CANARY AND ITS WILD ANCESTORS (*Serinus canaria*).

A HAPPY FAMILY.
Miss Slack's Aviary and Kennel combined at Stanwix, Carlisle.

FOREWORD

THE enormous development in the cage-bird fancy during the thirty years which have elapsed since Blakston's classic work, "Canaries and Cage Birds," was published from the Belle Sauvage press, forms the necessity for the present volume.

Following on much the same lines of treatment as Blakston in his deservedly popular book, and—save for the exclusion of foreign birds—covering the same ground, we shall treat of Canaries, Hybrids, and British birds, their management and exhibition, on lines abreast of the experiences of the most successful breeders and exhibitors of the day.

As Editor, the writer of this note has been fortunate in securing for this work the help of such an acknowledged authority as Mr. John Robson, the well-known judge of cage-birds and expert adviser to a leading fancy journal. Mr. Robson's wide experience will be reinforced by that of leading specialists. The historical chapter is from the pen of Dr. A. R. Galloway, of Aberdeen, who has not only made a special study of the literature of the subject, but has devoted years of experimental research to the many problems involved in the origin and variation of the Canary.

Allusion has been made to the work of Mr. W. A. Blakston, and in such measure as may be possible, considering the changes which have taken place, use will be made of the valuable material which his great treatise contains.

The coloured plates for the work are from the brushes of Mr. A. F. Lydon and Mr. E. F. Bailey, artists whose work needs no recommendation to lovers of cage-birds. They have necessarily aimed at showing ideal exhibition specimens, and the birds thus skilfully portrayed furnish useful guides to fanciers in their selection of show birds. The illustrations in the text have been chosen with the object of interesting and practically helping bird-keepers in the successful pursuit of their hobby, and in this connection the Editor is under no small debt of obligation to the many kind contributors to the journals with which he is so intimately associated.

Few hobbies are more easily available to town-dwellers than that of aviculture, and few give the same pleasure with so little expense. For the working man debarred by city surroundings from the pleasures of a garden or allotment, cage-bird keeping offers a welcome relief to the monotony of his daily toil. It is also essentially a home pursuit, and in this respect has its own distinct advantages over many other relaxations.

Our mission then is to help in the intelligent pursuit of such a humanising and elevating hobby.

S. H. Lewer.

Photograph by Mr. Allen Silver.

A PET MAGPIE AND ITS OWNER.

CONTENTS

CONTENTS

HYBRIDS

BRITISH BIRDS AMENABLE TO CAPTIVITY IN CAGE OR AVIARY

JACKDAW.
(Photograph by B. Hanley, Selby.)

INDEX TO ILLUSTRATIONS

INDEX TO ILLUSTRATIONS

LIST OF COLOUR PLATES

CANARIES

HYBRIDS

BRITISH BIRDS

LONG-TAILED TITS.
(*Photograph by A. J. R. Roberts.*)

"WE ARE SEVEN"
A Unique Photograph of a Nest of young Canaries belonging to Mr. Thos. Adamson.

CANARIES, HYBRIDS, AND BRITISH BIRDS IN CAGE AND AVIARY

CHAPTER I

INTRODUCTORY

THE longing for something to protect and care for is one of the strongest feelings implanted within us, and one outcome of it is the desire to keep animals under our control, which in its due place is, undoubtedly, one of our healthiest instincts. From what it arises, other than being a wise gift, we will not stay to inquire; but that the desire does exist, in a greater or less degree, in all of us, and that in many it is a strongly-marked peculiarity, few will venture to deny. It is true that the lower animals are all placed in subjection to man; but the disposition to which we refer is not born of any desire to subdue or destroy, but is rather the offspring of some tenderer chord in our nature which impels us to make friends of them, to break down some of the barriers which separate us, to study their habits and attend to their wants, subordinating the whole to their and our advantage.

We know that man is to a certain degree a predatory animal, and that an element in his character, different from the higher trait to which we have referred, enters into the case of those who indulge in what, for want of a better word, is known as "sport"; but even in the field something very like an intimate friendship and intelligent confidence is cemented between him and animals which are made to subserve the pursuit of what is, possibly, a legitimate end, though sensitive minds may question its morality.

We do not include within the ranks of sportsmen the man with the gun who brings to the ground every rare feathered creature he comes across, and by such ruthless destruction robs us and our country of many beautiful birds, which should be with us in numbers and even make this their breeding-place. Such reckless slaughter does not come within the scope of either sport or morality.

The Young Idea.

A feeling akin to this predatory disposition may be seen in the eagerness with which some village urchin expends his energies in the construction of snares or traps, or steals stealthily along through copse or by hedgerow, armed with catapult or other clumsy contrivance of home manufacture, knowing no fatigue and despising every obstacle, happy if only by the exercise of patience and skill he can compass the death or capture of even one small bird. To him, the advent of winter, with its frost and snow and long dark nights, means the arrival of his sporting season, when, impelled by hunger, his "game" leaves its usual haunts and seeks the homestead by day, or affords him by night all the excitement and glories of netting the sheltered sides of stacks, the overhanging eaves of barns, and the still richer preserves of ivy-clad walls. But the lad has a warm corner in his heart for all that. The friendly robin, enticed by crumbs, takes its morning meal at his window, and is allowed to come and go, hopping in and out from under the treacherous stable-sieve, delicately poised over the baited spot to which he wishes to lure other birds, and is a privileged visitor. The half-frozen thrush, captured in the snow on one of the lad's hunting expeditions, or some wounded sufferer with broken wing, appeals to his sympathies, is cared for, tenderly nursed, and, though a captive, becomes a pet. The young rabbits, taken from their downy bed—a short burrow in some fallow—find a home in his hutch, and when grown—well, the lad has not the heart to kill them, and so sets them at liberty, himself scarcely less happy than they. The nest of young birds, long marked down and daily visited with furtive steps lest other watchful eyes should discover them, carefully carried home in his cap, become objects of extreme solicitude, and are possibly actually killed with kindness. A strange medley is the lad—a compound of thought and thoughtlessness, but good at the heart. Nothing which appeals trustingly to his better nature appeals in vain; and so it is, we believe, that this desire to have something to love and care for overcomes the other and lower tendency. It grows with our growth and strengthens with our strength, and when satisfied teaches many a lesson of abnegation of self.

Nature Study.

The love of pets, indeed, insensibly leads us to the greater study of Nature. The volume lies open before us replete with interest, and the study is alike absorbing whether the subject be our own wonderful anatomy or the structure of a mollusc; the oak which has seen the summers and winters of a century, or the fungus which springs up in a few hours. Cage-birds are on our particular leaf of this inexhaustible volume, and we propose to look at them from a homely point of view—homely in every sense of the word. This will not be an abstruse work, but one in which the everyday life and management of the most popular and attractive cage-birds, foreign birds alone excepted, will be exhaustively treated. It is not intended for the naturalist or the ornithologist proper, though even they may, perhaps, dip into its pages and learn something of the domestic habits and economy of some feathered favourite; but it is intended as a practical guide, a *vade mecum* for all who take an interest in rearing and tending cage-birds, whether native, or coming to us from far-off climes during the migratory season.

One of our specialities is the Canary, the home-bird of England, and one more generally met with than any other. Other song-birds, each with its own peculiar

Cage-Birds.

quality, are found in many homes; but the Canary, most probably from his attractive appearance and friendly ways, is the bird of the people. Still, among popular favourites, there is the Linnet in his tiny cage, hanging outside the attic casement of some toiling artisan who sees but little blue sky except over tiled roofs and smoky chimney-tops, ever on the move and singing the day through of breezy hill-sides and blooming whin bushes; or the Skylark on his fresh sod, bought with hard-earned penny, carolling of green fields, new-mown hay, and skies all sun; the Blackbird or Thrush, in quaint wicker cage, chanting rich bursts of delicious music, wakening echoes of bygone days and carrying the listener back to some low-roofed, thatched cottage, with porch overgrown with woodbine, reminding him of early hopes and loves, and ambitions now tempered by stern necessities and manhood's cares. Every gush of melody floods his heart like refrains of angels' songs, and whispers perhaps of loved ones left behind sleeping peacefully under a little green mound in a far-off village churchyard.

The Favourite Canary.

But these birds are not everyone's property. Early associations and early surroundings have a great deal to do with developing a liking in any direction. Born in a woodland district, native woodland songsters are the early friends and companions of some; while others—and they are by far the greater number—unacquainted with these rustic beauties, make friends with the bird within reach of all, and install the Canary as favourite at home. And well he adapts himself to any circumstances. It matters not whether he be in a gilded cage in a drawing-room, tended by gentle hands, singing finished melodies acquired under expensive masters, or rolling out his own noisy, rollicking, untutored ditty in a cottage, he is equally at home. Cheerful and sprightly, companionable and docile, varied and beautiful in plumage, easily kept and easily bred, it is not to be wondered at that he is such a favourite, for not the least of his many virtues are his strongly-marked social disposition and domestic proclivities.

Canary Domestic Economy.

The way in which a pair of Canaries set up housekeeping and order their household is enough in itself to give the bird a strong claim on our sympathies. Other birds will, under favourable conditions, occasionally breed in confinement; but the hero of the first portion of our volume has for generations established itself in our families as one of us, and, regardless of prying eyes or inquisitive curiosity, builds its little homestead and treats us to all the interesting details of bird-life which can be seen nowhere else but in its little establishment. There is a strange fascination in a bird's nest, and few there are who cannot recollect with what emotions of delight and wonder they made their first discovery of the family chimney-corner of even the humble hedge-sparrow with its treasure of little blue eggs, carefully concealed in a quiet nook in the garden; and who has not then lifted the children one by one to peer quietly through the gently-parted leaves, and take stealthy glances at the little freehold? Who will say they were not wiser and better for each visit? If there be living poetry in songs without words, where look for tenderer sentiment, purer rhythm, or sweeter cadence? It is not often that with all our care and watching we are able to observe the whole of the daily routine of such a little household, or to learn how, without design or copy, and without ever having seen a model, a bird constructs its nest after an unvarying pattern peculiar to its kind. It is one of the mysteries of which creation is full, though some are of such everyday occurrence that we cease to regard them as mysteries. But our friend the Canary brings much of this home to us, and shows us with scarcely any reserve how the thing is done, busying about all day long, doing and undoing in a perpetual bustle yet with wonderful method, till the work is turned out in inimitable style. A breeding-cage is an

A FIND.
An Afternoon Ramble of the Border City Ornithological Society.

east, west, north, and south, devote their spare time to this interesting hobby. In almost every home where the music of the sewing machine or other adjunct to home industry is heard, there, above all other sounds, rises the cheerful but noisy music of the bird-room, for small though some of the cottages be the birds must have their share of them.

The young ones, as soon as they can take care of themselves, are sold by the score indiscriminately, or by the pair, the proceeds materially helping to fill the stocking-foot which provides for a rainy day or the claims of Christmas. There are but few breeding establishments in this country that are worked as business concerns pure and simple. It is one of those businesses which, perhaps, presents no better balance sheet than does a small poultry establishment maintained expressly for a supply of eggs. Half the profit consists in the pleasure; and the other half in money, which might go in more questionable ways, but which is saved in small sums, by every investment in seed or other necessary, and returned in the lump just at a time when it is useful. The occasional self-denial called into operation in ministering to the wants of creatures not able to provide for themselves, and the lessons of kindness thus taught, must also be written down on the credit side of the account. Few hobbies pay, except in the hands of larger capitalists than are the breeders of Canaries for the London market, for it is from cottage homes that the main supply of song-birds is drawn. The higher class birds hardly come under this category, and our remarks, therefore, apply more especially to the common singing Canary of the British home.

ornament to any house, and to almost any room in it.

An Important Industry.

It is not astonishing, then, that the demand for these birds is immense; that the breeding and rearing of them form no inconsiderable item in the minor industries of the country. The number of amateur breeders who adopt one or more of the many varieties of the Canary as their speciality, and make the development of its beauties their study, is very large, as the index of the catalogue of any public exhibition can attest, and the number is greatly augmented by the continuous stream poured into the bird markets of London, Manchester, Liverpool, Edinburgh, Glasgow, Preston, and other large towns, by those who make a business of it. The city of Norwich, with the surrounding villages and hamlets, counts its breeders by the thousand; while in Coventry, Derby, Northampton, Nottingham, and other towns in the midland district where labour is of a sedentary character, as well as in many towns in Yorkshire and Lancashire, the Canary is the poor man's savings bank; the substitute for the family pig where sanitary laws forbid the erection of a sty. A very large number of the working classes

The Development of our Canary.

Of comparatively recent admission into the ranks of domesticated birds, the Canary has, under man's care and skill, branched off into a number of distinct varieties. These differ in colour and form so widely from the original stock, that it is difficult to realise the fact that they proceed, one and all, from the same origin, and are simply divergences from one common type. The majority of them have existed for many years, but how they arose we know not. It is easy to guess at the mode in which some of them have been obtained, but when one comes to experiment in the way of crossing, it will be found that the results are generally very far from what was anticipated; the tendency to revert, as it were, to the early forms is manifested so strongly, especially in those breeds which are the farthest from the original type, that the hopes and wishes of the breeder to produce some fresh intermediate form are generally set at naught. As an illustration of this may be instanced the fact that the variety known as the London Fancy, one of the oldest and purest branches of the family tree, when crossed with other Canaries loses immediately its characteristic markings. At present there is no tendency whatever in any variety to retain permanently its peculiar characteristics without careful supervision. This subject is one, however, that need not be dwelt upon here, for in the chapter which follows Dr. Galloway goes very thoroughly into the history of the Canary and the origin of the many varieties which we find in connection with the bird to-day.

Varieties of Canaries.

These variations in shape and plumage are as marked as any that exist in the kindred fancies of poultry and pigeons—sections of the feathered creation to which apply the same general principles of development as those we have briefly referred to. It is this variation, with its endless ramifications, which renders the Canary an object of attraction to those who merge its naturally engaging ways in other considerations, and makes it worthy the attention of the naturalist as well as the fancier. Evolved from one common stock we have to-day no fewer than thirteen separate and distinct varieties, each

A WORKING MAN AND HIS FAVOURITE.
Mr. J. Thompson and his Clear Yellow Hen.

with strongly-marked and fixed characteristics. These are the Norwich, the Cinnamon, the London Fancy, the Lizard, the Belgian, the Scotch Fancy, the Yorkshire, the Crested, the Green, the Lancashire, the Border Fancy, the Dutch Frill, and the German; and each of these *varieties* is subdivided into many *classes*. It is a desire to produce each in its kind in perfection that has led to the present extensive system of scientific breeding. It is marvellous what improvement has been made during the past fifteen or twenty years, and although some few individuals differ regarding this progress, these are days in which individuals cannot raise standards of their own. The various specialist clubs have by thought and care worked out standards of the variety they represent, and it is right that they should supersede all individual opinions. Our object is to assist to the attainment of the ideals thus set out by an intelligent enunciation of simple principles, and detailed account of actual practice.

Hybrids.

Linked on the one side to the Canary-breeder's hobby, and on the other to that of the British bird keeper is the fascinating pastime of breeding hybrids between the Canary and many of our most attractive wild birds, such as the Goldfinch, Bullfinch, Linnet, Siskin, Twite, Greenfinch, and Redpoll, and in turn between these latter birds themselves. No branch of aviculture probably requires so much patience as does that of hybrid-breeding, and yet its followers are rapidly increasing; disappointment appears but an incentive to fresh efforts to attain some difficult cross, and the reward is often a bird of rare beauty, embodying in marked degrees the charms of its widely differing parents.

Since such mules, as these crosses are often erroneously called (hybrids being the correct term), are sterile, the objection has been raised as to the uselessness of raising stock that cannot perpetuate their race; but to the hybrid-breeder this matters little, for his delight is in overcoming the difficulties of their production, and, once secured, hybrids are hardy and long-lived, as well as, in the case of the rarer crosses, most valuable as show birds. In due course in these pages we shall, therefore, deal with this section of the fancy, and strive to remove some of the many obstacles which beset the path of the breeder of hybrids.

British Birds.

No section of a bird-show is so interesting to the general public as that which contains examples of many of our native birds, staged to perfection in health, plumage, and steadiness, and thus affording to the onlooker a closer study of their charms than is possible with the same birds in their wild state. Such an exhibition is the best reply to those who hold it wrong to cage a wild bird at all. They do not take into account the pleasure and the humanising effect of the study of birds under the only possible conditions open to workers in big cities, and also fail to realise the care and affection lavished on their birds by the thousands of enthusiastic keepers of British birds in these islands. Such fanciers yield to none in their detestation of cruelty to birds, whether in insanitary bird-shops, or at the hands of unskilled, careless bird-catchers, and ask only to be judged by the results they achieve in successfully keeping some of the most delicate of our insectivorous birds in full health and vigour, both in cages and the larger liberty of well-planned aviaries. British birds that some years since were considered almost impracticable as cage-birds are now frequently met with at exhibitions, and whilst adding to the delight and instruction of show-goers, also illustrate the remarkable advance made in the science of bird-keeping, and especially in the direction of providing the birds with the natural foods of their wild state.

As with the different varieties of the Canary and the many interesting hybrids already alluded to, so we shall hope in later chapters to deal with the various British birds judged suitable for confinement, and to furnish such hints as may help to a more intelligent appreciation of their needs and of the many *apparent* trifles which make up the difference between success and its reverse in their management.

A TYPICAL NORTH COUNTRY BIRD SHOW.

(From a flashlight photograph by G. Franks, of Gateshead.)

We say " apparent " trifles, for the smallest work of creative power cannot really be considered a trifle, nor are they triflers who give a careful attention to the many seeming insignificant works of nature with which they are surrounded. He is not a trifler who makes the " short-lived insect of a day " a life-long study, nor he who can find food for thought in contemplation of the lowest form of animal organism ; any more than he who makes the study of the higher works of creation his constant occupation. Nor is he a trifler who can read a page of the world's history in a fragment of rock which, cropping up by the roadside, speaks to him with a tongue that cannot lie of that distant beginning when this planet of ours was created ; any more than he who extracts from the bowels of the earth the treasures warehoused there for ages. Nor is he a trifler who carefully gathers the wild flowers in the hedgerow or the grasses of our fields, or notes forms of vegetable existence where the uneducated eye can detect nothing ; any more than he who cultivates broad acres, or who brings the flowers and fruits of the tropics under control in our latitudes. Neither is he a trifler who, from among the endless resources at the command of any thinker who goes through the world with his eyes open, selects for his special study the feathered portion of creation ; nor when, among other marvels of instinctive work, he finds his attention arrested by a simple little bird's nest is he any more a trifler than the men whose constructive genius designed the temples of old Egypt, who built the hoary Pyramids, who carved the solid mountains of the Nile into edifices of colossal proportions, or those who raised, brick by brick from their foundations, the more florid but less imposing structures of modern times. There is a time for everything, even for trifles, if such there be. Our trifle is the cage-bird of to-day—the fancier's Canary, hybrid, or British bird—and when we take into consideration the wonderful strides and improvements that have been made even within the past twenty years, there is much for us to advance for the consideration of the present-day fancier. We propose to deal with each bird by describing minutely its distinctive features, showing how to keep it, feed it, moult it, develop its beauties, improve its shape and feather, wash it, dry it, send it to the show ; how to get it there, what to do with it when it is there, and how to get it home again ; how to achieve success, how to profit by defeat ; as well as how to help each other, and so help ourselves.

CHAPTER II

HISTORY OF THE CANARY*

BY A. RUDOLF GALLOWAY, M.B., C.M., M.A.

THEORIES OF ORIGIN

All Derived from One Species.

AT the present day there is little doubt that all the varieties of Canary have been evolved from the Wild Canary (*Serinus Canaria*), of the Canary Islands, Madeira, and the Azores.†

It is comparatively easy for us, in these days of scientific progress, to come to this conclusion; but we can understand the great difficulty that writers on this subject, well into the nineteenth century, had in understanding the origin of a bird which, even in the commencement of the eighteenth century, had twenty-nine varieties placed to its credit.

It was impossible for them to believe that all those could have come from one ancestor, and accordingly many fanciful origins were given—some, no doubt, having a foundation on what was supposed to be fact, but which turns out to be fallacy, just as in the stories of the Chaffinch-Canary, Yellow-hammer-Canary, and other unknown hybrids of to-day.

A Fanciful Theory.

As an example of these false origins, which may be traced from the earliest writers, where sometimes the mistaken fact is given, through most of the later ones (who usually omit the fallacious foundation), let us quote from the article, "Canaria," in Rees' Cyclopædia, published in 1819:—

"These (29) varieties are not the spontaneous offspring of the common Canary finch, but of that bird crossed with the Venturon and Cini or Serin, two species very nearly allied to the Canary finch, and both which inhabit the South of Europe.

"It is by this means, as well as by pairing the Canary finch with the Goldfinch, Linnet, Yellow-hammer, Chaffinch, and even the domestic Sparrow, that so many varieties are produced. The Canary finch proves fertile with the Siskin and Goldfinch, but in this case the produce for the most part proves sterile. . . . The two birds with which the Canary intermingles its breed the best, as already stated, are the Serin or Fringilla Serinus, and Venturon or Citril, Fringilla Citrinella. The Serin is a bird of small size, being rather less than the Common Linnet. Its upper mandible is brown, the under whitish; the plumage above brown, mixed with yellowish green, beneath greenish yellow, and having the sides marked with longitudinal

* For permission to incorporate part of this paper, I am indebted to the courtesy of Professor Karl Pearson, editor of "Biometrika," in which (Vol. VII., No. 1 and 2, July and October, 1909) it originally appeared with illustrations and four colour plates, being also published separately as "Canary Breeding—A Practical Analysis of Records from 1891-1909," by the University Press, Cambridge.

† The Wild Canary is regarded as a sub-species of the Serin (*Serinus serinus*) which inhabits Central and Southern Europe, and occasionally visits the British Isles.

2

spots of brown; the wings are marked with a greenish band, quills and tail brown, edged with greenish grey, and the legs brown. This kind is found not only in Italy, but in Greece, in Turkey, Austria, Provence, Languedoc, Catalonia, and probably in all the climates of that temperature. There are, however, certain years in which it is very rare, even in the Southern provinces of France. Its song is agreeable and varied, but the song of the female is inferior to that of the male.

"The Citril finch is larger than the Venturon, and has a louder note; it is indeed remarkable for the brightness of its colour and for the strength and variety of its song. The female is somewhat larger than the male, has less of the yellow in its plumage, and does not sing so well, or rather answers him, as it were, in monosyllables. It is found in Provence, Dauphiny, Geneva, Switzerland, Germany, Italy, and Spain. In Burgundy it is known by the name of the Canary. The plumage on the upper parts is of a yellowish green, spotted or variegated with brown; beneath greenish yellow; wings dusky and greenish; and the legs flesh colour.

"We conceive it right to be thus particular in pointing out the characters of the two latter birds, since they have been most commonly confounded as varieties of the Canary finch, which alone is found in the Canary Islands, and from which they differ specifically, although in general appearance and manners of life they nearly assimilate. It is with these two primitive species that the Canary bird is commonly crossed with most success, and from the union of which many of the more esteemed varieties of the common Canary bird are produced."

The "Domestic Sparrow" Legend.

The "domestic Sparrow" origin I have traced to the following footnote to Buffon's description of the Canary:—"D'Arnault assures Salerne that he saw at Orleans a gray hen Canary, which had escaped from the volery, couple with a Sparrow and make her hatch in a Sparrow-can, which thrived." (From *Amusements Innocens, ou le Parfait Oiseleur,* 1774.)

AN EXHIBITION GOLDFINCH.

The female Canary mentioned here must have been a female Sparrow, with white in its plumage, a fairly common sport which we know had occurred before the date of the story, as Sparrows more or less white are mentioned by Brisson, Wilughby, and Aldrovandus. On no other explanation would such a mating in an open garden be possible. It is also quite likely that such a sport in the Sparrow would be called a Canary even at the present day by the majority of people.

It will be our object to prove that there is a much simpler and more feasible explanation of the great variability of the Canary than by supposing it to be due to crossing with allied species (the progeny of most of which we now know to be more or less sterile), or even to those influences included under the term "domestication," to which Darwin attached much importance.

Among the earliest references to the Canary must be noted the description of Gesner in his "Historia Animalium," Book III., p. 1, date 1555.

Oldest Canary Literature.

Although the figures in Gesner are somewhat feeble, not to say grotesque, the illustration here is an exception. A fairly good engraving of a Siskin with laced cap is given, and after some remarks about nomenclature and classification, the author says :—

"*Huius generis sunt quas Anglia aves Canarias vocat*" ("Of this kind are those birds the English call Canaries").

Gesner's description of the Canary may be here given (from Ray's translation, 1678, of Willughby's "Ornithology," 1676) :—

"It is of the bigness of the Common Titmouse; hath a small white bill, thick at base, and contracted into a sharp point; all the feathers of the wings and tail being of a green colour; so that it differs little from those small birds which our countrymen call Citrils, or those they call Zifels, and the Italians, Ligurini (Siskins), save that it is a little bigger than either of those, liker in show or outward appearance to this (latter), somewhat greener than that (former).

"Between the cock and the hen bird I have observed this difference, that the Breast, Belly, and upper part of the Head adjoining to the Bill, are more yellow in the Cock than in the Hen."

Gesner also gives another very interesting reference to the Canary at this date (1555)—Book III., p. 249, "De Citrinella."

THE SISKIN.
From Gesner's "Historia Animalium" (1555).

After describing the Citril as being similar to Chloris (Greenfinch), with yellow or citron breast, grey head, and excelling all of this genus in song, except the Serin, he adds :—

"*Similis huic est, ut audio, Canaria dicta avicula, quæ ê Canariis Insulis, sacchari feracibus, advehitur, suavissimi cantus*" ("Similar to this is, as I hear, the bird of sweetest song, called the Canary, which is brought from the Canary Islands, productive of sugar").

He further adds :—

"It is sold everywhere very dear, both for the sweetness of its singing, and also because it is brought from far remote places with great care and diligence, and but rarely, so that it is wont to be kept only by nobles and great men."

Gesner also says, referring to the Canary Islands :—

"Out of which in our age are wont to be brought certain singing birds which from the place they are bred, they commonly call Canary birds; others call them Sugar birds, because the best sugar is brought thence."

We learn from this that, in the first half of the sixteenth century, Canaries and sugar were imported into Europe (including England), and as the final conquest of the Canary Islands by Spain did not take place until the closing years of the fifteenth century we know that little time was lost in bringing the first Canaries to Europe along with the sugar.

"The Epitome of the Art of Husbandry," London, 1675. By J. B., Gent. (Joseph Blagrove). (P. 106.)

Later References to the Canary. —"The first I shall begin withal is the Bird called the Canary-Bird, because the original of that Bird came from thence (I hold this to be the best Song-Bird); but now with industry they breed them very plentifully in Germany, and in Italy also; and they have bred *some few here in England* though as yet not anything to the purpose as they do in other Countries."

He also writes (p. 107):—"Many Country-People cannot distinguish a Canary from one of our common Green Birds, etc."

In Ray's translation (1678) of Willughby's "Ornithology" (1676), the following quotation from a late English writer (probably modified from Blagrove) is given:—

"Canary birds of late years have been brought abundantly out of Germany, and are therefore now called German birds, and these German birds in handsomeness and song excel those brought out of the Canaries. . . . They are fed with Canary-seed, wherein they take great pleasure, which therefore is wont to be brought together with them out of the same Islands.

"Gesner, from the relation of his friend, writes, that they are fed with the same food with the Siskin and Citril, viz. Line seed, and Poppy seed, and sometimes also Millet; but particularly, that they delight in sugar and the sugar-cane, as also in that sort of Chickweed or Mouse-ear, which they commonly call Henbit. For, he affirms, that by this they are presently provoked to sing, etc."

In "Gentlemen's Recreation" (1677) Canaries in England are mentioned as being mostly of a green colour and imported from Germany.

"Traité des Serins de Canarie," par Hervieux (1713).—*See* p. 22.

Albin's "Song-Birds" (1759).—*See* p. 27.

HABITATS OF THE CANARY

The Canary Islands* were made known to the Romans in Augustus' time, by Juba, King of Mauretania, whose account is given by the elder Pliny, who states that at this time they were uninhabited, and that there were numerous birds: "*Omnes copia pomarum et avium, omnes generis abundant,*" etc. (Plin. VI., C. 32). They were rediscovered in 1334 by a French vessel. In 1400 a Norman gentleman, Jean de Bethencourt, sailed from Rochelle, landed at Lanzarotte and Fuerteventura, but was opposed by the natives. Having got a grant of the islands from Henry III., he, in 1404, mastered Fuerteventura, Gomera, and Hierro, but was repulsed at Palma and Canary. He returned home and died in 1408. His nephew sold his rights to Don Enrique de Guzman, and he, failing to overcome the natives, sold them to another Spaniard, Paraza. About 1461 his successors took nominal possession of Canary and Teneriffe, but the natives effectually resisted occupation. Meantime J. de Bethencourt's nephew had fraudulently made another sale to Portugal. Finally the islands were ceded to Spain. Canary, Teneriffe, and Palma being still unsubdued in 1476, Ferdinand and Isabella of Spain compelled Paraza's successors to sell the islands to the Crown. In 1477 one thousand soldiers were sent out, and after much bloodshed the Spaniards, under Pedro de Vera, became masters of Grand Canary in 1483. Palma, in 1491, and Teneriffe, in 1495, were conquered by Alonzo de Lugo.

The Canary Islands.

The approximate size of the main islands:—

Teneriffe, the largest: 60 by 30 miles.
Grand Canary: 24 miles diameter.
Palma: 26 by 16 miles.

* Mostly from *Encyclopædia Britannica.*

A STUDY IN EVOLUTION: THE WILD CANARY AND A DESCENDANT—THE MODERN CREST.

Lanzarotte : 31 by 5 to 10 miles.
Fuerteventura : 52 by 12 miles.
Gomera : 23 miles long.
Hierro : 18 by 15 miles.

In the case of the Canary Islands it is possible that the natives had domesticated the Canary many years before its introduction into Europe.

The Azores.

Although known to Arabian geographers in the twelfth and fourteenth centuries, the Azores were believed to have been uninhabited until annexed by Portugal, 1432–1457. Colonisation went on well, and in 1466 they were presented by Alphonso V. to his aunt, Isabella Duchess of Burgundy. An influx of Flemish settlers followed, and the islands were known as the Flemish Islands.

The area of St. Michael, the largest of the Azores, is 224 square miles.

Birds are so plentiful that 420,000, *including many Canaries,* are slaughtered annually (*Encycl. Brit.*).

It may be inferred, from the fact that Gesner in 1555 speaks of the birds which the English call Canaries, that a very early importation of the bird had taken place into England, and probably this came from the Azores into England, Belgium, and France some thirty years before the introduction to other European countries.

Madeira.

An island, thirty by thirteen miles, Madeira was not annexed by Portugal till 1420, although discovered long before 1351 by Portuguese vessels under Genoese captains.

The Elba Legend.

The advent of the Canary is thus seen to be independent of the usually given tale of a shipload of Canaries, bound for Leghorn, being wrecked on the island of Elba.

The extract from Olina,* who wrote in 1622 with reference to this, may be given, as illustrating an important feature in the Canary, viz. variability, which will have important bearings in the sequel.

"There are also found of this sort of birds in the Island Ilva a degenerate kind, descended originally from true Canary-birds, which were brought over from the Canary Islands in a certain ship bound for Lighorn, that was cast away near this Island, and after the shipwreck escaped and saved themselves on this Island, and afterwards propagated their kind here, breeding and multiplying greatly. But the difference of place hath wrought some change in the external figure of this Bird. For these spurious birds have black feet, and are more yellow under the chin than the genuine Canary-birds" (Ray, 1678).

We have, in this little experiment in Elba, a repetition on a small scale of what had previously occurred, in all probability, in the comparatively restricted areas of the three original habitats.

Early In-breeding, Sporting and Albinism.

There must have been in the history of the wild Canary from the first, owing to its comparatively restricted habitats, more than an ordinary amount of the in-breeding that takes place in most wild species.

An early instance of this interesting fact and its result is recorded by Gesner as follows :—

"For it is found by experience that by how much less they are, by so much are they more canorous. But the great ones shut up in cages turn their heads round about and backward, and are not to be esteemed genuine or right-bred Canary-birds. Of this sort there are brought from the islands Palma and Cape Verde, which they call fools, from that motion of their head which is proper to fools."

This is a most interesting and important reference to the occurrence of an early sport in the direction of albinism and increased size, for we know quite well at the present day the peculiar motion of the heads of some albinotic birds, especially when exposed to bright light, and of others with defective sight.

Dr. Latham (1823), in a footnote, quotes from "Adanson's Voyage," p. 20 :—

"The Canary Bird, which grows white in France, is in the Island of Teneriffe almost as gray as a Linnet."

* *Giovanni Pietro Olina. Ucceliera, overe discorso dell anatura e proprietà di diversi uccelli e in particolare di que che cantano. Roma,* 1622.

Adanson's reference clearly points to the occurrence of a grey variety, and Buffon states :—

" The grey kind are not of a uniform colour ; some feathers are affected by different shades, and some individuals are of a lighter or of a darker tinge."

THE WILD CANARY (*SERINUS CANARIA*)*

British Museum Catalogue Description.

As we intend to trace the variations in plumage of the Canary from their origin, and endeavour to discover their cause, it is important to give the accepted description of the original wild bird. In the Catalogue of Birds in the British Museum, under " *Serinus Canaria,*" the following is given :—

" Adult Male.—General colour above, ashy brown washed with yellow and streaked with blackish brown down the centre of the feathers ; rump, uniform olive yellow ; lesser wing coverts, olive yellow ; median and greater coverts, black, edged with yellow, the latter tipped with whitish ; bastard-wing and primary coverts, black, margined with ashy yellow ; quills, dark brown, edged with ashy brown, tinged with yellow on the primaries ; upper tail coverts, ashy brown washed with olive yellow, with darker brown centres ; tail feathers, dark brown edged with ashy brown, tinged with yellow ; crown of head, olive yellow, streaked with blackish centres to the feathers and slightly washed with ashy ; forehead, dull golden yellow ; eyelids and sides of face, dull golden yellow, with a dusky streak across the lower ear coverts ; cheeks, dull golden yellow with a dusky malar stripe ; throat and under surface of body, dull golden yellow ; the sides of the upper breast, ashy grey ; the sides of the body and flanks, more ashy and streaked with black, more broadly on the latter ; lower abdomen, thighs, and under tail coverts, whitish ; under wing-coverts and axillaries, pale ashy, washed with yellow ; quills below, dusky, ashy along the inner edge. Total length, 4.55 inches ; culmen, 0.35 ; wing, 2.75 ; tail, 2.2 ; tarsus, 1.65."

" Adult Female.—Similar to the male, but a little browner, and having the yellow on the forehead, sides of face, and under parts less vivid. Total length, 4.6 inches ; culmen, 0.4 ; wing, 2.6 ; tail, 2.1 ; tarsus, 0.65."

" Both sexes more ashy in winter."

*For coloured figure see my "Canary Breeding," which also shows the evolution of the different varieties.

Pennant's Description.

Writing in 1776, Pennant says :—

" We once saw some small birds brought directly from the Canary Islands that we suspect to be the genuine sort. They were of a *dull green* colour, but as they did not sing, we supposed them to be hens."

Gesner's short description (p. 11) best gives perhaps the general idea of the yellowish-green bird, but the British Museum detailed analysis is also important in view of the colour variations we must trace.

Latham also states, from Humboldt :—

" Canary finches in the neighbourhood of Orotave in Teneriffe said to be uniformly *green,* some with a yellow tint on their back."

CINNAMON INHERITANCE

Cinnamon Sports.

As the earliest form of Cinnamon Canary was called the Dun, or Quaker, and was closely allied to the grey and cinnamon types of pallid variation occurring in wild birds of the present day, it is necessary, in order to understand subsequent variations, to give some information concerning cinnamon sports and cinnamon inheritance generally.

As this has for many years been the puzzle of the fancy, it may be well to state as shortly as possible the known peculiarities of cinnamon inheritance before adding any fresh information.

Cinnamon colour of plumage in young birds can be obtained only by using a cinnamon, or cinnamon-bred, cock.

If a cock having no known cinnamon blood be mated to a self-cinnamon hen, the young have no cinnamon feathers.

If a cinnamon or cinnamon-bred cock be mated to a hen with no known cinnamon blood, all the young which show any cinnamon feathers are hens.

Recent Experiments.

In addition to these facts, I have during the season 1908 ascertained, from experiment and examination of past records, the following facts :—

(1) A self-cinnamon cock mated to a clear hen with pink eyes* (showing cinnamon descent) may have cinnamon variegated male progeny.

THE BORDER FANCY CANARY.

(2) Two clear pink-eyed parents, with no known cinnamon cross for at least two generations, may have cinnamon-ticked male and female progeny.

(3) My records also show that, if a pink-eyed male be mated to a dark-eyed female, all the clear, variegated, and green *dark-eyed* progeny are males; and the clear, variegated-cinnamon and self-cinnamon *pink-eyed* progeny are females.

(4) Moreover, in this mating the sexes occur in equal proportions.

The following is an extract from my records of this mating :—

PINK-EYED MALE × DARK-EYED FEMALE

14 matings gave	24 d.-e. males,	21 p.-e. females.
Sex unascertained in	4 d.-e. and	7 pink-eyed.
Total ..	28 dark-eyed,	28 pink-eyed.

In all probability 28 dark-eyed male progeny and 28 pink-eyed female progeny.

These results agree with those of Doncaster with regard to sex inheritance in the common Currant Moth (*Abraxas grossulariata*) and its pale variety (*lacticolor*).†

* The terms "pink-eye" and "dark-eye" are strictly reserved for those chicks in which these qualities were noted within two days of hatching.

† For an account of this interesting parallel case in moths to that of the Cinnamon Canary, and for its Mendelian explanation by Bateson and Punnett, see Report IV. to the Evolution Committee of the Royal Society.

Wild Cinnamon Sports and Cinnamon Hybrids.

For some years I have been collecting all the wild cinnamon birds of which I heard. Any rarity of this sort is nearly always called a cock, in order to enhance its value; and this remark applies also to many museum specimens. But I have now had a fair number in my aviaries, and have in every case succeeded in getting these cinnamon "cocks" to lay eggs. Some of these also have been examined *post-mortem* and the sex verified. I have also seen and examined several cinnamon wild birds belonging to other owners.

I have also bred six cinnamon hybrids of different sorts, and seen and examined several others.

All these cinnamon wild birds and hybrids I have found to be *females*. Therefore I feel confident in stating that all cinnamon wild birds are *females*, and that male cinnamon hybrids must be very rare, for, so far, I have seen none.

THE CINNAMON CANARY.

Basis of Statement.

These statements are based upon :—

(1) Twenty-five cinnamon wild birds and cinnamon hybrids seen at bird-shows and in bird-rooms.

(2) The following living examples at present in my possession :—

(*a*) Four cinnamon and very pale cinnamon (almost white) Greenfinches (*L. chloris*).

(*b*) One cinnamon Yellow-hammer (*E. Citrinella*).

SUMMARY OF CINNAMON MATINGS, DARK-EYED MATINGS, AND CROSS OR HYBRID MATINGS*

Terms.—p.e. = pink-eyed on hatching and pure pink-eyed bred so far as known. d.e. = dark-eyed on hatching and pure dark-eyed bred so far as known. F = hybrid nature of inheritance (males mentioned first, females second; *e.g.* ♂ × ♀). d.e. F × F p.e. means dark-eyed male from pink-eyed mother mated to pink-eyed female from pink-eyed father. ♂ = male, ♀ = female, o = sex unknown.

I.
p.e. × d.e.
Matings, 14. Progeny, 56. Dark-eyed: ♂ 24, o 4 = 28. Pink-eyed: ♀ 21, o 7 = 28.

II.
p.e. × p.e.
Matings, 9. Progeny, 35. Dark-eyed, 0. Pink-eyed: ♂ 9, ♀ 13, o 13 = 35.

III.
d.e. × p.e.
Matings, 33. Progeny, 110. Dark-eyed, 110. Pink-eyed, 0. Of the Canaries there were: ♂ 20, ♀ 21, o 9.

III. 1.
d.e. × F p.e.
Matings, 6. Progeny, 22. Dark-eyed, 22. Pink-eyed, 0.

III. 2.
F d.e. × p.e.
Mating, 1. Progeny, 3. Dark-eyed, 1. Pink-eyed, 2.

III. 3.
d.e. F × p.e.
Matings, 3. Progeny, 12. Dark-eyed, 4. Pink-eyed, 5. Doubtful, 3.

III. 4.
F d.e. × F p.e.
Mating, 1. Progeny, 2. Pink-eyed, 2.

III. 5.
d.e. F × F p.e.
Matings, 2. Progeny, 6. Dark-eyed, 5. Pink-eyed, 1.

IV.
d.e. × d.e.
Matings, 91. Progeny, 283. Dark-eyed, 283. Pink-eyed, 0.

IV. 1.
d.e. × d.e. F.
Matings, 4. Progeny, 16. Dark-eyed, 16.

IV. 2.
d.e. F × d.e. F.
Matings, 5. Progeny, 21. Dark-eyed: ♂ 7, ♀ 2, o 6 = 15. Pink-eyed: ♀ 3, o 3 = 6.

IV. 3.
F d.e. × d.e.
Matings, 3. Progeny, 12. Dark-eyed, 9. Pink-eyed, 3.

IV. 4.
d.e. F × d.e.
Matings, 4. Progeny, 10. Dark-eyed, 8. Pink-eyed: ♀ 1, o 1 = 2.

* *See* Summary of Conclusions, also "Canary Breeding," for full details of matings.

(*c*) Three cinnamon Canary-Greenfinch hybrids.

(*d*) One self-cinnamon Linnet (*L. cannabina*).

(3) The following, formerly in my possession :—

(*a*) One self-cinnamon Canary-Greenfinch hybrid.

(*b*) One self-cinnamon Canary-Linnet (*F. cannabina*) hybrid, bred by myself.

(4) The following preserved specimens, which died in my possession, the sex being verified *post-mortem* :—

(*a*) Three self-cinnamon Greenfinches (*L. chloris*).

(*b*) One self-cinnamon Goldfinch (*Carduelis elegans*).

(*c*) One self-cinnamon Sparrow (*Passer domesticus*).

(*d*) One very pale cinnamon (almost white) Sparrow (*P. domesticus*).

(*e*) One self-cinnamon Linnet (*L. cannabina*).

(*f*) Two silver-grey Linnets (*L. cannabina*).

(5) One very pale cinnamon (almost white) Blackbird (*Turdus merula*), shot in October, 1908; sent to me by Mr. John Dixon, Wigton, and examined *post-mortem*.

(6) One cinnamon Goldfinch (*C. elegans*), which belonged to Mr. John Hector, Aberdeen, was known to be a female during life; and has now been preserved and presented to me.

(7) One very pale cinnamon (almost white) Starling (*Sturnus vulgaris*), caught by a cat in Aberdeen recently, and now preserved and in my possession. It has every appearance of being a female.

All of these grey and cinnamon sports and hybrids are of the female sex.

Wild White Sports and White Hybrids.

While I have found all self-cinnamon sports in wild birds, and also all that show the faintest shade of cinnamon colour in their plumage to be females, I have also been impressed with the fact that most that show any noticeable amount of pure white plumage are males.

The following have been verified *post-mortem*, and most are in my possession. They are all males :—

(1) Two almost clear and one one-third clear Linnets (*Linota cannabina*).

(2) One half-clear mealy Redpoll (*L. linaria*).

(3) One white Corn Bunting (*Emberiza miliaria*). This bird has two or three ticked flights, all the rest of the plumage being clear.

(4) One almost clear Yellow-hammer (*E. citrinella*).

(5) One three-quarter clear red Grouse (*Lagopus Scoticus*).

(6) One three-quarter clear Blackbird (*T. merula*).

(7) An almost clear Chaffinch (*F. cœlebs*). This beautiful bird, unfortunately shot in Aberdeenshire during the severe snowstorm in December, 1908, when it might easily have been caught alive, is white all over, with the following exceptions: The eighth and ninth quills and three or four coverts of the right wing are of the normal dark colour; the left wing has the fifth quill "grizzled" or greyish; the seventh, eighth, and ninth, dark normal colour; and three or four coverts also dark. There are also three or four ticked scapulars on each side. The breast (upper) has a faint reddish-brown, and the dorsal region and rump a yellow tinge.

Dr. Henry, of Kemnay, Aberdeenshire, sent me on June 15th, 1909, a beautiful pure white male Wood Pigeon (*Columba palumbus*), which had been shot a day or two previously in the vicinity, after rearing a normally coloured young one, the mother being also normal in colour. The pigeon is perfectly clear (no dark feathers). The eyes were not noticeably abnormal.

I have bred hybrids (1908) from the following male birds :—

(1) One three-quarter white (clear) Linnet (*L. cannabina*).

(2) One one-third white (clear) Linnet (*L. cannabina*).

(3) From two others of a similar description in previous seasons.

I do not say that *all* more or less white

sports in wild birds are males, for I have at present two Linnets with one or two white spots about the size of 4–6 mm., and these are undoubtedly females; and I have seen a pure white female Pheasant (*P. colchicus*). Clear (white) and almost clear female hybrids also occur now and then. I believe, however, that the majority in this case is greatly on the male side, just as we have seen the preponderance in the case of cinnamon hybrids to be on that of the female.

Cock Cinnamon Hybrids.

It should be possible to produce cock cinnamon hybrids by mating a self-cinnamon cock Canary with, *e.g.*, a cinnamon Greenfinch. The nearest approach I have made to this is a cock Greenfinch mule of a peculiar greyish colour (neither the ordinary "dark" mule nor cinnamon) which I bred last year from a clear yellow cock Canary and a cinnamon Greenfinch, the Canary being bred from a clear yellow cock and a buff green hen, probably of cinnamon descent.

THE YORKSHIRE CANARY.

The question of correlation of sex with cinnamon colour is a most interesting one, and may explain the rarity of cinnamon varieties in wild birds. It also increases our interest in the origin of the cinnamon Canary. It would almost appear that we must look for and supply another sort of complementary sporting colour (probably greens) with cinnamon blood, before the cinnamon mother is capable of producing a son with sufficient cinnamon blood to prop-

Origin of the Cinnamon Canary.

THE GERMAN ROLLER CANARY.

agate the variety. In the case of the Canary it is possible that the cinnamon variety was propagated by the mating of original wild green cocks with the self-cinnamon (or grey) hen sports, the green cocks from this cross being capable, when mated with cinnamon hens, of producing cinnamon cocks for the propagation of the variety.

It will thus be seen that the establishment of a wild cinnamon variety is almost impossible, for even though such a conspicuous mother were allowed to live and breed, it almost means that she must mate with her own son before a male cinnamon bird could be produced.

The allied grey variation, being less conspicuous, and probably more vigorous, and with better eyesight, would be more likely to succeed; and this, as we shall see later, has probably been the initial stage in the Canary of the cinnamon variety. Since writing the foregoing, I have seen and examined a considerable number of additional sports and hybrids, and have bought a self-cinnamon female Linnet, a self-cinnamon female Chaffinch, and also a half-white male Goldfinch. I have also lately acquired from Mr. T. W. Hinson, Cambridge, a most interesting and rare bird, viz. a *silver-grey male* Linnet (*L. cannabina*), with cinnamon shaded back, reddish breast, and which is also a *ground tumbler*. This bird, caught near Cambridge in November, 1909, refuses ever to perch, and when excited (as when anyone approaches its cage) keeps turning head over tail on the floor. It has also the tremulous motion in its head and neck of the Fan-tail Pigeon. I regard this bird as corroborative of my theory of the albinistic origin of domestic varieties; it is also (if a male bird, which I believe it to be) the only partial exception I have seen to the general conclusion that all grey or cinnamon wild birds are females—an exception which, in all probability, proves the rule.

THE LANCASHIRE PLAINHEAD CANARY.

THE GREY OR CINNAMON CANARY AS THE FOUNDATION OF VARIETY*

Grounds of Belief.

As I believe this interesting Canary—the grey or cinnamon—to be the origin (after the wild green) of all our present kinds of Canaries, I shall give, at this stage, the grounds for this belief, which has been founded mainly on a study of my cinnamon wild birds, and on the cinnamon and other hybrids I have produced; for I have satisfied myself that cinnamon blood, wherever found, indicates the presence of a character essentially sporting, and varying not only in respect to colour and plumage, but also to type generally—*e.g.*, size and form of body.

(1) Three rich-coloured self-cinnamon Greenfinches, acquired in 1907 and kept in an outdoor aviary, in 1908 moulted pale cinnamon.

(2) One of my pale cinnamon Greenfinches of 1907 moulted paler still in 1908, and is now creamy-white, but still shows traces of her original cinnamon colour.

We learn from this to recognise several shades and intensities of the cinnamon colour, which occurs as a sport among wild birds, a fact which we must remember later when discussing the earliest varieties of the Canary.

(3) Two cinnamon-variegated Canary-Greenfinch hybrids, bred by me in 1906 and 1907, each with a small white spot on the nape and two or three white tail-feathers (the rest of the feathers being self-cinnamon), have in 1908 largely increased the white areas of plumage—the heads, tail-feathers, and coverts of both showing white areas which were previously cinnamon.

(4) A self-cinnamon Canary-Linnet hybrid bred by me developed several white tail-feathers at the second moult.

(5) The origin of the old Dutch Frill: One of the above cinnamon-variegated Canary-Greenfinch hybrids, after taking second prize at Bathgate, in perfect plumage, has moulted, in the second year, into a Dutch Frill hybrid, the body-feathers, although still cinnamon, showing the most extraordinary twists and turns. The father of this hybrid has no Dutch Frill blood, as I have bred the strain for many

*The chief types are illustrated in colours in "Canary Breeding."

CINNAMON CANARIES

1. Self-yellow Cinnamon 2. Self-buff Cinnamon 3. Evenly Cinnamon-marked Yellow

years, and never owned a Dutch Frill Canary.

(6) The origin of our birds of *shape and position :* The same hybrid, along with the frilled feathers, has assumed a semi-upright position, thus indicating the origin of our Canaries of shape and position—*e.g.*, Lancashire, Belgian, Scotch Fancy, which are supposed to have come originally from the old Dutch variety.

(7) The start of a Fan-tailed Canary: I have also noted that cinnamon Canaries and hybrids sometimes develop an extra number of tail-feathers. One cinnamon-variegated Canary of 1908 has thirteen. I have also two hybrids with fourteen each.

(8) The origin of the Lizard and London Fancy Canaries: I have bred and now possess alive two Siskin-Canary hybrids, one with a perfectly shaped golden-yellow cap (most of the rest of the bird being dark —heavily variegated) and the other with a beautiful silver-spangled back (most of the rest of the bird being clear).* The cap and spangled back are characteristics of the Lizard Canary—a specimen of which

THE LANCASHIRE COPPY CANARY.

I never possessed. The spangled back appeared at the first moult, just as occurs in the spangling of the Lizard Canary.

*Second prize, City of Glasgow show (1909).

I have also bred several other Siskin-Canary hybrids with irregular or broken Lizard caps.

The Canary parent in each case was of

THE FRILLED CANARY.

a strain with cinnamon blood, but with no Lizard cross.

In addition to these characteristics of the Lizard occurring in the hybrids from a cinnamon-bred Canary, we know the Lizard and London Fancy Canaries both show the same unstable character of plumage as the original cinnamon, both of these varieties being fit to exhibit only during the show season after their first moult, owing to subsequent changes in plumage, and both being extremely alike in nest-feather and again at three or four years of age.

Consequently we may safely infer that both Lizard and London Fancy have been derived from cinnamon Canaries.

THE EVOLUTION OF THE CANARY

Bearing in mind these points with regard to cinnamon wild birds and hybrids, let us now turn to the Canary and study the earliest authentic records of its different varieties.

We have already mentioned that the

first stage in the evolution of our favourite cage-bird from the wild green type described by Gesner was the occurrence of a grey variety. The colour grey occurs as a sport in several of our wild birds at present, and is closely allied to the well-known cinnamon sports.

Evidence from Hervieux.*

Of the occurrence of this initial grey stage we have ample evidence in the most interesting and instructive account of the Canary by Hervieux.† One is inclined to attach much importance to this author's statements, as they bear evidence of being founded on actual experiments and are not mere repetitions from other writers.

Indeed, many of the stories concerning the breeding of those mules, which we, at the present time, regard as impossible —*e.g.*, Chaffinch-Canary, Yellow-hammer-Canary—have probably arisen from the too free interpretation and misunderstanding of Hervieux's statements ; for he instances the above two hybrids, but only to illustrate his nomenclature: "A male Canary being coupled with a female Chaffinch, the young which come from them are named *Serin mulets de Pinçon*." And the others the same : "Canary mule of the Linnet," "Canary mule of the Yellow-hammer (*Bruant*)," "Canary mule of the Goldfinch."

Having stated this, he adds : "Of all those birds of which I am about to speak, those which one pairs most commonly with our Canaries are the Goldfinches, male and female, for the others are but seldom used above all at present, so that is an experiment which some new fanciers (*nouveaux Curieux*) wish to make, to see what sorts of mules are produced from these different birds."

This clearly proves that Hervieux had no personal knowledge of the Yellow-hammer-Canary and Chaffinch-Canary hybrids, which subsequent writers (*e.g.*, Buffon) state, on this inadequate evidence, to have been bred.

This prepares us to receive Hervieux's list of varieties of the Canary in 1713 with a considerable amount of assurance that we are dealing with facts which, being properly interpreted, are of the utmost importance.

But we meet in all translators, and in many subsequent writers (whether professed translators or not), with great errors even in the rendering of the variety names. For instance, the writer of the Canary article in Rees' Encyclopædia (1819) translates the term "Isabelle" as "pink," and gaily proceeds to speak of the pink Canary, and also the pink Canary with red eyes ! This translation occurs also in Buffon.

Subsequent Errors.

Before quoting the varieties, in order to understand the nomenclature it is desirable to give and carefully translate the following passage :—

"*Il faut remarquer qu'il y a bien des Serins dont je viens de parler, qui ont outre la queuë blanche, des plumes blanches à une aile, et souvent aux deux ailes ; mais malgré cette difference particulière, les Curieux ne leur donnent pas un autre nom, que Serin à queuë blanche, ou race de Panachez.*" ("It is necessary to mention that there are many Canaries, of which I am about to speak, which have, besides the white tail, the feathers of one wing, and often of both, white; but in spite of this particular difference, fanciers (*Curieux*) do not give them another name than Canary with white tail, or Variegated kind.")

It is evident that variegation, as we now know it, was just beginning at that time, and that it arose from the sporting types of which "Gris," "Jaune," and "Blonde" are mentioned. For Hervieux says that we know Canaries of these types, when they are of the variegated race, as having : (1) Several white feathers in the tail, (2) several white claws (*ergots*), (3) *le duvet.*

The transitional stage of the bird is also shown by Hervieux's uncertainty as to the kinds to include under the term

* *Traité des Serins de Canarie, par Hervieux* (1713). There are various editions from 1709-1785. The oldest most complete one is that of 1713, which I have used.

† C. L. W. Noorduijn, of Groningen, informs me that Hervieux was Inspector of Canary-breeding to the Duchesse de Berry.

"Variegated race," for he also adds (p. 272): "I say also that there are Canaries which are of the variegated race which have not, however, any of the three marks which I have given above, or which have not even one of them; so that it is necessary to leave it to the good faith of those who sell them to you for the variegated race."

These explanations prove that the term "*race de Panachez*" strictly means with white tail, with a few white body-feathers, or with both these variations from the self-grey or self-cinnamon in their different shades.

In our muling experiments we have shown that the first variations to occur are these particular ones—viz., white feathers in tail, a small white spot at the back of the head or on other parts of the body. Our term "Variegated" is denoted towards the end of the list ("which commences with the commonest and finishes with the most rare") by the single word, "*Panaché*"—*e.g.*, "*Serin Panaché commun.*"

To understand the list, we must also recollect, as I have shown in my experiments with wild cinnamon sports, that self-cinnamon is a varying colour, and frequently changes in the same bird through various shades of pale cinnamon to a creamy white, often with a gloss of yellow on the surface (*blond doré*).

A Grey Greenfinch.

We must also remember that the colour grey is, like cinnamon, one of the pallid variations which occur in Nature—*e.g.*, grey Greenfinch, a very beautiful example of which, a female, was shown at the Scottish National Show, 1909, and is the property of Mr. J. W. Bruce, Coldstream. This bird is said to be three years old, and not to have changed its colour; but it is quite likely that other examples might grow paler, just as the cinnamon type does, for present-day grey and grizzle crests invariably moult lighter each year until ultimately they become clear.*

* Two silver-grey Linnets (*L. cannabina*) died in my possession, were examined, found to be females, and are now preserved. A beautiful silver-grey Starling gained first prize in the Rare-feathered class at the Crystal Palace Show, 1910. This bird is also of the female sex.

The mottled or spangled type of variation (in my opinion, closely allied to cinnamon) also appears in the "agate" varieties.

Having considered these preliminary points, we are now in a position to interpret the list itself:—

Hervieux's List.

"*Noms que l'on donne aux Serins, selon leurs differentes couleurs.*"

"*Je croy qu'il est apropos de marquer ici les noms que l'on donne communément aux Serins, selon leurs differentes couleurs; afin que l'on sçache en quelle classe, on plûtôt en quel degré de beauté sont les Serins que l'on a, ou ceux que l'on souhaite avoir; pour cet effet je me suis proposé de les nommer par ordre, en commençant par les plus communs, et finissant par les plus rares.*"

1. *Serin Gris commun.* (The ordinary grey Canary.)

2. *Serin Gris aux duvets* * *et aux pattes blanches, qu'on appelle Race de Panachez.* (Slightly variegated Frilled Canary with white feet.)

3. *Serin Gris à queue blanche, race de Panachez.* (Slightly variegated Canary with white tail.)

4. *Serin Blond commun.* (The ordinary Pale Canary.)

5. *Serin Blond aux yeux rouges.* (The Pale Canary with pink eyes.)

6. *Serin Blond doré.* (The Pale Canary glossed with yellow.)

7. *Serin Blond aux duvets, race de Panachez.* (Slightly variegated Pale Frilled Canary.)

8. *Serin Blond à queue blanche, race de Panachez.* (Slightly variegated Pale Canary with white tail.)

* "*Duvets*" means the light feathers which adorn the under-surface of the body of birds, and may be translated downy or frilled—for it is this part of the bird that first shows the tendency to excess of feather seen in Dutch Frills. Hervieux's explanation of "*le duvet*," at page 271, may be translated as follows: "which shows itself, when taking your Canary in your hand, you find on it, on blowing it under the body and stomach, a little white down (*un petit duvet blanc*), and in consequence of a different colour from the natural plumage." He also adds: "There are some Canaries which have much more of this down than others. This is what one finds with the fanciers; one they call *Serins au petit duvet*, that is to say, those which show a little, and the others they call *Serins au grand duvet*, that is to say, those which have much; this down does not appear usually till near the moult."

9. *Serin Jaune commun.* (The lemon-yellow Canary.)

10. *Serin Jaune aux duvets, race de Panachez.* (Slightly variegated Frilled lemon-yellow Canary.)

THE NORWICH PLAINHEAD CANARY.

11. *Serin Jaune à queue blanche, race de Panachez.* (Slightly variegated lemon-yellow Canary, with white tail.)

12. *Serin Agate commun.* (The *original* Lizard Canary.)

13. *Serin Agate aux yeux rouges.* (The Lizard with pink eyes, showing cinnamon origin.)

14. *Serin Agate à queue blanche, race de Panachez.* (Slightly variegated Lizard Canary with white tail.)

15. *Serin Agate aux duvets, race de Panachez.* (Slightly variegated Frilled Lizard.)

16. *Serin Isabelle commun.* (The *original* cinnamon Canary.)

17. *Serin Isabelle aux yeux rouges.* (The cinnamon Canary with pink eyes.)

18. *Serin Isabelle doré.* (The cinnamon Canary glossed with yellow.)

19. *Serin Isabelle aux duvets, race de Panachez.* (Slightly variegated Frilled cinnamon.)

20. *Serin Isabelle à queue blanche, race de Panachez.* (Slightly variegated cinnamon with white tail.)

21. *Serin Blanc, aux yeux rouges.* (The white Canary with pink eyes.)

22. *Serin Panaché commun.* (The *original* variegated Canary.)

23. *Serin Panaché aux yeux rouges.* (Grey-variegated Canary with pink eyes.)

24. *Serin Panaché de blond.* (Pale cinnamon-variegated Canary.)

25. *Serin Panaché de blond aux yeux rouges.* (Pale cinnamon-variegated Canary with pink eyes.)

26. *Serin Panaché de noir.** (Green-variegated Canary.)

27. *Serin Panaché de noir-jonquille aux yeux rouges.* (Cinnamon-green variegated Canary with pink eyes.)

28. *Serin Panaché de noir-jonquille et regulier.* (The London Fancy Canary.)

29. *Serin Plein, qui sont à present les plus rares.* (Clear orange-yellow Canary, which is at present the rarest.)†

(30.‡ The Crest Canary—or rather, the Crowned—which is one of the most beautiful.—Buffon.)

THE LIZARD CANARY.

* *Noir.*—Such quills and tail-feathers are mostly black or smoky when spread out, but when in position show their yellowish-green edging mainly.

† Hervieux gives the Paris prices of Canaries in 1713; they gradually increase in price along his list from "Serin Gris commun" at 2*l.* 10*s.* (two livres ten sous—two shillings and fivepence) to "Serin plein et parfait" at 45*l.* (£2 5*s.*)

‡ In the 1793 London edition of "Buffon's Natural History," class 30 is included in Hervieux's 1713 list of varieties, where I have been unable to find it. All the varieties except 29 and 30 are mentioned in the 1709 and 1711 editions of Hervieux.

CHAPTER III

HISTORY OF THE CANARY *(continued)*

The study of Hervieux's most instructive list, which begins with the commonest and ends with the rarest, combined with a knowledge of the nature and behaviour of sports in wild birds generally, proves the "sport" origin of all the varieties of the Canary.

The "Sport" Origin Proven.

In classes 1 to 3 we have the grey Canary, varying in the direction of frilled and white feathers and white feet. In 4 to 8 the pale type (either of grey or cinnamon) shows the same variations, but in addition a more marked tendency to albinism (pink-eye), and towards the differentiation between "yellow" and "buff." In 9 to 11 the uniformly lemon-yellow Canary shows similar plumage variations. In 12 to 15 the original Lizard proclaims its cinnamon descent by having pink eyes, besides the plumage changes like the others.

THE LONDON FANCY CANARY.

In *Canary and Cage-bird Life* for April 16th, 1909, Mr. L. Butterworth's lecture to the Rochdale Ornithological Club on "The Lizard Canary Fancy, Past and Present," is given. In it, this lemon-yellow variation, with its tendency to become paler, is described in connection with the Lizard Canary of forty years ago. At the same time, the "*duvet,*" or frilled variety, appeared. As these statements from an experienced and observant fancier are important historically, I give them in full, premising that this lemon-yellow colour in mules is well known to be due to cinnamon inheritance.

"When I first started to breed the Lizard Canary there was a strain of Lizards which was very plentiful in and around Rochdale, known as the Lemon Lizard, or Lemon Jonque, on account of the cap being a pale yellow colour, somewhat the colour of a lemon. In its nest feathers it had a back full of straight, narrow rowing; but after its first moult the colour of its cap and the tips of the small feathers were of the same pale yellow colour, the spangle being not nearly so distinct as that of the orange-coloured variety. Breeders, seeing that it stood no chance on the show bench, refused to breed with it, and, consequently, in a few years the strain died out.

"About the same time there was another strain, known as the Flat or Hollow-backed Lizard. This was a class of bird with a back full of large, distinct spangling, or moons, as we called them. The moons were distributed all over the back and not in straight, regular rows, as you see them in the Lizards of to-day. This class of bird had very often a *split* or *parting* down the centre of the back, and as it very rarely got into the money at any show, gradually became scarce, until it has almost met with the same fate as the Lemon Jonque. I should never pair two golds or two silvers together without a special reason. . . .

"I remember experimenting in this direction many years ago. I paired a gold cock with a gold hen, and succeeded in breeding some decent young from the pair. Then I inbred with two of the young ones, also both golds. The result was the feathers on the young birds bred from the inbred pair, instead of lying close to the body, grew the wrong way about. They turned up over the back just like those on a *Frizzle* fowl, which convinced me that you can go too far in that direction."

In classes 16 to 20 the original cinnamon displays similar variations to those in previous classes. Class 21 is specially interesting to us, as the only white Canary* ever seen by British fanciers was exhibited, gaining 1st prize, at the Crystal Palace shows of 1909 and 1910, and is undoubtedly of cinnamon descent. (*See* page 33.) In 22 to 26 we have the start of our present-day variegated varieties. Class 27 is interesting, as indicating what I call a cinnamon-green variegation, for these birds, the produce of a cinnamon cock with a dark-eyed hen, are all males, and undoubtedly show more pinkness of the eye than other green-variegated birds. They also frequently show a tendency to the dark green, almost black, London Fancy markings.

In class 28 we have the start of the London Fancy—now almost extinct—and its occurrence immediately after class 27 may be of some assistance in re-establishing this beautiful variety.

In class 29 we have the appearance, of which I have had experience, of a rich orange-yellow bird. The special quality of rich colour which characterises the Norwich Canary has probably its origin here.

Class 30, mentioned by Buffon as being in Hervieux's list, whether there or not, at all events shows that crest was known about 1750.

In our cinnamon muling experiments we have shown that position is correlated with cinnamon sporting and frills. In this manner our birds of position—Lancashire, Yorkshire, Dutch Frill, Belgian, etc.—have arisen.

We have thus been able to trace the origin of all our present-day varieties, the subsequent perfecting of the different classes being due to the careful selection and skilful breeding of many generations of fanciers. It only remains for some enterprising breeder to follow out the experiments farther and introduce some new varieties, *e.g.*, Fantail, Trumpeter, Black, Tumbler,* Silkie, and many others.

In the English (1718) translation of Hervieux the term "*duvet*" is taken to mean "rough-footed," and "*Panaché*" and "*Race de Panachez*" are both translated "*copple-crowned*." The one interpretation is as nonsensical as the other, and quite as bad as that of the writer already mentioned who describes "Isabelle" as pink. But the reference to copple-crowns is interesting, as probably indicating the existence of a crested Canary in England before 1718. One feels, however, that in the case of this translator one has to deal with a poultry or pigeon, and not a Canary fancier.

I may mention that Temminck, in his *Histoire Naturelle Générale des Gallinacés*, describes the Silk Fowl under the name of the *Coq à Duvet*, and gives it the scientific title of *Gallus Lanatus* (Tegetmeier's "Poultry Book," 1867).

Also, in support of my interpretation of "*Panaché*," let me quote the following :—

"*Description des Couleurs d'un Canari Panaché, observé avec M. de Montbeillard.*"†: "The shades and arrangement of the colours of the variegated Canaries differ exceedingly; some are black on the head, others not; some are spotted irregularly, and others with great regularity. The differences of colour are commonly perceived only on the upper part of the bird; they consist of two large black spots on each wing, the one before and the other behind, in a large crescent of the same colour placed on the back, pointing its concavity towards the head, and joining by its horns to the two anterior black spots of the wings. Lastly, the tail is surrounded behind by a half-collar of grey, which seems to be a compound colour resulting from the intimate mixture of black and yellow."

* *See* "Canary Breeding" for coloured figure.

* Since writing this I have discovered a Tumbler Linnet as already mentioned.

† Buffon's "Nat. Hist. of Birds." London, 1793.

At this stage also, let me refer shortly to another old book on song-birds that agrees in every detail with my interpretation of Hervieux's list of varieties of the Canary, and also adds some additional information. The title is: "A Natural History of English Song-Birds and Such of the Foreign as are usually Brought Over, and Esteem'd for their Singing, etc." By Mr. Eleazer Albin. London, 1759 (3rd Edit.).

Albin's "Song-birds."

Albin's knowledge of the song-birds he mentions, and their proper treatment in confinement, is so complete and excellent (*e.g.*, his treatment of the Goldfinch with regard to hemp-seed) that this little book would be an up-to-date guide at the present day. On this account I attach much importance to his list of varieties of the Canary given on page 86:—

Albin's List of Varieties of Canary in 1759.

1. "Bright lovely yellow, with jet-black spots." This undoubtedly describes the London Fancy Canary, which, like the Lizard ("agate" of Hervieux), we believe to be derived from the cinnamon, and which is now almost extinct.

2. "The mealy-bird, so named from the mealy kind of colour which seems to cover his feathers." This is the buff bird of the present day.

3. "Mottled birds: their chief colour is white mottled with black or brownish spots." These are our green-variegated and cinnamon-variegated varieties.

4. "All yellow." Our clear yellow.

5. "All white."

6. "Grey." This is the original grey, the *Serin Gris* of Hervieux, which is closely allied to the cinnamon Canary.

7. Other varieties not named.

"The Epitome of the Art of Husbandry." London, 1675. By J. B., Gent.—At this date in England Canaries were green, and variegation had evidently not occurred, for the author, Joseph Blagrove, who is particularly well informed with regard to singing birds, says (p. 107): "Many Country-People cannot distinguish a Canary from one of our common Green Birds, etc."*

Blagrove's References.

The above reference would seem to indicate that, in spite of a probable early importation of the Canary into England, little progress had been made in its domestication, and it also lends colour to the legend that the initial varieties (including even the London Fancy) were introduced by immigrant Huguenots (*cf.* Hervieux's list of varieties).

COMPARATIVE EVOLUTION OF OTHER DOMESTICATED SPECIES

It will probably be found that in other domesticated animals a similar line of development has been followed, and I have mentioned one or two points of similarity in the domestic fowl. In it the Game varieties seem to form a more or less direct line from *Gallus bankiva*, while those which show greatest diversity in type generally and in plumage owe this variability to the original Cochin, which in 1867 not only included a definite cinnamon variety and a white variety in its family, but also had as its prevailing colour buff of various shades—*e.g.*, lemon Cochins, silver-buff Cochins, etc. (*vide* Tegetmeier's "Poultry Book," 1867).

The Evolution of the Domestic Fowl.

The Cochin shows the variability which we have seen to occur in cinnamon Canaries and hybrids.

1. According to Tegetmeier ("Poultry Book," 1867), this variety of fowl has the defect of "twisted primary quill feathers" much more frequently than any other. It is probably because this "defect" was made a disqualifying point in poultry shows that the Frizzled Cochin has not become an established variety.

2. The Silk Cochin, or Emu Fowl, is known.

3. Grouse and Partridge Cochins represent the spangled varieties.

4. "There is a tendency in Cochins to produce an extraordinary number of cocks in nearly every brood" (Tegetmeier). We

* *See* another reference to "The Epitome" on p. 12.

have thus a sexual peculiarity in Cochins just as in cinnamon Canaries (*cf.* "Mendelian Inheritance," p. 31).

5. Cochins are also peculiarly subject to visual defects, like albino birds. "The eye

CREST-BRED CANARY.

should be red. . . . In all cases of blindness pearl-eyed birds" (a further stage of albinism) "have been the sufferers" (Tegetmeier). This pearl eye is said to be "very hereditary" in Cochins (Wright's "Poultry Book," 1902). C. B. Davenport, in "Inheritance in Poultry," quoting McGrew (1904, p. 526), mentions the Buff Cochin as probably the oldest Chinese variety, and cites records of the oldest monastery—Hoangho—to the effect that this fowl was cultivated by the brotherhood 1,500 years ago.

From the same author a very important confirmation of our theory is obtained. Referring to the indigenous Buff Cochin of China, a traveller says that "no two can be found of exactly the same colour: some are a chestnut colour, others darker, and some quite light" (McGrew, 1901, p. 527). With regard to the Buff Cochins first imported into England, Wright agrees with Tegetmeier in saying that the colour varied from lightest silver buff and silver cinnamon, through lemons and buffs, to the deepest coloured cinnamons.

Thus we have in the Cochin the same variability that we have seen to occur in our cinnamon sports and hybrids, and we can understand how *Gallus bankiva*, through a cinnamon sport, might be the ancestor of all our present varieties without the aid of a separate ancestor for the Aseel-Malay Group, as invoked by Davenport. We have, moreover, evidence of the sporting tendency in *Bankiva*, for Darwin, quoting Mr. Blyth, says that the species varies considerably in the wild state, some from near the Himalaya being paler coloured than those from other parts of India.*

An interesting point also in connection with this cinnamon sport origin of all our domestic varieties (which sport occurs, as we have shown, from the female side) is the following statement by Blumenbach, 1813 (given by Tegetmeier):—"What we have observed above concerning the aberrations of the formative nisus—namely, that it occurs less frequently in animals of the male sex than in females—is confirmed by the examples of this variety of poultry, distinguished by the protuberance on the head; for of this deformity very slight traces indeed are found in the cocks, and those but seldom."

Darwin supports Blumenbach in his statement that this protuberance, with its accompanying crest, was originally confined to the female sex (*loc. cit.*, p. 270).

CREST CANARY.

Corroborative Evidence.

Since writing the above, Mr. Lewer has sent me a most interesting article on "The Origin of Our Breeds of Poultry," by Henry Scherren, F.Z.S., M.B.O.U., which appeared in *The Feathered World* for October 11th, 1907 (with coloured plate).

*Darwin, "The Variation of Animals and Plants under Domestication," 1875, Vol. I., p. 247.

This will be found to corroborate my theory. Aldrovandus' classification in 1599 is given :—

1. Common farm poultry, with Game characteristics, the female slightly crested.

2. Paduans, a crested variety with pale-coloured (yellow) beak and legs, and the wild plumage broken up with white, green, red and yellow.

3. A "buskined," or feather-legged race with similar characteristics. Evidently the original Cochin.

BELGIAN CANARY.

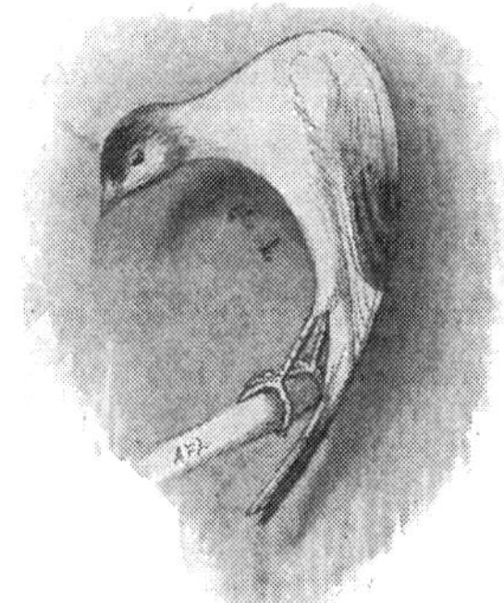

SCOTCH FANCY CANARY.

4. A dwarf race. The original Bantam.

5. Turkish fowls, in which Lewis Wright saw a fairly strong resemblance to the Pencilled Hamburghs. (Compare my origin of the Lizard Canary.)

6. Persians. Tailless or rumpless fowls.

Aldrovandus also mentions :—

7. Frizzled Fowl.

8. Woolly Fowl. The Silkie Fowl of the present day.

Buff Poultry and Cinnamon Canaries.

The term "Buff" in poultry indicates colour, not quality of feather. The buff colour has been grafted on to the different varieties of poultry exactly in the same manner as cinnamon in Canaries—*e.g.*, Cinnamon Norwich, Cinnamon Crests, Cinnamon-marked Yorkshires.

Davenport, after showing that the buff colour of the Cochin is of high antiquity, and stating that it has been transferred to many other breeds by crossing—*e.g.*, Buff Wyandotte—quotes McGrew (1901, p. 24) :—

"Two distinct lines were produced under different methods. One was formed from Wyandotte-Buff Cochin cross; the other came through the Rhode Island Red-Wyandotte cross. The Rhode Island Red is, however, as is well known, a direct descendant of the Buff Cochin. The Buff Plymouth Rocks were derived *directly* or *indirectly* from the Buff Cochin. The history of the Buff Leghorn is the same—the offspring of a yellow Danish Leghorn cock and Buff Cochin pullets mated with a yellow Leghorn hen. The produce—three-fourths yellow Leghorn and one-fourth Buff Cochin—gave (Wyckoff, 1904, p. 527) the first Buff Leghorns ever shown."

The Buff "Orpingtons," a highly modern and mongrel breed—have a similar history, being chiefly Buff Cochin and Dorking (Wright, 1902, p. 296).

The behaviour of the buff colour in these crosses is exactly the same as we have shown to occur in the cinnamon colour of Canaries; for the Buff Leghorns, for instance, were not obtained directly from the buff mother, but from her sons, in the same manner as we have demonstrated cinnamon feathers in Canaries to be inherited from the male side. We may safely assume that the buff varieties of poultry correspond with the cinnamon varieties of the Canary; that both are due to an original early cinnamon sport; and that this sport or mutation is, in all probability, the cause of the great diversity of all the varieties of the species.

Early "Sport" in the Pigeon.

In the case of the Pigeon also evidence is adducible which proves that the first change from the Blue Rock Pigeon (*Columba livia*) was one in the direction of albinism.

In "The Dovecot and Aviary" (Rev. E. S. Dixon, 1851), the author gives a passage in full from Varro, who lived from 116–27 B.C. He translates it thus:—

"If ever you should establish a Dovery, you would consider the birds your own, although they were wild. For two sorts of Pigeons are usually kept in a Dovery: the one belonging to rural districts, and, as others call it, a Rock Pigeon, which is kept in towers, and among the beams and rafters (*columinibus*) of a farmhouse, and which is on that account named 'Columba,' since from natural timidity it seeks the highest of roofs; whence it happens that the rustic Pigeons especially seek for towers, to which they may at their own pleasure fly from the fields, and return thither. The second kind of Pigeons is more quiet; and contented with the food given at home, it accustoms itself to feed within the limits of the gate. This kind is of a *white* colour principally, but the country sort is without white or variegated colours. From these two original stocks a third mixed or mongrel kind is bred for the sake of the produce."

SUMMARY OF CONCLUSIONS

All Canary varieties have arisen from a grey or cinnamon sport occurring in the female—the pallid type of variation which occurs at present among many wild birds.

This theory is advanced from a study of:

1. Wild sports generally, in nature and in confinement.

2. Cinnamon and cinnamon-bred hybrids, which frequently show characteristics of Canary varieties arising *de novo.*

4. The earliest Canary literature.

5. Collateral evidence of a similar nature in poultry and Pigeons.

Inheritance of Eye Colour.

"Dark-eye" and "pink-eye" are found to behave generally in Mendelian fashion, for from Group IV. (d.e. × d.e.), page 17, it is evident that there is a homozygous type of dark-eyed Canary. Also from Group IV., 2, 3, 4, it appears that there is also a heterozygous* or impure form occurring in the male as well as the female.

The pink-eyed birds being homozygous,* if we arrange our groups of matings according to Mendelian principles, we find:

Group III. d.e. × p.e. Matings, 33. Progeny, 110. Dark-eyed, 110.

In this group dark-eyed is dominant and pink-eyed recessive.

The following heterozygous matings:—

IV. 2 d.e. F × d.e. F.	Matings, 5	Progeny, 21	d.e., 15	p.e., 6	
,, 3 F d.e. × d.e.	,, 3	,, 12	,, 9	,, 3	
,, 4 d.e. F × d.e.	,, 4	,, 10	,, 8	,, 2	
		43	32	11	
The result closely approximates to:			3	: 1	

The following heterozygous × homozygous matings:—

III. 2 F d.e. × p.e.	Matings, 1	Progeny, 3	d.e., 1	p.e., 2	
,, 3 d.e. F × p.e.	,, 3	,, 12	,, 4	,, 5	Unknown, 3.
,, 4 F d.e. × F p.e.	,, 1	,, 2	,, 0	,, 2	
,, 5 d.e. F × F p.e.	,, 2	,, 6	,, 5	,, 1	
		23	10	10	

* For explanation of these terms see pp. 31-2.

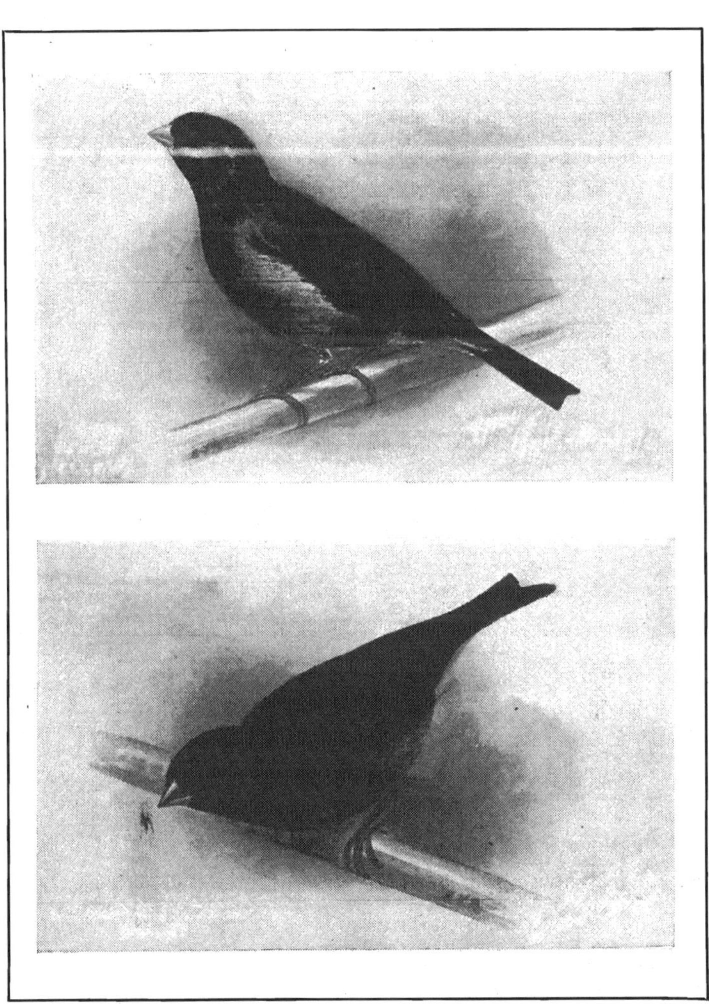

TWO OF THE OLDEST VARIETIES OF THE CANARY.

A Yellow London Fancy and a Clear-Capped Gold Lizard.

This result gives the required 50 per cent. of each.

One would expect the female of the homozygous type of dark-eyed Canary to be homozygous, as well as the male, and I have evidence of this in several of my females giving very large percentages of dark-eyed males when mated to pink-eyed males, the proportion of 6 to 1 occurring several times. It is probable that a homozygous dark-eyed female would be completely dominant over the cinnamon male, and that male dark-eyed progeny only would result.

A Suggestion for the Breeding of Male Birds Only.

I can prove the occurrence of wild heterozygous males by the following most interesting result, viz., a family of young Greenfinches which I bred in 1908. The father is a wild caught bird that I selected as being of the colour which I think indicates a heterozygous nature, not only in wild birds, but also in Canaries—viz., a colour I call cinnamon-green. To any casual observer, however, the bird would pass as a normally coloured Greenfinch. The mother is one of my pale cinnamon—almost creamy-white—Greenfinches already mentioned.

An Interesting Result.

The family of five consisted of four cinnamons and one of a greyish type, all much paler than the normally coloured young of Greenfinches. Unfortunately the whole family died from one to three months old, and on examination proved to be four cinnamon cocks and one grey hen.

Other characters which I have proved to behave as recessives are: (*a*) buffness, (*b*) crest-bred plain-headedness. Their contrasted characters—(*a*) yellowness, (*b*) crestedness—exhibit more or less imperfect dominance (*see* "Canary Breeding").

Inheritance of Other Characters.

It is essential in studying Mendelian phenomena as occurring in fancy varieties that the most strict definition of the characters under examination be made, and that their nomenclature, and behaviour under varying conditions be thoroughly understood.

A fancier is trained to detect differences which others are quite unable to see, and his success depends on the careful balancing of factors which to the uninitiated are unobservable.

It would therefore save much confusion if sharply-defined facts only were taken into consideration meantime, and if no assumptions were made with regard to technical "fancy" points, which the skilled breeder alone understands.

On the other hand, it may help the fancier in his breeding operations if I give the following short account of Mendelian inheritance with an explanation of some of its nomenclature. The term "gamete" is applied to the reproductive elements—male and female—spermatozoon and ovum. The cell formed by the union of a male and female gamete is called a "zygote." A zygote formed by the union of two similar gametes (*e.g.*, both with pure dark-eyed character) is called a "homozygote," while the term "heterozygote" is applied to the zygote formed by the union of two dissimilar gametes (*e.g.*, one with the pure dark-eyed, and the other with the pure pink-eyed character).

Mendelian Inheritance.

A simple and fairly typical case of Mendelian inheritance is shown by my dark-eyed male × pink-eyed female matings (Group III.). This may be more easily understood by the following diagram, where d stands for the pure dark-eyed character, p for the pure pink-eyed character, and (d) for the impure or heterozygous dark-eyed character.

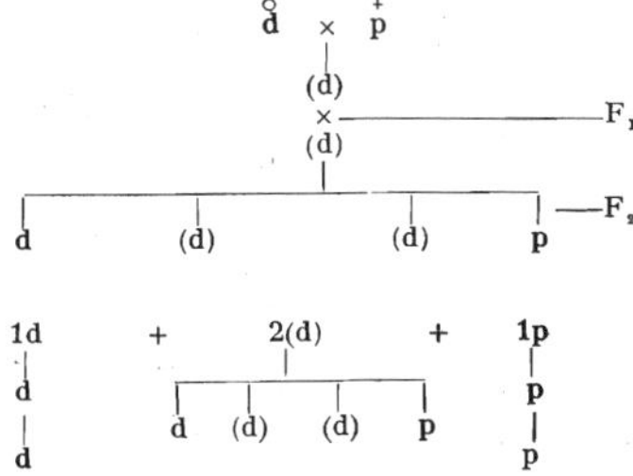

In the first cross (F_1) all the young are dark-eyed and heterozygous, d being dominant and p recessive. When these young are interbred, the proportions obtained are 3 dark-eyed to 1 pink-eyed, 3 to 1, 75 per cent. to 25 per cent. (Group IV., 2, 3, 4). The 3 dark-eyed on being tested are found to consist of 1 pure dark, and 2 impure dark, so that the composition

SILVER-GREY STARLING.
Exhibited at the Crystal Palace, 1910, by Mr. P. Walsh.
(See footnote p. 23.)

of F_2 is 1d + 2 (d) + 1 p, or 25 per cent., 50 per cent., 25 per cent., the typical Mendelian proportion. Of these the d breed pure, and the p breed pure, but from the 2 (d) the same proportions are again obtained, viz., 1d + 2(d) + 1p. The inheritance of eye colour, however, does not behave throughout in simple Mendelian fashion, being complicated with the question of sex as already explained in connection with cinnamon inheritance. In order to explain on Mendelian lines the results of the reciprocal mating to that already given, viz., pink-eyed male × dark-eyed female, it is necessary to refer to the interesting parallel case in the Currant Moth (*Abraxas grossulariata*) given by Doncaster in Report IV. to the Evolution Committee of the Royal Society, where the explanation of Bateson and Punnett with regard to this mating is given. They suppose that (1) femaleness is dominant; (2) that female individuals are heterozygous in respect of sex, having the constitution ♀ ♂, and producing male-bearing and female-bearing eggs in equal numbers; and that males are homozygous, of constitution ♂ ♂ producing only male-bearing spermatozoa; (3) that there is a gametic repulsion between femaleness and the dark-eyed character.

The following table gives their explanation of this mating of homozygous pink-eyed male × heterozygous dark-eyed female Canary :—

Parents.	Constitution.	Gametes.	Offspring.	
Dark-eyed female	d p ♀ ♂	p ♀, d ♂	p p ♀ ♂	= pink-eyed females 50 %
Pink-eyed male	p p ♂ ♂	p ♂, p ♂	d p ♂ ♂	= dark-eyed males 50 %

As the same result is obtained with a wild female, it is supposed that all wild females of the Currant Moth are heterozygous with regard to colour.

This theory that all wild females are heterozygous in colour is interesting from the point of view of my theory of the evolution of all our Canary varieties from the wild albinistic female, and, so far, in my Canary matings of this description (Group I.), my results are in accordance with the theory. Nevertheless, it is doubtful if *all* wild females are heterozygous in colour, just as it is probably not the case that the ordinary black-eyed hen Canaries are necessarily hybrids (heterozygous) in the pink-eye character, as supposed by Durham and Marryatt (Report IV., Evolution Committee of Royal Society, p. 60). For I have had long experience of the much inbred crested variety, pure dark-eyed both on the male and female side (Group IV.). If the females had been heterozygous in colour, some of the 283 young would certainly have shown pink-eye, or cinnamon

COLOUR, POSITION, FORM AND FEATHER VARIATION IN THE CANARY.
A white Canary and a Dutch Frill exhibited at the Crystal Palace, 1910, by Mr. W. Kiesel and Mr. C. I. Young.

feathers; this did not occur. I have also had experience of dark-eyed females being almost perfectly dominant over pink-eyed males—*i.e.*, the dark-eyed female is homozygous. In the fancier's view, also, it stands to reason that there must be a difference between a pure dark-eyed female, and one bred from a pink-eyed ancestry by a single dark-eyed cross. In like manner it is certain that although the majority of wild males may be homozygous in colour, heterozygous wild males occur (*see* account of my Greenfinch family on p. 31). The following table explains the constitution of the pure dark-eyed female, heterozygous in sex, and also of the offspring—all males—obtained from her and a pink-eyed male.

Parents.	Constitution.	Gametes.	Offspring.	
Pure dark-eyed female	d d ♀ ♂	d ♀, d ♂	d p ♂ ♀	= dark-eyed males, heterozygous in sex and colour, 50 %
Pink-eyed male	p p ♂ ♂	p ♂, p ♂	d p ♂ ♂	= dark-eyed males, heterozygous in colour only, 50 %

In the offspring d p ♂ ♀, dark-eyedness and maleness are dominant over pink-eyedness and femaleness. In the offspring d p ♂ ♂, dark-eyedness is likewise dominant over pink-eyedness, and the gametic constitution includes pink-eyed male gametes.

If we suppose the pure dark-eyed female to be homozygous also in sex, d d ♀ ♀, there would result 100 per cent. dark-eyed male progeny, heterozygous in colour and sex (d p ♂ ♀).

Unit Characters.

The above matings with their gametic constitution and the results obtained will be simplified by studying what are, after all, the chief points of importance in the Mendelian theory, viz., the conception of the *Unit Character*, and the principle of *Gametic Segregation*.

R. C. Punnett, in his "Mendelism" (Bowes & Bowes, Cambridge), says:—

"The heterozygote frequently exhibits the form of the pure dominant, from which it can only be distinguished by the test of breeding. That the recessive character is likewise carried is shown by the fact that when heterozygotes are bred *inter se*, one quarter of the offspring produced are recessive.

"There are cases, however, in which the heterozygote does not resemble the dominant, but has a character peculiar to itself.

"These facts led Mendel to the conception of pairs of unit characters, of which either can be carried by any one gamete to the exclusion of the other. A fundamental property of the gamete is that it can bear either one such a pair of characters, though not both. But the heterozygote is formed by the union of two dissimilar gametes, and consequently the cells of the individual into which it grows must contain both characters. To reconcile these statements it must be supposed that at some cell division in the formation of gametes a primitive germ-cell divides into two dissimilar portions. Instead of the dominant and recessive constituents passing in combination to the two daughter-cells, the whole of the dominant goes into one of these, and the whole of the recessive into the other. From this it follows that every gamete contains one only of such a pair of characters, *i.e.*, it is *pure* for that character. In other words, a simple heterozygote *produces gametes of two kinds, and produces them in equal numbers*. The characters are said to *segregate* in the gametes.

Gametic Segregation.

In this conception lies the simple explanation of the facts, that from the inbred heterozygote comes dominants and recessives in the proportion of 3 : 1, and that only one dominant in three is pure, the other two being heterozygotes. (*See* formula below.)

"A convenient system of notation is to denote the heterozygote by the letters D R, thus signifying that it gives off equal numbers of gametes bearing the dominant and recessive characters. On the same system the pure dominant and the pure recessive are represented by the terms D D and R R respectively. So far we have considered only the results obtained by inbreeding the heterozygotes.

$$\left.\begin{matrix} DR \\ \times \\ DR \end{matrix}\right\} = DD + DR + DR + RR$$

"The theory of gametic purity can be further tested by deducing from it the results which should follow from crossing the heterozygote with either of the homozygotes, and seeing how far such theoretical results accord with those obtained by experiment. When the heterozygote D R is crossed with the recessive R R each dominant and each recessive gamete arising from the former can unite only with a recessive gamete formed by the latter. Consequently, we should look for the production of equal numbers of zygotes of the constitution D R and R R."

This is what happens (*see* Group III., 2, 3, 4, 5). Half the offspring are pure pink-eyed recessives, and the other half are dark-eyed dominants which may all be proved to carry the pink-eyed character, *i.e.*, are heterozygotes.

$$\left.\begin{matrix} \mathrm{D\,R} \\ \times \\ \mathrm{R\,R} \end{matrix}\right\} = \mathrm{D\,R} + \mathrm{R\,R}$$

" Similarly, when the heterozygote D R is crossed with the pure dominant form D D we should from theory expect all the offspring to be dominant in form and one-half of them to be pure dominant. Here again experiment has borne out theory. The generalisation known as the principle of gametic segregation may be regarded as firmly established on the phenomena exhibited by plants and animals when strains are crossed which possess pairs of differentiating characters. Whether the principle applies universally or not can only be answered by subsequent experiments."

In this position we leave the important subject of inheritance in Canaries, with the hope that fanciers may be induced to study the theoretical side of their hobby, and invariably to make full notes of all their matings, for such points as we have discussed, besides being of value for breeding purposes, are full of significance with respect to *inheritance* generally, and details which seem valueless to-day may be the basis of the great discoveries of to-morrow.

DR. GALLOWAY'S CLEAR YELLOW SISKIN-CANARY.

Winner of many first prizes 1908-10 and also Championship Diploma for Best Hybrid, Crystal Palace, 1909 and 1910.

WELL-ARRANGED CAGES, SHOWING FITTINGS.
A corner of Mr. Barnett's (the noted Crest Breeder) Bird-room.

CHAPTER IV

THE BREEDING-ROOM

Site and Surroundings.

OF all matters connected with bird-keeping, that of the room, cage, or aviary is generally the first to be considered, for healthiness of surroundings is certainly one of the most important factors of our hobby. It may be well to state at the outset that pure air is essential, whether the birds be kept in a warm, cosy room or in an outdoor aviary; and there are circumstances which may make either of these general methods advisable.

A fancier's Canary room should be selected with some amount of care. Any room will not do, though too frequently any room *has* to do, on the "Hobson's choice" principle. The birds have to spend their lives in it, and it is only a question of common sense to insist that the conditions under which they live shall be as favourable as possible. We say "as possible," because a fancier cannot always have everything exactly as he may wish, but is obliged to make the best of things as he finds them. It is not every house in which there is a spare room, or in which the spare room is the most suitable for the purpose; but an effort should be made to secure one which has the full benefit of the morning sun, without, however, being exposed to the mid-day heat, which renders the atmosphere of any bird-room very uncomfortable.

Birds are the most practical exponents of the "early to bed and early to rise" principle we know of, and it is therefore not well to place them in circumstances which, to a great extent, subvert this order of things. The first streak of daylight sees them on the move, and long before the close of day their heads are tucked into their wings. Their day is not our day, but we are very apt to forget it. The value of the early sunshine to them is incalculable, for it enables them to begin work at a time that is in accordance with their natural instincts, not the least important part of which is to attend to the wants of their young.

Canaries will make a longer season in a room where they are not done up by the heat, which seems to fag them out, and throw them into moult before the proper season. With muling stock—*i.e.*, hens kept exclusively for breeding Goldfinch and other hybrids—this is a matter of the utmost importance, as their season does not begin till the Canary season is half spent, and the value of late nests will be sufficiently apparent. A cool room virtually prolongs a season, and the difference between losing a nest and gaining an extra one amounts to two, which is a valuable consideration. From these remarks it will be observed that a room with windows facing south-east is the most suitable for Canaries when breeding, while in the case of a room used exclusively for hybrid breeding windows facing full east are preferable.

The Question of Temperature.

Avoid a room that abuts on to the house, in the way that so many of the kitchens, with a room overhead, are built in the yards of small tenements nowadays. These rooms have generally very thin walls, and have at least two sides exposed, which makes them miserably cold in winter and as miserably hot in summer; the temperature out-of-doors is much more equable than in places of this kind. Sudden alternations are most injurious to the birds, and to these they are sure to be subject in rooms such as those to which we have referred. We have more than one such in mind while penning these lines, and have rarely known a really good season's work to have been carried out in any of them; knowing how sensitive the Canary is to sudden and frequent changes of temperature, we attribute the want of success as much to this cause as to any other. It is a cause, too, which affects the bird most at a time when it is least able to bear up against it; that is, during the breeding season, when the hens, at least, are not in a normal condition as regards health, but are more or less affected by the state of body natural to the period of incubation. Recollect that each pair of birds is boxed up in a house of about twenty inches frontage and not a foot in depth, and that some cages are placed where the occupants seldom get a gleam of sunshine, while others have no protection from the scorching rays of the summer sun. They have to make the best of their position, and have not the opportunities for exercise which aviary tenants have—they cannot plume themselves in a warm corner or retreat into the shade, but are entirely dependent upon the care and forethought of others for their comfort as well as for the necessaries of their mere existence.

Attention to these things constitutes the difference between a well-ordered room and one which, from floor to ceiling, shows at all points indications of want of thought. This question of aspect and general suitability is one on which we feel perfectly satisfied more depends than many imagine, and is probably the key to the solution of the question of varying success.

Ventilation.

The question of draughts and ventilation demands close consideration in connection with the breeding-room, and we may here indicate some arrangements which will be found useful. Something will depend on the room itself. If it be an attic with an ordinary lift-up skylight, it should be borne in mind that few of these windows shut closely, even if well made; they are constructed to exclude rain, but are very draughty contrivances. The ledge on which the frame rests ought to be covered with thin felt, or some such yielding substance, to ensure a close fit; and more especially during the blustering winter months. The aperture should be covered with wirework, through which the lever used to raise the window can act, and it can then be elevated or depressed at pleasure; the wired frame, too, presents an effectual bar to the escape of any birds which may find their way out of their cages, and also proves equally effective in preventing the ingress of any marauding cat. For a similar reason, if there be a fireplace in the room—one of the best ventilators—it should also be wired over; for where the chimney-pots are of primitive construction, or where there are none at all, cats not unfrequently gain access by the chimney.

In the case of an ordinary window a wire covering is still indispensable, and a perforated zinc contrivance, six or eight inches deep, may be adapted to the top for use when the state of the weather might render it unadvisable to allow it to be opened without some protection. A similar contrivance in the door or in the wall above it, and as near the ceiling as possible, will assist to keep up a supply of fresh air. A ventilating brick, or one of the many simple ventilators which can be opened and closed at will, may be inserted in the wall or door, instead of the perforated zinc, and any trouble or expense incurred in doing the work thoroughly will repay itself in the health and comfort of the stock.

As it is so near the roof, it might be imagined that an attic would be either uncomfortably warm or correspondingly cold; but the best breeding-room we ever had was what Johnson defines to be "the *topmost* room of the house," although he gives the meaning of cock-loft to be "the room *above* the garret": perhaps the current of air in the cock-loft acts as a gulf stream to the attic—a sort of atmospheric fly-wheel.

Methods of Heating.

A breeding-room can hardly be said to be complete without some kind of heating apparatus. To this it is probable some may demur, but we can only say in reply that those are fortunate who can do without it. Such a variety of circumstances combine to make the usage of one district different from that of another, that the "custom of the port," with its statistical results, must not be accepted as a standard rule calculated to produce the like elsewhere. Difference in latitude and variation in other physical relations make just all the difference between the natural productions of any two places, and a certain amount of artificial treatment must be resorted to in order to bring them on a level. We do not say that Canaries would feel the rigour of an ordinary English winter more in one part of the country than in another, but the critical time is when Nature begins to wake up from her winter's sleep. In some places she seems to slumber with one eye open, and in others to relapse into a state of such insensibility as to suggest no awakening. In the one instance she is quick in answering to the call, and balmy airs soon arouse her from temporary inactivity: in the other, pulse is almost dead and circulation is induced only by long and gradual effort.

So with occupants of our bird-rooms, who are soon affected by external influences; their awakening indoors is simultaneous with that out-of-doors, and every swelling bud or early spring flower is but the indicator of a corresponding spring-time in bird-life. When the one is late in being roused into life, so is the other; and we hear in some places of pairing, nesting, breeding, and all the excitement attending it, weeks, aye, almost months before those in a less favoured district dare even think of making any preparations for the campaign, lest too much haste might result in disaster. To obviate the evils arising from this, prudence would suggest that where a reasonably early start is contemplated, something should be done to assist in maintaining an equable temperature, so that breeding operations may be followed out independently of the weather. The way in which Canaries are affected by climatic alternations will be pointed out in our chapters on general management; our object here is to explain simple methods of warming the breeding-room, by which means the dangers attendant on early nests may be averted, and other discomforts which wait on a late spring considerably ameliorated. This last is the true object of artificial heating; not to force birds out of season, but to make the most of them in season—to combat adverse circumstances by means that most nearly approximate to those employed by Nature.

Hot-Water Pipes.

The best means of heating a bird-room is undoubtedly by hot-water pipes that pass along the side of the room, for which the water is kept hot either by a stove or gas jet arranged in a casing *outside* the room. But as such a construction is somewhat expensive, and as all houses are not convenient for equipment of this kind, the working-man is greatly handicapped in availing himself of it. There are, however, some handy hot-water coils which can be arranged in a room for heating with a gas jet which is enclosed in a small copper casing, and has a flue to carry off the deleterious products of combustion. Mr. H. Dewhurst, of West Kensington, London, brought out such an apparatus some years ago known as the "Economic Heating Apparatus," of which he is the sole maker. On this page is an illustration of the apparatus, and it will be seen that it takes up but little space. It can be stood either down the centre of the room or at one side—in any position, indeed, that is most convenient, for it can be fixed anywhere by screwing it to the floor through the flanges at the bottom of the two legs. *b* is the copper casing enclosing the gas jet and boiler, with the circulating pipes *c c* attached. This apparatus can be heated by oil, and we understand that an automatic oil tank will last from fifteen to twenty hours without re-filling. For ourselves, however, we certainly prefer to use gas. The tubes *d d* are of welded iron; *e* is a copper tank, from which the apparatus is fed; the water passes from it by means of the fine tube *f* into the lower large tube *d*; a condensing pipe *g* completes a most efficient apparatus. Mr. Dewhurst says of it: "It constitutes a great advantage in the utilisation of hot water for heating purposes, and is constructed upon the principle embodied in the well-known fact that radiated heat is the best and most healthy form of heat. The importance of this feature is evident, as the injurious products given off by most heating appliances make the atmosphere unpleasant and detrimental to health. By reason of the construction of the boiler and cover the heat is generated more quickly than with coal boilers. The absence of dirt, the saving in labour, and the facility of maintaining any desired temperature are some of the other advantages of this system which combine to render it superior to a coal fire, while its indisputable hygienic qualities make it superior to any existing gas stove. Without attention and without firing, and consequent risk of over-heating and explosion, a regular and uniform temperature may be maintained for hours at a time, by simply setting the gas tap. Another advantage of the heater is that the boiler can be fixed in an independent position outside the room,

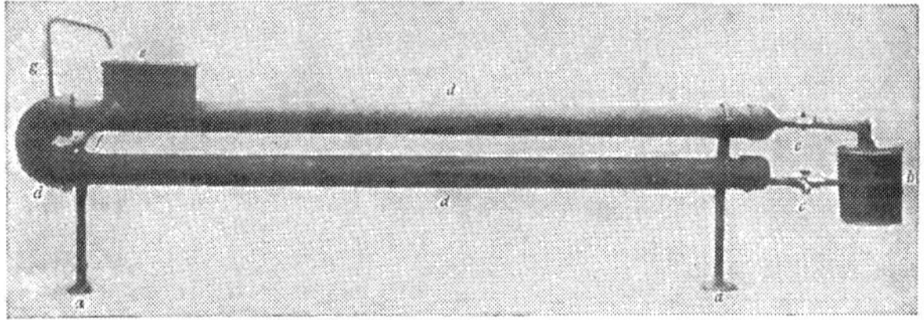

MR. H. DEWHURST'S "ECONOMIC" HEATING APPARATUS.

and connected through the wall to the radiator; as it is self-contained, an experienced fitter is not required to fix it. The boilers, tanks, and boiler cases are made of stout, hard copper throughout, which does not rust and will wear for years. The tubes are of heavy welded iron, and the fittings of best malleable iron. The burners are made of brass, and are adapted for atmospheric flames and cannot rust."

These heaters can be obtained in any size and constructed to suit any special place, either vertical or horizontal, or to fit any angle. No. 1 size, suitable for any ordinary room, has a length over all of 6 ft. by 1 ft. 6 in. by 7 in., and to keep the room at a temperature of say 60° or 65° will consume about 4 cubic feet of gas per hour. This would involve a cost of 1d. for 8 hours with gas at 2s. 11d. per 1,000, which compares favourably with any other means of heating. We use one of these apparatus in our own bird-room at the commencement of the breeding season, when the nights are cold, and have found it a most efficient means of maintaining a general temperature at a nominal cost.

Electric Stoves.

One of the latest heating apparatus by which a bird-room may be kept at a genial temperature is an electric stove patented by Messrs. Rorke Bros., of Barnes, London, a diagram of which is shown on this page. Messrs. Rorke's description of it is as follows: "A is the electric stove; no lamps are required in this, as the heat is produced by the passage of electricity through wires; it is therefore non-luminous. The electricity for the stove is taken from any source of supply at any ordinary voltage. One of the supply wires is broken at the automatic switch D, with the result that when the automatic switch is 'on' the electric stove is 'on,' and when the switch is 'off' the stove is 'off.' The movements of the switch D are governed by the maximum and minimum thermometer B. This thermometer is of the ordinary type, in which the mercury rises in one limb, say the right, for a rise of temperature and for a fall of temperature it rises in the left limb; as a consequence the two contacts (one on the right and the other on the left) shown in the illustration (which enter into the tube by thin platinum wires) are

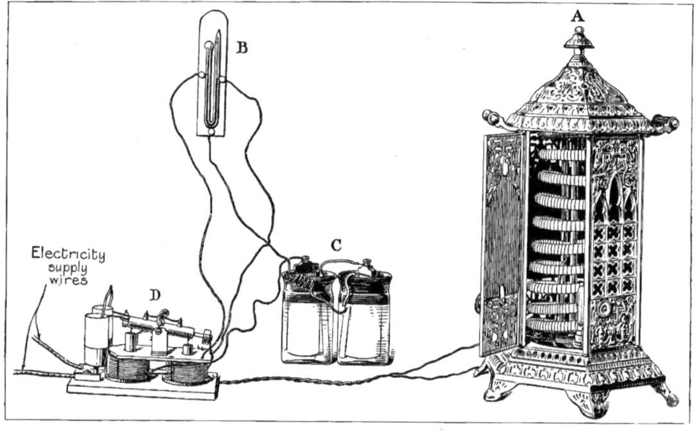

MESSRS. RORKE'S ELECTRIC STOVE.

NORWICH CANARIES
Clear Yellow (Colour-fed)
Ticked Buff (Colour-fed)
Even-marked Yellow (Natural Colour)

each alternately covered or left free from the mercury column. If now the contacts are put at say 55° F. on the left and 60° on the right, and a further contact is made at the bottom of the U, it is clear that an electric circuit can be established through the thermometer either when the temperature falls to 55° or when it rises to 60°. By using this fact the energy from two ordinary small bell batteries C is made to pass either round a small electric magnet on the front part of the switch D, which closes the switch, or round a similar magnet at the back part, which opens the switch. By an arrangement in the switch itself the small current generated by the bell batteries is cut off and left ready for the next movement. The general action of the system is as follows: Suppose the main supply is turned on and the temperature is at 54° or anything lower, the switch D will be found 'on,' and the current will pass through it to the stove A. The temperature will slowly rise in the room until it reaches 60°, when the right-hand side circuit in the thermometer will be made, and, as before explained, the switch will move 'off,' and the stove be disconnected, to come on again only if the temperature falls to 55°. It is obvious that the range of temperature can be anything required; for instance, 60° to 62°. Owing to the accuracy of the thermometer the system is quite infallible, and can be left practically without attention. The cost is cut down to its scientific minimum owing to the certainty that the supply will be cut right off the instant it is not required. Consequently the system can compete as regards cost with any other forms of heating without their attendant disadvantages. In some cases it is a good plan to stand the stove over or near a ventilating grating —if there be such in the room—as in this manner a supply of fresh air is drawn into the room and heated in its passage through the stove. Sometimes, also, it is worth consideration to place a small dish of water near or on the stove—not, as with gas or oil stoves, to endeavour ineffectually to trap the poisonous fumes, but in order to keep the air at a proper degree of moisture; but this, of course, is a refinement that in no way concerns the system described."

Messrs. Rorke further inform us that the cost for working the system from Christmas to April with electricity, at the "power and heating" rate of 1d. per unit for a room of 1,000 cubic feet, is under 20s. for an average winter, the temperature maintained being 55° to 60°.

Gas-Stoves.

We also know many fanciers who have used—and do still use—the Hygienic Syphon gas-stove as a means of heating their bird-room, and with every success. This stove condenses its own fumes into water. There are sundry other means of heating the room, such as a gas jet below several inverted flower-pots arranged one upon another, oil-stoves, and so on; but there is too great risk attached to them, and many have lost their whole stud of birds through mishaps with such arrangements. It is, therefore, needless for us to say more than that we believe either in using a means which is fairly safe or having no heat at all.

The Mouse Pest.

Such are the things to be borne in mind in selecting a good breeding-room, and we have but one more precautionary measure to which to refer. This relates to the exclusion of mice, which can make themselves troublesome in various ways if they once gain access to the room. There is no such effective mouse-trap as a cat, but the cat is not wanted in the very place where the mice are; if it clears the lower part of the house it does its duty very well, but it would never do to have it hunting about in the neighbourhood of the bird-room. The most effectual method of excluding mice is to nail strips of tin, bent at a right angle, on the floor and against the skirting-board. Perseverance and good teeth on the part of the mice will find a road through anything else, and it requires but a small hole to admit a regiment in single file. The bottom of the door should be protected by a similar contrivance. Should there be no skirting-board, as is sometimes the case in old rooms, a stout strip of wood must be nailed to the floor close to the wall, and a sharp look-out kept for holes that they may be stopped up at once with plaster of Paris or cement. Any holes in the floor itself must be covered with tin.

How to Poison Mice.

If mice should take possession of the room, summary ejection of the whole fraternity is better and more easy of accomplishment than tedious operations with traps. Poisoning can be resorted to without any risk of unpleasant results from the mice dying in their holes, for if one or two should do so their bodies are only very small. If the floor be well swept for two or three nights in succession and baited with a small heap of oatmeal, which must ultimately be mixed with some vermin poison, the entire colony can be cleared out without any trouble in one or two nights, when mice and poison should be buried. But if poisoning be objected to, examine the room for holes and stop up all but one. If the room be entered at night with a light, the mice will at once make for this one loophole of escape, which can be closed before even a single mouse has time to reach it; for unless the cages are so placed that the mice cannot by any possible means get into them, they will be found banqueting in the seed-hoppers. If a large box be previously placed on the vacant side of the room, about an inch from the wall, every marauder will run behind it. There need be no hurry to bring about the *dénouement*, and every long tail must be beaten out of cover; not one will attempt to leave the shelter of the box. A gentle squeeze, and that batch can be swept up, the box replaced, the hole unstopped, and the operation repeated in an hour. There will soon be no mice to squeeze. It is wholesale slaughter, but death is instantaneous and merciful. Dirty cages, filthy little tracks in their frequented runs, soiled seed, and perhaps a dead bird or two, are sufficient incentives to a massacre which need never occur again if the proper precautions are then taken to prevent the ingress of these pests.

We have referred to the cat as an effective mouse destroyer. Some persons succeed in training their cats in such a way

Cats *v.* Mice.

that they are allowed free access to the bird-room; indeed, not a few turn puss into the room every night to mount guard and protect the cages from the inroads of mice; and where the cat has been brought up to the work from kittenhood, it is astonishing how faithfully it will discharge its trust. We cannot but think, however, that the practice is fraught with great danger, and do not consider that a breeding-room containing valuable stock is the right place in which to commence "happy family" experiments. We say so in justice to the claims of the birds, which have no right to be exposed to such a risk. Our general experience of cats is that they are cats, and that, under favourable conditions, the cat nature will assert itself. It has to do so but *once* to entail disastrous consequences, and we think that the chance of that once should not be allowed. Granted that puss sits down to watch her favourite hole from which she has bagged many a mouse, and watches it as only a cat can; but a slight flutter in one of the cages breaks the stillness of the room, and she is there in a moment, and that unfortunate bird is either "killed fatally dead" or frightened to death. The cat's appetite thus whetted, she makes a complete job of the work before she tires of the amusement of putting her velvet paws through the wires. We have known it to happen in more than one instance, and think that shutting a cat in a room among birds is like smoking a pipe beside a keg of gunpowder with the head out: but one single spark is wanted to do mischief. "A place for everything, and everything in its place," is the motto for a well-ordered room; and the place for the cat is on the outside of the door.

We have spoken of mice only, as they are the most common depredators, and are *certain* to be attracted to a bird-room. But in country districts, where other kinds of vermin not unfrequently visit the homestead, the greatest care should be taken to exclude those known to be of a most cruel and bloodthirsty disposition. In old buildings in which the walls are none of the soundest, a weasel or stoat may easily secrete himself and play havoc. These gentlemen can squeeze through an opening something smaller than a crack; indeed, the how, when, and where of their ingress is often a mystery, and they must be guarded against with extreme watchfulness. We need only refer to a disastrous loss sustained by the late Mr. J. Yallop, of Cossey, near Norwich, when a stoat which obtained admission to his bird-room destroyed between sixty and seventy valuable birds, to show the necessity for vigilance in this direction. The lessons of such a catastrophe should not be lost upon thoughtful fanciers, who should ever study to reduce the *possibility* of an accident within the narrowest limits.

An Outside Bird-House.

On page 44 we give a sketch of the interior of a bird-room with a view to instructing our readers in the arrangement of the cages in the breeding-room to the best advantage. This sketch is of an outside bird-house the property of an enthusiastic Yorkshire breeder, Mr. W. Gladwin, of Catford, which for efficient arrangement would be difficult to surpass. The house is built of stout matchboarding with an inner lining of the same material; the space between the two is filled with sawdust, thus doubly protecting the house from the vagaries of the weather. The roof is of Gothic design, and is made of stout matchboarding covered with corrugated iron; the front, back, and sides of the house are also covered with this material, making it entirely weather-proof. Further, to ensure freedom from damp, the house stands some 18 inches above the ground, with two steps up into it. The floor is made of stout board, lined on the underneath side with thick zinc as a further preventive against damp and draughts. There are double doors, with a porch, so that when the house is entered the outer door is closed before the inner one is opened, thus preventing an inrush of cold air, or the escape of any bird which might by chance be out of its cage. There are two windows in the front, one on either side of the door, and a smaller one, high up near to the roof, in each side of the house. This arrangement affords an even distribution of light all through the house without the use of too much glass, which has a tendency to cause excessive heat in the summer and does not exclude the cold in the winter. The top panel of these windows works on a hinge, and when opened falls back into closed sides of sheet zinc cut on the slant, with a flange down the front on which the panel rests. This contrivance allows an abundance of air to enter the room through an aperture of about 12 inches at the top. The flange on the zinc sides prevents any possibility of draught, even to those birds that are close to the windows. The small side window on the left of the sketch is shown open. The whole of the interior of the house, including the ceiling, is varnished.

Interior Arrangement of Bird-Room.

The house has not been selected for notice because it is an outhouse, but on account of its neatly arranged interior, which can be adapted to any room of a house. In our sketch we are only able to show the back and a portion of each side of the room; the main windows are, as we have mentioned, on either side of the door in the front, and thus give ample light to the cages both at the back and sides of the room. The cages are all of uniform size, and stand in racks of which the uprights are of wood; the cross-bars, on which the cages rest, are lengths of small metal gas-piping. By the use of a rack in which to stand the cages, and by the adoption of a uniform size for the cages, every cage can be fitted into its place without the waste of an inch of space. One has only to look at the illustration to note the neat effect this system gives to a room, and how it sets off the birds. These racks will be fully explained later. In the room illustrated there are four tiers of cages; but the number of cages can be regulated according

A TYPICAL BREEDING-ROOM (*see page* 43).

to the size of the room. It will be seen that a stout wooden beading about 2 inches high is arranged round the floor about 1 ft. from the front of the cages. This serves to catch any seed-husks that may drop from the cages, and keeps them on the inside near the cages. The centre of the floor is thus kept tidy and free from husks.

Against the front, below one of the windows, a plain square table is required whereon to stand the seed, egg food, water, and other requisites when attending to the birds; below the other window can be placed a closed-in cupboard in which to keep the various utensils. A chair at one side is also desirable whereon one may sit to view and admire the birds in a spare half-hour when their wants have been satisfied. Then the room is complete so far as fittings are concerned.

THE MORNING ROUND.
(From a photograph by Mr. T. E. Batty.)

A CANARY BREEDER AND SOME OF HIS TROPHIES.
Mr. J. Trengrove, of Rishton, in his Breeding-Room.

CHAPTER V

CAGES AND CAGE-MAKING

It is quite possible to go to an extreme; to build with such strict regard to the line and plummet and to conduct our little establishment with such painful order and regularity as seriously to interfere with the comfort of the objects under our charge. We have a wholesome aversion to the whole family of antimacassars, and they are a large tribe. Yet we do not wish to be understood as objecting to a well-ordered breeding-room—anything but that; it is only French polish, and a sort of clock-work mechanism which admits of no deviation from a set line, that we object to when they obtrude themselves to the exclusion of the comfort and well-being of the birds. "Anything will do for a cage."

No; anything will *not* do for a cage. The anything-will-do system is bad from end to end, and is born of a careless slovenliness which goes about with holes in its stockings. There is a fitness in things, and a harmony which satisfies the judgment and pleases the eye as much as Dutch gold and stucco are repellent to it. If there be one place more than another in which we like to see handsome cages, it is in a working-man's cottage. They help to cover his walls, and amply repay any pains bestowed in making them and in keeping them clean.

The Use of Recesses.

In fitting up a breeding-room with cages, space can sometimes be economised by utilising recesses. We refer to this as belonging to the sphere of "contrivances"; and we are told that a good contriver is better than he that hath a large appetite. Recesses are also sometimes available in rooms other than those set apart for birds, and may even be the *only* available space at command. They can be adapted to—or rather converted into—cages with little trouble and not much expense. We must assume that there is no paper on the wall; if there be, it can readily be removed by wetting it, and the plaster laid bare. No better natural sides and back for a breeding-cage can be devised than a dry wall. The exact places to be occupied by the shelving should be set off with a square. The shelves should be 18 inches apart and made of half-inch ordinary yellow pine, planed, and the freer from coarse knots the better. If the recess be reasonably square, the shelves can be fitted in tightly without injuring the wall in any way, beyond the driving in of a few nails to support them or to fix small ledges on which the ends may rest. Each shelf must, in any case, be bevelled off to the exact angle of the particular niche into which it is intended to slide, and must be flush with the wall all round, especially at the back. Any spaces which occur between the shelf and the wall, be they ever so small, must be filled in with thin plaster of Paris, for the same reason that cage-bottoms must be made flush with the back and sides of the cage—viz., to prevent dry sand from running through, and also to prevent insects from harbouring in them. This is, perhaps, the most difficult part of the business, but it is of the utmost importance.

It must, however, be noted in passing that these contrivances do not allow of the insect pest being dealt with as effectually as it can be in cages which can be lifted about and removed from the rack on which they stand, or from the nails on which they hang.

However deep the recess may be, it is not advisable that the shelving be more than about 12 inches from back to front; but if it be not very deep, and it is wished to bring the cage fronts out in the same line as the jamb of the chimney which usually forms the recess, an inch or two is not of so much consequence as disturbing the uniformity desired; but we do not advocate deep cages. If there be width enough, the space at command may be divided into two or three compartments by permanent partitions or by slides, and the whole will then represent a large cage; and here we will leave it, to enter on the subject of cage-making proper.

Different towns and different schools of fanciers affect different breeding appliances.

Wire Cages.

Custom and long usage determine many fashions, quite irrespective of their suitability. The ancient, heavy, cumbersome, two-wheeled, four-horse plough can doubtless be found in use, even now, in some parts; while in most a light, effective machine, which a man might almost swing over his shoulder, is used. Each has its merits and demerits, and nobody will dispute either. In Scotland—and thousands of Canaries are bred beyond the Tweed—open-wire cages are used to a very large extent, while a few miles south of the old Roman wall such a thing is unknown. The "London" breeding cage, the ordinary sale article of wire-workers and cage-makers, in its early days was considered in the South to be the most perfect breeding cage ever produced; but it has since proved to be one of the most unsuitable it is possible to have. The various compartments arranged at the right-hand side of the cage for the hens to nest in, with a compartment below in which to place the young birds when they are first taken from the parents, become nothing but harbours for filth and vermin, and are quite unnecessary. Though they are still made by the ordinary wire-workers and cage-makers—who, as a rule, are not fanciers—no practical breeder would think of using such a breeding cage, or recommend the amateur or novice to do so. Of course, many beginners in London buy such cages, until their disadvantages are pointed out by some experienced breeder, when they are quickly replaced by the more common-sense cage of to-day.

The cage we recommend is one with the top, back, and sides of wood, and with the

The Best Cage.

front only wired—a business-like looking article not got up for show, but for practical use. It can be made in one, two, three, four, or any number of compartments. A cage of one compartment, intended for the use of one pair of birds only, is known as a single breeding cage. The illustration on this page shows such a cage fitted with a movable wire front, seed-hopper, glass drinking vessel, and earthenware egg drawer, all in their proper positions as used while breeding. A small glass vessel may also be fixed against the perch by passing a wire pin through the lip of the vessel. In this may be placed other tit-bits, such as a little maw-seed,

SINGLE BOX BREEDING CAGE, WITH WIRE FRONT AND FITTINGS.

bread and milk, or boiled rape, any of which are best given in a separate vessel. The only other article required in this cage is the earthenware nest-pan, hung either in the centre of the back of the cage, or at one end, whichever the breeder prefers. A small wire rack on the outside of the wire front, in which to place the nest-building material for the hen to pull through the wires, completes the fittings. It will be observed in the illustration of this cage that the turn-rail at the bottom is open; it is arranged thus to show its method of working. This cage is free from any fixed trappings inside in which insect pests may gather; the fittings are all movable.

Sand-trays can, of course, be used where preferred, but this cage has no sand-tray —simply the turn-rail in front, which is removed when the cage is cleaned out.

Compartment Cages.

A two-compartment cage is called a "double breeding cage," and affords accommodation for two pairs of birds, one pair in each compartment, and so on. In describing cages we shall adopt these terms. A "stack" of cages is simply a multiplication of compartments built either in one piece or in sections, though when built in one piece it is more generally spoken of as an eight- or sixteen-compartment cage, according to the number of pairs it is intended to accommodate, and is understood to be one piece of furniture. Thirty years ago it was quite a common thing in the North for fanciers to make long cages with eight or ten breeding compartments; others were made in a chest-of-drawers fashion, with a "stack" of twelve compartments. There were thus four compartments at the bottom, the top of which formed the base of four compartments above; the top of these again formed the base of the topmost four compartments. A little wood is saved by such an arrangement, but these large structures are awkward to move and handle when it is necessary to wash and repaint them, and altogether these disadvantages far outweigh the little gained by the saving of wood. The single-storey cages of somewhat smaller dimensions—not exceeding, say, four compartments arranged side by side with movable partitions—are very handy, and are as easily moved about for the purpose of cleaning or for arranging in order as are double cages; during the moulting season and winter months they are easily converted into flight cages by removing the partitions.

We only propose to deal with the double breeding cage, leaving it to the fancier to cut his coat according to his cloth in the matter of multiplication.

The Double Breeding Cage.

We will now proceed to construct our cage, which, to begin with, is nothing more than a box 40 inches long, 16 inches high, and 10 inches deep (for Yorkshires it might be 17 inches or 18 inches high), made of yellow pine wood about three-eighths of an inch thick. It must be planed smooth, rubbed down with fine glasspaper, and neatly and securely put together. Every joint should fit as closely as good workmanship can ensure. These dimensions allow reasonable space in each compartment for a pair of birds, but if it be wished to alter them let it be in the direction of the length, which may be extended an inch or two.

This " box " is then divided into two compartments by a central partition, which can either be the entire height of the cage or only half the height, the upper half sliding in and out in a groove. The advantage gained by this is that when the breeding season is over the slide can be withdrawn and the two compartments thrown into one; if an entire partition be used it can either be made movable or a fixture, but the former is preferable. If made a fixture, it must have an aperture in the centre, about 3 inches square, which can be opened or closed at pleasure by means of a door suspended on a screw to serve as a means of communication between the two compartments. In place of this aperture a small slide is sometimes used; the various arrangements are shown in the illustration on this page; but these and other minor fittings are entirely matters of taste.

Our preference has always been to have everything as plain as possible, and to have no sort of complications about a cage when a simpler appliance would answer the same purpose. We mention these things, however, at this stage of our work, because these details must be decided on before the front is made. While the box is still open and in this crude shape, we may as well direct attention to the fact that if a half-partition and large slide be used, the lower groove in which the slide works will have to be gouged out on the top edge of the partition, and the upper groove will have to be made in the same way, on the lower edge of a piece of wood nailed to the inside of the cage at the top. But we think this all means extra work, finished with a precision that the amateur joiner may not find it easy to acquire all at once. He has to choose, therefore, between an entire partition, movable or a fixture, with a central aperture or small sliding-door, and a half-partition with a large slide. The entire partition, with central aperture, is the easiest to make.

Many Yorkshire breeders prefer this kind of partition in their double cages; but the breeder must act as his fancy leads him. The movable partition is, we think, preferable, for the reason that when the partition is removed the cage makes a splendid "flight" for the winter months, while it will be found to be the simplest and best arrangement.

DOUBLE BREEDING CAGES, SHOWING VARYING ARRANGEMENTS.

In the drawing on this page the breeding-cage is divided into three sections, each intended to illustrate one or other of the various modes of construction we have described. The bottom section represents the unfinished cage, with wooden cross-bar and wooden framed door pierced ready for wiring. The illustration on page 50 shows this door wired, and the method of fixing. The front is a fixture; the wires are passed through the middle wooden cross-bar into the top cross-bar, into which they are forced to the depth of about ½ inch: this allows sufficient length for the bottom ends of the wires to be drawn down some $\frac{3}{16}$ inch into the bottom cross-bar, thus making the wires secure top and bottom.

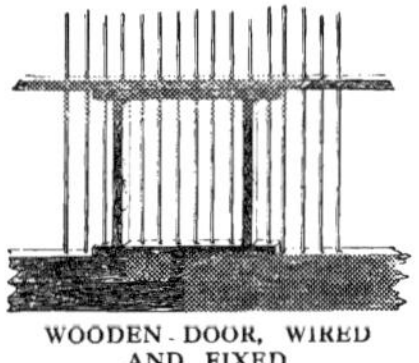

WOODEN DOOR, WIRED AND FIXED.

This cage also shows a fixed partition with central aperture, on the further side of which is supposed to be the small door hanging on a screw, and turned up out of sight to allow of communication between the two compartments. This door is round in shape, similar to that of the aperture, but a size larger. Suspended as it is by a screw over the top of the aperture, it is easily opened without flustering the birds. This is accomplished by the following very simple method: with a thin piece of wood, sufficiently long to reach half across the door of the aperture, the bottom of the door is raised until it has revolved far enough on the screw to fall against the back of the cage, when the aperture will be open. It is equally easy to close.

The middle section shows a wired front which can either be a fixture or what is known as a "loose wire front."

Loose Wire Fronts.

For the former it is inserted in the woodwork, and so becomes part and parcel of the whole. For the latter it is made in one piece, and fixed into the top and bottom front cross-bars. Four, or so, of the upright wires are made to project, say, ½ inch at the top and ¼ inch at the bottom, and fitted into holes in the top and bottom cross-bars. The doors swing on a stout upright wire. These fronts are easily removed by a little upward pressure of the fingers at the top, and are obviously a great improvement upon the fixed wire fronts. They afford easy access to the cage for purposes of cleaning, washing or re-painting. The upper portion of the partition in this section forms a slide which, when withdrawn, converts the cage into a "flight."

The top section illustrates the cage with a similar loose wire front, but with square, sliding, self-closing doors, which, though not so ornamental, are easier of construction, and answer their purpose equally well. We are inclined, indeed, to give preference to these doors, as they are not so likely to get out of order as the arched door shown in the middle section. The precise construction of the square door is more clearly indicated in the illustration at the head of this column.

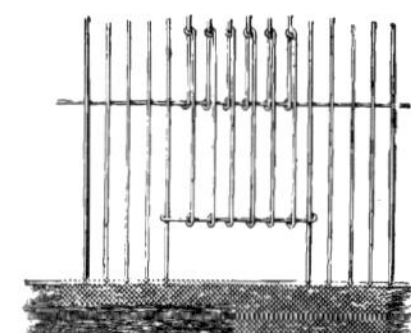

SLIDING WIRE DOOR.

The front is made in two portions, one for each compartment, which is much the easier way to make the loose wire fronts for double cages, and they answer equally as well as one large front to cover the two compartments. An illustration of a loose front for a single compartment is here given. The whole of the partition in this section is movable between the top and bottom front cross-bars. It will thus be seen that there are two kinds of fronts which may be used for our cage—the "fixed" and "loose."

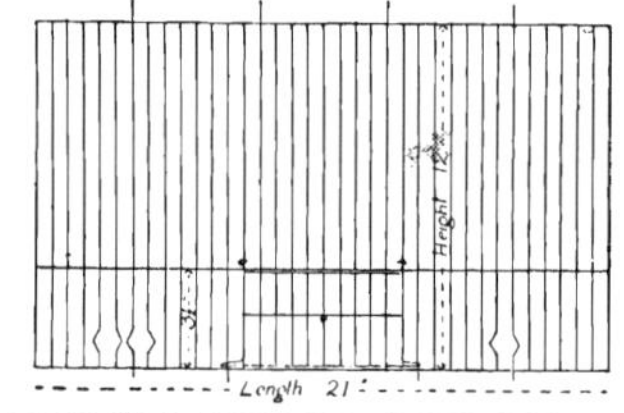

LOOSE WIRE FRONT FOR SINGLE BREEDING CAGE.

Fanciers who may prefer a fixed front should proceed as follows:—Plane up three pieces of yellow pine, American white wood, or mahogany, or whatever wood of which they wish to make the front, free from knots, the precise length of the body of the cage from outer edge to outer edge, and the exact thickness. That for the top bar must be ¾ of an inch broad, that for the bottom 1½ inches, and the third piece for the middle cross-bar should be ⅝ of an inch broad. Fit the top cross-piece immediately under the top of the box, cutting slots in the sides and centre partition (if a fixed one) to receive it. The slots should not be too wide or too deep ; it is easy to take off a shaving, but not so easy to put one on, and these cross-pieces and bar must fit close and tight, and be flush with the front edge. Fix the bottom piece in the same manner 1 inch from the bottom of the front. This will leave a space of 12¾ inches between the two. Now let the middle cross-bar in neatly, and exactly square, 4½ inches above the bottom piece, and having ascertained that everything fits just as it should, and that nothing requires altering in any way, take out these three pieces, and having marked off on one of them with a pair of compasses the position of the wire-holes ⅝ of an inch apart from centre to centre, clamp the three tightly together, and mark them across with a pencil and square, drawing the line through each point with the greatest care, for on this depends the accuracy of the wiring. Nothing looks more unbusiness-like than a badly-wired cage, and the operation is really so simple that there is no excuse for doing it otherwise than with the greatest exactness and regularity. Having set off the spaces, run a line down the centre from end to end, and prick the wire-holes on the cross-lines at the intersecting points, using for the purpose a bradawl one size smaller than No. 15 or No. 16 gauge tinned wire, and either shortened to ½ an inch in length or loaded with pieces of leather till but that portion of the bradawl remains. This ensures a uniform depth of hole, but after a little practice there will be no need to adopt the leather guide on the bradawl, the mere placing of a finger on the blade of the bradawl at the given depth will be sufficient. This, of course, only applies to the top and bottom cross-bars ; the middle bar must be bored right through. Anyone can prick a hole, but to bore it perpendicularly is another matter ; and it must be remembered that, in pricking the middle cross-piece, the awl must be kept perfectly upright, or the wires will enter the upper surface apparently in the right direction and come out on the lower in another, when it will be found that the more they are coaxed the more they will not go where they are wanted. But a little care will prevent any irregularity of this kind. The bradawl should be pressed gently as it is twisted to bore the holes, so as not to split the wood. In pricking the holes in the bottom cross-piece, it is better not to make any in the middle, on the portion over which the door will stand. It may seem unnecessary to call attention to such a trifling matter, but superfluous holes are the very places in which insects take up their abode. In the event of the Canary parasite—to which we shall by and by have to refer—getting into the cage, these unnecessary holes will all be found crammed with them. It is therefore wise to leave no holes.

Fixed Wire Fronts.

A quicker method of marking off these cross-bars for boring is to make a simple wire gauge. A piece of hard wood, such as ash or even oak, about 1 foot in length, should be planed down to about ¾ of an inch in width and ½ an inch in thickness ; on this spaces should be marked off on one of the edges with the compasses ⅝ of an inch apart, just as if it were being prepared for a cage-front ; a boring should then be made at each mark, in the middle, with a bradawl to the depth of ⅜ of an inch. In each hole should be inserted a short piece of wire a size larger than the bradawl with which the hole was bored, so that tightness is ensured, the end of which should project ¼ of an inch. When each projecting wire has been filed to a point, a simple yet efficient gauge is available for marking the cross-bars for wiring. All that has to be done is to stand it, points downward, on the edge of each of the cross-bars and give

A Simple Wire Gauge.

one slight tap on the wooden back. The places for the wires are thus marked with unfailing regularity and precision. If the marking is always commenced from the right of the cross-bars, with the first wire mark $\frac{5}{8}$ of an inch from the end, the marking is bound to come plumb on each bar. The bored cross-pieces can then be replaced and fixed with $\frac{3}{4}$-inch or 1-inch brads.

But what is to be done with the open space of 1 inch at the bottom, between the floor of the cage and the bottom cross-bar? There should be fitted into it on each side of the partition a piece of wood of the same thickness as the bottom cross-bar, or one piece the whole length of the cage may be made instead of the separate pieces for each compartment. In either case, it should fit tightly enough to need a little pressure to remove it. There should also be fixed on the front of this rail, about 8 inches from both ends, or in the centre if a separate rail is used for each compartment, a small brass knob by which to remove the rail when the cage is cleaned out. (An illustration of this turn-rail is here given.) The cage can be cleaned out through the opening thus afforded by means of a narrow scraper.

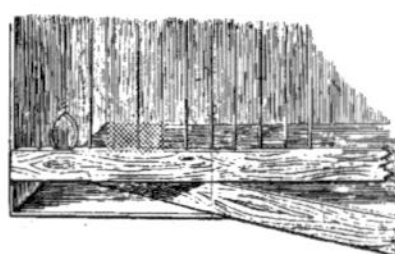

A SIMPLE TURN-RAIL.

In place of this turn-rail a false bottom or tray is sometimes used; but we do not favour false bottoms, as in our opinion they are cumbersome, liable to warp, and of no practical value. They are, indeed, distinctly disadvantageous, for they form a convenient harbour for red mite, and however well they may be made the sand or sawdust scattered by the birds is certain to get beneath them, in spite of any beading which may be put round. Thus, after the false bottom has been withdrawn, a scraper has still to be used to clear underneath. If this be not done the sand or sawdust will accumulate, and prevent the tray from shutting closely. The turn-rail obviates all this inconvenience, and has always been a special fancy of ours, as it is easily made, and in no way interferes with the appearance of the cage. It is a most efficient means to a necessary end.

The cage can now be painted or enamelled inside. A very good colour is sky blue or hedge-sparrow egg blue. The front cross-bars may also have a preliminary coat of black, and the cage is then ready for wiring. When this is done, the whole of the outside of the cage, including the front, should be painted black or any other colour that may be preferred; but the preliminary coat on the cross-bars must, of course, be of the same colour.

How to Wire a Cage.

It will be seen that the space to be wired is just $12\frac{3}{4}$ inches in the ordinary cage, or in one built for birds of position, such as Yorkshires, Scotch Fancies, Belgians, and Lancashires, $13\frac{3}{4}$ inches or $14\frac{3}{4}$ inches, according to the height of the cage. To ensure stability, each wire should be inserted at least a $\frac{1}{4}$ of an inch into the top and bottom cross-bars; the wires, therefore, must be cut not less than $\frac{1}{2}$ an inch longer than the space from top to bottom. If the middle cross-bar be kept well down, the birds will have plenty of head room when on the perches, a particularly important matter for birds of position.

Now to proceed with the wiring of the cage. In the old days the would-be cage-maker had to buy his wire in coils, which means that each length used had to be first straightened. This was partially done as it was drawn from the coil by passing it between a simple arrangement of iron pegs; but each piece had still a curve, and to make it absolutely straight was an art acquired only by long practice, and was accomplished by pressure between the finger and thumb. To straighten the hundred and fifty wires required for a cage was the work of only a few minutes for the man who had done the same with as many thousands; and when done they *were* straight. Much of the wire is now, however, straightened by machinery and sold in straight lengths ready for use by most wire-workers. It only requires to be

A TYPICAL NORWICH PLAINHEAD.

cut to the correct length for the cage with pliers.

In addition to this small bundle of wires it will be necessary to have a piece of No. 15 gauge wire for a strengthening cross-wire bar, a few yards of binding wire (technically known as "lapping wire"), and a pair of cutting pliers. The illustration herewith shows this strengthening cross-wire bar and the method of binding.

The actual operation of wiring is exceedingly simple. Pass the wire downwards through the middle cross-bar; it ought not to slip through, but should require gentle pulling with the tips of the pliers, by means of which — held near the end—it must be inserted in its proper hole and pushed down to the bottom, or till the other end is clear of the lower edge of the top cross-piece. This allows of the wire being inserted in the top hole without bending it, for though it has a certain amount of elasticity, it is better not to have to try it too much in that direction. This is our reason for directing the holes to be pierced ½ an inch in depth. Having pressed the end of the wire home the full ½ inch, place the other end in the hole in the top of the bottom cross-bar, pressing the end of the wire into it a ¼ of an inch. It will then be secure at both ends. The strengthening cross-wire must be run through behind the wires, midway between the cross-bar and the top; but before securing the wires to it we must see to the seed and water holes.

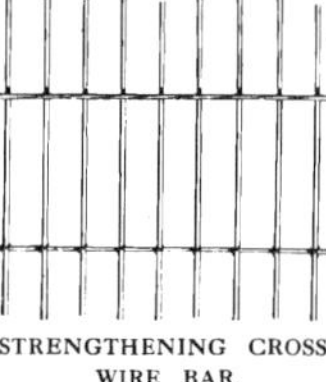

STRENGTHENING CROSS-WIRE BAR.

In wiring above the door the wires must come through the middle cross-bar to the under-side, so as to fill up the holes. It might be urged that it would be as well not to pierce through the cross-bar at this particular place; but by carrying the wires through, the work is materially strengthened at a weak spot; at the same time the bar need not be pricked *quite* through if care be used with the awl.

Our usual plan is to plane up a clean piece of wood, and having measured off as many bars as the width will allow, and set off the marks for the holes, to prick the entire piece before cutting it up. We have then several lengths all pierced with exactness, and then it matters not where it is cut, or into how many long or short lengths, for the tops and bottoms of doors or other purposes, the holes will always be found to correspond and make true work. The same method can be adopted with other cross-pieces; clamp as many together as can be managed, and mark them off for pricking on one scale; there is then never any risk of top and bottom holes not corresponding, or of the wiring getting out of the perpendicular.

Seed and Water Holes.

The wires must be cut a few inches longer for the seed and water holes, three of which are required for each compartment. The extra length is to allow for the wire used in making the round holes. They are easily twisted into shape by means of a round piece of hard wood; a ruler of lignum vitæ rather less than 1 inch in diameter answers well. The most approved twist is shown in the accompanying illustration.

Personally, we prefer a diamond-shaped hole, open at the top as shown in the illustration of a loose wire front on page 50. Such holes preserve the feathers on the back of the neck from damage, an ever-present risk when the round wire holes are used; owing to the daily rub of the feathers against the wire at the top of the hole, the feathers become quite thin and very soiled. The diamond-shaped holes are of especial advantage to crested birds, as they prevent the possibility of damage to the back of the crest.

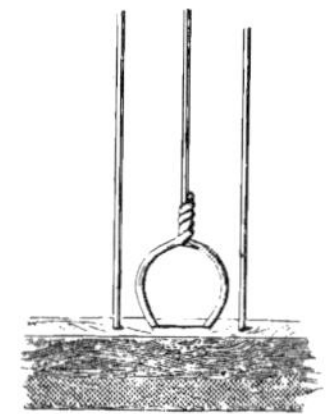

ROUND DRINKING-HOLE.

To secure the round holes in their places it is only necessary to hammer out the lower edge of the loop on any smooth, solid surface (nothing is better than that useful domestic appliance, a *flat-iron*), when it can be made sufficiently sharp to bury itself easily in the soft wood and remain securely fixed. For the diamond-shaped holes it is necessary for the wires to be only a little longer than the others, just sufficient to allow of their being bent into shape, one at each side, to form the hole. They are then firmly inserted into the cross-bar in the same manner as the other upright wires.

The water-hole wire or wires should be inserted about the third or fourth from the side, and the seed-hole wires should occupy the third and fifth places next the partition, according to the length of the seed-hopper intended to be used, which, as will be presently explained, can either cover both sets of seed-holes on each side of the partition or be fitted to each compartment.

We must delay binding the strengthening cross-wire bar until our door is hung—

The Cage Door.

and the door is a most important part of a cage. A great deal of work has to be done through the open door, which must be large enough to admit the hand easily. To harmonise with the cage the door must have a wooden frame; indeed, no other description of door would work well under a wooden cross-bar. It is, however, very simple in construction. It cannot be higher than the 4½ inches allowed for it, and the only question is as to the width. Assuming the compartment to be 20 inches wide, it will give us thirty-two wires, according to our plan of spacing out. If we make the door 5 inches wide that will take up the space of eight wires, so that if we leave the middle eight holes in the bottom cross-bar unwired, we shall allow the proper space for the door. One long wire by which the door is to be hung must be withheld until the door is placed in its proper position. This long wire is to be passed through the holes in the cross-bars and the last hole at the end of the top and bottom cross-bars of the door. When the wire is made secure it not only holds the door in its proper place, but acts as a hinge on which the door works freely. The door, of course, must be wired before it is hung.

The use of our lengths of pierced cross-bars will now be apparent. We have nothing to do but to cut off two pieces, each containing ten holes, allowing very nearly the whole half-inch before the first hole and behind the last—that is to say, we must not cut the length off directly through the first hole and through the tenth, but before and behind them—we want ten clear holes, and a small piece over at each end. Place these two pieces face to face, and it will be seen the holes correspond exactly—one is the top of the door and the other the bottom. The side-pieces are of the same dimensions with respect to thickness (but, of course, are not cut from pierced lengths), and must be cut of the precise length required. Place one of them exactly under the second hole of the top piece, and fix it in its place with a single brad driven through the hole; do the same with the other, placing it under the ninth or last hole but one; turn it up, and put the bottom piece on in the same way, and the door-frame is complete. Wire it, and it only then remains to hang it. The door of a right-hand compartment should be hung from its left side or end, and the door of a left-hand compartment from its right side. The inside of the top and bottom pieces of the door frame at the opposite end should be notched out where the last holes are bored, so that when shut the door may catch against the upright wire which finishes the wiring of the cage at that point. The door will thus be held in its proper position, and when closed will fit flush with the front. If this method of door-making be adopted when a set of cages is being made of uniform dimensions and uniform scale of wiring, any number of doors can be put together with the certainty of any one door exactly fitting any one cage. If one should happen to be a shade tight, the slightest tap under the middle cross-bar will give it liberty; or if it should be too slack, a downward tap between the wires will improve matters without putting the bar out of square in a way to offend the eye. The door can be fastened with a tiny button, or a wire, bone, or brass catch fixed on the front cross-bar of the cage. A glance at the illustrations will render these directions for door-making perfectly plain and easy of accomplishment.

The finishing operation of the whole is the binding of the wires to the strengthening cross-wire bar with the thin lapping material already mentioned in our inventory of necessaries. We give an illustration on page 54 of the orthodox twist which tightens the whole, and makes it impossible to displace any wire or widen the space between them so as to permit the escape of a bird.

If it be preferred, the cross-wire bar and upright wires may be soldered together instead of being bound with the fine wire; either method answers equally well. This strengthening cross-wire bar between the middle wooden bar and top of cage is, however, not absolutely necessary if a No. 15 gauge wire be used for the upright wires, and the cage is not of the loftiest dimensions. It is, however, advisable to have it for the more lofty cages.

A WELL-PLANNED INTERIOR.
(Photograph supplied by Messrs. Forse & Son, Leyton.)

Before dismissing the subject of cage-making, we must refer briefly to one other method of wiring, simply because it includes an excellent description of a self-closing door, very much in use, both in breeding and exhibition cages.

A Sliding Door.

This method consists in substituting for the wooden cross-bar a cross piece of wire, of the same gauge as the upright wires, or one gauge stronger, to which the upright wires must be bound in the manner previously indicated. The door, a pattern of which is shown on page 50, can then be made to slide up and down, and if carefully put together is a most effective self-closing arrangement, which, with its extreme lightness, constitutes its chief excellence. Even if it should not slide or fall freely, but have to be pulled

LANCASHIRE CANARIES

BUFF PLAINHEAD — YELLOW COPPY

down, it has the merit of not being able to swing open; for we have known birds play with the internal fastenings of doors and inadvertently open them. A reference to the illustration will show the construction and working better than any verbal description. It will be seen that after making the eyes to the several wires (which is done with a pair of fine round-pointed pliers), and bending them over at right angles, they must be kept in the same straight line while being turned up at the bottom and pinched on to the frame or short cross-wire bar on which the entire fabric works, for otherwise the door will not slide at all, or only with difficulty. The two ends of the bottom cross-bar of the door, which are turned round the upright wires in hook fashion, must not be nipped too closely on to the wires, but sufficient space allowed to admit of their running up and down the wires freely. Success depends entirely on true work. It is hardly necessary to add that the upper strengthening cross-wire of the front must be placed sufficiently high to allow the door to travel up.

Perches.

The perches, instead of being about the diameter of a lead-pencil, as is too frequently the case, should be twice that diameter, oval in section, and placed with the broad side uppermost. If the formation of a Canary's foot be considered, the reason for this will be evident. The perches should rest on the cross-bar, and fit firmly between two of the wires, so that they do not rock as the bird perches upon them. They should project ½ an inch so as to allow of their being drawn out at will for cleaning, etc.

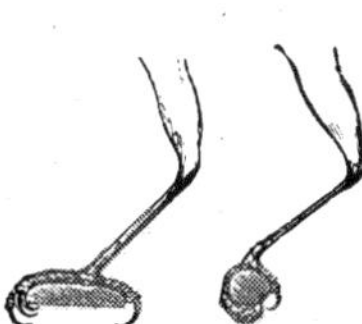

THE RIGHT AND WRONG SHAPE FOR PERCHES.

Another effective way to fix the front end of perches which rest on the cross-bar is to cut them to project just ¼ of an inch, and notch the centre of the perch with a pocket-knife so as to allow one of the upright wires to fit firmly into the notch.

Many prefer this method of fixing the perches, and we know from experience that it holds them securely and they do not work loose, as when fixed between two of the wires.

At the other end of the perch, which is to rest against the back of the cage, a brad, filed to a fine point, or a piece of wire, should be inserted so that it projects about ¼ inch. The perch should be cut full long, and the brad or wire rested against the back of the cage, where it can be wedged down firmly with but a slight pressure of the fingers. By this means the end of the perch will not touch the back of the cage, and will thus afford no harbour for insect life.

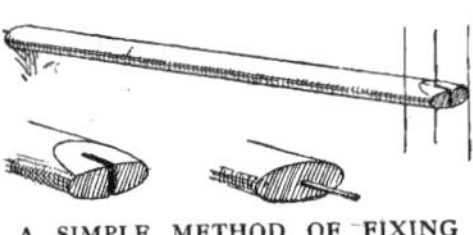

A SIMPLE METHOD OF FIXING A PERCH.

If a stock of these perches be kept they will often be found handy to push in here and there in various positions as occasion may require, or to replace others which are soiled and in need of a wash. Perches of various sizes may also be used in the same cage with beneficial effect to the birds' feet; the weakening of the hind toe is thus often prevented.

SHORT PERCH WITH WIRE ARMS.

To enable the birds to get at the seed and water easily, a perch may also be put lengthways. This is the common method, but we prefer a couple of short cross perches about 3 inches long, one fixed in front of the seed hopper, and the other before the drinking vessel. These are kept in position by means of wire arms hooked on to the top of the bottom cross-bar as here illustrated.

Egg-Drawers.

Some, to whom the construction of a breeding-cage is no novelty, will perhaps observe that we have made no reference to egg-drawers and a few *et cœteras*, which sometimes are united to it. We prefer to supply them by inside attachments, though we by no means object to their being made fixtures. One way is as handy as the other. We always like to see the front of a cage cut up as little as possible, though sundry useful contrivances, such as neat earthenware egg-drawers, can be inserted in the front, and are very convenient for general purposes. Experience will suggest many things of this kind, which it is quite unnecessary to enter into here, their adoption or rejection being matters of taste and ingenuity.

Two appliances only are now necessary to make our cage tenantable—the seed-hopper and water-vessels. On this page is shown a double seed-hopper, which supplies the two compartments of the cage. A wooden partition, fixed in the centre of the hopper, gives it two advantages. In the first place it prevents the birds from quarrelling with each other, should one in each compartment be feeding at the same time, and in the second place, should it be necessary, it enables the seed mixture for the two compartments to be varied. For instance, in one compartment may be a pair of birds which are feeding their young, and in the other a single bird or a pair nesting; in such a case it is obvious that a variation in the seed would be necessary for the two sets of occupants. Therefore, though the double hoppers are convenient, we prefer a single hopper (half the length of the double one) for each compartment, and in our opinion they are much handier and easier for the amateur to make.

The Seed-Hopper.

DOUBLE SEED-HOPPER.

It is not necessary to furnish any specific dimensions for a hopper, but when we say that a double one must be made long enough to cover both sets of seed-holes, it will be obvious that to fit our cage and system of wiring it will require to be 7 inches or even 8 inches in length. The depth is immaterial, but from $1\frac{1}{2}$ inches to 2 inches is ample, with a width of, say, 2 inches. Nothing is gained by increasing these dimensions, except that more seed is required to fill the hopper. It makes no difference in the consumption. There is a fashion in hoppers as in many other things, the front being sometimes carried round in a curve, or cut off at an acute angle; the one we illustrate, we think, is as easy to make and looks as well as any. The two sloping ends are grooved for the reception of a piece of glass, which prevents the birds from throwing out the seed—a thing they will do apparently in sport, or in wanton waste, whenever a fresh supply is given.

The middle partition in the double hopper is made just sufficiently high to allow the glass top to slide over it. This glass also affords light for the birds to feed by, and enables them to see the seed without difficulty, even in a cage to which they are not accustomed.

The old-fashioned seed-drawer, with the holes inside the cage, is now almost obsolete. As a method of supplying food it may be as good as any other, but the trouble of making and fixing the inside box, coupled with the facilities it affords to insects and the difficulty of getting at them, have caused the hopper to supersede it.

Some old-fashioned fanciers, however, have a liking for old-fashioned contrivances, and still stick to this seed-drawer. We have no wish to try to persuade them to the contrary, but would simply point out that the seed-hopper is much the better, if only for the reason that the seed is kept clean and free from the birds' droppings.

Water-Vessels.

Of water-vessels there is an endless variety of patterns and materials. We will not undertake to recommend one as being superior to another, but generally we use the ordinary open-top round glass vessel, illustrated on the next page. It is egg-shaped inside, so has no corners at the bottom; it is consequently easily cleaned out and kept clean. It is easily adjusted to the cage, as it requires only a piece of wire bent round to its size with the ends made hook-shape in a similar manner to the ends of the wire arms for the short cross-perches previously described. These, when pressed over the top edge of the bottom cross-bar, hold the round wire frame firm; the glass drinker cannot slip through owing to the flanged edge of the top. In the list of open water-vessels will be found, too, the glass and earthenware cups, which also require to be suspended in wire loops.

OPEN TOP ROUND GLASS DRINKING-VESSEL.

The covered-in round-topped glass bottles are still used for both seed and water in song cages, though not to such an extent as they were. We have a great objection to them, for while they may be handy for the seed they are anything but suitable for the water; they are most difficult to clean, and as the edges round the opening are very rough, one's fingers are often cut in the effort to clean the inside of the vessel. Great care is also required to fit them so that the mouth of the bottle is exactly opposite to the wire hole, and very little is sufficient to displace them; the bird is then deprived of water or seed, as the case may be, until the mischief is discovered.

Another glass drinking-vessel in general use in many parts of the north of England is the half-moon shape (shown in the next column). It will be observed that the flat side of the vessel rests against the front of the cage, and that the wire loop is passed through the front bar with the ends bent inside to hold it in position. A better method of fixing the wires is to make the ends into hooks, so that they grip over the top of the bar. The wire loop can then be removed when the cages are washed, etc.

The well-known conical glass fountain with projecting lip is a rather expensive but admirable reservoir, which furnishes a continual supply of clean water. We know of no better water-vessel than this, if the wire hole be placed above the cross-bar and adjacent to one of the perches, so that egg and other soft foods which soon decompose are not likely to be thrown into the mouth. When used in connection with large flights, where a group of birds are flying together, it is not so quickly cleaned as the open-topped drinking-vessels, and two or three of the latter placed a little apart along the front of a flight would answer the same purpose. If, however, the water holes are limited in the flight, then the conical fountain will well supply the need, as more than one—if of fair size—will not be required unless there is a great number of birds, and the flight is very large.

HALF-MOON SHAPED DRINKING-VESSEL.

It is not necessary for the amateur cage-maker to have a complete kit of joiner's tools. He should have two saws (one a panel and the other a tenon or back saw), a "jack" and a smoothing plane, a couple of hammers (one very light and the other a little heavier), two bradawls (one to carry No. 14 or No. 15 gauge wire and the other to carry No. 16 or No. 17 gauge), a marking gauge—which we fully described, and which he would make himself—a square, a couple of sharp chisels, differing in size, a medium-sized screw-driver, a pair of cutting pliers, a pair of round-pointed pliers, a 2-foot rule, an oil-stone, and a soldering iron. Additions can be made to the kit as they are found to be helpful, such as a brace and bits, files, different sized chisels, compasses, etc.

Tools for Cage-Making.

CONICAL GLASS FOUNTAIN.

Apart from breeding purposes, all varieties of canaries and hybrids may be kept in box-shaped cages, though they may, as we shall describe, differ a little in size and arrangement.

CHAPTER VI

NESTS AND OTHER APPLIANCES

In following out the plan of our work we propose to deal with the appliances belonging to the bird-room as occasions for their use may present themselves.

Fixing the Cage.

We have built our cage and fitted it with the three absolute necessaries, and now proceed to hang it up or place it against the wall in some way. There are more ways than one. Perhaps, instead of a single cage, it may be one of four or six compartments, and it may be proposed to stand it on a small table, in which are drawers for seed, and tins, and all kinds of neat little arrangements. It is difficult to disabuse anyone of the idea that such things are dangerous in the bird-room. We do not object to them in the breakfast-room or library, or in any room into which the idea of furniture enters as an element, but while such tables are valuable adjuncts to the bird-room as stores for accessories, it is advisable not to stand large flight-cages on them. If this be done there is a possibility that the drawers may become infested with red mite, through the connection with the cage. It is much better to stand flight-cages on a pedestal similar to that shown in the diagram on this page. Such can be made any height and length. The cage rests on the four uprights, and thus no harbour for insects is afforded beneath it. With such an arrangement, too, three or four flights can be placed one above the other with perfect safety. A small block of wood, about half an inch square, should be placed at each of the four top corners of the first cage for the second one to rest upon, and so on, for the others. This arrangement prevents the

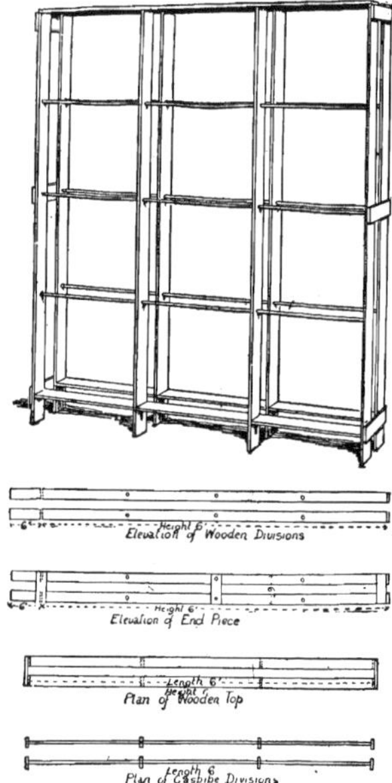

A SIMPLE CAGE-RACK.

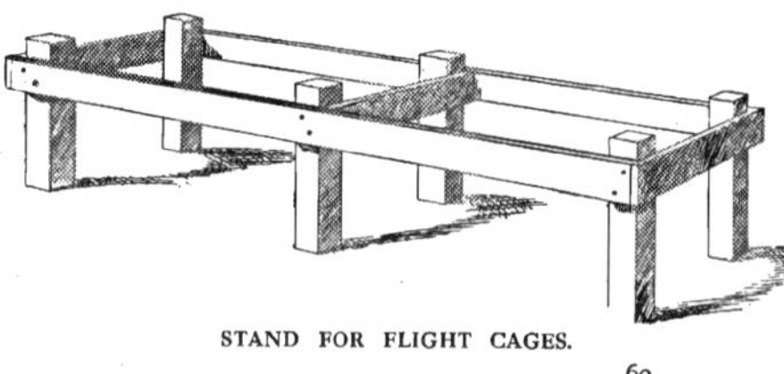
STAND FOR FLIGHT CAGES.

bottom of one flight-cage touching the top of the one below it, and again there is no harbourage between for insects. Should, as sometimes happens, a colony of mites form on the top of one of the flight-cages the advantage of this system is at once apparent. A sharp look-out will soon reveal the pests, and with the space between the cages they can be destroyed without much difficulty.

With such a stack of "flights" before him, the wisdom of adopting uniformity in size and arrangement of parts will now be apparent to the fancier. Seed-hoppers and water-vessels will be seen to be in rows, one above the other, and apart from the pleasing effect to the eye, the convenience of the whole will be manifest in many ways.

The Advantages of the Rack.

For single and double breeding-cages the use of the rack described in connection with the sketch of a room on page 44 is far preferable to hanging them on the wall. In the first place the possibility of insects congregating between the back of the cage and the wall is prevented, for when stood in a rack a space of about an inch can be allowed between the cages and wall. The cages can also be arranged in a much more uniform manner in the rack, for the regularity of the hanging is dependent upon the unevenness, or otherwise, of the chinks between the bricks, wherein the nails have to be driven. An illustration of one of these racks ready for standing the cages in is given on page 60, together with sectional and other diagrams.

The Question of Cleanliness.

Bird-rooms should be thoroughly cleansed and renovated once a year, in the early spring for preference, just before the birds are paired up for breeding. The walls and ceilings should be distempered, and tables, drawers, and any other accessories scrubbed down in the same manner as the housewife carries out her spring-cleaning. Have a real turn out. The cages should all be taken into the yard and given a thorough good scrubbing inside and out. When they are dry any that may be getting bare should be re-enamelled or painted both inside and out. It is a good plan to re-enamel or paint them all over every second or third year, but in any case they should be washed every spring before breeding commences. Much slavery is thereby avoided during the breeding season in attempts to keep down the insect pest, and precautionary measures secured against the attacks of epidemics.

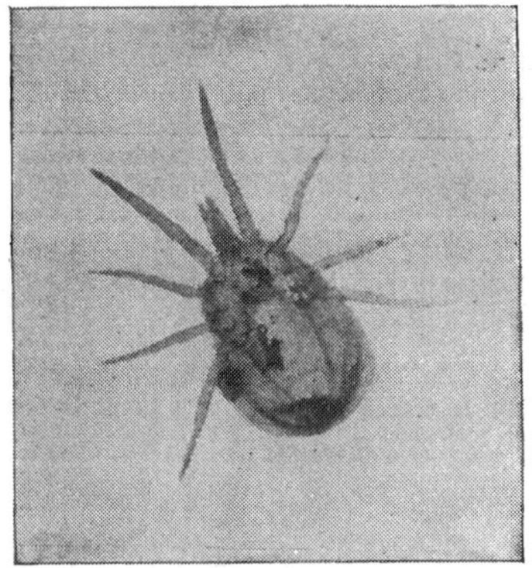

MICRO-PHOTOGRAPH OF RED MITE, MUCH ENLARGED.
(Photograph supplied by Mr. S. Dean.)

When cages have become greatly soiled during the breeding season, as they so often do, from the droppings of the young birds, it is always advisable to scrub them out directly after the breeding season, especially if it is intended to keep birds in them during the autumn and winter.

Nest-Boxes.

Nest-boxes play an important part in the economy of the breeding-cage, and the contrivances and arrangements for them vary greatly in actual practice. Square wooden boxes are largely used in some districts even now, and some breeders maintain that they are warmer for the birds than those of earthenware. We ourselves are glad that this old-fashioned nest-box is fast falling into disuse, and giving place to the more sanitary nest-pan, which forms much less harbourage for the red mite pest than the ordinary wooden box. That the latter is warmer for the birds is pure imagination ; for the earthenware becomes equally warm from the heat given off from the body of the bird. For our own part, we should hesitate now to use either a square wooden nest box or nests of wickerwork, chip, or any similar material, simply on the ground that every crevice would appear to us to be an advertisement of " Apartments to let," and an invitation to the first stray parasite to wander no farther, but to take up his abode in such a cleverly contrived residence.

The Insect Pest.

We have several times referred to this possibility of " insects " becoming a nuisance, but have preferred to keep it out of sight as long as possible. It would have to be explained sooner or later, so we may as well out with it at once and be done with it. Perhaps it will be policy also to represent the case as being much worse than it really is, and then the beginner will be agreeably surprised if he finds things are not so bad as he expected. The Canary, or, indeed, any cage-bird, is liable, under certain circumstances, to become infested with parasites much in the same way as other animals are similarly plagued. The preventive in each case is the same, viz. cleanliness and fresh air ; that is the beginning and the end of the dreadful story. But lest any may find themselves beset by an army of these pests, we give a little further account of them and show how to deal with them. Without entering into any question as to what the little parasite is, it will be sufficient to say that if a sharp look-out be kept on the ends of the perches, the tops of wooden doors, where they touch the cross-bar, the inside of wooden nest-boxes, between the nest and the back of the cage, or any similar hiding-place, the first signs of the pest can always be traced. These consist of a white floury substance, which, if examined closely, will be found to be replete with life, and, if disturbed, will move about in precisely the same way as do the mites in cheese. It is, in fact, a colony of mites—using the word to signify a very small insect and not as a strictly correct scientific term.

Another indication of the presence of the pest, and a sure guide to its hiding-place, are minute white specks dotted along the cross-bar of the cage, along any crevice, or along the top of the cage.

There cannot be the slightest doubt concerning the close connection between this peculiar organism and the bird, since the presence of the latter is a necessary condition of its existence, and probably of its production. How it is generated it is not in our power to say definitely, though many theories have been advanced. We only know that the fact of its existence stands and that it is a very disagreeable fact. Now, if these small settlements of mites be left undisturbed, they will increase and multiply at a rate which leaves blackbeetles and cockroaches far behind in the race. In the early stages of their existence they are white, but when they reach maturity they are of a bright red colour. They then feed upon the birds by abstracting their blood, and to this is due their change of colour. Definite proof of this can be obtained with but little trouble by removing the birds from an infested cage. Let the cage remain empty, and do not disturb the insects. They will not die for a considerable time, but change colour on being deprived of their natural food.

These pests do not, like the larger grey louse, remain on the birds ; but simply go to them, chiefly at night, and then return to their hiding-place. If the cages be examined by candle-light, the insects will be observed running over the birds in great numbers with extraordinary speed, disappearing beneath the feathers in a twinkling. They are essentially nocturnal creatures, and only display this lightning-like agility when running about on the feathers of the birds; for if a nest of them be disturbed during the day, they certainly run off in all directions, but only in a comparatively sluggish way, and are easily killed. It must be admitted that these insects are most undesirable tenants for a breeding-cage; but while fully admitting that they are troublesome and irritating to the birds, we are by no means prepared to go so far as to support the assertion sometimes made, that they suck the blood from the young ones, and cause their death by literally draining them. We can call to mind several nests of exceptionally strong birds which, when we had occasion to remove them into more commodious lodgings, we found had been reared over a perfect ant-hill of insects that lined the under part of the nest in a moving mass. One would have thought their numbers sufficient to have effected a massacre of the innocents in a single night, but the young birds had never shown the slightest ill effects. It is hardly necessary to add that this happened before earthenware nest-pans were made. Nor are we, on the other hand, prepared to support the theory of many old breeders that birds are never so strong and healthy as when infested with these insects—that they are, indeed, positive indications of robust health. Candour, however, compels us to state that though we would rather be without them, and would, and do always, use every precaution to prevent their appearance, they would have to congregate in very great numbers indeed to prove fatal to a bird. We are, though, firmly of the opinion that if not taken in hand they will, and do, in time impair the health and affect the plumage of a bird. The latter effect is due in a large measure to the efforts of the bird to rid itself of the irritation.

The Remedy.

And now, what is the remedy for this evil? If when the cages are cleaned a close look-out be kept for the first appearance of the insects, much anxiety and trouble will be saved. Should, however, a condition of affairs be reached such as we have described, drastic measures must be taken. Clean perches must be supplied, and the dusty spots painted over with turps or equal parts of carbolic acid and water. This will secure the instantaneous death of the pests, and the danger is over. Some fanciers use paraffin, with a piece of camphor in it, in the same way, with good effect, but either of the two former is preferable.

It will now be seen why we have been so very particular to condemn cracks and crannies in the cages. There is no doubt that the smaller the crevice the greater is the likelihood of its becoming occupied.

When cages are whitewashed instead of enamelled inside a loose flake of whitewash will form a certain cover for insects, while unused wire-holes and similar minute recesses are preserves which should regularly be beaten. One thing is certain, the insects must go *somewhere*, and it is as well to know where they *do* go; hence some breeders prefer to keep open one crack that they may know where to find them. Short work can then be made of them by drawing the blade of a knife through the crack. In a sound cage, however, the places we have indicated are about the only ones accessible, and a weekly examination will do the rest. Should the floury appearance show itself on the outside of the cage, round bad joints, or in similar places, nothing is better than to pass over it a small paint brush, which has been dipped either in turps, carbolic, or paraffin. This is a simple method, and does its work quickly, for the moisture soaks into the crevice should one exist.

It will be seen that this nuisance is preventible by the exercise of reasonable care. It is only by neglect of ordinary precautions that it attains formidable dimensions, but if a cage should be found to be infested, it is best to remove it and give it a thorough washing with soap and water, after which it should be rinsed in clean water. Should there be any joints or cracks which afford hiding-places for the pests, they should then be well dressed with a solution of bichloride of mercury, or either of the solutions already mentioned. If the cages have been previously enamelled or painted inside and out they should now have a fresh coat of enamel. No livestock will then be left, as these measures make a clean sweep of them, and destroy their eggs also. One word of caution: old rickety cages should not be allowed in the breeding-room, for it is almost impossible to keep them clean; burn them.

These remarks have followed on our reference to wooden nest-boxes, basket-work and similar nests, and we think that the reason of our objection to them is now patent. Possibly none of our objections is very serious, but we are staunch believers in the old adage — "Prevention is better than cure." We do not assert that the wooden nest-box is not used successfully; indeed, we shall now endeavour to show that it is.

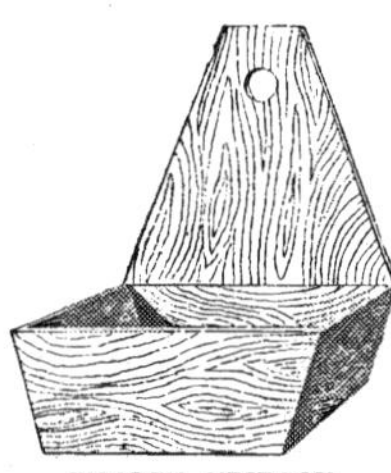
WOODEN NEST-BOX.

It is strange that some people should adhere for so long a time to early teachings in the face of a newer and better creed. In Norwich, the city of Canary breeders, a wooden box shaped something like a kitchen soap-box (as can be seen by a reference to the illustration) is considered the correct thing, and scarcely anything but dried moss is supplied for building material. Yet who shall say that the Norwich men are not successful breeders? We believe that the same methods are applied in certain of the Midland districts, Northampton in particular, another stronghold of Norwich breeding. This doubtless arises from the fact that the example of the Norwich breeders was followed in the early days, and continued as a matter of custom.

The Wooden Nest-Box.

In fact it is only necessary to furnish a hen Canary with some niche or other, and she will soon occupy it; all else failing, she will take possession of the egg-drawer, or even deposit nesting stuff in the seed-hopper, or in the corner of the cage bottom. She *must* build.

The wooden box requires no lining at the hands of the fancier. A more skilful architect than he will weave her own felt, and furnish it in a way compared with which all other attempts are but the most clumsy bungling. We are quite prepared for the statement that years of domestication have done their work in impairing the architectural skill of the Canary, and that it is necessary for their comfort to assist them in this respect. It may be so; and yet if the offspring of a wild bird, which never in its life saw a nest built, can construct its own habitation, why should not the offspring of a tame one, which in its turn never saw one built, be able to do the same thing? The fact is, many of the finches build very slovenly nests as compared with other birds, and birds of the same family vary much in the display of a knowledge of the art of nidification, as every schoolboy knows. The character of the nest is there, but the finish is frequently wanting. And so it is with our caged Canaries. One will do its work in the most masterly way and turn out its nest with exquisite finish, while another will content itself with a mere apology scarcely worth the name. No two build their nests exactly alike: one makes the most perfect cup, so deep that you wonder how she will manage to sit in it; another fills up her box, or nest-pan, leaving barely the slightest depression in which to deposit her eggs; another makes an oval cavity; and another invariably selects the corner of her box, leaving the wood exposed on two sides, much in the same way as we sometimes find a wild bird's nest built against a branch, part of which positively forms a portion of the inside of it. And these birds always do the same thing if they build half-a-dozen times in the season, and yet somehow always manage to take care of their eggs and their young ones if left alone. Perhaps with all our consideration and well-meant endeavours to assist them, they know as

GRASSHOPPER WARBLER. SEDGE WARBLER.
REED WARBLER.

much about it as we do, and, it may be, a little more.

On this page is given an illustration of a tin nest-pan, which has rendered good service in days gone by; some breeders, indeed, use it even now. It is cup-shaped, with a zinc bottom, perforated for purposes of ventilation. It is attached to an upright back, precisely similar in construction to the old-fashioned sconces in vogue before the days of gas, which, containing a spluttering candle, were hung against the wall to render the darkness visible. It is suspended against the back of the cage, on a strong flat-headed tack or nail, driven in at a very acute angle; the hole in the tin is shaped like an inverted keyhole, through the enlarged eye of which the head of the nail passes, the narrow cut allowing the tin to fall on the shank. The inclined position of the nail generally affords sufficient grip to prevent the nest being pulled to one side by the bird. This will constantly happen if the tin be suspended on a screw, as there is then nothing but the friction of the nest against the back of the cage to prevent its oscillating freely, unless the head of the screw be sent well home so as to bite the edges of the slit, in which case it sometimes bites too much, and it is not easy to lift the nest off and on.

Tin Nest-Pans.

TIN NEST-PAN.

Some breeders use these tin nests unlined, but they are much better lined with soft felt procurable at any saddler's. There are two kinds of this felt, white and brown; the white is the better of the two, but is a trifle more expensive than the brown, which is harder and much tougher. The latter is an excellent quality, however, for some birds never leave it alone, even while sitting, but peck away at it till the bottom of the nest is completely perforated. The tougher kind is also to be had black; the texture of the material is the same. We have no choice as to selection, but the white looks cleanest, and has a comfortable appearance about it suggestive of warmth. The felt should be cut into circular pieces, as shown in the accompanying diagram, according to the size of the tins; the diameter of the felt must be much greater than that of the tin, to allow of its being pressed into the cup, flush with the top edge. Each piece must then be split into two, like a muffin. It will be found that the white will split easily, but the brown requires a good pull. In order to fit it into the tins, a deep angular-shaped piece must be cut out of the edge; this should not be cut too large at first, but if the felt will not fit smoothly without any ridges the notch can be enlarged till the desired shape is obtained. The remainder can be cut to pattern. We have always found one deep notch to be amply sufficient, as the stuff is very easily worked into shape in the tins. It must be firmly secured by a few stitches of stout thread passed through the perforated zinc bottom, as the hens will pull away at it in a resolute manner, sometimes biting through the thread and turning the bed out on to the floor. Our reason for making only one notch is that there is only one rent to close, and so the less chance is afforded for insects to find their way into the stuff. When a lot of these felts have been cut they should be threaded on fine strings, according to size, and hung up for use. They will all be wanted before the season

FELT LINING FOR TIN NEST.

is over. Clean nests mean healthy birds, while dirt and filth engender discomfort and disease.

The nest to which we give preference over all others, and which we have now used for many years with the greatest success, is the modern unglazed earthenware nest-pan, lined with either swansdown or felt. The lining is fixed into the nest-pan by means of a stiff paste made of rye flour. If the linings are fixed in overnight they will be firm, dry, and ready for use in the morning. When the nest is soiled by the young birds the linings are easily removed by soaking the nests in water for half an hour, when they will lift out. The nest can then be scrubbed and cleansed from any adhering excrement, rinsed in clean water, and allowed to stand until dry. They can then be relined with new swansdown or felt, and will be equal to new. The zinc pattern by which new linings can be cut, shown in the accompanying diagram, will be found most useful in cutting the swansdown or felt without waste.

Earthenware Nest-Pans.

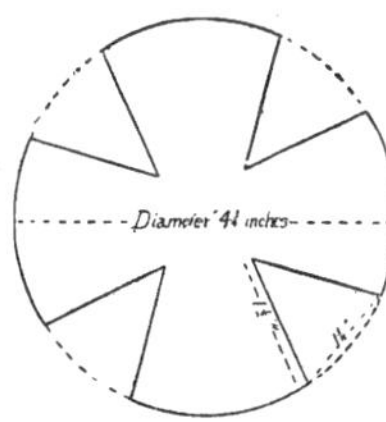

ZINC PATTERN FOR CUTTING LININGS FOR EARTHENWARE NEST-PANS.

This nest is fixed in the cage by means of a wire bracket (*see* diagram), which is hung in the centre of the back of the cage between the two perches, or at the one end, whichever is preferred. This is done by means of a small wire hook, which is screwed into the back of the cage at such a height that the top of the nest-pan, when placed in the wire bracket, hangs about an inch above the level of the perches. This is a nice height for the hens to hop to and from the nest, while it also serves to check the habit, which some hens have, of flying off the nest on to the perch, if the perches are just above the level of the top of the nest. This habit is frequently the cause of young birds or eggs being pulled out of the nest by the hens. The advantage, therefore, of having the perches arranged just below the level of the top of the nest will at once be apparent. When the young birds are about ten days or a fortnight old, the perches can be raised to the level of the nest, or 1 inch above the top if it is desired, as there is then no fear at that age of the young birds being pulled out of the nest by the hen. With the perches fixed above the nest in the manner we have described, the old birds have a greater command, and can feed the growing youngsters much easier, as they in turn stretch up to be fed.

EARTHENWARE NEST AND WIRE BRACKET FOR HANGING.

The round frame of the wire bracket which holds the nest-pan projects about a quarter of an inch at the back, and is finished off with two sharp points which imbed themselves into the back of the cage just sufficiently to hold it firm and prevent the bracket oscillating on the points. These projecting points also keep the nest from touching the back of the cage, thus preventing any possible harbour for insect life. This is a distinct improvement on the arrangement of other nests.

The nest itself is of the most approved shape, it spreads gradually from a nice roomy bottom, rounded inside, with good expanse, thus allowing ample room, for the growth of the young brood. It will be observed from the illustration that there are three or four small holes round the side of the nest-pan as a means of ventilation. The thick round rim at the top not only prevents the possibility of its dropping through the wire bracket, but also affords good perching accommodation on which the old birds may stand to feed the young. As the wire bracket and nest are entirely separate, the nest can be lifted out of the bracket without the slightest difficulty when necessity arises to attend to the eggs or young.

We cannot say that these nests are entirely free from the insect-pest, but, inasmuch as they offer the least amount of shelter, insects are not found in them in such numbers as in the ordinary nesting contrivances.

Slovenly Hens.

There is one difficulty to contend with in breeding domesticated birds, such as the Canary, which does not occur in connection with wild birds: this arises when the hen is given to slovenliness in building her nest. In those circumstances she will often fill the nest with all manner of rubbish that is within her reach, and that may have accumulated in the cage. This must be removed from the nest by the breeder, or otherwise the hard substance would be liable to damage the fragile shell of the eggs while the hen is sitting, and so render them useless. It is well known that there are many British birds who make no nest at all, but simply lay their eggs in a depression in the ground; but the shell of such eggs differs entirely in strength and thickness from those of birds like the Canary, whose general instinct is to build a nest wherein to deposit their eggs. We can only conclude, therefore, that the hen Canaries which build slovenly nests, or no nest at all, are of a slovenly disposition. For these hens a nest must be shaped out as a means of protection for the eggs. It is, however, useless to attempt to form a nest for them until they have laid their full clutch of eggs. Should the nest be placed in the cage before this time, the hens, in nine cases out of ten, will immediately pull it to pieces. This, however, will not happen when the full complement of eggs has been laid, as the hens are then broody, and desirous of sitting on their eggs in the nest.

All that is necessary to make a good nest is a little doe-hair placed in the nest-pan. It should be shaped out with the fingers, and finished off by making the inside smooth and firm. This is best done by twisting a hot boiled fowl's egg round and round a few times. If the eggs are then placed in the nest and returned to the cage the hen will immediately take possession and commence her duty concerning them.

Egg-Drawers and Troughs.

We have digressed a little, and allowed ourselves to trespass slightly on what is, strictly, in the province of "general management," but we have found it difficult to say all we wished about the various kinds of nesting apparatus without doing so in some degree.

We find, on referring to our inventory, that there are not many appliances left to describe; and we may as well dispose of the most important of those which remain, and then dismiss this portion of our subject. It is well not to have anything to make, or to get, at a time when it is wanted for immediate use—a fact the truth of which we all of us experience at some time in our lives.

Egg-drawers, or troughs, must be our next consideration. These are shallow pans in which is supplied the egg-food. There are various kinds: some are made of tin, others of glass, and others again of white glazed earthenware. Those of tin we do not care for, inasmuch as egg-food, being of a moist nature, does not keep sweet for so long a time in a tin vessel as it does in one of glass or earthenware. We therefore recommend the breeder to use either the earthenware or glass trough, or drawer, for this purpose. One of the most handy of these for use in a cage of which the doors are all wire, and slide up and down, is illustrated herewith. This drawer is made of white glazed ware, is of

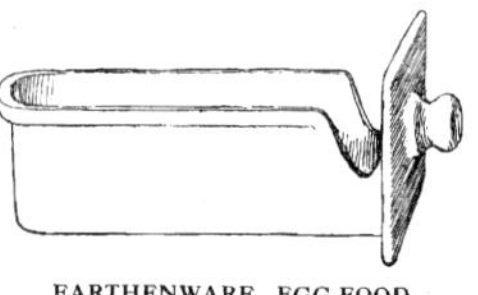

EARTHENWARE EGG-FOOD DRAWER.

nice size and depth, and is notched out at either side just behind the front, so as to allow the door to drop down close upon it. This arrangement makes it impossible for the birds to escape beneath the door, and at the same time the egg-drawer is securely fastened. By means of this efficient trough the breeder is enabled to give his birds their fresh supply of egg-food in a very short space of time and without disturbing them in the least. He simply has to raise the door a little, lift out the egg-drawer, turn out any stale food which may have been left, wipe the drawer dry with a cloth—this should always be done when fresh egg-food is given—put the required quantity of egg-food in the drawer and replace it.

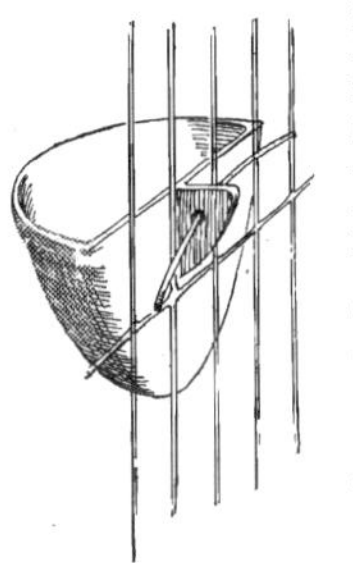
GLASS OR EARTHENWARE EGG-TROUGH WITH LIP TO FIX BETWEEN WIRES.

Where the cage door does not slide up and down, but opens outwards, a very useful trough, made in both white glazed ware and glass, is here shown. The bottom of this vessel is oval, so that there are no corners for the egg-food to lodge in, and consequently it is quickly cleaned out. It is fixed to the front wires of the cage inside, against one of the cross-perches, and has for this purpose a lip with a hole through it. This lip is passed through between two of the wires, and a piece of wire about three inches long is slipped halfway through the hole in the lip, which holds the vessel securely in its place.

A SHALLOW EARTHENWARE EGG-DRAWER.

Shallow earthenware drawers, such as that illustrated, are also largely used, but are not recommended. They are so shallow that much of the egg-food is wasted by being knocked out with the bird's beak. There is a possibility that this stale egg-food may lie on the floor of the cage and form a dangerous attraction to the young birds when they are able to leave the nest. Should they pick about amongst it diarrhœa quickly supervenes.

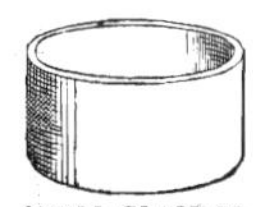
SMALL GLASS OR EARTHENWARE VESSEL.

For this form of drawer, too, the front of the cage has to be cut to allow of its insertion. It will therefore be seen that the deeper drawers and troughs before described are not only more advantageous but more convenient.

Another useful little vessel, made in both glazed earthenware and glass, is also illustrated. In this may be given a supply of boiled or soaked rape-seed when the birds are breeding. It does not occupy much room if stood on the bottom of the cage, and holds as much as should be given at one time. These vessels are also useful for supplying the young birds with a little egg-food while they are in the nursery cage. Crushed seed can also be given in one of them if so desired, or a little bread that has been soaked in scalded milk. It will thus be seen how useful a few of such vessels are in the bird-room during the breeding season. In point of cleanliness nothing equals these earthenware or glass vessels.

As we have dealt with the most suitable vessels in which egg-food can be given, it will not be out of place if we now treat of the best way of preparing the egg-food itself. Various methods are adopted. One, which we remember when quite a boy, was simply to cut in halves a cold hard-boiled egg, unshelled ; the two halves were cut through again, and each pair of birds that was feeding young, was supplied with a quarter, being allowed to feed from the solid piece of egg. This was, of course, a very ex-

Egg-Food.

pensive method of giving egg-food where a large number of birds was kept, and led to the adoption of another that was less extravagant. This plan was to cut the egg into slices after it had been shelled, and mince it up fine with a knife on a clean piece of board kept for the purpose. By this method the egg was given in smaller quantities, and one egg served more pairs than when it was merely cut into quarters. Experience led to still greater improvements, and a very simple but effective utensil was adopted for the preparation of the food. This was the egg-sieve, as it was sometimes called, or the egg-box. It consists of a wooden frame about 3 inches high, and 8 or 10 inches square, with a top of perforated zinc through which hard-boiled eggs are squeezed by pressure with the blade of a dinner knife or a small wooden spatula. It is a most simple and effective contrivance for accomplishing the purpose desired, doing more thoroughly in a few seconds what could scarcely be done in half an hour under the old system of chopping, though the egg when thus manipulated is still always spoken of as "chopped" when referred to in the dietary.

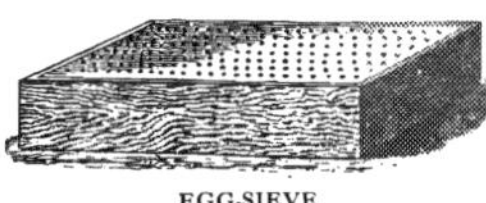

EGG-SIEVE.

It is better to cut the egg up into slices, so as to relieve the perforated zinc of a great deal of pressure which would otherwise have to be exerted to force the uncut egg through.

An adjunct to the egg-sieve is a board to place underneath it, on which to receive what is passed through, for the purpose of mixing—one clamped at each end to prevent warping will be found most serviceable.

There is now an even more rapid means than the sieve by which to prepare our egg-food—an egg-mill. The type illustrated is a mill which has a cylinder perforated with holes of different sizes, and toothed. The shelled egg is placed whole in the receiver on top, with the required amount of biscuit, whole, or broken just sufficiently to go into the aperture. The ram is placed on the top, the handle of the mill given two or three turns, and the egg and biscuit will pass round the cylinder and be ejected on to a board which is placed ready to receive it. The whole process does not occupy more than a couple of minutes. The food may, of course, need just a little more blending with the point of a knife, after it has passed through the mill.

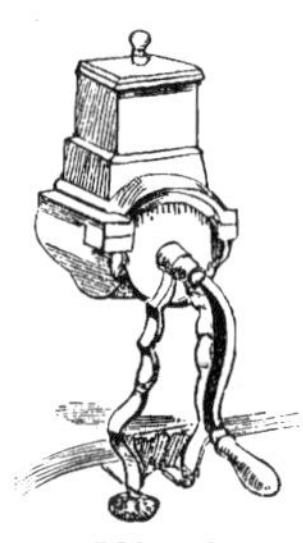

EGG-MILL.

The Bath-Cage.

The bath-cage is a *sine qua non*, and can be purchased in a variety of shapes. It is practically a small cage, the bottom of which forms a trough about 2 inches deep, and may be had either in the form of a zinc trough wired over, or with a wooden bottom containing a zinc or earthenware basin. This bath-cage has a wooden top and bottom and four uprights, and is wired in the form of a cage, with one side entirely open. Two strong hooks in front serve to attach it to the open doorway of the bird's cage. In the illustration of the bath-cage given, a projecting wire from one of the uprights will be observed which comes in front of

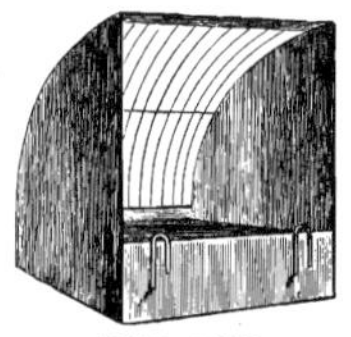

ZINC BATH.

WOODEN BATH-CAGE.

the open door of the cage, about two or three inches from the top of the bath-cage. This wire—which projects about an inch—forms a rest for the sliding wire door of the cage to rest upon. There is thus no possible fear of the door dropping down when the bath is in position, and so shutting the bird in the bath-cage or, what would be worse still, dropping on to the bird as it passed through the doorway into the bath.

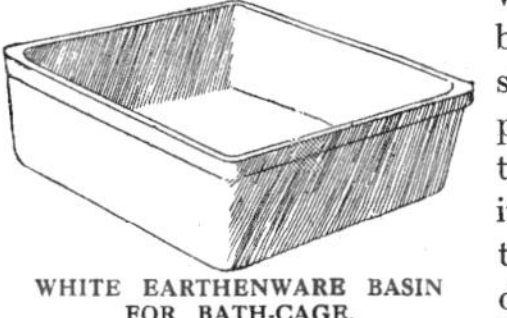

WHITE EARTHENWARE BASIN FOR BATH-CAGE.

Several of these bath-cages will be required, according to the size of the establishment; for birds have their own ideas as to the right time of the day for a wash. The replenishing of the water-vessels is generally the signal for a dip while the water is clean; and the Canary can manage a very fair shampoo through his water-hole. A thorough wash is another thing, and it frequently happens that when one wishes the birds to wash they will take no notice of the bath; but at length, after a few preliminary sprinklings, in goes one bird with a splash, and then out pops every head through its water-hole, and there is a general commotion in the cages. This is washing-time, and the advantage of having several baths at hand to indulge the birds while they are in the humour will be seen as soon as the baths are suspended from the doorways.

A square white glazed earthenware basin suitable for use in the bath-cage is illustrated herewith.

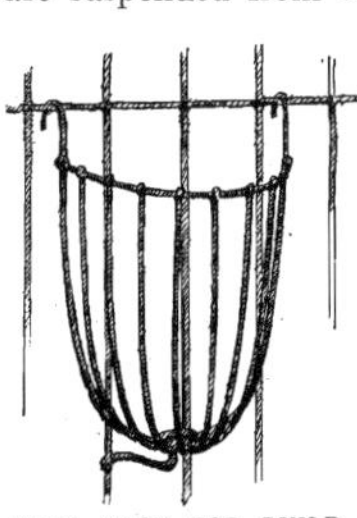

WIRE RACK FOR BUILDING MATERIAL.

Another most useful accessory to the breeding-cage is a small wire rack to hook on the front of the cage, in which doe-hair or other building material may be placed. The birds will pull this through the wires of the cage, and use it to build their nest with.

Miscellaneous Requirements.

Where coarse-cut sawdust is used for covering the bottom of the cages a supply of sharp, gritty sand must be given in a tin or earthenware vessel stood in the cage. A very useful earthenware vessel for such is here illustrated.

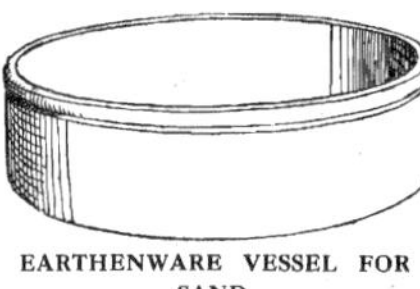

EARTHENWARE VESSEL FOR SAND.

Nursery cages, the use of which will be explained later, must not be overlooked.

Nursery Cages.

These can be bought much cheaper and better than they can be made, unless one is very handy indeed with tools. The cheap rate at which small cages can be manufactured is due to its being a home industry, in which the work of many little hands is turned to account. The cages we use as nurseries can be bought at about 9s. a dozen, and a handy size is nine inches long, seven inches wide, and nine inches high. They have light wooden frames, with the bottom, top, and one end of wood, except for a space of about two inches, between the top of the

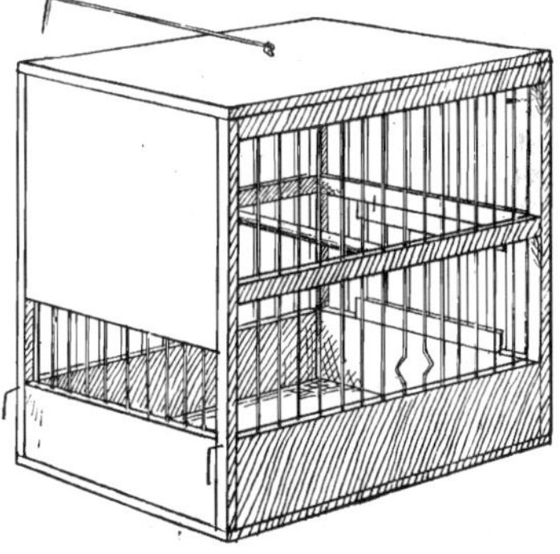

THE NURSERY CAGE.

lower wooden cross-bar and the bottom of the wooden end, which is wired (*see* illustration). Both sides and the other end are wired. The door is made in the wired end, as that is the most convenient place for it when the cage is in use. The framework of wood round the bottom of the cage should not be less than two inches in height. There should be only one perch in the cage—placed in the middle, and resting on the middle cross-bars which run along either side. A turn-rail is also made in the bottom cross-bar, usually at the same end as the door. A water-hole is arranged in the wire-work at one side of the cage so that a drinking-vessel can be hung for the use of the young birds. Two wire hooks shaped thus ┓ are forced, one at either side, securely into the lower portion of the wooden end, by which to hang the cage on to the breeding-cage. A long loose wire catch, arranged from the centre of the top of the nursery cage to fasten on to the front of the breeding-cage, makes the nursery cage complete and ready for use. It is hung in front of the open door of the breeding-cage by these two hooks, and held securely in position by the top wire catch.

METHOD OF CLEANING A CAGE NOT FITTED WITH SAND-TRAY.

A stock of these cages is both useful and necessary in the breeding-room. A few single cages, more or less are never in the way, and cannot well be dispensed with. They are required for the cocks, which should always be separated off singly, and also for the cocks which have to be removed while the hens are incubating their eggs. A spare cage is useful, too, when a bird is taken ill, and indeed in many emergencies. A rolling-pin of hard wood for crushing biscuit, hemp-seed, or other hard food, is necessary to the equipment, as is also a small mill—an ordinary coffee-mill—for crushing seed for young birds until they can crack it for themselves.

Cage-Cleaning.

A simple but effectual method of cleaning out cages which are not fitted with sand-trays is here shown. The turn-rail is removed, and the edge of the dust-pan placed just below the bottom of the cage and held in that position with the left hand; the soiled sawdust, or whatever the material with which the bottom of the cage is covered is then drawn out with the iron scraper into the dust-pan.

Canisters for different kinds of seeds, and a fine sieve for cleaning them should also find a place in a well-ordered room. Where the requirements of a large establishment demand that seed should be bought by the bushel, or even by the sack, canisters for storage are, of course, out of the question. In these circumstances, provided the store-place is dry and free from mice, the seed will keep just as well standing in the sack as it would in a bin; but if mice or other vermin are in evidence then the seed is better stored in a galvanised bin with a lid.

Seed-Canisters, etc.

Seed should always be sifted before it is supplied to the birds, and the contents of the hoppers should also be sifted at intervals—say once a week—as a certain amount of dirt always finds its way into them. If not cleaned out at intervals this accumulatcd dust at thc bottom of the hopper will become a moving mass of mites. Sieves can be procured in varying sizes, but one of the smaller is most generally useful.

Miscellaneous Hints.

A judicious manager will gradually confiscate such articles as a water-can, a galvanised pail, a brush and dust-pan, a scuttle, and other useful articles which he may find about the house, and carefully lock them up in his bird-room to prevent their being again "lost" or mislaid. He will find a use for them all. If he be wise he will also have a small lock-up store-chest, in which he will from time to time stow away medicines and other small sundry articles which are required to be in readiness when occasion necessitates.

If a stout little table, with a nest of drawers, and a comfortable chair have been quietly carried upstairs, there remains nothing for the fancier to do but to lock his bird-room door, put the key in his pocket, and, calling his household together, proceed to the enactment of the most stringent laws with regard to the pains and penalites which will follow any attempt to pry into the secrets of his *sanctum sanctorum.* It will be well for him to remember that he will have to be his own servant and charwoman, and will have to practise carrying his scuttle downstairs in a way calculated not to disturb the amicable relations existing between himself and the guardians of the neutral territory through which he has to travel. There is an art in filling a scuttle and an art in carrying it, and our practical experience leads us to suggest, in the interests of domestic peace, the wisdom of studying both. Bird-seed and chaff have a natural affinity for stair-carpets, and have a way of their own of working into them in defiance of any combination of bristles with which we are acquainted; and Paterfamilias will soon see the value of our hints and the desirability of carefully effacing all signs of his trail.

EXTERIOR OF AVIARY SHOWN ON PAGE 56.
(Photograph supplied by Messrs. Forse and Son, Leyton.)

YOUNG COMMON CANARIES IN AN AVIARY.

CHAPTER VII

INDOOR AVIARIES

THERE are two methods of breeding canaries and other cage-birds, both of which have their own peculiar merits, though the objects desired by each are as widely different as, generally speaking, are their results. The one has been dealt with in the preceding pages of this book, viz. breeding in cages with the view of producing some particular point or points in the birds by scientific pairing. This object can only be carried out successfully by keeping the suitable pairs of birds together in cages, so that other sires of their variety, which are quite unsuitable for certain hens, are unable to get to them while breeding. The other method is followed where the breeder has no particular object in view except to keep a few birds in an aviary; the birds are allowed to fly together and pair up indiscriminately if they desire to breed. The exhibition of birds or the production of stock for the purpose have no charm for this kind of fancier.

To suit his purpose there are outdoor and indoor aviaries. Each is intended for a similar purpose, but from the very nature of things each is of a somewhat different character. For instance, a much higher class of bird can be kept in an indoor aviary, even though indiscriminate breeding be allowed, than in an outdoor one. This would apply equally to some of our British birds.

Danger of Draughts.

Let us, then, first proceed to consider the arrangement and fittings of an indoor aviary. We will suppose an empty room or small conservatory is to be devoted to the purpose. To begin with, it should have a warm aspect and be well protected from draughts; if a conservatory or similar glass erection, it must be well shaded from the strong sunlight. As far as possible all extremes, must be avoided, for it should be remembered that the birds will to a certain extent lead an artificial existence and be more liable to feel the injurious effects of external influences. The most important consideration of all is to effect thorough ventilation with complete freedom from draughts—a more frequent cause of death to Canaries than many people imagine. Too much attention cannot be paid to this, and our instructions on the point are most emphatic. A bird which can be acclimatised to almost any extent can be killed in twenty-four hours in a draughty room.

HIGHEST TYPE OF INDOOR AVIARY.

Trees and Plants for the Aviary.

Having selected a suitable room, proceed to furnish it by placing in it a number of "Christmas trees"—small firs—of various sizes. These, if obtained at a nursery, can be lifted in the autumn, and will, if carefully raised and well potted, live the year through, by which time they will be about done for; as, apart from the unfavourable circumstances in which they are placed, the birds will make sad havoc of them. In their selection substantial plants with flat, spreading branches, should be chosen. They should be tastefully arranged on such stands as can be extemporised for the purpose, singly or in clumps, filling up corners—arranging them, in fact, in any way and every way to suit the individual taste. Avoid, however, placing them so that any part of the room cannot be got at if necessary; for old birds as well as young are apt to flutter away into inaccessible corners, and make no effort to release themselves from positions not dangerous in reality, but from which the birds seem to think escape is hopeless. For instance, if a bird, when frightened, should happen to flutter about and scramble between a tree-box and the wall, the chances are that it would remain there and die without ever trying to get free again. It is this sort of contingency that must be guarded against as far as possible. These are simple matters, but the result of experience shows them to be important. Nothing jars more unpleasantly on sensitive minds than to find that any creature under our care has suffered through circumstances which we might have prevented by the exercise of a little forethought; one such death in the little household is quite enough to leave behind it unpleasant memories which detract greatly from our pleasures.

One would think that, to use a common expression, birds would "have more sense" than to behave so foolishly; but it is not exactly the want of what we call sense which induces such misfortunes. The bird from some cause or other becomes frightened, or perhaps it leaves its nest before it is able to take care of itself, and naturally betakes itself to the quietest corner it can find, where, removed from observation, it remains till the little heart ceases to beat.

The most unaccountable accidents from the most improbable causes will happen at the best of times, and it certainly behoves us to use every precaution against them. There is no excuse for leaving water-jugs and similar traps standing about. The bird has no intention of committing suicide, yet it finds its way into the jug and cannot find its way out. This and many other misadventures have happened to our knowledge, and we are anxious to save others the pain and vexation they cause, for if an accident does occur it is usually to one of the best birds or a particular favourite.

In addition to the firs, trees and shrubs of various tints of foliage, may be used, for they not only give a set-off to the birds, but a pleasing effect to their surroundings. Ferns, too, may be introduced, and so may many of our flowering pot-plants, hung in wire baskets at various heights and positions, or from brackets at the sides.

The Question of Perches.

A few fantastically-shaped branches (from which all loose bark must be removed, for reasons which will hereafter appear) may be arranged in rustic fashion, and any old gnarled stumps or roots may be utilised in a similar way. The branches are not intended for nesting-places, but only as perches. Nothing is more out of character in a room such as we are describing than long, straight perches ; but substitutes must be provided. Canaries are not always on the wing, but will not often visit the floor, except to feed or on other matters of business. The trees themselves are not suitable for perching on, unless any should have fairly substantial branches, and some comfortable resting-places must, therefore, be provided. The birds will soon find these out, and the object of using the supplementary branches is that the whole may look as natural and attractive as possible. If, in place of such an arrangement, one or more long perches be used, the result will be that the birds will generally be seen sitting in a row, in not very picturesque fashion, on the topmost bar, to which they will also immediately retreat when anyone enters the room. To obviate this, all ledges over doors and windows, must be rendered untenable, and more tempting places offered. The birds will most certainly please themselves in their selection of favourite resting-places, and the thing is to make their choice comfortable for them and pleasing to our own taste. It takes a great many birds to fill a small room, and a place may appear tenantless while a score or two of birds are perched up aloft somewhere out of sight.

Another commendable arrangement for such aviaries is to have a number of short perches, about three—but not more than four—inches in length, on which only one bird, or not more than a pair can rest, fixed end-ways into the sides of the room at various heights. This is easily done by driving a wooden peg into the wall, and then screwing the end of the perch to it, tight up to the wall. The positions of the perches must be so regulated that the droppings or excreta from the birds resting on the higher ones do not fall on to the backs of those perching on the lower ones. These short perches prevent much fighting, as they keep the birds well distributed about the room. It will be found that each bird—or pair, as the case may be—will claim its own perch, and always make for it.

Nesting Arrangements.

Ordinary nesting-boxes are out of place in a well-furnished aviary, though they might be cast in a rustic mould. The birds will select their own nesting-places in which to build, and not a little amusement will be derived from noticing the impossible corners some will choose. The slightest projection will suffice for one, and it will spend a great amount of time and labour in constructing its nest under circumstances of self-imposed difficulty. Not unfrequently, some place will be chosen on which it may seem almost impossible a nest could rest ; but it will be found that the Canary is not a bad architect, and generally turns out to be the best judge of a site. Domestication, however, has impaired this wonderful instinctive faculty, and it will be seen that some will make attempts

INTERESTING HYBRIDS.

GOLDFINCH-BULLFINCH. LINNET-BULLFINCH.

CLEAR GOLDFINCH-CANARY.

which turn out perfectly futile, while others will commence to build on a foundation manifestly sandy, in which case it may be well to supply a nest-box, if the bird has shown a determination to settle in that spot and no other. Constant ministration to its daily wants seems to have affected the bird's self-reliance; and though it is wise to leave well alone, it is advisable to maintain a careful watch. Draw a line between watchfulness and inquisitive interference, and there need be little fear for the results.

The small wooden wicker travelling cages, in which the German Canaries are imported to this country make excellent nesting-places, and are greatly favoured by the birds. The whole of the wicker should be removed from one end, so that the birds can pass in and out freely, and the cages hung in various parts of the aviary. They may be placed so that all the outer parts are covered by the foliage of plants growing in the aviary, with the open end left exposed for the entry of the birds. A few birch brooms placed upside down amongst the shrubs with an old Blackbird's or Thrush's nest placed in them are quarters quickly taken possession of; the birds will build their own nest inside the old one. An earthenware nest, similar to those used for the breeding-cage (*see* page 67) may also be hung here and there amongst the foliage, without spoiling the general effect.

A good supply of nesting material should be furnished, such as fibrous roots, where they can be obtained; long, fine, dry grass from the hedge-side; hay; plenty of moss, and, if it can be had, the coarser kind of lichen; soft cow-hair makes capital material for nests, and is always kept in stock at the better class of bird-shops; a supply of soft feathers will be appreciated, as will, also, some rabbit-down and doe-hair. The hair and these latter materials are best packed in small nets, and suspended in positions where the birds can get a good pull at them.

Building material which a bird has some difficulty to obtain, to pull from a net or other enclosure, is much more appreciated than that which it can pick up from the floor. The former is carried off to the nest with much greater triumph, as though a great feat had been accomplished. This provision of material also prevents birds from plucking each other.

If building material be allowed to lie about, the finer stuff will nearly all be wasted. We have mentioned the materials which ought to be supplied, but there are some which ought *not* to be admitted on any account—such as cotton, wool, or other long, tough stuff, which can become entangled in the birds' feet. Wool becomes twisted round the feet in a most dangerous way, and, as it cannot be so readily perceived in a room as in a small cage, a bird may suffer exceedingly, and even lose its toes, before the cause of the misfortune is discovered.

Pleasures of an Aviary.

To complete the furnishing we might arrange in the centre of the room, or some other convenient part, a fountain which could be kept continually playing, thus insuring the birds a constant supply of fresh drinking and bathing water. A small rustic chair, placed in the most retired corner, in which the observer can sit quietly and watch the busy world at work around him, will provide a large fund of interest to the bird-lover. The only requirement really necessary is that the observer *does* sit quietly. It matters not then if there be a nest within a foot of his elbow, or even built on the back of his chair; things will go on just as regularly in his presence as in his absence. Such an aviary is illustrated on page 75. Look which way we will, we continually find something fresh to attract the attention and interest the mind, and the aviary is voted the best room in the house.

Sand and Lime.

A few items, all-important in their way, have to be included in our inventory. The floor should be strewn with clean sand, and a supply of old lime rubbish will be found conducive to the general health of the birds, as well as furnishing a necessary element in the formation of egg-shell. This need not be crushed so small as to become dust ; that will accumulate quickly enough without any assistance ; but if pieces of a crumbly nature are accessible to the birds, they will not fail to avail themselves of them, and with beneficial results. This should be renewed at very short intervals, say weekly, or at most, every two or three weeks. When the birds have picked it over and it begins to get soiled it may still serve as a covering for the floor, but nothing further, for it is virtually dirt, and it is well to remove it from the aviary altogether. In sweeping it up there is no occasion to flourish a long handled brush and create as much terror as possible amongst the occupants. It should be done gently and quietly, and then the birds will take no notice of either brush or sweeper. It is, in fact, only necessary to use a broom at intervals when the aviary is being given an extra clean-out, as a square-mouthed shovel, spade, or scraper, will, in the ordinary way, remove all that is necessary.

It will soon be seen, too, that the supply of fresh sand will be as eagerly looked for as a supply of fresh food, and every bird in the room will be down on the floor in a moment to turn over the fresh stuff and take in a supply with which to assist his little mill to grind its seed.

Clover-Sods.

In country places, where they can easily be obtained, thin clover-sods will be a great acquisition, and almost every part of them will be turned to some good purpose. All work and no play does not suit a Canary any more than the youth in the legendary poem, who is reported to have been made very dull by the process ; and birds are as fond as other creatures of amusing themselves. Nothing entertains them more than picking and pulling to pieces something of this kind, which they will do with many a resolute tug. It is this attention to *little* wants, which may not perhaps be absolute necessaries, that goes far to make up the sum of their happiness.

The Food Supply.

The subject of feeding will afford matter for special consideration. It is no part of the fitting-up of an aviary, though the receptacles for food and water, we think, have to do with it. We do not advise the scattering of much seed on the floor, as a great portion of it would by that means be wasted. Canaries do not scratch and search for their food like the *gallinæ*, or feast till the dish is empty and then pick the bones. Throw a handful of corn to poultry among loose gravel, and not a single grain will be allowed to hide itself ; but the natural habits and instincts of the Canary do not lead it to search in this way, and unless the quantity of seed thrown down be very trifling, it will only be trodden in and hidden under the sand, to be scraped up with droppings and soiled sand. We are satisfied that sweet seed, supplied to the birds in a receptacle which protects it from the contamination of dust and the birds' droppings, is a preventive of disease. All seeds, except those which are given in very small quantities, should be placed in self-supplying hoppers, by which plan there will always be food at command, and the waste will be reduced to a minimum. What is scattered from the hopper falls in one place, and may be collected and sifted without so much probability of its being crushed and trodden into the floor. All our sweepings go to the poultry ; but the fact of having poultry to pick over waste food is no reason why food should be wasted.

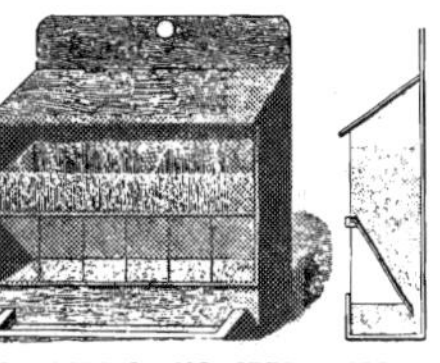

SELF-SUPPLYING SEED-HOPPER.

We show a handy form of self-supplying seed-hopper on this page. The top part of the front is of glass, so that the state of the supply can always be seen. These seed-hoppers are generally made of zinc or wood, some are of mahogany. It will be observed that there is a hole in the back at the top by which the hopper can be hung up. It should be hung in a prominent, bright position, so that the birds have no difficulty in finding the seed; not too high up, but well away from the floor. If it is stood on the floor it is not only likely to become very dusty and dirty, but should there be any mice about it is they and not the birds who would feast on the seed.

Three or four of these self-supplying hoppers should hang in different parts of the aviary if it is a large one and contains a good number of occupants. The seeds which are given in small quantities as tit-bits may be placed in a small earthenware vessel such as is illustrated among the breeding-cage utensils (*see* page 69). The earthenware vessel used for the sand in cages may likewise be brought into use.

Water-Vessels and Baths.

Water, plenty of it, fresh and clear, can be supplied from a large fountain, an illustration of which is here given. It is simply a glass globe with a long neck inverted in an earthenware pot open at the top, and furnished near the bottom with apertures, the lower edges of which are slightly higher than the bottom of the glass neck. Smaller editions may be placed on suitable brackets, the only thing required being that there shall be some kind of perch or other resting-place from which the birds can have free access to the water-holes. Let it be borne in mind that though a bird's instinct leads it to build its nest, to look for food and water, and to be in many respects of a very inquisitive character, it has no intuition which teaches it that water exists for it, not in brooks or pools, but in a glass globe inverted in an earthenware pot which may look to the bird as much like an engine of war as anything else. Many Canaries, when changed from one cage to another and required to put their heads through a hole into a formidable-looking covered-in receptacle in search of what they had been accustomed to find in an open vessel, have never found their water, and have died before the matter could be remedied. It is therefore necessary, in using covered-in vessels in the aviary, to see that young birds and new-comers find their way to them; a "general management" hint, but not out of place.

DRINKING FOUNTAIN.

The drinking-fountain illustrated has an advantage over the conical drinking-vessel with a lip, as the glass globe can be lifted out of the earthenware jar and thoroughly cleaned, likewise the inside of the jar. Water keeps much cleaner in a jar of this description with apertures through which the birds can put their heads to drink than in vessels made with the lip, which catch much dirt, and even the droppings from the birds.

A bath is the last requisite, and nothing is more suitable for the purpose than a large shallow dish, which should be introduced every day for an hour or two. If this be done before sweeping-up time, there will not be much dust. There is no danger in leaving a bath in the room constantly, provided the water be not more than one or two inches deep; but not much is gained by it, because unless nearly all the birds bathe at the same time, those which are not in the humour to do so while the water is clean will not bathe after it has become soiled. Familiarity with the bath also seems to do away with the desire to use it; whereas, if it be introduced only for a short time during the day, the birds splash into it "head over ears" almost before it can be placed on the ground.

A Simpler Aviary.

On page 81 we illustrate a room which is fitted up in a much simpler manner for the successful keeping and breeding of cage-birds flying together in groups. Though it lacks the elaboration of the high-class indoor aviary, birds can be kept and bred successfully under these plainer conditions if the room be not overcrowded—a reservation to be borne in mind under any conditions. In fitting up such a room all that is necessary is first to distemper the walls and ceiling, and then arrange the necessary fittings which are to make the room comfortable for the birds. No. 1 shows a shapely dead tree with a goodly number of branches shooting out in all directions, but with the leaves stripped off. This is fixed firmly into a large garden pot of mould or a square box stood on the floor of the room. The branches are made good use of by the birds as perches. No. 2 is a shallow dish for the birds to bathe in; it can be as large again in circumference as suggested in the illustration, or even larger, provided that it is not more than two inches deep—a depth that prevents any possibility of birds getting drowned. This bath can also be combined with a fountain. The water trickles into the bath from a smaller pan or saucer, into which the spray from the fountain first drops. There must be an outlet near the top of the bath to carry off the surplus water into some convenient receptacle, or possibly it could be carried out of doors by a small waste-pipe—a plan which would be much the better.

The arrangement is shown in the accompanying diagram 2*a*. Such a fountain could either be supplied with water direct from the pipes laid into the house, or from a small cistern, which could be placed close to the ceiling of the room, and from which the water could be conveyed through a small pipe, as shown in the illustration. The cistern will be seen on the right side of the room near the ceiling, with the small pipe running down the side of the wall and across to the fountain.

No. 3 is a single-legged table on which may be placed the birds' soft food and other tit-bits. As the leg fits into the centre of the table-top it is impossible for mice to gain access to the table, and thus the birds' food is kept free from the contamination of these pests, even should they gain access to the room. The bottom of the leg of the table can be fixed into a wooden box about six inches in depth by putting a strong screw, or a couple of screws,

A SIMPLE INDOOR AVIARY.

through the bottom of the box into the end of the leg. The box should then be filled with garden mould, and, if desired, a little rape-seed can be scattered over the surface. This will soon shoot up and keep the top of the box of mould green with its young foliage. As this is devoured by the birds fresh supplies of seed can be sprinkled, and a continuous crop secured. The box with the table can be stood upon the floor in any part of the room, as the weight of soil will keep it firm and steady.

If the box of soil is not considered desirable, the leg of the table can be screwed to a piece of board about two inches wide and a foot long, and by this be fixed securely to the floor of the room by means of two or three screws.

No. 4 gives an illustration of an earthenware tray suitable for giving soft food, or sand, if the floor of the room be covered with rough-cut pine sawdust. In the event of its being used for soft food it would, of course, be stood on the small table already referred to. No. 5 walls. No. 10 is a wire flight built outside the window. When the weather is genial the window may be thrown wide open, and the birds allowed access to the flight. During inclement weather, of course, the window must be kept closed.

A single-storied house built in a garden

A GREENHOUSE INDOOR AVIARY: BREEDING-CAGES ABOVE, FLIGHTS BELOW.
(Photograph supplied by Mr. Percival Lane.)

shows a green shrub, of which there should be several standing about the room in large flower-pots. No. 6 shows receptacles for building-materials, hanging on different parts of the wall. These are wire racks, and take the place of the nets which were referred to in connection with the other aviary. The birds pull the material between the wires of the racks, which answer their purpose well. No. 7 is a self-filling seed-hopper hung in a bright position on the wall. No. 8 are sundry nests hung in different parts; they are all of the open kind; but small wicker cages and box-pattern nests can also be used. No. 9 are perches; but a good number of the shorter ones, three or four inches in length, which were described in the earlier portion of this chapter, should also be placed along the

can be fitted up in a similar manner to either of the aviaries just described.

Garden Aviaries.

If it is lighted from the roof all sides of the house can be brought into use. Such a house in winter-time can be heated by hot-water pipes if desired, just as easily as an indoor room. In this more simply constructed aviary polygamous breeding is more encouraged than in the aviary shown in our first illustration, for there is not the cover and seclusion for individual pairs of birds that is afforded amongst the shrubs and evergreens in the better-class aviary. Consequently, to avoid much fighting amongst the male birds during the breeding season, and while they are in breeding condition, it is advisable to allow two, or even three hens, to every cock.

We have known of even a larger number than this to be allowed. With these extra wives the cocks are kept too busy to fight much. This has reference more especially to Canaries, as male British birds flying together in an aviary during the breeding season are not of such a spiteful disposition.

Such a room as this could be divided off, if of good size, by means of a fine ½-inch mesh wire netting partition, thus making two aviaries. The wire should be fixed on a wooden frame and a door made either at one side or in the centre of the partition to connect the two aviaries. The wire partition will in no wise obstruct the light, whatever may be the arrangement of the windows.

Canaries could then be caged in one side, and British or foreign birds in the other, or, if Canaries are not kept, British birds could occupy one side and foreigners the other. We are strongly of the view that insectivorous and seed-eating birds should have separate aviaries, and from experience we are certain that they do best when so classified.

Then again, if desired, such a room may be divided off down each side, into a number of smaller aviaries, of, say, three or four feet in length, the same in height, and about eighteen inches or two feet deep from back to front. Under this arrangement the aviaries could be made one above the other, and carried up to within eighteen inches of the ceiling, or the ceiling may be allowed to form the roof of the topmost one—the top of one aviary forming the bottom of another. The centre of the room could be reserved for a table on which to prepare the birds' food, and a chair, or other convenience for the fancier's accommodation.

Aviaries arranged in this manner round a well-lighted spare room are excellent for hybrid-breeders who wish to try a number of different crosses at the same time. Such an indoor aviary may be carried out to the utmost extent of elegance and elaboration. What it may be made is suggested by the illustration on page 75. But even in such an ornithological paradise, the essential matters for attention will be just the same, and no more, than those that have already been mentioned.

Such we take to be the leading features of the aviary system; which, it will be manifest, is rather a means of general interest and source of pleasure to the general observer, than a method of carrying out any specific system of breeding with the object of bringing about definite results. It has been our aim to present it in this its true light, and we feel assured that those who make it their study will discover in it many beauties we have failed to point out; they will find it a world which insensibly becomes peopled with creations of which they once knew nothing, with which they can hold converse and enter into companionship. Their own world of observation will be considerably enlarged by even this small peep into the vast domain open to the inquirer who, at every step, recognises the evidences of a Wisdom "past finding out."

LIZARD CANARIES.

OUTDOOR AVIARY AND FLIGHT.
The property of Mr. Holmes, Carlisle.

CHAPTER VIII

THE OUTDOOR AVIARY

THE aviary method of keeping birds, as we have already explained, is best adapted for those who have no definite purpose, other than the pleasure derivable from general observation—a pleasure of the highest order, though confined, in a considerable degree, to the simple lover of Nature who regards all her manifestations with a delight into which no question of how or why intrude. To such the outdoor aviary opens up a new world of interest, peopled with forms whose outer adornment is of less moment than the beauties of their inner life. These equally charm the fancier, who nevertheless is more exacting in his demands in other respects. His admiration of the general economy of the aviary is not lessened if to it he unites other aims, and seeks to clothe its tenants in higher forms of beauty. It may be, and probably is the case, that any one ruling passion has a tendency to crowd out others; but there is no reason why one healthy feeling should absorb more than its due share of attention, and we fail to discover any reason why the interests of the true naturalist and the genuine fancier should not be combined.

We have said that each of the methods of breeding indicated has its advantages and disadvantages. We may sum up the advantages of the aviary system briefly, by saying that it involves only a small amount of care and attention; the birds are left pretty much to take care of themselves, to choose their own mates, and make

YORKSHIRE CANARIES

1 Clear Yellow 2 Clear Buff 3 Ticked Yellow 4 Cinnamon-marked Yellow

their little world inside the wires as much as possible like that outside. This putting the reins of power into their own hands removes all the responsibility from the observer, who has nothing further to do than to keep the birds' abode clean, supply the necessary sustenance for existence, and to watch the goings-on of the little republic. There will develop, among much that is beautiful, certain forms of government which the conservative fancier considers subversive of all order.

Indiscriminate Breeding.

Among these disadvantages is indiscriminate pairing, which renders it impossible to breed any distinct variety—if more than one be kept—though this may not be a disadvantage to those who, so long as they breed *something* and have the pleasure of seeing it reared, do not care what that something may be. It would perhaps be scarcely fair to charge the Canary with habitually pairing with more than one mate; indeed, the idea is foreign to the natural habits and instincts of the Finch family in a wild state. Half the poetry that attaches to the mere name of nest seems to consist in the halo of quiet and purity which surrounds it. Still there are now and then evidences of a contrary state of things even among wild birds, and no doubt the commotion which sometimes takes place in the ivy is nothing more than a noisy public meeting to take into consideration the desirability of turning out of the community some ill-conducted member. The occasional capture of a hybrid, too, is evidence of an alliance having taken place between members of different families. These, however, are manifestly exceptions, and there are many keen observers who assert that such alliances have never taken place in the wild state; that they have been accomplished under the influence of man, and that wild hybrids so caught have either been liberated, or have escaped from an aviary; with which assertion we agree. The wild bird in her beautiful little home demands all her mate's care and attention, and receives it. He spends his entire day in ministering to her wants, and is not more exclusively devoted to her in all his delicate attentions than is she to the precious treasures nestled so closely to her breast. But in the aviary things are different. Although preserving many natural instincts almost unimpaired, the Canary has had some of them modified, or even materially affected, by generations of domestication. Notwithstanding that he may, in the early spring, select some one particular bird, and that matters be arranged to the entire satisfaction of both, he yet no sooner sees his mate comfortably settled down on her nest than—though he does not forsake her—his attention is drawn away in other directions. This is all very pretty and all very well for those who only wish to study bird-life generally, and to keep the aviary well stocked; but it is, for obvious reasons, not the fancier's way of going to work. We must, however, say, for the credit of the sex, that such an erratic disposition is not shared by the hens: as a rule they remain true to their first selection, till a lengthened separation and entire seclusion wean them from their original mate.

Quarrelsome Males.

We must not forget that in an aviary the birds are in a limited space, and on that account it is not advisable to have too many male birds flying together during the breeding season; much quarrelling is otherwise likely to ensue, with possible injury to birds of a fierce disposition. This is, in a measure, guarded against when the aviary affords an abundance of secluded shelter with a plentiful amount of thick foliage. It is in this direction that an outdoor aviary can be made so much more advantageous than one arranged indoors. The wired or netted open space, or fly, of the aviary can be arranged in such a manner as to induce the growth of bushy shrubs and evergreens, which prove a paradise to the birds. They serve both as a means of shelter from the interference of other birds, and for the building of their nests. We have known as many as forty to fifty young Common Canaries to be reared in one season in a thick privet hedge that ran along one side of the fly of an outdoor aviary.

In cases where twice, or even three times, as many hens as cocks are in the aviary—a state of affairs which is often advisable, where good shelter cannot be afforded—polygamy is directly encouraged among the cocks. The repeated calls for attention from the various hens is more than they can resist, for a time at any rate, and meanwhile the first choice of the season sits quietly incubating her eggs. Polygamy, of course, is rarer among those males whose duty it is partly to incubate the eggs. I am not prepared, indeed, to say that any such species are polygamous, for they are kept too busy during incubation time, taking their turn at sitting on the eggs.

Communal Nests.

Another outcome of the complete domestication of the Canary is seen in the fact that all nests become common property. The birds seem to want a *place* in which to lay, and nothing more, and select their favourite nest much in the same way as do domestic poultry. All are at one time or another affected by the desire to set up house for themselves, and go about it very energetically, evidently impressed with the importance of having, according to bird building-society maxims, a roof-tree of their own. This once done, and the instinct satisfied, nothing further seems to be desired. There is no idea of privacy, nor the slightest regard for property rights. Two or three, or as many hens as can possibly find a resting-place, may be seen occupying the same nest and even sitting on each other's backs, anywhere and anyhow, so long as they can only find some means of squeezing in, like hens in a poultry-yard, taking possession of the same eggs, too anxious to cover them to think of quarrelling. The young even become common property, and we have frequently seen two hens, one on either side of a nest, assisting the cock bird to feed a family which could certainly be in no way related to one of them, and which she had taken no part in hatching

These, of course, are exceptional cases. At times some extraordinary instance will be found in a wild bird at liberty, for we have more than once on our rambles seen an old Blackbird feeding a young Thrush which kept fluttering after it and crying for food. We have also seen an old Thrush feeding a young Blackbird which kept crying for food in the same manner. In neither case would the adult bird be the parent of the young one it was feeding, but it is evident that the pitiful appeals of the young birds, who had apparently got astray from the nest, appealed to the parental instinct of the adults.

Unfertile Eggs.

There was a time when we had the impression that only Canaries and other birds kept under domesticated conditions had unfertile eggs and neglected their young. This delusion was largely due to our not having been observant enough in our travels in Nature's realm. For, as time went on, we found many wild birds' nests which contained not only unfertile eggs, but whole broods of young dead in their nest, without a particle of food in their crops. Whether the parents had met with an untimely death by some marauder or other we do not know, but the fact remains that we have frequently found nests of dead young, and also deserted nests of eggs. The unfertile eggs were not always occasioned by non-sitting, as we have found them in nests with a young brood being tenderly cared for by their parents. In some instances flustering the mother from the nest will cause failure in breeding amongst birds in their wild state, as well as with birds in captivity. Then, of course, they have the ill effects of unfavourable seasons to contend against, just as birds indoors have, with this difference, that the captive birds have shelter and food provided, and are thus relieved of much misery and discomfort.

The illustration on page 87 is a pretty design for an outdoor aviary of simple construction by Mr. A. C. Horth. It could, of course, be built on a large or small scale, and with or without sleeping quarters—

we prefer the former. Nesting and sleeping accommodation can be arranged in the roof and over the porch of the doorway if none can be afforded adjoining the aviary. The structure should be boarded in on two, or even three sides, so leaving only the front open. It should

A Simple Outdoor Aviary.

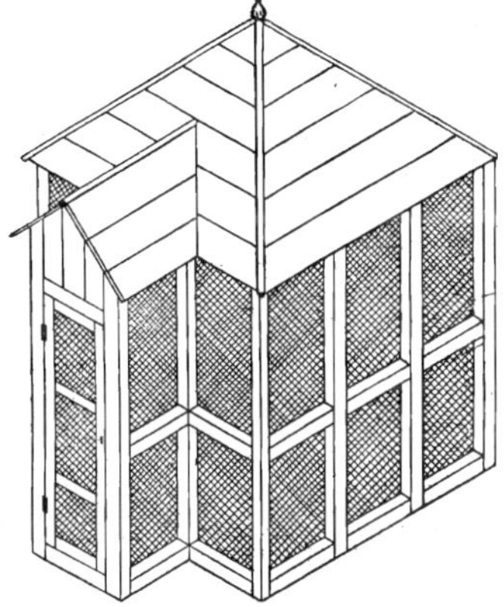

MR. A. C. HORTH'S OUTDOOR AVIARY.

be so planned that the open front escapes the east wind. The design shows two sides of the aviary boarded in, and for the sake of simplicity in their description we will call them the offside and the back. In building such an aviary some yellow deal quartering $2\frac{1}{2}$ inches by $2\frac{1}{2}$ inches would be required for the framework, or if it is intended to build it on a large scale it might be better to use 3-inch by 3-inch; but the $2\frac{1}{2}$-inch would be sufficient for a strong aviary of good size. Some battens, 3 inches by 1 inch, would also be required for the framework of the roof, and a further supply of battens of the same size for the framework of the door. Some $\frac{5}{8}$-inch match-boarding, tongued and grooved as shown in the accompanying diagrams, completes the wood requirements. The quantity required would depend entirely upon the size of the aviary it is proposed to construct, and could easily be arrived at by measuring up before the building is commenced. Various sizes of nails or screws would also be wanted, but the latter are preferable, for if the aviary is built in sections, it can be easily taken to pieces for erection elsewhere if it is so desired. With the necessary quantity at hand of galvanised wire, or $\frac{1}{2}$-inch mesh wire netting, building operations can at once be commenced.

MATCH-BOARDING, TONGUED AND GROOVED.

After the rough quartering has been planed smooth and square, the four corner uprights should be cut and then the top and bottom rails or cross-bars These

CORNER UPRIGHTS, MORTISED AND TENONED.

are mortised and tenoned at both the top and the bottom, as shown in the diagrams on this page. Into this square frame the other uprights should be housed in the manner shown. Care must be taken to get a good fit at this point. The cross-bars for the centre should next be prepared, planed, etc., and the ends tenoned into the uprights. The two joints in the centre are quite simple, as may be seen from the diagram. When the framework of the aviary is completed the roof-frame should next claim attention. The 3-inch by 1-inch battens are used on edge, with the sides sloping at an angle of about 45 degrees. Two opposite pieces should first be securely fixed by nailing, or screwing them on to the top of the corner uprights and at the open ends. The other pieces can then be fixed. Though this roof is not scientifically constructed it will be found quite suitable to the purpose of the aviary. The framework over the porch should next be put together with the $\frac{5}{8}$-inch match-boarding, of which also the roof is built. The latter is completed by nailing some $1\frac{1}{4}$-inch round or cornice lengths over the joints of the boards at each angle, and not forgetting some kind of ornamental knob or spire for the top.

ARRANGEMENT OF ROOF BEAMS.

The roof can be made thoroughly water-tight if it is covered with sheet zinc before the rounds or cornices are nailed in their places, or the cornices could be covered with the sheet zinc as well.

The Aviary Doors.

The double doors yet remain to be made, one for the entrance into the porch—which should be strong and well put together—and an inner one, which is fixed at the other end of the porch and admits directly into the aviary. This need not be of quite such stout material as the outer door, as it is really only placed here to make the aviary doubly secure against the escape of birds. The outer door should, of course, always be closed before the inner one is opened, so that should a bird dart past as this inner door is opened it can get no farther than the porch, where it can be easily secured or driven back into the aviary. For convenience' sake it is better to make both doors the same size. The cross-bars should all be mortised and tenoned into the uprights, and if it is desired to make an extra strong job a diagonal piece should run from top to bottom, housed into the cross-bars.

There now remains only the galvanised wire or fine-mesh wire netting to fix on to these frames, and the doors will be complete. The wood for the fillets can be sawn out of any odd pieces that are left over. The strength of the hinges to be used in the hanging of the doors depends entirely upon the weight of the latter. It is well, however, to remember that it is always better to have them a little on the strong side than otherwise. They not only last longer, but the doors hang more true; weak or slender hinges are a source of trouble from almost the commencement, for they quickly allow the doors to drop out of their proper level. Of locks for securing the doors there are plenty, but the good ones are the cheapest in the end, for the cheap forms soon get out of order. A wire catch or hasp should be fixed on the inner side of both doors, so that they can be securely fastened from within the aviary, without any fear of their flying open.

Wiring and Painting.

The flight portion of the aviary may be doubly wired as an extra precaution against cats. This is done by wiring the inner side of the wooden frame as well as the outer; this allows a space between the two, so that when the birds cling to the wirework—which they usually do—they are well out of reach of any marauding tabbies.

Two or three coats of good paint on both wood- and wirework should be given as a protection against the ravages of bad weather, and a coat at intervals afterwards, for the sake of keeping the structure in good preservation and appearance, should never be neglected.

Fittings.

Such an aviary can be fitted up, in a similar manner to that recommended for the indoor aviary, with nests, perches, food vessels, fountain, etc. The green shrubs are much more easily kept green in the open flights than in an indoor aviary, and if the earth forms the floor a hedge of privet may be planted on the inside of the wirework either partly or right round the flight. The birds will much enjoy this to fly into, and will even build their nests in it. Where the earth forms the floor it is advisable to run a border of concrete right round the outside of the aviary, to a depth of at least 6 inches—if it is 10 or 12 inches deep so much the better—to prevent the ingress of vermin. If a covered-in house in which the birds may roost is built to an aviary it is best to let such a house have either a concrete floor or one of boards raised six or eight inches from the ground, as a preventive of damp.

A Simple Outdoor Aviary.

Below we give an illustration of a very useful outdoor aviary different in shape, yet simple in construction. The flight sides and roof are entirely open, with nice, cosy covered-in sleeping quarters attached. The wooden framework of the flight is covered with lengths of close

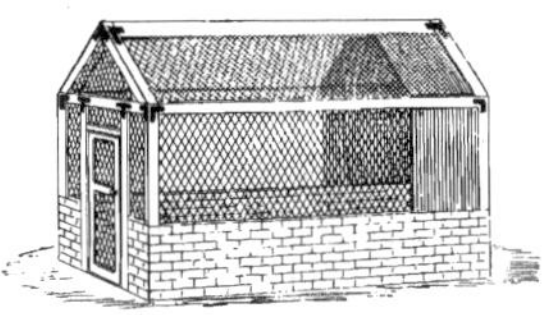

A SIMPLE OUTDOOR AVIARY.

galvanised wire, or ½-inch mesh wire netting may be used instead. The joints of the framework may either be mortised and tenoned into each other or fixed by strong angle-irons securely screwed over each joint. Our illustration shows the framework of the flight fixed with these angle-iron plates. The strength of the framework must be regulated according to the size of the aviary, but it is always well to have the woodwork sufficiently strong. This to some extent guards against much warping, especially if well-seasoned wood is used. Our illustration also shows the lower portion of the flight, built of brick to a height of about two feet. Match-boarding could be used instead of brick, though, of course, it is not so durable.

Some aviculturists prefer a single door to their aviary, and for their convenience we show this flight built in that manner. The porch and double doors could, if desired, easily be adapted to such an aviary.

Although the illustration shows this flight with an open wire roof, there is nothing to prevent its being built with a covered roof if it is preferred. It is simply a matter of continuing the boarding of the sleeping quarters over the flight instead of covering it with wire. It can be made weather-proof with a covering of good tarred felt, corrugated iron, or sheet zinc —one of the two latter for preference. The little extra expense which would be incurred at the outset would be more than saved in the end, to say nothing of the labour in attending to the roof at intervals when felt is used, or the boards simply tarred.

The sleeping quarters, or house, as will be seen, is a wooden structure closed in all round, the roof being covered with corrugated iron or sheet zinc. There is an entrance into this house from the flight, which can either have a door to close when the weather is cold and damp, or be left without one. This apartment can be made very comfortable for the birds even without a door if it is well sheltered. If preferred, a door can be made into the sleeping quarters from the outside, either at one of the sides or at the end; but a house which has the entrance to it from the flight is, as a rule, much more cosy. The interior fittings can be arranged to the builder's own taste.

A Lean-to Aviary.

Our next illustration shows the form of outdoor aviary, known as a "lean-to," of which a wall or wooden fence forms the back. They are not at all difficult to erect, and are put together and jointed in a similar manner to those with which we have just

A LEAN-TO AVIARY.

dealt. Where a good wall or fence can be utilised as a back a great saving can be effected in material. The highest point of the roof should be kept some six or nine inches below the top of the wall. By this means the work can be made more complete, while the edge of the roof which joins the wall can be made more waterproof than if it were taken up to the level of the top of the wall. A little cement well mixed with sharp sand placed along this line will secure this result. As an alternative the roof can be taken up a little above the wall, so that the back-edge can be covered with a strip of sheet zinc and thus made damp-proof. The doors and other arrangements can be made on the same lines as those for other aviaries.

It will be seen by the illustration that this aviary has a covered-in house for sleeping and breeding quarters, which is made nice and light by means of a sky-light in the roof. This arrangement would naturally encourage the birds to take up their nesting sites in this secluded spot during the breeding season. The wood-work of the roof can be covered with tarred felt, corrugated iron, or sheet zinc; of the two latter the zinc would make by far the neatest job, as it can be made to fit closely round the glass skylight. It is, of course, not absolutely necessary to have the glass skylight. A small window fitted in the side would answer the purpose so far as light is concerned, and would be easier for the amateur to construct, but it would not afford so much light. The doorway into the sleeping quarters of this aviary opens into the flight, and this flight differs some-what from the other examples. The top is covered in, and one half of the front and end have glass windows, with the lower half closely boarded. These windows are made to open outwards, like casement windows, with a closely fitting frame of fine wirework inside, so that in the summer-time the glass windows can either be removed or fixed widely open night and day. In the winter they can be kept closed. With the protection thus afforded many birds can be kept in this aviary during the winter which it would not be advisable to attempt to retain in one of the more exposed flights. The top of this aviary has to be covered as shown—the zinc, corrugated iron or felt fitting closely round the skylight, the end glasswork made all alike, and the door built just one half of the end.

A Model Aviary.

On page 91 is an illustration of a charming aviary on a large scale in the grounds of that well-known lady aviculturist, Miss R. Aldersen. The flight has a glass roof, and runs off flat at the front; to prevent the birds injuring their heads should they fly up against the roof, it has an inner lining of "strainering" stretched lightly across an inch or two below the glass. This "strainering" is a transparent material which practically obstructs no light, and does not injure the birds when they fly against it. This large flight and covered-in shelter or house are divided off into sections—the flight by means of fine-mesh wire netting partitions. In these compartments groups of the different birds can be kept together, and allowed plenty of space, both for shelter and flight. There is no need for us to go into details of this aviary as the illustration plainly shows its construction.

The site selected for this aviary is, however, worthy of a note, as it clearly reveals the careful thought that has been given to the welfare of the birds. The aviary is surrounded by trees, and so arranged that while the trees do not obstruct the light, they afford protection and shade, and thus assist to keep the aviary cool during the summer weather, and in the winter afford protection against the fierce winds. In such an aviary little or no difficulty would be experienced in getting the shrubs to grow inside the wirework of the flight.

To all, therefore, who desire an all-the-year-round pleasure, and have the facilities wherewith to carry it out, we say set up an outdoor aviary and keep it well- but not over-stocked. The time spent in looking after the needs of the occupants is well rewarded by the lessons learnt and pleasure gained.

We have illustrated several types of aviaries from the simplest to the most ornate form, and as large numbers of bird-keepers are town dwellers, conclude the series on our next page with a range of lean-to aviaries built against the stone wall of an Edinburgh suburban garden, which may furnish useful hints to fanciers whose dwellings are similarly situated.

An outdoor aviary, for general purposes, is, we think, quite as useful as the indoor, and where pairs or groups of British birds for hybrid breeding are to be the chief occupants, it is certainly the more desirable.

As to whether the Canary can, under reasonable conditions, withstand extremes of temperature, there is not the slightest doubt. He is one of the most easily acclimatised birds we have, and there is no difficulty in housing him so that he shall care nothing for either winter or summer. We will not undertake to say what might or might not be accomplished in this way very far north, or in situations exposed to long-prevailing east winds; but we repeat that, under reasonable conditions, or even under circumstances which might, until tried, be thought too adverse, the question of being able to establish an outdoor aviary and keep Canaries in it throughout the year, need not cause the slightest apprehension as to its perfect practicability. Indeed, we are of opinion that it is *the* method of keeping any number together indiscriminately, and that birds once acclimatised are as proof against the attacks of the weather as our native wild birds. In thus expressing ourselves we, of course, refer to the Common Canary, and not to high-class exhibition stock.

FRONT OF MISS ALDERSEN'S AVIARY.

SUBURBAN GARDEN, WITH AVIARIES.
(*Photograph supplied by Mr. A. Cochrane, Edinburgh.*)

CHAPTER IX

THE EGG AND DEVELOPMENT OF THE YOUNG BIRD

BEFORE entering upon the subject of nesting and hatching, it will be well to give some account of the structure of an egg, and to do this simply we propose to trace the egg throughout its development.

The Egg and its Production.

The late Mr. Lewis Wright, the ablest of modern writers on poultry, gave in his "Book of Poultry" a most explicit account of the structure of an egg and its development into a living chick, from which, since the remarks are equally applicable to cage birds, the following extracts are taken.

"Every animal, of whatsoever kind, is developed from the egg-form, or, as physiologists express it, *omne animal ex ovo.* But the mode of that development differs, in one detail especially. In mammalia the egg is retained throughout within the body of the mother, which is its sufficient protection, and the development is uninterrupted. In oviparous animals, such as birds, the egg is enclosed in a hard protecting shell, and at a certain stage of development extruded from the body of the mother; in this case development is arrested at that point, and may or may not be resumed and completed.

"The ovary of a hen during or near her laying season presents an appearance much like that of a cluster of fruit [similarly arranged to a bunch of grapes, and varying in size; of course, in fowls the number is much greater than in the case of cage birds]. There are, strictly, two such organs in every bird; but one remains merely rudimentary and undeveloped, the fertile one being almost always that on the left of the spine, to which it is attached by means of the peritoneal membrane. By the ovary the essential part of the egg, which consists of the germ, and also the yolk, is formed, each yolk being contained within a thin and transparent ovisac, connected by a narrow stem or pedicle with the ovary. These rudimentary eggs are of different sizes, according to the different degree of development, and during the period of laying they are constantly coming to maturity in due succession.

"As the yolk becomes fully matured, the enclosing membrane or ovisac becomes gradually thinner, especially round its greatest diameter or equator, which then exhibits a pale zone or belt called the *stigma*. Finally, whether or not fecundation takes place, the sac ruptures at the stigma, and the liberated yolk and germ, surrounded by a very thin and delicate membrane, is received by the funnel-shaped opening of the *oviduct* or egg-passage, whose office it is to convey it to the outer world, and on its way to clothe it with the other structures needful for its development and preservation. . . . It will easily be seen how *two* yolks may become detached and enter the oviduct at nearly the same time; in which case they are likely to be enveloped in the same white and shell, causing the 'double-yolked egg' [so well known to every breeder of cage-birds].

The "White" and Shell.

"Thus received into the oviduct, the yolk becomes enveloped in a glairy fluid called the white, or by chemists, *albumen*. This is secreted by the mucous membrane of the oviduct, and added layer by layer as the egg passes on. The uses of the white or albumen are manifold. It is eminently nutritious, forming, indeed, the chief nourishment of the chick during its growth in the shell; as it becomes absorbed by the little animal, and forming as it does by far the greater part of the egg when laid, it gives the fast-growing little body the needed increase of room; it is a very bad conductor of heat, and hence guards the hatching egg against the fatal chills which would otherwise occur when the hen left the nest; and, finally, it preserves the delicate yolk and vital germ from concussion or other violent injury.

"At a still farther point of the oviduct the egg becomes invested with the skin or parchment-like covering which is found inside the shell. In reality this skin consists of two layers, which can easily be separated; and at the large end of the egg they do separate entirely, forming the air-chamber. At first this chamber is small, but as the egg gets stale it becomes larger and larger, so that even in eggs stored it fills at length a large portion of the space within the shell, the egg itself drying up in proportion. In eggs on the point of hatching it usually occupies about one-fifth of the space. It has been proved by experiments that the perforation of this air-chamber, even by a needle-point, is an effectual prevention of successful hatching.

"In the last portion of the oviduct the egg becomes coated with that calcareous deposit which forms the shell, after which it passes into the cloaca, and is ready for expulsion."

Coloration of Egg-shells.

The majority of the shells of eggs contain colouring pigment, or are coated with it, hence the varying shades. "All these things obviously depend on some peculiar condition of the secreting organs, as does the shape of the egg of each bird when finally laid." At the time of laying it is expelled from the uterus by violent muscular contractions, and passes with its narrow end downwards along the remainder of the oviduct to reach the exterior.

Variations of Eggs.

"Occasional departures from the ordinary type of egg will now be understood. If the latter portion of the oviduct be in an unhealthy condition, or if yolks be matured by the ovary faster than shells can be formed by that organ, 'soft' or unshelled eggs will be produced. If, on the contrary, the oviduct and its glands be active, while the supply of yolks is temporarily exhausted, the diminutive eggs which consist of only white and shell, and which not infrequently terminate the laying of a long batch, may be expected to occur."

This, however, more particularly applies to fowls, though we have known of some isolated instances of yolkless eggs being laid by Canaries.

"Disease, extending to the middle portion of the passage, may result in eggs without even the membranous skin; and if the entire canal be in an unhealthy condition, yolks alone may probably be dropped without any addition whatever, even of white. This last occurrence, therefore, denotes a serious state of affairs, and should be met at once by depletic medicines,

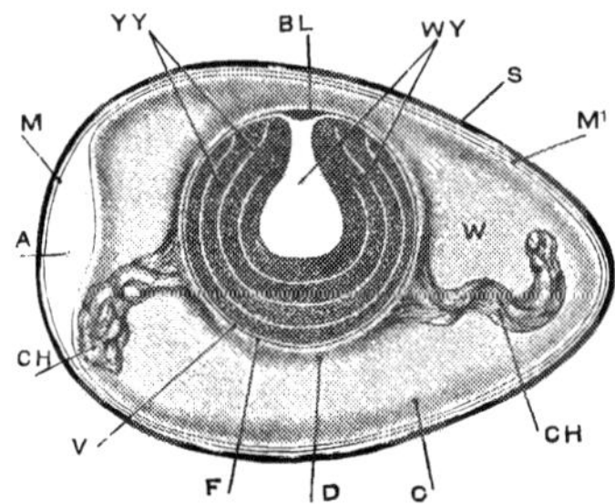

DIAGRAM OF AN EGG (*Magnified*).

BL, Blastoderm; WY, White yolk; YY, Yellow yolk; V, Vitelline membrane; F, Layer of very fluid albumen round the vitelline membrane; D, Dense albumen enclosing the yolk, with preceding envelopes. In this envelope D are incorporated the ends of CH, the chalazæ; W, Body of the albumen; C, Somewhat denser layer of albumen, surrounded by a fluid layer; M, M[1], outer and inner shell membrane, separated at A, air chamber; S., Shell.

or it will probably be followed by the loss of the bird.

The Egg and its Structure.

"Let us now consider the egg itself, which is a much more complicated organism than many people are aware of. There is much even in the shell, S [*see* diagram], to excite our interest.

"It is composed chiefly of prismatic particles [carbonate of lime, with a small quantity of phosphate of lime and animal mucus, so arranged as to allow of the shell being porous]. For its thickness and texture its strength is phenomenal.

"As hatching proceeds, however, the carbonic acid and dioxide formed by the breathing of the chick, dissolved in fluid, gradually dissolve a portion of the material, and thus the prismatic bodies are slowly softened and disintegrated. The shell thus becomes far softer and more brittle as hatching approaches; and so great is the difference that if the edge of a fracture made across a fresh egg-shell, and another of one hatched or hatching, be examined under a microscope, it will be instantly seen that the two are in a quite different molecular condition. Were it not for this beautiful provision of Nature, the bird could never break the shell.

"The outer and inner shell membranes, M and M[1], separating the air-chamber, A, need no further explanation. Proceeding inwards, we come next to the white or albumen, W. This is composed of a denser and a more fluid kind, arranged in layers, which can be peeled off in a hard-boiled [fowl's] egg, like the layers of an onion. A layer of the more fluid kind is always next the shell, and another thin one, F, next the yolk, but enveloped by another layer, D, of the dense kind. If an egg be broken into a basin, there will further be observed attached to two opposite sides of the yolk two slightly opaque and rather twisted thick cords, C H, of still denser albumen, termed the *chalazæ*. They are not attached to the shell, but to opposite sides of the dense layer of albumen, D, which envelops the inner fluid layer and the yolk. They are so attached at opposite sides, rather below the centre; thus they act as balancing weights, keeping the side of the yolk which carries the germ always uppermost, and very nearly in floating equilibrium. If the egg be turned round, therefore, the yolk itself does not turn with it, but retains its position with the germ on the upper side.

"It will be seen how elaborately and beautifully the yolk, bearing upon its upper surface the tender germ, is protected within the egg. Itself rather lighter at the upper part, it is further balanced by the *chalazæ*, so as to float germ uppermost in the albumen. It is usually very slightly lighter than the albumen, but scarcely perceptibly so; thus it floats near the upper side of the shell, but always separated from it by a layer of albumen of more or less thickness, and oscillating gently away from the shell on the least motion. In a few cases it probably floats more strongly up against the shell, and these are generally the cases in which adherence takes place, or the yolk is ruptured during hatching; but an exquisitely delicate floating balance is the rule. Nevertheless, it will be readily understood why it is inadvisable to leave an egg, and above all a hatching egg, lying on the same side for any length of time.

"The shell being porous, and permitting of evaporation, such a course keeps the germ close to the portion of albumen which is slowly drying up, and may cause a tendency to adhesion." [The eggs should be turned by the breeder at least once a day until they are returned to the birds to incubate.]

The Yolk.

"Turning now to the yolk, this is contained within a very delicate vitelline membrane, V. It is composed of both white and yellow cells, and if an egg [fowl's] be boiled hard and cut across, it can be seen that there is a flask-shaped nucleus or centre of white yolk, W Y, round which are several concentric layers of yellow yolk, Y Y. Under the microscope additional thin layers of white yolk - cells can be distinguished amongst the yellow layers. On the top of the yolk rests the *blastoderm* [germ-skin], a small disk shown at B L. The difference between a fertilised and unfertilised egg is solely to be found in this small disk, and much of its detail can only be distinguished under the microscope; but with a pocket lens it can be discerned that whilst in an unfertilised egg the little disk is whitish all over, except for small clear spots very irregularly distributed over its surface, in the fertilised egg an outer ring or margin is whitish, while in the centre is a smaller clear circle, in which are very small white spots. This central clear space is the germ from which the chick will be developed.

"It should be clearly understood that, at the stage when thus examined, after the egg has been laid, development or 'hatching' has *already been carried on* to a certain extent, due to the eighteen or twenty hours it has been subjected to the heat of the hen's body whilst traversing the oviduct. As it entered the oviduct the germinal disk consisted of only a single cell. During its passage this cell becomes traversed by successive furrows or divisions, dividing and subdividing it into many cells—the first stage in developing a real *organism* out of the *single cell.* This process goes on not only on the surface, but beneath, so that by the time the egg is laid the blastoderm consists of two sheets or layers of cells. At about this stage the egg should be laid, and with the cessation of warmth the process ceases, or nearly so, but not exactly at the same point in every case. Perhaps the most wonderful thing about an egg is the power it has of keeping the development, already commenced, suspended for a time when warmth is withdrawn, to be resumed and carried on whenever the necessary warmth is restored.

Weakly Embryos.

"Several points which puzzle many people will now be understood. It may happen that an egg is retained for a day or two beyond the natural time; in that case the development or hatching will be continued, and the new-laid egg may contain a visible embryo. Again, since even the new-laid egg is already an *organism,* which has attained a certain stage of growth, it is subject to disease, or weakness, or accident, like other organisms. Thus an egg may be fertile, and the germ may begin to develop, but may perish at any stage from sheer lack of strength, precisely as a weakly baby may die at any age. Quite apart from accidents or injuries whilst hatching, there is no doubt that in many eggs the embryo is not strong enough in itself ever to come to maturity. Such deaths at various stages, within the shell, are in no essential respect different from deaths of weakly chicks at various early stages after leaving the shell; the necessary vigour may fail the infant creature at any particular time, so also the embryo can be injured within the shell in various ways; and while it might be fanciful to say it can be 'frightened,' there is much evidence to show that it may suffer from some kind of nervous shock, as in a severe thunderstorm."

Such shocks, however, would be more likely to affect the eggs of birds which build their nests upon the ground, such as poultry, of which Mr. Wright treats, than the eggs of those which build in a bush, or which breed in captivity in cages. In fact, we have very little faith in the idea that eggs incubated by birds that build some distance from the ground are affected by storms, and after years of close study of the subject we have not found any authentic record of hurt resulting, other than that of the purely imaginary kind, of which we have heard of many.

"Whenever the egg is again subjected to a heat analogous to that of the hen's body, the process of development is resumed, if the interval has not been too long. There can obviously be no definite limits to such an interval."

Much depends upon the strength of the germ; it is only natural to presume that a weakly germ would perish sooner than one which was strong and healthy. In cases of hens refusing to sit we have kept eggs a week, lying on bran in the dark, turning them daily, and have had them successfully hatched, and the young reared. We have, however, also been unsuccessful with fertile eggs kept a similar time, the weaker germ having doubtless perished. There might be other causes for the failure, but it is only reasonable to say there is a difference in the strength of the germ, just as there is a difference in the strength of birds, though we have again and again seen puny youngsters grow into fine robust birds. Obviously it is well to get all eggs under the hens, and on their way to incubation as soon as possible after the full clutch is laid.

Development of the Chick.

"It is needless to describe in detail the development of the chick when steady incubation has been commenced. A few hours enlarge the central pellucid spot, which becomes oval, with a furrow down the centre, and blood-vessels appear round it; then begins to develop a double membrane called the *amnion*, which at a later period entirely encloses the embryo, along with what is called the amniotic fluid. By the second or third day the tiny embryo enclosed in the amnion can be clearly seen, as in the accompanying illustration, surrounded by a patch upon the surface of the yolk which is covered by

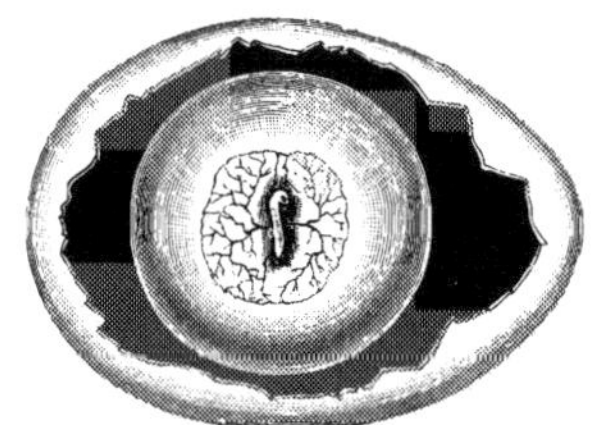

CHICK ON SECOND OR THIRD DAY (*Magnified*).

fine blood-vessels. The eyes can also be seen with a magnifying glass, as dark spots, and even the pulsation of the heart. At or soon after the third day another growth, called the *allantois*, begins to push out from the digestive canal of the embryo between the two coats of the amnion, and

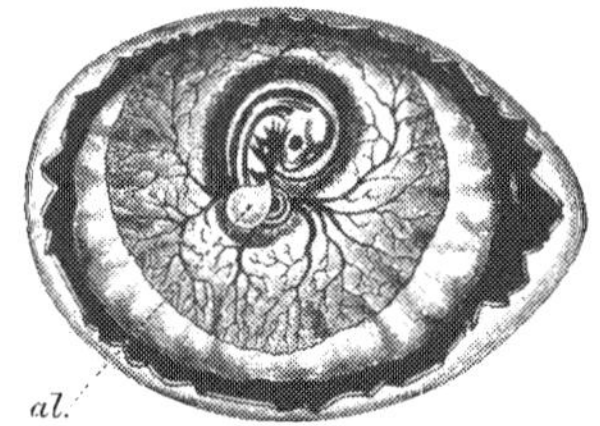

FIFTH DAY: *al.* Allantois (*Magnified*).

at a later period also encloses the embryo. By the fifth or sixth day the allantois can be clearly seen as a bag or sac protruding from the navel, independent of the yolk-sac (*see* illustration). By this time rudiments of the wings and legs can be clearly seen as buds or small clubs standing out from the surface of the body, which has grown a great deal. The network of blood-vessels has also extended, and the yolk-sac is larger and more defined. This and the developing allantois, at about the seventh day, are more clearly shown in the next illustration.

"The allantois is, however, flattened and spread out in reality between the outer and inner layers of the amnion, where it gradually extends till it entirely surrounds the growing chicken close to the outer shell and membrane of the egg. It is furnished with a beautiful network of blood-vessels, extended under the porous envelope of the egg, while at the umbilicus they are in connection with the

SEVENTH DAY: ALLANTOIS, *al*, MORE DEVELOPED. Yolk-sac shown in connection with the navel. (Magnified.)

young chick. The allantois, with its capillary blood-vessels, thus serves as a temporary lung by which the blood is oxygenated from the outer air, the chick not being able to use its true lungs till the very eve of hatching. The allantois is thus a structure of cardinal importance to the life of the growing chick."

In a Canary's egg at the seventh or eighth day signs of downy-like feathers are faintly discernible, and a movement of the young bird is often perceptible if the egg is opened at about the ninth or tenth day.

Just before hatching "the beak ruptures the membrane which divides off the air-chamber, and the bird for the first time breathes air through the lungs, after which the chick's blood gradually ceases to flow into the veins of the allantois, which has completed its work, and is no more needed."

Finally the young bird, by the force of its rapid movements within the shell, breaks from its prison. The first part of the thin brittle shell to chip is that toward the thick end of the egg, with which the tip of the beak comes in contact. The constant tapping causes the shell first to crack, then the fractured part rises slightly with the pressure of the beak, that portion directly over it dropping off, and the movements of the young bird gradually increase the crack round the egg, thus giving freedom for the head, wings and legs to move, and complete the young bird's escape.

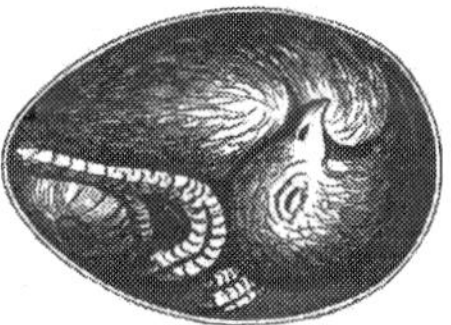

NEARLY READY TO HATCH.

The arrangement of the young bird the day before hatching is shown in the accompanying illustration, while the next diagram shows the bird forcing its way from its prison with the egg fractured half-way round. The other part of this illustration shows how the two portions of the shell are forced apart as the young bird escapes from it.

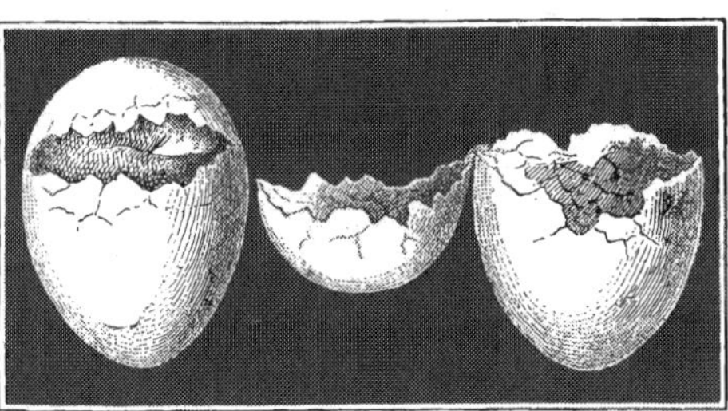

EGG FRACTURED BY YOUNG BIRD. POSITION OF SHELL AFTER ESCAPE OF BIRD. (*Magnified.*)

Nourishment of the Chick.

"During this process of development the embryo has at first been lying as a small object on the upper surface of the yolk; later on, as it increases in size and definiteness of form, it is clearly apparent that the neck of the yolk-sac is in connection with the umbilicus or navel (*see* illustration). The material needed for growth is therefore derived primarily through the yolk ; but as the original yolk-matter is absorbed, it is replaced by fresh material from the albumen, drawn through the delicate membranes. The albumen comprising much of the bulk of the egg, it is manifest must furnish much of the nourishment for the young bird ; but it passes through the yolk-sac in this process. Shortly before hatching, the entire remaining nutritive material of the egg is gathered within the considerably shrunken yolk-sac, communicating with the umbilicus of the young bird, as in the above illustration; and during the last few hours it is rapidly drawn into the abdomen, where it furnishes food for the newly-born chick during the first day of its independent existence."

YOUNG BIRD TWO DAYS BEFORE EXCLUSION, SHOWING SHRUNKEN YOLK. (*Magnified.*)

This matter is fully explained here in order that the reader may quite understand the entire independence of the young bird with regard to food for at least twelve hours after its birth, or even longer. Nature has furnished it with full provision, though it is rare that the parent allows the nestlings to go so long before giving them a meal. The old birds are usually busy attending to their wants an hour or two after hatching. In fact, as soon as the downy feathers—which are damp when hatched—have been dried by the heat of the mother's body, she is busying herself about her chicks. She, however, gives them but very little food the first few hours, and that which she gives them the first day is of quite a creamy consistency.

When young birds are hatched the abdomen is much distended, and greatly outweighs any other portion of the body. This is observable in the illustration on this page, though the yolk-sac has not been quite absorbed. Nature truly displays her handiwork in this arrangement, as the weighty distended abdomen acts at first as a support and balance to the young bird before it has much strength in its legs, when holding its head up to be fed by the parent. As it gets older this abnormal state of the abdomen gradually disappears, and the bird is able to rise up on its legs in the nest to be fed. The next illustration shows a young Yorkshire canary when four days old, and though the abdomen is still large, it gradually assumes more normal proportions with the body, and continues to do so as the bird becomes well feathered.

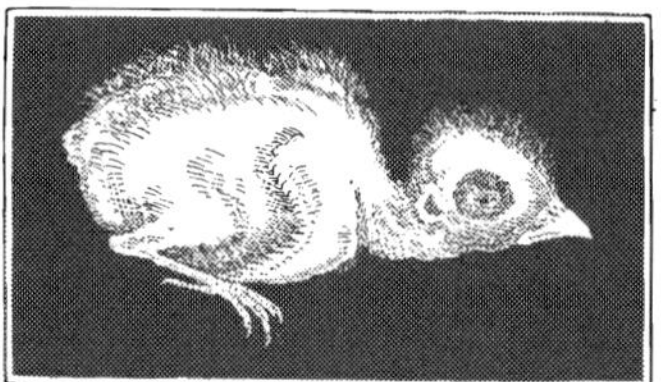

YOUNG YORKSHIRE CANARY, FOUR DAYS OLD.

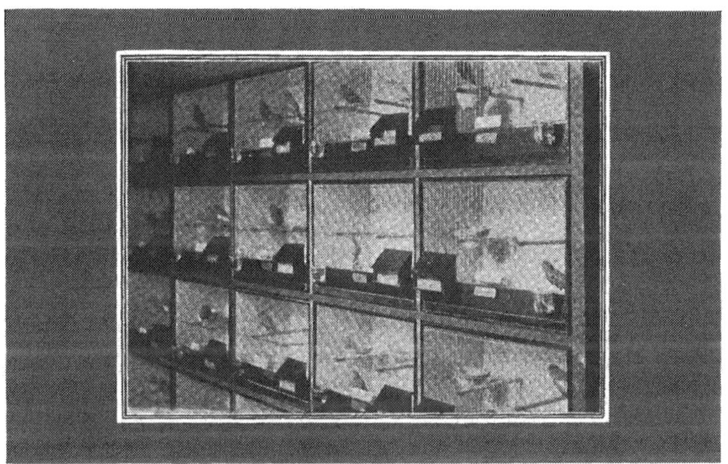

CAGES WITH NESTS IN POSITION, SHOWING ARRANGEMENT OF PERCHES, ETC.
(Photograph from Mr. W. R. Dunn, Portobello.)

CHAPTER X

PAIRING AND SITTING

In preparation for the housing of the birds the bottoms of cages should be furnished with a good covering of sand, or rough-cut pinewood sawdust. If sand is preferred nice sharp sea sand, free from dust, or good sharp river sand should be used. It is a good plan to mix powdered egg-shell with the sand, for the birds are particularly fond of this limy substance, and will pick every particle of it out of the sand. The shells of all fowls' eggs used in the kitchen should be dried in the oven until they are crisp—but not brown—and then powdered up finely, though not into dust.

Personally we like, and have used for the past twenty years, the pine sawdust for the bottoms of the cages, preferring it to anything else at all times of the year, and have supplied the sand in a shallow earthenware vessel, where it is always clean for the birds to help themselves to. Then, with our seed- and water-vessels filled, the cages are ready for the stock.

Of the different varieties of Canaries, and the method of breeding them with a view to producing each in perfection, we shall treat *in extenso* by and by. We purpose devoting this and the succeeding chapters to the subject of General Management and the discussion of the best means to employ in Breeding, Rearing, Feeding, Moulting, and Preparing for Exhibition.

The first question that suggests itself is as to the selection of breeding-stock.

Selection of Stock.

We do not mean as regards quality, or the best variety for a beginner to make a start with. One kind is no more difficult to manage than another when once a little experience has been gained, but the raw recruit would do well in his first year not to go in for stock that is too expensive. Let him instead keep cheap but pure-bred stock until he has had a season's experience and knows the ordinary routine of bird management. This accomplished, he can launch forth carefully, remembering that good birds eat no more than bad ones.

It is only too easy, even when at the top of the ladder, to make a false step and slide down to the bottom; but next to impossible to begin at the bottom and reach the top if the bars be rotten; and we therefore urge the fancier to buy the very best his means will permit. The only question we shall enter into in this place, in speaking of the selection of stock, is as regards age, and we shall dismiss it summarily by saying it is perfectly immaterial, except when a bird is past breeding. There is, however, no definite age when a bird ceases to breed; this entirely depends upon health and stamina. Many are only fruitful for three or four years, while others will go on for several years longer. Therefore a bird must only be discarded for breeding purposes when it fails to perform the necessary functions. Secure good birds, but never mind the age if they are only healthy. A Canary at twelve months old, notwithstanding it still carries a portion of its nest-feathers—viz. wings and tail—may still be said to be matured, and displays all its natural instincts. The cock birds look out eagerly for mates, and the hens are equally anxious for the duties of maternity, and, if left to themselves, would lay nests of unfertile eggs and sit on them till hope died out with declining health and strength. We have never found that age added one iota to their experience, or that youth was connected with any lack of knowledge. The exercise of maternal duties is the outcome of natural instincts, native and deep-rooted, and as strongly developed and true in their action when the first nestling emerges from its shell as when great-grandchildren are performing like duties. We have heard various theories on this subject of age, but do not consider any of them worth a second thought.

The Time for Breeding.

The time of the year at which the birds should be put together varies according to circumstances, as we briefly indicated in a previous chapter. There is nothing in the whole round of Canary-breeding that requires such a cool head and the capacity for resisting temptation as the itching desire everyone has in the early spring to make a beginning. It is only experience which makes the breeder wise in this respect. Nature, if we would but study her, has regulated all things well for the protection of both old and young birds, and, as we have pointed out, the breeder is often wont to run against her, with disastrous results

A warm temperature practically annihilates egg-binding, and there is nothing gained by being too anxious to pair the birds up early in the year during the cold period. Even supposing one succeeds in getting the hens to lay, and the eggs prove fertile and hatch out, there are odds against rearing the young. It must be remembered that though young birds are bountifully covered with a fine silky down-like feather, which is quite sufficient for the first few days, while the mother keeps them closely covered, and leaves the nest only at intervals for a second or two to get a few picks of egg-food with which to feed the young, this down each day becomes thinner, and just before the feather appears the young birds are practically bare. At this time the hen comes off the nest more frequently, and remains off for longer periods, and it is then the danger occurs if the weather be cold, as the featherless young get chilled, inflammation sets in, and quickly carries off the brood. Of course, if artificial heat is available, this can to a great extent be avoided. Scores of unfertile eggs are another result of pairing the birds too early.

The Call of Spring.

The symptoms of this desire to pair the birds up early are pretty much the same in every case, and generally show themselves on a sunny day after a short country walk. Perhaps we have picked a sprig or two of chickweed or young dandelion leaves, and have given our birds a taste all round, and next day find some of the hens carrying the bare stalks and roots about the cage. It seems to have infused fresh life into the whole room and into the fancier also. The weather continues open, and another stroll is taken to gather fresh moss, and unless the fancier knows the folly of giving way to this unexpected early snap of fine weather, he gets as restless as the birds, and must be doing something; he cannot help it. The smell of newly-turned earth in a ploughed field through which he has to pass only aggravates the complaint, while the early spring song of the Thrush or Blackbird tells us that "the time of the singing of birds is come, and the voice of the turtle is heard in our land." But one Swallow never made a summer, and several fine days do not make spring. The return of inclement weather produces a reaction in ourselves and in the birds too, and we feel glad that we proceeded no further than a general furbishing-up of cages and examination of *matériel*. "More haste, less speed," should be written over every bird-room door. We have known breeders lose half their hens by disregarding this precept; deaths from inflammation of the egg-passage, and consequent "egg-binding," being the penalty for rousing the birds into action before the dreary days of winter were fairly past. Our rule is never to put our birds up till they can see to feed at six o'clock in the morning. They retire to roost early in the day, and during the early part of the season the long nights should be made no longer than necessary. From six till six is a long fast, even supposing the young ones go to sleep on full crops. The policy of waiting till the spring is fairly advanced will, therefore, be obvious. A safe rule, and one based on common sense and long experience, is to wait at least until the middle of March—even if the weather is open—in southern and south-western districts, and until the beginning of April in the midland and northern districts.

Preparing the Birds.

Where a number of birds have been living together through the winter, hens in one cage and cocks in another, they should be looked over early in the spring, and those intended for breeding purposes set apart and kept as quiet and free from excitement as possible. They should be fed on nothing but plain diet, such as canary-seed with a little German rape added two or three times a week, and a small piece of sweet apple, or cold boiled carrot, on the intervening days. Later on, of course, other green foods may be given. The cocks will gradually be growing "fresh," and will require to be caged off into separate compartments, though when they have been kept together in flights for a lengthened period they will remain good friends till one or more of them begin to come into high condition and full song, when the troublesome ones, at least, must be taken out, or constant skirmishes will ensue. But we will assume that things have gone on in an orderly fashion, and that no jealousies have sprung up, and the breeder finds himself landed into March with a nice stock of healthy birds. We should advise him at once to put a match to his gas-stove, or put his hot-water apparatus into action, for, at the best, March is but a blustering month, and April is not to be relied upon. East winds continue to harass us, and winter does not depart without a struggle. With the quarters thus made comfortable the birds will soon show a desire to pair.

Treatment of Cocks.

Many fanciers at this time make a grave mistake by feeding their hens up too freely with egg-food and neglecting the cocks. Because the cocks are in song their owners are under the impression that they do not require any feeding up, the consequence of which is that unfertile eggs follow the mating. Our experience shows that as a rule hens are in breeding condition before the cocks. The cocks, however, should not be overdone with egg-food. A safe rule to follow is to allow them half a teaspoonful twice a week, and the hens the same amount once a week. The cocks will then be ready to pair at the same time as the hens. A pinch of maw-seed, too, may be added to the egg-food, especially to that given to the cocks, and a pinch of niger-seed to the hens' seed diet on days other than those on which rape is given. A pinch of niger will do the cocks no harm.

The Nest-Pan.

When the birds are seen to be ready the nest-pan or box should be hung at the back of each single breeding cage, or of each compartment if double or larger cages with partitions are used. Place the nest between the two perches, with its bottom on a level with them, or nearly so, letting the top of the nest be about one inch above the perches, with about an inch to spare between the nest and perches. This will allow the birds good standing-room when engaged in feeding. But this is not very material, as the birds can, and will, stand on the nest-edge as often as on the perch when so engaged; indeed, some breeders never place their perches on the cross-bar, but support one on the upper cross-wire and the other below the middle cross-bar, on a small transverse wire between the door-frame and the side, so compelling the birds to fly up to the nest whenever they have any business to transact there. All these perch arrangements, however, are entirely matters of taste, for it really signifies but little whether Canaries take their everlasting hop, hop, treadmill-exercise on the level or with a rise and fall.

There is, however, an advantage in keeping the top of the nest just above the perch, as it compels the hen to leave her nest more steadily, and with less likelihood of dragging her young out with her, than if the perch is arranged a little higher than the nest. In the latter case many hens just rise from their sitting posture and fly direct on to the perch, and thus frequently drag some of the young ones out with them, especially if they are but a day or two old. When the top of the nest is just above the perches the hen usually rises, and steps on to the edge of the nest and then hops on to the perch.

A first-size nest—a No. 1—is best; for although a hen will gather her eggs under her in a large nest as well as a small one, she has a forlorn look squatted at the bottom of one that is two or three sizes too large for her, and which she would fill up to suit her own ideas of comfort if material were furnished her.

The Nest.

If the nest be lined with felt or swansdown—which we recommend—nothing else in the way of nesting materials need be supplied at first, except a few sprigs of dried moss, or short lengths of meadow hay, with which the hen will amuse herself until, after a few days, she settles down to work in real earnest. Then a free supply of the usual building material should be given, such as meadow hay cut into short lengths of about three inches, dried moss, and doe hair, placed in a small wire rack hung on the cage front so that it does not come in contact with the food and water.

There is a new building material now sold called "chirpy," which is used largely among Canary breeders in Germany; this is really shreds of white linen, very similar to the white "cops" which fanciers used to procure from the mills in the North of England some thirty years ago. The Germans maintain that "chirpy" is superior to other nesting materials, as it is softer and of a cooler nature. Birds are fond of it as a building material; but not more so than of the moss, hay, and doe hair, and we think it simply a matter of taste, and so long as it is clean either material will do equally well.

Pairing the Birds.

Having furnished the lodgings thus far, a pair of birds should be put into each cage or compartment. Our instructions on this point must necessarily be general in their application: what kind of cock, and what kind of hen, manifestly belonging to later chapters. There is not the slightest necessity for any previous acquaintance, and as for putting the cock in one cage and the hen in another and allowing them

EVENLY-MARKED YORKSHIRE CANARY.

to scrape acquaintance through the wires—the thing, in a large establishment, would be practically impossible. We have read somewhere that the cock should be placed face to the wall, opposite his hen, in a cage with a wooden back, having a circular hole in it just large enough to allow of his putting his head through, when he will commence his love-making across the room, and must be conducted in the most gradual way to his hen, until she is made acquainted with his entire personal appearance, from his head to his tail. We really have not patience to comment on such nonsense; it is simply the veriest twaddle. The probability is that when the birds are first put together they will quarrel, but it is not always so. It arises from the fact that the cock bird is always the first to make advances towards a more intimate acquaintance, and the hen, as is fit and proper, with becoming modesty repels them.

If he be wise he will commence by admiring the nest, and will coax his hen with presents of dainty morsels and a display of polite gallantry; but if he begins at once to be too familiar, and the first song he sings is "Oh! name the day, the happy day," she will thrash him, or try to do so. He in turn will drop his wings, dance from one end of the perch to the other, with head feathers elevated, then dash after her round and round the cage as she tries to evade his pursuit, singing the while as he chases her till they can go no longer. The sequel is usually the same old, old story. In a few days they settle matters to their mutual satisfaction, and then begin their family duties.

It is not, however, *always* so. Some hens take a settled aversion to a particular cock and will *never* pair with him; but these viragoes are very rare, and though they may succeed in knocking all the spirit out of one cock, and may have to be introduced to another, they generally meet their match in the end. There are also badly behaved cocks that are just as spiteful with the hens. This occasionally results from a cock being paired to a certain hen by her continued call to him from her cage, and may be termed "pairing by voice." The two birds may not have seen each other, but they know one another by voice, and should the hen introduced to the cock not happen to be the hen to which he has responded he can tell in a moment. Such cases, however, furnish no reason why valuable time should be wasted in pairing birds on the gradual introduction system alluded to.

Still, we have known cocks that would literally scalp their hens, and the late Mr. Blakston once had a Lizard hen that half-murdered her mate, and would have finished him if he had not interfered. She used to drive him under the egg-trough, on which she would sit like a cat watching a mouse, and say, as plainly as she could say it, "If you put your head out, I'll have you as sure as you are a Lizard"; and she did "have" him frequently, by stooping from the perch and picking him up by the top of the head and swinging him backwards and forwards underneath. But ninety-nine per cent. of Canaries pair as naturally as possible, and the breeder will not have long to wait for evidence of their having properly paired. The first indication of this is the cock feeding his mate, for the Canary belongs to a class of birds which feed from the crop.

Food for Paired Birds.

We should have mentioned that, as soon as the birds are put together, they must be supplied with a mixture of chopped hard-boiled egg and bread-crumbs, or egg and crushed biscuit, with just a little maw-seed mixed with it as a stimulating diet. This should be given in small quantities of a teaspoonful every other day for each pair of birds. A mill can now be procured for a shilling or two for mincing up the hard-boiled egg and bread or biscuit together expeditiously, and the preparation, after being stirred a few times with a fork, is ready for the birds. The cock will, in reply to the invitation of the hen, made by a rapid fluttering of the wings, accompanied by a low twittering, constantly feed her by disgorging the contents of his crop. If, in

BORDER FANCY CANARIES

THREE-POINTED BUFF — YELLOW GREEN

CLEAR YELLOW — EVENLY CINNAMON-MARKED YELLOW

addition to the soft food and the canary and rape-seed, already alluded to, a small teaspoonful of equal parts of niger, gold of pleasure, and maw-seed be given twice a week, and a little chickweed, watercress, young dandelion leaves or lettuce be furnished, the cock will be all the more assiduous in feeding his mate.

Nest-building.

Meanwhile the hen will begin to show signs of a desire to build. If she have only a felt or swansdown-lined nest, she will pull and tug at it the day through, constantly getting into it and "scuffling" with her feet and wings in her endeavours to adapt it for use. Now is the time to supply nesting-stuff, but only very sparingly, because till she begins to build in real earnest she will only waste the material to an unlimited extent. So long as there is any hair or moss to be had from the rack by pulling it through between the wires, so long will she continue to pull at it, carry it to her nest, throw it out again, and scatter it about in the cage bottom. To allow this is to countenance sheer waste, for this stuff, when once soiled, will never be used for its intended purpose. It seems as though, for a time, her object were nothing but amusement. This activity, however, is beneficial to the hen while her eggs are developing, and a small piece of building material, as explained earlier, will answer the purpose as well as a bunch; indeed, a single feather will occupy her constant attention, and this she will carry backwards and forwards to her nest all day long. Something of the kind she *must* have, or she will purloin a feather from the cock's tail or disfigure him by plucking him whenever she can get a sly pull. Some hens are very ill-mannered in this respect.

When it is seen, however, that the hen is really beginning to construct her nest, remove all soiled stuff and give a fresh supply, and the fancier will be rewarded in the course of a few hours by a wonderful display of skill. She takes a mouthful of moss, pulling it from the bunch a sprig at a time, hops away to her nest, pops it in, and then pops herself in on it, with a quiet pantomimic expression that seems to say, "There is no deception, I assure you. I take this small piece of moss and drop it into my nest, so; then in I drop, so; three turns and a scuffle, and where is it now?—the quickness of the foot deceives the eye. Now I take a small piece of hair, so, and I drop *it* in—there's no deception; three more turns and another scuffle. Now take a peep; you see I have woven a piece of tapestry. Richard! a mouthful of egg, if you please, and don't forget a bit of maw-seed this time." And so the work goes on, the cock occasionally popping up to see how it is progressing and looking very wise over it, till at length the little nest—we cannot use a prettier word—is completed and lined out daintily with the snowy-white hair, encircled by a fringe of curly moss, behind which the little hen settles herself down full of happy pride, her shining black eyes glistening with love while her mate bursts into song, answered in a chorus which makes the room echo by half-a-dozen friends, who are just as busy as themselves, and are also having a house-warming. Some hens continue building until they have laid their first egg, and in some instances even the second and third, but in the general way the nest is completed before the first egg is laid.

Laying-time.

There will not be much alteration in the position of affairs for a day or two, but by that time the hen will have become more sedate and matronly, and indications of the little event which is shortly to come off will be manifest; indeed, what may be expected in the morning can generally be foretold with tolerable certainty the night before. The situation is not now entirely free from danger, and the first duty of a breeder on visiting his room in the morning is to notice whether all his hens which ought to have laid have done so, or if any are making heavy weather of it. Some phenomena, however, occasionally present themselves, startling in appearance, but which need not cause serious apprehension. It will sometimes happen that the day before a hen lays she will be seen in the morning in the most complete health, going about just as usual, her feathers close and compact, wings tucked up, and showing nothing to indicate the presence of any disarrangement whatever; but in the afternoon she will be found apparently about to "go home." She seeks a corner of the cage, panting violently, and squats on the ground with wings outstretched, feathers all ruffled, head thrown back, eyes closed, in a state of the most entire prostration, the picture of complete misery. A more pitiable object cannot well be conceived. She seems to have lost the use of all her bodily powers, and if taken in the hand offers no resistance; indeed, she is too ill to think of it. When replaced in the cage she scuffles away to her corner, and appears to wish for nothing but to be left alone in quietness to die. You think she might be warmer in her nest, and gently place her there. But it is no use; she tumbles out, or, rather, hops out, falling heavily, and shuffles away to her comfortless corner again. There you leave her and begin to mourn over hopes apparently nipped in the bud. You cannot rest at night for thinking about her, and go upstairs to see if she is dead or alive. Somehow she has managed to scramble into her nest, which is to her a sick-bed in real earnest. We will not enter into any discussion as to the cause of all this fuss. A probable cause will suggest itself, and as in similar cases of an equally interesting character, we can only say, "My dear, I'm afraid you'll have to be worse before you're better." Do not interfere with the bird, and Nature will do all that is necessary. Next morning, instead of finding her a subject for a *post-mortem,* you will find an egg in the nest, and the little hen going about her business quite at her ease.

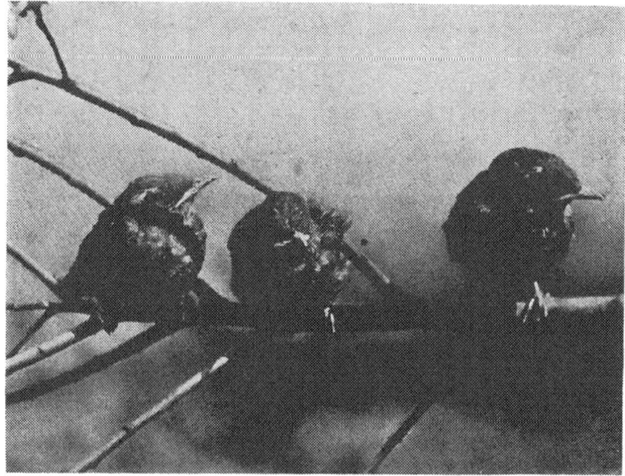

YOUNG BLACKBIRDS.
(Photograph by J. Williamson.)

Egg Difficulties.

But if she should *not* have laid her egg, something will have to be done. That something is so very simple, and so efficacious when it is done, that anyone can manage it, and nobody should hesitate about trying. Take the hen gently in the left hand, with her head towards the little finger and the tail projecting between the thumb and first finger, and hold her in this position over the steam of boiling water in a narrow-necked jug. The jug should not be quite full of water, and a piece of fine muslin should be laid over the top just slack enough to allow of its dropping slightly into the neck of the jug, so that if the egg passes from the hen during the operation—as sometimes happens—it is caught by the muslin, and so saved. Expose the vent freely to the action of the steam, and let the hen have a good vapour bath in this way; then, with a small bluntly-pointed thin stick, drop one or two drops of sweet oil on the vent, holding the bird practically upside down, so that the oil penetrates well into the vent. On no account insert the stick; the parts are too small, and will be too much inflamed to allow anything of the kind, and also the egg, being so near expulsion, might be damaged. One drop of equal parts tincture of ergot and olive oil may also be given direct into the beak. Gently replace the hen in the nest, and the egg will soon be laid, even if it be not dropped in the muslin covering the jug.

Extreme Cases.

Some cases, however, may prove very obstinate; for some there is no relief, and death inevitably follows. In such cases a *post-mortem* carefully made will reveal the internal economy, and explain the difficulties of the position. Heat is an important element in bringing obstinate cases to a successful issue, and when things look bad the hen should be wrapped in warm flannel and placed near the fire or on a wire frame over a jug or basin of hot water. *Early* attention also is of the utmost importance, as every minute increases the difficulty and lessens the chances of success. If, therefore, after the treatment mentioned the egg is not laid in half an hour, hold the bird's vent over a jug of boiling water with the muslin cover, and, with the finger and thumb placed gently on the bird's sides behind the location of the egg, use a slight pressure, but with great care. This often assists delivery, but it must be remembered that the egg must on no account be broken, or the consequences will be fatal, unless the whole of the shell and its contents come away at once. We have known this to happen, and the hen immediately recover; but it is well to avoid such risk. The ultimate saving of the egg, also, is a matter of no moment compared with saving the life of the bird, and she should not be placed in her nest too soon, simply with that object in view.

One lesson to be learned from this not unfrequent episode in bird-life is the importance of an early visit to the bird-room. Canaries soon get to know those who have charge of them, and will not be at all put out by a quiet visit, when a glance round will show whether things are going on well.

Further Treatment.

Many of these troubles can be avoided, even during severe trying weather, if half a teaspoonful of niger-seed, with a pinch of maw-seed added to hens about to lay, is given daily, and until the completion of the whole clutch of eggs. This tit-bit, moreover, will not be detrimental to the cock bird who is running with the hen.

In instances where a hen has had difficulty in passing her egg, and shows signs of weakness afterwards, bread and milk, given on the day of the attack, and for the next day—but not longer—will be beneficial. The bread should be soaked in the milk until it is cold, then lifted out in the solid piece; most of the milk should be squeezed out, and three drops of tincture of gentian and a pinch of maw-seed should be sprinkled over it. Milk, instead of water, to drink should be given, but it should be seen that this does not turn sour before it is renewed.

In no circumstances should a bird be tampered with whilst laying, except to save her life; let Nature have her full play before resort is made to artificial means. Many a hen has been lost or ruined through needless interference and impatience on the part of the owners. We have even known of their interfering and tampering with a hen which appeared quite well, but had not laid on just the morning they thought she ought—with disastrous results, entirely due to their own folly.

Is it necessary to point out the importance of entering the bird-room quietly? As regards a clumsy, noisy manner of opening and shutting doors, some persons have a gift that way; but if that gift be practised on the bird-room door, the consequences will be "claw-holed" eggs. Quiet, and the entire absence of everything like fluster, are essentials demanded of visitors. Gesticulation may be the soul of oratory, but we object to having our birds pointed at with an umbrella.

The removal of the eggs as laid is a practice on which there is some difference of opinion. Our own mind has long been fully made up on the matter, and our advice is to do so invariably. Ivory, bone, or china eggs, obtainable from any bird-shop, should be substituted when the hen's own egg is removed from the nest. Not that it is absolutely necessary, but some hens are offended if their eggs are removed without dummies being substituted, whilst others are quite the reverse. It is better, however, to use the dummy eggs in all cases, and remove them when the real eggs are returned to the nest.

Should Eggs be Removed?

The only argument we have ever heard adduced in favour of allowing a hen's own eggs to remain is that those of wild birds are untouched till the full complement has been laid. But there is not the slightest analogy between the two cases. The wild bird does not become broody until she has laid her complement, and consequently does not even remain near her nest; and we do not think any schoolboy ever found one or two or even three eggs in a nest which should on the average contain four from which he had occasion to disturb the parent bird. But a Canary confined in a box eighteen inches square can scarcely be said to be in a natural state; indeed, some of her after proceedings would almost support the theory that her nature has been modified by circumstances to an extent we are loth to acknowledge. From not being allowed to lose sight of her nest and eggs, she has every inducement to sit, and will frequently become really broody and begin to sit with the first egg. The chances of her wishing to do so are increased on the appearance of the second, and if she should really begin to sit in earnest, the result is simply that the young ones are hatched at intervals instead of simultaneously; the elder rapidly outgrow the younger and literally smother and starve them. They get the lion's share of the food, reach up above their younger nest-mates, and thus keep in advance of the smaller, later hatched ones, which are often found crushed flat on the bottom of the nest.

We are aware that some breeders who never interfere with the eggs assert that it makes no difference in the time of hatching. This we do not admit, and are perfectly satisfied that where such may have been the case it has resulted from the hen *not* having begun to sit as was supposed. We do not call sitting for an hour, or two hours, and then coming off the nest for as long a time, *sitting*, any more than playing with building-stuff is *building*; and it is only when this fast-and-loose, on-and-off sort of sitting has been indulged in and has been mistaken for genuine business that the hatching has been simultaneous, and the possible evil results have been averred to be a myth. No one who practises the let-alone system can say that simultaneous hatching is the general rule; and that is just our point. We fully admit that it may, and does sometimes occur, under the conditions and circumstances we have described; but it ought *always* to happen, and that can only be ensured by removing the eggs, and then setting the hen as we would a broody fowl.

Record of Eggs.

Our mode of procedure is this: we number or letter all our cages, and have a shallow tray divided into compartments, like a seedsman's box, lettered in a corresponding way, as shown in the accompanying illustration. Each compartment is three-parts filled with bran, than which there is no better or more suitable material for the purpose ; it is soft, and the eggs lie securely in the little impressions or dents made in the surface of the bran with the tip of the finger. A lid to the tray lessens the possibility of injury to the eggs. As the eggs are laid we transfer them to the tray, placing them in the compartment bearing the corresponding letter or number to that on the front of the cage. Each morning the first thing we do is to turn all the eggs in the tray, then go round and take all those laid that morning from the nests, placing them alongside those already in the tray corresponding with the letter or number on their respective cages.

We keep a breeding record as well, in which we write a description of each pair of birds, number of nests taken and of eggs laid, with the number hatched, and a description of the young. Some fanciers indicate the fact of a hen having laid by a chalk-mark on the front of the cage, and

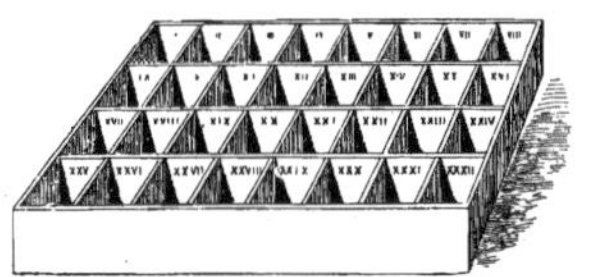

NUMBERED EGG TRAY.

post up their record from these chalk-marks, in which they believe most devoutly. The book is for detailed items, but the chalk-marks show the whole state of affairs at once in a thoroughly practical way which we will explain. We will suppose the fancier going into his room between eight and nine o'clock in the morning, by which time his hens will all have laid. If he have any method in him, he will begin at the beginning and go steadily through. The information given by the marks on a few cages will suffice to explain what we wish. Here is a cage without a mark. The hen was expected to lay this morning, and has done so ; we put the egg in its place in the tray and chalk the cage. Here is one with a single mark, or two marks, as the case may be ; that means we may look for more eggs, which we do, and add a mark to those already on the cage. We pass on to a third, the chalks, bear in mind, telling at a glance, without any reference to a book or comparison between it and the tray, just where we have to look, and what we may expect to find when we do look. In the next cage, which has two marks, we anticipate finding the third egg, but we do not. We know from the marks that it *ought* to be there, and that it is *not ;* so we add a cross or a cipher, or some such distinguishing mark, which tells us the hen has missed a day, and if the third egg be not there to-morrow we shall not sit her on the two she has laid, but give one to each of two hens on the other side, whose marks indicate that they are likely to stop at three, as they have not laid on the fourth or fifth morning, and are sitting close to their nests.

Short Clutches

A hen that has laid but two eggs rarely sits out her time. Some do not attempt to sit at all, others sit close for two or three days, then suddenly desert the two eggs, and commence to build again on the top of them. The cause is easily understood. The hen has only laid part of a clutch ; something unseen temporarily checked Nature's progress ; the machinery, so to speak, has now righted itself, the other eggs are coming along, and the hen is busying herself for the happy event. The effect of this is temporarily to destroy all tendency to brood the eggs previously laid. She may now lay another three or four, when she will settle down to brood them in right earnest in the normal way. But the two previous eggs, having been partially sat on, would be useless unless they were transferred to another hen as soon as deserted. It is, therefore, much better to transfer such eggs at once to another hen which has just started sitting on a small clutch. A very good plan is to mark the two eggs transferred with a small spot of ink so that it may be known by this mark whether the eggs have hatched or not. Another good plan, wherever possible, is to put them under a hen of a different variety to that which laid them. There is then no difficulty in distinguishing the young birds from the foster-parent's young when reared.

This is amply sufficient to explain our system of marking, so far as regards the point of practice we are detailing. We remove the eggs, then, one by one, till there are three in the tray, and on the evening of the third day we replace them. The hen then goes on to her nest at night, lays her fourth egg in the morning, and at once commences to sit so closely that the date of hatching may be reckoned from that fourth morning with certainty; they usually hatch on the thirteenth day counting from the evening when the hen was set. The reason why we replace three eggs, and date from the fourth, is because, though five is a common number, and six not unusual, four is an average nest. If a fifth egg be laid it must take its chance; but the fancier soon gets to know the peculiarities of his hens in this respect, and acts accordingly. Before setting the hen we generally make it a rule to clean out the cage, or at any rate to give it a rough scrape and supply some fresh sawdust or sand, for it will be a fortnight before it can again be disturbed, beyond removing any excreta which may accumulate during incubation.

Time of Hatching.

The hen will have much more confidence if not disturbed during incubation. Some hens are so nervous, although good mothers, that the moment an attempt is made to clean out their cage, either while they are sitting, or when the young are a few days old, they will rush off their nest in such an excited manner that they bring either eggs or young out with them. The temperament of the birds should be studied, and action taken accordingly. If they are too flustered when the cleaning operation is attempted, then simply remove quietly any collection of excreta, and let the proper cleansing wait till the nestlings are older. Many a fine nest of youngsters has thus been saved.

The Sand Question.

We should have remarked, in speaking of the sand required for the cages, that it should *be* sand—gritty sand, and not earthy matter, capable of being compressed into small lumps. All birds are not alike, but some are apt to get very dirty feet, and if the sand be of a binding nature, they will be continually gathering it up under their toes in a ball, which will eventually grow so large as to inconvenience the bird seriously, and must be removed. It is easily managed by moistening the ball with water, but no rough usage must be attempted. See also that the claws are cleaned at the same time, for it is more than likely that each will have a small tip of dirt attached to it, and when such is the case, it is evident a hen cannot have much command over them, and is very likely to injure her eggs in consequence. It is possible, too, that the bird's feet may be permanently injured, with the loss of a claw or two into the bargain. Much of this clogging of the feet is avoided if rough-cut pine sawdust be used on the bottom of the cage, and sand provided in the manner suggested on page 99. The sawdust not only gives off a pleasant odour, but dries up the excreta as it is dropped, thus keeping the bird's feet clean and in good condition.

Food for Sitting Hens.

Egg-food and green food should be discontinued while the hen is sitting, and seed only be given. A very small quantity of egg-food can be included in the bill of fare at intervals of three or four days during incubation without any bad effects, if the allowance be but sufficient to be eaten up quickly. It should not exceed about a quarter of a teaspoonful, and if the weather is chilly a pinch of maw-seed may be added to it. If egg-food is given every other day while the hen sits inactive on her nest her health is sure to suffer from such stimulating food. But apart from this question of health it is certain that a liberal supply of egg-food to a sitting hen has a tendency to bring her on to lay again before her young brood can manage for

GROUP OF HYBRIDS.

1. TICKED SISKIN-CANARY. 2. UNEVENLY-MARKED GOLDFINCH-CANARY. 3. REDPOLL-GOLDFINCH. 4. BULLFINCH-CANARY.

themselves. Indeed, this is not unfrequently the case even when the hens are fed on plain seed diet while incubating the eggs.

Green food, if given during this period, is apt to cause inflammation of the bowels and diarrhœa, a condition which every breeder is always anxious to avoid. The advantage of feeding sparingly and plainly while the hen is sitting is thus evident.

The Cock's Duties.

The hen will leave her nest occasionally to feed, but after cracking a few grains of seed, and taking a fly round the cage to stretch her wings and legs, will soon hop back on to her eggs. Where the cock is left with her he attends to her needs, carrying food to her as she sits on her nest—a duty in which he never fails. Indeed, during the whole period of incubation, his life is one incessant round of attentions to his mate. During fine weather the luxury of a bath may also be indulged in, and though the hen may sometimes appear to remain off her nest longer than prudence might suggest, we have never known any but good results attend a free use of the bath.

Restless Hens.

There is, as we have already suggested, a marked difference in the temperament and disposition of hens and their deportment during the time they are sitting. Some, nothing seems to disturb; they are like broody fowls, and if at any time an inspection of the nest may be necessary, they require to be lifted off by putting the finger under the breast, and even then will often do no more than stand up or, at the most, hop on to the nearest perch, and wait the first moment to settle down again on the precious eggs. Others appear to be sulky, and if disturbed will not return to the nest so long as they are watched. They will sit on the edge of the nest, in the very act of hopping into it, but as rigid as if stuffed, and not a hair's breadth will they budge until they are alone again. Others are restless and fidgety, especially if the cock has been removed, and are everlastingly leaving the nest without any apparent reason, really seeming to spend as much time in looking out of the windows as in maternal duties. The remedy in this case is to "draw down the blinds," by tacking a strip of brown paper in front of the cage, just where the nest hangs, so that the hen cannot see out of her cage without leaving the nest; a couple of drawing pins will keep the paper in position, and it can easily be removed when not required. This will often keep restless hens quiet, and closer to their nest and eggs. Many breeders adopt this plan in every instance, especially when the arrangement of the cages is such that the birds in some of the compartments can see those in others.

We, however, only recommend that the cage should be covered where a hen is found to be restless, and is continually leaving her nest.

Fertile and Non-fertile Eggs.

Such, we think, are the principal features to be noticed during incubation, which we will assume has gone on for five or six days. At the expiration of this period the eggs may be examined, to see how many are fertile, for it sometimes happens that it may be found necessary, with a view to saving time or obtaining a final nest late in the season, to combine two nests, due at the same date, into one. We do not, however, recommend this procedure for the mere sake of getting an extra nest from a hen, for experience has long ago taught us that an overworked hen will as a rule do little or nothing in the next breeding season. Unless, therefore, another nest is desired for some special purpose, we would recommend that a hen should be allowed to sit through the full period of incubation even on a nest of unfertile eggs, as this will prevent her next clutch of eggs coming along too quickly. It is a common thing when a hen is not allowed to sit the full period of incubation for her next clutch to be unfertile, too, due to her having been forced to lay again too quickly.

A practised eye can detect at a glance the fertile from the unfertile eggs, without taking them in the hand; but if they be held up to the light the former will be found to be one-half opaque, or rapidly becoming so, the dividing line being drawn diagonally. A day later, and, in a strong light, the network of blood-vessels can be distinctly traced spreading over the inner surface of the shell; and a day later still the fertile egg becomes entirely opaque, while the unimpregnated ones remain perfectly transparent. In a nest of four or five an unfertile egg should not be removed, as the young ones, when hatched, will cluster over it, and it serves as a support for them; fragile as it is, they will not break it, though it be allowed to remain till they are full grown.

But the fancier must not, even at this advanced stage, begin to practise that simple elementary arithmetical process which experience has shown frequently results in erroneous conclusions; he must wait patiently till the morning of the thirteenth day, before which arrives he may have learnt a practical application of another wise saw: " Many a slip——" We all know the rest and have often experienced it. The proverb is stale but very true. A man, to become a successful Canary-breeder, must have the quality of patience strongly woven in his composition.

Risks of the Final Stage.

The principal dangers to be apprehended in the later stages of incubation are the misfortune of the hen forsaking her eggs, or the young birds dying in the shell—" going back," as it is called. The former may arise from the sitting-fever subsiding, which may be occasioned by a sudden change in the weather, such as the advent of a second winter, or any marked fall in the temperature. Sitting hens do not like the long, cold nights, and this is when the value of some heating apparatus will be realised. Similar causes may have a fatal effect on the young ones in the shell, but most probably the decline in the natural heat of the hen's body has most to do with it. It is the steady decline, the gradual dying out of the fire at a time when the flame ought to be kept up, that does the mischief.

Young birds, when within a day or two of hatching, can, however, survive several hours of exposure, and if the eggs be found to be quite cold they should still be persevered with.

This would not, of course, apply in a case of gradual decline, but in one of accidental exposure, as, for instance, when a hen has deserted her eggs, or has been inadvertently shut off from her nest. We have known many instances of hens deserting their eggs a day or two before they were due to hatch, in some of which the eggs were left for six and eight hours before another hen could be found to take them, and yet every egg was successfully hatched. In cases where a second hen is not available, and it is necessary to draw on the services of a friendly breeder, the eggs must be carried in the nest, covered with wadding, a layer of doe hair, or other similar material.

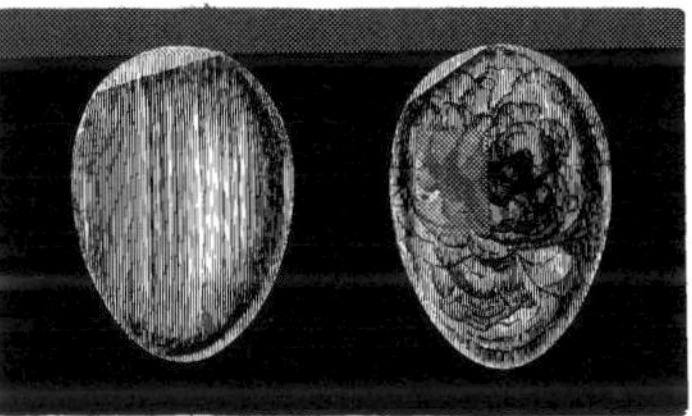

BARREN EGG. FERTILE EGG.

We draw attention to this matter so as to warn the breeder against being too hasty in breaking open eggs which do not hatch out to time.

Delay in Hatching.

The Canary sits thirteen days, and hatches almost to the hour with commendable punctuality. If eggs do not " chip " at the time expected, and yet are evidently fertile, they should on no account be interfered with for at least eight or twelve hours, and if early in the season even longer. The eggs of the first nests in the season are sometimes a day late in chipping, and occasionally as much as two or three days. This probably arises from the hen not having got the full incubation heat up when commencing to sit, or else through not sitting closely during the first two or three days. If it is finally decided to break the egg, it should first be slightly dented with the thumb-nail toward the thick end, and then placed for a few seconds in a cup of water, a little more than lukewarm. After this it should be returned to the nest. In most cases this will be sufficient to enable the bird to escape from the shell if it is alive. Should it not hatch out in a couple of hours, and there is a certainty that it is alive, the egg should be taken in hand again. After dipping it in warm water as before, the eye-end of a sewing needle should be inserted into the skin or membrane which adheres to the inside of the shell, and gently drawn half way round, thus slitting the membrane. Great care must be taken to insert only the tip of the needle, and to keep it close up to the skin so as not to touch the body of the young bird within. Having split the membrane the egg should be placed in the nest again, and the hen allowed to return to it. In all probability, and in less than an hour, the chick will be hatched. I have known this means to be entirely successful in many cases.

Such an operation must, of course, be carried out most carefully; it is usually found to be necessary in the middle of the breeding season if the weather is hot and dry, and the hen is not a free bather. We prefer that the eggs should hatch naturally, for the ability of the young bird to break its shell denotes strength, and generally where they do not the reverse is the case. A young bird which cannot liberate itself on account of the membrane which lines the shell having become dry and tough usually chips the egg where the tip of the beak lies, but makes no further progress. It is this indication of life which justifies the rendering of assistance before the young bird becomes exhausted in its struggle for liberty.

FIRST LESSONS IN BIRDKEEPING.
(From a photograph by Mr. J. E. Reeves, Canning Town.)

THE WILD CANARY AND ITS NEST.

CHAPTER XI

HATCHING AND REARING

In anticipation of the thirteenth morning ushering in a successful hatch it should be seen that the egg-food pan or drawer is cleaned out overnight, and replenished with a little fresh food in which the yolk of a hard-boiled egg must predominate. The question is often asked, "Which shall I mix with the egg—biscuit or bread?" Many breeders use Osborne, tea, thin lunch, or milk biscuits, whilst others use good, sweet bread-crumbs with equal success. But whichever is adopted should be adhered to; there should be no changing from one to the other unless matters are not progressing favourably.

Some Canaries feed their young largely on seed, and give them but little or even no egg-food; in such cases it is well to remove the seed for several hours each day, and so compel them to feed more freely on the egg-food, as it is rare that nestlings make such good progress when fed on seed alone as they do on equal parts of seed and fresh egg-food.

The Hatching. On the thirteenth day of incubation, when the breeder looks into the cage in the morning, he will probably see half a shell in the bottom and will hear a little chirp. In ordinary circumstances he will not think of disturbing the hen, but we will excuse him if, on this occasion, he takes a peep, though we would strongly recommend him instead to watch his opportunity when she is feeding, as hens as a rule come quickly off to any dainty bit of egg-food put fresh into the pan. The curious breeder can attend to the other birds and keep an eye on the cage for the chance of a glance. Then in the bottom of the nest he will see something which looks like a cluster of hairy caterpillars, and he is sure, as, instinctively, he gives a little chirp on his own account, to see the bunch open itself out, and untwist four little heads on four long necks out of a knot in the middle, which will raise themselves up and open out four little mouths. If he then looks farther he will probably see that each little neck has a yellow spot of egg on its side, which shows that already, almost before the down on the youngsters is dry, the hen has given them their first meal—a good omen for the future. The breeder must not allow this to act as an incentive to interfere with the hen more than possible; for, strangely enough, most hens will feed their brood for the first three or four days; it is after that time when many begin to fail in this respect, and interference has not a little to do with this neglect.

The breeder should now add a little German rape and hemp to the canary-seed, and give the egg-food in small quantities, *fresh*, twice a day, or even three times if convenient to do so. From the time the young are three days old, the white of the egg may be used as well as the yolk in the composition of the egg-food, and a little fresh green food should be supplied daily; and if the mother is attentive the young will grow apace.

All stale food should be taken away when fresh supplies are given, excepting the seed, which only requires the husks to be blown off and the vessel replenished each morning. Once a week the seed should be sifted so as to free it from any dust that may have accumulated.

Colour Identity.

From the time the young birds are a day old, or even at hatching, the breeder can indulge in a little speculation as to the colour of the young. If he notes that the down on one youngster is dark it will develop into a green or else a heavily marked bird; or if the parents are, say, Crested Canaries, and he sees that a nestling has a dark crown, it will turn out, in all probability, a dark-crested bird. Of course there are dark-capped Crest-breds as well.

Nest Cleaning.

Among its other maternal duties the hen frees the nest of any excreta which the young have passed, which at this period is practically undigested food. This the mother swallows, and, with other food, gives again to the young; she continues to do this until the chicks are seven days old. After the seventh day it is only waste which passes through the young, and this the hen instinctively ignores. At this age the nestlings are able to expel their excreta over the edge of the nest, and the hen, after feeding them, usually stands on the nest edge until they have done this, and then tucks them in beneath her, and so makes them comfortable for a nap. The mother, even if a bad feeder, will usually keep the nest free from the droppings of the young, but should she not then the excreta must be removed from the nest each time the nestlings are fed, so as to prevent their vents from becoming covered by adhering excreta. No young bird will thrive, however well fed, unless it is kept clean either by the mother or the breeder. The adherence of excreta round the top of the nest is of no importance, for all nests get into this condition before the young broods leave them; it is the cleanliness of the interior of the nest that is essential.

The Feeding Question.

These are the actions of a good mother, but there is no guarantee that it will be continued. It is a very disagreeable truth, but it is only too true. If all should go on well, the young birds will grow under the eye almost hourly, and the next morning will find them nearly double the size, plump and fat, and like little balls of down. But it may be that the mother will positively refuse to feed them at all, or only at such long intervals and in such a half-and-half sort of way, that the experienced breeder can tell at the end of a day or two what are the future prospects of the nest. If in place of full crops, plump breasts, and heavy abdomens, he finds every feature dwarfed, it is then time for him to step in and assist by artificial feeding, in the hope that the want of attention on the part of the mother—which can only result from unhealthy action of some kind or other beyond our ken—will presently give place, under healthier conditions, to the exercise of the constant attention on which depends the well-being of the nest. Understand that our rule is, in dealing with our breeding hens, to leave well alone, and to content ourselves with the best they feel inclined to do, if that best be only a reasonable display of care sufficient to keep things moving.

Hand-Feeding Young Birds.

But for young birds to stand still is for them to retrograde, and we generally find ourselves every morning not "doing something in a temporary way with a teapot," but with a hard-boiled egg in one hand and a little spatula of wood in the other. And our mode of procedure is this: We cut a hard-boiled egg in halves, and having moistened a little of the yolk with our saliva in the palm of our clean hand—if a smoker use a tiny drop of warm water instead—mixing it into a thick creamy substance, which is kept warm by the heat of the hand. We then visit the nest of the doubtful ones, and where we find any empty crops we give the young birds a good feed of the paste, putting it gently into their mouths with the tip of the spatula. They will swallow it as fast as it is given to them, but they should not be overfed. Just sufficient should be given to fill up the right side of the neck, which it will be found quickly rises up like a yellow bladder. They should be fed in this way about every half-hour.

There is no difficulty in making young Canaries open their mouths; it is almost the first thing they do in this world, and they never seem to forget the way; the difficulty is to fill them fast enough. When the hens do not immediately commence their duties never interfere with the young birds till they are twenty-four hours old, because the yolk absorbed into the stomach is sufficient to sustain them for that time, and we like to give the hen a fair chance of feeding for herself; but after that time the very youngest birds can be fed in this way, and if attended to at intervals, can frequently be kept going till the hen takes the work in hand. It will be seen that the breeder who has the opportunity of visiting his birds frequently has a great advantage therein. The man of business is perhaps compelled to leave them from morning till evening, or, at the most, is able to snatch a few minutes in the middle of the day. But in most households there is some person who can be trusted to attend to these matters, and when once it is taken in hand, the interest felt in the little things, dependent on our attention for their lives, grows immensely, and no bird will be allowed to die without a struggle having been made to save it.

When the young are two or three days old just a little powdered biscuit should be added to the yolk of egg, but the creamy consistency should still be maintained, and when they are four or five days old a little canary-seed, German rape, and hemp-seed should be added. These seeds should be first prepared by passing a rolling-pin over them to crack the husks, and these can then be separated from the kernels by gently blowing them aside. What remains should be ground into a fine meal with a pestle and mortar, and then egg-food should be added in the proportion of about one-fourth seed to egg. The whole should be mixed into a thick paste. The spatula should be dipped into water occasionally, so that the food will leave it freely when put into the bird's mouth. A little more of the powdered biscuit and seed in the meal form should be added to the egg as the birds get older. The mixture must be given in a moist state, as long as it is necessary to hand-feed the young brood. They will be able to do for themselves when four weeks old, though some hand-reared birds will allow themselves to be fed as long as their owner likes and will only look after themselves when they are fairly starved to it. In any case hand-feeding must not cease suddenly; it should be dropped by degrees, by feeding at longer intervals until the birds are weaned from it, and feed themselves freely.

We have referred to this possible feeding difficulty arising thus early, because it requires to be met at the outset, and is one of the first disappointments the fancier may have to encounter. When all is plain sailing, the business of the bird-room will run on wheels, the birds will take the reins in their own hands, and astonish even the most sanguine breeder by the way in which they will work out the problem we are endeavouring to show him how to solve. There are so many phases in Canary life, as seen in the nursery, that it is almost impossible to arrange the various pictures in a very methodical manner, and our plan will be to present them as we think it probable they may pass before the breeder's observation in some cage or other in his room. So far as we have gone we have only dealt with the nest in its very earliest stage, pointing out the dangers which beset it, and indicating the best methods of tiding over them.

Cocks and the Young.

The fancier will have noticed by this time that the cock where he has been allowed to be with the hen can usually be depended upon as a feeder. This is generally the case; the exceptions in our own experience have been where the cocks appeared to be too nervous to carry out their instinct of attention; though their demeanour and movements told us plainly they wanted to do so. There are, of course, other instances where cock birds will suddenly fall sick, and in consequence fail in this duty; but with these exceptions they are most diligent in their attention.

Apparently the cock knows as well as possible when things are not going on properly, and when he flies up to the nest with his crop full of food, he will stand on the edge and say to his mate as plainly as a Canary can say it, "You know you are not doing your duty; those young ones under you are starving, and you know it. No, it's not a bit of use your fluttering in that way; I don't intend to give you another mouthful. If you don't mean to feed them just turn out, and I will do it, but don't sit there in that unnatural way, starving the family, or there will be a coroner's inquest shortly." And then he looks round and round the nest so wistfully, the very picture of affection and loving attention, twittering and doing all he can to induce some youngster to pop its head out. Presently one pops up from behind, and in a moment the cock has him, and stuffs him as quickly as possible, knowing the value of every moment. And this he will do all day as patiently as possible, though every visit to the nest generally ends in his ultimately giving the hen a great portion of the meal intended for the young ones. Perhaps he does so in the hope that she will disgorge some of it; but that hope is too often disappointed.

Refractory Hens.

In cases where hens have neglected their share of the duty to an inordinate extent, we have dealt with them successfully by taking the cock away for six or seven days, and so compelled the hen to leave the nest for food. The young thus get fresh air—which assists to revive them—and their necks are outstretched for food the moment the hen hops on to the edge of the nest; by this she is induced to give them food, and gradually she becomes an attentive mother. When the young are seven days old the cock bird may be returned, for by that time the hen has become active, and the young have grown bigger; they will not allow her to sit so close on the nest. As a consequence the two will attend conjointly to the wants of the brood without further trouble. Should the hen again show signs of lagging in her duties, the cock must at once be removed, and the hen left to do the work by herself.

Green Food.

We will not make the picture more dismal than there is occasion for, but suppose that the hen is a model mother, and that from the first she settles down to her work in that earnest way the breeder likes to see. The egg-food trough in that cage will require filling two or three times a day, for *fresh-and-fresh* is the rule, and fresh dainties will often induce a hen to feed when nothing else will. A supply of green food is most necessary, such as a small bunch of chickweed, spray of watercress, or leaf of young lettuce; but whichever is commenced with must be continued until that brood or broods are reared. *Fresh at least once a day* is imperatively the rule here, for there is nothing so fatal to a young brood, or even to old birds, as stale green stuff.

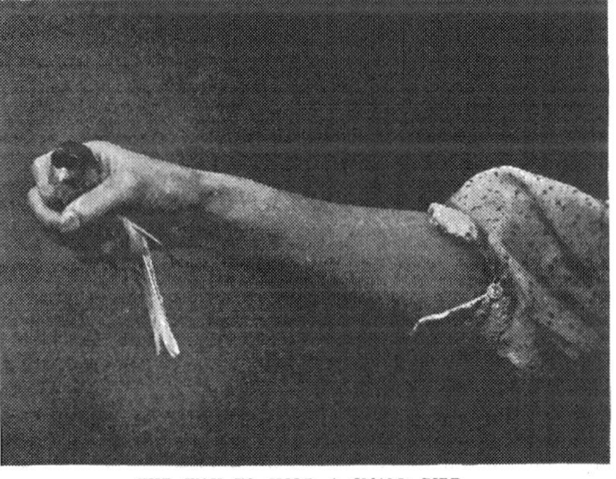

THE WAY TO HOLD A SMALL BIRD.

To hold a Canary, or other small bird, securely, and at the same time not injure it, the hand should control the whole of the bird's body up to the shoulders, with the wings lying close in their proper position. A sufficient grip should be taken of the bird to hold it firmly, so that it can neither slip backwards nor forwards, but on no account should any pressure be put on the bird's body. Whilst the hand encircles the bird let the pressure be in the tips of the fingers, which should rest on the thick part of the palm towards the wrist. This forms a stay and support to the fingers, and prevents possible injury to the bird by too great pressure should it struggle to escape.

Some breeders give green food in unlimited quantities. We have seen handfuls placed in a gallipot in the cage for the bird to feed from, and while such a method may be successful, it is always fraught with great risk of contamination, and we do not recommend the practice. We believe in giving green food in moderation, and a spray of watercress or a small bunch of chickweed or a young lettuce leaf or two placed between the wires of the cage are quite sufficient at a time, and will soon be eaten.

Egg-Food.

As regards the composition of the egg-food, there are almost as many recipes as there are breeding-rooms. The staple commodity is hard-boiled egg, with the addition of bread-crumbs, dry, or soaked and squeezed dry; milk-biscuit, water-biscuit, sweet-biscuit, stale sponge-cake, or other kind of farinaceous food, mixing two parts of hard-boiled yolk of egg to one part of whichever you use. After the third day mix two parts hard-boiled egg yolk and white combined, with the biscuit or bread; but it must be noted that one combination should be adopted and continued unchanged. The egg-food must not be mixed with bread on one day and biscuit another, nor should even the kind of biscuit be changed. When the youngsters leave the nest and are getting about the cage, the egg-food may be prepared in the proportion of bulk for bulk, decreasing the quantity of egg somewhat as the birds get older.

We have tried all the methods. Our best results have been obtained from either home-made bread—loaves four or five days old—crumbled up fine, or Osborne or thin lunch biscuit powdered fine, and mixed with the egg, while the late Mr. Blakston said he obtained the best results by feeding largely on egg and crushed hemp-seed. The fact is that each method is good, but every breeder naturally, and wisely too, recommends the particular mixture he has found produces the best results.

So much, however, depends on the birds themselves that it is unfair to condemn one food or praise another unduly, when it is quite probable the experience of some other breeder is at direct variance with our own as regards the effect of using some particular diet. What succeeds in one bird-room is certain failure in another, and what one swears by another proclaims to be poison. The same remarks hold good with respect to green food. One gives chickweed and nothing else, avoids groundsel above all things, and can tell you stories by the yard of how it killed a lot of young birds. Another will walk miles to find a few plants of groundsel, and will pass acres of chickweed as worthless. One eschews lettuce and gives dandelion, and each gives a satisfactory reason why. A *reason*, even if a poor one, entitles any statement to respect. In the rearing of young Canaries dogmatic assertion should never be listened to. We ourselves recommend hemp-seed—in limited quantities, of course—as having been a good servant to us, while another fancier will say it is the forbidden fruit, the unclean thing, the abomination of abominations, and he would not have a grain in his room; his diet is egg and ——, it matters not what; we may have tried the mixture, and our birds would not look at it. Our advice is to use any of the mixtures we have mentioned, but not all at the same time, and hold fast to that which gives you the best results. The way should be felt when trying a fresh food; all the stock should not be plunged madly on to it; it should be tried on one or two birds first, and the result, whether satisfactory or otherwise, carefully noted.

Feeding Experiences.

To the egg-food can be added a pinch of maw-seed (poppy), or a little German rape in its raw state. If the hen is troublesome and is not attending to her brood as she should, scald the rape seed well, or boil it for five minutes, then strain it off, as dry as possible, and give to the birds when cold. Some hens are passionately fond of rape-seed given in this way when feeding the young; it is good for them and they will often feed on this and egg-food when they will feed on nothing else. But whatever is used, let it be fresh and sweet, and when one diet is found to be working well, go on with it, and make hay while the sun shines. Our experience has ever been that when birds mean feeding, they will feed if they have reasonable attention and proper food given them; and that when they do not intend to feed, nothing will tempt them to do so freely; in short, it is a question of the health of the hen rather than biscuit *v.* hemp-seed.

Preparation of Seed.

Sanguine men and born theorists will say all this indicates defective knowledge and wrong treatment. We assert that an unsuitable diet will bring about trouble, and thinking men of our acquaintance, who dislike groping in the dark and search deeply for the how and why, have come to the same conclusion as ourselves. The first step, therefore, is to try to regulate and improve the condition of the hen; give a little cooling medicine, such as a teaspoonful of fluid magnesia, in the drinking water for a few days, and a temporary entire change of diet is capable of working wonders, and reviving all the lost vigour and activity. The whole question finds a solution in the fact that the Canary is neither wild nor tame; we do our best to reconcile the two conditions, and sometimes succeed, and sometimes do not. Especially is this latter the case with the inexperienced fancier, as a comparison between the number of eggs hatched and the Canary bills of mortality will show.

Dangers of Unsuitable Diet.

Let us suppose that everything has gone on swimmingly under the usual method of feeding, and that we have been voted a croaker by the reader—too fond of looking on the dark side of the picture. The birds are now four or five days old, and are as fat as moles. But on looking at them one morning, the breeder may find the down all tangled and matted with moisture. This is the first indication of the hen having begun to "sweat" them, as it is not very elegantly called in the vernacular of the fancy, which she does by sitting on

"Sweating."

them very closely, seldom leaving the nest even for a few moments. This, of course, means two most unpleasant prospects—viz. starvation and suffocation.

We know of no effectual cure for this sweating in all cases, though experiments which have been tried have in some instances worked wonders. We have seen all manner of cures prescribed, even to the extent of rigging up a contrivance which obliges the hen to "sit" standing; but we cannot call to mind an instance where a cure has been effected by such a method. We have known of fanciers who have washed their hens' breasts in salt and water, of others who have ducked them in a pail of water, and done other silly things in their vexation and hasty moments, but with no result, except that the hens continued to "sweat," and so did their breeders in their endeavour to combat the evil which promised to take off their promising broods of youngsters.

This ailment, however, is sometimes not of long duration, and the ill effects may then be combated successfully by removing the cock, and thus obliging the hen to leave her nest to feed, or else starve. This, at all events, affords the young ones an opportunity of getting partly dried, besides relieving them from the suffocating pressure of the hen; and to induce her to come off as often as possible, it is well to put the cock in an adjoining compartment, if there be one vacant, or into one of the spare nursery cages we have described, and suspend it against the front of the cage in which the hen is sitting. The consequence will be that he will incessantly call her to come to feed through the wires—an invitation to which she will frequently respond; and the chances are that, on returning to her nest, she will sometimes be inclined to feed the young ones, whose importunity it is not easy to withstand, and so this unpleasant feature is occasionally so far ameliorated as to allow of the brood being saved.

We ourselves at one time were under the impression that hens really did "sweat" their young, but we have for some few years now altered our opinion, and question whether any hen really does do so. From close observation we have found this sweaty, clammy appearance of the young is not caused by the hens sweating, but by the young suffering from an attack of diarrhœa, caused possibly by the parents having given them something in their food which has temporarily upset their bowels. The consequence of which is that the excreta, instead of being in its normal state and dealt with by the hen as previously explained, is soft and watery. The hen is then unable to clear it from the nest, and the heat of her body when sitting, combined with that of the young, draws this moisture up and causes the sweating appearance of the nestlings. Another point is that the young birds affected by this diarrhœa do not take their food so freely, and the hen, becoming

MRS. C. H. ROW AND HER YOUNG JAYS.
(Photograph by Mr. Allen Silver.)

Is "Sweating" a Reality?

anxious, crams herself with food, and not getting rid of it to the young is herself upset, and sits yet more closely on them, and so is wrongly branded as a "sweater." It is true that by taking the cock away matters will improve at times, and this naturally leads the unobservant fancier again to the conclusion that the hen is responsible; but it is quite possible that the cock has fed the youngsters too freely on one kind of food—possibly seed—and that this has set up this irritation in the young birds' bowels. His removal often remedies the evil, and the young brood rapidly become their normal selves again.

Other Remedies.

A hen will also sometimes feed too much on seed and give the young little or no egg-food, with the same bad results. In such a case, we advise changing the brood over to a hen that feeds her young on a good portion of egg and green food, as well as seed. This quickly puts matters right, provided the brood is not too far spent; they require taking in hand at once.

We have also found that a very little raw arrowroot mixed with the egg-food works wonders in some cases in a very short time. An additional pinch of maw-seed has also had beneficial effects; and in other cases the temporary withholding of the green food. Without exception, whenever we have succeeded in stopping the diarrhœa in the young, the supposed "sweating" has quickly disappeared, and the hen's feathers have become dry again. There *may* be genuine cases of sweating, but we are dubious as to their existence, and in every instance where supposed "sweating" is present, if the bottom of the nest inside be examined, it will be found to be covered over with watery excreta, never present with young birds in a healthy condition.

A hen *can* at any time bring up her brood without assistance from the cock, and the plan of separating the parent birds is frequently resorted to in the case of an indifferent feeder, with a view to compelling her to work harder. There is always a hopeful chance of saving a nest if the fancier only has the time to devote to the room, because so long as the hen will keep the young ones warm, the cock will always feed them if the hen be driven off the nest to give him the opportunity. But should a hen forsake her nest altogether, there is nothing left but to break up the establishment, and distribute the young ones among the charitably disposed occupants of other cages, who will take kindly to the foundlings. When two or three nests, each containing three youngsters about the same age, are possessed, one of the foundlings should be added to each; by this arrangement no nest will be overcrowded.

"Feeders."

This general uncertainty as to feeding, it will at once be inferred, is the great drawback to success, and in the case of valuable birds it is not advisable to make success entirely dependent upon such a contingency. It will be found most useful to put up a few pairs of the commoner kinds of Canaries, in the hope that among them may be found a few good feeders, whose services will then prove invaluable. The commoner the birds for this purpose, the less reluctance is felt in destroying their eggs, and sometimes, unavoidably, their offspring, to make way for those of greater value. No breeding-room should be without a number of these "feeders," who certainly earn their food in the important work they discharge. We have, indeed, heard many an old breeder say "they are worth their weight in gold in the rearing of high-class stock."

Feathering Time.

Surely we are out of danger now, if by one means or another we have got our young birds up to eight or nine days old? The risk certainly lessens every day, but a strange mortality sometimes attacks birds at this age, just when they are going to begin to cut their teeth—or rather, form their feathers. We can do nothing further than mention what *may* occur, and what has occurred under our observation more than once. We will suppose there has been positively no drawback, and that the young birds are even exceptionally fine and strong; yet, just at this age, a sickly, jaundiced colour comes over the flesh, and brood after brood will die, plump and fat, and with their crops quite full. We are apt to say they have died from surfeit; but up to within a few hours of death every function has been healthy and the digestive powers unimpaired, and we are rather disposed to think the cause lies in another direction, probably in that we hinted at—some obstruction in the feather-forming functions which at this time are called into action.

Other youngsters waste away until they are gaunt, miserable objects, and these cases may be the result of surfeit as well as of the feather trouble. This wasting arises from no neglect, but is evidently an internal ailment, for which we can prescribe no remedy other than an entire change of food for the parent birds directly the colour of the young ones changes as described, or wasting sets in. In such cases a little bread soaked in scalded milk and given when cold to the birds, instead of the egg-food, is excellent, if the old birds will feed the young upon it. A couple of days free feeding on this, with maw, canary-seed, and a little German rape—but no hemp or green food—we have repeatedly found will bring things back to their normal state. It is only by this means that one can try to save them, as they are too young to administer drugs to direct. Such a case may not, of course, occur in one's experience for years, but it is well to be prepared as to the best means to adopt should such a misfortune arise.

Nest Accidents.

It may be said that we have presented the life of the young Canary as consisting of a series of struggles against adverse circumstances. We are glad if our object has been so clearly understood—that is just what it is. We have before said it is easy to sail with the tide, and anyone can float down with the stream. The difficulty is to steer clear of the rocks and shoals, and we know there are plenty of them. We have endeavoured to point them out distinctly with all their bearings, and we mistake greatly if the experienced fancier does not recognise them as places where he has either come to grief, or escaped shipwreck by a good look-out and careful navigation. There may be other dangers ahead, but we will not now anticipate them and meet trouble half-way. We must, however, call attention to a very common accident which will happen in some nests. It is that of the young ones being pulled out by the hen in hopping out or flying off the nest. It is well, when this occurs, to examine the hen's claws, and if they are very long just to shorten them with sharp scissors, taking care not to cut so close as to induce bleeding. Some hens are naturally clumsy and habitually do this sort of thing; all such should be furnished with a deeper nest than ordinary. It is quite possible, when not suspecting such a mishap, that the young thing in the cage-bottom may be overlooked; but with a knowledge of these and like contingencies, the breeder gets into the habit of keeping a sharp look-out. This accident generally occurs when the birds are very young, and consequently additionally liable to suffer from exposure; but so long as there is a spark of life left in the little naked thing, there is every chance of its recovery. This can be speedily effected by placing it on the warm palm of the hand, covering it with the other hand, then gently breathing on it through one side of the closed hands. As soon as it begins to move freely and wriggle about, pop it under the hen, and it will soon be all right again.

Crest and Crestbred hens are very liable to pull young birds out of the nest with them, even when leaving it in a quiet way; their bodies are so heavily feathered that the little mites get nestled up amongst the long feathers, and so are carried over the side of the nest. Very close watch should be kept on the cage-bottom when these birds are rearing young, especially during the first week.

It is worthy of note that, kind and attentive as is the cock while the newly-hatched birds are in the nest, he seems to forget all his duty to the sprawling youngster on the floor of the cage. Perhaps it represents to him in that position something to play with, or something to eat, for he will frequently bite off the extremities—the toes, tips of the wings, and the little beak. Some fanciers maintain that these mutilations take place through the cock bird trying to carry the young bird back to the nest; but if this is the case, how is it that the hen never does this kind of thing? A young bird will never be found mutilated on the bottom of the cage where a hen is rearing a brood by herself, and one would naturally think her instinct to get the youngster back to the nest would be quite as strong as that of the cock. Be the cause what it may, it is only too true that not one young bird in twenty escapes mutilation if the cock is in the cage, unless it is discovered almost as soon as it has been pulled out of the nest. We have even known very rare cases where this mutilation by the cock has occurred in the nest.

Mutilations by Cocks.

We have done our best to suggest the various means to be employed to keep things in a healthy state and prevent mishaps, but there is a point beyond which we cannot go, even with the exercise of all the skill we can command, and a not very extended experience will soon indicate that line to the breeder. It then becomes a mercy to destroy such young ones as we know we cannot possibly save. It seems cruel to kill a little, blind, helpless fledgling—we say "blind," because a young bird's eyes do not open until it is seven days old—but it is more cruel to allow it to linger on in weakness, till the end we can foresee comes. It destroys the pleasure we derive from keeping animals to rear sickly, puny specimens. Our utmost energies should always be given towards alleviating sickness when it overtakes anything in our charge, but the same wisdom which dictates the policy of destroying the weakly young of rabbits, dogs, or any other animal we desire to rear in the beauty of its strength, will tell us when it will be a kindness to put a whole nest out of the way if we can see no reasonable chance of rearing it. It is one of the disagreeablenesses of the position, but we must accept it, and by prompt action make it as little painful as possible.

Treatment of the Unfit.

What is the sum of all that we have advanced? Is it that the bird-room, instead of being the pleasant place we described, is nothing better than a hospital, and the occupation of Canary breeding one in which half the pleasure is lost in trouble and vexation? Not a bit of it. Disappointment lurks at the bottom of our best pleasures, and vanity and vexation of spirit have ever been found to wait on many legitimate enterprises. Difficulty and opposition act as a stimulus to endeavour, and it is best to know we have these things to grapple with. The Canary-room is a little world of itself, and we can no more expect to find it free from cares and ills than the great outside world, in which we have to take things as we find them, and do our best to make as much sunshine as possible. Despite all the misadventures to which we have called attention, it is just as likely the breeder may go through a season without troubles as with them, and we now return to our nests as though there were no such things as failures in eggs, or failures in hens, or failures in anything. Nothing seems to come amiss to our birds: they are all feeding well, and several nests contain four and five young ones which are rapidly feathering.

The Brighter Side.

At this period of their growth it will be of advantage to notice the principal portions of the body on which the feathers grow. It does not follow, because a bird is covered with feathers, that the covering sprouts from every part of the surface of the body, and such will be seen not to be the case by reference to the illustration on page 126 of a young bird just developing its feathers. This is knowledge to be turned to account when we

How the Feathers Grow.

HEDGE SPARROW.

TREE SPARROW. HOUSE SPARROW.

come to speak of washing for exhibition. Briefly, a strip of feathers will be observed to run down the back of the neck; two broad bands, one on either side of the breast, with two smaller ones on the side of the back, and one down the centre, will be found to be the principal plantations from which will eventually depend feathers covering otherwise bare places. The head and wings, too, show

YOUNG BIRD, SHOWING ARRANGEMENT OF FEATHERS.

the formation of the feathers which cover these parts, and the shafts of the tail feathers are just beginning to expand. This growth of feather represents a bird ten or twelve days old. It is on the fifth or sixth day that the first signs of the appearance of real feathers, other than down, are visible to the naked eye. This is the time, too, when the fancier is able to note whether his expected clear birds are going to be disfigured with dark feathers, or his dark ones with clear feathers; for every individual feather is discernible, and in nearly every variety, and every class of that variety, the future character of the bird is to be read at this early period of its life with tolerable certainty.

Nothing further need engross the attention of the breeder for another week or fortnight, except to see the birds grow and feather. As the feathers grow and open out of the sheath-like scales which encircle them, the web expands, and so the whole of the body is covered by the feathers. By comparison between a brood that is doing well, or better than well, and one which, though safe, is not quite up to the mark, the breeder will be able to learn, better than any words can describe, the difference between the results of *good* feeding and attention not so constant. The difference is so marked that those who may think this portion of our subject tedious will, when they come to see the importance of it, wish we had even gone more minutely into it, seeing that on it depends, in the first place, the very existence of the bird, and subsequently its growth to mediocrity or advance to high excellence.

It is at this time that the indifferent attention of some old birds—though they may have reared them well to this point—causes so many youngsters to be much inferior in size to their parents.

Insect Pests.

It is at this early stage of growth, too, before the young bird has any idea of using its wings beyond a continuous flap, flap, while being fed, that the nest should be examined for insects and if any be found at once condemned, and a clean one substituted. A nest over-run with red mite is a cause of stunted growth in a young brood, as well as otherwise upsetting them. There is no occasion to study how to make the clean nest a facsimile of the old one, for when young birds have reached the age of feathering the parents will attend to them just as well in a nest they did not construct as in one of their own building, so long as it is of the same shape. It is advisable to line it even though the young are feathering; it not only keeps them warm but also prevents the possibility of their getting their toes fixed in the small ventilation holes in the nest pan, and thereby getting the nails or claws torn off or otherwise injured. A little building material can also be put in and moulded into shape with the fingers, and then settled down firmly by rolling a hot boiled fowl's egg round in it for a few seconds. It is also a good plan when changing the nest at this stage, especially if there are four or five young, to use a nest a size larger than the one taken away, as it gives the young brood more room to stretch and grow in comfort.

If for this cause a wooden nest-box should have to be replaced by an imitation of a natural nest, the best plan is to shape a nest with moss inside the box, then line it with a little hair, and finish it off by working the cup or hollow in the centre of the nest by pressure with a hot hard-boiled egg as described. Mark that the hen will not destroy such a nest. If she were wishing to build, she would soon put it to rights; but when her object is to lay, or, having laid, to sit, or, having hatched, to feed, she accepts each position in the full exercise of the reigning instinctive faculty of the hour. It is not a time for play now, but rather for duty, and instinct regarding that duty is stronger than mischief.

Leaving the Nest.

Having furnished a clean nest, the young ones must not again be interfered with, but be kept absolutely quiet, for if they are once frightened from the nest it is very difficult to make them take to it again. There is, of course, no danger of this occurring now, but a week hence such a thing might easily happen. A breeder is always very glad when his young ones are strong enough to leave the nest, and is glad to see them go, but he is always desirous to keep them there as long as possible, snug and comfortable, and well cared for. Extreme care is necessary at the last when the birds are just over a fortnight old, when a startled sort of restlessness pervades the nest. So long as they squat and keep their heads well down, there is not much to fear; but as soon as one youngster, more venturesome than the rest, lifts up his head and turns himself round, you may look out for a jump. When one goes they had better all go, for they will still stick to each other a little longer, and, acting in concert, may even determine to return to the nest at night. But a single young one, if he persists in refusing to return to the bosom of his family, fares rather ill the first day or two of his liberty, and it is best to take every precaution to prevent premature flight, which ought not to take place till the birds are nearly three weeks old, by which time they will be almost as large as their parents.

Hens and Second Laying.

We are exceedingly loth to hint at the possibility of any more misfortunes, but by the time the young ones have reached this age it is more than probable the hen will begin to show indications of wishing to sit again—an event which can scarcely be looked on in the light of a misfortune, but which requires nice management. Sometimes she will lay in her old nest, depositing her eggs among the young birds, who will not injure them, although there may be as many as twenty-four or thirty sharp little claws in the nest. In any circumstances it is advisable to supply her with a second nest-pan of the small No. 1 size, which may be suspended on the side of the cage, opposite the partition, if it be a double cage, or if there be room at the back it can be placed there, bearing in mind that as the perches are all movable, they can be removed at will to suit the new arrangement, or additional ones brought into use. It may be that the building fever may not be very strong, and the hen may be content to take such accommodation as is offered, but a small portion of new building material should invariably be furnished in the rack for her use, as its presence may be the means of giving her employment at a time when she is apt to illustrate the truth of the aphorism that "somebody" makes it his business to find mischief for idle hands to do. By giving her a new nest and fresh moss and other material—for it is better to give her a mixture so that she can find that which she fancies most—she will not be tempted to pluck the young birds.

If each pair of birds has a double cage—that is, one with a partition in the centre—a wire partition can be inserted and the young birds kept in the one compartment and the cock bird and hen with her clean nest in the other. The old birds will then attend to the wants of the youngsters and feed them through the wires of the partition, while the hen will also go on building her new nest. Such an arrangement answers equally as well as having a nursery cage. When the young can do for themselves they can be removed to another cage, and the wire partition removed.

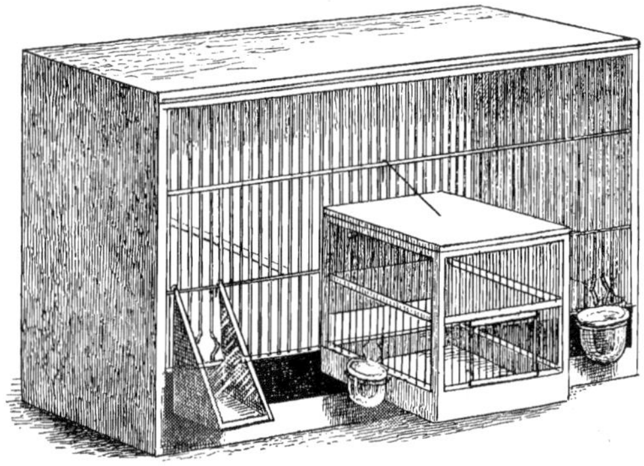

NURSERY CAGE IN POSITION, WHEN IN USE.

The Nursery Cage.

If single breeding cages are used, then this is the time to use a "nursery" cage, into which the young brood can be placed, and the whole hooked on end-ways to the open door of the breeding cage, as shown in the illustration herewith. The old birds will feed the young through the wires, which must be sufficiently far apart to allow of the young birds getting their beaks well through so that the parents can give them food. Five-eighths of an inch is ample space to allow between each wire along the end of the nursery, as if a wider space is allowed young birds are apt to get their heads through the wires, and there is then danger of their heads being plucked. The cock which has just been introduced to the hen, if he has not helped to rear the young, may feel spiteful toward them, and will scalp them if opportunity arises, even though the mother is continuing to feed them. It is where one cock is working with two hens that scalping is likely to occur, as he must be returned to the hens, as a rule, a few days before the young are able quite to do for themselves; but the space we recommend to be allowed between each wire will keep the young ones safe from attack, and at the same time allow ample space for them to be fed.

Plucking by Hens.

The reason for not having a perch across the end of the nursery cage for the young to sit or perch on is to prevent them getting too near the wires, and so giving the hen an opportunity of plucking out a few of their feathers, which she is very liable to do. By standing on the bottom of the nursery cage to be fed, the young birds offer no such opportunity to the hen. Breeders will thus at once recognise the necessity of keeping a sharp look-out for small feathers in the new nest when once the young birds have left their nest, and before they have been transferred from the mother's breeding cage to the nursery; for this disposition to pluck becomes, apart from the pain and inconvenience to the young birds, a positive calamity in the case of birds in which it is imperative that the original wing and tail feathers should remain intact. It will be seen, when we come to treat of varieties, that there are at least two in which this is one of the show conditions, and it is not pleasant to find one's prospects in this direction clouded so early. Moreover, now that we have unflighted classes given at

YELLOW PIEBALD SCOTCH FANCY CANARY CLEAR YELLOW BELGIAN CANARY
CLEAR BUFF SCOTCH FANCY CANARY

most shows, it is of the utmost importance that the ycung flight feathers of most varieties should be kept intact and as perfect as possible. It is likely that one of the best young birds from the season's work might have half or more of his young flights plucked out, and thus spoil his chance of competing in these unflighted classes owing to the new flight feathers coming longer than the original ones, and so making the wing feathers appear uneven in length.

This disposition to pluck is, perhaps, one of the most vexing incidents of the breeding-room. We spoke of it as commencing at a comparatively matured age; but it is sometimes begun when the birds are very young, and not sufficiently fledged to be left all night without the protecting covering of the mother's wing, and it is then very distressing and painful to witness.

Remedy for Plucking.

In such cases, if the birds be, say, ten or twelve days old, the best plan is to take a shallow square or slightly oblong wooden nest-box, and shape out in it a nice warm nest with moss and hair. The young brood should be placed in this and transferred to a nursery cage. The nest should be put close up against the end of the nursery cage through which the old bird or birds have to feed the young, and the cage hung in the usual way in front of the open door of the breeding cage. As the old birds stand to feed them, the youngsters will rush up out of the nest and push their beaks through between the wires. When the old ones have fed them a few times in this way, the youngsters can be covered over with a piece of flannel, three or four ply thick, or a piece of swansdown, made just large enough to cover the nest, but not quite to the edge; the young birds will nestle beneath this, and with the heat from each other's body will be kept warm and comfortable. Every time the parent birds come down to feed them, and they are hungry, they will stretch their long necks out to the wires to be fed, and when satisfied will quickly draw back again beneath the cover. The cover, however, must not be placed over the young until the old birds have fed them a few times in their new nest, or they would not come near it with the cover on. There will be no difficulty in keeping the nest clean, as the young birds at this age will pass their droppings over the edge.

This is the only effectual remedy we know of where hens take to plucking the young before they leave the nest, and if not adopted, all the hen will do, so long as the young brood is with her, is feed them and then sit on the edge of the nest and pluck every quill or feather out of their young bodies until they are as bare as the back of one's hand. When hens acquire this propensity, not only do they pluck every feather, but the new quills also, just as they shoot from the skin; and if the youngsters survive such a trying ordeal they generally grow up miserable-looking objects. More often, however, they are eventually found one cold morning all dead, with the hen sitting over them, or flying about the cage frantic for another nest-pan in which to start to build and lay again. Though we have known a hen pluck one brood and never touch a feather again, as a rule they are feather-pluckers and eaters of the worst character, and continue their nefarious game. Happily, such desperadoes are few, and where one does turn up, the method we have described is the only efficient remedy.

Removal of First Brood.

Whether plucking takes place or not, it is always advisable to remove the young birds when the hen has laid again, either into a nursery cage or to a partitioned-off compartment of a double breeding cage. For although, as we have said, the young ones will not break the eggs when climbing over them, they make the clean nest in a deplorable mess with their droppings. Sometimes the eggs will be found covered with excreta and sticking together, and in the endeavour to clean them one or two generally get broken. Moreover, if the hen has commenced to sit again, it is anything but pleasant to her to have four great youngsters, perhaps bigger than herself, sitting in the nest with her, or even on top of her, as they will do. Some mothers will put up with it, but such cases usually end in the clutch of eggs being "addled," if they are not broken when being cleaned.

Useful Cocks.

The plan recommended as a remedy for plucking should also be adopted with forsaken nestlings for which no foster-mother can be found, where the cock bird has been assisting to rear the brood. He will keep at it like a Trojan, to all appearances liking the job. Worth his weight in gold is a good cock bird of this description, and if very fond of his bairns he will attend to them through the wires of the nursery and at the same time drive the hen—which has been left in the cage with him—off to nest again, giving her a good "hiding" now and then for deserting her young and not helping him to rear them. Such cases are most interesting to watch, though it is much better not to be troubled with them. Such a good-natured cock bird may also be turned into a "flight" with the young birds, and he will keep his eye on them, and will always "ken his ain bairns." He will, however, not only look after his own, but any that may not be quite able to look after themselves in the flight, even though he may have never seen them before. It is very amusing to see the performance when the cock has been away for a while, and the young are hungry. They pounce upon him in a body, and drive him into a corner, or perhaps he retreats thither on strategic grounds; and ensconced there, supported on his tail on strictly scientific principles, taking care to keep his centre of gravity well within his base, he dispenses his charities to the clamorous applicants, giving each his fair share, and never, in any circumstances, losing his temper.

Cocks as Pluckers.

The mischievous practice of plucking is not confined to the hen, for we have known a few cock birds guilty of the practice, and they have usually, though not always, learnt the wretched habit from a hen. In such rare cases the same precaution must be taken, with this difference: if plucking is going on, and it is thought that the hen is not the culprit and she is a good feeder, remove the cock bird, and let the hen rear the brood by herself until they leave the nest, then place them in the nursery, and return the cock to the hen. In many such cases he will again resume his duties and assist to feed the young until they are able to look after themselves.

Young Birds and Plucking.

Again, this mischievous habit of plucking is not peculiar to the parents, but is frequently indulged in by the young birds among themselves when turned into the flight cage in groups. With them it takes, if possible, an even worse form, inasmuch as they do not content themselves with plucking the small feathers, for which they have no use, but make the strong quills of the wings and tail the object of their attack. Anyone whose acquaintance with feathers has been of even the most superficial character will have noticed that when the stronger quills are growing they are full of liquid, and if accidentally drawn, the blood follows in considerable quantity. When the quill becomes matured, this ceases to be the case. It is when the young birds are first turned into the flight, and before the wings and tail and stronger feathers of the wing-coverts are grown their full length, that the persecution is carried on. The mode of action is beautifully simple. A bird may be observed quietly seated at the end of a perch, close to the back of the cage; he is a bird of a retiring disposition and meditative turn of mind, is very young, and the proprietor of about one inch of tail. Some of his companions are older, and versed in the ways of a wicked world by at least fourteen days more experience. One of them sidles up to him in an insinuating sort of way, betokening mischief, and looks him over in an impertinent manner. He is a bird of delicate tastes, has a sweet tooth, and knows what is nice; and will, if he goes on at his present rate, probably be soon a candidate for the sick ward. The way in which he puts his head down and peers under and over little Verdant Green's tail is the embodiment of cool impudence; and before one can see how the thing is done, out comes a juicy feather, which he turns over in his mouth like a choice cigar, evidently with a keen relish, and having finished it, marks his man down in a remote corner and repeats the operation. The appearance of the latest arrival's tail naturally attracts a considerable amount of attention, and the force of bad example is quickly apparent. There were but twelve feathers in the inch of tail to begin with, so as there are now two missing from one side, some friend commences on the other side to restore the balance; and as birds do not usually do things by halves, they soon finish him up entirely, stripping him bare, literally not leaving him a feather to fly with—a most pitiable spectacle, bleeding profusely from every wound. This is not in the slightest degree over-drawn, and it does not take long either to bring about the catastrophe. When a bird begins to be so maltreated, it must be removed at once, for its feathers will *never* be permitted to grow. It will live in a state of chronic nakedness, absolutely more bare than when it issued from its shell.

Evils of Plucking.

The trouble, too, will not stop here, for once the habit is acquired by one or two, the whole group in the flight become depraved, and, unless checked, every bird in the flight will be practically stripped of feathers. Such a condition of affairs, if allowed to go on, has often a disastrous ending, for many of the birds die owing to their nude condition. Even when they do not succumb to such treatment, many malformed feathers grow in the tail and wings; a tail feather grows wrong side up or turned half side-ways, through the cell from which the feather grows having been injured by repeated plucking. This misplaced tail feather throws all the others out of their natural fold, and the bird is rendered totally unfit for the show bench. The same deformity will occur at times in a wing, and therefore an equally sharp eye must be kept on young birds in flights, and any attempt at plucking nipped in the bud, by removing, not the bird that may have lost a feather or two, but the bird that plucked those feathers out. The scamp must be isolated, for when once he has had a taste of the blood in the feather he will continue the habit, and his removal to a cage by himself will not only effectually stop the plucking, but prevent others acquiring the habit, which, in young birds, one sex is just as guilty of as the other. Possibly another may take up the running as soon as one culprit has been removed, so a sharp look-out should be kept. This vice is a common one until the moult is over, and a bunch of shepherd's purse or seeding chickweed—with practically no leaves on it, but just full of seed—or a number of plantain seed stalks fixed between the wires of the cage in various parts for them to strip, will often prevent plucking amongst young birds. Another remedy is to tie a number of short lengths of twine or tape to the wires of the cage. Young birds must have something to play with for the first few months of their lives, and they will spend hours pulling and tugging at such things as we have mentioned instead of their companions' feathers.

The Second Brood.

This digression on plucking has thrown us off our track a little, but remembering that our hen going to nest for her second "round" was the occasion of it, brings us to our starting-point again. As at the close of autumn the seasons appear to overlap each other, and the gardener in the pursuit of his calling seems to wish to do two things at the same time, and occupy the same piece of ground with two crops, so we seem to want to do two things at the same time in our cage. We want the hen to be attending to one brood and laying the foundation for a second; and we want the cock also to be in two places at once —that is, with the nest of youngsters as well as with the hen. The only way to effect a compromise is by running him in with his hen for a short time, night and morning. For once a hen has gone to nest, and had a clutch of eggs and a young brood, she will continue to lay at regular intervals, so soon as the broods can do for themselves or nearly so, if a nest is allowed her. This is the case whether the cock be with her only at intervals or permanently. Many hens, in fact, would continue to lay at regular intervals right through the season, when once they have started, without seeing the cock, but of course the eggs would then be unfertile.

Cocks and Young Birds.

If the cock is run into the hen's cage night and morning as advised, her eggs will be fertile; half an hour each time will do, or even less, and then he can spend the rest of the day with his young family in another cage, attending to their wants until they can pick up food for themselves. Where a hen goes to nest a second time before the young can thus fend for themselves, some cocks, unless so shut off with the youngsters, though the very best of feeders while the hen assists to feed, stop doing so when the hen does, and frolic about with her, building the nest instead of attending to the hungry brood.

By this method both cages can be kept going successfully, and the hen can give all her attention to her new nest without having the care of the young brood. This, of course, refers to where a cock is running with one hen only, and remains with her while she is rearing the young. When she has laid the third egg of her new clutch he can be removed altogether, and put in constant charge of the young birds, which, by the time the hen is ready to hatch her new brood, will be quite able to do without him altogether, and he can be allowed to return to the hen.

One Cock—Two Hens.

This is, perhaps, the best place for a few hints on the common and sometimes necessary plan of running one cock to two hens. To do this some breeders use a three-compartment breeding cage, of which the end compartments are 18 or 20 inches long, the centre one 14 inches; height, the usual 15 or 16 inches, and depth from front to back 10 or 11 inches. The two wood partitions which separate the compartments are movable, and have two smaller slides or partitions cut in them at the front, just above the level of the perches, which can be closed with a small wooden slide or have a small wire partition inserted as occasion necessitates. These cages are otherwise put together as was described in the chapter on cage-making.

The object of having these two small partitions cut in the large ones, and fitted with small wire as well as wooden partitions, is, that when running a cock with two hens the cock at the commencement of the season can be put in the centre compartment, with a hen in each of the end compartments. By this means the cock can see both hens that he is intended to run with through the wires on either side of him, and so get familiar with both at the same time, before being placed with either. After a week or so of this separation he is let through to the most forward hen of the two. The small wire partition is removed that separates the other hen, and the wooden one inserted in its place, so that hen No. 2 is shut off entirely from the sight of the cock. Thus his whole attention is devoted to the hen with which he is running until she has gone to nest.

When No. 1 hen has laid, and commenced to sit, the cock is then run into the centre compartment for a day, and the small wire partition inserted between him and hen No. 2, so that he may again become familiar with her. He is, of course, now shut off entirely from hen No. 1, and on the following day is let through to his new love.

It is maintained by many fanciers that this arrangement prevents much quarrelling between the cock and the two hens. This is doubtless the case where the cock's nature is to cling to one hen, for birds' temperaments differ, but where such little differences take place they are as a rule not of long duration if both of the birds are in good breeding condition. Many cocks will allow themselves to be transferred from one hen to another without showing the slightest resentment. It is where a cock is inclined to be spiteful that the three-compartment cage will be found very useful for obviating friction.

When No. 2 hen has laid her complement of eggs, and commenced to sit, the cock is then run back into the centre compartment by himself, and the small wooden partitions kept closed on either side. Our illustration of this specially constructed cage shows its excellent arrangement for the work it is intended for. The compartments at either end of this cage are, of course, fitted up with nests and other breeding requisites in use in ordinary breeding cages.

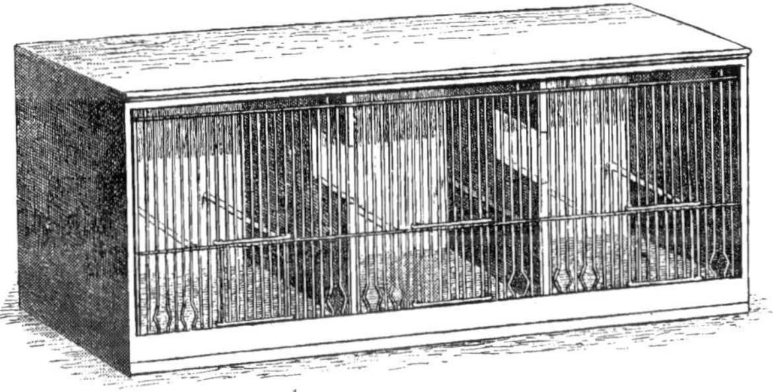

THREE-COMPARTMENT BREEDING CAGE.

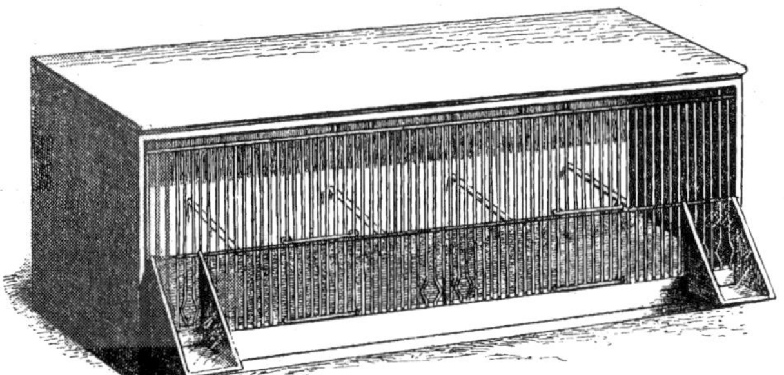

THREE-COMPARTMENT BREEDING CAGE WITH PARTITIONS REMOVED, MAKING A USEFUL FLIGHT CAGE

All that has been previously written will now apply to the future management. The cock may either be allowed to take part in feeding, or not, as circumstances demand; if the hen feeds badly, run in the wire slide, and repeat the arrangements already described.

Arrangement for a Double Brood.

The cock will be equally ready for any other emergency, and can be run in, first to one and then to the other, to assist in feeding, and will eventually take charge of one or both nests in the centre compartment, from which they will in due time be transferred to a larger flight, and the business begun *de novo*. With the partitions removed one of these three-compartment cages makes an excellent flight, as shown in our next illustration.

This method of working may have suggested itself if the reader has carefully read our previous instructions; but we give it in detail, because it is a useful plan when there is but one cock of any particular variety, and it is desired to make the most of him, and most cocks will readily fall in with such duties. Of course, there are occasionally birds that will do more mischief than good by maltreating the young. When any show such a spiteful disposition they must be debarred access to the young birds.

We have mentioned the mating of one cock to two hens only, but he may be paired with three or even more under similar methods; but it is advisable not to over-work a bird, and whenever a cock is called upon to run with more than two hens, he should not take any part in rearing the young.

From the time that the young Canary leaves the nest, it makes rapid strides towards independence.

Nursery Feeding.

It must of necessity spend some days in a nursery cage before being turned into the flight to shift for itself, as it has to pass through a sort of intermediate stage, and undergo what is equivalent to a weaning process. To carry this out the utility of spare cages, in which groups of young birds, equally advanced, can be placed, will be obvious. Hitherto their food has consisted almost entirely of the egg-mixture, with just a very little crushed hemp-seed sprinkled over the top of some canary-seed, and a pinch of German rape, which must still be continued, though the quantity of egg must be gradually decreased, the object to be attained being to get the birds on hard seed as speedily as possible. As soon as they are on the perch they will begin to pick at the soft food, though at first they will not be able to attend entirely to their own wants, hence the value of the nurseries attached to the breeding cages. It is not, however, desirable to keep them in leading-strings a day longer than necessary, but at the same time they must not be allowed to starve.

Young birds with but few exceptions can feed themselves well at the age of four weeks, and many even a day or two before this, provided egg-food and the little crushed seed just mentioned be supplied them in shallow vessels in the nursery cage from the time they are placed in it, though it may be some few days before they can really do entirely for themselves. Never forget to give fresh water daily, hanging the glass on the outside of the nursery cage in front of the water hole.

The youngsters will even in the early days make a very respectable attempt at picking up for themselves;

The Hunger Cry.

but after a while comes the noisy chirping and begging. If not attended to they soon feel the ill effects of neglect, and ruffle up their feathers in a way indicative of much discomfort. Just in proportion as they have still the craving to be fed will they evince but small desire to assist themselves; and when once they feel the pinch and begin to clamour, they will refuse to help themselves. Hunger at this stage of their lives *will not drive them to search for food*, but to beg for it; and the demand must be satisfied. By degrees, and rapid degrees, they clamour less and help themselves more, and every hour then makes the matter easier; but up to the last, no young bird must be allowed to cry for food without the cock being at once permitted to give it a meal. When its hunger is satisfied, it is much more likely to visit the egg-food than before; and the philosophy of the whole thing consists simply in the bird being ultimately able of itself to keep its appetite in check, and hence it cries no more. But remember that so long as it does cry, it must have that cry attended to in the way Nature intended it should be, the cry being indicative of a still existing necessity. The whole process does not last long, and the visits of the faithful cock will soon be few and far between.

A Variable Rule.

It will be seen that we have all along been supposing a brood to have been removed from the breeding cage at a comparatively early age, in consequence of apprehended ill-treatment; but this is not the invariable rule, by any means. The hen as frequently as not goes to nest quietly, and the cock has then nothing to do but to continue his attentions to the young ones, either in the nursery or in another cage, so that the hen may sit in peace, and also for the safety of her eggs, and by the time the cock has educated the previous brood to provide for themselves the hen will be on the eve of hatching the next.

This is the way to make fine birds; they never want for a moment, and never seem to feel the isolation which attends their being put on the other side of the front door, while poor old paterfamilias tells them as he drops the portcullis: "You see, there is a second family coming on. If you require anything, call to me and I will supply you; but you must do your best to shift for yourselves entirely as soon as possible." Canary life has its parallels.

Preparation of Seed.

Canary-seed is, of course, the staff of life, but a variety of other seeds can be used in moderation with benefit. The coffee-mill will come into use now; it can be set to grind fine, or merely to crush, doing, in fact, little else than crack the husk—a feat the young bird cannot accomplish for itself for the first week or so, even though it is feeding freely on the egg-food. Some fanciers crush all the seed—canary, rape, and hemp alike; but we have never adopted such a method, as if the canary and rape are crushed they usually go to a meal, and in this condition it simply lies in the seed-hopper, and the young birds only pick over the top of it. Indeed, they do not like the hemp-seed even crushed into a meal, but prefer it with the husk just cracked, so that they can nibble out the kernel.

Our plan is to give the canary-seed with a pinch of German rape uncrushed, and just crack the husk of a little hemp-seed as described. It should be crushed fresh each day, as, if a quantity of it is done at a time, it is liable to become rank, and so set up inflammation of the bowels in the birds. We sprinkle a little crushed hemp-seed fresh daily over the top of the canary and rape—though some fanciers we know give it in a separate vessel. We have, however, found our method excellent for inducing youngsters to learn to crack whole seeds, as, after they have devoured all the crushed hemp in the hopper, they go freely on to the canary and rape, and from almost the first day peg away at it until they manage to crack it.

In the event of a small coffee-mill or other seed crusher not being among a breeder's possessions, the husk of the hemp can be cracked by spreading some seed on a table, and passing a stout, round glass bottle or the good housewife's rolling-pin, over it, using a little pressure. A few split groats may also be added to the seed at this early period; in fact, they will do no harm if continued in moderation.

One lesson is sufficient for the youngsters to learn at a time, so their egg-food and seed should be placed in a prominent place, and the water vessel, though hung on the outside, should be placed in a good light and where the birds can get to it without difficulty. After a couple of weeks' careful treatment in this way in a cage of the size of a single breeding cage—until, indeed, the young birds get fairly well on to the seed—they can then be transferred to the larger flight cage, where they will have more room for exercise.

Before taking this final step, the different broods should be marked so that each bird can be recognised at a future day. This can be done by using numbered rings, either open or closed. We prefer the former, which should be placed on the birds' legs on the first day they leave the nest, or when they are twelve days or a fortnight old. To ring the young birds, gently lift them one at a time from the nest, place the ring round the leg, close it with a little pressure of the finger and thumb, and return the bird to the nest. By putting the rings on at this early age the birds do not try to get them off to the extent that they do if the operation is deferred until they are older. They will then often peck at their legs and feet until these become inflamed by the endeavours to get rid of the rings.

Marking the Broods.

If closed rings are used, these must be put on when the birds are about six or seven days old, as they have to be slipped over the toes on to the leg, and it requires great care and skill to put them on even at that age. The three front toes should be gently held close together and the ring slipped over; as the ring is passed over the ankle, the hind toe is carried up the back of the leg until the ring is beyond the length of the toe and has allowed the latter to come back to its normal position. The ring will then drop down quite easily, resting just above the ankle. It is because the young birds have to be handled at such a tender age that many fanciers object to the closed ring; but we have never heard an objection against the use of the open ring.

If, of course, the breeder prefers not to use any kind of ring, then he must mark the birds by some other means, such as the simple system of notching the inside web of the wing, which in no way interferes with the appearance of the bird, and is not discernible until the wing is examined in the hand. With two wings at disposal, and not less than, say, ten feathers in each to mark on, the breeder requires nothing more than a sharp pair of small scissors to enable him, with the exercise of a little ingenuity, to contrive a set of notches representing numbers corresponding with the number of the cages, and to indicate also the fact of the bird having belonged to the first, second, third, or fourth nest, thus giving its age to a week. The notched wing becomes, in fact, the private index to the stock-book.

Another method is to stamp the inner web of the wing feathers with a number by means of a small rubber stamp in which the numbers can be regulated as required.

Some such method is necessary in a room in which breeding means something more than putting up so many pairs of birds every year without any regard to their parentage, and with no more definite end in view than producing as many young ones as possible. Such is not what a fancier means by breeding. He will have been endeavouring to build with material of which he knows something, and in that endeavour has not been groping in the dark and trusting to chance. He has been keeping before him one object, and all his work tends in that direction. He has planned to produce certain results, now and in the future, and these results must be chronicled in some way to guide him in his work. Here are several birds which, to anyone else but himself, simply mean Canaries. They are very much alike, so much so that he can scarcely tell one from the other; but to him each represents some link in a chain he is forging, some stone dressed and carved into shape, and destined to fill a particular niche in the little edifice he has designed; and each should be duly marked and numbered, so that, when required, it can at once be put in its proper place and to its proper use. They are

The Necessity for Marking.

LIZARD CANARIES.

BROKEN-CAPPED. CLEAR-CAPPED.

more than this: they represent certain elements evolved from raw material he has been passing through the crucible, and are intended to be combined with other elements, also duly labelled and marked with sundry hieroglyphics—indicating their character, whence sprung, and what capable of effecting. There must be no confusion and no mistakes—nothing left to memory; every bird's pedigree and age should be registered on the bird itself.

The reason we prefer the ring is because it is handy for reference at all ages of the bird, whereas with both the notching and marking of the wing feathers, since these feathers are shed by the birds, the marks are lost after the first season. It is then difficult to recognise special birds, particularly those with clear plumage.

Flight Cages.

Some fanciers use enormous flight cages, 7 or 8 feet long, 3 or more feet high, and of like width, into which they turn thirty or forty youngsters. These may serve for common Canaries to frolic about in (though we are not convinced that they are best even for these), but we long ago decided that smaller flight cages with fewer inmates are preferable for high-class stock. By smaller flights, we mean cages 4 or 5 feet long, 16 or 18 inches high, and 10 or 11 inches wide. If ten or twelve youngsters are put in such flights they will do much better. The habit of plucking is also not so prevalent amongst small groups as when larger numbers are kept together. They can get plenty of exercise to develop their frame, without it being exhaustive, and a backward bird, moreover, stands a much better chance of gaining strength and general condition where numbers are limited. In the first eight weeks of young birds' lives these two factors are essential.

We are not alone in our views on the advantages of the smaller flights. Mr. R. L. Crisp, of Chelsea, the well-known breeder and exhibitor of Yorkshires, and Mr. J. Tyson, of Chelsea, the noted Crest fancier, not only share our opinions on this point, but have backed them up by having their very large flights made smaller. Mr. C. L. Quinton, of Great Yarmouth, one of our oldest breeders of Cinnamons, Norwich, and Crests, also adopts such flights for the young, and also for moulting his birds in. The reader must remember that when we refer to large flights we do not refer to aviaries proper.

Over-crowding.

Over-crowding, too, must be avoided, in either large or medium size flights, and ample perch accommodation provided. Perches, however, should not be too close together, as if one bird can reach the tail of another standing on an opposite perch, the temptation will often induce it to pluck the tail feathers out. It is the want of ample perch room that frequently leads to quarrelling and mischief. Birds like their own particular corners and places to sit and roost in, and commence early in life the business of elbowing their neighbours who get in their way. When there is space at command, another kind of construction is often arranged called by many fanciers a "flight," but which in reality is an aviary. A portion of the bird-room is partitioned off and enclosed with wire netting. Such a place requires no description, as it must be left entirely to circumstances; but a little ingenuity, a few strips of wood, and a few yards of fine galvanised netting, mixed up judiciously, ought to do a great deal. Of course, in such a construction the door must be made large enough to allow a person to pass in to catch birds, clean out and perform other duties; but young birds ought not to be turned into even such a place as this until they are well on to hard seed, and strong on the wing. Birds of a quiet, kindly disposition, that will not defend themselves, are better kept in cages.

The aviary or flight, whether large or small, should be kept scrupulously clean; the perches should be arranged so that the birds, when they alight on them, or are roosting, cannot soil others on the lower perches with their excreta. If this evil is not guarded against the whole of the birds will soon wear a dejected appearance, and poor health quickly follow.

Give plenty of good sound seed, and note that stimulating, fattening food may be given more freely in aviaries, where the birds have plenty of space for exercise, than in the more limited area of small flight cages. There should be a supply of ripe seed heads without green leaves, including bunches of white flowering dandelion heads and plantain stalks, which, when almost ripe, are of a deep reddish colour, and are then at the best stage for the birds. Two or three of these stalks should be interlaced in the wires at distances apart, and at a convenient height for the birds, so that several can partake of them at the same time, which they cannot do if given in one large bunch. The seed heads are not only quickly devoured, but they also make a valuable addition to the birds' dietary, and assist to check plucking by keeping them occupied. A bunch or two of shepherd's purse may also be given to the youngsters after they are taken from their parents. These ripe wild seeds are perfectly safe so long as the green foliage is not given as well, for the latter may cause diarrhœa.

Feeding in Flights or Aviaries.

A little egg-food can be given once a day at this stage, and clean sand or sawdust, at least once a week, must be sprinkled on the bottom of the cage. All soiled stuff must be removed, and clean drinking water be given with the addition of a bath every morning, while the weather is warm. In any case, birds must have drinking water fresh daily, and the bath at least once a week. This is quite often enough when the weather gets colder, even if time permits of it being given more often. Everything will then have been done to develop a hardy constitution and robust growth.

The self-supplying seed-hopper and water fountain shown on pages 79 and 80 are the suitable furnishing for a portion of a room wired off as an aviary; or a drinking fountain such as Jones's Hygienic Fountain, illustrated herewith, and obtainable from Messrs. Trower and Company, Caledonian Road, London, we consider preferable to that illustrated on page 80, because the Jones fountain is all glass, and will consequently attract the young birds more readily than the earthenware bottom which completes the fountain shown on page 80.

For large flight cages, two or three seed-hoppers, hung at intervals along the front of the cages, will be sufficient for the seed supply, and the ordinary drinking vessels, or a couple of the conical fountains shown on page 59, may be arranged in like manner.

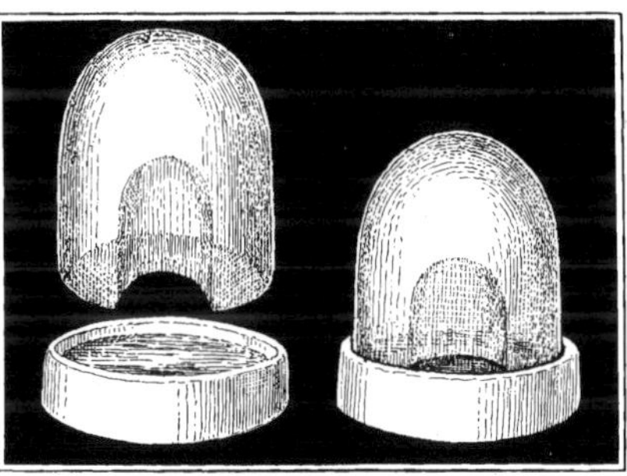

JONES'S HYGIENIC GLASS WATER VESSEL.

We wish we could at once go to the next part of our subject without a "but." The flight cage, however, is often the scene of a malady which carries off many young birds. It is not our intention in this place to enter on the subject of diseases, but we refer to this particular form as belonging to management and rearing. During the earlier part of their existence young birds spend a good deal of time in sleep; but a healthy sleep must not be mistaken for unhealthy listlessness. Our reference to sleeping applies more particularly to the young bird when it first leaves the nest, any time between the age of seventeen days or a month; after

Ills of Young Birds.

A SIMPLE FORM OF AVIARY OR LARGE FLIGHT FOR YOUNG BIRDS.

that age much less time is spent in sleep, and as they get older less still. When a bird is observed to sit thick and lumpy, with its feathers at all ruffled up, it should at once be caught and examined by blowing up the feathers of the breast and lower part of the body, when, in place of a plump breast, there will most probably be found indications of wasting, and more or less of inflammation about the abdomen, arising from the presence of unwholesome and undigested food, causing general derangement of the system. This may have been induced, in the first place, by the bird eating stale or sour egg-mixture, or from partaking too freely of such delicacies as may have been introduced into the flight from time to time. And it means "going home" speedily, if some prompt remedial measures are not applied. Young birds are more susceptible to these attacks from the age of five or six weeks until they have got nicely away with the moult than they are at any other period, and we have found from long experience that much of the mortality during the period mentioned can be warded off by a little regulation in feeding. If egg-food be given every other day instead of daily, and bread soaked in scalding milk—allowing the bread to lie in the milk in a solid piece until cold, and so absorb as much of the milk as it will—is given on alternate or every third day, and the egg-food on the intermediate days, with the seed, of course, daily in addition, much can be done to ward off the malady. The bread and milk has a relaxing but not purgative tendency on the young bird's bowels, and, consequently, is soothing to the tender internal parts, and at the same time is nourishing.

The late Mr. W. A. Blakston spoke of the great mortality among young birds at the age we mention, but recommended as a remedy purgatives and cod-liver oil, the efficiency of a bread and milk diet to combat the malady not being then known. We were among the first, if not actually *the* first, to advocate, through the columns of *The Feathered World* and its offshoot *Canary and Cage-Bird Life*, this method of feeding, experience having taught us its great benefits; thousands of young birds have been saved where it has been adopted.

If any young birds in the flight or aviary go wrong they should at once be removed to a cage by themselves, and put on bread and milk entirely for three or four days; no other food or seed should be given, but a sufficient supply of the bread should, of course, be allowed for the daily consumption. It should be made fresh each morning. In very severe cases we have found one drop of syrup of buckthorn, given direct into the beak, and five drops of tincture of gentian, added to two ounces of drinking water fresh daily, in addition to the bread and milk diet, assist in a wonderful way to bring the patient back to good health. The bird can then be gradually put on to the usual diet again. If the weather is cold and chilly, the removal of such birds to a warm room has a most beneficial effect.

Further Treatment.

As a general precautionary measure we may say that, in our opinion, the principal ailments of young birds arise from derangement of the digestive organs and inflammation, and that is our reason for emphasising the need of careful attention to their dieting.

A LOOK ROUND.

An Interesting Photograph of a Hand-reared Thrush by Mr. J. Brighty, of Clapham.

BIRD-ROOM OF MR. T. IRONS, NORTHAMPTON.
The lower cages are eminently suitable for flight cages for moulting.

CHAPTER XII

THE CANARY'S PLUMAGE AND MOULTING

The next great event in the life of a young Canary is its first moult, indications of which begin to present themselves at about the age of two months, though, no doubt, preparations have been going on unseen for some time, and indeed may, as well as the food, have had something to do with the troubles to which we referred in the previous chapter. Undoubtedly the first moult of a young bird determines its future life for better or for worse, so that it is an important period which the fancier cannot afford to treat lightly. A keen oversight must be maintained of the birds daily to see that all is progressing favourably.

In adult birds moulting commences about July, but the time varies greatly according to circumstances, the whole period extending over the next three months. With the decline of vigour the moulting begins; indeed, the latter is always accepted as an index of the former, and the breeder notes the presence of a few feathers in the bottom of his cages as sure indications of the beginning of the end of his breeding season. We are referring now entirely to adult birds, and may say here that the first sign of incipient moult—the shedding of one or two quill feathers—is to be regarded as the signal to discontinue breeding with such birds as show it.

The First Signs of Moulting.

Singularly enough, it is usually the cocks that first drop into moult, and this often results in the last clutches of eggs being unfertile where breeding has been carried on too late. The birds may not at first manifest any disposition to give up the duties of domestic life, but desire is sure to fail as the drain on the system consequent on moulting progresses; and even if it be found that the hen is sitting on fertile eggs at the time when the moult begins, it is better to remove them at once and not allow her to exhaust herself in endeavouring to discharge two duties at once.

If she has commenced to drop a few feathers the chances are greatly against her sitting even her thirteen days; and it is certainly too much to expect that, with failing energies and a constitutional sickness coming on, she will continue for a still longer period to perform duties which are born of a physical condition altogether different from that incident to the moulting period.

Preparations for Moulting Season.

We cannot do better now than take this opportunity of dismissing our breeding stock for a while, and leave them to moult and recruit their exhausted energies in their winter quarters, which we prepare for them by opening all partition-doors and drawing out all slides, and after giving the cages a thorough autumn cleansing, turn them, as far as such arrangements will permit, into flights. Now will be the time to go over the old stock, with a view to putting aside for further use such as have answered our expectations by accomplishing fair results, and putting into the sale cage those we intend to dispose of; and having done this roughly, by making a comprehensive selection which will bear further thinning out, the old hens may all be run together, in suitable numbers not to overcrowd any one particular flight. They will require no further attention beyond a supply of good, nourishing food, their cages kept clean, and an occasional bath.

We do not advocate the indiscriminate use of the bath during moulting, but an occasional dip is beneficial. Such hens as possess show properties, and are wanted for exhibition, must be caged off separately, not necessarily singly, to be put through the mill on the special diet of which we shall treat presently. The same with the cocks: many of these may have show properties of a permanent character, and may be required to travel the circuit again. To do them justice they ought to be put into separate cages, or kept in couples, as they will not be likely to quarrel now, especially if the cage allotted to them is of the same size-dimensions as a single breeding-cage; in fact, one of these will answer splendidly for the purpose. The remainder will do well enough in groups in a roomy flight as described for the hens, and as the blood in their veins is not so hot as it was in the spring, they will soon be tired of quarrelling.

How to Distinguish the Sex of Young Birds.

The young birds will also require to be drafted over, and most probably a selection of hens made from them; and the question at once arises: How are they to be distinguished from the cocks? If the fancier has been in the habit of spending much time among his birds, the greater number of them will have declared themselves; for the cocks begin to sing in their way at a month old, and some precocious youngsters even earlier. But he must learn to distinguish them by other signs. In some varieties the plumage is a slight guide; and in the case of moulted birds, of any variety, the brilliancy of the plumage alone is an almost unerring indication. But it is one of those things which can only be learned by experience. Where there is a marked difference in form and structural points, or in the general character of the plumage, verbal description becomes easy, and a novice can readily learn from it. For example, we think that anyone who can write his own language could not fail to describe the difference between a cock and hen in game fowls, so that a child could not possibly mistake the one for the other. It is not so, however, with some birds, and the best judges are liable to be deceived in certain instances. The difference between the appearance of the sexes in some varieties of the Canary is so slight, that although an experienced eye can detect it, it is not easy to define clearly in what that difference consists.

Distinguishing Features.

All knowledge of this kind is comparative, and if we say, of any one feature, that in the cock it is found larger or broader, or differs in some other respect from the corresponding feature in the hen, we do not see how that conveys any very definite idea, if the feature, as it exists in the hen, is not familiar to the person we are endeavouring to teach, beyond emphasising the fact that differences do exist. When two closely similar objects are placed before the eye, a comparison between relative properties can easily be instituted; but it is only by long acquaintance with each individual object that the knowlege of its ruling feature can be so impressed on the mind that one is able to recognise it at a glance, without the necessity of having the other object before us to enable us to arrive at a conclusion by actual comparison. If we say of a Canary that the cock is more sprightly and vivacious than the hen, we must have a correct idea of the native sprightliness or vivacity of each before we can recognise one or other by this quality. Then, again, vivaciousness differs to a marked degree in varieties. Crests, to wit, do not display the sprightly movements of the more lightly feathered varieties, but then the sex of this variety is easily recognised by the experienced breeder by the marked difference in the texture of the feather in each. For this reason we feel that the best description we could give would necessarily be obscure to the general reader in the absence of living specimens to illustrate it, and the breeder himself will at first, perhaps, fail to discover some of the more subtle distinctions. If the breeder be a close observer, however, experience will make even these little differences easily discernible to him.

Colour Distinctions in Sex.

There will not be found much difference in regard to the colour of the nest feathers of the young birds of either sex in the flight, though the cocks generally show better in this respect, and especially the Yellows, where the brighter shade of colour is more discernible than among the Buffs. The use of these two terms almost lands us in another digression, which, however, we will avoid by a simple general statement — viz. that with the exception of one or two varieties of Canaries in which the colour is certainly not what even a novice would call yellow or Canary colour, or anything like it, every bird in the flight, whether clear in colour or variegated with green or a shade of green, will be found to be in its body-colour what we will, for the sake of simplicity, call either yellow or white; not exactly, perhaps, but sufficiently so to meet our statement. The yellower coloured birds are what are technically known as "Yellows," and the whiter ones as "Buffs." But this whitish buff colour is faintly shaded or tinged with a lemon shade of yellow over the surface, especially on the shoulders, cheeks, and forehead, the general body colour being of a whitish buff. Whereas those called "Yellows" have a distinctly richer shade of yellow all over the body, though in their nest feathers the yellow shade is by far the richest on the butts of the wings and head, but at the same time the general body is free from the whitish buff shade found on the Buffs. The flight and tail feathers of both colours are a buffish shade; it is the short body feathers that form the guide to the colour of the bird, though the outer fringe of the web of the wing feathers is, as a rule, a shade richer in the Yellows than in the Buffs.

The inexperienced person usually calls these different shades of colour "rich yellows" and "pale yellows"; the breeder's term is "yellow" and "buff." And we say, in resuming the thread of our description, that though there is a difference in the colour of the sexes even in their nest feathers, it is not so easily seen in the Buffs or whiter birds as among the Yellows, and is not at any time a good criterion as to sex at this stage of their growth. And as we are verging somewhat on the domain of feathers, we may say parenthetically, that the colour of any bird in its nest-plumage is not always a guarantee of its future excellence, any more than the absence of colour indicates a permanent want. No fancier who knows what moulting means ever thinks of disposing of young unmoulted stock, lest he might unawares dispose of a gem in the rough. We discard the colour test, then, as being unsatisfactory in regard to a young bird's sex at this stage of its life. Though, after it has left the nest, and before it has moulted, an experienced eye can tell the sex of three out of every four birds with tolerable certainty. When they are in the nest, just as they commence to feather, the heads of the cock birds appear much bolder, and the colour of the feathers just breaking from the sheaths is much richer than that of the hens in the same nest; but as the birds mature and become fully feathered, these distinguishing marks are less discernible. Hence, we discard colour at this stage, and prefer shape, style, carriage, action, and voice as more reliable data to work on.

WHICH SHALL IT BE?

Mr. R. B. Falconer, a veteran Scotch Fancy Breeder, studying two favourites.

Size and Carriage Distinctions.

The cock is, as a rule, larger and more massive than the hen, is bolder and more energetic in his movements, and, in the flight, bustles about in a commanding sort of way, as if anxious to impress the looker-on with the idea that he is a superior being. Put him in a cage alone for a few minutes, and his carriage is bold and defiant, his chirp clear and ringing, his action quick and decisive and full of fire. The hen is, on the contrary, smaller and more delicately built—there are exceptions, but we are speaking of the rule—and has a neater head. By "neater" we mean that she is not, as a rule, so massive in head (this refers to plainhead varieties), and has a softer and quieter eye; there is none of that glistening defiance of the cock about it. The hen is less demonstrative in her movements, and when put into a cage alone, hops backwards and forwards in a quiet way with a soft, plaintive chirp. The cock in similar circumstances seems to pull himself together, buttons up his coat as it were to show fight, and with a ringing voice calls out again and again, as much as to say, "I'm here." Perhaps the boldest of our hens is the Yorkshire, owing to this variety being of such a swaggering character; though even the

Yorkshire hens lack the boldness of their mates. Their voice soon betrays them, and the experienced fancier can tell a hen immediately by her hop and soft "cheep"; or, failing that, by her head and eye.

Possibly much of this may seem to the uninitiated to point to distinctions without a difference; but, as we stated at the outset, some of the distinctions *are* subtle, and such as only experience and accurate observation can determine. They exist, however, and to the educated eye are palpable enough, and in mastering them lies the difference between judge and no judge. In young birds these distinctions develop more prominently after the moult; but in the case of adult birds a mistake need scarcely ever be made, especially in the spring, or when the birds are in condition, as an examination of the vent will quickly decide the question. That of the hen is small, and in the same straight line with the body, while that of the male bird is more prominently developed, and as a rule has a tendency to curve inward, especially when a bird is in full breeding condition.

Adult Differences.

In this connection there is an art in catching and holding a bird when any examination is required. There should be no hurry or fluster, but a sharp, decisive pounce, and when you have him be sure you keep him. But do not grip to injure him; better let him go and have another try than do this. To examine either back or breast, lay the bird in the palm of the hand, with the thumb across the neck; it cannot escape, and if the pressure of the thumb is on the forefinger, allowing just sufficient space for the bird's neck, but so that it cannot slip its head through, the body can be given perfect freedom, letting the palm of the hand bear its weight.

How to Hold a Canary.

If two birds be held in this manner it is the best, and, indeed, the only way, to arrive at a correct estimate of the relative colours. To hold a bird securely without ruffling the plumage, take the tips of the wings and the root of the tail between the thumb and fingers, in which position he is powerless to escape.

There is no way of determining the true age of a Canary, except of young birds of the current season's breeding. They are distinguished by their paler-coloured wing feathers, the greater portion of which they do not moult in the first season. These wing feathers, called "secondaries," "primaries," and "spurious quills," are indicated in the diagram of the body of a small bird on page 148. The paler colour of the wing feathers referred to is more pronounced after the young bird has had its autumn moult, though an observant eye may even then be deceived in natural-coloured birds. So pronounced, however, is the difference between a young and old colour-fed bird—unless the youngster has had its flight feathers plucked out—that the merest novice need have no difficulty in detecting which is which, once the difference has been pointed out to him. After their infantile moult these young birds are called by fanciers "unflighted" birds until the next year's moult, when they shed the wing feathers as well as the short body feathers, and come under the category of adult birds, though they have then done their first season's breeding.

Age Distinctions in the Wing Feathers.

The mark of age follows with this; after the first year the scales on the legs become larger and coarser, and a year-old specimen of any variety which does not carry signs of its age in its plumage can generally be told in this way, though some birds would puzzle the best judges. Year-old birds with their second moult are looked upon as being at their very best, for while they moult out as primly as those that are a season younger, they (the over-year birds) are more furnished in plumage, having attained their second flight feathers and tail feathers with their richer tint of colour, which gives a finish not possessed by the bird which has only had its infantile moult.

The Leg Age-mark.

The reason, by the way, why "unflighted" classes were introduced into exhibitions, was to do away with the barbarous practice of drawing the flight and tail feathers of young birds. This was done for the purpose of obtaining the richer tint in these feathers in the first season, instead of waiting for its advent in the natural way with the second moult, and to make it possible to compete in the first year on a level footing with older birds.

A Cruel Practice.

Happily this cruel practice is now looked upon with horror by most breeders, and we are certain it will never be revived by anyone possessing a spark of humane feeling. The pain caused to the birds, no matter how skilled the operator, was beyond description, while many of the poor things had to hobble about the bottom of the cage until the flight feathers grew sufficiently long to enable them to use their wings again.

Turning again to our leg-guides to age, it is not easy to define clearly in what the difference actually consists, but we think a judge could pick out the two or three matured specimens in a group of twenty, and feel pretty sure he had hit the right nail on the head in every instance.

Leg Differences.

As a rule, the skin of the leg and toes of a young bird is much finer in texture, and has a more tender, fleshy appearance than that of a year-old or older bird, which has a more horn-like surface, that almost verges on a scaley roughness, especially on the top of the toes. The toe-nails of a young bird are also much finer and brighter flesh-coloured than those of an old bird, while the blood vein down the centre (called the "quick") comes farther down the nail of a young bird than in the case of an old one. There are exceptions, however, and some old birds carry their age with such juvenile smartness and finish that they puzzle the best of judges. On the other hand, some youngsters very quickly develop these marks of age. In judging age, therefore, it behoves us to move with caution, and, above all, to take the bird's health into consideration, as this at times very materially alters the appearance of the legs in regard to increased roughness.

We now come to the main subject-matter of this chapter—viz. moulting. We have preferred to explore some of the small by-paths as we have come to them, knowing that when followed to their termination we should have to turn back, and there was no chance of our losing ourselves or coming out upon the main stream lower down, and leaving some portion of it behind unexamined. We think the questions we have just discussed would be most likely to arise in the mind of the fancier at this stage of his experience, and have, therefore, endeavoured to dispose of them in furtherance of our plan, rather than leave a number of miscellaneous items for after-discussion.

Moulting.

The phenomenon of moulting is a wonderful provision of Nature, common to all animals whose outer covering consists of hair, feathers, or other analogous forms. The bare mention of this fact seems to open out at once a wide field for thought, upon which, however, we must not venture to trespass one inch. We use the word in its generally accepted significance, as referring to the annual shedding of the feathers of birds, which, besides being of use as an outer covering, are destined for other purposes, for the accomplishment of which they require to be kept in a state of constant repair and efficiency. As a livery, only one suit is allowed in the year, and this suit is apt to get much injured by wear and tear, as well as in the broils and vicissitudes through which it has to pass. Some parts of it will bear patching and repairing; but as it gets old and worn-out there appears to be a limit even to this, and the wearer has often to go in rags and tatters, with portions of his body none too well covered. One condition on which the new livery or coat of feathers is granted is that the old one shall be entirely cast away; and in the exercise of much kindness and wisdom it is supplied just at the time when it is most required.

We naturally inquire: What is this covering formed of, what are its constituent elements, and what its component parts? Mudie, in his "British Birds," says that "the feathers of birds, the coverings of the featherless parts, and even the beak

Composition of Feathers.

ORNITHOLOGICAL REGIONS OF THE BODY OF A SMALL BIRD.

1. Upper mandible.
2. Lower mandible.
3. Nostrils.
4. Ridge, or culmen.
5. Commissure, or cutting edges of the mandibles.
6. Apex or point of the beak.
7. The chin.
8. Upper throat.
9. Keel, or gonys.
10. } Coloured bands usually
11. } called Bridles and Stripes.
12. The forehead.
13. The gape, or rictus.
14. Space round the eye.
15. Lower throat.
16. Superciliary region.
17. Crown, summit, or vertex.
18. Hind head, or occipital region.
19. The nape, or nucha.
20. The ear, or ear feathers.
21. The throat.
22. The breast
23. The neck above, or upper neck.
24. The back, or mantle.
25. Scapular wing coverts.
26. Lower back or tergum.
27. The shoulder.
28. Body, or lower breast.
29. The belly.
30. The vent.
31. The tail feathers.
32. The under tail-coverts.
33. Spurious quills.
34. Secondary quills, or secondaries.
35. Primary quills, or primaries.
36. The shoulder margin.
37. Wing-coverts.
38. Under-surface, or under-part of body.
39. The tarsus, or leg.
40. The front toes.
41. The hinder toe, or hallux.
42. Upper tail-coverts.

and claws, are all, chemically speaking, formed of nearly the same materials; and nearly the same with the hair and cuticle of all animals, and even with the epidermis which covers living shells. This material is coagulated albumen, or nearly the same substance as white of egg when consolidated by heat, in which state it better resists the action of water than almost any other flexible substance. This substance is, especially in the upper or more coloured and glossy part of the feathers, combined with oils and metallic substances in very minute proportions; but in the down and light-coloured feathers it is nearly pure."

In giving definitions of the component parts, Mudie refers to the "*ear-coverts*, which consist of certain soft feathers covering the external organ of hearing. The *scapulars*, or feathers which cover the shoulders and shoulder-bones, and the places where the *humeri*, or first bones of the wing, answering to the bones of the human arm above the elbow, are articulated. They unite without much distinction with the common feathers of the back, and along with those of the wings and the sides. The scapular feathers serve only as a clothing to the parts they cover, but they form a thick and comparatively downy covering, which, while it admits of easy motion, preserves the important joints which it covers from the changes of the weather. The *bastard wing* consists of a greater or smaller number of feathers, bearing some resemblance to the quills of the true wing. They grow from a little bone which is united to the third joint of the wing. The *lesser wing-coverts* are the first part of the plumage of the wings, which in all birds take the form of definite and firm feathers. There are generally several rows of them; and there are the *under-coverts* which answer to them, and line the under or inner side of the wings; but these are more slender and downy in their consistence, and,

Various Feathers.

generally speaking, have less colour. The *greater wing-coverts,* which lie under the lesser ones, and are still larger and stronger, stretch a considerable way over the quills or flying feathers, and are supports to these for a greater part of their length than the lesser coverts. They are also much stronger in proportion to the coverts which answer to them on the under sides of the wings. The *primaries,* or principal quills, which form the termination of the wings are the strongest feathers in the bird. They rise from the hand, or that position of the wings which is below the wrist-joint, and which, though it sometimes contains three distinct bones in its length, is frequently called the first bone of the wing. These feathers are numbered in order; the outer one, or that which is foremost in the expanded, or lowest in the closed wing, is the first. The *secondaries,* or second quills of the wing, arise from that part of the wing which is commonly called the second bone, and which answers to the forearm in man. They come from it towards the wrist-joint, and admit of a folding of the wing between them and the primaries, when the wing is closed. When the wing is open they sometimes appear a combination of the same curve with the primaries, 'as is the case in the wing of the Canary,' and at other times they form a distinct curve of their own. And the *tertiaries,* or third quills of the wing, arising chiefly from the same bones as the secondaries, but nearer to the elbow-joint.

"From the manner in which the several coverts support each other, and the quills, the wing is a finer combination of lightness, strength, elasticity, and stiffness than could be produced by any other means. These coverts support and admit of motion upon each other, not unlike that which takes place in a coach-spring."

Continuing the description of the remaining portion of the feathers, we have the "*Rump-feathers* and *upper tail-coverts,* the first being a continuation of the covering of the back, and the second the support of the tail-feathers on the upper side, being strong in proportion as the tail-feathers are adapted for action in flying; the *vent-feathers* and *under tail-coverts,* which cover the hinder part of the bird; and lastly the *tail-feathers,* which require no reference beyond saying how well Nature has ordered everything for use, in that the tail and longest wing feathers have by far the strongest stems to enable them to carry out the work intended for them, the wings for flight, and the tail as a rudder.

"The other feathers are to be considered rather as the clothing of the bird than as active instruments in its flight. These ordinary feathers are imbricated—that is, placed one over the edges of two—as slates are in covering a roof. The lines in which the several rows of feathers are placed form very curious curves, and their shafts diverge or converge so naturally, and with such perfect agreement, to the surface they cover, that no line of separation can be traced."

We have given these definitions and interesting descriptions in full, and would strongly advise the fancier who has not already done so to familiarise himself with them, and, by comparing them with the features presented by his own specimens, verify their accuracy; feeling satisfied that the little scrap of knowledge thus gained will prove of service by and by, and enable him to follow closely descriptions in which the use of recognised nomenclature may be adopted. Our book is essentially homely, and we have no intention of taking a very scientific view of any question, but it is as well to call things by their right names, and to know what is meant when we use them.

Treatment in Moulting.

We have already briefly pointed out in our remarks at the commencement of this chapter that no special treatment is necessary in general moulting. It is a provision of Nature; and though instances will occur in every breeding-room in which the functions are impeded, and the operation retarded and sometimes altogether checked, yet these cases are not frequent enough to justify us in characterising the moult as being such a critical period in a bird's history as to cause any serious apprehension as to the result.

We have already alluded to the fact that "the first moult is the making or otherwise of a young bird," and there is no doubt truth in the statement, as a bad or impeded first moult is detrimental to the bird's final stage of maturity. So that a good free moult is desirable, and this is greatly assisted by good health, which is largely assured by sanitary surroundings, roomy cages, and judicious feeding.

Moulting Diet.

The dietary at this period should be canary-seed as a staple food, with a little German rape added two or three times a week, a little linseed, and occasionally just a pinch of niger-seed. These two latter seeds assist in giving a satin-like polish to the new feathers, which all add to the finish and appearance of the bird. A little egg-food should also be given two or three times a week right through the moult, mixing with it a little maw-seed. It may be given daily—if in such small quantities that it is eaten up in, say, the space of half an hour—with beneficial results.

In regard to diet it should always be borne in mind that our birds are in a limited space, and we must regulate our food supply accordingly; stimulating foods can be given much more liberally where birds have large aviaries for flight, as the exercise counteracts the ill-effects which would follow such liberality in the restricted area of a cage or ordinary flight.

Where birds are not being colour-fed, a little green food is also beneficial daily in small quantities, such as young lettuce or seeding chickweed. This latter they are very fond of, and devour the seed with voracity. A few of the ripe seed-heads of knapweed and plantain may also be given whenever procurable; there are plenty to be found on railway banks, in the hedges, and on other waste ground during the summer months. The birds are very fond of the seed of these plants, and they are beneficial to all Canaries, as well as hybrids and British birds.

The Bath.

During the moult the bath may be allowed weekly; but let the birds take it of their own free will; do not force them into it, or attempt to spray them if they will not bathe, or you may cause them to faint, which many birds will do, if excited during the moult and period of new feather production.

A point to remember is that at no time of the year does the red-mite pest require such diligent suppression as during the latter part of the breeding season and moult.

Moulting Difficulties.

Birds previously healthy will, it is true, sometimes die at this time, but the percentage of deaths is very small; and although the moulting season may claim a few victims, and may be, in the case of ailing birds, the last straw which breaks the camel's back, we do not think that the number of deaths in previously healthy subjects is greater than those which can be directly traced to other causes. Personally, we never experienced the least difficulty in carrying our birds through this period; though, of course, we keep a sharp eye on them, and carry out our regulations to the letter; and we are of opinion that the idea of death is about the last which enters the mind of the experienced breeder when he finds it time to take his young stock in hand. Beyond doubt there must be a strain on the system to produce the plumage, but it is all perfectly in obedience to settled laws, and Nature does not call on the bird for the effort without furnishing the munitions of war in abundant supply, and doing her best to maintain the healthy conditions necessary for the successful carrying out of the work. This process is sometimes spoken of as the moulting "sickness," but we think the term misapplied; for the disposition to incubate and perform other duties is just as much a sickness, inasmuch as the bird requires to be in an abnormal state of body at the time. By sickness, we usually understand a derangement of certain functions; but we do not consider the phenomenon results from any such cause; it is a most perfect and healthy recognition of certain laws in the bird's economy.

We furnish on this page an illustration of the interior of a great Norwich firm's moulting-room—a most complete house for the purpose for which it is intended. The "room" is a detached house in the garden, on the outskirts of Norwich, and is a wooden erection about 12 feet high, standing on six substantial posts, about 2 feet 6 inches from the ground, with a view to guarding against damp. It is weather-boarded on the outside with 1¼-inch stuff, and the space between that and the ¾-inch boards with which the inside is lined is filled with sawdust, which acts as a non-conductor. It is warmed by hot-water pipes, and the perforated covering seen at the bottom is contrived so as to admit fresh air from outside as well as the heated air from the pipes.

A Moulting Room.

The entrance—which is approached by two or three steps—consists of double doors, the rule being to close the outer one before opening that immediately leading into the room, in case any birds should have escaped from their cages. It is lighted from the roof, and is well ventilated by means of six patent contrivances, the foul air being carried off by a 4-inch pipe through the roof, which is tiled. There are two hundred and forty-eight cage-compartments, separated by sliding partitions. Each compartment is the same size, and each front slips and unslips by a very simple arrangement of small brass buttons. The doors are all framed, and swing on beads, so as to afford no hiding-place for parasites between the door-frames and the cross-bars, and each fastens with a neat brass button. The seed-hoppers are all made of one pattern, and fit any set of holes. The water-vessels are of glass and the egg-drawers of one pattern—to push through a hole made for them in the middle of the bottom front rail.

A NORWICH MOULTING ROOM.

The building is thoroughly cleaned out at the commencement of the moulting season in the following manner:—The birds having been removed into another room, each front is unslipped, and every compartment is well scraped—top, sides, back, and bottom—and as much whitewash as possible removed. The fronts are then placed inside, each in its own place, and every aperture being closed, the place is well "stoved" by burning a quantity of sulphur—a process that is twice repeated. This destroys any pests that may have taken up their abode in the cages or on the wooden walls of the house. All wooden structures should undergo this process once a year if possible, for it is certain death to insect life and germs of all kinds. The cages are next washed with diluted carbolic acid from top to bottom, and afterwards limewashed twice.

All glasses, egg-drawers, and seed hoppers are laid in soda and water, together with the fronts, and well washed; when dry the wires of the front are coated with japan black. The hoppers and outside woodwork are then repainted black and varnished, and all other accessories washed scrupulously clean. The fronts are fastened in their places, and all is ready for the stock to be moulted.

When the room pictured is in full operation, it contains as many as 1,200 birds. Twenty cages are cleaned out and sanded each day, so that the entire room is gone through once in a fortnight; cleanliness is one of the leading principles in the government of this interesting establishment.

It is not, however, necessary for the ordinary breeder to have a room specially arranged to moult his birds in, for the breeding room answers equally well, the double breeding cages being converted into flight cages by the removal of the partitions.

A NOTED CRESTBRED HEN.
From a photograph kindly supplied by Mr. R. Rhodes.

BROKEN CAPPED SILVER LIZARD CLEAR CAPPED GOLD LIZARD
JONQUE LONDON FANCY

YOUNG COMMON CANARIES IN A FLIGHT.

CHAPTER XIII

MOULTING ON COLOUR-FOOD

WE propose now to consider the question of moulting from a point of view which clothes it with a profounder interest than that felt by the fancier when regarding it as a simple, natural phenomenon common to bird life. He divides the whole Canary family into three principal groups, comprising the colour section; those having distinctive plumage; and the birds of shape and position. With the first of these, as well as some of the others, moulting has everything to do; and the specific treatment and special dieting practised while the operation is going on, with a view to inducing the development of colour, has ever occupied the closest attention of those breeders who have made the colour section their specialty; and such are by far the larger number of the body comprising the great world of the Fancy.

The Colour Problem.

The problem of what is colour, how produced, and how affected, is one which breeders have long tried to work out, each in his own way, according to his own theory, with varying success. That some Canaries have the native property of developing it to a greater extent than others, is patent. We know why some violets are blue, and why some are not blue; why grass is green, and how it is that flowers are painted with parti-coloured tints. And there must be a reason why some birds are decked with all the colours of the rainbow; some law which governs the change in the hues of the summer and winter plumage of certain of our native birds, as well as the more strongly marked changes in those coming to us from tropical climes. What colour really is, what are its chemical constituents, can all be clearly defined; but how, when fed from the same fountain, we find it existing in so many separate hues in one and the same member, a single feather to wit, is a seemingly incomprehensible mystery.

This, however, is not a treatise on the mysteries of creation, but on the more practical matter of moulting Canaries.

Early Theories.

A thoughtful consideration of the fact that in the earliest stage of their growth the feathers of the Canary, as of all other birds, are *not* feathers, but simply little tubes in which the blood circulates, and which eventually develop into what we call feathers, the web of which is nothing more than an expansion and minute ramification of the material of which the whole is composed, led to the supposition that the colouring matter must be manufactured in, and deposited by, the blood; and various theories were propounded and methods devised for bringing about this result. The fact that certain food is known to have the direct effect of colouring the fat, and even the bones of animals, seemed to support the theory; and the notion of feeding the feather from its birth, and while in embryo before its birth, took a strong hold on the minds of breeders, though the idea was but very imperfectly developed, and, we should imagine, in many cases worked out in a very clumsy way, and without any clear perception of the principle involved. Anything "yellow" that the bird would eat was supplied to it; no matter what it was, or whether it was a substance the bird could digest and assimilate: so long as it was yellow, that was sufficient; and we have heard of the most extraordinary compounds having been administered in the shape of pills, powders, draughts, anything and everything, any way and every way, no matter what or how, if colour might only be born of it.

Colour-feeding.

From among this diversity of modes of feeding and widely varied practice, however, one truth was extracted, and it became no secret that certain food *would* affect colour in a sensible degree. Each breeder, with the most commendable selfishness, kept his particular nostrum a profound secret, but the existence of the fact was demonstrated over and over again by fanciers buying high-coloured specimens, and utterly failing to moult them with anything like the same results. Certain towns with their schools of breeders apparently had the game in their own hands, and the secret, such as it was, was jealously guarded for years. The difference between the colour of a bird moulted on ordinary diet and one fed on *extra*-ordinary diet in its very earliest days was not so marked as now or as it was thirty or thirty-five years ago, simply because the agents employed were not so powerful in their action as those now in use; but it was sufficient to give the feeder an advantage over the breeder—an advantage he has ever held when both have started in the race on the same terms as regards the quality of the birds.

From what we have said it will be gathered that the verb "to moult" is both neuter and active, and that we use it in the latter sense as signifying the indirect doing of something on the part of the breeder, rather than expressing an action entirely confined to the bird. It includes in it the idea of feeding by rule; and we are quite prepared to be met at the outset with the question: "Is feeding, then, the whole secret of colour in the colour section of the Canary family?" We are very much inclined to answer that question by another, and ask: "Why not?" And we might ask one or two more questions, such as: What *is* the natural colour of the Canary? Is not the assumption of the fact that the colour in which it usually appears is its natural or proper colour rather an arbitrary assumption? If various descriptions of vegetable food, all of which it might find in a state of nature, and which it eats with avidity, affect its colour in as many degrees, who shall say that any one shade of colour is *the* colour, and that all other shades are improper and unnatural because novel and comparatively unusual? Is not the word "unnatural" wrongly applied? For how can anything be unnatural which is in direct accordance with Nature? If any description of food be literally unnatural, it is the *artificial* food which the bird could not find in a natural state; for Canaries do not gather hard-boiled eggs among the seeds and fruits of the earth, nor do they find port wine in the brooks and pools by the wayside. Our idea of unnatural food would be the mixing up of some diet nauseating to the bird and forcing it down its throat. The results produced might be strictly in harmony with natural laws, just as natural results follow a dose of strychnine. Remember that the Canary has been a domesticated bird for centuries, is dependent upon us for everything, and has no chance of showing us, by any voluntary act of its own, what it would eat, drink, and avoid, if it had the opportunity of unlimited selection. For generations we have followed the traditions of our forefathers, and have acted as if we believed that canary-seed was created only for the Canary, and the Canary for canary-seed, and that to supply it with anything else of which it is fond, and which does it good, is—the meaningless term over again—unnatural. Unusual, we admit, but most certainly not unnatural.

Is Colour-feeding Legitimate?

Suppose a Canary to have escaped into a conservatory, and to be observed feasting on some berries growing there in profusion, acrid and poisonous to ourselves, but of marked benefit to the bird, improving its health, and, by the action of certain properties inherent in them, beautifying its plumage—what lunatic would call such food unnatural, and such results unnatural, because, among other reasons, these berries happened not to agree with ourselves? The force of this and previous arguments will be seen presently.

Our original proposition we put into the form of the question: "Is feeding the secret of colour?" We now answer: "Yes." And we have anticipated some of the objections which might arise by asking the questions above propounded—questions which we think require no reply. It is altogether foreign to the subject to stay now to inquire *how* the colour is affected; indeed, no philosophical reason has yet been assigned, though no doubt it will ultimately be shown to result from the deposition of colouring matter in the cellular tissue through the action of the blood. It is perfectly immaterial whether it be brought about in this way, or whether it be due to the development of colour native to the bird, though latent, by calling into vigorous exercise existing functions. So long as the agent employed is no more than the active principle of a natural diet, the process is strictly natural from beginning to end, and is not to be condemned as unnatural simply because it is the development of a phenomenon which has been hidden from our view by force of circumstances for centuries.

It has been openly proclaimed by some that there is no difference between *colour-feeding* and an outward application of dye to the feather; that the one is simply an outward application and the other passed through the system of the bird with a view to producing the same effect. If that were the case then the practice of colour-feeding would be fraudulent, which in no circumstances can it be proved to be. It is a well-known and established fact beyond dispute that iron is an excellent tonic both to man and beast, and it has also been proved beyond dispute to have an enriching effect on the colour of a bird's plumage, and we believe also on the coats of animals, in districts where iron-ore abounds. Would anyone even suggest that birds or other live stock taken from such districts were fraudulently improved in their colour? How then is a distinction to be made? Is it not just as legitimate to give a captive bird iron, or other tonic, when it is proved that such tonic improves the bird's colour and plumage when at liberty?

Then still further proof of the effects of these tonics is to be observed in the Canary's egg. The yolk of an egg from a bird given an iron tonic in its drinking water or food is much richer in colour than the yolk of an egg from a bird not so treated. This can easily be proved by practical experiment. The yolk is still further enriched—almost to blood-red—if colour food be given as well as the iron. This we have proved beyond doubt, having examined the yolks of many eggs from birds we have kept under the conditions cited.

Interesting results obtained by direct scientific experiments were communicated by Dr. Sauermann to the Vienna Ornithological Association (*Die Schwalbe*, April 30 and May 15, 1890). He ascertained definitely in regard to cayenne that the piperine, or hot ingredient of hot peppers, had no part in the result; that the colour component given pure had also very little effect, and that it was most efficacious when given in chemical combination with albumen or fat.

The difficulty becomes greater still when we consider the general law governing colour in animals; for there is such a law traceable. If we heat a coloured oxide we are expanding it, and also, as a scientist would say, "adding energy" to it; and even in this simple case, the usual result is to change its colour towards a tint nearer what a physicist terms "the red end of the spectrum." If a globule of copper borate, which is blue, be heated, it turns green. If yellow oxide of mercury be heated it gradually turns orange, red brown, and finally almost black. Now, very curiously, it seems as if a general rule can be traced by which animal colours also, starting from the highest degree of vitality or energy, tend, as we diminish this, to change in the converse order of black (the highest), brown, red, orange, green, blue, white. This law explains most changes, just as an infant gains strength, and again declines in energy with old age or from privation. Children's hair generally changes from very light or yellow to red or brown or black; while with age comes grey and white. Thus it seems that richer colour may probably be the effect of either more vitality or greater heat of the blood. Eastern breeds of fowls lay brown eggs, and the early native Cochins were darker, more cinnamon, than the colour attained by the birds in our colder clime. Canaries were green—our warm rooms and more stimulating food have doubtless assisted to make them yellow. The nest feathers—that is, the first feathers which appear on the body—are much paler in colour than the second feathers, which come after the first moult, even if the birds are not colour-fed; but if colour-fed on still more stimulating food, many become orange red. This shows at once that it is not a question of stain, but the action of the food upon the blood, and subsequent feather of the bird.

Colour Laws.

Instead of a "food," it would be more correct to call it a tonic mixed with food, for the capsicum is nothing more nor less to the bird, and requires to be mixed with other nourishing food in some form or other. It has also been said that the colour-food or tonic must be given each time the bird moults, otherwise the rich shade of colour is not reproduced. This is quite true, and it is only reasonable to expect that we must again give the colour-food whenever the bird changes its coat. If we would have the new coat the same rich colour, we must have the blood in the same condition as when that rich colour was first produced. Herein lies the secret of success. For imparting a gloss to the feathers linseed has few equals. There was a time when this was a guarded secret amongst the experienced breeders. Would anyone be insane enough to say it is fraudulent to give this seed to a bird with the object of obtaining gloss on the feathers? Where is the difference between giving this for one special end, and heating tonics for another?

What is Colour-food?

We said that the use of *something* to produce colour became a common practice with all breeders; perhaps we had better say nearly all; and among the many "somethings" were included marigold flowers, strong solution of saffron, cochineal, port wine, beetroot, dragon's blood, turmeric, annatto, mustard-seed, and other comestibles, the principal feature of which, it is evident, was the possession of colour.

But the entire exhibition world was destined to be revolutionised by one important discovery which was made in 1871. In the search after the philosopher's stone an explorer "struck ile." We have read how some of the Australian

BORDER FANCY CANARIES.

CLEAR. EVENLY-MARKED.

settlers stared at each other in speechless amazement when, after washing their first pan, they found the little shining lumps of gold in the bottom; and though, to anyone not in the great Fancy, it may seem absurd to draw any comparison between the two events, we do not know which of the discoverers felt the greater delight, for each had found gold. To whom belongs the honour of the discovery to which we refer we are not in a position to say. It has been said it was first found out by an old lady giving her singing canary, which was not well, some cayenne pepper with its food, to see if it would do the bird any good, and the bird, being in the moult, began to show the effects of the cayenne in its plumage. A fancier noticing this asked the old lady what she had been giving her bird. Having ascertained this, he experimented further.

A Great Discovery.

This statement, however, must be taken for what it is worth; there may be truth in it, but we do not know the actual source from which it originated. No one has to our knowledge set up a definite claim to the honour of the discovery, but the fact of its having been made came out in this way.

The First Effects.

Towards the close of the moulting season of 1871, rumours were rife in the Midland districts that in the neighbourhood of Sutton-in-Ashfield some extraordinary birds had been bred—candour compels us to state that for a long time the superior quality of these birds was asserted to belong to the breed or strain which it was alleged the discoverer of the grand secret had in his possession. Had it been openly stated that a new "feed" had been discovered, it is very probable that that fact would have been accepted more willingly than the assertion that the breeder had hit on a superior combination of blood, which story was altogether discredited; the new birds were received with the gravest suspicion on some hands, and avowed unbelief as to their genuineness on the part of others. Some of the best breeders of the day examined them; and though all known tests failed to show that the colour was due to any outward application, yet one mysterious fact stared them in the face—the birds were of *two colours!* An explanation of the fact that the colour was owing to the feed, and not to the strain, would still have cleared up this difficulty, which is now understood and will be explained presently; but this valuable strain (?) would then have lost its market value. As the colour section, however, had always ruled in the market according to the depth and purity of the colour of its representatives, and such colour had always commanded its price as representing breed or strain—a fiction of which the many outside the feeding circle we have before mentioned had been the victims for years—we can scarcely be surprised at the discoverer of a new feed endeavouring to make his market in the same way. This may all seem very naughty, and convey the idea of a lax code of morality, but it is nevertheless true. We ourselves, and a large circle of friends, had been breeding colour birds for years—and this at a time, bear in mind, when Canary shows were not reported, and when the Canary had no literature of its own—and we had never heard of feeding as influencing colour. We well remember the knock-down blow we received when a fancier in a high position, whose status in life and official position—for he was a magistrate—forbade the idea of anything but the exercise of any but the most honourable conduct, told us to give up trying to breed colour-birds, as the secret lay in the feeding and not in the breeding. In the present existing state of things, when the doings in the Canary world are chronicled weekly with as much accuracy as the rise and fall of the money market, it would be next to impossible for intelligent men to grope in the dark as we did; but we are giving a true account of Canary society as we found it in the 'seventies, when some, who ought to have known better, persistently followed out the questionable policy of preaching *breed,* while all the time taking infinite pains to conceal the necessary adjunct—*feed.*

A Curious Situation.

The line of policy, therefore, adopted by the discoverer of the new thing, the miraculous feed, was only an extension of the system of morality in which he had been educated. By ignoring the existence of the true agent, however, it will be seen that he laid himself open to the suspicion of foul play, which was strengthened by the then remarkable feature of his birds being, as we have already said, of two colours—not two shades of one and the same colour, mark you, but, as asserted, two distinct colours—viz. yellow, and a shade of yellow it is true, but with a distinctly green tint, which it was at once affirmed was the consequence of unskilful *dyeing.* And really it looked funny. Fanciers who knew that the best show-birds were the exceptional specimens selected from large numbers, and who were content to produce one or two in a season, would not have it at any price that a dozen could come out of one breeding-room, and from the same pair of birds in one year, much less five or six stars out of one nest, as was alleged of these extraordinary specimens. But the existence of the two colours on the same bird was the pill no one could swallow, and it was all adjudged a fraud. Every breeder, however, now knows that this appearance arose simply from the presence of feathers which had grown before the birds had been put on the colour-producing diet, which, even in the very best specimens, appeared absolutely *green* beside the rich, ruddy orange now so common. But our friend in Sutton-in-Ashfield kept his own counsel, and was content to sit and grin and bear the sneers of a virtuous world, strong in his own integrity. We have said this occurred in 1871; but we have reason to believe that birds fed in this way had been exhibited one or two years in succession at one of our largest shows, and had been disqualified on the ground of being artificially coloured by means of outward applications, and that the original discoverer pocketed the opprobrium and bided his time.

Early Experiences.

The late Mr. W. A. Blakston related that his first introduction to these birds was at Cheltenham, where he was judging the same year. "At that time," he wrote, "their fame had not reached us, but one or two of them were sent to Cheltenham, and one, we well remember, a heavily Variegated Buff bird, beat a large class. We were attracted by its extraordinarily rich colour, which fairly took away our breath; but an examination showed us sure indications of its genuineness, and we gave our award unhesitatingly."

Mr. Blakston further related that at a show which was held shortly afterwards he was solicited to exhibit. The usual clause in the rules, that "all specimens shall be *bona fide* the property of the exhibitor," was purposely expunged, and a silver cup held out as an inducement for large entries; and six of the then notorious Sutton-in-Ashfield birds appeared in the catalogue in Mr. Blakston's name. Some of his best friends—and one in particular, whose name will appear presently, a gentleman who subsequently became the champion of the new school, and who, with him, fought its battle and won—severely censured him for having anything to do with these dangerous birds. The judges, however, were satisfied with them, and they were duly gazetted winners. Then came the *dénouement.* The committee, in the fullness of their zeal, tested (?) the birds in a way perfectly unjustifiable, literally scrubbing off the web of the feathers in one bird's tail, leaving it with twelve almost naked quills; and shortly after charged Mr. Blakston formally with having exhibited painted birds, at the same time producing, as evidence, a handkerchief which was alleged to be stained with the colouring matter from this mutilated tail. It is not necessary to refer to the amusing incidents of the protest, but the following copy of a certificate Mr. Blakston obtained from an analytical

CHILLI (AMERICAN RED PEPPER).
Capsicum Annuum Longum (Hot).

chemist to whose examination he submitted the birds will speak for itself:

"226, High Street, Sunderland.
"There is not the least trace of a pigment or foreign colouring matter of any kind on any of the feathers I took from the birds numbered respectively 1, 2, and 3.
"JOHN J. NICHOLSON, F.C.S."

This portion of our subject has had rather a personal character, but we have detailed it as an historical fact, and as furnishing the first published account of the first chemical test to which these birds were publicly submitted, and their satisfactory passage through the ordeal.

Mr. Bemrose's Exhibits.

We next find these same birds figuring at the Crystal Palace Show, in February, 1872, by which time our mutilated friend had grown a new tail, which everyone said had been painted for the occasion; and though he was passed over as a suspicious character, some of his companions went through their examination and obtained the diploma of V.H.C., which is perhaps a rather significant comment on the knowledge of that day. The year 1872 passed away, and the memory of these ill-fated birds died with it, till February, 1873, again brought round the Crystal Palace Show, when, to the astonishment of everybody, the late Mr. Edward Bemrose, of Derby, one of the keenest fanciers of the day, and a man on whom no one could lay the finger of suspicion, but who was the very friend of Mr. Blakston's to whom we have referred, brought out two specimens of the same school, which he asserted, on his word of honour as a gentleman, he had moulted himself in his own house, and which owed their extraordinary colour to nothing but the peculiar diet on which they had been fed. Despite Mr. Bemrose's dignified asseverations, however, he left the Palace Show under the imputation

NATAL PEPPER.
Capsicum Annuum Acuminatum (Hot).

A COLOUR-FED YELLOW NORWICH PLAINHEAD AND NON-FED YELLOW BORDER FANCY.

of being in league with the naughty men of Sutton-in-Ashfield; but not before he had delivered himself of a promise, which he fulfilled almost to the letter, that next season he would bring out, not two, but a string of birds which he would send to every show in England, and with which he would take every prize, from Whitby in September, round to the Palace Show again in 1874, and that when he had thus vindicated his character he would give the secret to the world.

And he kept that promise. Next season he was invincible, and the exhibitors in the Colour section of the Canary family lay under his feet. Some accepted their defeat like men, and others writhed and wriggled like worms. In some directions confidence began to grow, while the now historical birds fearlessly travelled the country. In others the opposition was bitter, and every means that blind prejudice or petty interest could devise was called into operation in the endeavour to injure the reputation of the exhibitors of these birds. But the climax was reached at the great Norwich Show, held in St. Andrew's Hall in October, 1873, on which occasion several of the Norwich breeders protested in a body against the genuineness of a consignment of these birds, which, "under our own judging," said Mr. Blakston, "had taken almost every prize within their reach. From among a large number, seven were selected for analysis, of the result of which we append a copy." It was his lot to be connected with similar birds on their *first* examination by a qualified analyst, and he was officially concerned in them in his capacity of judge on this the *last* ordeal they were ever to undergo, and which established their reputation on a basis nothing could ever afterwards shake:

Colour-feed Vindicated.

"County Analyst's Office,
"Eastern Counties' Laboratory,
"Norwich, October 17th, 1873.

"CERTIFICATE OF ANALYSIS.

"*Of* Seven Canaries.

"*From* the Bird Show in St. Andrew's Hall, Norwich.

Mark. $\frac{70}{5}$ $\frac{112}{7}$ $\frac{28}{2}$ $\frac{40}{3}$ $\frac{54}{4}$ $\frac{88}{6}$ $\frac{13}{1}$

"I hereby certify that, in the presence of the Chairman of Committee and other representative persons, I have examined these birds with a view to ascertain the presence of artificial colouring matter upon their plumage.

"My opinion is that no artificial colour has been used. "(Signed) FRANCIS SUTTON."

Shortly after this the secret began to ooze out, and the first use made of it by some who had been loudest in their denunciation of the new school of birds was to *sell* it, which was not discovered until one, smarter than his fellows, boasted of having netted £50 by the *sale* of a *gift*.

"This coming to our knowledge," said Mr. Blakston, "we put Mr. Bemrose in possession of the fact, and on December 11, 1873, he published, in the *Journal of Horticulture*, the grand secret of the extraordinary colour of the birds which had so completely demoralised the whole Canary world; and when he stated that the agent employed was nothing more than CAYENNE PEPPER, we must say in justice to the Fancy that half of them did not believe him. But in searching after hidden things how frequently does it happen that we place our hands near them, or even on them, and yet are not aware of it; and it was almost too much for fallen humanity to be asked to believe that in the cruet which stands *next* to the mustard, which some of them had been using every day, lay the solution of the whole mystery. The wonder is that it had never been discovered before, for cayenne pepper had long been prescribed as a comforting spice; and it is probable that its administration in excess first led to a knowledge of its remarkable properties. There is also not the slightest doubt that it had long been used in very small quantities simply as a condiment, and that it then produced effects which were not attributed to it, but to some other vehicle in use at the same time. Years ago we were recommended to use a patent pungent condiment as being an excellent agent in conditioning certain birds, and though we have not analysed it, we

The Great Secret.

think there is every reason to believe that it contains the pepper in a large proportion, and that the effect attributed to it as a whole was, in the main, traceable to the presence of cayenne in its composition."

Such is the history attending the introduction of capsicum as a colour-feeding agent into the bird-room. Well does the present writer remember his father sending for two pairs of these colour-fed birds—the first introduced to Carlisle. They certainly were the most wonderfully coloured birds we had ever seen, similar in tint to that rich orange red one sees in the deepest-coloured common garden marigold; they were, indeed, rather a shade richer than the marigold. Those two pairs of birds were a secret to be kept strictly private from fanciers, and were placed in a back room in cages covered with fine muslin to keep them clean. Some rumour, however, had got afloat amongst the bird-men—as they were then usually called—that we had got something *special* out of sight. So one day an old fancier, by name Joseph Sowerby (now deceased), called to see a bird which we had in the back room, and when my father and I went to fetch it, he very quietly followed us, and the first we knew of his presence was the remark, "Hullo! what have you got here?" pointing to the muslin-covered cages. "Ah, it is them I want to see; I heard there was something special in this room, and I want to see them."

Early Colour-fed Birds.

When he did see them he never spoke, but simply opened his mouth and eyes and glared as if he had had a fright, for he had never seen the like before. The news quickly spread to the old school, and each year more colour-fed birds were brought into the Border city until they became general; though, of course, "common" Canaries—now called Border Fancies—as well as birds of position, such as the Scotch Fancy and Belgian Canaries, were then much more extensively bred there, just as the Border Fancy continues to be to this day.

Effects of Capsicum.

During the two or three years when it was first in practice it is only natural that the peculiar characteristic of the capsicum should occasionally have caused some speculation as to whether its pungent heat was not distressing to the birds. It has been accredited with many ills that bird life is heir to; but the fact that the birds eat it greedily without apparently suffering the slightest inconvenience would seem to answer the question satisfactorily, that no ill effects accrue therefrom.

Collateral proofs also are not wanting that some varieties of birds, though not belonging to our family, are inordinately fond of the capsicum. We may mention the instance which was recorded by the late Mr. Blakston: "A cockatoo of ours escaped, and was captured in a conservatory, where it had lived over again an hour of its old sub-tropical existence. We expressed our regret at the circumstance, fearing it might have done some injury, but were glad to know it had done no mischief, though the gardener expressed his opinion that 'the bird had a queer taste,' for it had '*stripped all the capsicums of their ripe pods.*'"

We have introduced the question of the influence of food upon colour in this place as forming part of the practical business of moulting, though it is evident its application will lie chiefly in the direction of those classes we have indicated as forming what we have described as the Colour section. Our reference to them has been necessarily somewhat vague, since we have not as yet minutely described any particular variety, and do not presuppose any knowledge of them. We will, however, exhaust the subject so far as its general principles and practice will carry us, reserving any remarks upon special treatment till the occasion offers to present them.

We say feeding is the secret of colour, because this certain class of feeding will intensify the colour of a good-coloured bird, as also that of a poor-coloured one, though not to the same extent as in the case of the former; but we shall have more to say on this when dealing with the breeding of the birds.

We will now return to our flight cage, where our birds are about eight weeks old, by which time it will be necessary to put those intended for a colour-fed moult on to the "feed." The breeding compartments that are at liberty should be thoroughly washed with soap and water with which a little carbolic or some other disinfectant has been mixed, to make sure there are no insect pests to torment the birds, and then well rinsed. Then, when dry, two or three birds should be placed in each compartment, but they should not be overcrowded. It should be remembered that the work can be done as efficiently by utilising these cages as by using a set of small moulting cages. Specially contrived cages for certain kinds of birds will be described in their proper place.

Moulting Cages.

Some breeders, however, like to have a stack of small moulting boxes, so as to allow each bird a cage to itself. These moulting boxes are about 10 inches square and 15 inches high, and can be made in the flight style in groups of six; that is to say, a flight can be made sufficiently long to partition off into six 10-inch compartments. The turn-rail for cleaning out can be made in one length to fit across the six compartments. Such moulting boxes usually have one perch arranged in the centre, as there is not room for two from front to back, the ends of the perch being wedged firmly against the sides or partitions of the compartment. Another perch is arranged in front of the bottom front rail of the cage for the bird to stand upon to feed, and so keep his tail and plumage clean. There is no fear of the bird soiling this bottom cross perch with its excreta, as the arrangement of the top perch prevents this. The bird can also hop from the one perch to the other without inconvenience.

Small Moulting Boxes.

Each compartment is fitted with a small seed-hopper and drinking vessel in front, as well as the usual egg-pan or drawer for the supply of egg and colour-food.

Such cages are put together in a similar manner to the ordinary breeding or flight cage. They are, of course, best enamelled, or painted, both inside and out. A very good colour for the inside is Hedge Sparrow-egg blue, and for the outside black. Care must be taken that the paint is quite dry and hard before the birds are put in. The cages can be arranged very neatly in stacks, in racks, in the same manner as other cages, and fifty or sixty of these boxes, each containing a bird undergoing the process of transmutation (for it is little else) is a sight a breeder may be proud of when he lifts up the clean sheet—thin white calico answers well—with which they should be covered. We have given details of these moulting boxes, as several large breeders use them, though by far the greater number of birds are moulted in flight or ordinary breeding cages, and they do equally well in them, though, of course, they should be sheeted over in the same manner.

We must here say that at the head of the Colour section stands the Norwich Canary; and we take that bird to illustrate our mode of going to work. It is, in fact, *the* colour bird. Two others of the family have also the power to develop colour in a remarkable degree—viz. the Lizard and London Fancy. The Lizard is, probably, at least its equal in this respect, while the London Fancy is, by its admirers, considered its superior. But each of these has *other* properties which rule above colour in them, and which are their strong points, while in the Norwich Canary colour is one of its leading characteristics. The Cinnamon Canary is another member of the colour family, but is of an entirely different shade, and this peculiar property practically rules, or at least is the leading characteristic of this Canary.

The Colour Section.

We have heard the question asked with wonder and amazement, as if it were a mystery past human comprehension: "Why is it that in the same nest, all fed on the same diet, one bird out of three or four will sometimes be found to show no colour ?" *Why?* Simply because the machinery is defective, and the bird would have exhibited the same deficiency, and in precisely the same degree, on any feed. Viewed in this light, colour is nothing more than the manifestation of certain physiological functions which we can search for and *test* by the use of particular food. The deposition of colour is the result of possessing these functions and having them in healthy working order; and by supplying food from which colour can be secreted, we ascertain which birds have and which have not the capacity of doing that, the manifestation of which constitutes their distinctive character in a fancier's eye. The capsicum, instead of being the enriching agent which has to hide all defects, the cloak to cover a multitude of sins, really becomes the most reliable guide we have, indicating the character of the birds submitted to its test, and showing pretty clearly the direction in which we should look in selecting breeding stock likely to carry out to a practical issue the theory of like producing like in regard to colour.

Colour-food.

We take our representative bird, then, to illustrate the business of moulting, and we note, first, that we put it on "feed" thus early at the age of seven or eight weeks, because it is necessary that the colour process should be commenced while the feathers are yet in embryo. And what is "feed"? We have no doubt that half a dozen breeders would give as many different recipes, but the active agent in all of them in the early days of colour feeding would have been cayenne pepper, now known by fanciers under the name of "hot Natal pepper." But to-day the chief condiment is a species of the capsicum plant, the fruit of which, though slightly pungent, is quite free from any heat-giving properties, though it contains a powerful colouring agent. The knowledge thus gained by research since those early days has revolutionised the whole cage-bird fancy in the matter of colour feeding, yet we have no richer colour-fed birds to-day than we had in Mr. Blakston's days. In fact, it is questioned by many old breeders whether the birds are as deep in tone now.

After trying the fruits of several species of capsicum, dried and ground into the form of pepper, it has been found that the "cold" or "sweet red pepper" (under which names it is advertised) imparts a splendid colour to the birds' plumage equal to that of the hot pepper. This latter is obtained from a fruit of oblong shape, similar to a peapod, called *Capsicum annuum acuminatum,* grown extensively in Natal—hence the name "hot Natal pepper"—while the capsicum fruit from which the cold or sweet pepper is obtained is very like a tomato in shape. We have seen various samples of this fruit, some of quite a pale colour, but those used for colour-food are of a deeper, richer shade than a tomato. One of the chief fruits from which the cold pepper is produced is *Capsicum annuum grossum.* This has been found to yield a good colouring agent, and this colour-food is given in a more humane way than in the early days of its introduction—that is, from the casual observer's point of view; for, as we pointed out, the birds ate the hot pepper feed with such relish and with apparently no ill-effects that it is still questionable whether it entailed any cruelty on them—but there certainly were hardships inflicted by some of the other ingredients tried, which, after all, gave little or no result.

How to give Colour-food.

The colour-food can be mixed with the ordinary chopped egg and biscuit or bread-crumbs, or with any of the soft food compositions of which birds are fond. It may also be administered by mixing it with "cake," made of eggs, flour, and sugar, or any similar sponge-cake foundation. The pepper should be given in the proportion of one of pepper to two of cake, with a small portion of "hot Natal pepper" added, just sufficient to give it a nice warm flavour. The capsicum, or cold red pepper, is supplied by vendors of colour-feeds under various names, such as "Pure Tasteless Red Pepper," "Royal Red Pepper," "Sweet Tasteless Red Pepper," etc., but they are all one and the same thing. Some breeders use the cold red pepper alone with the egg food; but we have always obtained better results by adding a little "hot Natal" in the proportion advised, and we know hundreds of other breeders of long experience who are of like opinion. This small fillip of hot pepper apparently assists to maintain heat in the body, and thus encourages a quick moult.

We are well aware that there are other foods in use as adjuncts to the ordinary capsicum, for the Fancy still has its little secrets, which may or may not be of value; but, thanks to the Fancy Press, lectures before societies, and the many handbooks published, knowledge of essentials is now widely diffused. The thoughtful breeder can still investigate the relation between cause and effect for himself, and great discoveries have been made by chance; but earnest research tells in the long run and is a source of pleasure as well.

The present system of feeding may as yet be only in its infancy; but the rule is that the brightest and richest-coloured pepper usually produces the best results. But it must be a genuinely rich-coloured pepper and not a faked one. In the old days, through ignorance, the birds were forced to eat as much colour-food as possible; their seed was removed, and they were only allowed a very little at intervals, and some, indeed, got practically none. This practice was a mistake, and any bad effects from colour feeding then were probably rather owing to the removal of the birds' seed than to the pepper. Even now there are obstinate birds from whom it is necessary to remove the seed for a short time each day until they have had a feed or two of colour-food and become accustomed to it, after which they will take it quite freely even when seed is present. Such cases will rarely occur if the colour is added to the egg-food in small quantities at first, gradually bringing it up to the full strength. To compel birds to consume the colour-food in excess is, we think, unnatural and wasteful. It hinders the healthy action of the various organs without any gain in colour of plumage, for the surplus passes through the bird's system, and the colour-food is blamed for causing the disorder, whilst in reality it is the foolish system of administration which is at fault.

Dangers of Excess of Colour-food.

TASTELESS PEPPER.
Capsicum Annuum Grossum (Cold).

It does not follow that because the bird is fond of the capsicum, and eats it greedily, that it can live on it, any more than we ourselves could live and thrive upon mustard, horseradish, and pickles, without a reasonable share of beef. We have seen very poor results obtained from over-feeding, and we have seen most satisfactory ones from the use of barely a tithe of the colour-food wasted in the other case. A judicious use of colour-food is becoming more common every day, and we are happy to say that the process is now carried on in a more rational way and with less harmful effects than ever before.

To begin with, we recommend one hard-boiled egg, chopped fine or passed through the egg-mill or sieve, with its equal bulk of a good plain biscuit or breadcrumb, mixed with a teaspoonful of colour-food. Of course, if more than one egg is required to serve the number of birds to be fed the bread or biscuit and colour-food must be increased in like proportion. The colour must be well mixed with the egg-food until it presents a red tint throughout, and each bird should be allowed a small teaspoonful of the mixture per day, or this quantity per head where a group of birds are flying together. The strength of the colour should be gradually increased by adding more to the egg-food until it presents a rich deep-red tint throughout. To gain this depth of colour it usually takes about two heaped teaspoonfuls of the colour-food to one egg, and its equivalent bulk of biscuit or bread. Some eggs, of course, are a little larger than others, and it may be necessary to add a little more colour-food before the necessary rich-red tint can be obtained. In mixing the food, the two tablespoonfuls of colour should be blended well with the egg-food, as the more it is worked into it the deeper the tint becomes, and it is easy to add additional colour if the tint is not quite of the required depth. The birds should be fed with the mixture at this strength right through the moult until their new suit of feathers is complete.

How to Mix Colour-food.

Another method is gradually to increase the colour-food up to the proportion of four teaspoonfuls of the colour-food to one egg, and its equivalent bulk of bread or biscuit, and then to give the birds but half a teaspoonful of the more concentrated mixture. Our experience of this plan is that the birds thus get quite as much of the colour-food into their systems as they do by the previous method of feeding. Moreover, as we have not to give so much egg-food it is of advantage to the health of many birds, which must be our first consideration.

An Alternative Method.

It is well for the birds for the food to contain a percentage of oil and sugar, as both are helpful to their feather and colour. The oil also keeps the bowels right whilst the birds are being fed on the stimulating colour-food. Some breeders add the sugar and oil each time when preparing the egg-food, but by far the better and easier plan is to mix them with the peppers in bulk at the commencement of the moulting season, so that all that has to be done later is to add the colour-food thus mixed to the egg-food each day. There is really no difficulty in doing this, for supposing that about ten pounds of colour-food are required to moult the stock of birds, seven pounds of the cold red pepper (also called Tasteless or Royal Red pepper) and one pound of Hot Natal should be procured and placed in a large bowl or pan; a pound and a half of soft brown sugar (not Demerara) should be added, and the whole well stirred together through and through until they are evenly blended; then fourteen ounces of the finest salad or olive oil should be added and well mixed until it is evenly distributed. One medium-sized wineglassful of good brandy should then be stirred in thoroughly; this keeps the food sweet and good. The mixture should be stored in a large covered earthenware vessel in a cool, dry place. It is then ready for use, and all that has to be done is to add the required quantity to the egg-food daily. This is a much better plan than adding the oil and sugar each day as required, as the component parts become far more thoroughly blended, and the flavour of the sugar in turn impregnates the pepper and makes it very palatable to the birds, besides giving most satisfactory results as regards colour and the good condition of the birds.

Oil and Sugar.

The peppers supplied for colour-feeding have a certain amount of natural oil, but some of the samples we have had submitted to us from time to time have contained more than their own natural oil, so that should a pepper be found to be very oily, it will not be necessary to add the full two ounces

Oily Peppers.

of oil that we advised to each pound of pepper; one ounce per pound will be sufficient.

Seed Food.

There is no mistake about the birds being fond of a good well-prepared colour-food, but whilst on this diet they should be given seed as well; that is, canary as a staple seed—of which the birds should always have a supply—together with a little linseed, and occasionally a sprinkling of German rape. A few ripe seed stalks of plantain may also be allowed, which should be fixed between the wires of the cage two or three times a week as long as they are procurable. The birds are particularly fond of them, and they are beneficial during this period if fresh-gathered in their ripe, succulent state.

Importance of Linseed.

The breeder should see that his birds have a supply of linseed during the moult. It may be given as a seed with the staple canary-seed already mentioned, or a little of it may be ground up in a coffee-mill and mixed with the egg and colour-food two or three times a week. Some birds will not eat linseed when given as a seed; but they should have a little in one form or the other, as it is of great assistance in giving lustre to the new feather. If given in the meal form, only as much as is required should be ground each time, so that it is fresh and sweet. A teaspoonful to one egg is sufficient at a time.

Drinking Water.

To each two ounces of drinking water should be added a piece of sulphate of iron the size of a small split pea every other day right through the moult, or four grains of the sulphate of iron can be dissolved in a quart of water in a jug, and, after the drinking vessels have been well washed, they can be filled from this supply. Clear water should be given on alternate days. If it is preferred, a very little saccharated carbonate of iron may be mixed with the egg-food instead, in the proportion of one grain to one egg and its bulk of biscuit or bread.

The Bath.

The bath may be allowed once a week on bright sunny days, but care should be taken to keep the cages shaded from the bright rays of the sun. The experience of a season will do more towards teaching a fancier the actual routine of this part of his business than a volume of instruction. We have explained what we believe to be the principles involved, and it is for the fancier to regulate his feeding to suit his birds, but ever bearing in mind *never to overdo it.*

Many other things are used to facilitate the moult, as well as to assist the deposition of colour by acting as precipitants; but we refrain from mentioning them, as from experience we know that they are not beneficial to the birds' health, in spite of their great assistance as colour agents.

Sand and Sawdust.

At the time when sand was in general use for covering the bottom of cages the birds were always deprived of it during the moulting season, the cage bottoms being covered with chaff, oat husk, or similar clean material so as not to soil the new feathers. This was a great mistake, for gritty sand is necessary to birds as an aid to the proper digestion of their food. Good, clean, rough-cut pine sawdust is now in general use for the bottoms of cages at all seasons of the year, and the sand is supplied separately in an earthenware vessel or some such receptacle. Pine saw-dust is one of the best coverings we can have for the cages at all times, and the sand should for preference be *clean, gritty* sea sand.

Flight and Tail Feathers.

We note, in the next place, that by a provision of Nature the Canary does not shed its eighteen flight-feathers, nor the twelve tail-quills, till it is a year old—that is, till its second moult; and it must be evident, therefore, that our moulting feed can have no effect on these feathers, since they are already quite matured. They are, at any time, the whitest feathers in the bird, having only a faint tinge of colour on the outer edge of the web, occasionally barely perceptible, and when the smaller body-feathers have all been renewed under the most favourable circumstances, these original "nest-feathers" will appear a yellowish-green in comparison with the golden glory of the new ones. This difference in colour was not so marked in the olden time before colour-feeding came into vogue, but even then breeders, in their endeavour to make the most of the bird, were accustomed to pull out the flights and tails of their young birds before placing them in their moulting cages, in order that they might be put on an equality with adult birds and have the opportunity of developing a deeper colour.

THE GOLDEN-CRESTED WREN.
A brilliant bit of Nature's coloration.

Tailing and Flighting

There are many operations performed on animals under subjection to man which, to the superficial observer, savour of cruelty, but which are really acts of kindness, rendered necessary by the circumstances in which they are placed. We have not the slightest intention of entering on this question, though our idea of what is included in the notion of subjection is very broad. It comprehends, however, not the vestige of an idea of abuse of power for selfish ends, and we fail to find any justification in our own mind for certain operations which, doubtless originating in abuse, not use, of power without any *necessary* end in view, have come, in the course of time, to be regarded by sensibilities blunted by frequent contact with questionable practices as things not worth a thought. It is just this very want of thought that keeps them alive.

We quite recognise the wisdom which, by momentary or, at the most, short-lived pain, can secure permanent immunity from trouble; but we must have an end worthy of the means—not a mere whim or fancy, or subservience to a prevailing fashion, but an imperative necessity. We must therefore frankly admit that, although keen fanciers, rigid and exacting in our demands, we cannot conscientiously say we see any necessity to disarrange the provisions of Nature to such an extent as to pull out these thirty-six feathers in a bird's wing to satisfy our eye in the matter of uniformity of colour, or, as in the case of a Yorkshire, to gain a little length.

We candidly admit that in days gone by we have "tailed and flighted" many birds without a thought; but sitting down quietly, as we do now, to look at every feature of our subject from as intelligent and philosophical a point as we can, we feel that we should not be true to ourselves if we placed it on record that tailing and flighting, as understood by the Fancy, is a means justified by the end sought. It is with a settled conviction that we pen this, so much so that we scarcely like to advance anything in palliation of the practice lest we should find ourselves fencing with a subject on which our mind is fully made up. But there is just one feature in the case to which we feel bound to refer. The same authority we quoted in giving the definitions of the various feathers says: "The feathers of birds, while they remain perfect and firm in their connection, are really parts of a living animal, and as such they must be regarded as organs of feeling. They do not, probably, in themselves feel pain, but they are in intimate connection with parts which do. The epidermis in no animal appears to feel pain, even in those parts of the animal which are regarded as being more immediately the organs of sensation; but they very speedily transmit impressions to the parts that do feel."

WING OF A BIRD PARTIALLY STRIPPED OF FEATHERS TO SHOW THE INSERTION OF THE QUILLS.

The Tail Feathers.

A good deal seems to depend, then, on the feathers being "perfect and firm in their connection," and the experience of every breeder will point to the fact that very frequently they are *not* so. The entire nest-tail, for instance, is no sooner fully matured in some birds than it requires some care to prevent its being knocked out by the bird fluttering about in its cage, and the occurrence of the tail coming out in the hand when a bird is caught is so frequent as to cause no surprise. This seems to suggest anything but the idea of "firm connection"; and whether it be that from confinement and non-exposure to the effects of a free atmosphere the tail-feathers become prematurely matured, or that the ground in which they are planted is less tenacious than the more muscular covering of the framework of the wing in which the flights are placed, there is no getting away from the fact that the tail is so easily dislodged that, in the case of the London Fancy and Lizard varieties—in which the presence of the nest-tail is an indispensable show condition—prudence suggests not only that they should not be handled, but that, if possible, specially contrived cages should be furnished to reduce the possibility of accident to the tail to a minimum. We do not mean to say that the tail is always in this loose state, but when we find it so we believe we cause the bird not the least pain, but do it a positive service, by pulling it all out. We say "pulling" it out, but we might have said "blowing" it out; for in such case a puff will scatter it, and it requires more care to keep it in than trouble to pull it out. Even tail feathers, "firmly fixed," as we would term it, come out with the exercise of but little force.

The Wing Feathers.

This, however, does not apply to the wings, in which we find the quill-feathers more securely fixed, as they have a much heavier share of work to perform than the appliance rigged aft, and there is no denying that it *does* take a good jerk to pull them out. The wing, moreover, has to be very carefully held to avoid the dislocation of the joints of the wing. It is possible also even to break some portion of the bony substance when flight feathers are pulled out in any number. Even breeders who are most expert in drawing flight feathers have had such things happen. We cannot tell what is the amount of pain inflicted, but surely there must be some—possibly less in some cases than others, for even flight feathers are apt to come out in a most provoking way when they are not wanted to, as the experience of an hour's washing of dirty birds will confirm. Yet if we take a score of young birds two months old, we do not think there would be a loose wing feather found in the lot. The pain of extraction may be much, or it may be as imperceptible as that occasioned by pulling out a hair, and the statements of those who talk of quivering flesh and broken bones are met by dispassioned counter-statements that the operation is perfectly safe, and the pain, if any, instantaneous. We agree that the pain may be instantaneous, but at the same time, if we are to judge by the conduct of the bird during the operation, it must be acute. The bird calls out as each feather is pulled from the wing—we are speaking, of course, of the extraction of firmly fixed feathers—just as human beings call out and flinch at a sharp shoot of pain. Our illustration of a wing (page 169), showing how the flight feathers are imbedded in the gristle-like substance which coats the bones, must confirm this opinion.

Is the Practice Justifiable?

We cannot think, then, considering the end to be accomplished, that the operation can be justified on the ground of necessity, more especially as there is a doubt in the case as to the amount of pain inflicted and the extent of its duration. Even if we give the defenders of the practice the benefit of this doubt, the helpless condition of the birds after the operation is sufficient to condemn it. In some instances the perches have to be lowered so as to enable the bird to get on to them until the new wing feathers have grown a fair length again. If the giving of classes for unflighted birds at shows has done nothing more than to discourage this cruel practice and render it unnecessary, a lasting benefit has been conferred on the Fancy.

Broken Feathers.

In the case of broken or frayed feathers, however, we think the bird is as much benefited by their removal as inconvenienced by the operation, and all that is necessary is to hold that portion of the wing from which the injured feather springs firmly between the finger and thumb, and then the smarter the twitch the less will be the pain. A few of the small body feathers can be pulled out in the same manner, and they are really so small in the quill that the probable pain is not worth a moment's consideration. It would be hard lines to have to keep a good show bird at home throughout the show season because it has a couple of broken flight feathers; but only in such circumstances should even a single wing feather be drawn.

The first place on which the new feathers will be observed is on the breast, where a rapid growth takes place, the feathers on the longitudinal strips on either side quickly expanding and covering the whole, giving the breeder a fair opportunity to judge as to the future character of his bird. With regard to depth of colour, very unlikely looking specimens in the flight cage may, perhaps, bid fair to become gems; a sharp look-out should therefore be kept on the groups in the flights, as well as on those moulting in couples. Any such promising birds should be removed at once into single cages, or placed in couples. It is this early promise, indeed, which eventually determines which birds are to remain to be moulted in company and which are to receive special attention, for, as we have already said, the nest feathers are not a sure criterion of future merit.

Early Colour Evidence.

The back next begins to throw out its new covering; but the breeder will notice that there is a vast difference in the rate at which the work progresses in different birds. Some seem to go into it with a will, and there is a simultaneous casting of the whole plumage; others are very lazy over it, and, in some cases, the moult is lingering and protracted in a most tedious manner. Our experience has always been that a rapid moult is better in every way, and we believe this opinion is shared by the entire Fancy, not more for the sake of the bird than for the character of the results, which are always more satisfactory. We cannot help the "Why?" coming in on the presentation of any natural phenomenon, and we think the "Because" which answers it in this case is, that the same amount of vital force which enables the bird to throw off its old feathers enables it to produce its new ones with corresponding vigour. Or, inverting the reason, we would say that it is the speedy production of the new growth that displaces the old; and where we find healthy action at work in one direction, it is only natural to infer it is going on in others. Vigorous growth is therefore accompanied by vigorous feather-action of every kind. A lack of ability to produce new feather will, in the same way, be attended by corresponding inability to carry on the other part of the work, and a slow moult, therefore, generally means deficient colour. We may extend this yet a step farther, and say that in cases in which birds are late in going into moult, or show signs of not being able to moult at all, it is no cruelty to do our best to set the machine in motion, in the hope that when once set going it may gather impetus and finish a work it had not the power to begin. The bird has to moult or die.

Advantages of Quick Moult.

In the olden days a common remedy was to pull out the tail feathers of such birds and then turn them into a very large flight; but a much better plan is to give them saffron tea to drink. This is made by placing a few shreds of hay saffron in half a teacup of boiling water and letting it stand until cold. The bird's drinker should be filled with the liquor, which should be prepared fresh daily. The cage must be placed in a dark corner of a warm room, with its front half covered over, and to the small allowance of egg-food should be added on every third or fourth day a slight sprinkling of flowers of sulphur, until the bird gets well away with the moult. Very little sulphur must be added, or the bird will not eat the food. When once the overdue moult is thus started the bird usually goes right through without any further interruptions, though, of course, its vigour must be maintained by light, nutritious feeding.

Accelerating the Moult.

Desperate diseases require desperate remedies, and if we had a bird which, after going so far, seemed to have no power to go farther, leaving the head with the feathers uncast, we should add the flowers of sulphur more frequently to the egg-food—just the slightest dust daily for five or six days. At the end of that time we should only give it every third day, or even at longer intervals. In obstinate cases there may be added to the water in an ordinary sized drinker half a teaspoonful of liquid cochineal, fresh daily. The bird should be kept very warm, with the front of its cage three parts covered with brown paper.

Finger Plucking.

Some fanciers whose lengthy experience entitles them to respect do not hesitate to finger-pluck the parts in such cases, but we should only advocate this practice when all other remedies had failed. In most cases a week or two of the treatment we have advised will assist Nature to finish her temporarily suspended work.

Influence of Heat at Moulting Time.

The importance of maintaining the moulting action will be obvious. Heat is a powerful means to this end, and its application is absolutely necessary when birds are late in completing their moult, and are overtaken by an early, cold, damp autumn. A hot-water coil, or any other generator of heat at disposal, should be set going so as to keep the temperature up to 65 or 70 degrees until the moult is completed.

When all the birds have finished getting their new coats the temperature can gradually be lowered to normal. This will in no way make the birds delicate ; but, on the contrary, tend to preserve them in good health by assisting Nature to perform her functions just at a moment when colds and chills are more than usually fatal in their effects, as the bird is in a state which renders it very sensitive. As a precautionary measure it is well to cover the front of the cage with a substantial screen, and particularly at nights, when it must be remembered the bird has to sleep with a short allowance of clothes, until the new feathers have grown their full length. Obviously this will not be required where birds are being colour-fed, as they will already have been sheeted down.

Influence of Light on Colour.

A covering also serves to keep the new plumage from being soiled by dust or smoke, which will find its way into rooms in towns, despite every effort to exclude it. What may be the chemical effect of light upon the colour we cannot explain, but it has been proved beyond doubt that the direct rays of the sun do affect colour induced by vegetable feeding to a greater or less degree, until the colour is fixed by the maturing of the feather. It is well, therefore, to shade against the harmful effects of bright light. It is said that to darken the cages is detrimental to the bird's health. This is in a measure correct, but there is no need to do this ; it is sufficient if they be shaded from the full glare of daylight. Again, the material should not be heavy, so that it makes the cages close and stuffy ; it should hang an inch or two from the front of the cage, and thus allow ample ventilation. Another way is to shade the window of the room so as to prevent the direct rays or bright light of the sun falling on the birds; but we have always found the cage covering to be the better method.

Nothing can exceed the spotless beauty of a bird when fresh moulted, before anything can have affected the bloom on its feathers; and for this, if for no other reason, we recommend covering up—together with perfect quiet—so that the bird may literally have nothing to do but to moult.

The End of the Moult.

The whole process of moulting occupies about a couple of months, of which period, frequently, a considerable portion is occupied by the reclothing of the head and neck. So long as a single pen feather is visible protruding through the others, so long is the moult going on, and so long must the colour-food be continued. Even when the bird appears " fine," if it be caught and " blown," it will be seen that there are still an astonishing number of young feathers enveloped in their little sheaths not yet expanded. This formation can be most clearly seen on the head of a Crested Canary, and we have known exhibitors on the eve of a show open one by one with a sharp pen-knife the skin-like sheaths which encase the feathers, and blow them out so as to produce a respectable crest. Anyone attempting such a feat needs to be very careful not to damage the feather, and it is better not to try it unless quite unavoidable.

WHAT THE MOULT DOES FOR A POPULAR BRITISH BIRD

A Greypate Youngster and an Adult Goldfinch.

As the moult approaches completion the birds begin to regain their sprightliness, and their appetite—which in some will have been rather fastidious—returning they will demand a supply of substantial food. The more dainty regimen must now be gradually discontinued till the bird is once more on its hard seed; and what colour-food it still has should be given in the form of cake, or, if mixed with soft food, only at longer intervals. A day should at first be missed, then a little later two days, and so on. This enables the system to get gradually accustomed to the hard seed and plainer diet again.

After the Moult.

The metamorphosis the bird has undergone will be seen to be truly wonderful. Wherever there exists a tiny pigment cell there will the subtle action of the blood have conveyed its complement of colouring matter, while the theory that the leg-scales and other featherless parts are composed of the same material as the feather, and are physiologically but cell developments, will receive verification from the evidences they will present of being also receptacles of the pigment matter which, for the last two months, has been playing such an important part in the moult, and developing in their case to a rich flesh colour.

Little remains to be said under the head of general management; but the gems of the season should now be transferred to separate cages, because, as they continue to freshen and come into song, they will turn jealous and pugnacious, and if left together may mutilate each other and thus spoil their chance of success in the show room. Of course, where they do agree, leave well alone, for there cannot be separate accommodation for every bird, and after the best have been drafted off into separate compartments or cages, the remainder can go into winter quarters—the cocks, half a dozen or more, in roomy flights or in the double breeding compartments, and the hens in numbers to suit the cage room at command. Casual quarrelsome birds should be isolated, or they will cause continual strife amongst the fellow occupants of their flight.

WASHING A CANARY (see p. 185).

Mr. James Johnston, Kilmarnock, with Apparatus, Drying and Show Cage.

CHAPTER XIV

EXHIBITING AND WASHING

Owing, in some degree, to the remarks of a few exhibitors and to the advice of certain writers and lecturers desirous of giving an impression of their special ability to impart supposed secrets, it is thought by many that two or three weeks of more or less occult "conditioning" is the main secret of successful exhibition. In many cases special treatment for "condition" is useful; but it cannot be said too plainly that it all amounts to nothing in comparison with that success in rearing and moulting already described. Many birds require no further treatment, and such as do not are those which, as a rule, make the best exhibition birds. First-rate show condition means simply perfect health, cleanliness, and just that amount of flesh which gives a finish to a bird's shape and does not approach an over-fat condition, which mars the symmetry of any variety.

Norwich Show-cages.

Uninjured plumage is of the utmost importance, and for this reason a bird must be steady in its cage to show off well, and also not to damage or disarrange its plumage. It is also essential that birds be shown in the recognised show-cage of its variety. Of those for Canaries we give illustrations in this chapter, and shall deal with those for hybrids and British birds later.

The illustration on this page depicts a Norwich show-cage, a shape that also answers admirably for Greens and Cinnamons (Norwich type). No cage displays these birds to greater perfection. The cages differ slightly in their inside colour, those for the Norwich and Cinnamons being hedge-sparrow egg blue and that for the Greens being a light bluey-green, quite flat in tone—that is, without gloss. The outside of all and the wires are coated with black enamel or wood Japan-black. In size, roughly speaking, a Norwich show-cage measures 12 inches long, 11 inches high, and 5 inches deep from front to back, outside measurement, though some makers may vary them ½ inch. Double cages of this description are also made for showing pairs of birds in; they are just twice the length, with a wire partition in the centre, one bird being placed in each compartment.

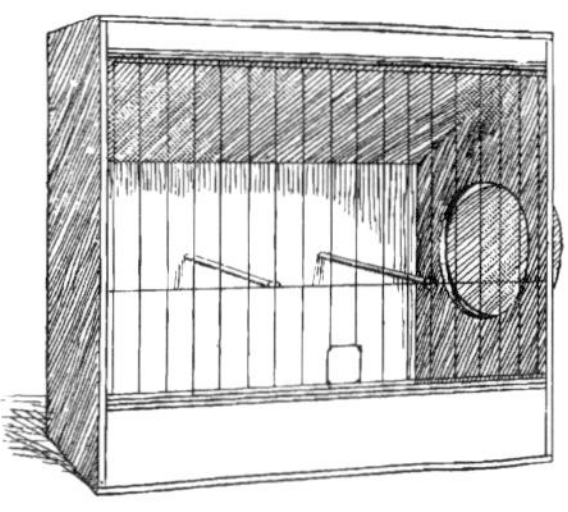

A NORWICH SHOW-CAGE.

Cages for Lizard and London Fancy.

The Lizard and London Fancy are shown in a cage of similar type, but a size smaller, about 11 inches long, 10 inches high, and 5 inches deep. The top of the cage is slanting, like that of the inner lining of the Norwich cage, and has no outer roof like the latter. The inside of the Lizard cages is azure blue for "golds" and moss-green for "silvers." Azure blue answers well for the inside of London Fancy show-cages, the outside of all being black, as for the Norwich.

Crest Cages.

On this page we give the recognised show-cage for Crests and Crestbreds. It will be observed that it is of the same shape as the Norwich show-cage, but larger, on account of the size of the bird. Its dimensions are 13 inches long, 11½ inches high, and 5 inches deep from back to front, outside measurements. Again, some makers may vary the size a ¼ inch. The wire cross-bar, on which the perches rest, is also lower in this cage, to enable the crested birds to get on their perches without difficulty. Low perches also have another advantage: they permit of a full view of the expanse of crest, and also show off to greater advantage the large heads of Crestbreds. The water hole in this cage is necessarily much larger, so that no damage or disarrangement of the crest feathers may occur when the birds drink.

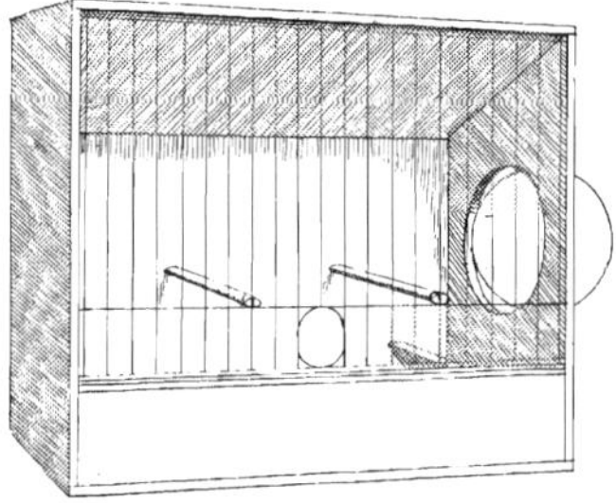

SHOW-CAGE FOR CRESTS AND CRESTBREDS.

Some fanciers show Crests and Crestbreds in a similar cage, but with the front portion of the cage top made of wire to a depth of 2 inches back instead of wood, the top of the wire front being bent over thus: ┌, and let into the narrower wood on top. These cages do not protect the birds from water or soiled seed dropped from cages above so well as the all-wood top, and they can be seen equally well in the recognised cage which we illustrate. Hedge-sparrow egg blue answers well for the colour of the inside, the outside and wires being black. Double cages are also made, in which to show pairs of this variety. They are just twice the length of the single ones, with a wire partition in the centre, a water hole in each compartment, and a door at each end, as in the Norwich cage. Such a cage is essential in pair classes for this variety, as the wire partition prevents any possibility of a bird's crest being damaged by the other, as a mouthful or two of feathers taken out will ruin a crest for show purposes for at least six weeks, until the feathers have grown again.

Cages for Birds of Position.

Birds of position have an entirely different pattern of show-cage, the entire top portion being all wire, with a wooden bottom and framework round. On this page is the latest pattern of a Belgian show-cage, largely used by exhibitors of the Belgian Canary and adopted by the United Kingdom Belgian Canary Association as their standard show-cage. It is much neater and lighter than the old clumsy dome-shaped cage in use many years since, and shows the birds off equally well. This cage measures 9 inches long, 5½ inches wide, and 12½ inches high, which height includes the wooden legs, 2 inches in length, on which the cage stands.

BELGIAN SHOW-CAGE.

WING-MARKED BUFF DARK CREST AND CLEAR YELLOW CRESTBRED.

A similarly shaped cage answers well for Dutch Frills, but a size larger, say 10 inches long, 6½ inches wide, and 13 inches high (including the 2-inch wooden legs), the actual height of the body of the cage being 11 inches. The Belgian cage is painted or enamelled black, or covered with a coating of wood Japan-black, both inside and out, wires as well. Either enamel or Japan-black is better than paint, and when dry and hard is very durable and gives a nice finish. The same colour answers equally well for the Dutch Frill show-cage.

YORKSHIRE SHOW-CAGE.

Above we give an illustration of the generally recognised show-cage for Yorkshire Canaries, and a more suitable cage to enable this bird to display its standard properties it would be impossible to find. The measurements are taken from a cage now before us, 9 inches long, 6¼ inches wide, and 14 inches high to the highest point of the dome, the dome rising from 11 inches at the sides.

On this page, too, is a Lancashire show-cage. This is squarer than the Yorkshire, and larger, owing to the size of the bird for which it is intended; it also has a flat top. The size of those we have measured is 9 inches long, 7½ inches wide, and 14 inches high outside measurements. For many years these cages had four wooden legs 4 inches long, which made the total height 18 inches. It was maintained by many of the old breeders that the legged cage gave the bird a more commanding appearance and showed it off to greater perfection. Be that as it may, these legs were a source of expense to exhibitors who sent birds by rail to shows, owing to the large cases required to pack them in, and to relieve this unnecessary expense the Lancashire and Lizard Fanciers' Association decided some few years ago to do away with the legs and to adopt the cage illustrated. We believe the Lancashire Canary Association also adopted the same cage, though there are still some few exhibitors who keep to the old form. These cages, too, are coloured black, both inside and out, though when those with legs were in general use the wood frame round the bottom and the legs were made of mahogany, either French polished or varnished, and very attractive they looked. It is, however, much better to have all show-cages for any one variety of the same uniform size and colour.

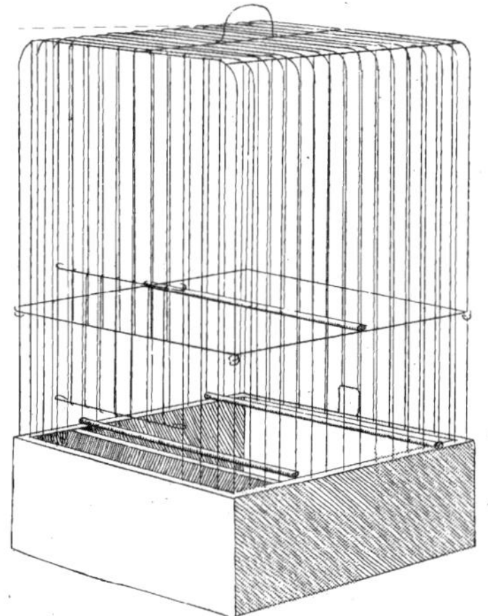

LANCASHIRE SHOW-CAGE.

The present-day Scotch Fancy show-cage is illustrated on this page. The top portion of the cage is all wire; the bottom and the four corner uprights are of wood extending half-way up, finished off with a fancy turned bone spiral. The top portion of the corner uprights is of wire passed through the bone spiral and forced into the top of the wooden upright. In some the middle cross-bars are of wood, and in others of wire, with a sliding door at the end. Some have, besides, a small door in the front below the middle bar. Some of the cheaper kinds are coloured all black, but the better-class cage is made of mahogany, either French polished or varnished, while others have the front bottom cross-bar beautifully inlaid with various fancy woods. As will be observed, two perches are arranged on the cross-bars so that the birds can take a regulated hop of about 7 inches, a characteristic we shall deal with fully in the chapter on this bird The cage is oblong in shape, with the top slightly domed. In length it is about 15 or 16 inches, 5 or 5½ inches wide, and 11 inches high at the ends, rising gradually to 13 inches in the centre of the dome.

On this page is also shown a Border Fancy show-cage, similar in shape to the Scotch Fancy, but smaller. The middle cross-bars are made of wire, and drop at

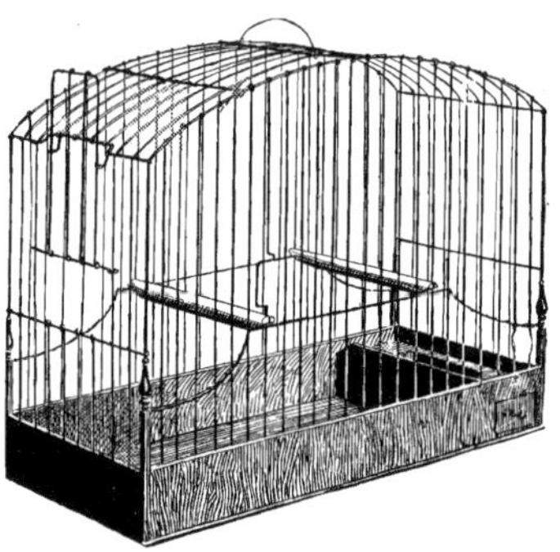

BORDER FANCY SHOW-CAGE.

the ends with an artistic curve. This kind of cross-bar is also used in some Scotch Fancy show-cages. With either variety it gives a set-off to the bird, though, of course, it will not make a poor specimen of a bird into a good one. The Border Fancy cage has only one door at the end; the cage is 13 or 13½ inches long, 5 inches wide, and 9 inches high at the ends, rising gradually to 11¼ inches in the centre of dome. It is coloured black both inside and out, the wires as well, and has two perches resting on the middle cross-bars.

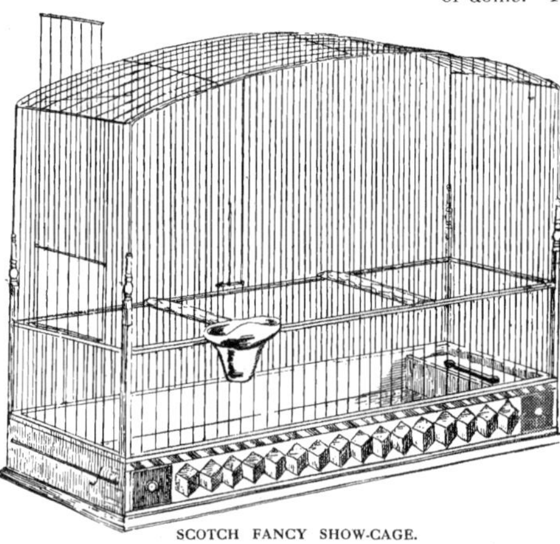

SCOTCH FANCY SHOW-CAGE.

Cleanliness in Cages.

Show-cages require to be kept in just as good condition as birds, they should also be spotlessly clean every time the birds are run into them to send to a show, or otherwise the plumage will be soiled. To avoid this it is essential to wash the show-cage each time it is required, so that good work in preparing the birds may not be undone. The task need not be a long one; a good sluicing in water is the work of but a few moments, and the cage soon dries. The paint should also be kept in good condition, and if the cage be given a fresh coat of enamel just before each show season it will look as good as new. Cages thus kept set off the good condition of an exhibit just as a dirty cage has a tendency to detract from the bird's value.

If the exhibitor is desirous of making his own show-cages, he can do so by following the directions given in Chapter V. relative to ordinary cages. Those for Norwich, Cinnamon, Norwich-type Greens, Lizards, London Fancies, and Crests and Crestbreds are all made with loose or movable wire fronts, and when first enamelled or painted will require at least two coats, both inside and out. When the first is thoroughly dry and hard it should be rubbed down smooth with fine glass-paper; the second coat will then cover with a smooth, even surface. It should be remembered that enamel should be applied thinly, as if it is put on thickly it will run and give a bad finish to the work. The cages should be thoroughly dry and hard before the birds are put in them. We have known birds' plumage to be literally ruined for the whole show season through lack of this precaution.

How to make Show-Cages.

We said early in this chapter that a bird must be at home and steady in its show-cage, otherwise it will not display its good qualities and plumage before the judge to the best advantage. This is where careful "training" comes in; that is, running the birds into the show-cages frequently until they become reconciled to them. Some birds are born show birds, and from the time they leave their parents can be run into the show-cage and will move about in it with all the grace and confidence of an old show bird. Such specimens give practically no trouble. But there are others—good birds, too—that have not the same nerve with regard to strange show-cages and faces, and require very careful handling until they gain confidence. Specimens for exhibition should therefore not merely be run into the show-cage, but accustomed to seeing people in front of their cages, to having their cages lifted and handled, and to be "run" from one cage into another. The last is very important, and is easily taught, its use being to save unnecessary catching, which soils the birds and frequently damages their plumage. A good plan to adopt is, when a friend calls to have a chat and look at the birds, to run all nervous birds out into the show-cage and let him take them gently in hand as well as yourself, and look them over. It is surprising how soon even birds that are nervous become steady with a little such training; the start, however, should not be made about a week before a show, but from the time they are able to feed themselves, or soon after. Of course, birds which are born steady show birds will only require an occasional run into the show-cage, as it does not do to make them too tame, or they will want to play instead of show off their good qualities, a fault just as bad as not being steady. What is wanted is that birds should not flutter about in the show-cage, but move about their perches with an air and grace as if they were of some importance. It is, of course, not necessary to use newly painted show-cages for training, so long as they are scrupulously clean. Some large exhibitors reserve their new cages exclusively for the exhibitions.

"Training" the Birds.

At the beginning of the show season most birds that have just finished their moult and have been kept in a room by themselves and sheeted down, as explained in the chapter on moulting, will be fit for the first shows without being washed, as they will then be in that spotlessly clean condition which has very much to do with success in exhibiting. A few weeks later, however, the new coat becomes soiled, and hence most light-coloured birds have to be washed before being shown. "Tubbing," indeed, is an absolute necessity in these days of close competition. A few

Washing.

favoured fanciers living in some of those sweet villages still left to us may be exempt from the necessity of washing birds, for in such pure air, if properly attended to and allowed to bathe freely, Canaries can surpass in brightness and bloom all that the best washing could do for those bred, say, in London, Bradford, or Manchester. Most Canaries, however, are town-bred, and such must be washed occasionally to have a chance of success. One good wash will often suffice for more than one show if the birds are able to have a day between at home so that their show-cages can be cleaned out or the transfer effected to a fresh one. The process of washing, however, is very exhausting to the birds, and should on that account not be abused.

Over-washing.

The result of too frequent washing is a kind of giving way of the feathers, which might almost be called a rubbing-out, and which is very apt to display itself about the back of the neck especially. By these or similar signs a bird which has been subjected to much tubbing can often be recognised at good shows. In spite of all this, however, washing being a necessary evil, let us see how it may be made the best of, for with care much can be accomplished without injury to the feather for a number of times in succession. We have long ere this hinted at the propriety of enlisting the active sympathies of one's "better half" in all experiments in Canarydom; and now that we reach the final stages of getting our birds into proper condition to show, this course is more than ever advisable, since the domestic domain is almost necessarily invaded. If breeding, and rearing, and moulting have been successfully surmounted, it will be strange if hopes and sympathies are *not* excited by this time as to the ultimate result.

If the operator has not seen a bird washed by some experienced exhibitor—which we advise him to lose no chance of doing—he should not attempt to wash his best birds first. A common one, or even a sparrow, is good enough to practise on at first, and if successful with one of these confidence is gained, and with it half the battle, enabling the operator to tackle the good birds aright.

Preparations for Washing.

First of all, before operations are commenced, if there are children in the house it will generally be best to see them safely to bed. There are some little treasures, born fanciers, who know how to abide still as mice until need arises, when a little hand will pass a warm cloth or other necessary, neither one moment too soon nor too late—no one would think of sending *them* to bed. But average children are sadly in the way, and all the space by the fire is badly wanted. Moreover, washing a small bird requires care, and chatter by no means assists the process. While this is being managed, then, let a good fire, *free from ash and dust,* be made up, and some large vessel full of hot water placed upon the hob so as to keep simmering. Boiling is not necessary, but if many birds are to be done, plenty of hot water will be wanted through the evening.

Drying Cages.

A drying-cage is also required. There are various forms of such, but when at all possible birds are best dried by air heated by hot water. This is accomplished by having a hot-water tank, about 3 inches deep, 16 to 20 inches in length, and 10 or 11 inches broad. It can, of course, be larger or smaller as desired. This tank is made either of copper or block tin, and stands on four legs, 4 inches high, thus admitting of a small gas ring or spirit lamp being placed beneath the tank. There is a small funnel-shaped opening in the top at one corner whereby to fill and empty the tank, and also act as an outlet for the steam if the water gets very hot. This tank can be placed on any convenient firm piece of furniture, and on it should stand a box-shaped cage made of wood, with a wire bottom and front. To form this bottom, first make a wire frame the size of the inside measurements of the cage, and stretch a piece of stout flannelette over it; then fix this firmly in the cage at

1 inch to $1\frac{1}{2}$ inches from the bottom of the sides and back. A very good plan is to nail a narrow strip of wood along the inside of the two ends 1 inch from the bottom, so that the wire frame can then rest on them and be quite firm. The reason for thus raising the drying cage floor level is to prevent the bird's feet or body touching the hot tank. The front of this cage is a movable wire one, with a door in it, or a door can be made in one of the wooden ends. Over the wire front a sheet of glass is made to slide in grooves, to keep the heat in the cage and at the same time not obstruct the light. This cage should be made slightly shorter and narrower than the top of the tank, the heat from which rises through the flannelette. The temperature is regulated by a ventilator in the top. It is well to have a thermometer hung inside the cage at the back so that the temperature can be seen at a glance, and it should be remembered that 90 degrees Fahr. is a suitable heat to maintain.

On this page is illustrated such a cage ready for use, with the glass front over the wires. The advantage of drying birds in a cage of this kind is that it is impossible for the birds' feathers to dry "harsh" by heat generated by hot water; furthermore, owing to there being plenty of light, as soon as the birds get partly dry they begin to plume and preen out their feathers.

In *Canary and Cage Bird Life* there appeared, on November 5, 1909, another pattern drying cage, heated by a hot-water tank, the work of Messrs. J. E. Reeves and A. Mallett, and we are indebted to the Editor of that journal for her kind permission to reproduce an illustration of this cage (p. 182), with Mr. Reeves's description of it, which is as follows: "When about to wash the birds the cage can be stood upon the table and the tank filled with boiling water. When the birds are washed after being rolled in the flannel they are laid on the perforated tray over the tank. After they have been there the necessary time they are taken out of the flannel and put into the flight, with a perforated tray, above where they had been lying. This is repeated until all the birds are washed. The flight has a glass front, which protects the birds from draughts. The heat from the tank and the vapour from the birds can be regulated and ventilated by a thermometer inside and two 2-inch discs on the top. The birds can remain in this state till the next day without any fear of getting a chill or of the feathers drying too sharply as before a fire. The idea is that, after birds have been washed and allowed to remain in a space where there is a moist heat, by flying and preening themselves the feathers gradually dry and retain their natural sheen and tight position, as by the ventilation the heat and vapour leave as the birds dry. Anyhow, it has proved so after the many successful trials we have made. Work worth doing is worth doing well. The following are the dimensions, inside measurements: Case, 21 inches square and 10 inches deep; flight, 12

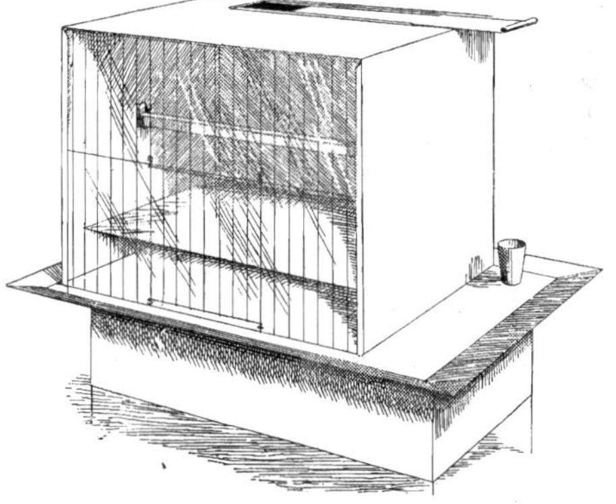

DRYING CAGE, WITH HOT-WATER TANK.

inches high, with perforated zinc bottom tray; drying compartments, 5 inches high with tray as above, which is directly over the tank; tank space, 4 inches high. The tank is made of copper, covered with flannel to retain the heat. It slides in at the back on 1-inch blocks screwed to the bottom of the case, and has 1 inch space

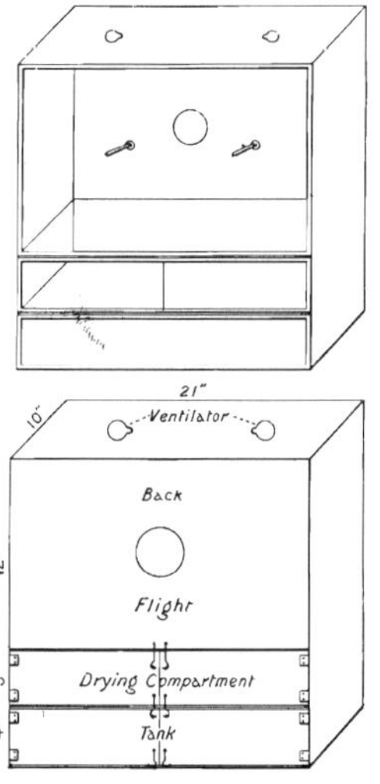

ANOTHER FORM OF DRYING CAGE.

all round, so as not to come in contact with the case, which also gives a good surface of heat. The back of the flight is 11¼ inches, with a 4-inch round hole for the door in the centre, with two stump perches screwed on from the back, the ¾-inch perforated tray which slides in from the back making it up to 12 inches for flight and acting as a block for the two doors of the drying compartment; in the latter another tray slides in and acts as a block for the two doors of the tank space. There are two folding doors, hinged and opening outwards for the drying compartments; also two more for the tank space which can be opened singly if required. When cleaning, the doors are opened and trays taken out, giving the whole a clear space. The cage was designed and made by Mr. A. Mallett, of West Ham, London."

Drying before the Fire.

If it is not convenient, however, to have a drying cage heated by hot water, then the old-fashioned way of drying the birds in an ordinary box cage before the fire must be resorted to, but an arrangement far superior to an ordinary box cage can now be obtained for use under these conditions. That is, a box-shaped cage about the size of a single breeding cage, with the top, bottom, and sides of wood, and with flannelette or stout calico stretched tight across the back and tacked to the wooden frame all round. The woodwork inside and out is left unpainted, and the front of the cage is of glass. A small ventilator is made in the top—so that the heat can be regulated—and a door at one end. A couple of perches are placed fairly low down, say 3 inches from the bottom, so that the birds can get on to them easily before they are dry. The inside of the bottom must be covered with clean flannel or some handy woollen material. The cage is then placed where a good heat from the fire can reach it, with the flannelette back towards the fire, though not near enough to scorch. By this means the birds get the warmth of the fire through the material, and at the same time can have a good light from the room through the glass on the reverse side, and thus are able to get about and preen their feathers as they dry.

Other Preparations.

The mistress of the house having been propitiated as aforesaid, we next beg a few clean, soft cloths—*clean and soft*, mind—about 18 inches square; and lastly, from the same or other source, three good-sized basins. Washing-basins are very suitable for the purpose, as they are less liable to be overturned; but better than all are the round white pans to be had in some parts of England, of equal size at bottom and top; these, when procurable, not only stand firm, but without occupying any more room, hold double the quantity of water, which consequently keeps cleaner and needs less attention.

The first basin or pan should be half-filled with warm water of about 50 degrees. If clean rain-water is procurable for the purpose so much the better for both washing and rinsing, as this needs no addition to soften it. Failing this, a piece of lump borax should be dissolved in the ordinary hot water; a piece the size of a small haricot bean will be quite sufficient to soften a quart of water, and will be beneficial to the bird's feathers. Certainty should be made that borax is used, as we know of two instances where fanciers were given alum in mistake for borax, with the result that the plumage of several of their most valuable birds was ruined for a whole season—until, indeed, they moulted again; the feathers were stiffened, and many of them caused to stick up like porcupine quills, while the plumage was given a bleached appearance.

After the water has been softened it should be thoroughly impregnated with soap by means of a badger-hair or other soft shaving brush, rubbed over good yellow or white soap. The other basins should be half filled with water maintained at a temperature of 90 degrees. A small piece of borax should be added to each of these waters. The soap should be placed where it is handy. A good plan is to bed it in the soap-dish with flannel, so that it will not slip about while passing the brush over it when washing the birds. These preparations completed, the actual washing of the birds can be begun.

How to Wash Birds.

Take your first bird and place it along the palm of the left hand, as shown on this page, the head towards the wrist, and the tail projecting between the thumb and forefinger, while the other fingers hold the bird lightly but firmly, the little finger securing the head, and the others the shoulder or side of the wing. It will be readily found that in this position the bird can be held lightly yet with perfect security, and that the position of its body can be changed at convenience, according as the back or sides are being done. Immerse all but just the head in the suds for a few seconds, whilst the lather-brush is being plied with

FIRST POSITION FOR WASHING.

telegraphic speed over the soap; as soon as a good free lather is obtained in the brush, lift the bird out, remove the thumb or second finger out of the way, and wash well with the brush the lower part of the body, the wings, and tail; always work in the same direction as the feathers lie, occasionally dipping the parts that are being washed into the soap-suds. Do this until the dirt appears gone, and when satisfied that the back up to the shoulders, sides, and top of tail are clean, turn the bird over in the hand as shown in the

SECOND POSITION FOR WASHING.

next illustration, with its head coming under the little finger towards the wrist as before, and commence brushing the under side of the wings and tail, opening the wings as much as possible; and finish off with the throat, breast, and belly. Having done this, reverse the bird, holding it in the hand as at first, except that the head and neck should now be between the thumb and forefinger; it can be held quite securely in the palm of the hand with the other three fingers, thus allowing the operator to open the forefinger and thumb, and giving full scope to wash the head and neck, which are always best done last, as they can then be quickly rinsed from soap, and so prevent undue irritation to the eyes should any soap perchance get into them. With the bird in this position it can be held with forefinger and thumb round the neck while the head is washed, opening the finger

ANOTHER METHOD OF HOLDING A BIRD FOR WASHING.

and thumb as explained, and securing the bird with the other fingers while the neck is dealt with, and removing the other fingers sufficiently and alternately like those of a violinist, to give space as head and neck are washed, taking care that the dirt is well removed round the beak and nostrils, and finishing off with the shoulders. The third finger, placed under the throat, will readily raise the head for its wash. It is no use attempting to be too particular about the eyes; it is better to forget that the bird has any, except, of course, that care will be taken that the brush does not come against those delicate organs, and this is best accomplished by passing the side of the brush over them. The soap will affect them for the moment, but this cannot be helped: its effect soon passes off, and it is no use fretting; most sensible birds shut their eyes.

Should the foregoing method of holding a bird be found awkward or difficult —and different hands seem naturally to fall into different methods—there is another we have seen practised with good results. In this method the head is passed between the thumb and forefinger of the left hand, and the three other fingers spread out so as to support the flights and tail whilst they and the back are washed with the brush, as shown on this page. The bird is then reversed and laid on its back in the palm of the hand, while the throat, breast, belly, and under parts of the wings and tail are washed; it is then reversed as before and the last three fingers closed over the back with the thumb and forefinger opened sufficiently to allow the head, neck, and shoulders to undergo the operation. Should this method be pursued, care must be taken not to press the neck feathers too tightly with the fingers, or they may become "frilled."

So far all is fairly simple; but at first, until the operator gains confidence and masters the task, he is almost as afraid to handle a Canary as average men are to meddle with a new-born baby. It is difficult to avoid a fear that the legs will come off, or the bird collapse, or something equally dreadful happen. Once get over this and remember that the object is simply to get the dirt out of the feathers, and that there is no danger so far, or any great particularity as to which way the brush moves so long as it moves in the general direction of the feathers, and that is enough. Of course, it should be seen that there is no particular pressure on any part of the body, especially on the belly.

We will suppose that the birds are now clean. The next thing to do is to squeeze the soap from the brush, dip it in the water in the second basin—making sure that this is of the temperature advised—and with it wash out the soap left in the bird's plumage. Finally, hold the patient (by this time reduced to comparative tameness) in as perpendicu-

Rinsing.

CRESTS AND CRESTBRED

Evenly Wing-marked Yellow Dark Crest — Clear Buff Dark Crest — Yellow-Green Crestbred

lar a position as possible, and scoop the water in the third basin over it with the right hand until it is perfectly free from soap. A small cup can be used to run the water over the feathers, allowing it, of course, to run in the direction in which the feathers should lie. In either case too much water should not be placed on the head, as this exhausts the bird—about three sluicings over the head are quite sufficient. After this the flights and tail should be gently drawn through the fingers to remove as much water as possible before proceeding to the drying stage. Care must be taken not to use much pressure, or a portion, or possibly the whole, of the tail may be pulled out. If preferred, a sponge may be used for the final rinsing, and the bird may even be dipped and freely moved in the clean warm water—with the exception, of course, of the head. In whatever way it is done it should be remembered that the great point is to get every particle of soap completely out of the plumage, for if any is left in it will proportionately hinder a good result.

At this stage a heavy sigh may probably be heard from the " better half," and an anxious face be seen watching the proceedings. Very likely the operator feels badly too, as he beholds the miserable little object he has produced; few men have ever " smole a smile " at this crisis of their first wash. Never mind; but having first " wrung out " the bird, as it were, with the fingers (some people draw the wings and tail through the lips instead), take one of the soft cloths, previously *well* warmed at the fire, which the good wife will have all ready for you; place the bird on it, and " dab " it gently between the hands until the worst of the wet is soaked up by the cloth. Be especially sure that the water is well absorbed from about the belly, vent, and under the wings. An excellent method of " towelling " for effecting this purpose is to place a second dry and hot cloth *over* the whole left hand; then take the bird with the right hand, with the two first fingers under the belly and the thumb over the root of the tail and ends of the wings, when the patient will open its wings a little at the shoulders. At once the covered left thumb is popped under one wing (extending between wing and body), and the left second and third fingers (also covered by the warm cloth) under the other wing (see illustration), which will, with a little judicious manipulation, rapidly soak up the wet all along the belly and under the wings. After this the left forefinger, brought up over the right side of the bird's neck, holds it securely while the right hand takes up the loose end of the cloth and wipes over the head, down the back, flights, and tail.

How to Dry the Bird.

The wet being, in the main, soaked up, another hot, dry cloth, doubled this time, is taken in the right hand, and the bird gently rolled in it, so twisting the cloth at the end where the head lies that the bird cannot slip out, but at the same time allowing free access of air to the beak, so that the bird can breathe quite freely. Let it lie in front of the fire in this position for a few minutes—not too near, but just to keep nice and warm—to recover somewhat, and then take it out of the cloth, see that its plumage is all lying in its proper position, and place it in the drying cage—on the perch if it has recovered sufficiently to stand; if not, put it gently on the cloth which covers the bottom of the cage. If it is one of the hot-water drying cages, close the door and slip down the glass front, and that is all that is necessary. If a cage is being used so as

POSITION FOR DRYING.

to dry the birds before the fire, place it in front as previously explained, and leave the bird alone. The bird may appear half dead, in which case some think it best to hold it quietly in a cloth near the fire till a good pulsation can be felt in the heart again, and then place it in the cage. But very few—not one in hundreds—really do die, and it is as well to place the bird in the warm flannel-lined cage at once, with the tail pointing towards the fire. It will generally lie there till about half dry, when it will give a bit of a roll over, stand up suddenly, and hop on to the perch, taking care of itself till the feathers assume their natural appearance.

Words of Caution.

Here a word of caution is necessary. The drying cage must be very warm, for the danger of chill is considerable. On the other hand, if too hot there is a possibility of the birds becoming faint. Hence the advantage of having a small thermometer in the cage, as it can then be watched and the temperature not allowed to rise above 90 degrees. Throughout the washing the heat of the water should be kept up by judicious changes or additions, and it should be renewed as often as dirt or soap make it necessary. The cloths should be regularly dried and heated after each use on a bird, so as to be always ready for the next; a towel should also be kept for the sole purpose of wiping the wet hands after each bird is done.

If a bird gets cold and shivers after it is put in the drying cage, it should *always* be taken in hand and carefully wrapped in a fairly warm cloth for a minute or two, when another warm cloth should be applied. This operation repeated two or three times will soon thoroughly warm the bird, when it can be returned to the drying cage, where it will soon move about and commence to plume itself.

In conclusion, we may remark that one practical lesson from a good practical washer will be more effectual than a cart-load of instructions; but if it cannot be obtained it is well to practise, as we said at the beginning, on a few common birds before those of value are operated upon.

After the Wash.

As the birds get thoroughly dry—if being dried before a fire—they should be gradually moved farther from it. When there are many to be washed, they are generally moved into another cage as they dry off; this is quite safe, as the room will have got fairly warm. It need hardly be said that the cage into which a washed bird is put should be scrupulously clean. When the washing is done and the bird is dry it is essential that it should have a drink and feed. After this it is best to draw a linen cloth over the cage and leave it for the night. If the bird does not look as well as it might in the morning, it is a good plan to put a flannel or other clean cloth over the bottom of the cage and give it a natural bath; this is the surest and best way of getting the feathers quite right and restoring the natural bloom. Some birds' attire looks so perfect after they have been washed that it is well not to offer them the bath, as in that case it does not improve them, rather the reverse—so the fancier must be guided by circumstances; but if a bath would apparently improve the finish of a bird, and it will not bathe when it is offered, it should be sprayed with tepid water, though not over-done, or the bird, instead of preening itself, will sit sulkily huddled up in a lump. Such a spray may be purchased from any chemist or vendor of bird requisites for a shilling. When the bird's plumage is made nicely damp all over, remove the flannel (put into the cage to absorb the wet), wipe the perches, feed the bird, and leave it again to dry; or it may, after the bathing or spraying, be run into a clean, dry cage. We lay great stress on clean cages, since the birds begin operations at once after a bath of any kind, and any dust on the wires or perches is at once transferred to the head near the beak and spoils all. The cold bathing or spraying process is called "fining down," and is very necessary for showing some birds in good bloom. They generally look their best a day or two after washing, and on this account it is well to wash all, or nearly all—there are a few exceptions—three clear days before they are to be shown. They ought to be covered up to keep them clean and from knocking themselves about in the meantime.

General Condition.

A word is necessary about the general condition of birds irrespective of their plumage. We have already explained the wisdom of having them in a plump, but not over-fat, condition. It is equally essential that they should not be in a too forward condition. Life and sprightliness have their good qualities in assisting a bird to show itself off well; but a bird fed up until it is practically in breeding condition is a mistake, for then he thinks more of peering through the wires of his show-cage at his next door neighbour, or, if in an all-wire show-cage, dancing from one side of the perch to the other, singing, than he does of showing off his good points. This is what we mean by a too forward condition. Great care should be exercised in the use of stimulating foods, such as egg and maw-seed. If a bird is a bit down and backward in condition, these may be given it fairly frequently in small quantities until the bird is fit enough to show itself off well, but not mad to be through the cage wires at the other birds. That high concert pitch should be avoided. Very backward birds, which are wanted ready for a certain show with time going apace, may occasionally have two or three drops of Parrish's Chemical Food mixed with a little egg-food. This has most beneficial effects, as has also a pinch of niger and linseed with a little maw; but these must not be over-done. Daily use of the bath for a week, if the bird will bathe, also assists to the desired end. A tonic in the water, too, is beneficial; say 10 drops of tincture of steel and 5 drops of tincture of gentian on alternate weeks in 2 ounces of drinking water, fresh daily, are good, given at intervals during the show season to birds doing a lot of travelling, especially the gentian. In some cases a teaspoonful of good port in the drinking water works wonders in keeping a bird in condition when travelling.

Selection for Exhibition.

In selecting birds for exhibition it is always well to choose several, and place each separately in a show-cage and stand them side by side, for some birds show themselves off better in the box or flight cages they live in than they do in a show-cage, and vice versa. This method of selection will often prevent the leaving of a good show bird at home.

"Grooming" Crests.

In the Crested variety some of the crests are apt to get a little untidy. The wash will put some of them right, and they require nothing more. Others require their crests "groomed" or "dressed"—that is to say, the feathers trained to lie neatly in their proper place. There are many supposed secrets held by fanciers for dressing the crest feathers, but we have found nothing to excel taking such birds in the hand, blowing the feathers into their proper position, and then placing a small piece of sponge, wrung out in moderately hot water, over the crest. This should be held on the crest, the feathers being in their proper places, until it is thoroughly warm and soft with the vapour from the sponge; the tip of the warm sponge should then be worked round the crest and the feathers smoothed into their proper places. A few dressings of this kind usually have the desired effect. Some fanciers use a fine tooth-brush for this purpose, made warm by dipping in hot water and then shaken almost dry; either plan answers well. Of course, there are some unruly feathers in rough crests which nothing will bring into subjection, and unscrupulous persons pluck these out and then tell fanciers they have a secret for making such feathers lie down. This is "faking" or "trimming," and not legitimate dressing of a crest.

In almost all varieties a bird will at times twist or fray its tail feathers. These can be straightened and put right again

—providing they are not broken—in the following manner. The whole of the tail should be dipped into a cup of almost boiling water and held there for a few seconds. The wet tail feathers should then be drawn gently between the fore-

Straightening Tail Feathers.

A SIMPLE PACKING TRAY.

finger and thumb, and most of the water so abstracted. The feathers will then become quite straight again. Of course, when the tail is held in the hot water, care must be taken that the water does not touch the bird's body.

Final Preparations.

Both birds and show-cages now being clean and ready, the birds are transferred to the latter (presuming the time has arrived for their despatch to a show) and the water-tins are hung outside, so that the birds can have a final drink before being packed, care being taken that the tins are sound and do not leak. Seed vessels are useless; the better plan is to throw about equal quantities of seed and oat or rice husk on the floor of the cage, and with just a very little egg-food and maw-seed in addition, this will provide a good feed before the journey is begun. Care should be taken also to see that the show labels are properly fixed to each cage: they are usually tied to the front wires at the left-hand corner on such cages as Norwich; to the middle cross front bar at the left-hand corner in such as Scotch Fancy; and to the Yorkshire cage at the top in the centre at the highest point of the dome, at the end on which the water-tin hangs, these being the most convenient places on which to tie them. All labels should be checked by the schedule to see that the right label is on the cage for each bird, according to its class. The birds should then, if possible, be left for a couple of hours to settle down.

Despatching the Cages.

Next comes the packing, the mode of which will depend upon the kind of cages. In the olden times of exhibiting, Belgian and Coppy cages were often put in a bag of coarse linen made to fit, and drawn with a string round the top; then a stick was placed through the rings on the top, which were tied to the stick, say four in a row, and made a handy package. The Norwich or similar cages were often packed in wrappering. They were put face to face in pairs with two pieces of paper between them, the paper being large enough to turn over a little and thus prevent draught, each pair being tied round the middle with string. Then three pairs were placed end to end on the wrapper, which was sewn up tightly by the aid of a packing-needle, leaving a corner or ear by which to carry it.

Then an improved method for packing such cages was adopted, as shown in the illustration on this page. The cages fit end to end in the double tray along the bottom and rest against the centre rails *b b* and *c c*. Through the bottom and end rails holes are bored for ventilation, and canvas is tacked along the bottom *a a*, projecting somewhat at the ends. This,

TRAVELLING CASE FOR CAGES.

being laced up tightly at the top and both ends, makes an admirable package. But by far the best, easiest, and safest way to send birds by rail or other means to an exhibition is to pack the cages in light boxes or baskets, like poultry baskets, lined with unbleached linen, made square or oblong instead of round, to suit the shape of the show cages. We give an illustration of such a case on page 188. They can be made any size, to hold two, four, or six cages as desired, and make capital packages. They are now in general use by all experienced exhibitors, and can be obtained from all makers of show-cages. Such appliances save secretaries and committees much trouble, as well as being far more secure for the birds than mere canvas. In any case, before finally fastening the package up, it should be seen that the water-tins, rolled in a couple of thicknesses of paper, are put inside the packages, and also that a good supply of the proper food is included.

The words "LIVE BIRDS" should be painted as conspicuously as possible on the canvas or other package, independently of the show label. This last is now sent reversible by all the best-conducted shows; but it is as well to have the owner's address legibly *painted* on the box or basket. This tends to prevent cases or birds going astray should the official show label by chance come off the case. The exhibitor has now done with his birds when he hands them over safely packed to the officials of the railway company or carrier, who has to take them to their destination. But let us impress one more point on his mind—the last connected with this chapter, but not the least. *Always* despatch the birds, no matter by what means they are going, so that they arrive at the exhibition in good time. It is to the exhibitor's advantage: the birds get reconciled to the strange surroundings, and have a feed and rest before being judged, and consequently stand a much better chance of showing themselves to advantage than birds arriving late, with only time to be unpacked and placed right away in front of the judge, as some are, by no fault of the show officials, but entirely through that of the exhibitor and owner of the birds himself.

JUDGE AND STEWARD AT WORK.
A Snapshot at Brackley Show.

A MEMBERS' SHOW.
Photograph by Mr. Jas. A. Talbot, Leyton. *For arrangement of a large open show see page 7.*

CHAPTER XV

SHOWS, JUDGING, REPORTING, AND TECHNICAL TERMS

Bird shows are now of such frequent occurrence that there is little need to enter into the details of their management except to give a few general hints to those responsible for their promotion.

Show Management.

A well-lighted, roomy hall, free from draughts, is most desirable for the well-being of the exhibits, and attention to or neglect in the selection of such a place frequently has the effect of increasing or decreasing the entries at future shows. The hall selected should, if possible, be situated in a good thoroughfare, so as to attract the attendance of the public and thus make the exhibition a financial success. The secretary or manager should have some experience of the work he is undertaking, or else be supported by an experienced staff. He should possess a complete set of show account books, so that the details of everything connected with the exhibition can be at his finger-ends. Good temper and tact are also valuable assets in tiding over difficulties and getting the best out of the working staff.

At such events *every member* of the society, whether on the committee or not, ought to render all possible assistance, and not, as is too often the case, allow the lion's share of the work to fall on about half a dozen willing workers.

Members of the committee do not always realise the responsibility incurred through their names figuring on the official list; and whilst we well know that "too many cooks spoil the broth," this is only true if all want to be *head* cook, not if each is willing to take the place allotted to him under a director.

Staging the Birds.

Of late years great improvement has been made in regard to the staging or tables for standing the cages upon, and this has been of the greatest assistance to judges in carrying out their duties, as exhibits staged at a proper height are seen more easily and to greater advantage. It is all the better for the public, and perhaps of even greater importance for the birds themselves. Picture what must be the nervous strain on birds, even if steady and used to the excitement of shows, when staged on low tables about 2 feet 6 inches high, with a throng of people peering over the top of them the whole day through for two or three days, to say nothing of the probability of several of them getting knocked over.

The best staging is that on the two- or three-tier principle—that is, one tier above another. It saves space, and gives the show a neat appearance. The bottom tier, or shelf, should be about 3 feet from the floor and 7 or 8 inches wide for the cages to stand on, this width affording greater protection to the birds and cages than a narrower shelf. The next shelf is arranged behind and about 10 or 12 inches above the first one, and the third a similar height above this; the rests, or arms, for the shelves being arranged on the lean-to principle. Two shelves can be placed on the opposite side in like manner, with the third as apex or top for both sides. This arrangement permits of staging a large number of birds in a small space. On the two lower tiers on either side such varieties as Norwich, Crests, Cinnamons, Lizards, Hybrids, British, and all birds other than birds of position should be placed. Birds of position, such as Belgians, Scotch Fancies, Yorkshires, Lancashires, Border Fancies, and all varieties which are exhibited in open-wire cages, show better when staged on the topmost tier. If the front of the staging is draped with red or green baize from the bottom tier to the floor, a neat finish is given to the exhibition.

In the North of England and Scotland the staging is often arranged in the form of long shelves directly above each other, with just sufficient space between each for the cages to stand. At some shows three of these shelves stand one above another, and at others, where space is at a premium, we have seen four, five, or even six rows of cages thus placed. The shelves are raised on upright single-legged trestles, a 2- or 3-inch lath being nailed across the top of each upright from one end to the other, and the bottom of the legs of the trestles being fixed to the floor. This staging is quickly erected and as quickly removed after the show. Mr. D. Kinlayside, of Edinburgh, has adapted a collapsible principle to this form of staging. It is fixed up with thumbscrews, and it answers well.

Question of Space.

Whatever form of staging is adopted, sufficient space must be allowed in the aisles between the exhibits so that several people can pass each other without inconvenience and the staging arranged so as to get the greatest amount of light thrown

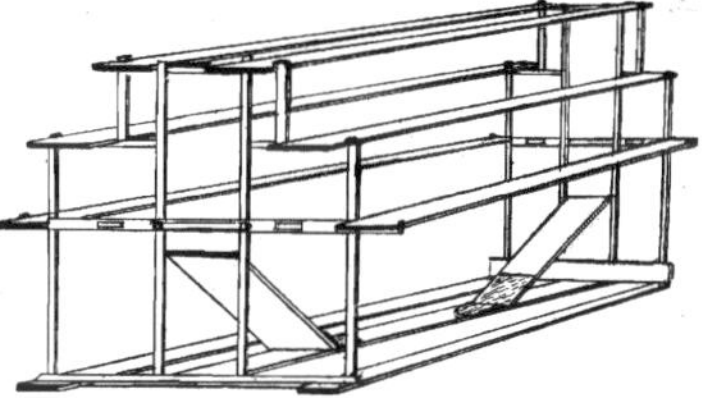

MR. KINLAYSIDE'S COLLAPSIBLE THREE-TIER STAGING.

upon the birds both by day and gas light, and thus prevent unnecessary handling of the cages by visitors. All should be erected before the birds arrive, and the space measured off for each class. This can easily be calculated by taking the number of entries in each class and allowing for the average sized show-cage of the variety. As each class is thus measured off, its class number should be affixed, so that as the exhibits are unpacked they can at once be put into position.

How to Deal with Exhibits.

The exhibits should be unpacked in a place free from draught, and as each cage is taken out its number should be called over to the official in charge, who should check it by his list and direct where it is to be staged. For this purpose he should be familiar with the arrangement of the classes, and in this way one checker can keep several unpackers at work without confusion, and save much time. It is most important to check the birds off as they arrive, so as to know if any birds are absent. As soon as each package is emptied the label should be reversed, so that the *exhibitor's address is outside,* and then put away in the appointed place.

If food is sent, another person ought at once to see that the cages are supplied with this and also water given, taking care that none is missed. It is most important that every bird should have water before leaving the unpacking table, and not be kept without it until after judging. The neglect of this makes judging most difficult, for the birds are restlessly searching for a drink instead of showing themselves off before the judge. In giving water, care should be taken to but half fill the tins at first. If more is allowed, the chances are that the birds will begin to splash and drench themselves, and probably not be dry when the judge comes round. Many a prize has been lost through neglect of this precaution, which is unfair to exhibitors. After the class is judged the tins may be filled up.

Careful packing and quick despatch of the birds at the close of the show, prompt payment of prize money and despatch of specials, all augur well for greater support at a future event. A good schedule, with reasonable classification and a good list of specials, all assist to bring a good entry, and whatever the value of the specials mentioned in the schedule, it should be seen that the winners of them receive that value.

Advertising.

To advertise a show may seem to some an unnecessary expense, but this is a grave mistake. A few good, well-worded advertisements in the Fancy Press two or three weeks before the show takes place acquaint the would-be exhibitor with the good things in store for him, and also bring the show before the notice of bird keepers, not only increasing the entry, but inducing fanciers and others to attend. A few good posters and handbills distributed locally by members do much to secure the attendance of the general public. The outlay on advertising, if done properly, will undoubtedly be well repaid.

Judges.

We know from experience that the liability attached to a show makes its officials study expenditure carefully, and this is quite right; but still, cheapness should not be their first consideration, and qualified judges, whose decisions meet with the general approval of exhibitors—even if costing a little more for their services—are usually the cheapest in the end, for they secure a good entry. Again, while no proper judge will complain of a good day's work, he should not be over-taxed. Let him, as far as possible, have a good start in the morning whilst fresh and when the light is good, the show-room quiet, and the birds not excited. The duty of a judge, it should be impressed, is to judge to the recognised standards, and not to "pet" notions of his own.

Reporters.

Then press officials have as important a duty as the judge, provided we are to have a *reliable* report. If not, then better have no report at all than a false criticism, misguiding to inexperienced exhibitors and worse than useless to readers unable to attend the show. It has been suggested by some that judges, as well as reporters, should be supplied with a catalogue while officiating. We should be sorry to see such a practice in vogue, for we maintain if a judge cannot pick out the most perfect exhibits for the prizes without the aid of a catalogue to tell him to whom those exhibits belong, then he does not possess the necessary ability to act as a judge. We say the same of the reporter. When taking our notes at a show we use a schedule from whence to get the headings of the classes, then write our critique and afterwards secure a catalogue for the names of the respective exhibitors. Two points need constant care as regards critical reports—viz. impartiality and competence. Reports thus written are of immense value to all concerned, and the journals we have been and are connected with, we are happy to say, have always made these their leading principles. It is sheer presumption—almost impertinence—for a reporter merely to say that an award is wrong, or that some other bird ought to have received it, and not support the statement by well-reasoned argument. An honest expert's report upon a class, differing from the judge, may often start a discussion on important points that may clear away difficulties and perhaps affect breeding operations through the following season.

Catalogues. Catalogues showing the prize-winners should be on sale soon after judging is completed, but until these are ready there should be a supply without the awards.

A certain number of stewards should always be about the show, keeping a watchful eye on the exhibits and seeing that all is well.

Fancy Terms. Before passing from these general chapters to detailed treatment of various breeds and varieties, it will be convenient to present a glossary of some of the terms employed by fanciers and breeders in descriptions of birds, and a reference to the diagram of the ornithological regions of the body of a small bird on page 148 will assist our explanations.

Action. — This applies particularly to the regulated hop of the Scotch Fancy from perch to perch and the tremulous motion of the neck of this bird and of the Belgian Canary as they pull themselves up into position when their cage is taken in the hand.

Awry.—A twist in feathers which ought to lie straight, or an unnatural twist of the neck or other part not characteristic of the bird.

Bald Face.—A patch of light colour running into the dark colour of the cheek of a Lizard Canary, often encircling the eye.

Blaze.—The red on the face of a Goldfinch or Hybrid.

Boaty.—An expression applied to Yorkshires with a falling away at the sides of the breast, giving a boat-like appearance to the under body.

Bottle-shaped. — A term applied to Yorkshires when the body lacks symmetry of cut and has too much of a sameness all round.

Braced-wings. — Wings carried close to the body in a neat, compact manner, giving a smart, even finish, and good carriage.

Breast.—This term refers to the extreme point where the breast-bone terminates and the lower part of the neck begins.

Breed.—Any variety of bird in all its distinct characteristics. The breed includes all the varieties of colour which are found in it.

Broad-tail. — A tail which is wide at the root, or base, as well as at the end or tip not closely folded.

Broken-cap.—Dark feathers intermingled with light crown or cap of a Lizard Canary's head; it matters not whether there is only a dark feather or two, or the greater portion be dark.

Broken Green.—A bird with the greater portion of its colour green, but with a light patch or patches in wing, tail, or on body.

"**Broken-lafter.**"—A term used freely in the North of England for a broken eggery; that is, when a hen lays part of a clutch of eggs, say two, and then misses several days or possibly a week, then does not sit, and then lays the other portion of the clutch or another complete clutch; afterwards settling down to sit in the usual way.

Brood.—A family of young birds from one nest.

Browed and Beetle-browed.—Terms applied when the feathers over the eyes have a pronounced overhanging appearance, giving a frowning, sullen appearance. A term freely used in describing the head and head feathers of Crestbreds and Lancashire Plainheads.

Bull-necked.—Indicating a short, full neck, an important characteristic in some varieties.

Burnished.—When the surface of the feather possesses a rich, glossy surface, as if polished.

Carriage.—The bearing, attitude, or style of a bird.

Centre.—Applicable to the centre of a Crested Canary's head, from which the feathers of the crest radiate evenly all round the head and over the beak.

Cere.—The soft, pliable skin immediately round the eye which acts as a shutter or lid to that organ.

Chick.—A newly hatched bird.

Cinnamon.—Indicating the colour of certain birds after that name.

Cinnamon-green.—A shade of green in Canaries produced by crossing birds of cinnamon colour with birds not cinnamon colour or cinnamon bred, some of the offspring from which carry a distinct cinnamon tone in their green colour.

Cinnamon-marked.—A bird with markings of a cinnamon shade of colour.

Circle.—Indicating the convex outline of a Scotch Fancy when in position.

Circular-crest. — The desired round, even shape of a good crest for show purposes.

Clean-cut.—A term used freely in describing a neat, harmonious finish to the shape of a bird; the outline clearly defined.

Cleaned-out.—Applicable to the breast of a Scotch Fancy, showing no prominence at the breast, but arched out as if to give the necessary curve to the body.

Clean-front.—Indicating close, smooth-lying breast feather.

Clear.—A bird absolutely free from dark feather, marking, or flue.

Clear-cap.—A term used in describing the light patch on top of a Lizard Canary's head, which should be quite free from dark feathers from a marginal line of thumb-nail shape. The light patch should cover the whole of the top of the skull.

Close-feathered.—Showing no looseness on any part of the body, the plumage fitting the body close and compact throughout.

Cloudy.—Applied to the spangling on the back of a Lizard when not clearly defined.

Coarse-head.—Lacking neatness according to variety.

Cobby, or Chubby.—Short, stout body, having a plump, chubby appearance.

Compact.—Neat, smart appearance. *See* CLOSE-FEATHERED.

Condition.—The state of a bird as regards health, beauty, and perfection of plumage, the latter especially.

Contour.—The defining outline characteristic of a variety.

Coppy.—Indicating the crested bird of the Lancashire variety.

Crest.—A crown or tuft of feathers on the top of the head, drooping evenly all round from the centre.

Crest-awry.—The centre of the crest misplaced more or less to one side, causing the crest to have a tilting tendency.

Crestbred.—Indicating the plain-headed bird of the Crest variety.

Crossed-flights.—Applied to the long flight feathers of the wings when they cross each other at the tips instead of just meeting.

Crouch.—To display a squatting appearance when on the perch, as if afraid to stand up.

Cushion-shaped.—A term applied to the head of a Crestbred when the head displays a convex shape of the skull from front to back or side to side.

Dark-capped.—A green patch covering the whole of the top of the skull of an otherwise clear bird.

Deep-chested.—Possessing a broad, deep, full, prominent chest.

Double-buff.—Pairing two Buffs together, or the produce from two Buffs.

Double-yellow.—The pairing of two Yellow birds together or the produce from two Yellows.

Drawn.—A term used to denote the fine, slim, symmetrical appearance of the body of a Yorkshire.

Drive.—The forward carriage of the head of a Scotch Fancy when in position with neck fully extended, as if sighting some landmark to make for.

Droop ("a good droop").—Applicable to the feathers of a crest when they fall with a graceful curve from the centre over the eyes and beak, falling evenly all round.

Ear-coverts.—Fine feathers covering the ear, a little behind the eye on either side of head.

Entrance.—That part of the skull immediately over the base of the beak.

Evenly-marked. — Having similar dark marks on either side of the body; that is, on the eyes, wings, and a feather or two on either side of the tail. Also see definitions of "two-pointed," "four-pointed," and "six-pointed."

Eye-cere.—*See* CERE.

Finger-moult.—To assist a bird to moult quickly by plucking out portions of its plumage—a very undesirable practice.

Fish-tailed.—A term used to describe a bird with the tail nicely folded at the base, opening out wide at the end like the tail of a fish, the tips of the feathers being inclined to turn outwards a little.

Flat-backed.—Chiefly applicable to a Yorkshire whose back is inclined to a slight depression toward the shoulder, and a Scotch Fancy lacking curvature of the back.

Flighting.—Plucking out the secondary and primary quill feathers of the wing.

Flights.—The primary quills, or long, strong feathers of the wings.

Flow.—A term often used in describing the feather when covering the body gracefully (" a nice flow ").

Flue.—The soft down-like feathers next the skin which are covered by the more solid and exposed portion of the feather.

Foul.—A term used to denote one dark patch on an otherwise clear bird, largely used in describing such a mark on a Scotch Fancy.

Foul-feathered.—A term used in describing a bird with a light feather or feathers in an otherwise dark wing, or a feather or feathers with grizzly, dark streaks in an otherwise clear wing.

Foul-green.—A green-coloured bird with one or more small light patches on some portion of the plumage.

Foul-tailed.—The presence of light or grizzle-marked light feathers in the tail of an otherwise dark bird, or such birds as those whose standard properties demand a dark tail.

Four-pointed.—An evenly-marked bird, marked on both eyes and both wings. *See* EVENLY MARKED.

French Moult.—A term often used in connection with birds in an unhealthy condition which lose their feathers and fail to reproduce others; the body in time becomes practically nude, except that the primary and secondary feathers of the wing and the tail are retained.

Frontal.—That portion of a crest which comes over the beak.

Furnished.—Has assumed the full characteristics—i.e. when a bird has attained its full adult plumage (which it does with its second moult), and its coat has a more complete finish.

Gait.—The free-and-easy movement with which birds move from perch to perch.

Go.—Often used to describe birds of position; possessing a nervy, quick movement, the whole body being on the move.

Grey.—Applicable to a light-coloured crest, the light feathers of which are dappled or faintly streaked with dark. Such crests are sometimes called "grizzle crests."

Grizzled.—This has reference to feathers that are streaked or intermingled with light and dark, giving a greyish appearance.

Grizzle-tail and Grizzle-wing. — *See* GRIZZLED.

Ground Colour.—The general colour of the body feather which intensifies, or otherwise, the finish on the surface.

Gutter-backed.—A hollow running down the centre of the back between the wings from the shoulders downwards, most noticeable in Belgians and Scotch Fancies. Some Yorkshires, too, have a similar tendency. The term "gutter" is also frequently used in describing a "split" or vacancy in the feathers at the side of a crest.

Hairy Crests.—A common way of describing the texture of the feathers of a crest which is fine and thin in web, especially towards the tip of each feather.

Harsh Colour.—Lacking softness and tone.

Headgear.—The plumage on the top of the skull; chiefly applied to crests.

Heavily Variegated.—A bird the greater portion of which is dark.

Hollow-necked.—A too great falling away at the back of the neck in a Yorkshire, giving an unsymmetrical finish to the neck.

Horned.—A term applied to feathers which have a tendency to curl up slightly on either side of the back of the skull in both Crests and Plainheads. In Plainheads forming a pair of small horns at the back of the head, but in some instances only curling up on one side.

Hot-colour.—Very deep, colour-fed bird.

Hugs Perch.—Synonymous with CROUCHING (which *see*).

Jonque. An old name for Yellow, and at one time used to describe a yellow Cinnamon, London Fancy, or Lizard.

Jonquil.—Another old name for Yellow; of French origin.

Laced, Lacing.—A stripe or edging round a feather of some colour different from its ground colour, as in the Lizard Canary. The word "laced" is also often used to describe the darker stripes on the breast of a Linnet or birds similarly marked, the back of a Green Canary, or Cinnamon.

Lashing.—A term used in describing the heavy eye-brows of a Crestbred when the feather droops somewhat over the eye.

Leggy.—Used freely when describing good length of leg in a Yorkshire.

Level-colour.—Pure and even in colour all over.

Light-throated.—A defect in a Self-Cinnamon or Green, the throat-colour running too light.

Lineage.—The spangling of a Lizard's back, running down the back in straight lines one after the other, closely packed together.

Long-in-barrel. — A term often used in describing a Norwich that is too long in body.

Lustre.—Depth and brilliancy of colour; having a glistening surface.

Marked.—This abbreviation is applicable to either evenly or unevenly marked birds.

Mealed.—A pale covering over the surface of the richer ground colour of a buff bird, as if coated with hoar-frost.

Mealy.—Another term for "buff."

Mixed-wing.—Applied where a light feather appears in the midst of the dark feathers of an evenly wing-marked bird.

Mooning.—The moon-shaped white tippings to the flights of a Goldfinch's wing.

Mop-crest.—Disorderly arranged feathers of a crest, often minus a proper centre and lacking radiation.

Nervy.—A term applied to highly-strung birds of position.

Non-capped.—A Lizard Canary without a light cap, the whole of the head being dark and spangled like the body, but with finer spangles.

Non-fed.—Referring to the colour of a bird which has not been given colour-food during the moult.

Norwich-breasted.—Applied to Yorkshires with a too prominent and broad breast.

Open-centre. — Applicable to the centre of a crest, showing the skin in a greater or lesser degree, owing to the centre not being well filled with feathers.

Open-plumage.—The feathers on the body lying loose and untidy.

Oval-crest.—When the crest is oval instead of the desired circular shape.

Over-capped.—Applied to the cap of a Lizard when the light patch on the head runs too far over the back, verging into the neck.

Over-lapping Flights.—The lower feathers of the wing overlapping each other, giving the wing an untidy, ragged appearance, due largely to a stagnant moult.

Over-shown.—A bird which has been sent to a large number of shows, and as a consequence is showing the effects by its plumage becoming jaded or losing its usual sprightliness.

Patchy-colour.—A bird uneven in colour; rich and pale colour on the same bird.

Pencilling.—The narrow lines of darker shade on the back of such birds as the Green and Cinnamon Canary. The breast and sides of the Linnet, Twite, Redpoll, and birds similarly marked.

Piebald.—A common phrase in the North when describing a variegated Scotch Fancy.

Pied-cinnamon.—A cinnamon-coloured bird whose colour is broken up by patches of clear yellow or buff.

Pied-tail.—*See* Foul-tailed.

Pinched-skull.—Applicable to the entrance or back of skull when the head runs off narrow at the front or back—i.e. lacking normal width.

Pink-eyed.—The eye of a decided pink shade all over, not only the pupil; indicating the presence of Cinnamon blood, though the bird may not show a cinnamon feather.

Pipe-tail.—The feathers of the tail closely folded, having a narrow, solid appearance, similar in shape to a pipe stem, with the faintest indication of a V-shaped notch at the tip, owing to the shape of the feathers: a desirable feature in Yorkshires, Scotch Fancies, and other varieties.

Polish.—*See* Lustre.

Pose.—*See* Position.

Position.—Carriage of a bird characteristic of its variety.

Primaries.—The flight feathers of the wing.

Quality.—A term applied chiefly to the silk-like texture of the feather; it may be good or otherwise.

Quick-action.—A bird smart in movement when in position, such as the Scotch Fancy.

Racy.—A term used to describe the long body and alertness of a stylish Yorkshire.

Radiation.—Applicable to the feathers radiating from the centre of a bird's crest, falling evenly all round.

Reach.—Length of neck in a Scotch Fancy or Belgian when the bird is in position and the neck is stretched to its full extent.

Roughness.—Plumage fitting the body in a slovenly manner; apparent more or less in all long-feathered birds.

Rowing, or Rowed.—A term applied to the marking and work on the breast of a Lizard.

Rudder.—Used by some when referring to a bird's tail.

Saddle.—That portion of the back immediately below the shoulders.

Saddle-marked.—A bird with mark on the saddle and the remainder of the body clear.

Secondaries.—The upper half of the flight feathers in the wing: those resting upon the bird's back, the lower half of the flight feathers being called the Primaries.

Self.—A term applied to Cinnamons and Greens whose uniform tints are unbroken by the intermingling of any other colour.

Sheen.—*See* Lustre.

Shield-crest.—A crest inclined to be shaped as a shield: wide at the back, running off gradually to a point at the front.

Sib-bred.—The progeny of relations bred in and in for a year or years.

Side.—A term often used in describing a Scotch Fancy, Belgian, or Yorkshire, as "length of side," this adding to the merit of these birds.

Six-pointed.—Marked on both eyes, both wings, and either side of tail. *See* Evenly Marked.

Slack.—Plumage hanging loose, often in a pronounced way, about the thighs.

Slip-toed.—The hind toe turning in below the foot in a forward direction, the nail sticking up between the front toes as the bird stands upon the perch.

Smoky.—Colour not clear and bright in tone; dull and cloudy.

Snaky.—A term applied to the finely moulded, neat head, and long, thin neck of a Scotch Fancy or Belgian.

Snipy-head.—Applicable where the forehead is unduly narrow and the back of the head of the normal width.

Soft.—An indication that the bird is not quite in its usual bright, sprightly condition.

Soft-moult.—Continual dropping of feathers other than at the proper moulting season.

Spangle.—The marks produced on the back of a Lizard Canary owing to each feather having a dark eye in the centre, the fringe of the feather being a lighter shade, giving the spangling effect.

Spectacle-eyes.—The desired eye marks in evenly-marked birds.

Splashed.—A common phrase used when referring to a marked bird.

Split-crest.—The circular formation of the crest, marred by a gap or gaps, as if feathers were missing; sometimes caused by a slight twist in one or more feathers.

Sprightly.—A bird of lively disposition, full of life and activity.

Squatty.—Not standing up ; stomach often resting on the perch as if legs were weak.

Stamina.—Indicating health, strength, and vigour.

Steady.—Applied to show birds ; indicates confidence, shown by the bird moving about the cage freely, with no tendency to flutter when the cage is taken in hand.

Stiff-tailed. — The tail carried straight and stiff ; a desirable trait in a Belgian.

Stilty. —A term applied to Scotch Fancies when straight-legged like a Belgian, and to other birds longer in leg than is characteristic of their variety.

Strain.—A race of birds which have been carefully bred by one breeder or his successors for years, and which has acquired individual characteristics the reproduction of which can be more or less relied upon.

Style. — Smart movement of the body, or any part which gives a set-off to the bird's characteristics.

Substance.—Denoting bulk of body.

Surface-colour. — That portion of the feathers exposed to view. *See* UNDER-COLOUR.

Sweating.—A term used when the feathers of hens and their young have a damp, sweat-like appearance.

Symmetry.—Perfection of proportions, the shape and form of the bird fitting harmoniously, giving a neat finish to the whole.

Tailing.—Plucking out the tail feathers.

Texture.—*See* QUALITY.

Thick-set.—Refers to shape of body, being of good, stout build in birds which should have this characteristic.

Thin-crest.—A crest having only one or two layers of feathers instead of several.

Ticked.—A bird with a small, dark mark on an otherwise clear body. According to the standards of some specialist clubs, it may also have a mark on one eye, wing, or tail, but not more than one such *technical* mark, separately, or in addition to, any other variegation on its body.

Tilted-crest.—*See* CREST AWRY.

Top-knot.—Another name for crest.

Travelling.—A Scotch phrase referring to the regulated " hop " of a Scotch Fancy from one perch to another and back again, when in the show cage and while the cage is held in the hand.

Two-pointed.—Marked both eyes or both wings ; body otherwise clear. *See* EVENLY MARKED.

Type.—The general characteristics of a bird in accordance with the respective standards.

Under-colour.—That portion of the feathers below the surface only seen when they are parted with the fingers or blown apart by breathing heavily upon them. The fluff of the feather differs greatly from the surface colour.

Under-flue.—*See* FLUE.

Under-work.—Applicable to the lacing on the breast and flanks of a Lizard.

Unevenly - marked. — A bird similarly marked to an even-marked, but minus one or more of the marks, making it uneven ; or it may have a dark patch on the body in addition to the even marks, thus making it uneven.

Unflighted.—A young bird having its first flight feathers after the first moult.

Variegated Cinnamon.—*See* PIED-CINNAMON.

Variegation.—Another name used for " unevenly marked," with this difference : most birds so termed have dark patches, more or less, all over the body, some considerably more than others ; these are called " heavily variegated." Those showing more light than dark are " lightly variegated."

Variety.—Some definite division of a breed known by its colour, marking, or shape. Thus the breed includes all varieties.

Veiny-crest. — Indicating a dark stripe down the centre of each feather of a dark crest, the stripe being darker than the other portion of the feather.

V-shape Head.—*See* SNIPY-HEAD.

Wastrels.—A breeder's term for the throw-outs from his breeding-stock, having many more faults than good points.

Web.—The flat or plume portions of the feather projecting from the centre stem.

Wedgy.—The body inclined to wedge-shape.

Weeping-crest. — Indicating droop ; the feathers fall evenly and neatly all round over sides and back of head as well as the beak.

Wing-bar.—Any line of darker or lighter colour than the general colour of the wing, arranged partially or wholly across the wing.

Wing-butts. — The corner or ends of the wing ; the upper ends are more properly called the shoulder-butts.

Work.—A term often used to describe good back-spangling on a Lizard.

Wry-necked. — A deformity of the neck, causing the bird to carry its head more or less to one side, with a slight twist.

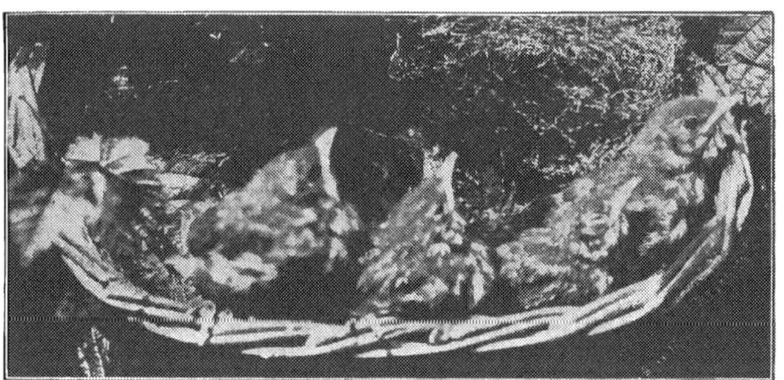

YOUNG THRUSHES.
From a photograph by Mr. J. Brighty, Clapham.

CHAPTER XVI

PEDIGREE OR LINE BREEDING

IN all highly-bred live-stock the chief points which characterise a particular race or strain are the result of repeated and continuous selection, year after year, of breeding stock possessing those particular qualities in more or less perfection. This is equally true of such purely "fancy" points in our Canaries as shape, position, certain kinds of markings the spangle of a Lizard, to wit—or a particular shade of colour, such as cinnamon. Such points may sometimes occur occasionally, as if by accident, in some individual bird, but if it occurs habitually, as one mark of a strain or family, it has been bred into it by many generations of selection.

Natural Selection.

Some people think that this is not the case with wild birds or animals; but in reality it is sometimes even more true in their case. Darwin has taught us that the "natural selection" induced by surroundings, food, struggle for bare existence, and competition amongst surplus numbers is most severe; it is unmodified by pity or caprice; and Nature does not vary her methods save in long periods and by imperceptible degrees. She does not select like man, making one choice this year and another the next, but her conditions are the same for generations, and often for ages; hence the wonderful uniformity and permanence of her patterns, as in the plumage of a Goldfinch or Bullfinch when uncrossed by any foreign strain. It is in this sense that the proverbial phrase of the breeder—"Like produces like"—is true. They are all of the same pattern as regards colour and structural points, though some may be better developed specimens than others.

Breeding to Points.

It is the ambition of every breeder to produce the most perfectly developed specimens possible, and it is only reasonable to expect by far the greater number of well developed young from those specimens which best display the desired characteristics.

In requiring size, for instance, we should naturally expect to get it to greater perfection from a bird possessing size than from one which had been bred from good-sized parents but had not developed that quality. The same applies to colour, shape, position, feather, or any other desired quality. We have again and again had this confirmed in the breeding of crests. We have paired a long-fronted crest cock to a crestbred hen, and have paired a brother of the said crested cock without such a long frontal crest to the same hen, and have produced good birds from both, but far more valuable specimens from the crested cock with the longest frontal. Instances of this kind furnish pretty conclusive proof that specimens with the desired structural developments as a rule are the more potent in ensuring their reproduction.

The same developments can be brought about by the use of other stock, in which the desired points are not so pronounced, by careful selection; but the progress is slower, although there may be—and, indeed, are—instances where rapid improvement comes from the happy blending of imperfectly developed stock. Still, we are not speaking of isolated cases; our reference is general, and to lasting results rather than fortunate hits or sports.

Sir Ray Lankester once wrote in the *Daily Telegraph:* " Selection, whether due to survival in the struggle for existence or exercised by man as a ' breeder ' or ' fancier,' is the only way in which new characteristics, good or bad, can be implanted in a race or stock, and become part of the hereditary quality of that race or stock. This applies equally to man and to animals and plants. And this selection is no temporary or casual thing. It means ' the selection for breeding ' of those individuals which spontaneously, by the innate variability which all living things show (so that no two individuals are exactly alike), have exhibited from birth onwards, more or less clearly, indications of the characteristic which is to be selected. Nothing done to them after birth, and not done to others of their family or race, causes the desired characteristic; it appears unexpectedly, almost as an inborn quality. It may be a slight difference only, not easy to take note of; but if it enables those who possess it to get the better of their competitors in the struggle for life, they will survive and mate, and so transmit their characteristic to the next generation.

Sir Ray Lankester on Selection.

" Selection is not a thing once done and then dropped; natural selection is continuous and never-ending, except in rare and special circumstances, such as man may bring about by his interference. The characteristics of a race or species are maintained by natural selection just as much as they are produced by it. Cessation of selection (which is sometimes brought about by exceptional conditions) results in a departure of the individuals of the race no longer subject to selection from the standard of form and characteristics previously maintained."

[This we have efficiently borne out in the Canary family where they are allowed to pair up indiscriminately.]

" To understand this we must consider for a moment the great property of living things, which is called ' variation.' No two animals or plants, even when born of the same parents, are ever exactly alike; not only that, but if we look at a great number of individuals of a race or stock, we find that some are very different from the others in colour, in proportion of parts, in character, and other qualities. As a rule, it is difficult to look at such a number, because in Nature only two on the average out of many hundreds, sometimes thousands, born from a single pair of parents, grow up to take their parents' place, and these two are those ' selected ' by natural survival on account of their close resemblance to the parents. But if we experimentally rear the offspring of a plant or animal to full growth, not allowing them to perish by competition for food, or place, or by inability to escape enemies, then we see more clearly how great is the inborn variation, how many and wide are the departures from the favoured standard form which are naturally born, and owe their peculiarities to this birth-quality—called innate or congenital variation—and not to anything which happens to them

"Variation."

afterwards differing from what happens to their brothers and sisters.

"Of course, we are all familiar with this 'congenital or innate variation' as shown by brothers and sisters in human families. How and why does innate variation arise? It arises from chemical and mechanical action upon the 'germs' or reproductive cells, contained in the body of the parents, and also sometimes from the mating in reproduction of two strains or races which are already different from one another. When an animal or plant is given unaccustomed food or brought up in new surroundings (as, for instance, in captivity), its germs are affected, and they produce variations in the next generation more abundantly. The best analogy for what occurs is that of a 'shaking up' or disturbance of the particles of the germ or reproductive material, somewhat as the beads and bits of glass in a kaleidoscope are shaken and change from one well-balanced arrangement to another. The same analogy applies to the crossing or fertilising of one 'strain' or 'race' by differing from it. A disturbance is the consequence, and a departure in the form and character of the young from anything arrived at before often takes place. These variations have no necessary fitness or correspondence to the changed conditions which have produced them. They are, so to speak, departures in all and every direction—not very great, but still great enough to be selected by survival if occurring in wild, extra-human nature, and obvious enough when produced in cultivated animals and plants to be seen and selected by man, the stock breeder or fancier. Indeed, the stock breeder and horticulturist go to work in this way deliberately. Thus they get offspring produced which show strange and unexpected variations of many kinds—new feathers, new colours, length of limb—all kinds of variation. From the congenital varieties thus produced by 'stirring up,' 'breaking down,' or disturbing the germ matter (germ plasm) of the parents, the breeder next proceeds to select and mate those which show the character which suits his fancy, whilst he rejects the others. Thus he establishes and, by repeated selection in every generation, maintains, and, if he desires, increases the characteristics which he values.

"Birth-variation is, then, an inherent quality of living things (including man) as much as heredity, which is the name for the quality expressed in the resemblance of offspring to parent. What happens, then, when there is a cessation of selection? All sorts of birth-variations appear and grow up."

This is yearly verified in the breeding of our Canaries. The great power of this principle of selection is not hypothetical, it is certain; an animal's organisation is something quite plastic, which can be modelled almost as one pleases, within reason, in the hands of careful breeders who know their work.

Lewis Wright on Selection.

Mr. Lewis Wright, in his "Book of Poultry," clearly showed the force of selection. In dealing with pedigree he took as an illustration the appearance of a fifth toe in one or two chickens, in a variety in which that peculiarity does not naturally exist, but which might have arisen from some remote taint, and showed what might be done by breeding from one of these chickens. "If one of these chickens be bred from, it is probable that a few of her progeny, but still few, will also show this fifth toe; the greater part, however, reverting to what we may call the usual type of the yard. If we mate this hen to a cock showing the tendency in the same way, the number of five-toed progeny will be somewhat increased; but still, supposing there is no appreciable taint in the yard, they will not be many, and the four-toed chickens they produced will have little tendency to breed birds with five toes. But now suppose we select from the chickens produced from these two five-toed parents a pair also five-toed, and breed *them* together. We shall now find the tendency vastly increased—so much so, that very likely a full half of the produce will be five-toed,

SCOTCH FANCY CANARY.

and even those which are not will show an evident tendency to breed five-toed birds. We have accumulated into one direction—that of producing five toes—the transmitted powers of *two generations*—parents and grandparents. If we breed from this third generation again, still selecting five-toed individuals, the tendency to produce the peculiarity will be increased enormously, and in a generation or two more a bird *not* five-toed will be as rare as the five-toed specimens originally were. We have now what is called a *strain*, so far as regards this one point of five toes; that is, we have produced a race of birds which we can *depend upon* with almost absolute certainty to produce nothing but five-toed birds. . . . The first pair have scarcely any tendency that can be relied upon to produce the desired five toes; the other pair can be depended upon as regards nearly every one. The first pair presents nothing to a breeder save the foundation upon which he may, by care and perseverance, found a structure hereafter; the other represents work fully done, and a 'strain' which, as regards the one point we have considered, is perfected and established, and only needs ordinary care to preserve in the same perfection for an unlimited length of time."

Inbreeding.

Mr. Wright, in this clear and concise description of work begun and accomplished, illustrates the result of the inbreeding of relatives, but he does not suggest the mating of birds simply because they are related. He merely cites a case where a variation from the usual type appeared, one that might almost be called an individual variation, as it was so long since there was any sign in the stock of a tendency to five toes, and having no material at hand possessing the feature he desired to perpetuate except the stock from which this bird sprang, he had necessarily to inbreed. For the fancier to pair two relatives together in order to produce points which neither possesses, nor have shown any tendency to develop, is the height of absurdity. Yet we have met breeders who have been foolish enough to do so, led away by the craze for "inbreeding" through mistaken notions as to the real object of mating relatives—viz. the fixing and perhaps accentuating certain known characteristics in a strain.

That most skilful breeder, Sir John Sebright, used to say with respect to pigeons, "that by selection he would produce any given feather in three years, but that it would take him six years to obtain head and beak."

Even in a state of nature the evidence we have adduced proves beyond doubt that selection leads the way, and that the mating of wild creatures possessing the same characteristics in a greater or lesser degree is not the outcome of relationship, but rather the natural instinct of adaptation for each other, which is their controlling power.

Inbreeding, no doubt, goes on to a considerable extent under natural conditions, but such a system cannot be safely carried on indefinitely with domesticated stock, such as Canaries. There is not with birds in captivity the natural law as to the survival of the fittest, and hence with close inbreeding under these artificial conditions a slight taint in related parents becomes emphasised and fixed in a few generations of inbreeding with close-blooded relatives, and physical weakness and deterioration result. Hence, in producing such properties as are desired in our stock, close breeding should never be carried so far as to produce evils of this class, but must be modified so as to prevent them.

On this account it is necessary to provide at the outset *several pairs* of birds to form the ancestors of our stock in order to avoid any necessity for a cross out until the new strain is thoroughly blended together, and the desired properties established.

Difficulty of Breeding to Points.

This is all-important to everyone who means to have a "strain" of his own, not only for the general reasons already given, but to avoid the danger of unwittingly dropping the "link in succession," which we have seen to be so important. As an example of this we selected the production of the five-toed fowl; but to any other feature the same reasoning would apply, such as the production of any particular shape, marking, crest, long or short feather, position, or size in a Canary—"all are subject to the same laws, and can be 'fixed' in the same manner. But it will readily occur to most of our readers that every animal is bred for *many* points, and not solely for *one*, such as we have been considering, and that here the difficulty in successful breeding begins, and the inexperienced breeder usually finds that, as he attempts to deal with any one point, he is very apt to deteriorate in some other previously attained.

"The chief reason of this is, that the *faults* as well as the good points of any parent tend to be perpetuated. When, therefore, it is considered that it is almost impossible to tell *when* all tendency to revert to the features of any particular animal in a pedigree shall for practical purposes be lost, the complication of the problem becomes apparent. At each step in the process of breeding towards some given point, the parents have to be chosen in reference to it; and in each such case the parents introduce tendencies to produce other points which are *not* wanted. Nay, not only do they introduce tendencies which can be known or surmised, but it will be evident at once that unless their own pedigree and course of breeding are known for generations back, they must introduce tendencies which, not appearing in themselves, are *not* known. When, therefore, we consider the changeful and capricious manner in which most amateurs —in the first instance, at all events—conduct their breeding, often trusting to pedigree alone without the necessary qualification, and in many instances not giving even that meagre attention to their selections, we shall cease to wonder at the anomalous nature of the results they often obtain, and that they retire from breeding in despair before they have learnt that better things are possible, and how they are to be achieved."

Thus, supposing we are at any time paying great attention to obtaining a good crest, and some evident fault in another point appears as a result of the season's breeding, to correct this new blemish a cross with another family will, perhaps, be necessary. We then select a bird strong in the point in which our stock fails, and with an exquisite crest, and thus apparently unlikely to interfere with our aim of breeding for crest while correcting the other fault; yet this new purchase *may* be the *only* good-crested bird in a room of inferior crests, and in that case may spoil the progeny from the hens paired to him. In such a case the best course is not only to turn him out from the stock, but all the offspring as well, and thus "nip the evil in the bud." There are occasional cases of this kind, but they are very few indeed, as really good birds with well developed points are not likely to have such detrimental effects; in fact, the selection of good birds and their influence for good has demonstrated this over and over again. But withal we have a continual battle to wage against points we do not want, and if a breeder can get to know something of the pedigree of any new bird before introducing it to his stock, and thus by careful selection obtain a bird that will "hit" or blend well with his strain, it will assist him to secure the properties aimed at. The necessity for too frequent recourse to such an outcross, with its attendant difficulties, is in large measure obviated by attention to our caution as to starting with a sufficient number of pairs of birds of known characteristics at the outset. If several pairs of birds are kept purely for the production of stock birds from which to draw when occasion arises, the task of maintaining the upkeep of the strain is made easier.

Attention to Faults.

In breeding there is a tendency in all animals, as Darwin clearly showed, to revert to apparently long-lost character, and this tendency is developed by *crossing*. To make ourselves quite clear, supposing two strains

The Tendency to Throw Back.

of Crested Norwich to have been carefully bred, but one to have been bred first for feather and afterwards for crest, while the other was bred first for crest and afterwards for feather; the result of crossing two such strains would be that many of the progeny would throw back to the first or faulty points of both. Hence it is important that the outcross selected should not only be good and have been carefully bred, but also be the produce of a similar course of breeding to the birds with which it is to be mated; unless it be some characteristic—such, for instance, as "swagger," also called "breed," in a Yorkshire Canary, which is the product of a foreign cross. It will thus be seen what an advantage there is in knowing something of the true pedigree of any new bird introduced to a strain.

Pedigree, unless backed up by good development of the property desired, is, of course, useless, and it is obvious that the *surest* way of securing what we want is to obtain our stock from a breeder who can show both, and has what we shall call, for the want of a better word, a "stock corner" in the breeding room, from which to draw building material as necessity requires, and who can tell pretty nearly the latent tendencies of each bird therein.

The Necessity for a Record.

It is in this way, also, that we secure the advantages of an intelligent plan, or a definite object steadily pursued without the evils of in-breeding. If three strains have been started from three nearly-allied and similar pairs of birds, and the same plan of breeding pursued with all, the advantages of a cross can be had for many generations, without its evils, by keeping a record of pedigrees.* Where another must breed together brother and sister, or else resort to a foreign cross, a breeder thus armed can take a bird out of one of his other families, or "stock corner," as the case may necessitate, which in the course of breeding has arrived at precisely the same point, and will produce similar effects, yet with nearly all the advantages of a cross.

The Case of the Lizard Canary.

In following out the extracts on "Pedigree Breeding" to their conclusion, as indicating the general principles on which the breeder should act, we take, as the illustration for the final quotation, the Lizard Canary, as best exemplifying the admirable instructions given by the late Lewis Wright for "commencing any strain or race in which *fancy* points are the chief object sought." The fancy point in this case is distinctive character or marking in individual feathers, and is nearly on a par with that assumed by Mr. Wright in establishing the fifth toe in a strain of fowls, the *modus operandi* is nearly identical, the principle involved—and that is what we are here considering—absolutely so; and we will suppose the object desired is to found a strain of well-spangled Lizards. "We would provide, then, for breeding several hens perfectly spangled. If we could only afford a couple of such birds we would rather have them than a dozen even only a little worse in this quality, since every shade *now* saves much trouble afterwards. We wish especially to show the folly of this far too common plan, which stands in the way of success with scores of amateurs. Supposing the cock to be a well-bred bird, it is; very likely he may 'throw' some well-spangled young ones from these poor birds; and many people think this is a gain. To a certain extent, and in a certain sense, it is; where the pocket will not permit the procuring of the best it is the only resort, though a longer road, and from a breeder's point of view it is a serious loss of time and ground gained, and 'puts back' the strain, since if these birds in turn are bred from they '*throw*' *back to the poor parent.* Of course the cocks will also be selected with all practical care. From such pairs, breeding *only* from well-spangled birds,

* *The Breeding Record*, published by *Canary and Cage-bird Life*, London, is an excellent register for keeping pedigrees. It is mapped out in such a plain, concise way that the merest novice in Canary breeding cannot well err in keeping a true record of his stock.

there will be the very first season some equally well-spangled young hens. If the proportion is good, it shows that the cocks, too, are of good breeding quality, and have 'hit' well with the strain of the hens, in which case they should be kept. And so the first season's breeding comes to to an end.

"Next year's breeding will show a *marked advance,* the proportion of well-spangled birds being very good—so good, that out of them, if ordinary judgment has been employed, we can now have little difficulty in finding the few we want to breed which are also good in caps and other matters." And here will be seen the advantage of the plan we have insisted on, of fixing upon the one *most* important point, whatever that may be, and never dropping it. If this plan has been followed it will be found that we have now—imperfectly, it is true, but still to a very great extent—made it *certain* already in our new "strain," and can to a moderate degree, without dropping it, already begin to select our birds for other points as well.

The next season the proportion of purely-spangled birds will be very large indeed (we will suppose *only* the perfectly-spangled to be bred from), and there will probably be no difficulty whatever in selecting those which show also other points required. Every variety has some point or points which demand long breeding and patience to acquire. Some points are obtained with comparative ease, and are readily transmitted even from parents, so that a single mating will produce them in a fair proportion of young, others will need years of work, and one unhappy mating may upset much work already done.

Four Points.

Comparing many breeds or varieties, we have found that about four points will in nearly all of them cover those which cause real difficulty and require serious breeding for, those beyond four giving little anxiety or trouble. Let us consider these, therefore, and suppose that, taking all things into account, we have determined their order in difficulty and value. In perfecting our bird by selection a difficult point must never be sacrificed to obtain a minor though necessary point, and on these should attention *first* be fixed and kept there, gradually giving attention to others, *not by turns,* but just as fast, and no faster, than the increased number of birds (good in the first point and therefore admissible to breed from) enables selection for the second and subsequent points to be made. One thing, however, is obvious. The best birds, *from the breeding point of view,* must never be sold, but kept for the breeding room; for a man cannot reasonably be expected to make any marked progress who is constantly selling what represents nearly all the ground he has gained, as the breeding which is to succeed in producing valuable birds consists in throwing *all* these tendencies into one desired direction, so that the influence of remote ancestors, of great-grandparents and grandparents, as well as of the parents, combine toward the desired point. And as Darwin rightly says: "The key is man's power of accumulative selection. Nature gives successive variations; man adds them up in certain directions useful to him. In this sense he may be said to make for himself useful breeds. Over all these causes of change I am convinced that the accumulative action of selection, whether applied methodically and more quickly, or unconsciously and more slowly but more efficiently, is by far the predominant power."

Clearness of Purpose Necessary.

In commencing to breed with a view to producing the highest class of canary, of whatever breed or variety, we cannot impress too distinctly upon the mind of the beginner the importance of having a clear notion of what he intends doing, and of following out some definite plan such as we have fully explained. That success can be achieved by such a process can be amply proved by a visit to our exhibitions. Desultory breeding is not "breeding," but only an amusement that frequently goes by that name.

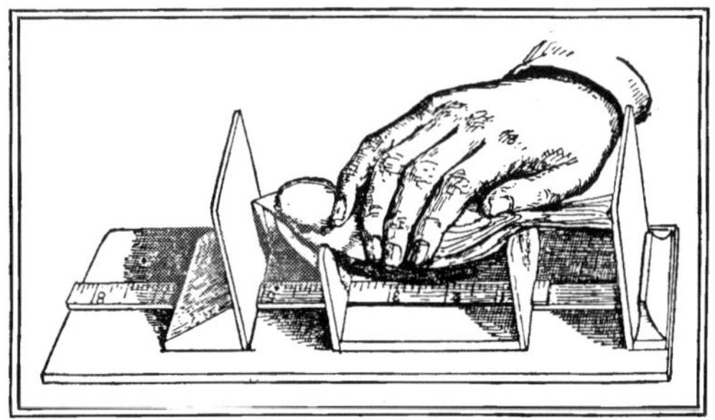

A CANARY MEASURE.
Of use in connection with varieties for which a standard length is adopted.

CHAPTER XVII

THE NORWICH CANARY

WE now turn from these details of general management to a description of the different varieties of the Canary, and the classes into which they are divided, with specific instructions as to the method of breeding them, and such further remarks on management as may be special in their application. We propose to arrange them in three sections, each based on some distinguishing feature. This, we think, is the most natural course to follow, and we accordingly divide them into (*a*) Colour Birds; (*b*) Distinctive Plumage Birds; (*c*) Shape and Position Birds. At the head of the colour group stands the Norwich Canary, perhaps the most general favourite of the entire tribe, and certainly one of the most extensively bred, being the embodiment of the popular idea of the bird, and the fountain from whence spring three-fourths of the drawing-room cage-birds in the country. It is easily recognised as a brilliantly-illuminated edition of the every-day Yellow Canary. It took its name from the city in which it has for generations been cultivated, and where it doubtless built up for itself a character so decided as to cause it in early times to be recognised as possessing features sufficiently distinctive to identify it with the name of the place in which it had become localised, and to distinguish it from other varieties already established.

Hervieux speaks of the clear orange-yellow Canary as far back as 1713, and, as will be seen by this early description, colour was the first and leading characteristic of the bird, and continued to be so for many generations; but to-day, whilst colour is still looked for and is essential in a good bird, we must have type and other points as well.

Order of Norwich Points.

The relative importance of points has been entirely reversed by new standards drawn up by the specialist clubs representing the breed, and the order of merit as it now stands may be cited as: *first*, type; *second*, quality of feather and general properties; and *third*, colour. We shall deal further with these points when describing the present-day standard of the bird.

History of the Breed.

It is more than probable that the cultivation of this bird as a speciality began in the latter quarter of the sixteenth century, when the Flemish, driven from their country by the persecutions of the Spanish under the Duke of Alva, took refuge in our "right little, tight little island," indirectly repaying us for the protection afforded them by the impetus they gave to some of our manufactures. A great number of these refugees settled in the county of Norfolk, where they found congenial employment in the woollen manufactories which had been originally established at Worsted by their kinsmen more than four centuries before, under the fostering care of the first Henry, just in the same way as the silk-weavers, driven from France by the Revocation of the Edict of Nantes in 1685, found their way to London, and, by their skill, gave an impulse to our silk trade. Canary-breeding, we know, had by this time spread through a great part of Germany, and was extensively engaged in in the Netherlands; this view is borne out by Dr. Galloway's able treatise on the Origin and History of the Canary in Chapter II. of this work. It is only natural to suppose that the refugees, in escaping with their little all to find a new home, would not leave behind them all their home associations and pleasures, but would carry with them their tastes and likings for natural pursuits, which could not fail to commend themselves to, and spread rapidly among, the population round about them. From that day to this—for the introduction of steam-power into many of our manufactures is only an event of a little over half a century—the nature of the occupation and the character of the inhabitants has changed but little. Though the iron horse now waits at the pit's mouth, ready to run his heavy load across streams bridged for his convenience, over valleys filled up to make him a highway, and through hills levelled or pierced to remove every obstruction from his path on the iron road, and deposits it by thousands of tons where the noise of machinery, replete with life and giant power, has displaced the modest loom and the music of the shuttle, still there may be isolated here and there a rose-covered cottage by the roadside, where may still be heard the quiet click, click of the primitive machine which yet has a poetry of its own, and in which some exquisite textile fabrics are still woven by delicate fingers that know no other handicraft. It is not to be wondered at that such sedentary employment, carried on generally in the 'sixties of the nineteenth century under the domestic roof, should have a tendency to induce a love of quiet home pleasures; and it is under such favourable auspices as these that the Norwich Canary has for so many years been nurtured, till its fame has spread far and wide, the world over, and other towns vie with the old cathedral city from which the bird takes its name in producing—nay, even excelling in the production of—the most perfect specimens.

Size.

Regarding the size of the Norwich Canary, it is difficult to give exact measurements, except of the length that the bird must not exceed, for it is practically impossible to find any two birds to measure alike in bulk of body or size of any particular part. An exact standard of measurements has been proposed by some fanciers, but the very thought of such mathematical definition of the bird's proportions sends a shock to our nerves, for we know too well the confusion which would follow upon the adoption of such a suggestion.

The shortest and best description is for us to say that the bird is similar in size to a German Bullfinch. It is plump, chubby as opposed to length and slimness, and is stoutly built and bold of carriage; quick and active in its movements, and lusty in its song, and when at rest stands at an angle of about 40 degrees, measured from a base line drawn from the tip of the tail.

The Head.

The head should be broad across the skull, not round, but with a gradual rise from the base of the beak right over the crown, then falling away gradually at the back of the poll into the neck in an even curve, with a good expanse throughout. A bird with a small, narrow head shows to poor advantage, and has a peculiar expression when seen face on, giving one the idea of being out of drawing. The richest colour, too, is found on the crown, and the larger the surface, the better the effect. No idea of coarseness should attach to it, but neatness and elegance and delicate close feathering should be its characteristics; coarse feathering and overhanging eyebrows indicate a cross in the direction of size not bred out. The eye is dark, full, bright, and sparkling; the beak should be neat and finely finished, free from any appearance of coarseness, and of a clear pinkish-white, free from discoloration, though the whole or half of the upper mandible is sometimes dark. This is no disqualification; but other points being equal, the clear beak would win. We are speaking now of the "clear" bird, which is one in which the whole of the feathers are entirely free from any dark marks whatever. The discoloured mandible is indicative of hidden marking somewhere or other, which should be searched for, for reasons which will presently be explained.

The Body.

The neck should be short and full, the under part forming in profile a perfect line of beauty with the breast, which should be broad and full, and feathered as smoothly as it is possible to conceive. Any departure from either of these properties is a defect of some moment. The back is broad, and rises very slightly immediately after the junction with the neck, forming a very delicate curve, and must show most compact feathering without the slightest disposition to open in the middle, which is not an uncommon feature in some varieties. Between the shoulders it is slightly convexed. Looked at from any point of view, the bird's outlines present a series of subtle curves of singular beauty—a feature common to all birds, in fact, the presence of a hard line being nowhere visible.

Wings.

The wings should not be long, but should harmonise in length with the chubby-built body; they must be carried firmly closed, without a symptom of drooping, and tucked in close to the body, the flights matching feather for feather on the back, the primaries meeting in a point over the rump-feathers without overlapping each other. The closer the flights are packed the better will the colour of the wing show itself, as only the extreme outer edge of each feather is tinged, and close lamination is necessary to maintain the continuity. The same holds good with the arrangement of the larger coverts and the small feathers of the bastard wing, any slovenliness here interfering most materially with the compact appearance indispensable for the uniform distribution of colour throughout the entire member.

Body Feathers.

The shoulders should be well covered by the scapular-feathers and show no projection of any kind, the feathering throughout the whole of this part being of the closest possible character, compactness and perfect imbrication being the most necessary conditions for the exhibition of colour. The rump-feathers are the finest and most silky in quality in the entire bird, and as they merge in the upper tail-coverts, become longer and narrower, the greater portion of their length being clothed with snowy white flossy under-flue. Any coarseness here, or in the vent-feathers and under tail-coverts, is a blemish interfering with the gradual tapering which constitutes what is known in the Fancy as a neat "waist," and is one of the blemishes it is necessary to breed out of any cross which may have been made with a view to obtain size, which it usually accompanies. It is the presence or absence of this coarseness and want of general compactness which indicates the possession or lack of "quality"—a term almost undefinable, and applied to individual parts or to a balance of good properties considered as a whole.

The Tail.

The tail should harmonise in length with the body and wings, and be inclined to shortness. The shape of the individual tail-feathers—i.e. narrow at their base and slightly increasing in width in the direction of their length, the outer ones being the longest, and each of the six on either side gradually decreasing in length—will, of itself, determine the correct shape of the tail, which cannot better be described than by comparing it with a closed fan, narrow at the junction with the body, and slightly, but very slightly, radiating, the lengths and arrangement of the feathers causing a V-shaped indentation at the extremity. Here, as in the wing, carriage is everything, the closed fan, so neatly folded together, showing the gilt edges as one feather, but which, when partially spread, spoil the effect.

The only remaining parts of the body covered with feather growth are the thighs, which should be well-covered with silky flue right down to the hocks; this flue should be short, close, and compact. The legs, which Nature generally makes of a proportionate length, should be inclined to shortness rather than length, as if too long they raise the bird too high from the perch. On the other hand, they must not be too short, or they will give the bird a squatty appearance as it stands on the perch; but be such as to give the bird full command of its body, the muscular power of the legs and feet taking a firm grip of the perch, and they should be free from malformation or defects of any kind, even to the toes and claws. It seems scarcely necessary to mention a matter of this kind; and the points, as described in several printed standards, " toes and nails entire and not twisted awry," always seem to us superfluous. Malformations are malformations wherever we find them, and it seems absurd to point them out as things not to be desired in a perfect specimen; still, for the enlightenment of the inexperienced, we have done so.

The Legs.

In summing up the whole under the head of general appearance, we should say the Norwich Canary is a jolly, comfortable sort of bird, not of the extremely graceful school, but inclined to *embonpoint* rather than to sylph-like proportions. Though not the largest variety of Canary, the Norwich is a bird of good size, and this property has its value when combined in a marked degree with type, quality, and colour—a combination rarely found in very large birds. Mere size alone is not sufficient, for whilst size is a feature in almost every variety, yet, where it is not *the* property, it has to give way before the particular feature sought. Hence, where that feature is found to develop itself prominently in any specimens, they are sure to be selected for future breeding operations, whatever other minor properties, even though they may be desirable ones, are absent; and thus size has, no doubt, been over and over again relinquished in favour of the three *sine qua non* properties mentioned above.

General Appearance.

Size, however, should never be lost sight of, especially in the breeding-room, though we must admit that the best Norwich are almost invariably of a medium size, and there seems to be a point beyond which it appears impossible to go in attempting to unite the properties aimed at in the standard. Still, some breeders have made strenuous efforts to do so, though with only partial success, and have only desisted when they found that their birds, though grand and imposing, were palpably deficient in the more valuable points. Other things being equal, the larger of two birds wins; but in the struggle for size, it is evident the chances of other things being *un*-equal are greatly increased. This view of the question will hardly admit of the supposition that size is a property which has been lost and might be regained, since it rather goes to show that the extreme development of quality of feather and colour has only been brought about by a compulsory relinquishing of size to an extent which almost indicated the incompatibility of their co-existence in the breed. Still, of recent years great progress has been made in maintaining fair size combined with type, quality, and colour, although the grafting of size into this variety from other sources brought into it many objectionable characteristics. These caused many a battle royal between the older and younger breeders of the bird, even to the extent of holding conferences at some of the Crystal Palace shows, with a view to arriving at a common understanding as to a standard for the breed, and following upon the conference of 1890 held at the Crystal Palace, great strides were made in

Size.

improving the all-round properties of the bird. The objectionable points alluded to have and are still being gradually overcome, without sacrificing to any extent the size gained, and this is of great importance, for in conjunction with the other leading features of the bird, size helps much to give a noble and commanding appearance.

In these general remarks on conformation we have been obliged to mix up the question of feather to some extent, but it must have a place to itself, as forming one of the most important features in this variety.

Feather Qualities.

The texture of the material cannot be too fine and silky, nor can the feathers be too short and compact. Nothing can atone for coarseness, for which there is no excuse in the eyes of a Norwich breeder. We are speaking now of the points of a show or ideal bird. We say " nothing," for even colour cannot compensate for a marked deficiency in close, soft feathering. Notwithstanding this, colour is the first thing looked for by many breeders after type, and is supposed to be the beginning and the end of the bird, " all over, underneath, in the middle, outside, overhead, on top, on all sides, and at both ends," it cannot stand unsupported on the show-bench, but must have shape and feather to sustain it. No true fancier of the variety but would accept an average display of colour combined with high quality, in preference to simply excess of colour without them, or with only a moderate share of them. When they are presented in this way, it is not easy to arrive at a correct estimate of their combined values by the application of a numerical scale, because the sum of the three values is really increased by an indeterminate number representing the effect of the combination. For instance, supposing two birds to score 20 and 30 points respectively under the head of colour, and 20 and 10 respectively for shape and quality of feather; then the value of the first would appear to be 20 + 20 = 40, and that of the second 30 + 10 = 40; but in reality the value of the first would be 40 + an indefinite number expressing the value of the effect of such a balance of power, and that of the second 40 − a discount for loss of effect occasioned by such disparity in the proportions of the combining parts, assuming, of course, the relative stand and values of the properties to be equal.

We have left the property of colour to the last, because the revised standards of the various specialist clubs representing the Norwich have placed it below type and quality; but though thus placed at the bottom of the scale, we should be indeed sorry to see colour neglected, because it is an important characteristic of the breed, which rightly heads the list of the colour family of Canaries.

Colour.

Though colour, as we have shown, has no right to over-rule all other properties, it is noteworthy that the principal characteristic of the Norwich is the capacity it has to develop colour. A long-continued application of the principles of selection has doubtless fixed this feature. The ultimate colour of all " clear " Canaries is what is generally understood by the word " yellow." But there are many shades of this colour, and it ranges from pale lemon to the deep hue of a Seville orange. Well, then, the Norwich bird is the Seville orange among a basket of lemons—the difference in colour is quite as decided; and if a further illustration be necessary, we think we could not make a happier comparison than by reference to the difference between the rich chrome of the dark African Marigold and the pale lemon-coloured flower of the same variety. We have endeavoured to describe its shape and its feather, and these two illustrations will serve to give a general idea of its colour, which is measured for depth and purity. The idea, however, is but general, and we will now go into details.

The entire Canary family is divided into two colour-classes, Yellow and Buff, which are synonymous with the terms Jonque and Mealy; but inasmuch as these terms do not express the real colour, they

CINNAMON CANARY, NORWICH TYPE.

must be regarded as purely technical. For example, we speak of a Yellow Green or a Buff Green, a Yellow Cinnamon or a Buff Cinnamon, when it is patent neither of these colours can be yellow or buff in reality; and the words, therefore, taken in their general application, are technicalities. The explanation is simple. Whatever be the body-colour of a Canary, whether it be literally yellow, or green, or cinnamon, or whether it be in a Lizard or even a dark Self-coloured Canary hybrid, it has two forms in which it manifests itself. One is bright and, for want of a better word, we will say luminous, polished, and glittering; the other, dull and flat, and is by comparison what frosted silver or dead gold is to the burnished metal. The first is the yellow form, and the other the buff; and one or the other presents itself in every Canary or Canary hybrid. In speaking of the Norwich Canary, the terms Jonque and Mealy in years gone by were generally adopted, and are both expressive of the general character indicated. The word Jonque is originally pure French, and may be taken to signify jonquil-coloured, which speaks for itself. The very word "mealy" indicates a pale shade of colour. These appellations are rarely used now in connection with the Norwich Canary, the usual terms being "yellow" and "buff."

Colour Terms.

Having thus cleared the way, we will endeavour to show how the Clear Yellow Norwich Canary, to which we have alluded, has been produced, and, from our investigation of the subject, deduce the laws which govern the recognised system of classification and the nomenclature adopted with regard to it. We remark, in the first place, that the fountain of colour in the entire variety is the original green. And this word "green" requires some explanation, for, after all, it may turn out not to be green. That it is a form of green we think is admitted on all hands; and the fact that the corresponding type in some other varieties is green, pure and simple, seems to support the idea. The one green, however, does not eventually resolve itself into the same form of yellow as the other: from the pure green we get lemon-yellow, and from the Norwich green we get a rich orange shade. The foundation colour of our bird is of a rich bronzy tone; so much so that whenever a bird of this type comes into competition with a pure green in a *bona fide* Green class it is invariably passed over as *not* being green, and such birds usually run very light on the breast and under-part of the body, though rich in colour pigment. Then what is it? It has always seemed to us to be no inapt comparison when we say it resembles a piece of gamboge, or some of the deep yellows in an artist's colour-box. Outwardly it shows but little indication of the delicate tints lurking within, but can be diluted and toned down to almost any shade. So with our bird: we have every gradation of tint, from the semi-opaque bronzy specimen, down to pure rich yellow, which we can further tone down to a pale straw colour. In the case of the so-called "pure-green"—which we have admitted to be so, as much for the sake of argument and illustration as anything, as this bird shows much black pigment on certain parts—we find the same diluting process possible, with this difference, that it ends in a lemon-yellow with a decided green tinge, capable again of being toned down to a greenish-white.

The Evolution of the Clear Yellow Norwich.

These Self-coloured Norwich Greens (we will adhere to the name) having a disposition to break or sport, advantage is taken of this, and it is cultivated to its ultimate issue. The first step in the direction of albinism gives us the "Heavily Variegated" class, as it is called in show language, or the "Broken Greens" of the breeding-room. We might also say here that classes are now provided at shows exclusively for Self and Broken Greens, and that they are bred as a separate variety of the Norwich Canary. These, with other greens, will be dealt with in a separate chapter.

Proceeding with our Norwich and the

Broken Greens, we include those birds which, although showing a fair amount of light colour, still carry a preponderance of the original green in irregular blotches or patches; one condition usually insisted on by a number of the old school of breeders in the 'sixties was that the bird should not have a "clean breast"—in which case it was said to be "Lightly Variegated." These distinctions were, however, not recognised by some schools of breeders, but they are important as indicating two separate and distinct bars of the colour-ladder, and we regret that more attention is not given to such marking to-day, though it may be merely a form of variegation. In open shows the distinction was seldom acknowledged, but the birds were united under the comprehensive term "variegated," though in clubs where the members understood their business (and we are bound in justice to admit that in those days they gave more thought and attention to markings than the majority of the present-day fanciers), an annual exhibition was held among the members for the purpose of comparing notes. What object-lessons those shows were! It was usual to keep every link in the colour-chain separate. A Lightly Variegated bird, whilst carrying a clear breast, had to be more or less marked on the back or neck, either or both, independently of carrying the green on the wings, which was a feature common also to the Heavily Variegated bird, which had, however, the marked breast in addition.

"Lightly Variegated" Class.

From this brief outline it will be seen that the difference between "Heavily" and "Lightly" variegated was entirely a question of degree, the conditions being the existence of body-marks, and the dividing line the presence or absence of a clear breast; but under all conditions a Lightly Variegated bird's body shows more light than dark, while the order is just reversed in a Heavily Variegated specimen.

Such stands good to-day, though no attention is paid as to whether the bird has a clear or marked breast in either form of variegation. The question arises: Would it define matters better for the breeder, in deciding as to which is a Heavily and which a Lightly Variegated bird, to adopt the marked and clear breast definition, with other markings as described, to distinguish the two classes of variegation? There has been much misunderstanding from time to time on this, and as to what constitutes a ticked bird, and in this way there certainly would then be a definite class of marking for each of the two forms of variegation, the Heavily Variegated having the marked breast and the Lightly Variegated possessing the clear.

The Separation of the Variegated Classes.

The most advanced form of light variegation is when the entire bird, including wings and tail, is perfectly clear with the exception of a few dark feathers interspersed here and there, or in the form of a grizzly patch on the head, neck, or back; such feathers usually being not dark from the quill to the end of the web, but grey or grizzly, showing a tendency to an entire fading out of the native green. When a bird shows but one small patch of such dark feathers on any part of the body surface, or dark under-flue only, they are known as "ticked" birds. Some club standards admit of more than one small dark patch on a ticked bird, with the result that novices become puzzled, and enter their birds in wrong classes at shows, entirely owing to this difference of definition. Other clubs, in order to avoid this confusion, have added a clause to their rules that a bird with two small dark patches is not a "ticked" bird, but lightly marked, and must be shown as such. This certainly is a clearer definition, but if it could be universally adopted that a ticked bird is one with one small dark or grizzle patch on any part of the body surface or dark under-flue, how much better it would be, and the veriest novice could not then well make a mistake.

"Ticked" Birds.

Such a definition need not in any way interfere with the exhibition of birds with dark under-flue and a perfectly clear body surface in classes for clear birds, where it is desired to do so; the wording of a schedule to that effect at the head of any such class would make that perfectly clear. This question as to what is a "ticked" bird and what is not has been a vexed one for a long time. If we adhere to the true meaning of the word "tick," then one small mark is the most consistent definition, and had our esteemed friend Mr. W. A. Blakston been with us to-day, we are sure this interpretation would have had his strongest support.

The question next arises as to the size of that small mark. After a moment's reflection it must appeal to any reasonable mind that whilst the same rule cannot be applied to all parts of the body, yet a definition can be drawn up to apply so closely to the various parts that no one need err — viz. any mark on the surface of the body, other than the flight and tail feathers, shall not exceed the circumference of a sixpence; that the extent of dark flue constituting a "tick" be unlimited so long as it does not show on the surface; dark thighs—one or both—to count as a "tick"; not more than four dark flight feathers in one wing shall constitute a "tick," or not more than four dark tail feathers shall constitute a "tick." But a "ticked" bird shall only carry one such mark on wing, tail, or body; the feathers constituting the "tick" may be entirely dark or of a grey or grizzle colour, and may be smaller than the specified size; or the dark feathers in flight or tail fewer in number than mentioned, but not more. Though with any one marking such bird may in addition have dark under-flue so long as that dark flue does not show as the bird stands on the perch.

Size of the "Tick" Mark.

One feature in connection with Variegated birds, and more particularly the Heavily Variegated section, must be noticed as bearing on our theory of gradation of colour, and showing that the yellow really seems to be one form of what we have designated green. It is the fact that in some parts of the bird the gradation is so delicate that the edge of the green merges in that of the yellow, so that the actual dividing line cannot be discerned. This is most noticeable on the lower portion of the breast, the stomach and the region of the "waist" among the soft, silky feathers of the sides and top of the rump, where some of the richest combinations of hues are to be found. We do not yet know what is the precise character of the pigment matter in the cells of the feather formation, except that a Green Canary's plumage contains a blending of black and chocolate melanin, and a pure yellow—or what we call "clear" yellow—plumage owes its difference of colour to the presence of these pigments in a modified degree only.

A Curious Feature.

We must observe, however, as having much to do with the colour question generally, that the Greens are the strongest as regards colour, and have the greatest power of developing or depositing it—a physiological property that breeders are not slow to acknowledge and avail themselves of, by having frequent recourse to the Green as a source from whence to derive fresh vigour and colour-producing power. This must not, however, be abused where the desire is to breed a preponderance of clear birds. The first remove from the Green always produces the greatest depth of yellow, wherever the clear patch of yellow shows itself; and so it is throughout the whole scale—so long as there is a vestige of a green feather, or even the dark under-flue attaching to it, it is the evidence of a colour producing power not possessed by the clear bird, for reasons already stated. Remember that the direction in which the breeder travels is *from* dark *to* light, and a clear bird once produced is the culminating point. Continue the diluting process, and colour recedes; and we must go to our colour-box for a fresh supply. This is the enunciation of a recognised principle in breeding to which we shall hereafter refer.

The Influence of the Green in Breeding.

We resume our classification, and remark that the introduction and maintaining of

GREEN CANARIES

YELLOW YORKSHIRE GREEN | BUFF YORKSHIRE GREEN

YELLOW NORWICH GREEN

the Green element have produced Pied birds, and this immediately opens up a field for the fancier, in the form of a desire to fix this Pied character in certain directions and render it permanent—a task of great difficulty. It is easy to account for this if we regard the Pied or Variegated bird as being in a transition state, somewhere on its journey from a dark self-colour, with feathers dark in stalk, flue, and web, towards the "Ultima Thule" of the fancier—the Clear bird, with spotless feather and snowy white underflue. Any exactness or regularity of marking which may appear can, therefore, only be regarded as a fleeting beauty, difficult to arrest and invest with the character of perpetuity, for, owing to our desire to produce clear birds, we take no steps to keep marking under proper control. It is by no means an hereditary quality, and the aphorism "Like produces like" is here applicable only to a very limited extent, simply because the work is tedious and patience on the part of the breeder short.

Pied Birds.

It is no more unreasonable to think of "setting" markings than it is to set the various types, provided the work is followed up in a business-like manner, which up to the present has not been the case. There are men, however, who are always doing wonders. To breed birds that are marked feather for feather with mathematical exactness is child's play to them; only the disappointing part of the business is that the world never sees them—they invariably *die in the nest.*

It is not an easy task under even the most favourable conditions, and we question whether an *evenly* marked bird has ever been bred that possessed absolutely the same number of dark feathers in each of the dark marks constituting its even marks. But the task of breeding a bird with its markings so well balanced that they appear even to the eye as the bird stands in its cage is not an impossible one. We shall have more to say on this when dealing with the breeding of birds with evenly balanced markings, commonly called "Even Marks."

The Differences of "Marked" and "Variegated" Birds.

What constitutes a "Marked" bird, and what is the difference between it and a "Variegated" bird? It is manifest that any Pied Canary is Variegated, and therefore what is known as a "Marked" bird is as much a Variegated bird as any other. The literal meaning must, it is evident, be discarded at once, and the terms regarded as technicalities, viewed in which light the matter is simple enough. There are certain places on the body of a bird in which the original dark colour seems to love to linger. In some places we often wish it would *not* stay, and vexing is the pertinacity with which it maintains its hold. But the last resting-place seems to be on the eyes, the wings, and each side of the tail. These marks most frequently appear in company with many others, but they are *there;* and as the objectionable patches or blotches disappear, largely by careful breeding or in obedience to chance, the eye, wing, and tail marks remain. These, and *these only,* are technically *marks,* and a bird is two, four, or six-marked, according as he possesses each or every pair. Such a bird is a "Marked" bird proper, and any bird which is marked in any *other* place than those indicated is a "Variegated" bird, even though it possess, in addition to its splashes and blotches, any or all of the marks the locality of which we have described, and which are the acknowledged standard "marks" recognised as such by the Fancy. A mark on the top of the head, however regular in its formation, or on the back (and some saddles are most exquisite in shape and characteristic pencilling of each individual feather), is not a "mark" proper; and hence it may be accepted as an axiom that a "Marked" bird must have a clean run, over and under, from the beak to the tail. And since dark feathers on each side of the tail constitute "marks," and further, since there are twelve feathers in the tail, it might be demonstrated from these premises that an entirely dark tail is a "marked" tail. But, if admitted, it would be of no value, because such marking is invariably accompanied by so much of a detractive character that the value of the whole would be subtractive instead of positive; indeed, it is by common consent tacitly agreed that a dark tail constitutes "variegation," and not "marking," because the absence of light feathers in the middle destroys the idea of a clean run from stem to stern, with the marking on each side. When the clean run is obstructed, above or below, the marking ceases and becomes variegation, and this criterion applies as much to the head as to the tail.

It will be plain that "marking" is a question of *locality*, and that there are but six places in which marks can possibly exist: elsewhere they are not marks. The perfection of marking consists in evenness and exactness—two separate and distinct things, though the latter idea is included in the former. Nothing is more common than to hear that a certain bird is not evenly marked, because one wing or one eye mark is heavier than the other; but if it be marked on *each* wing or *each* eye it is evenly marked, although the marking may be so irregular and badly balanced as to lay but small claim to be called exact. To be exact, the marks should correspond in shape and feather, one side of the bird being the counterpart of the other. It may seem unnecessary to have to explain this, but, simple as the thing is, a misapprehension as to the meaning of the terms gives rise to nearly as much misunderstanding as the "ticked" question already referred to.

Uneven Marking.

Uneven marking should define itself; but that there may be no mistake, we say that a bird with only one eye or one wing or one side of the tail marked, is unevenly marked; or, to put the definition in a concise form, if any one of the three marks is not repeated on the other side the bird is unevenly marked. A three-pointed bird may have both eyes marked and one wing, or vice versa, or a five-pointed bird may have both eyes marked, both wings, and one side of the tail, or both sides of the tail, both wings and one eye. Such markings are of common occurrence. Such birds are not technically "Variegated," because there is the absence of the necessary body-marks; but inasmuch as they cannot win in a class in which the desideratum is evenness, they are allowed to be shown in the "Variegated" class by sinking the technical character of their markings and considering them as of no value, and thus allowing them to compete with the irregularly-pied birds, whose variegations also are of no value, on the common ground of colour, quality, condition, and all other good properties except marking. This grouping, though sometimes convenient, is not defensible on any other ground except convenience—not always the safest foundation on which to build; and a very little inquiry into the character of the special feature of each of these two classes will show the truth of our position. The birds are representatives of different classes, to begin with, and have been bred with different objects in view. The one must be considered as approximating closely to that standard of excellence which consists in the entire absence of body-marks and the retention of those representing evenness and exactness, to retain and fix which has been *the* aim of all others, in the prosecution of which the production of colour has had to give way in some instances as being only secondary in the endeavour to produce even markings. The other represents a class in which marking or variegation of any kind is valueless, as such, and only exists as evidence of an admixture of the native green element essential to the development of colour.

The Old and New Methods of Classification.

The result of mixing up these unlike things in one competition, as was done years ago when colour was the ruling passion, was that the unevenly marked bird had no chance of winning on a colour basis in what was essentially a colour class, a thing which ought not to be; while, if it did happen to win by sheer force of sympathy, on account of it being so nearly perfect, then an injustice was done to the variegated birds to whom such approach to perfection of marking is of no value whatever. Since those days all things have changed, some for the better, and some not. To-day we have not the careful, observant breeders we had thirty years ago. Breeders then *studied ;* they studied type, studied quality, and studied colour and markings as well. It was common in the 'eighties to have a class of twenty or more Evenly-marked Norwichs at a good show. Not so to-day. In the " rage " to " win," these ideals of Canary culture have been thrown to the wind ; no thought or consideration is given them by the multitude of present-day breeders ; with the result that now we never see a class of Evenly-marked Norwichs, and casual specimens of this handsome ideal of a Marked Canary are usually consigned to the " Any Other Variety Class."

It may be *convenient,* as we said, to adopt such a system of grouping, and, considering the comprehensive character of the class, to give and take a little on both sides ; but in investigating the principles of correct classification we must have something more definite than convenience to guide us. The lack of this may have had something to do with causing the decline in breeding evenly-marked birds, which, given proper classification, might in a few years be brought to the front again. A very detailed classification may not be possible at once with the present multitude of shows ; but if it could be gradually improved, and breeders encouraged to produce the various colours and markings, and thus bring out more attractive birds, a greater interest would be created in our exhibitions. With this object in view we will explain the true principle of classification, so that it may be extended or contracted in the right direction.

With respect to the unevenly-marked birds, our contention is, that inasmuch as the breeder has aimed at getting " marks " at all hazards—with colour, if possible, but without it rather than lose the marking—it naturally follows that it is not in this section that we must look for the richest colour ; and it is, therefore, hard for these birds to be called upon to sacrifice what they have gained at great trouble, and be measured by a property which their opponents, the variegated birds, have been bred for alone and possess in excess. The simplest way would be to give these unevenly marked birds a place by themselves, or in the event of such an extension being considered impracticable, to group them with the evenly-marked birds in one section under the comprehensive name " Marked." They would then at least have the opportunity of competing on the merits of their distinctive feature. There naturally arises the question : " Would you then, give a prize to an *un*-evenly-marked bird over an *evenly*-marked one ? " It would depend entirely on the quality of the marking. There is a description of marking, to which we shall presently allude, which is next to worthless. We will assume we have before us a class of " Marked " birds, which will, therefore, contain Marked birds only, but marked in every degree of evenness and exactness, as well as all degrees of unevenness. The *best* marked would then win ; and we put the case of an unevenly-marked specimen being found among them to inquire into his chances. Given a bird with exact wings and one beautifully pencilled eye, and another with two respectable wings, one good eye, and, on the other side of the head, a mere blotch, which happens to include the eye ; given, also, that the first is equally good in type and superior in colour and quality, in our opinion it is the better bird, and should win. In all shows the percentage of really exquisitely marked birds would, at any rate for some time, be small, and among the so-called evenly marked ones are always to be found many which it requires a great exercise of charity to recognise as such. They may just come within the pale of the law, and, being there, claim the rights and privileges of citizens of the district. But they are worthless members of society ; even the very qualities upon which they

True Classification.

base their claim to notice are of negative value; there is an absence of good breeding about them, and all they can do is to flaunt their credentials in the face of birds which, slightly defective, are yet in other respects superior, and, after allowing a liberal discount for the defect (*blemish* there is none), could, in our way of thinking, win easily.

If evenly- and unevenly-marked birds were classified together in this way at shows, it would stimulate breeders to breed birds with evenly balanced markings, much more than they do at the present, as then there would be classes for them at all shows in all varieties, and they would not have to go into the "Any Other Variety Class," as at present. As their numbers increased, the even-marked could be separated from the uneven, and given separate classes.

Before going on to say in what consists good marking, we must draw attention to the thighs of the bird. The covering here is so scant that no decided character can be given to any marking thereon. When it is present it is generally in the form of dark flue, which shows itself upon any movement of the bird. It always has a negative rather than a positive value, and more frequently turns the scale against a competing specimen than places any points to its credit, and rightly so, especially if the dark colour shows through to any extent. The presence of dark feathers in the tail also is frequently accompanied by more or less dark colour in the rump feathers; this is not considered as a body-mark unless the dark colour is on the surface of the feather, and is a consequent disqualification in a "marked" class if not showing on the surface, simply counting against the bird to its extent. Some clubs allow greater latitude in this matter than others, and the birds have in consequence to be judged accordingly.

Thigh and Rump Markings.

The mark most difficult to obtain good is that on the eye, where it only too frequently assumes the character of a mere blotch or patch. There is a wide difference between a clumsy patch which happens to enclose the eye within its limits, and the delicately-pencilled spectacle-mark which gives such a distinctive style to the head of an Evenly-marked Canary. Sometimes a mark is found immediately in front of the eye, extending no farther. When this is the case it is, in the majority of instances, clear and decided, though only small; but such a mark is, in our estimation, of infinitely greater value than one of the blotch type. Sometimes the front of the eye is clear, and the marking runs off from behind it; this is also a good mark when clear and decided. But the perfection of marking should commence in the front of the eye, and, passing above and beneath with a clearly-defined edge, continue its course in the same curve as the outline of the head, and run away to a point behind the eye. This gives us a short, rounded mark in the front and a long pointed one behind. Such pencilling can occasionally be met with as perfect as if put on with a brush; but the general form is by no means so regular, and perfection is so rare that any decent approach to it is valuable. There should be no break in it, and no disposition to enlarge into a cheek-mark, any tendency in that direction detracting much from its merit. Neither should it reach so far above the eye as to threaten the crown; but whatever the character of the mark, clear outline is absolutely imperative. We do not object to a heavy mark, if it be only decided and have no tendency to the posterior enlargement we have referred to as constituting a cheek-mark. Equally objectionable is anterior enlargement, which, when it reaches the beak and begins to creep up the skull, ceases to be a "mark." It sometimes happens also that the mark runs round in the direction of the back of the skull; this also is objectionable, and of little worth.

Eye Marks.

The wing-marking should be confined to the flights, and there is no fixed limit to the number constituting a show-wing; it is all a matter of taste, and the value of an exact wing is too great to afford room for disputing as to the extent of the marking. Some fanciers

Wing Marks.

like the entire half of the wing dark; but we think seven feathers in each wing the extreme limit for beauty, and prefer only five or six, especially in a yellow bird. We need scarcely say they must be the inner feathers or secondary quills, and must form a perfect V, the point of each feather meeting its fellow, and the lighter brownish colour of the outside edge matching exactly with the corresponding bar on either wing. Slovenly wing carriage is fatal to a telling display, and the heavier the marking the worse such carriage makes it look. Though we say the dark feathers should be confined to the flights, many wings we have taken notes of have had the corresponding coverts dark also; indeed, it is sometimes astonishing, on expanding a wing for the purpose of counting the feathers, to find how large a portion of it is dark. But this is not of so much importance except in close competition, in which the nearest approach to exactness must win, other points being equal. The worst blemishes are the presence of occasional light feathers among the dark ones, and the opposite; and also an obstinate very black feather, which sometimes grows in the most provoking way among the bastard quills. Dark feathers will also frequently appear among the smaller coverts, the first row often being wholly dark, and though these are hidden by the scapulars when the bird is at rest, they show themselves when the wing is raised, and the bird is said to have black "butts."

Tail Marks.

A dark feather on either side of the tail is an addition to the markings, but a questionable advantage to a Norwich bird, because it is so frequently accompanied by dark flue at the base that what is gained one way is lost another. A bird with a marked tail and clear flue would beat one with a clear tail; but the difficulty is to get the gain without its equivalent loss. And when, in addition to this, we consider that the dark tail-feather is scarcely visible unless the bird be examined for it, so much so that its existence is not unfrequently overlooked and would sometimes not even be suspected but for the tell-tale dark flue, its value as a show point cannot be much. The most that is seen of it at any time is the extreme outside edge, and unless there be a sufficient number on each side—which should not exceed three—to give a decided character to the marking, we look upon it as worthless, the six centre feathers, of course, being clear.

"Clear" Birds.

The highest point of development attainable by the Norwich Canary is the "Clear" bird, which, as its name implies, should present a uniform clear colour throughout. Not the slightest tinge should be observable in a single feather, nor should the under-flue of its spotless golden plumage show any trace of its native green. This latter point is not always insisted on even by the best judges, provided a bird be absolutely externally free from the slightest suspicion of a stain; but the possession of dark colour *anywhere* may become a most dangerous property to a show specimen, since it is seldom entirely confined to those places where it is entirely hidden, but is apt to develop itself in certain feathers, which, though they do not take a more substantial form than mere down, are very liable to carry at their extremities the colour of the dark under-flue, the slightest indications of which, in a severe competition, would disqualify a bird. The most usual place in which it crops up to the surface is on the downy covering of the thighs, indicative of the fact that the native green still lurks within, and is doing the work of depositing colour in a way that never occurs in the absolutely Clear bird. The question as to what *is* a Clear bird is generally answered by the definition: "One which *shows* no green"; and it is probable that it will remain there, in the face of certain difficulties in carrying it any farther. But we think the definition is open to objection, and serious objection too. We have shown how the native green is the fountain of colour and how it has the capacity for development; and the object in breeding from dark to clear is to maintain that capacity to as full an extent as possible, and at the same time eradicate all trace of the original colour. We have also said that so long as there is a vestige of a green feather remaining, the colour-work goes on with greater energy; and it is only fair to consider whether the presence of dark under-flue in any quantity is not indicative of a considerable amount of the green element still at work, and whether such a bird really has bidden good-bye to the green and is perfectly clear.

We do not desire to take a one-sided view of the question, and are quite prepared for the inquiry: If a bird *shows no green,* where else can it be put except among the Clears, or the externally clear, since every other class *does* show it? But the plan of combating objections by asking questions is generally open to being itself met in the same way; and we would reply by asking: If birds with dark under-flue are stronger colour-producers by virtue of that taint, are not the absolutely clear practically as much at a disadvantage in being brought into competition with them, as they would be if made to enter the lists with the *bona fide* Ticked birds, which are considered the first remove from Clear, and have one leg already inside the door? Difficulties always commence when we hesitate about drawing a clearly-defined boundary line. When we have marked out our ground, we have nothing to do but to drive in our stakes and go ahead with our fence on the line; but if we begin to diverge here and there to include something without our circle, we at once lay the foundation of trouble. Now, it is not the breeding up to almost-but-not-quite clear that is difficult, but it is the putting the finishing touches to the work and turning out perfection, without a taint of imperfection, that shows the master-workman; and we have seen really clear gems, clear throughout, with snowy-white silky flue, that it would be a sin to put into competition with birds carrying dark under-flue which "blow black" all over, especially round the waist. And here we draw our line and define "Clear" to mean: not having the remotest tinge of dark colour in quill, flue, or feather; birds from which every trace of the green has been eliminated so far as the colour of the feathers is concerned; the feathers have a clear, silky, snowy-white under-flue, and show by it that they have arrived at the goal. There is not a fancier who has ever exhibited a high-class *bona fide* Clear of his own breeding that would not object to be beaten by a bird with dark flue; and "doing as you would be done by" is not a bad plan to follow, even in the matter of a simple question on Canary classification.

The "Ticked" Class.

We have no desire to turn the dark-flue birds out of their companionship with the Clears without finding a place for them, and we submit that their proper place is the *bona fide* "Ticked" division, which we define to mean: *not* lightly "variegated" in the sense in which we have explained the latter, but simply as having a small patch of dark, or grey, or grizzled feathers, or dark flue. Nineteen out of every twenty of them *are* ticked, for a "smoky" thigh and dark flue are first cousins. It is frequently only the delicate flue of the silky, downy covering of the thighs that is dark; and so long as the thighs remain in good repair, and the bird sits still, the discoloration is not perceptible without looking twice at it. But the bird flies up against the wires and uncovers his thighs, and then it is plain enough: the colour is *there,* and the bird owes his deep, rich tone of yellow to it, and is not clear, and his grizzled thighs are as much ticked as is the head or neck of the bird in the next class, which may blow almost perfectly clear, and have not more than half-a-dozen grey feathers in it. Birds of this kind are all on an equality: they are in one and the same stage in the march towards *freedom from the trace of green,* the possession of which, be it ever so slight, groups them in one class.

Our arrangement of the whole in order of colour-gradation is—first, Green; second, Variegated; third, Clear. Subdividing them further for the purpose of more detailed classification, and arranging them again in complete order, we have—(*a*)

STONECHAT. WHINCHAT.
WHEATEAR.

Green, (*b*) Heavily Variegated, (*c*) Lightly Variegated, (*d*) Evenly-marked, as it is from the previous three we produce these—(*e*) Unevenly-marked, (*f*) Ticked, (*g*) Clear. This is the extreme extension, and includes every form. There are, of course, yellows and buffs of these grades, and to classify the two colours separately—which it is usual to do—that is, yellows in one class and buffs in another, would give just double the number of classes. The classes which may be united on a common footing are (*b*) and (*c*), which contain practically identical birds, differing only in the amount of variegation. Classes (*d*) and (*e*) can also be united under the inclusive term "Marked," as we have shown. It is also usual to group (*b*), (*c*), and (*f*) into one, as representing more or less variegation; but we have endeavoured to show that there is a closer affinity between (*f*) and (*g*) than between any other, and that (*f*) should be used as an adjunct to (*g*) for the reception of birds perched on the top bar but one, where it is desired to curtail the classification.

Colour Classes.

We supplement these notes on classification based on the natural gradations in colour by a few remarks on the difference between the Yellow and Buff. We think there is no occasion to say anything of the Yellow, other than that it is of a pure bright hue, with all the colour on the surface like an exquisite orange-coloured satin. The Buff bird is of the same hue, but the colour does not appear to glisten on the surface; it is still a ruddy orange satin, and sometimes ruddier even than the yellow, but the satin is covered with a delicate white gossamer veil by which its gloss is clouded, though rendered, if possible, more beautiful by the veil-like hoar-frost covering it. The colour is softened in places where the lace covering seems to lie in thicker folds, but a movement of the bird brings a fresh gleam of light to play on its beautiful dress, and from under the silvery cloud shines out the golden yellow.

Difference between Yellow and Buff.

The word "Mealy" is very expressive of the appearance of the bird, though the idea is not very poetical: we have seen Norwich Canaries which appeared almost as if the white bloom on them would come off in the hand like that of some fruits. This silvery frosting is occasioned by the extreme edge of the feathers being fringed with a margin of white, and the effect produced is greater or less as it is presented in places where the growth is dense or otherwise. The feathering on the Buff birds is much denser than on the Yellows, the under-flue being very thick and long, as the fancier will be able to observe when he makes his first essay in washing. This dense feathering gives the Buff bird an altogether larger and stouter appearance, and it is, as a rule in every respect the lustier bird of the two. By this we do not infer that the Yellow bird is not robust in health; we refer more particularly to appearance. Every fancier, said Mr. Blakston, has his own particular liking. His was for the perfection of development in a Buff bird. Personally, we have no hesitation in saying that a Yellow of equal merit with a Buff would, and does, take precedence over the Buff on account of the greater difficulty to produce such a Yellow.

Such is the Norwich Canary of which we have endeavoured to furnish as complete a description as possible.

Judging the Norwich Canary

Negative Properties

A Clear Yellow Norwich Canary should not appear dull in colour, however deep the tone may be, nor show any signs of meal on the back or breast, nor be patchy, nor white on the outside edge of the flights or wing-coverts, nor show dark under-flue or discoloured thighs. It should not be loose or coarse in body-feather, nor carry its wings looselv or crossed at the tips, nor spread its tail like a fan. It should not have a coarse head nor overhanging eyebrows, nor be long and narrow, nor be in any way of puny build. It should not show any discoloration on either mandible or on the legs (though to show this is not a disqualification, but a blemish in an otherwise clear bird), and should never be shown dirty or with broken patches.

A Clear Buff Norwich Canary should not be deficient in meal, nor look like a bad Yellow, nor be unevenly frosted, nor show any indications before referred to as foreign to Clear birds. It should not be coarse, shaggy, nor open-feathered, nor other than as if cut out of boxwood, nor in the slightest degree puny in build.

The *bona fide* Ticked birds are judged for precisely the same features as the Clears, with the exception that the unavoidable presence of dark under-flue entails no subtractive value, the points which would otherwise be allotted to white flue and clear beak and legs being distributed between the two all-important features—viz. colour and quality of feather.

These remarks apply equally to the lightly and heavily variegated birds; of course, a *well*-marked bird usually scores an advantage over a badly-marked one, owing to its attractive markings displaying its other points of merit off to greater perfection. By kind permission of the Norwich Plainhead Club, we publish their Standard and Scale of Points, which is the standard recognised by all Norwich Plainhead Specialist Clubs throughout the country.

The Norwich Plainhead Club Standard

Colour.—Deep, bright, rich, pure, and level throughout.

Shape.—Head, round, full, and neat; neck, short and thick; body, short and chubby; with wide back, well filled in, deep, broad, full chest.

Feather.—Soft and silky, with brilliancy and compactness.

Wings and tail.—Short, compact, and good carriage.

Size.—Well proportioned.

Beak.—Short and stout (clear).

Legs.—Well set back (also clear).

Feet.—Perfect.

Condition.—Health, cleanliness, and sound feather. Streak beak and marked legs not to be a disqualification, but count against the bird to its extent.

Length.—Not to exceed 6½ inches.

Scale of Points

	Points
Head.—Round, full, and neat, with short beak **Neck.**—Short and thick	25
Chest.—Deep, broad, and full	15
Back.—Broad and well filled in	10
Wings and tail.—Short, compact, good carriage	15
Feather.—Soft, silky with brilliancy and compactness	15
Colour.—Deep, bright, rich, pure, and level throughout	10
Staging and Good Condition.	10
Total	100

In judging, the maximum total of points in all standards is 100.

It might be urged that 10 points of 100 is too much to assign to the vague property of "Condition," which is no positive part of any bird; but health, cleanness, and soundness of feather are such essentials on the show-bench that no scale of show-points would be of use unless the value of this item were expressed in the terms at which it is assessed by every practical judge.

A REPRESENTATIVE GROUP OF BIRD-KEEPERS.
Photographed at the Hull Show.

CHAPTER XVIII

BREEDING THE NORWICH CANARY

THE first thing to be mentioned in connection with breeding the Norwich or any other variety of Canary is that, in pairing, the general rule is to put a Yellow and a Buff together. It is immaterial which sex is the one colour or the other; but, except in special circumstances, the arrangement must be as we have said. The first object is to ensure the production of good feather; the Buff supplying the close, compact element, and the Yellow the silkiness of texture and the colour. There is no rule that has not its exception, nor are there wanting occasions when this order of things is not adhered to; but it is only departed from when specific results are desired. It may be, perhaps, that some particular strain, good in all other points, has, from some necessary line of procedure in breeding, become too thinly feathered or the contrary, in which case it may be advisable to pair two Buffs or two Yellows to counteract this tendency in either direction; and it may even be found necessary to continue such treatment for one or two generations, till the required texture has been obtained.

In the case of double buffing, a Buff can be selected to pair with birds that have been double buffed, bred from Yellow and Buff, if it is found necessary to double buff more than one season in succession. By this means undue sacrifice of colour and silkiness of texture in the feather is avoided.

Difference in Feather.

There may be other causes for such pairing—as, for instance, to avoid too close consanguinity; but it must be understood that the rule, as applied to *feather*, is, pairing two Yellows induces thinness, and pairing two Buffs has just the contrary effect, and we do not wish to apply it, at present, in any other direction. It will be seen that there is here scope for the exercise of a considerable amount of skill on the part of the breeder, who, in the pursuit of the many points of excellence recognised by fanciers of this variety, must maintain, from end to end, fine quality of feather. It is in this respect that Canary-breeding differs so materially from poultry-breeding. We have two distinct descriptions of feather, which we are bound to mingle; to maintain, as it were, both *surface* and *grain* of the page to be printed; and this it is which renders our work doubly difficult. We have the same ends in view as regards the production of certain fancy points in feather, but we have to work with these two distinct qualities of material, which we cannot always get. The one object we may be keeping steadily in view may be rapidly assuming its desired proportions; but we require, from the time of laying the foundation-stone, that the same property which we are seeking to develop shall be present in the *two* birds we pair. This it may not be so difficult to find, but these birds must, as a rule, be one *buff* and the other *yellow*, and we have no guarantee that we shall find such in the nests we have reared with such strict regard to the development of the fancy points sought. We have to search for these points in two different *forms* of birds, and we have no rule by which we can determine the way to produce these two forms with anything like certainty. The success of our operations may depend upon an even balancing power in the direction of Buffs and Yellows throughout our nests; but the result of the season's breeding may show such a marked difference in their respective numbers as to puzzle us how to pair them the next season without imminent risk of injury to feather, which, in the Canary, is a serious matter, because many of the fancy points sought depend entirely upon that display of feather caused by the union of Yellow and Buff.

For this reason we recommend pairing a Buff bred from Yellow and Buff to a Buff bred from two Buffs, if this mating of like colours is necessary for more than one year. The balance is, we admit, pretty evenly maintained; but the difficulty is at the root of much of the failure of some breeders through lack of thought in pairing.

The Source of Colour.

The pairing of Yellow and Buff also affects colour most materially. The Yellow is undoubtedly the fountain of colour, for though good Buffs frequently display it in great purity, yet the tendency of an ordinary Buff is in the opposite direction. This is sometimes a reason for pairing two Yellows, the philosophy of the thing being nothing more than a concentration into one channel of the power to produce yellow. Occasionally it is found necessary to do this, owing to some peculiar feature in the colour of the feather, arising from too much concentration of Buff blood at some previous stage, through which the brilliancy of the yellow has been clouded by a decided leaning towards the semi-opacity of the duller shade. Its lustre must not be dimmed by the suspicion of even the fringe of meal, shown of late years in many Yellows owing to abuse in double buffing. Where such Yellows occur we have found that the pairing of "double Yellows"—i.e. the offspring of two Yellows—showing this extra proportion of Buff blood restores the proper balance of colour. Buffs bred from loosely-feathered high-coloured Yellows similarly paired have the same effect, and the tendency to closeness of feather is also intensified.

These observations apply simply to the general way in which colour can be affected by systematic pairing. The whole thing lies in a nutshell, so far as the simple principles involved are concerned. The Yellow bird represents brilliant colour, the Buff bird subdued colour; the former fine, delicate feathering, the latter excess of feather. The elements in each case are simple, requiring nothing more than the exercise of the most ordinary common sense to control them, their mixture being almost mechanical in its action. These remarks are strictly general in their bearing; and when we refer to the pairing of two Yellows or two Buffs, or the uniting of these opposites, the question of the degree of colour in either is not taken into account in laying down a rule applicable not only to the Norwich variety, but to all Canaries, and which is intended to do nothing more than indicate what is required in the first place, whatever may be the quality of the birds so put up for breeding, whether as regards colour, distinctive plumage, shape, size, or any other feature. The distinctions which are peculiar to Buff and Yellow birds respectively are possibly entirely the result of selection in breeding, and are not native to birds in a wild state, though there are different degrees of colour in some of these. They are, therefore, properties which can be retained or lost, improved and made thoroughly distinct in character, or allowed to deteriorate by neglect.

The necessity which exists for working with two sets of birds, if we may so express it, may make the business of breeding sometimes rather complicated; but the pairing of the two produces each in its beauty, and even here the principles of pedigree breeding can assist a thoughtful breeder in directing the course of the channel in which he may wish any stream to flow.

The Value of Greens.

We will assume that to produce Clear Norwichs is the aim of the breeder, and the question is how to do it. Pair Clears in the way we have mentioned, and Clear offspring will be the result. There may, perhaps, be one here and there not quite clear, but the tendency is decided, and the direction of each succeeding season will be towards perfect and complete uniformity of colour if everything of a contrary character be excluded. But, with this plan, depth of colour will certainly decline. This then, evidently, is not what we want to be at, and the inference is plain that we have begun at the wrong end. We have selected parents in which are concentrated the tendencies of generations of families all bred and selected for the one purpose of getting rid of the native green, which is, perhaps, only one form of the paler colour we call yellow; and we have been pushing this tendency still further, and paling our birds still more. In fact, we have begun just where we ought to have left off; our colours have been carefully blended and toned down till the required shade has been obtained, and to maintain this we cannot dilute further without loss, which must be replenished from some source or other. We will go to the fountain for it, and remark that it may be laid down as a maxim worth remembering that a breeder of high-class Norwichs should never be without a good Green bird in his room: not a dull, flat, smoky-looking Buff, but a brilliant Green, in itself a beautiful bird, which we will for our present purpose consider in its character of a colour-fountain. We do not say to beginners, commence with Greens and plod on patiently till they break; that might never be—though never is a long time—but it would certainly be a tedious process, and more especially if the Greens come from a fixed strain not much given to sporting.

Knowledge of Pedigree.

It is, therefore, eminently desirable that something should be known of the constituent elements of the material with which it is proposed to work. A good Green will often be thrown by parents themselves very lightly variegated, and well advanced in the journey up the Hill Difficulty. It is natural that such a bird should occasionally present itself, as the eradication of the dark self-colour is not accomplished without an effort and a struggle on both sides; and such are valued accordingly as they emanate from a branch of a family more or less remote from a known starting-point. Greens bred immediately from Greens may, as we have indicated, be reluctant to produce anything else, and may hesitate before they unlock the door of the warehouse containing their wealth of colour; but a Green thrown by comparatively light parents is, in most cases, almost running over with colour, which seems only seeking an outlet to diffuse itself through many channels, all of which it will tinge with something of its own brilliancy. Mixed with itself, it probably would have a tendency to become more fixed, but poured out upon the rich yellow or equally rich buff of a Clear strain, it adds to their lustre, and infuses fresh, vigorous, colour-blood. This is called "taking a dip into the Greens," and the benefits to be derived are in proportion as we dip into the *right kind* of green at the *right time* and in the *right way*.

Of course a Variegated bird (providing it possesses the necessary rich brilliant colour) will answer equally well to pair with a strain that have been Clear bred for generations, *not* descendants of Greens of the previous year. This fact must never be lost sight of, as a Ticked bird, or even a Clear not far removed from the Green, is more suitable to pair with a bird of immediate Green descent that yet lacks depth of colour, which the breeder wishes to strengthen. Every breeder should know the nature of the material in his possession, for every bird in his room should represent to him something more than it would to a casual observer. He knows what it is made of and what it holds as plainly as if it were a glass phial duly labelled with the registered strength of its contents. It is to an intelligent man of this kind that we should apply for our first pair of birds; and, whatever else we got, we would take care that at any rate we did our best to be supplied with tubes from which pure colour could be extracted by careful manipulation, rather than with empty ones which had been squeezed dry.

The late Mr. W. A. Blakston, in writing on the breeding of Norwichs, cited an excellent illustration of this. "One of the best birds," said he, "of this kind we ever saw was a Clear Yellow exhibited by Mr. Edward Bemrose, of Derby; it was in the last show held in the Tropical Department at the Crystal Palace, and was claimed by Mr. John Young, of Sunderland. In those days we, perhaps, didn't know so much about Greens as we do now, but we had a glimmering of the truth. This bird was paired with a Clear Buff hen, as was then our wont in our endeavours to produce high-class Clears; but the produce was a marked preponderance of Heavily-Variegated birds. Among the offspring were one or two Clears, which were fully up to the standard of the day, and, notably, a Buff. The hens were, most of them, very heavily marked, some of them being only slightly broken, but all could be relied upon for producing first-class Clears when mated with Clear cocks; and one cock, a Variegated Yellow, was equally reliable for producing pure Clears when paired with Clear hens. Clears from this strain were also pretty sure to throw one or two birds more or less marked, the balance of Green blood being such that by careful mating, so as not to harp too long on one string, it could be diverted into certain channels with a degree of certainty we never knew surpassed by any strain which came under our observation." This clearly shows the value of careful selection and pairing.

Breeding Clears.

The immense number of birds of the variegated form which find their way into our exhibitions cannot be accounted for by any supposition that they are bred in that direction from any desire to produce the infinite variety of marking which we find in them, for the sake of any value which may attach to them on account of such irregular variegation. They are in reality the exhibition of so many intermediate links in the long chain, the value of each link being in exact proportion to its known tendency towards progression or retrogression; and all goes to prove the existence of a recognised system by which the peerless beauty of the Clear bird is developed.

The Use of Variegated Birds.

It is important, then, in selecting breeding-stock, that the Variegated birds chosen should be taken from the upper branches of the tree and not from too near the root; and so long as they are of known pedigree, and can be relied on not to play unaccountable pranks as regards colour, it is not of much moment on which side, male or female, the green is found present or latent —for it is possible that it may not always be present, though very near the surface. Some breeders prefer to pair Variegated cocks with Clear hens, and others the reverse; but in actual practice it is found necessary to mate them, not as one would wish, but as they are to be obtained; for with all the care in the world they cannot be bred to order, though the experienced breeder can, with a fair amount of certainty, anticipate what he will get from a carefully selected pair of birds. Some breeders recommend the pairing of two Variegated birds together; but this defeats our object of transferring the rich colour of the dark to the surface of the Clear. We could understand such pairing if our object were to breed a few dark-coloured stock birds or Greens, and it should only be adopted in such a case.

A breeder who wishes to work with his own stock must take it as he finds it. Much has been said about the danger attending the introducing of fresh blood into a strain through the admixture of blood of which the constituent parts are not known; and a breeder who may find himself short of Clear or Variegated cocks or hens, may have some of his carefully-arranged measures completely upset by the introduction of a foreign cross which appears to be what it is not—viz. an established Clear, when it may in reality be nothing more than the chance issue of an obstinate dark strain. Whilst this risk is not very great, there are few good birds that are not the result of previous careful

Risks of "Fresh Blood."

breeding, and good Clears are not so easily bred as to be the frequent produce of dark pairs; yet we must emphasise the fact that indiscriminate buying at shows of birds of unknown pedigree, unless the desired points are very pronounced, is not free from risk, and is not the best road to success.

THE NORWICH PLAINHEAD TO-DAY.
(An interesting contrast with the bird portrayed on page 233.)

Cardinal Points.

In our chapter on Pedigree Breeding we pointed out that four points practically summarised all those which give the breeder real difficulty in most varieties. We have now shown the importance of colour, and its effects even on feather, as to whether this fits the body closely or otherwise. Another difficulty in the Norwich is the maintenance of a bold and neatly moulded head, harmonising with the stout body of the modern Norwich, for nothing looks worse than a small, puny head on a standard sized body. We need no stronger proof of the importance of head than to say that 25 points are given for it, combined with beak and neck, out of the total of 100 points allowed for the whole bird.

The head should not only be bold, but nicely arched, and free from browiness over the eyes. We must have a good full eye brow, but no loose feather or resemblance to the Crest-bred. Shape is another important point, and it includes several minor points which are easily controllable as we proceed in the breeding of good birds. Our fourth point, and one not so easy of control, is compactness of wings and tail. These should harmonise with the build of the body, and the wings be carried close to the body and just meet at their tips.

Minor Points.

If we keep all these characteristic points well in hand, those which naturally follow in their train are not difficult to handle. We can include under this heading such as coarse beak; a tendency to browiness giving the head a coarse appearance;

untidy waists, that is, feather hanging loosely just behind the legs, marring the neat finish of a bird; standing a little too high on leg, and too erect carriage, are all faults that can be eradicated by pairing birds free from such blemishes to those possessing them. Large hens are not, as a rule, so finely moulded and nicely cut away as medium and smaller hens, and where this is the case a medium-sized cock is a suitable mate for such a hen, for generally such a bird is active and smartly moulded, and will thus correct in the progeny the points which the hen lacks. On the other hand, most breeders know that it is desirable to pair up a large cock to the medium or smaller hens.

Out-crosses.

In the gradual building up of the modern varieties breeders have had to introduce certain out-crosses, and thus all varieties of the Canary owe something to each other. This crossing would seem at the outset to strike directly at the root of the theory of "pure" breeds of any kind; but fanciers generally know how extremely difficult it is to maintain what is understood by purity of breed, or to refute the truth which seems to speak out occasionally in the persons of their different specialities, hinting at a remote impurity, imported for useful ends, which has not quite died out. That, we take it, is the purest breed in which the most desirable properties are most securely rooted, and perpetuate themselves with the most constant fixity; and we might almost go so far as to say that, in some fancies, the demand for ultra-excellence has induced systems of breeding which would make a reversion to some of the "old," "original," "pure" (?) types anything but satisfactory, few of them having reached our day without having been vastly improved upon and materially altered, to their manifest advantage.

In the early days, when the Norwich was a much smaller bird than now, the Lizard cross frequently gave good results, for the Lizard possessed the sought-for colour in an eminent degree, and its shape and texture of feather harmonised well with the Norwich of those days. In the effort to get colour in our stock we must never overlook the fact that no plan is more surely fatal to future prospects than a persistent endeavour to make colour feeding supersede breeding for colour production. It is here that the *careful breeder for colour* will always leave the fancier behind who trusts to the colour pot to make up that which he forgets when pairing his birds. The Lizard cross is not now the most suitable for our purpose, since the Norwich of to-day is a much larger bird. This difference in size is due to the introduction of Crest blood through the Crest-bred—a cross which we have used with success.

Introduction of Crest Blood.

At that time the Crest Canary was much closer in feather and nearer in type to the Norwich, but larger, and of better colour, as Crests were then paired Yellow to Buff, like Norwich Plainheads. This cross was at first much bewailed, and yet, but for its introduction, we should not possess the present-day grand type of Norwich. The desire was for more size, and this the Crest possessed, and, moreover, it was the nearest approach in type. What then could be more natural than to use it to introduce the desired size, and afterwards, by careful selection, to retain this increased size, and get rid of the other properties not desired in the Norwich? The real trouble was that breeders were in too great a hurry to put the changed type on the show bench before the birds were properly fined down, and had got rid of all Crest-bred characteristics. This impatience gave the opponents of the introduction of any foreign blood their opportunity, and crossing with the Crest was given the credit of every evil, and particularly of loss of colour. This latter was true to a certain extent, for double buffing had been much resorted to with the view of further increasing size, trusting to the colour-food pot to make up for the colour thus lost by the abuse of double buffing. To double buff occasionally is an advantage when it assists to complete some work or point desired, but excessive double buffing generation after generation is ruinous both to colour and quality of feather.

In the end, however, all things came right, and we now have a noble bird, and plenty of material for the breeding-room. If there were any lack of this we should not hesitate even now to use a Crest-bred cock to make stock or building material, provided we could get hold of the right type of bird. Such a Crest-bred should have a large broad head, a bulky body, with feather as tight as possible, that is, too sparse for crest-breeding. We should also endeavour to get one with short tail and wings, and as near as possible to Norwich type, and a Yellow for preference, though we should not hesitate to use a Buff of the same description. Such a bird we should pair to one of the tightest and richest opposite-coloured, short, chubby-built birds we could select. The young from these we should pair back to pure Norwichs, and also the following season, when, having gained the desired size, we could by selection refine the stock and develop standard properties. We have seen many birds exhibited as Norwich which carried more feather than the type of Crest-bred we have described as suitable for crossing; but just now there is no need to use this cross, as there are plenty of large stock Norwichs available, the chief faults of which are a little coarseness in head, and excessive length in body, wing, and tail. Birds of this class should be mated to others of chubby, neat, good all-round properties. We have also an ample supply of large, rich-coloured Norwich type Green and Green Marked birds, from which to draw for colour as necessity demands, without having to resort to the Lizard.

Type of Crest-bred for Crossing.

The first nests from a Green and a Clear Norwich will be, for the most part, more or less Pied, showing in a marked way a combination of the distinctive features of each variety; but by judicious mating of these Pied birds with others from Clear strains—selecting for the purpose those most lightly variegated—the dark markings will soon vanish, and Clear birds of good feather and rich colour appear.

Crossing with Greens.

Its departure will be characterised, as the Clear blood gets stronger hold, by slight markings of grizzly appearance on the feathers, the whole having a faint, undecided character about it suggestive of its inability to stand before the continued infusion of Clear blood. The use of the Green is not so much in vogue in some breeding centres as in others, but its introduction cannot be dispensed with for long in any methodical breeder's room, though it should be kept under proper control, so that a good number of Clears are always produced in the progeny.

While enunciating the theory of the intimate connection between the Clear Yellow and the Self-coloured Green, we do not mean to say that very pleasing results may not be obtained from mating Clear pairs, especially such as are nearly allied to the Greens, but in such pairing much " sporting " power is left on both sides, and whilst some very beautiful Clears are bred in this way, many darks often verging on Self-Greens are also produced, both parents being Clear. The breeder has more control over this Green tendency where he pairs Clears of this sort to others that have been Clear-bred for a generation or two.

Mating Clears.

Our theory is that the natural high orange colour is but one form of the normal green plumage arrested at a certain stage of its decadence, when at its greatest beauty, and the art of maintaining it at this point consists in a careful selection and pairing of birds showing the least tendency towards retrogression, and in checking any decline of colour, when it sets in unmistakably, by use of Green blood as indicated.

Experience of the breeding-room and knowledge of the stock must be our guide in pairing, and whether it be Clear with Clear, or Clear with Variegated, there should be a reason for each mating, and this should be coupled to an accurate noticing of results each season, and a weeding out of such birds as show no progress.

It is the attention to such details, and the surmounting of the obstacles met with, which yield the chief pleasures of the breeding-room.

Mr. Irons on Breeding.

Northampton has long been a stronghold of Norwich breeders, and Mr. T. Irons of that town has bred and exhibited the Norwich Canary successfully for over forty years. Writing of his breeding experience, this fancier says:—

"I have tried various ways of pairing, double buffing and double yellowing, but not to excess. In the early days before Cayenne feeding was in vogue I bred for colour, and the best that I ever produced was when I took a cross from the London Fancy with my Norwich. The colour of the young was simply marvellous. I bred one real good Norwich from two Buffs about thirteen or fourteen years ago. It was a 'topper,' but unfortunately for me the bird was stolen from a show. When pairing up I always study size. I like a bit of this in my breeding stock, both in cocks and hens, and I also like them tight in feather. From such pairing I usually have good results, and have bred most good birds from Buff cocks and Yellow hens. I have not tried a Cinnamon cross with my Norwich; I prefer a *good* Green for improving colour, and like a bronze shade of green, as from this I have got rich Yellows, and the Buffs have been beautifully mealed over a rich under colour."

Mr. E. Baker, of Cowes, Isle of Wight, another well-known breeder and exhibitor, writes:—

Mr. E. Baker's Experience.

"When selecting my stock for breeding I always try to pick out the best. I do not believe in putting a big, indifferent cock to a little, good hen, or *vice versa*, for, depend upon it, the bad points of the big, indifferent cock will predominate over the good points of the little hen. Experience has taught me that the more perfect the stock birds are the better the results. Many fanciers say that show birds do not always produce show youngsters. True; but I venture to say that the progeny of two really good show birds will produce a far greater percentage of show specimens than of those I have previously mentioned. I like birds of good medium size, the nearer perfection in type, quality, and colour the better. If a good Yellow lightly Variegated cock, with a good head, short flights and tail, with a good bold front, teeming, if possible, with colour, be paired to a good bold, lively Buff hen, with type and quality, the former must be especially conspicuous if good results are to be attained. If the hen be a Clear, or if the cock is only very lightly marked a Clear Buff hen, bred from lightly marked parents, can be used with good result.

"I like colour in stock. Many say that colour should not count too much, but it does, and will count. Let three birds of equal merit for type and quality be placed side by side for judging, and let one be of good colour, and the other two indifferent in colour, and it would be a poor judge who would not put the best coloured one first, and rightly so, as in many cases colour means quality. Try how you will you cannot get colour in a harsh, coarse-feathered bird.

"My reason for selecting good medium-sized birds is, that as a rule they are more lively. I like to see them go from perch to perch, full of life and energy, and these properties are not frequently found in big, heavy birds. Nothing pleases the judge's eye more than to see a 'tip top' specimen looking the very essence of health and activity. Equally good results can be obtained by pairing Buff cocks to Yellow hens in the same way as I have described for Yellow cocks and Buff hens. Whatever you breed from let the stock be the best. Should colour be lacking, select the best heavily-marked Yellow cock, and pair to a Buff hen bred from Variegated parents; the progeny from these should be either very heavily marked or quite Green, what the Norwich breeder calls stock birds, for the breeding-room. By Greens I mean a rich Bronze Green, not what is called 'Liverpool Green.' Almost all fanciers know what is meant by a Bronze Green. Pair the young from the Variegated pair to Clears that have been bred from Clear birds; should there be very Lightly-marked birds from the Variegated pairs, put them to Lightly-marked mates, in this way one can intensify colour to a very marked degree.

"We are living in an age when size seems in great demand, and suggestions for obtaining such are given by many fanciers. Of these doubtless the most popular is double buffing. This can be resorted to at times with good results, but I should strongly advise novices not to try it. The experienced breeder can select a good Lightly-marked Buff cock of good medium size, with good soft, silky feather; the hen also should be of good medium size, well mealed, but very tight in feather. In no circumstances should either a cock or a hen be put up for double buffing which shows a superabundance of feather, especially at the thighs. For double yellowing I always select the largest-sized, Heavily-marked cock—one with a good head and very short, thick neck, and plenty of fibre in feather. The hen must also be of good size, not marked so heavily as the cock, and she, too, must be very thick and short in neck and body. Double yellowing has a tendency to produce young that will look thin and weak in neck unless great care is taken in selecting the stock. From such a pair I once bred a Clear Buff of the best quality I ever saw, and this bird sired some of my best youngsters.

"Whilst admitting that good results can be obtained by double buffing and double yellowing, yet I am certain that until a breeder has had a great deal of experience, more certain and better results will be obtained by pairing Buff and Yellow or Yellow and Buff. It is true that freaks will sometimes crop up, and a fair specimen appear from a poor pair; but to be successful always select the best. If good medium-sized birds are paired together, there will be no occasion to double buff to get good bold birds. Weakly or delicate birds should never be paired up, for disappointment is sure to follow."

Mr. S. Gill's Advice.

Mr. S. Gill, of Plymouth, another old Norwich breeder and successful exhibitor, furnishes us with these interesting notes:—

"In selecting birds for breeding size is not my only consideration; one must have type and quality. I always select birds with good round heads, short neck, full chest, well-filled-in back, good wing carriage, short legs and tail, as near the Bullfinch type as possible. I believe in pairing Yellow cock and Buff hen, or *vice versa*, preferring plenty of substance and colour on the cock's side. I have always found that size and colour are better conveyed from the cock's side than the hen's. I like hens of medium size, but they must be full of quality and type. As regards in-breeding I am a firm believer in it, bearing in mind that the birds used for in-breeding are strong and healthy, and as near perfection as possible. I should not recommend the in-breeding of birds with faulty points, as I fear it would only help to fix the bad points. I have practised in-breeding for years with good results, and this year (1910) have paired a Ticked Buff brother and Clear Yellow sister together, both show specimens. I have never found careful in-breeding weaken the birds in any way."

It should be clearly noted by those who adopt in-breeding that Mr. Gill only recommends it as a means to an end—i.e. for fixing points obtained, and that he would not in-breed with faulty birds. The case of close in-breeding which he cites, of pairing brother and sister, was of two birds most perfect in points—in fact, two show birds, which had both won—and this pairing was with a view to fixing these good all-round properties. From these two birds he bred five young, three Yellows and two Buffs, which promised to be quite as good as their parents; beyond this, further description of them could not be given at the time of getting our notes, as they were then deep in moult.

Mr. Gill writes further:—

"I have paired Yellow to Yellow with very good results, I have also double buffed with good results, and my partner, Mr. Pethick, has on more than one occasion bred winners from double Buffs. At the same time I do not believe in double buffing, as it tends to shorten the number of Yellows. My past experience has taught me that the best results are obtained from pairing Yellow to Buff, or *vice versa*. As regards Cinnamon blood for the improvement of quality of feather I have never tried it, and I fear it would be a step in the wrong direction. I have never seen a Cinnamon in this part with a head good enough for a Norwich. Besides, I do not think it at all necessary to introduce Cinnamon blood into the Norwich. The 'Chubby One' is full of quality in itself, and with careful pairing is, I am sure, quite independent of all other sources. To retain colour I always resort to the Green or Heavily-marked, and breed only from good specimens to retain size."

Mr. F. Beardall's Notes.

Mr. Fred Beardall, of Hucknall Huthwaite, Nottinghamshire, a most successful breeder and exhibitor, gives the following experience:—

"I have never used Crest blood with a view to increase size, and I think it would be disastrous for any Norwich breeder to do so. It might have been used to advantage some twenty years ago, as the older fanciers tell me there were Crest-breds then almost as good in quality as Norwich, besides, there was plenty of Yellow blood amongst the Crest and Crest-breds at that time. I have had very good results from double buffing with a view to increasing size and tightening up feather. One season I paired a Heavily Variegated Buff cock, good type, quality, and size—in fact, a show bird, but being heavily-marked told against him—to a good Clear Buff hen, except that she was a little slack in feather on the back. From them I got three birds; one a Clear Buff cock of grand type and excellent quality, he also came out a grand colour, and did a good bit of winning; the other two were hens, one a Clear Buff, good type and quality, from which I bred a winner, and the other a nice Buff-marked hen. I sold the latter to a friend, who bred some good birds, with plenty of size; in fact, he said one was the largest he had ever bred. The following season I had another nest from this same pair, and got another Clear Buff cock. This bird was never exhibited as an unflighted; but he did a good bit of winning for me afterwards, taking 1st at Nottingham, 1905 and 1906. In the latter year I showed this bird eight times, and he took seven firsts, and an H.C.

"As another instance of double buffing, Mr. Vardy, of Hucknall, bred a Buff Green from two Buffs; it was a cripple in one foot. Mr. Vardy thought it was a hen and sold it as such;

THE NORWICH PLAINHEAD OF TWENTY YEARS AGO.

but it proved a cock, and was again sold for a singing bird. I afterwards bought it, as I knew it was bred from two good birds, and I paired him to a nice Clear Yellow hen which I had bred from a Ticked Yellow that had done some winning for me. From this pair I bred a grand Ticked Buff, and when he was eighteen months old the late Mr. John Sandiford, of Preston, claimed him for £10 10s. at Pendleton show, and afterwards named him 'The King.' This bird was well known to show-goers as one of the finest Ticked Buffs that had been seen in the show seasons of 1901 and 1902. Altogether, then, I have had excellent results from double buffing, but it must not be done too often, or colour will be lost. If there is plenty of variegation in the stock, and double buffing is not resorted to too often, no harm will be done. I may say I have never failed to get good quality from double buffing, besides getting shorter, thicker birds. With regard to Green blood, I have never been without one or more of this class of bird in my room for the past fourteen years.

" I think the best way to get Green birds is to pair two Variegated birds together. One season I paired a Yellow Variegated cock to a Buff cap and wing-marked hen—both good in type and good size—for the purpose of getting some good dark stock birds. I got a good Buff Green hen, and a Heavily Variegated Yellow cock; both these birds were large and of good type, with a good amount of feather, but they carried it tight, and in its proper place. Now these two birds did me a lot of good. From the hen, paired to a Clear Yellow cock, tight in feather, I bred a Clear Buff cock that bred me the best Yellow-marked hen I ever had. From the Yellow-marked cock, paired to a Clear Buff hen—a nice, close-feathered bird—I bred two Buff hens both in one nest, and both show birds. One was slightly marked on each wing, which I showed in 'stock pairs,' and she won when she was six months old. Unfortunately, however, she died when nearly dry, after being washed for the next show. The other hen was a grey-tailed one, with clear body; she did a good bit of winning, including 1st at the International Contest, held at Pendleton between the English and Scotch Norwich Plainhead clubs. I also bred a Buff Green hen from the same Yellow-marked cock, and to this I paired my old saddle-marked Yellow, which won at the Palace for me when an 'unflighted.' He also won at the L. and P.O.S. Show, held at the Palace, previously being shown amongst the old birds, as there was not an unflighted class. He was bred from a Yellow Green hen. From this pair I bred a good Yellow Green hen, also a Variegated Buff cock—the one which I exhibited so successfully in 1905 and 1906, taking 1st at Nottingham, in a class of thirty-one unflighted. I also bred from the same pair the year previous a Ticked Yellow which proved a winner.

" By this it will be seen I have had good results from using plenty of Green blood. I do not think that success would have followed from double buffing if I had not had plenty of Green blood in my stock, though, of course, it must be regulated with Clears so as to breed a good percentage of Clears as well as Green marks; but Green blood is an advantage when double buffing.

" I tried Cinnamon blood in breeding Norwich Plainheads about ten years ago, and found I could get plenty of colour in the young from it; but the type of birds I bred from them did not suit me, so I discarded them.

" The plan that I have found best to get rid of long wings and tail and undesirable carriage is, when I have had good stock birds with plenty of substance and fairly good type, but possessing these faults, to mate them to small hens that have been bred from good typical birds. These hens being small, and bred from typical birds, are short in wings, tail, and body, and when paired to these long flighted and tailed birds have produced good show birds. I have bred show birds from these little hens—hens that some fanciers would not look at a second time. One I remember in particular—I think the smallest hen I ever paired up. She was a Yellow, and I paired her to a large cap and wing-marked Buff cock, which had plenty of substance, but was rather long in wings and tail. From this pair I bred as typical a Buff cock as I ever had, with fair-sized, short wings and tail, and the best of quality; his only fault was that he was a little pinched at the back of the head. He won for me at Leeds; I believe it was the first Norwich Club medal the present Norwich Canary Club gave.

" I should not advise breeding with hens that have long wings and tail. Nearly all small hens bred from good stock have good wing carriage and short wings and tail, so by breeding with these hens one gets short wings and tail and good carriage as well. If long wing and tailed hens are used for Norwich breeding, they must be paired with cocks that are short in wings and tail.

" As to in-breeding, the breeder is quite safe in practising this while he has plenty of size and stamina in his stock, and has a special object in view. I will just give one instance. One season I paired my old saddle-marked Yellow for one nest to a Clear Buff hen to which he was grandsire; this hen was bred from the two Buffs that I mentioned in connection with double buffing, and was sister to my Clear Buff Nottingham winner, but a year older.

DARK CANARY MULES

Yellow Siskin — Yellow Goldfinch

Yellow Linnet — Buff Twite

From grandsire and granddaughter I got three birds all Yellow—i.e. an Evenly-marked hen, an Unevenly-marked hen, and an Unevenly-marked cock. The cock proved a great winner, amongst his honours being 1st at Manchester and Nottingham. This bird was not shown as an 'unflighted,' as he was a very late-hatched bird, and did not get fined down in the first moult; his winnings were secured after the second moult. I only bred with him one season, as he died a week before the Palace Show, being then only nineteen months old."

This shows the effects of in-breeding and the importance of not sacrificing stamina; but as Mr. Beardall points out, he had the consolation that this bird bred before he died the largest Buff hen he ever had, and from his sister, the Unevenly-marked hen, he bred a good Dark bird that won for him in a Dark class. Mr. Beardall's experience is another demonstration of the fact that in-breeding with blood relations should only be adopted as a means to an end, to fix work accomplished. If pursued indiscriminately with any strain or stud of birds there is no surer road to ruin for that said stud, for loss of stamina means eventually loss of the stud; this is fully explained in the chapter on Pedigree and Line Breeding.

Mr. John Trengrove, of Rishton, near Blackburn, another successful breeder and exhibitor, favours us with a summary of his experience. He says:—

Mr. John Trengrove's Notes.

"It is now about sixteen years since I first took up this interesting hobby. I started like most novices, in a very humble way, with only about two pairs of Norwich. For a time failure seemed to dog my every footstep, but still I kept plodding on until better luck knocked at my door. My breeding stock for the last few years has varied from twenty to twenty-five pairs, pairing up in the old-fashioned way, Yellow cock and Buff hen, or *vice versa*, but I do not make any hard and fast line in respect to Yellow and Buff. I have not derived any benefit from double yellowing, I tried this method for a few seasons, but always found that the young bred in this way were very thin in feather, and also failed in type. With double buffing my experience is quite the reverse. By pairing in this way I have been fairly successful, having bred some very good birds that have held their own on the show bench. My Clear Buff 1st and Special for best Norwich at the Crystal Palace show in 1905 was bred from a Buff cock and Buff hen. My Clear Yellow, which held an unbeaten record in 1905, and was 1st at the Crystal Palace in 1906, was bred from a Buff cock bred from Buff parents. But great care must be used when pairing two Buffs. I always use birds of medium size, with good type in the hen, and showing plenty of meal. I am a firm believer in Green blood, and always keep a good supply on hand, Green blood, in my opinion, being the very fountain of colour. Much has been said both for and against in-breeding; but if this method is tried with care the result will be found beneficial both in regard to type and quality of feather, I have had good results in this way; even when pairing son to mother the result has been most satisfactory. Care must be used, however, not to pair the young bred in this way with each other, or the result will be disappointing."

With these notes we take leave of the Norwich Canary. We have endeavoured to indicate the principal steps to be taken in breeding it, but the fancier will discover as he goes on that there are many little by-paths in which he will be able to wander with pleasure, and will find that the general principles we have enunciated will throw ample light on his path, and enable him to make his way with as much of certainty as attaches to a pursuit in which there is a great deal of speculative uncertainty, an element in which perhaps consists much of its charm.

EYE-MARKS ON EVEN-MARKED BIRDS.
The heads are drawn simply to show markings, and not as types of any variety.

CHAPTER XIX

BREEDING EVENLY-MARKED CANARIES

It was natural that the varied forms of marking should arrest fanciers' attention, and that particular shapes should be fixed on both for beauty and difficulty of attainment. This has been the case with all light coloured varieties except Belgian, Scotch Fancy, Lancashire, Dutch Frill and Roller Canaries, whose breeders as yet have placed little value on exact markings.

Our object is to endeavour to show how to produce the highest form of marking—viz. Evenly-marked—and the advice will apply to all varieties of the Canary, as the principles involved in developing and fixing the marks are the same. These Even Marks may be either Green or Cinnamon colour, and beautiful specimens of both have been produced.

We are afraid we shall offer a rude shock to some of our readers when we say that we know of no established strain of Evenly-marked Canaries which will reproduce all their progeny more or less evenly-marked. Indeed, so far from Even Marks being a fixed "variety," there are to-day only a few rare specimens which make their way into our shows. We can assure our readers that the small number which do appear in the category "Evenly-marked" will bear a liberal discounting when carefully examined, even though it cast a reflection on the exhibition morality of the day.

How to Breed Evenly-marked Birds.

The truth is, that even-marking is not the permanent feature of an established strain —though that is no reason why it should not be. Owing to the fact that such markings have been produced by experimenting in pairing evenly, or almost evenly-marked birds together, we are not only convinced that this is the way to perpetuate even marks, but that it is the *only* way by which Evenly-marked strains of birds can be established. Moreover, the task is not impossible. Failure in the past has been due to selection not being pursued far enough owing to lack of patience after the result of the first year or two. Until characteristics become fixed, much sporting is bound to occur, and a large proportion of the produce be disappointing; but with care and perseverance control can be obtained, and each year show in the produce a larger proportion of birds well balanced in markings.

The breeder must enter upon his task with the idea that he is going to arrest a very erratic beauty. And what is this beauty? In itself it is nothing extraordinary, being simply the dark pencilling encircling the eye, a description of marking common to many foreign Finches, and which we think is perhaps the counterpart of a somewhat similar feature native to the wild Canary. This may or may not be so; but it is worthy of note that when the domesticated bird has lost every other trace of dark plumage, here it seems frequently to linger, as if it were hard to eradicate entirely this old family mark.

The Beauty of Marking.

These eye-stripes are referred to in the Editor's Introduction to the "Book of Birds" from the text of Dr. Brehm. "There are many birds which have stripes of variously coloured feathers situated above, before, and behind the eye; while others sometimes occur at the base of the lower mandible. To all these distinct names have been appropriated. A *superciliary* stripe is situated *above* the eye, occupying a position analogous to that of the human eyebrow. An ordinary eye-stripe is either *anterior*, *posterior*, or *entire*. It is called *anterior* when it only occupies the space between the eye and the bill; *posterior* when it commences behind the eye and advances or unites with the ear-feathers; and *entire* when it is both posterior and anterior. A *maxillary* stripe commences at the base of the under mandible and descends on the sides of the neck."

We referred on page 218 to that form of marking which is considered by the fancier to be *the* correct thing, and which may be seen in the Evenly-marked birds on the coloured plates; also the Evenly-marked Yorkshire on page 103, and also to other forms not so highly prized, all of which find their counterparts in the description given above, and which a reference to the illustrations on the opposite page will make sufficiently plain. The heads portrayed are not typical, but serve the purpose of showing the forms of marking. In Figs. *a* and *b* the anterior and posterior stripes will be recognised, and in Fig. *c* will be noticed a combination of the anterior and superciliary marks, the latter when it occurs really as a mark and not in an exaggerated form, being usually very clearly defined in outline. Figs. *d* and *e* represent enlarged forms of anterior and posterior marking, the latter not only advancing towards but uniting with the ear-feathers, where it loses its character and eventually breaks into an objectionable patch, which sometimes almost breaks the heart of the fancier. That considered the most perfect eye-mark, called the "Spectacle Mark," is shown in Fig. *f*.

To fix this feature with exactness is the object in view. And is this all? No; there is a corresponding exactness in the marking of the flight-feathers to be secured; but this is not a matter of so much difficulty, the wings appearing to be much more tractable and open to impression than the much-coveted eye-mark of the fancier. Whether or not our theory as to the probable origin of this mark be correct, is, perhaps, not much to our present purpose; but we might say further in its support that this particular form of eye-mark, a long streak from front to back, frequently appears with more or less regularity of form in the most heavily and irregularly variegated birds, which have *never in any way been bred with a view to its production*, and it will also occasionally appear in lighter strains, in which, if any attempt has been made, it has been in the direction of *entire obliteration*.

Evenly-marked Canaries at present are thus, with but a few exceptions, chance productions, and this is evident from the statistics of our largest shows. Take the Crystal Palace, for instance; there were in 1877 two hundred and forty-three Clear and Variegated birds

Modern Apathy.

staged as against forty-eight Evenly-marked, many of which had only very slight claims to the title, while some did not belong to the class at all ; and to-day less attention is apparently paid to Evenly-marked Canaries than in 1877, for while the Clear, Ticked and Variegated birds at the Crystal Palace show in 1910 had increased to more than five times the number of 1877, the Even Marks did not reach a dozen. The reason is that most breeders now pay little attention to markings so long as they can breed a bird that can win. It was not so with the old fanciers of 1877, who knew the value of an Evenly-marked bird too well to allow it to slip through their fingers. They never lost sight of good markings in the pairing of their birds, though they did not pursue their course long enough to secure their object permanently. We were sinners ourselves in this respect, but of late years have given the subject closer attention, and with most satisfactory results. It is an advantage to the exhibitor to endeavour to breed Evenly-marked birds, as, through paying careful attention to markings, those birds which are *not* Evenly-marked are much more attractive than the Unevenly-marked bred in a haphazard way, as the marks are neater, and more evenly distributed. Many such neat Unevenly-marked birds were to be seen at our exhibitions thirty years ago, but to-day most Marked birds are of the ordinary Variegated type. We are glad, however, to see that, of late, in some varieties, the Border Fancy, to wit, the Evenly-marked bird is growing in popular favour, and a few breeders have given it their special attention, though we do not think the results are as yet so fixed in their character as to warrant our saying that any reliable strain has been established. Yet if such Evenly-marked birds are the outcome of careful breeding for several years, and are paired to others that have been equally carefully bred, much will have been accomplished, and it is only a matter of following the system up to establish the points explained under "Pedigree or Line Breeding."

As proof that in endeavouring to breed Even Marks we improve the neatness of the uneven marks we have only to refer to the classes of Border Fancies for the latter at our shows ; many of them are almost even, certainly none of them badly marked, as seen in other varieties. There was a time when the Yorkshire Canary could boast of more Even Marks than any other variety, and it played no small part in assisting to establish the good markings in the Border Fancy of to-day. It is a great pity that the Yorkshire Canary does not hold the proud position to-day it did thirty to forty years ago for good Even Marks, and we hope that some of its admirers may yet be induced to follow those old breeders who made this branch a special study, and bring the Evenly-marked Yorkshire back to the proud position it once held. There is plenty of material to select from, for in this variety there are some of the most beautiful of Uneven Marks, both Green and Cinnamon. We know that fraudulent practices were much indulged in by some in the old days to make birds appear Even-marked which really were not, and that such was not elevating to the hobby, but that is no reason why we should cease to strive to breed Evenly-marked birds in a legitimate way, and at the same time stamp out any attempt otherwise with a strong hand.

The Necessary Marks.

In enunciating a few general principles which must be observed in trying to produce these beautiful birds, we must direct the attention of the breeder to the fact that there are some things he wants and must have, and other things he does not want and must endeavour to eradicate. He wants chiefly well-formed and decided eye-marks. Every fancier knows the value of these, though it would be equally correct to say he does *not* know their value, for their worth cannot be over-estimated. He also wants lightly and exactly-marked wings, and he who has had any experience knows he can breed a hundred good wings for one good eye. If we add a correspondingly exact marking in the tail to the extent of a feather or two on each side—which, by the way, owing to their not adding much to his beauty, the bird is as well without—we have indicated the necessaries. Then he does *not* want, and must not on any account have, any body-marks, which are the great bugbear to be exorcised. The great difficulty, indeed *the* difficulty, will be in making a beginning, because, select what stock he may, and let it look ever so promising, the probability is that, unless it really has been bred for some length of time with due regard to the principles of selection and rejection, the offspring will show surprisingly little of the points desired. In commencing, therefore, the first thing we should insist on is that the birds chosen should be entirely free from body-marks of any kind, except those desired, because when it is remembered how intimately these are connected with irregular variegation, liable at any time to make its appearance in the most provoking way, it will be plain that any trace of this should be studiously eschewed. The accompaniments of this sort of thing, also, and the indications of its presence not far beneath the surface, such as any considerable amount of dark flue, dark legs, or dark beak, must be considered as dangerous concomitants to an otherwise promising-looking bird, and will represent shoals and quicksands the dangers of which will be patent to those who have read carefully our remarks on development of clear colour from the normal green in breeding the Norwich Plainhead. Fully satisfied as we are, both from practical experience and extensive observation, that our theory on this point is correct, and based on sound premises, we should select birds which, as regards the body, fulfilled all the requirements of Clear birds, although the *bona fide* marking on them was not strictly even, but was really marking, as technically understood, and nothing more —that is to say, we should not hesitate to breed from birds having nothing further than one good eye-mark, or good eyes and only one wing, or any similar defective arrangement of the feathers we do want, provided only there were the entire absence of those we do not want. Birds having eye-marks only, or wing-marks unsupported, we should regard as valuable material so long as they were clear in the body; and even these will, when paired together or with absolute Clears, throw quite sufficient irregularly-pied birds severely to try the patience of the most patient breeder at first. We need scarcely say that birds showing all the desired points in a high degree of perfection would of course be valuable allies; but it may be accepted as a fact that the greater the amount of the marking, the greater the risk of reverting to the variegated form; and we know that this risk is so great that we would, in beginning, *prefer* breeding from the lesser degree of marking and take our chance of getting it reproduced in an improved form, to breeding from birds in which the heavier marking, if not established, would be almost certain to land us in a wilderness of blotches and irregular patches. That is, instead of putting two such birds together marked on eyes and wings, pair one such up to a bird marked on both eyes, and the rest of the body clear or even one marked on one eye only, and the rest of the body clear, or a Clear bred from Even Marks. The strength of dark blood is thus reduced, the tendency to variegation averted.

How to Proceed.

Unevenly-marked birds, such as we have referred to, are not difficult to find; they frequently occur in large stocks, and some, not being exhibition birds, are not generally much valued, and the breeder who is on the lookout for them will be able, in the course of a season, to pick up many such. These opportunities should not be neglected, always having due regard to the quality or character of the marking, and not gathering up indiscriminate rubbish, but neat birds, free from objectionable features and showing some one desirable point clearly developed.

This, we think, will show the description of raw material we should select, and our reasons for so doing; and anyone who has rushed into breeding Marked birds in a blind faith in the like-producing-like creed will admit that we have not one whit exaggerated its difficulties, nor made one mole-hill into a mountain. We know only too well what it means and how it is usually set about; and though a slice of luck may occasionally accompany a turn of the wheel of fortune, or nearly the whole hand turn up trumps, yet we know how hit-or-miss breeding ends in the long-run.

This carefully-selected stock will require equally careful pairing; and in doing so we should, at starting, make colour a secondary consideration—that is, we should not for one moment allow any rule as to pairing Yellow and Buff, or *vice versa,* to interfere with our main object, which is marking. If we found the necessary combinations existing in the opposite forms of colour, well and good, but we should not be diverted from our purpose for the sake of keeping up perfection of colour or feather. We fully recognise the truth that "extremes are dangerous," and would certainly do our utmost to maintain these desirable requisites; but it is marking we want, and marking we must have—note the "must"—with colour, if possible, but marking at all events. And bearing in mind that while we are endeavouring, by mating marks, to concentrate in one channel the tendency to produce them, as we are, at the same time, concentrating two forms of development of native Green or Cinnamon, we should be very careful to avoid pairing two Heavily-marked birds, lest the combination of two streams of Green or Cinnamon blood, as the case might be, should cause an overflow on the body; we would mate a Heavily-marked hen with a Clear cock, and *vice versa,* the Clear being bred from the technically or Evenly-marked stock. This is an excellent plan with birds from an established stock when there is a tendency to get too heavy markings; the Clear bird reduces the weight of marking in the offspring. Here we could mate Yellow and Buff, and maintain colour and feather. Very lightly-marked birds we would pair; but not if both had dark legs, or we should not be astonished to find a speedy reversion to heavy variegation.

Birds with eye-marks only we would couple occasionally, as they require more nursing to maintain than wing-marks. We would also pair an only eye-marked bird to one with wing marks. You then have in the two birds the combination of a desirable Even Mark. An odd wing is very apt to be repeated, but knowing how certainly heavy wings will produce what we do not want, we would prefer one wing, if containing only three or four dark feathers, and run the chance of getting a neat V by pairing it to a bird with the opposite wing marked in a similar manner and the eyes marked on one or both birds.

We should not be disappointed if we obtained a lot of odd wings, provided they were neat; on the contrary, we should be pleased, as it would indicate some tendency towards fixity, and we would wait patiently for duplicate marks. We should never expect to produce accurate marking in any quantity, and should be more than satisfied if we simply held our ground. To do that would be virtually to advance, for one step made good means protecting our rear, and security from retrogression.

Wing Marks.

The illustration on page 241 represents an expanded wing, in which the six inner flights alone are dark, the larger and smaller coverts, as well as the bastard flights attached to the thumb, all being clear. This may be accepted as a perfect wing from a fancier's point of view. There are one or two features in the formation of the wing worthy of note. When expanded to its full extent it will be seen that the marginal outline formed by the extremities of the feathers is practically a straight line: the stalk or midrib of the outer flights is close to the outer edge of the feather, and the ends of these feathers are pointed; but as we proceed towards the inner portion of the wing the midrib is found nearer and nearer the centre of the web, the dark feathers are fringed with a lighter margin, and the extremities alter in shape from pointed to round, becoming squarer and squarer in each succeeding feather till the tip is merely rounded off at the corners, the inner flights or concluding portion of the secondary feathers, however, again becoming more ovate and less substantial in their structure. When the wing is folded and at rest the marginal line is entirely changed, being almost as irregular as is that of the human hand when the fingers are extended and consequently at rest. Close the hand, as when in the act of grasping, and the tips of the fingers will be found to be as much in a straight line as is the margin of the wing when in action.

A PERFECTLY-MARKED WING.
(The six inner flights alone are dark.)

A WING SHOWING SEVERAL DEFECTS WHICH ARE LIKELY TO BE PRODUCED EITHER SEPARATELY OR COMBINED.

The second illustration on this page represents a type of wing to which we made reference on page 219. We insert the cut here to show the breeder in one view *several* defects that he will be sure to produce either separately or combined. There is the otherwise perfect wing, but that the larger coverts corresponding to the dark flights are dark also. Note, this is not exactly a blemish, but the wing is better without them, for we have just shown how apt the green or cinnamon colour is to *run over,* and the next step would probably be a few green or cinnamon feathers in the margin of the saddle. There is also the *mixed* wing, an unfortunate white feather intruding itself among the dark ones, or *vice versa.* Observe, also, that the bastard quills are dark, and that the first row of small coverts is also dark—serious blemishes which it must be sought to eliminate.

The breeder will have to content himself with very slow progress on the journey, and even approximations to what he desires must be accepted and made the most of. Where we found that any particular pairing had the direct effect of fixing the point aimed at, we should again pair the birds so bred, either among themselves, by selecting cocks and hens from the same nest, or with their own father or mother, for once, if the stock was tolerably robust and free from any weakly tendencies, or with others from nests in which similar results had been obtained, and so endeavour still further to unite the various streams and concentrate the same tendencies in one channel. This would, it is obvious, necessitate some departure from the regular beaten tracks of everyday practice, but it must not be forgotten there is a specific object for doing so.

We have known of an Evenly-marked bird being produced from a Green and a Clear. We have also produced a really good Even Green marked bird from an almost Self-Cinnamon cock, having only a light feather in one wing and the tail, paired to a Clear hen. It is only reasonable, then, with a force of dark colour immediately behind such even-marked birds, to anticipate much sporting in their offspring until the dark colour is gradually reduced to its proper strength and place by careful selection and judicious pairing of not only one, but several generations, even then continuing to select, as described in Chapter XVI., in the direction from which one is getting the desired results. It would also be folly to pair two birds together so bred, both marked eyes and wings; such would be preferable paired to Clear birds bred from marked stock, and then select the best marked birds of their progeny to pair back to marked birds as described in our first selection.

The Cinnamon Cross.

The question may naturally arise: Are there any other reliable sources from which to draw in breeding Evenly-marked Canaries?" The reply is: "Yes." We have referred to cinnamon colour, but not to its virtues, and whether it be owing to its well-known tenacious characteristics when crossed with birds of colour other than its own, and the sexual influence necessary to reproduce this colour, it is quite unnecessary here to discuss. But suffice it to say no bird has or does play a more important part in breeding Even-marked Canaries than the Cinnamon, and we have little hesitation in saying that nineteen out of every twenty Evenly-marked Canaries, be they green marked or cinnamon marked, are bred from the introduction of Cinnamon blood either directly or indirectly. Its tendency to fix eye and wing marks are indisputable, and a little of this blood should always be kept in the strain even when breeding green Even Marks. It is not necessary to introduce a pure Self-coloured Cinnamon, for a cinnamon-marked bird answers equally well, or a clear pink-eyed bird which, though clear, is bred from Cinnamon blood. There are plenty of these and Cinnamon-marked birds to select from, either in Norwich or Yorkshires or Border Fancies. In fact, cinnamon-marked birds are to be met with in almost all varieties, except perhaps the Lizard and London Fancy. But the three varieties previously mentioned are the chief ones in which Even Marks are bred. Therefore selection can be made without difficulty from the type of bird one is breeding, and it rests entirely with breeders to make even marks as permanent a characteristic of our canaries, either in the green or cinnamon colour, as other points already fixed by selection.

Scale of Points for Judging Evenly-Marked Canaries

(*a*) EVENLY-MARKED NORWICH

Points of Merit

Marking	*Maximum*
Eyes.—For neatness and regularity of outline—Anterior mark, 10; Posterior, 10; Entire	25
Wings.—For exactness, decreasing in value as the marking extends beyond the secondary flights or encroaches on the wing-coverts	15
Tail.—If not accompanied by discoloured tail-coverts—for exactness	5
Shape and Size.—That of the recognised Norwich Standard.	15
Feather.—For compactness of body-feather and carriage of wings and tail . . .	15
Saddle.—For width and clear margin . .	5
Colour.—For depth and purity of body-colour	10
Condition	10
	Total, 100

Negative Properties

An Evenly-marked Norwich Canary should not have broken or ragged eye-marks or irregular patches on the side of the head, nor marks running towards the top or front of the head over the beak, nor should it have a dark cap, however symmetrical. It should not show any light flight-feathers mixed with the dark, nor any marking on the greater or lesser wing-coverts, nor on the still smaller coverts fringing the upper margin of the wing, which, when the bird is at rest, are hidden by the scapulars, nor should the feathers of the bastard wing be dark. It should not show any dark feathers on the margin of the saddle where the feathers merge with those of the wing-coverts, nor any discoloration in the upper or lower tail-coverts, nor should there be any mark whatever to interfere with a "clean run," above and below, from the beak to the tail.

(*b*) EVENLY-MARKED YORKSHIRES

Points of Merit

Marking	*Maximum*
Eyes.—For neatness and regularity of outline, and for distinctness	25
Wings.—For exactness, decreasing in value as the marking extends beyond the secondary flights or encroaches on the larger wing-coverts	15
Tail.—For exactness free from discoloured coverts	5
Shape and Position.—That of the recognised Yorkshire Standard	20

Marking	*Maximum*
Feather.—For compact body-feather, and close carriage of wings and tail	20
Colour.—For pure body-colour and brilliancy of markings	5
Condition and sound feather	10
	Total, 100

Negative Properties

An Evenly-marked Yorkshire should not have broken or ragged eye-marks, nor any of the irregular forms not recognised by the laws governing eye-marking, neither should it have a dark cap, however symmetrical. It should not have a "mixed" wing, nor should any feathers attached to the wing be dark, excepting the necessary number of flights; and specially, the feathers of the bastard wing should not be dark. It should not show any discoloured feathers on the margin of the saddle or where the feathers merge with those of the wing-coverts, nor any discoloration in the upper or lower tail-coverts, nor should there be any mark whatever to interfere with a clear run, above and below, from the beak to the tail, nor any other violation of the simple law which determines the difference between technical "marking" and variegation.

(*c*) EVENLY-MARKED BORDER FANCIES

Points of Merit

Marking	*Maximum*
Eyes.—For neatness and regularity of outline and distinctness	25
Wings.—For exactness decreasing in value as the marking extends beyond the secondary flights or encroaches on the larger wing coverts	15
Tail.—For exactness free from discoloured tail coverts	5
Shape and Position.—That of the recognised Border Fancy Standard	20
Feather.—For compact body-feather and close carriage of wings and tail	20
Colour.—For pure body-colour and brilliancy of markings	5
Condition and sound feather	10
	Total, 100

Negative Properties

An Evenly-marked Border should not have broken or ragged eye-marks, nor any of the irregular forms not recognised by the laws governing eye-marking, neither should it have a dark cap, however symmetrical. It should not have a mixed wing, nor should any feathers attached to the wing be dark excepting the necessary number of flights, and especially the feathers of the bastard wing should not be dark. It should not show any discoloured feathers on the margin of the saddle, or where the feathers merge with those of the wing coverts, nor any discoloration in the upper or lower tail-coverts, nor should there be any mark whatever to interfere with a clear run, above and below, from the beak to the tail, nor any other violation of the simple law which determines the difference between technical "marking" and variegation.

CHAPTER XX

THE GREEN CANARY

THE name of this breed—or even that of "Grass-Greens," as they are sometimes called—singularly fails to convey a correct idea of the colour, for we have yet to see a true Grass-Green Canary. We shall, perhaps, not make matters much clearer if we say the colour is a very green green, and that in the purity of the green and its freedom from any tinge of orange or yellow consists its value.

There are, of course, Yellows and Buffs among these Canaries, just as in their lighter coloured relatives. As a race they belong almost exclusively to the North, which was their early home, and still remains so. Certain forms of them peculiar to certain districts almost constitute, indeed, a separate colour family, and at one time no schedule issued in the North would have been considered complete without a class for the popular "Green Canary"—a somewhat vague definition, it must be admitted, and attaching it to no particular variety. As regards shape, it would have been difficult to assign some of them a definite place, as the fanciers of the colour in the old days developed it on any base according to taste, and the bird appeared in all shapes, from indifferent Belgian down to the nondescript type known as "Common." In most instances, however, length, erect stand, smart build, and other characteristics of the Yorkshire indicated, if not the probable source of the main stream, at all events the direction in which it was wished to divert it.

For many years the Yorkshire type was the only one given serious attention by breeders of the Green Canary, and so well did they progress in that direction that to-day the Yorkshire Green compares favourably as regards shape, carriage, and quality with other branches of the Yorkshire Canary. But fanciers of the Green Canary have advanced beyond this, and to-day we have three distinct types of the bird for which classes are provided at our shows. They are the Yorkshire, Norwich, and Border Fancy, to say nothing of many that are bred in the Scotch Fancy variety of this colour. Each section continues to make splendid progress in type and colour, and the adoption of the various types to breed to has greatly increased the number of breeders and birds by giving a wider scope for individual taste, and this in time will ensure the Greens being taken up more generally throughout the country.

Types of Greens.

We cannot see our way clear to pronounce the Green Canary a distinct variety on the ground of its colour, which is simply the basic form of several varieties from which clear plumage has been gradually developed. If we accept that theory as the foundation of its claim, then must we admit Green Scotch Fancies into competition with any Green form, simply because they are green —a most absurd proceeding. More in accordance with the principles of natural arrangement is it to classify under each variety the different forms of colour in which that variety appears, but such strict attention has been paid, and continues to be paid, to the breeding of Greens as a speciality in the three varieties named, that we think the breeding of the Green Canary worthy a chapter to itself; leaving, of course, their classification in accordance with the various types of bird bred to. That is, a Green of the Yorkshire type

Not a Distinct Variety.

must be the counterpart of the recognised Yorkshire standard in every particular except colour; and the same holds good as regards the Norwich and Border Fancy types.

Colour Points.

The colour points of a Green Canary are the purity and brilliancy of the green, its uniform distribution, and the absence of black stripes in the feathers of the back—for, the heavier the black stripes are on the back the heavier as a rule are they on the flanks; the narrower and fainter these stripes are the better the shade of green that is obtained, and the more even is the green colour on the back as well as other parts. This is due to the absence of the black pigment from which these black stripes are derived, and which is so much stronger than the green.

The flights and tail feathers should be a glossy black, edged with a delicate margin of green. Nowhere must there be seen any indications of running or breaking in the colour, which must throughout be characteristic of a genuine dark rich green self.

These remarks apply to Yellow and Buff alike; the Buffs, of course, do not display the lustre or depth of colour on the feather so vividly as do the Yellows; but in a good Buff the green is very pure in tone.

Dark coloured beak, legs, feet and toe-nails are also desirable features in a Self Green Canary.

We like size in both Yorkshire and Norwich type Greens, though, of course, in the case of the Yorkshire size refers to good length without bulk, as the body of a Yorkshire is slim and of upright carriage. The Norwich type should be stout in build and stand well across the perch.

Colour the Chief Consideration.

While size is to be desired in both types, colour must be the ruling feature. Get size with colour if you can, but good colour must never be sacrificed for size. Purity and brilliance of colour, shape and quality, are the first essentials of a good Green Canary, whether it be of the Yorkshire, Norwich, or Border Fancy type.

Breeding.

The principal thing to be kept in view in selecting breeding stock, then, is good sound colour, and in the Yorkshire type to secure length, shape, and style without coarseness—features not always procurable on demand, or good Yorkshires would not be so valuable as they are. It is the difficulty of producing, or we had better say approaching, the ideal that enhances the value and lends pleasure to our hobby.

In selecting breeding stock of the Norwich type, colour must again lead, followed by shape, combined with size without coarseness, for freedom from coarseness as a rule ensures good quality. The same applies equally to the Border Fancy. Sound, brilliant colour, and good shape and quality are required; coarseness in any shape or form mars the combined finish.

Variations in Progeny.

In our description of the bird it was stated that there must be no break in the colour, which must be throughout characteristic of a genuine dark Self. There are many otherwise good coloured birds that run just a little light on the flanks or at the throat, and this tendency often appears in the progeny where one of the parents is a variegated or foul-marked bird, and the other, of course, self green. The partial light coloured bird is sometimes used to enrich the colour, and at other times to brighten the tone. The light blood in the variegated birds reduces the strength of black pigment in the green. The progeny of these light-throated and light-flanked birds, if otherwise of good colour, can be improved by pairing them back to good Self Greens that have been bred from pure Selfs for two or three generations.

When striving to get the dark stripes—or "pencilling," as it is called by many breeders—as fine as possible, with a view to obtaining a richer green, the breeder at times gets some birds light on flanks and throat. Such should be paired to birds that are somewhat heavy in the dark striping on the back, as these are usually a dark shade of colour—a very deep rich green—on the neck, breast and flanks. The pairing of a light-throated and flanked bird to such a partner usually produces offspring that are superior to either of the parents, both the over dark shade, and the light throat being improved.

A Green produced from Cinnamon blood is also an excellent partner to pair with a view to improving these too light shades or patches. It is always well to pair foul-marked birds to Self Greens that have been bred from self-coloured birds for two or three generations.

Two Buff birds are also paired together at times, especially in the Norwich type, with a view to improving size and thickening the web of the feather. On the other hand two Yellows are sometimes paired together in the Yorkshire, Norwich, and Border types with a view to gaining richer and purer colour in the offspring or refining the feather.

Experience and a glance at Chapter XVI. will show the breeder when these departures from the usual pairing of Yellow Green to Buff Green, or *vice versa*, is advantageous, or when a foul-marked bird will be better than a Self to pair to a Self. A careful breeder is always watching how the tide of his stock is flowing, and acts accordingly in future pairing.

Cinnamon Blood.

A dash of Cinnamon blood introduced at times on the hen's side has an excellent effect, enriching and deepening the tone of colour as well as greatly improving the quality of feather, and we have already cited one instance where such is the case. In taking a cross from the Cinnamon we should pair up a good rich coloured foul or variegated Green cock to a rich coloured Cinnamon or cinnamon-marked hen; the cock Buff and the hen Yellow, or two Yellows, if one is not of the richest shade. In fact, it is often an advantage to pair two Yellows at this stage, and from their progeny select two or three of the best and richest coloured Green or green-marked Yellow hens to introduce into the Green stock. Some breeders are opposed to this, while others uphold it and produce proof that some of their very best and most successful show-birds were produced by the use of a little Cinnamon blood. We propose to cite experiences on both sides of the question. Personally we have always upheld it as necessity occurred, because we have produced some of the finest Greens by using it judiciously. The greatest objection we have heard raised against Cinnamon blood in the breeding of Greens is that it produces a bronze shade. With this we entirely agree if the Cinnamon blood is used too freely; but if the offspring is paired back to Greens free from Cinnamon blood for several generations, the bronze shade is avoided, and the beneficial effects are maintained for some years without further introduction of the Cinnamon direct. We write this from experience, for birds of the best and purest of grassy-green shade we ever bred were from Green hens three times removed from the Cinnamon paired to pure Greens. And it is just possible some of those who do not believe in Cinnamon blood may have purchased such Green hens, from which they may have bred some of their good Greens, not knowing that the said hens were bred from Cinnamon blood.

It is not advisable to use Cinnamon blood on the cock's side, as this would produce some cinnamon-coloured young, which, of course, would be hens, as explained in the chapter on Cinnamon breeding; thus when taking a cross from the Cinnamon it is only necessary to retain a few of the best young hens from the cross for future use. Care must also be exercised in the class of Cinnamon selected, for crossing any kind of a bird will not do, and here possibly is the cause of some of the trouble complained of by those opposed to its use. It is useless to introduce a poor coloured Cinnamon with a dull smoky tendency; the bird *must be* a bright, rich colour. Again, the introduction of the Cinnamon blood may have been at an inopportune time or made too frequently. Any one of these mistakes would account for the objection raised against it.

When introducing Cinnamon blood the type of bird selected must be either Yorkshire, Norwich, or Border Fancy, according to the variety it is to be paired with.

In all pairing, the endeavour should never be lost sight of to produce good dark beaks, legs, feet, and toes, by pairing any birds which are not good in these properties to those which are good, at the same time correcting other weak points, such as coarse beak, coarse or flat head, lack of smartness of finish, size, slackness of feather and other faults in a like manner. With the Yorkshire type "breediness" or style must be bred for by selection just as other points.

GREEN CANARIES.

Yorkshire Type. Norwich Type.

We are indebted to Mr. John Abbott, of Liverpool, a breeder and exhibitor of Yorkshire Greens, for the following notes on the breeding of Greens :—

"In breeding the Yorkshire Green Canary I have found the following method the best :

purchase the best birds you can get hold of, not necessarily show birds; but good stock ones, bred from show birds. The cocks to be of good size and colour, with good dark legs and beak, about 7 ins. in length, and smart carriage. The hens to be of good type and quality with a bit of breed and style about them, as near the standard length as it is possible to get them. I pair a Yellow Green cock with a Buff Green hen or *vice versa*. I like to pair a Self with a foul or marked bird, if the Self is a little too dark. But if the Self Greens are not too dark I pair two Selfs with good results, if they are suitable for one another—that is, where one fails the other must have the required points.

Mr. John Abbott's Notes on Yorkshire Greens.

"With regard to crosses, I always introduce fresh blood from the hen's side. I have used both Cinnamon and green-marked birds when the Greens were getting a bit too dark, but I get the best results from green-marked Yorkshires, as I find by introducing Cinnamon blood I get the greens too smoky, or mouse-coloured; whereas by using the green-marked Yorkshire hen I get better colour, type, and quality."

Mr. John Walker on Norwich Greens.

We are also indebted to Mr. John Walker, of Liverpool, a most successful breeder and exhibitor of the Norwich Green, for the following notes:—

"I know of no other variety of the Canary that has made greater strides during the past six years than the Norwich Green. From the small bird of old times it has now become a big, bold bird, and almost perfect in other points. To win on the show bench to-day the bird must be of good size, colour, type, and quality. In breeding the Norwich Green we must never forget that size is wanted. If a bird is almost perfect in other respects, and has not size, judges as a rule are loth to put it forward. I usually like size on the cock's side, also colour and good head properties. The hens must be good type, have good wing carriage and quality of feather. By size I mean birds that possess a good frame, which is quite distinct from birds that look big owing to the amount of feather they carry.

"Before saying anything about matching the birds for breeding, I should like to emphasise the importance of this. I consider it to be *the* most important point in Canary culture. It is that which determines progress or retrogression. One may purchase first prize winners, but if not matched correctly they will only produce indifferent looking specimens, whereas moderate looking stock, properly matched, will produce birds very much better than themselves. I myself have bred some of my best birds from birds for which I could only get songster price. I like in pairing one of the birds to be a 'foul'—that is, one with a light patch on the body or light feather in the wings or tail of an otherwise green bird—because by this means we are able to keep a brighter yet rich shade of green. I prefer the cock to be a Self Green, because there is then a better chance of getting Selfs in the progeny, which is the ideal at which we are aiming. To produce size, I have already said I usually like big cocks, the exception being when I want big hens; I then use medium size cocks with big hens. I have not yet bred a big hen from a small one.

"For colour I insist upon the cocks being level in colour, and of the correct shade, which is a rich deep grass green, with no foul throat or foul mark of any kind on the body; the pencilling to be distinct, and, if possible, the beak, legs, and feet dark.

"For type I look to the hen. She must be as near to the 'ideal' as possible. At the same time the cock must not be overlooked in this respect, and he must on no account be weak in head.

"Matching for feather or balancing the feather when pairing is the most important point of all. It is here that the novices sadly fail; they will pair birds together which look big, due only to the amount of feather they carry, when the resulting progeny will be small framed birds. Then again two fine feathered birds will be paired together, the result being narrow necks. I like plenty of feathers providing they are well carried, and fit the body closely, and are of good quality; to such a bird I should pair another possessing a good frame. In breeding for Yellow birds I allow a little more bulk than when breeding for Buffs. I occasionally double-buff, but the birds must be suitable; they must be clean cut and show no looseness at the thighs. Double-buffing tends to give the tail a shortened appearance, owing to the thickening of the web of the feather filling up round the vent and base of tail, while it improves the neck. Double-yellowing has a contrary effect, making the web of the feather finer—and so giving it a lengthened appearance; while it also tends to produce a narrow neck. With regard to crosses, they are not so much required now as formerly, and it is much better for the novice to start with the ready-made article.

"I have tried three crosses to produce the Norwich Green—the Variegated Norwich, the Cinnamon, and the Crest. I first started with the Variegated Norwich, and I obtained some typical Norwich Greens, but they failed in size. A feature of this cross is that the green offspring are, as a rule, smaller than their variegated parents. From two Variegated Norwich I bred what I consider was the best Norwich Green that has graced the show bench, but it failed in size, and with two exceptions had to take second place to a bird that beat it in this respect. One of these exceptions was at the Welsh National Show, Swansea, where it took first prize.

"The Cinnamon cross has been the most useful to me; by it we gain quality and size, although we lose a little in colour at first, and are apt to get long-sided birds with weak heads. I find the Cinnamon hen to be the best for the purpose; but the one selected must be as chubby and as short in wings and tail as possible. The Norwich Green which won the Diploma at the London Cage Bird Association's Show, held at the Horticultural Hall, Westminster, 1909, was bred from a Variegated Green cock paired to a Buff Cinnamon hen. The Buff cock which won first and special at the Scottish National Show in 1908–9 was bred in a like manner, and, what is more, a son of this last bird won first and a similar special in 1909–10. These results prove the worth of Cinnamon blood if used with care.

"Crossing with the Crest has not been of much service to me; what has been gained in size and colour has been more than lost by undesirable features in the young, such as coarse feather, long wings, tail, and sides, and flat heads.

"I am a great believer in inbreeding, and consider it is the only way to make a definite strain; but the birds must be suitable for inbreeding. Birds to be inbred must have some particular point of excellence which the breeder wishes to establish; not only this, there must not be any really weak points, because if there are these weak points would be established as well as the strong one.

"To sum up my experience, I should say to the beginner in breeding Norwich Greens: Start with the ready-made article, getting the best possible birds that the purse will allow, then, by selection, careful attention to matching, and judicious inbreeding, endeavour to produce better birds than those started with. I may conclude by saying that these notes have been written chiefly to aid the beginner; but if by chance they prove of benefit to older fanciers the pleasure of having written them will be all the greater."

Mr. Thomas Harrison, of Altrincham, another most successful breeder of the Norwich type Green, to whom we are indebted for the following interesting notes on the breeding of this variety, says:

Mr. Thos. Harrison on Norwich Greens.

"During the last few years the Norwich Green has made good strides towards the shape of the Clear or Ticked Norwich, and compares very favourably with the winners on the show bench to-day. The method of pairing should be carefully thought out before commencing the breeding season; success on the show bench more often than not depends upon this important point; never pair up at random. The method I usually adopt is as follows: Self Yellow cock, Self Buff hen, No. 1 pair; Self Buff cock and Self Yellow hen No. 2 pair; Self-Buff cock, Foul Buff hen, No. 3 pair; Self Yellow cock, Self Yellow hen, No. 4 pair; Self Buff cock twice double-buffed, Foul Buff hen twice double-buffed, No. 5 pair; Foul Buff cock very slightly foul and Variegated Yellow hen, No. 6 pair, and so on throughout the room.

"The use of Cinnamon blood I do not care for, nor the crossing with any other variety. In my opinion the careful selection of the *real* thing—viz. the Norwich—is quite sufficient. With reference to pairing as above, it will be noted that No. 3 pair will be double buffs; the reason for this is to increase size and colour. I use the Foul hen for the purpose of getting the body a little lighter colour. No. 4 pair I put up for the express purpose of hens only which I pair up the following year to the cocks from No. 5 pair (twice double-buffed). No. 6 pair is very useful with which to produce stock birds.

"When selecting birds prior to pairing, I select hens that are short and stumpy, heads nicely rounded, with tail and flights as short as possible, and neatly carried; cocks with broad chest and good broad skull; and when placing two foul birds together, I like the beaks, legs, and feet to be as dark as possible, and in the case of two selfs the hen's legs not so dark as the cock's.

"I may say my Greens have been bred by the careful selection of variegated birds from my strain of Clear and Ticked Norwich; so that it is possible for any Norwich breeder to produce good Greens in a few years if the stamp of bird is right from the start. My winner of the Championship Diploma for Best Norwich Green at the Crystal Palace, 1910, was bred in this way. Of course, what you are deficient of in one bird must be made up in the other when pairing, and last but not least allowing the birds plenty of bathing facilities forms one of my best burnishers."

Mr. Thos. Arnot on Border Greens.

Mr. Thomas Arnot, an old breeder of the Green Border Fancy Canary, who exhibits with his colleague Mr. Jamieson, under the joint names Messrs. Arnot and Jamieson, of Hawick, Scotland, has been good enough to favour us with some notes on his method of breeding the Green Border Fancy. He says :—

"The first pair I had was a Yellow Green hen, very dark in colour, and a Buff Green cock of fairly good colour; but both were very deficient in type and quality. So to improve the type and colour I purchased a Yellow Self Cinnamon hen—which in those days were a long way in front of what they are even now. This hen I put up to a Buff Green cock from the old pair and bred some very nice young Greens, one of which won several firsts. The next season I paired a Yellow Green cock and hen together, both very low set birds. I bred from them what was reckoned one of the best coloured Yellow Green cocks in the North, and one extra good coloured Yellow Cinnamon hen; both these birds did a lot of winning. After this I paired up Yellow and Buff in the usual way.

GREEN BORDER FANCY.

"I always depend on the hen for getting type, quality and pencilling, and the hens which breed the best young are those that are very dark on back with good sound colour down the front running right into the ven', with plenty of pencilling on the flanks. A hen such as this paired to a Buff Green cock even failing in colour down front or rather scarce in pencilling with 10 per cent. light blood, and 5 per cent. Cinnamon, will be almost certain to produce young which will be a credit to any fancier. I never use a Yellow cock that is smutty in colour, as they always seem inclined to get dark, and whenever I see my birds getting dark or bronzed on the back I pair them with a Cinnamon hen bred from Greens. I find I always have the best and finest pencilling off this cross, and fine pencilling goes a long way to improve the ground colour, because there is much more green feather left than there is when too heavy pencilling is obtained.

"As for arguments put forward regarding Cinnamon blood being the cause of light feet, legs, and bill, well, my experience is that age alone causes the feet and legs to become light, and I never have had occasion to try to improve my stock in that respect. Some people seem to think that dark feet and legs are the only sure signs of their being Green-bred. I have a young Yellow Green cock that is double-green bred that was bred from stock double-green bred for this last ten years, and it has light feet and legs, while its sister's are nearly black. These people would turn round and say there is 30 or 40 per cent. Cinnamon blood in the cock, and the hen Green-bred. Time alone is what is wanted to learn about Greens. As I said before, rely on the hen for colour and pencilling, and never use a cock that has a smutty or bronzed back.

"Of course, the first consideration in Green Borders is type and quality, the same as in other colours of the Border Fancy; only one has sometimes to temporarily overlook type for the sake of getting colour, which is why, as a rule, Greens do not come up to the standard of Clears; although there is a great improvement amongst Greens and Cinnamons this few years back, and in time no doubt they will equal the other colours in type."

Standard for Greens

The Green Canary Association have drawn up standards for the Yorkshire, Norwich, and Border Fancy Green Canaries and by their kind permission we herewith publish them.

Standard for Yorkshire Greens

Points of Merit

Marking	*Maximum*
Colour.—Rich deep grass green, sound and level throughout; pencillings distinct, beak, legs and feet dark	35

DARK MULES.

GREENFINCH-CANARY. GOLDFINCH-CANARY.

Marking	Maximum
Shape.	
Head—Small and round	3
Neck—Moderately long and straight . .	3
Shoulders—Narrow, round and well filled .	3
Back—Long, straight and level . .	3
Breast—Round, smooth, body gradually tapering to a neat waist . . .	5
Legs—Long, straight, without being stilty .	3
Wings and Tail—Long, compact and well carried	5
Position.—Attitude—erect and fearless . .	15
Feather.—Soft, silky, and compact, showing plenty of that characteristic called quality	15
Condition.—Health and general smartness .	10
	100

N.B.—Light beak, legs or feet are not a disqualification, but count against a bird according to their extent.

Standard for Norwich Greens

Points of Merit

Marking	Maximum
Colour.—Rich deep grass green, sound and level throughout; pencillings distinct; beak, feet, and legs dark	35
Shape.	
Head—Full and round	4
Neck—Short and thick	4
Body—Short, chubby, well filled in back, and deep full chest	20
Legs—Well set back, short, feet and claws perfect	6
Wings and Tail—Short, compact and smartly carried	6
Feather.—Soft, silky, and close fitting, showing plenty of quality	15
Condition.—Health and general smartness .	10
	100

N.B.—Light beak, legs, or feet are not a disqualification, but count against a bird according to their extent.

Standard for Border Greens

Points of Merit

Marking	Maximum
Colour.—Rich deep grass green, sound and level throughout; pencillings distinct, beak, legs and feet dark	35
Shape.	
Head—Small, round, and neat looking; bill, fine; eyes, dark and bright; neck, rather fine, and proportionate to head and body.	6
Body—Back, well-filled and nicely rounded, running in almost a straight line from the gentle rise over the shoulders to the point of the tail; chest also nicely rounded, but neither heavy nor prominent, the line gradually tapering away to vent . .	8
Wings—Compact and carried close to the body, just meeting at the tips . .	5
Legs—Of medium length, showing little or no thigh, fine, and in harmony with the other points; feet corresponding . . .	3
Tail—Close packed and narrow, being nicely rounded and filled in at the root . .	3
Size.—Not to exceed 5½ inches in length, measured in the usual way	
Feather.—Close, firm, and fine in quality, presenting a smooth, glossy, silky appearance and free from frill or roughness .	15
Position.—Semi-erect, standing at about an angle of 45 degrees	10
Carriage.—Gay and jaunty, with a fine free poise of the head	5
Condition.—Health, cleanliness, and general smartness	10
	100

N.B.—Light beak, legs, or feet are not a disqualification, but count against a bird according to their extent.

Negative Properties

A Green Canary should not be of a dull shade of colour, neither should it show any tinge of yellow or bronze, nor should it lack lustre. It should not show heavy dark stripes on the back, nor on the undersurface of the body—the narrower and finer the pencilling on the back the purer the green shade of colour—nor in any other place should there be any departure from the genuine character of the pure green; neither should the marginal edging of the flights or tail be wanting in colour. It should not be small in size, slovenly in carriage, or loose in feather. These properties should each be well maintained in accordance with their respective standards. Nor should a good specimen have light coloured legs, feet, or beak, though these are not a disqualification.

Disqualification

The presence of a white feather in any part of the body, or a decided "break" in the colour.

CINNAMON CANARY.
(Modern Norwich type, an interesting comparison with page 257.)

CHAPTER XXI

THE CINNAMON CANARY

THE name of the Canary at the head of this chapter surely tells its own story. It is the colour of, and takes its name from, the ordinary cinnamon of commerce. This name, however, is of comparatively recent date, though now generally accepted and firmly established. The original Cinnamon bird was a sober, quiet, unpretentious-looking Canary, and in the olden time was more generally known as the Dun; and as the meaning of the word "dun" in our "Walker" is "of a dun colour," we must leave it there as expressing in very intelligible terms a correct idea of what the colour really is. Many of the old school still call the bird by this name, which was certainly more appropriate as regards the old style of bird than the modern one, and it may be that with an improvement and alteration in the colour the name has gradually altered, and as the quiet dun has given place to the richer and warmer cinnamon, so has the one name displaced the other. The Yellow Cinnamon of old times (remember that the technical terms Yellow and Buff run through the whole Canary family) was a bird in which the prevailing pale brown, such as it was, was tinged with a greenish-yellow — or perhaps yellowish-green would convey a better idea—and the more general or "level" this pale dun tone, and the more evenly distributed, the better the bird. In Buffs, the dun was more decided, more true to name and character, singularly soft and mellow in tone and covered with a delicious bloom; in fact, the whole bird had more of the dove-colour about it than anything we can compare it with, and we are not surprised at the name "Dun" being then given to it.

We have heard it said that by breeding from Greens, selecting those with the brownest tinge and following up the work closely, the result will be Cinnamons, and have also read some account of work carried out in this way, the end of which was alleged to have been the advent of Cinnamons; but we entirely discard all such theories: no combination will produce them. We should be sorry to dispute the fact of Cinnamons having been born from a pair of Greens, but there was gold in the crucible to begin with: Cinnamon blood lurked in the veins of the Green to a certainty.

Cinnamon Characteristics.

What may have been the origin of this Canary, as a variety, we can only surmise; but that it is a distinct variety, its peculiar characteristics not common to other Canaries, and certain native properties not elsewhere discoverable which seem to cling to it in spite of the endless crosses to which it has been subjected, abundantly testify. Most prominent among these is the *pink eye,* which no other Canary, not having Cinnamon blood in its veins, possesses. That the bird is traceable to the common stock we must take for granted, and we think its distinctive plumage is referable to the peculiarity many wild birds possess of assuming a cinnamon garb. This is by no means a feature of rare occurrence with many of our indigenous birds, such as the Jackdaw, Starling, Blackbird, Goldfinch, Greenfinch, Redpoll, Skylark, Sandmartin, and others; and this colour may have been prized and perpetuated in the case of this Canary by the selection of those bearing it, and Dr. Galloway, in Chapter II. of this work, confirms our views on this point with some excellent illustrations.

The Cinnamon variety, when fixed, having probably little to recommend it beyond the unobtrusive singularity of its originally homely plumage, would not become a very popular favourite, and so would remain comparatively unrecognised and be thrown into the shade by the more strikingly beautiful varieties which engrossed the attention of the fanciers of a century ago. Indeed, the bird appears to have been regarded with disfavour rather than otherwise; why, we are puzzled to know.

The Pink Eye.

In a very old book lying before us, containing a deal of sound information on Canary matters, but which unfortunately has neither back nor title-page (and we are not sufficiently versed in bibliography to fix its date), it is said, in a very quaint phraseology, in speaking of the different varieties and referring particularly to the *pink eye,* the hall-mark of the Cinnamon:—

> "Some are all Yellow, which are Cocks,
> Some the Colour of Buff, & some of an Ash Colour.
> Some have Red Eyes, & the Cocks of this Sort Sing as well as Others, but the Hens are good for Nothing at all, being always Dim Sighted, and can not See to Feed their Young Ones (if Ever they Should have Any) and so Starve the Whole Nest."

Brehm also says: "Such as have red eyes are weak"; and Bechstein speaks of Canaries which "have often red eyes and are not strong." True, neither Brehm nor Bechstein refers the red eye directly to the Cinnamon; but we know that none other has it, for although in some instances not a trace of a single cinnamon-coloured feather is to be found in certain pink-eyed birds, yet they are to all intents and purposes Cinnamon in character, having all the peculiar traits found only in the family. There seems to be some doubt also as to what was meant by "ash-coloured" Canaries, though we take it to mean dove-coloured.

Our experience of the Cinnamon Canary is that it is neither short sighted nor more weakly than any other high-class Canary, that it is a prolific breeder, and the hens as a rule are good mothers.

Hervieux, in his work translated and published in London in 1718, speaks of "Ash-colour Canary-birds with red eyes," and also "Buff-colour Canary-birds with red eyes"; though he afterwards connects the red eye with almost every form of colour in the most perplexing way, which would lead one to suppose that the Cinnamon must have been crossed more extensively a couple of centuries ago than now. Brent, in his little treatise, refers to this vague definition of colours and says: "The principal difference consists in the names given to the colours. For instance, what the translator of Hervieux, 1718, calls 'ash-colour,' P. Boswell names flaxen, and buff is designated yellow *dun* colour; thus rendering the obscurity of the first translator doubly confounded." Sufficient, however, is adduced to show that the red-eyed Canaries of the olden time bore a bad character for stamina, rightly or wrongly, and hence, probably, the bird which we imagine to have been the Cinnamon, and nothing else, did not rank high in the fancier's estimation.

Types of Cinnamons.

But what do we find the bird to-day? We have three types varying as widely as the three stems on which the pink-eyed bird has been grafted — viz. the Norwich Cinnamon, the Yorkshire Cinnamon, and the Border Fancy Cinnamon. There are also birds wholly or partly cinnamon coloured to be found in almost all varieties of the Canary. It is our province here to describe the first of these forms, belonging as it now does pre-eminently to the colour section of the family—a section we purpose exhausting before dealing with birds of shape or position, or distinctive plumage. We have certainly referred to the distinctive plumage of this bird, but have done so more with the intention of calling attention to one peculiarity—viz. its colour —than with any idea of classing it with those having many peculiarities, each in itself a feature of consequence.

Forty years ago it would have been open to us to have ignored the bird altogether as a separate variety (for it was then very seldom found pure and free from some cross, unless it was in the pit districts in the North, where, next to a mule-breeding strain of hens, the "Dun," as it was then called, was the bird of birds), and have referred only to the effects of crossing it with such pure tribes as we may from time to time treat of; but we prefer to give it the place we consider it deserves, as it is now bred pure in almost all parts of the world (though not, we regret to say, in the large numbers we should like to see it), and we propose to discuss both its general character, and, so far as we can without departing from our plan of arrangement, the effect produced upon it by being crossed with other varieties, as well as the effect it produces upon them.

Evolution of the Colour.

Considering it, then, as a colour-bird, we accept the modern Norwich type as a much improved form of the old bird. It is not so very many years ago since it was comparatively rare, and the winning strain was supposed to be in very few hands. It is in too few even now; the more a bird is distributed the more popular it becomes. How the colour had been so intensified was a matter of some speculation, but the great family resemblance the new bird bore to the Norwich variety, and the unmistakable stamp of the variegated birds, soon indicated the fountain from whence came the hot blood. The Variegated Cinnamon of that day was essentially a bird of shape and markings, until some of the southern breeders, by sending *their* notion of a variegated bird northwards, opened the eyes of the admirers of colour to the fact that there were other valuable crosses besides birds of the position school. Many of the heavily-variegated birds exhibited were hens, and, being claimed or sold into the North, soon told a tale which, in the course of a few years, produced the remarkable Cinnamon of to-day, capable of developing almost as much colour as the Norwich bird itself. Everyone who is learned in Canary lore will remember the consternation caused in the ranks of the Cinnamon breeders—a consternation almost amounting to demoralisation—when Mr. Bemrose added to his then mysteries the still greater mystery of two or three Cinnamons which put all competition at defiance. Great discoveries have been made by accident or while in quest of something other than the thing found, and it may be that it was when in search of variegation the new vein of colour was struck. In describing it we say, first, that in size and shape it is almost the counterpart of the Canary with which it has been so systematically allied, though there is more than the average disparity between the size of the Buff and Yellow birds, the former being, as a rule, much the larger, and carrying their size without the corresponding increase in coarseness of feather which would be looked for in any other fine-feather variety. This does not infer that there are no coarse feathered birds.

The Yellow Bird.

The colour of a highly-improved specimen is in the Jonque (Yellow) a brilliant chocolate, the deepest shade being found on the top of the head. There is some very pretty pencilling on the cheeks, and the back, like that of a Green Canary, has always more or less of a striped appearance, owing to the saddle-feathers being much darker near the midrib than on the margin. Excess of this marking is considered a defect, and the uniform distribution of the chocolate, forming what is known as a " level " back, is one of the strong points of a show-bird. Therefore, the lighter the pencilling the more level the cinnamon colour, though it is extremely difficult to get the brilliant colour without the pencilling. The throat and breast should show none of this, as anyone who has paid attention to the character of the breast-feather of most Self-coloured Canaries will understand. It is here, perhaps, that the purest and brightest shade of colour is to be found, the whole surface of the breast being unsullied by a single streak, and being free from the comparative dullness caused by the darker midribs of the saddle. Here, too, the rich Norwich blood seems pent up, inducing a ruddy glow startling in its warmth when compared with the quiet, old-fashioned vest of years ago. The ambition of the careful breeder is to get this warmth of breast colour as even as possible right up to the base of the under mandible.

Where the breast feathers merge with those of the side, it is not unusual to find in the very best specimens indications of stripes more or less decided in their pencilling; and where this is the case it is invariably connected with rich warm colouring throughout the region of the waist. When they are not present, their absence is a tolerably reliable indication of the desire of the Norwich blood to break bounds and tinge the waist with a lighter but very brilliant colour, which, though not always discernible, is but one remove from yellow proper, and is as prejudicial to the winning chances of a Cinnamon as a yellow waist is to a Green Yorkshire. A Cinnamon, in fact, however rich in Norwich blood, must be true in colour, whatever the depth of shade. It must also be bright and glossy: mere depth of colour counts but little in the show-room if it be dull and unpolished, requiring burnishing to bring out its true quality, and a good judge will allow a balance of points in favour of shining silk as against a rusty, coffee-coloured suit. The feathers of the wings and tail are paler on the broader web than the rest of the bird, but the outer margin is full of colour, and on its development and a good carriage depend much of the effect to be derived from equal distribution. The underflue is dark; beak clear, and legs and feet usually so, but sometimes inclined to be dark. The thighs, we have omitted to mention, should be well clothed, and the colour of the livery well maintained. All that has been said of the Norwich Canary with regard to texture and compactness of feather attaches to the Cinnamon with equal force as a necessary condition for an effective display of colour.

The Buff Bird.

The Buff bird differs from the Yellow with respect to colour more directly than does the corresponding form in the Norwich. In the highest types of the latter the body-colour of the Buff is, where most exposed, and even under the gossamer frosting, equally as rosy as the purest Jonque (Yellow); but in the Cinnamon it is duller and of a different cast, even in the old, unmixed—we were going to say unadulterated—strain, being softer and greyer, and showing the chocolate or cinnamon of an entirely lighter shade, the entire bird, and more especially the hens, being shrouded in a most delicate dove-colour, so quiet as at one time to have obtained for these birds the name of "Quakers." But, in mixing with gay company and feasting on its dainty meats, it has shown itself not averse to throwing off its quaint attire, and appears now in a vestment which perfectly bewildered the Fancy when the cayenne regimen first developed its latent beauty. We do not wish to convey the idea that the Buff Cinnamon is not cinnamon-coloured, but simply to call attention to the fact that, whereas in the improved Jonque the bird is in every part some shade or other of the rich cinnamon, in the improved "fed" Buff the intensified colour is accompanied by a ruddy glow which is not so plainly a chocolate as some of the corresponding enriched portions of the Jonque. This is most noticeable on the breast, which, in the Buff, is remarkably fiery, contrasting strongly with the polished walnut hue of the breast of the Jonque when placed side by side. On the top of the head, too, this is observable, despite the intensely deep brown, and also on the scapular feathers, where the play of colour, assisted by the meal, is very pleasing. This feature is doubtless an immediate result of the strong infusion of Norwich blood. Any disposition to run light in colour in the waist or in the region of the vent or under tail-coverts is, as in the Jonque, a weak point, and a single bona fide light feather—i.e. white in the shaft, flue, and web—is a fatal defect in either form of bird. The level back, which, in the Buff, shows less of the streaky marking before referred to, and also the closest feathering, is indispensable.

In order to explain the classification of Cinnamons it is necessary that we should assume that the old form, the veritable Dun, is, for all practical purposes, *non est*, having been entirely supplanted by the type of bird we have described in detail, now so firmly established and so universally recognised as *the* bird, that no other form is tolerated in the show-room except the Border Fancy. And a fancier of the variety, in referring to it by its generic name, has no other ideal in his mind—albeit the very bird he accepts as a type of the purest form is only one of the many crosses which have resulted from grafting Cinnamon scions on other stocks; and no flower of the show-room has been worked on so many bottoms. But colour being the primary feature, it will at once be understood why, in the pursuit of a fancier's fancy, that stem should be selected in which flowed the strongest sap. Unlike the dark Self-coloured Green Norwich, with its inborn disposition to sport and change to brilliant yellow, the Cinnamon is born a Cinnamon, and, like the members of the estimable society whose name it once bore, its children follow in the footsteps of their fathers, dressing in the same quiet garb with but slight variation. There is occasionally found, even in the oldest and, therefore, we infer, purest strains most remote from foreign taint, some slight tendency to break into a colour which, so far as it may be regarded worthy to be called colour, is little more than a greenish-white, and, having nothing special to recommend it, has never been deemed worth cultivation. To check such disposition, indeed, has ever been the object of the Cinnamon breeder: to produce whole, sound colour is his aim, and light feathers are as much his *bête noire* as is the obnoxious tick vexatious to the Norwich breeder. The infusion of Norwich blood, however, renders this not always a matter so easy of accomplishment as in the days of really pure Cinnamons, when the only departures from the self-coloured form—which, bear in mind, was not crossed in any way for colour purposes—were to be found in the variegated offshoots of crosses made for other purposes. But now we

Trueness to Colour.

A NOTED WINNING CINNAMON OF 1888.

(Selected to portray pencilling only. For present type see p. 252.)

A WINNING CINNAMON OF 1891.

(Selected to show good level back colour. For present type see p. 252.)

have not only the rich whole-coloured bird known as Self, which, it need scarcely be explained, must here be regarded as a technical term meaning absolutely free from light or non-cinnamon-coloured feathers, but we also have the variegated *colour-offshoots* thrown off in working upwards from the Norwich cross. This gives us, therefore, the key to a natural classification of what we call the modern Cinnamon, which is, (*a*) SELF, (*b*) VARIEGATED, always recollecting that the Self bird is the self-coloured form, and that the order of progression is from light or parti-coloured up to dark, the two birds we have described being the representatives of Class (*a*). It must also not be forgotten that the original Cinnamon, which we have assumed to be defunct—practically, it is so—we are regarding only as a base, having indelible traits, on which have been reared three superstructures, and that we are dealing with the first of the three, the Norwich Cinnamon or Cinnamon Norwich, as representing the bird from a colour point of view in harmony with our original plan of arranging the Canary family in groups.

The Variegated Cinnamon.

We will dismiss Class (*a*), then, without further remark, except to say this class can be, and is, subdivided into Yellow and Buff, and proceed to the Variegated or Class (*b*), which is subdivided into *Variegated* proper and *Evenly-marked*, the first including every possible pied form, not being evenly-marked, from the bird which has but one light feather in it down to that having but one cinnamon-coloured feather. Between these two extremes it is obvious there exists every degree of variegation, its extent counting for nothing, though, as in the Norwich, the greater the quantity of clear feathers and the less of the green, the nearer is perfection ; so, in the Cinnamon, the larger the distribution of cinnamon colour and the fewer the light or white feathers, the nearer the bird is to the goal. In judging a class, however, in which the definition "Variegated" is meant to convey nothing further than its purely technical meaning, and no idea whatever of marking, the amount of variegation is not of so much value as the quality of the colour which rules paramount. Slight ticks in an otherwise whole-coloured bird are easy to detect, a frequent form being a very small patch on the back of the head, one of the many trials which sorely exercise the minds of some fanciers. The safest way to inspect such birds is with the hands deep down in the trousers pocket ; for, if handled, these foul feathers are so apt to—for want of a better word we will say apt to come out. Canary and cage-bird morality, let us say here, even if it be scarcely the right place, to its credit be it written, is governed by no fast and loose policy. We do not say its laws are never broken by the unscrupulous ; but nothing is allowed, or recognised, or understood, in the sense of "they all do it," to make a bird *appear* what it *is not ;* and the wretched sophistry which argues that a bird must be good to begin with, to bear "making"—the fertile cause of deception and fraud among some classes of fanciers—has no rest for the sole of its foot in the Canary and cage-bird show-room. Some reader may ask, smiling : "How about colour feeding ?" To answer the question is, perhaps, to admit its reasonableness. Our reply is : that it neither adds to nor subtracts from, *mechanically*, but develops *naturally*, and shows what a bird *is*.

Concluding our remarks on Variegation, we observe that another common and very vexatious form is the presence of a white feather in the wings or tail—a defect which, as an item of breeding information, it is much more difficult to eliminate than mere body ticks.

"Foul" Marked Bird.

We regret that classes are not given at shows for this class of Cinnamon, for we are perfectly satisfied that such classes would be patronised by breeders to a greater extent than those for "Self," and without the slightest detriment to the self-coloured birds, and they would materially assist to make the Cinnamon more popular. Some say such foul-marked birds are only stock birds; *but*—and it is these "buts" that make all the difference—some of the most beautiful specimens are amongst the foul-marked birds, so why should they be hidden in the breeding-room? If the Cinnamon Canary is to be saved, and hold the position it ought in the Canary world, some such classification will have to be adopted in addition to that for self-coloured birds. We hope these remarks may be the means of a trial being given them. It was once tried, but not continued for long enough.

The Evenly-marked birds are judged in precisely the same way as in the Norwich variety, due regard being had for the richness of the Cinnamon marking, and extreme care being required to detect any small ticks, which are not so discernible on the deep orange ground as are the green feathers in other varieties.

Evenly-marked Cinnamons.

Evenly-marked Cinnamons of the Norwich type (we might even include other types) are as yet entirely in their infancy, and we do not remember ever having seen a class set apart for them; indeed, we question whether there are enough birds of the kind in the country to make a respectable show, even if Yellows and Buffs were grouped, those claiming to be evenly-marked being found either in the comprehensive Variegated division or among the Evenly-marked specimens exhibited as such without regard to their being Colour, Shape, or Position birds. This is one of the anomalies of our cut-and-dried system of show classification, and yet, at the same time, an arrangement which can scarcely be prevented when it is remembered that there are not *many* of either of the three types, and that, until each is more extensively bred, financial considerations compel them to be so grouped and judged for one common property—viz. even-marking—although each has a separate and distinct property, apart from the marking, for which it has been especially bred. The bringing of birds having dissimilar properties into competition in the same class is defensible only as a matter of policy. It is an incontrovertible axiom that it is impossible to compare unlike things. We may compare colour with colour, size with size, shape with shape, position with position, or any like with its equivalent, but when we endeavour to institute a comparison between colour and shape, or any other dissimilars, we attempt an impossibility, and the result is an absurdity out of which springs as much unpleasantness as is possible to be born of such a Babel of confusion of ideas. Yet such, we fear, must remain for a time, at least, until more of this class of bird (except in the Border Fancy variety) are bred. At many shows a class is now given—at some, two—where evenly Green and Cinnamon-marked birds only compete together.

The few Evenly-marked Norwich Cinnamons which have from time to time appeared—doubtless, to a great extent, chance productions—have been birds possessed of beauty enough, one would have thought, to fire the enthusiasm of the most unimpressionable fancier; but the bird has as yet failed to take any great hold of the show world, and up to the present time we have seen but little indication of its occupying the prominent position it might. With all the lustrous beauty of the clear plumage of the Norwich bird, it has a softness and delicacy peculiarly its own. Granted that the contrast between green and gold is more striking than between chocolate and gold, and that the dark pencilling of a Norwich eye is more effective than the softer auburn; but it is in the quiet, soft expression that the beauty consists. The marked Buffs have a chaste refinement about them that cannot be gainsaid. Whether it arise from the admixture of the Cinnamon blood, bringing with it a softness and peculiar tone in the colour of the clear portion of the plumage, or from some other cause, we know not; but there is that about the texture and colour of the Buff which is found nowhere else, and this beautiful quality is so patent that even in the case of an almost perfectly clear pink-eyed bird, or one having so few cinnamon feathers that they require to be sought for to satisfy one as to their existence, there is no difficulty in at once determining from the very "something" which surrounds it that the bird is Cinnamon-bred, and a fancier has seldom to appeal to the pink eye to confirm his opinion, so clearly is the character of the bird stamped upon it.

In addition to these standard classes there is the Crested Cinnamon, in which every class of Norwich Crest, as detailed in the chapters on that variety, has its counterpart. Very few, however, are bred, and on one or two occasions only within our knowledge has even as much as a solitary class for the entire variety and one for Cinnamon Crestbreds been provided at any show.

The Crested Cinnamon.

The present place, indeed, of one of our prettiest Canaries is that home for the houseless, in which *new* varieties of sterling merit are perhaps not so often recognised as are the representative specimens of standard forms, which, for want of a special class, are, for the occasion, sent into the "Any other Variety." This is to a large extent the breeders' own fault, as, when a class or classes are provided, they are not supported as they should be. There is too much timidity of meeting Tom, Dick or Harry's best bird, and so the classes are allowed to pass into oblivion. A few very fair specimens, chiefly Buffs, have made their appearance from time to time, but nothing possessing more than average merit, with the exception of two birds, one of which was owned by Mr. T. Heath, of London, and the other by Mr. T. J. King, of Cheltenham, whose Crests compared favourably with many good specimens of the Green Crest variety. The principal defects are, apart from the lack of that striking crest development which can only result from continued careful pedigree-breeding, want of purity in body-colour, and also lack of depth of colour and consequent failure of contrast between the colour of the cinnamon crest and the clear body-feathers, in which must consist much of the beauty of the bird. We do not think that the endeavour to produce this bird in perfection has ever been very persistently followed out, but we are fully satisfied that were but a few gems to appear it would set the Fancy in a blaze, and create as widely-spread a taste for Crested Cinnamons in every form as for Crests of the Green, Grey, and Clear colours. From the nature of things, we know that high-class Crested Yellows of any variety must always be more rare than Buffs; and we think that a rich, clear-bodied Buff, with well-formed cinnamon-coloured crest, or a bird with good cinnamon-marked wings and cinnamon crest, is one worth trying for, and deserving of a leading position in our schedules.

Our description of the Cinnamon as a member of the Colour section must here cease. We shall have to refer to it again when we come to speak about one or two varieties with which it has been crossed for other than colour purposes, here only asking our readers to keep in mind our line of arrangement—viz. to consider the bird, first, *per se*, and then to treat of the use made of it. Its connection with the Norwich variety, with the effects produced, and the intimate mutual relations existing between the two, we have exhausted, and shall devote the next section to the subject of breeding the modern Cinnamon.

As the name indicates, Norwich typed Cinnamons should be the type of the Norwich Plainhead Canary, with this difference, that the Cinnamon Club have decided that no restriction be put on size—the larger the better—so long as they are of the Norwich type, sound Cinnamon colour, close in feather, and good quality.

By the kind permission of the Cinnamon Canary Club we herewith give their

SCALE OF POINTS FOR JUDGING CINNAMON CANARIES

	Points
Colour	35
Quality of feather	15
Good wing carriage and compactness of tail	10
Shape and Type, good round head, showing no lashing	20
Size	10
Condition, Health and Cleanliness	10
Total,	100

Negative Colour Properties

A Self Jonque Cinnamon should not show any tinge of green, nor be dull and rusty or semi-opaque, nor should it be patchy in colour or show dark stripes on the back or saddle, nor should there ever be any doubt as to the soundness of the cinnamon colour throughout, or any suspicion of a break.

A Self Buff Cinnamon should not show any shade of green, nor have the expanse of colour on neck and breast hidden by meal, nor have dark stripes on the back. Neither Yellow or Buff should be coarse in feather, nor have a slovenly carriage of wings or tail, nor have a narrow skull.

VARIEGATED CINNAMONS

Here the assessments correspond exactly with those in the Norwich scales, due regard being had to the depth of the cinnamon colour in the Evenly-marked class, as well as to the purity of the clear body-colour. This applies especially to the irregularly-pied birds, in which the 35 points allotted to the items "depth, purity, and brilliancy of colour" must be understood here to apply to those properties as attaching to the cinnamon colour, which is *here* the *body-colour*, the position of things being inverted.

CRESTED CINNAMONS

The ordinary Crest Standard could be very well adapted in judging these, with this difference, ten points might be given for purity and richness of sound cinnamon colour on the parts of the bird so marked.

BREEDING CINNAMONS

Note that we say breeding, not producing—a distinction with a wide difference. How originally produced we have endeavoured to investigate; how to breed we will show.

In the whole round of canary-breeding there is not a bird subject to such remarkable peculiarities as the Cinnamon, in whose blood abides an influence so subtle as to make itself felt in a very astonishing way. Were it not that these peculiarities are certain in their action and invariable, they would prove as perplexing to the breeder as their cause is puzzling. Instead of proceeding to enumerate them in detail, we will begin by putting a case to which probably many a fancier will find a parallel in his own experience. We will assume that a breeder of the variety, roused to enthusiasm by the rich colour of specimens he may have seen in the show-room, and having heard of the potency of a Norwich cross, has determined to import that blood as a means of bringing his birds up to the standard of the day. He doesn't believe in working with ready-made stuff, but prefers to mix his own paint; and what more natural than that he should procure one or two of the richest yellow Norwich cocks he can find to pair with his Cinnamon hens?

He has gone on long enough pairing Cinnamon with Cinnamon, and has bred birds beautiful enough in themselves and apparently able to cope with anything he remembers to have seen, but has found himself a long way from the front when his pet specimens have been compared with the celebrities of the year. The Norwich blood is to perform the necessary transmutation, and his very best hens are paired as we have described. His first nests rather surprise him: the young ones are nearly all Greens or broken Greens, but never a Cinnamon has he. These Norwich cocks must have been bred from a very strong Green strain surely? Try again. And he does try again, with the same result, and again without producing a single Cinnamon feather. The season is fast waning, and his room is full of Greens, and many of them only very indifferent in colour, but his Cinnamons are still *in nubibus*. All this comes, he thinks, from having neglected the advice given in a previous chapter about ascertaining the pedigree of the birds before introducing a cross; because it *must* be the new cocks. He puzzles his brain over it till he can think of nothing else, and becomes a silent man. The wife of his bosom, from whom he has never concealed anything since they twain became one, begins to be uneasy, and wonders whether he has been accepting a little bill.

It isn't often she goes into his bird-room; but she did yesterday, and there lay his diary full of mysterious memoranda and a note about something "falling due" in a few days. The little affair, when due, brings with it only a repetition of his disappointment. He has another Yellow bird, however, a Norwich bird, or at any rate he bought it for such, and he resolves to try what it will do, and pairs it with one of his Cinnamon hens. Hope has nearly died out of his breast, and he awaits the "chipping" of this nest with some anxiety, but to his great delight finds there are at least two or three pink-eyed young ones, which, while they puzzle him the more, lead to mutual explanations and restored domestic confidence. The solution of the enigma is very simple. Cinnamon blood cannot be introduced with direct results, *except from the male side;* or, to use a simile we have frequently adopted, no scion whatever can be grafted on a Cinnamon stock, but the Cinnamon can be worked on any bottom. If a cock Canary, not being a Cinnamon or crossed from the variety, be paired with a Cinnamon hen, the produce will not show the pink eye or any cinnamon feathers, but will consist of Self-coloured Greens, cocks and hens, and Variegated Greens. If, however, we invert the order of things, and infuse the Cinnamon blood by mating a Cinnamon cock with, say, a Norwich hen, we obtain altogether different results. The progeny will, for the most part, consist of Self-coloured and Variegated Cinnamons, with an occasional Green or Green-marked bird, and with this strange result also, that all the Cinnamons, Clear or Variegated, will be hens.

A Curious Fact.

This is a fact not generally known, but our own experience has shown it to *be* a fact, while inquiry on every side has never in any one instance led to a knowledge of any other result. Some breeders will only declare positively as to the Yellow Variegated, but our experience is that every bird which shows one cinnamon feather will be a hen. Among our northern breeders, who above all things in the early 'seventies of the last century delighted in a good "Dun-marked" bird, the Green and Green-marked birds from this cross were not recognised for ordinary breeding purposes as Greens proper, however brilliant they were, but, as bred from, or "off," the Duns, and, when their pedigree was known, were much valued for the results to be obtained from them. The Green or Green-marked cocks so bred, paired with clear birds of any variety, will throw both Green-marked and Cinnamon-marked, as well as pink-eyed, clear-bodied offspring, which last are Cinnamons in their acts and deeds. The Green or Green-marked hens will produce like results if paired to cocks descended from Cinnamons, though these cocks may show no cinnamon-feather or pink-eye. A friend of the late Mr. Blakston once, writing to him from Darlington, said: "I have bred this season from a Green-marked cock, the son of a Cinnamon, which I have paired with two well-bred Norwich hens, having no trace of Cinnamon blood in them, and have got both pink-eyed Clears and Cinnamon-marked produce."

To anyone not acquainted with their peculiarities, it might seem strange to find Cinnamons preponderating in a nest bred from, apparently, ordinary Greens. But very frequently it is so, and some admirers of the variety obtain their Evenly-marked Cinnamons from these Variegated Cinnamon-bred Greens. Many of them, indeed, will throw decently-marked young ones with such certainty as to be almost as valuable in their way as are the "muling" hens which produce the wonderful hybrids, so mathematically exact in their marking, between the Goldfinch and Canary; some of the very best and most reliable of these muling hens being, in fact, full of Cinnamon blood, which, when united with any other, seems to have the property of appearing either in the Green or Cinnamon form in the eye-stripes, and other regions where native marking is probably latent. We referred to this in our remarks on breeding Evenly-marked Norwich, but prefer rather to deal with the peculiarity here in the character of a property of this variety, which, beyond any doubt, will be developed to an extent hitherto not dreamt of when the breeding of Marked Cinnamons of the Norwich type, persistently followed up, will throw the *Green-marked* birds so produced into the Norwich classes, just as the *Green-marked Cinnamon-bred* birds of the Yorkshire type are thrown into the Yorkshire classes—many of the best Evenly-marked examples of which are greatly indebted to Cinnamon blood for the accurate pencilling of their beautiful eye-stripes.

We have said that the pink-eyed Clear-bodied birds also are Cinnamon in their functions. We knew a dealer who was in the habit of making rather extensive purchases of Norwich birds from an exhibitor in the South, who, at that time, had also one of the best strains of Cinnamons in exhibition. Our friend, the dealer, not having disposed of all his stock, put up his surplus pairs in the spring, mating a Clear Yellow *Norwich* (?) cock with a Buff hen of the same variety. The result was, that in every nest there were some fine *Cinnamons;* and an inspection showed the *Norwich* cock to be *pink-eyed.*

Some Curious Experiences.

We had a similar experience in our early days of Norwich breeding, though the birds we were breeding with had neither pink eyes nor a cinnamon feather, yet we produced Cinnamons in every nest from two pairs. Inquiry elicited the fact that the birds we were breeding with had all been crossed with the Cinnamon, which fact dispelled the mystery.

The Breeding Principle.

The principle involved in breeding colour-Cinnamons is easy of deduction from what we have advanced, and is analogous to that on which the production of Clear Norwich Canaries is based, in so far as it consists in improving colour by the infusion of a foreign element, every trace of which ultimately requires to be eliminated, leaving only its active agency behind. In the Norwich, we operate on the Clear plumage by infusing the strong Green; and in the Cinnamon, we work in the same way by adding the Clear element in various stages of its development, and striving in each case to maintain the plumage operated on intact, and changed only in regard to the brilliancy and depth of its colour. The two processes may appear to be the reverse of each other in their practical operation, but they are nearly identical in principle. To breed whole-coloured Cinnamons, pair the purest and richest-coloured Selfs together, Yellow to Buff. The improved bird is full to the brim and running over with colour-blood, as the constant recurrence of light ticks and pied forms attests.

We mention this plan first for the encouragement of those who, altogether inexperienced in Canary-breeding, may see difficulties in our exhaustive details which, possibly, may debar them from commencing with a variety requiring so much building up and maintaining in a high degree of excellence. All varieties require this building up: in it consists the art of breeding; but we think this string can sustain its present tension long enough for the amateur to acquire some proficiency before it will require tuning afresh. In pairing Yellow cocks with Buff hens, select, if possible, male birds having some size: such are not always procurable, as the tendency of the richest-coloured Jonques is to run small. We only mention this as a disposition it is desirable to keep in check, but do not advise sacrificing any material point in doing so, but by selecting birds of good size, at the same time not neglecting quality of feather and colour, the three essentials of the bird are retained.

Mating.

The head of a Cinnamon, too, is of the utmost importance. A fine large head on a good body, covered with the richest of pure colour, is the ambition of every Cinnamon breeder, and this is why dips have had to be taken into the Norwich, and even the Crestbred and Lancashire, to get these various properties, but the best results have been obtained from the Norwich Cross. It should be remembered that the true Norwich is a bird of fair size, and also that the Jonque Cinnamon cock need not be allowed to become even smaller. Bear in mind, also, that size and colour are difficult to bring out in the same bird, and, therefore, be cautious. We deem it well to refer to this in all its bearings, inasmuch as the acknowledged want of size in Jonques is so far admitted by the Fancy as to warrant large birds of high-class "all-round" properties occupying leading positions in the most severe competition. Plenty of length can always be obtained in the Jonques; it is the stoutness of body which is difficult to get and retain, and it is this we require; the present Norwich standard of type demands it.

In mating the other way, that is, Buff cock to Jonque hen, there will be no difficulty as regards the size of the cock, the Buffs having, by some means or other, managed to carry a full share of colour with size. But care must be taken in the selection of a Yellow hen, many of which, though very dark, are singularly dull in tone, and lack the lustre which gives finish to a bird when in high condition. Such hens are generally very compact, and we would sooner pair them with Jonques than with Buffs, which in some feather points they resemble, though in such pairing there is a liability to lose considerable substance of body in the offspring. A hen should be chosen, therefore, which, if not so brown, is brighter and purer in colour, and in every instance, whether male or female, Yellow or Buff, birds which have a greenish tinge should be avoided, for it often betokens a common extraction.

The first and simplest cross to restore declining colour is with the richest Self-coloured Green Norwich hen; and we would not in this instance insist on the rule for mating Jonque and Mealy being carried out, preferring rather to use a compact Yellow cock. This cross, being less likely to sport than any other, will give least trouble, and is one to be recommended if there be any tendency on the Cinnamon side to throw occasional white feathers. From this cross will come some improved whole-coloured Cinnamons direct, while such Greens as may be produced will be invaluable colour-fountains. Not one should be sold till tested, for a Green cock from this cross may, when paired with a Cinnamon hen, throw Cinnamons of the purest water; and if one or two foundation pairs have been mated as directed, the Green cocks from the one when paired with the Green hens from the other *may* also produce a preponderance of Cinnamons, which are certain to be of high character. Where a breeder is working with but one or two pairs there is not scope for much interbreeding of this kind, but if the same cock be mated with two or three hens, Yellows and Buffs, it will be plain that from the offspring two or three threads can be twisted into one, and desirable forms concentrated, at the same time that the admixture of Yellow and Buff will afford material for keeping up the texture of the feather.

To Gain Colour.

When one finds their birds becoming a little dull, and too dark in colour, a little rich clear blood from the Norwich brightens and brings it up again.

It is unnecessary that we again enunciate the general principles which should guide the intelligent breeder in gathering up his threads. Concentration into one channel is the leading idea. All that is requisite is to have shown how to spin the threads out of a peculiar material.

To detail the working of a cross in which the vehicle for introducing colour is a Variegated hen would be merely to repeat the instructions given in the chapter on breeding Clear Norwich from the Variegated form. It might be asked: Why make use of Variegated birds and court difficulties, when the same result may be obtained from Self, that is Greens, with less trouble? We do not say the same results, or rather such good results, *will* follow the cross with the Green as will eventuate from pairing with a rich Yellow Variegated hen, having the pure Yellow well developed. The Green cross will make a marked improvement, but an infusion of brighter blood from a variegated or clear spring will do still more in producing a brighter and warmer hue. This cross will also furnish the breeder with several classes of birds, all of which are valuable for different purposes. There will probably be Self-Cinnamons, at once, which will show the highest and purest form of colour, and which may be mated with the original strain without more ado. It must not be expected that such mating will produce nests entirely free from blemish, because the Clear Norwich blood is very near the surface, and will, in all probability, bubble up; but it is a very safe cross, and one from which very little trouble may be expected. Then there will be others in all degrees of variegation, heavy and light, which will require dealing with according to the extent and quality of the cinnamon marking. Some may be merely ticked, some have nothing more than pied wings or tail, and others may be irregularly splashed. For every one there will be a place. Some may be green or broken green: these also can all be treated as Cinnamons, and worked accordingly. But some will probably show very fair *marking*, either cinnamon or green, and one or two may be clear from cinnamon-coloured feathers entirely, but yet have the *pink eye*, which, we may remark, can be discerned by the merest novice directly the young birds leave the shell, and is the distinguishing mark by which the breeder can determine at once the character of a mixed nest in which he anticipates finding Cinnamons. The existence of this pink eye as the infallible tell-tale of Cinnamon blood does not appear to be so well known as it should be. Many instances have come under our notice of persons having pink-eyed birds without having the slightest idea of their descent, any knowledge of of the fact being further kept out of view owing to many of these birds having been bred for one purpose or another perfectly clear, without as much as a single cinnamon feather being discerned in them. Having thus passed from hand to hand they have come into the possession of persons who were quite unacquainted with their character, and, not suspecting it, have mated them with birds of other breeds, with some of the perplexing results to which we have referred. Young birds of this class, when feathered, it will be well to mark by a distinguishing notch on one of the flight-feathers, or in some similar way, or by placing a numbered Canary marking-ring on one leg, taking note of the number to ensure identification at a future day. The value of those found to have good technical marking, or even a decent approach to it, cannot be over-estimated. We have in them the starting-point of a *marked* strain, and there are many ways of pairing, a few of which only need to be suggested in order to indicate the direction in which the work can be carried out. The Cinnamon-marked birds, *being all hens,* may be mated with Clear-bodied pink-eyed cocks, with the tolerable certainty of having marking of some kind reproduced. The Green-marked cocks might also be similarly mated with these hens, and by that means two like tendencies would be concentrated in one channel, even at the risk of producing a heavy form of marking, or a leaning towards irregular variegation through the infusion of two streams of Cinnamon blood, followed up as explained in the chapter on breeding Evenly-marked Canaries. Or these valuable Green-marked cocks might be paired with Clear hens of a fresh Norwich strain, with a reasonable expectation of throwing lightly-marked Cinnamons or a further supply of pink-eyed Clears, both cocks and hens, if these Norwich hens have any Cinnamon blood in them, to be made use of in the almost endless ways in which the principles of pedigree-breeding can be brought to bear upon this remarkable Canary.

Mr. C. L. Quinton, of Great Yarmouth, one of our most successful Cinnamon breeders, writing to us, says:

A Personal Experience.

"I have been breeding Cinnamons for the past twenty-four years, and have always found the Norwich cross the best with which to increase size and colour in the Cinnamon, when I found it necessary to take a cross. I breed my birds pure so long as they retain good size and colour; but if I find I am losing size, colour, or quality, I select the largest Clear or Ticked Yellow Norwich hen I can, with good shape, colour, head and quality. I pair such a hen to one of my best Cinnamon cocks, and select the best of the young from these to pair back to my pure Cinnamon. I have never used any other cross, and have found such most successful in yielding me the points I crossed for. The young hens from this cross I have sometimes paired back to their father, or birds of the same strain, with good results, fixing the points I required—of course selecting from their young only those possessing the improvements I required for future breeding with. Some of these young ones so bred have given me splendid results in their progeny. My object in in-breeding, when I do resort to it, is to fix points I desire."

Crested Cinnamons.

We do not think it necessary to devote a separate chapter to the subject of breeding Crested Cinnamons in all its detail, because the line of operation can be deduced from our foregoing observations, the chief point for consideration here being how to introduce the crest in the first instance—this, of course, implying the assumption that the breeder has no Crested Cinnamon of any kind at command. The most direct method, it is obvious, will be to import it through the hen, since in that way the object sought is obtained at once. It is not material what class of hen we select, but we should prefer a Grey-crested or a Clear-bodied Dark-crested. Hens of this description, paired with a rich Jonque Cinnamon cock, would produce—what? In accordance with the law of Cinnamon first-cross we should expect to find Greens, Cinnamons, Variegated birds of either kind, and also Clears with pink eyes, the nests containing, as a natural consequence, both Crests and Plainheads, probably by far the greater number Plainheads; this, however, could to an extent be checked by using a Crested hen which has been bred from two Crested parents, not Crest and Crest-bred as usually paired. Of these young, bred from the Cinnamon cock and Crested hen, the Cinnamon-marked Crested birds must, at least, be hens, whatever the amount of their variegation, be it merely a few cinnamon feathers mixed in the crest or a more widely-distributed form of variegation. And the Green-marked Crested will be—what? Cinnamon-bred, of course; the cocks being a medium through which cinnamon crest can be planted on any variety, just as the corresponding form in the Plainhead can produce cinnamon marking. Similar forms of feather will also be found among the Plainheads, and there will also probably be the pink-eyed Clear body. What are we to do with these varied products? If we have put up several pairs, or have mated the same Jonque Cinnamon to two or three hens, we shall have material at command to carry out our pedigree-breeding efficiently, without forming a series of alliances too far within the prescribed bounds of consanguinity; though, in commencing, we should mate irrespective of such laws if any two streams ran in the direction wished, only too glad to unite them in one. Take the Green-marked cocks first, Crested or Plainhead: a Crested bird we would pair with a lightly Cinnamon-marked hen, and expect to find among the produce Variegated Crested Cinnamons of either sex, more or less evenly-marked according to the marking of the parents. If our Crests were very few in our first cross we should not hesitate to pair these Cinnamon Green-marked Crest cocks to lightly cinnamon-marked Crested hens or pink-eyed Clear Crested hens (the same way bred) with a view to increasing the number of Crests in the next generation. A Plainhead from our first year's work we would mate up with a Clear-bodied Cinnamon-crested hen, and expect them to produce the same as the previous pairing, with probably lighter marking; we would also pair a Green-marked Crested bird with a Clear Crest-bred hen, and a Green-marked Plainhead with a Crested hen, and look for similar results, with the addition of more Green-marked and pink-eyed Clears, in all of which we should expect to find increased depth of colour. So far we have worked only with the produce of the pairs put up for crest-breeding, but in any room in which the breeding of colour-Cinnamons has been carried on there will be Plainhead cocks and hens in every stage of development, both Buff and Yellow, with which suitable mating can be effected when once the crest has been introduced and developed in the cinnamon form.

We need not pursue this farther; it is simply a matter of following up the work begun; but it should be borne in mind that the largest and densest Crests possible should be selected to commence with, continuing such selection; also the more feathery the Cinnamon cock, the better, so long as he has good colour with it.

Use of Greens in Cinnamon Breeding.

There are many forms in which the results of crossing in the way we have endeavoured to explain will show themselves, to which we think it unnecessary to refer. The presence of any such form will at once suggest to the breeder a method of dealing with it in accordance with the laws which regulate Cinnamon-breeding, and the law of common-sense, which directs all breeding operations, apart from special considerations arising from peculiar conditions. There is one feature, however, to which we must refer before dismissing the Cinnamon. What is to be done with the house full of Green birds, the produce of the Norwich cock and Cinnamon hens, to which we directed attention at an early part of this chapter? Are they useless for the purpose of Cinnamon-breeding? On the contrary, they are very valuable; but when we left them there was nothing in the breeding-room to which they could be mated with such effect as with some of the birds resulting from the combinations we have suggested. But bearing in mind that Cinnamon blood infused from the male side will assert itself in *any* cross, it will be evident that if the hens, at least, of this batch of Greens—which now contains an addition of strong Norwich blood—be paired with the original Cinnamons, the result will be an improved edition of the bird, deeper in colour and richer in tone, but not so rich and bright as when obtained in the other way. In the same manner, if it be thought advisable, for the sake of some exceptionally superior crest formation, to import that feature through a Crested cock, it can be done in that way, although the direct result will be, not Crested Cinnamons, but Crested Greens, which can, in the next generation, be made Cinnamon by mating with pure Cinnamon cocks. Birds of singular beauty, however, can be obtained from these Plainhead and Crested Greens by mating with pink-eyed Clear Yellow or with Variegated Yellow Cinnamon cocks—a plan which must be adopted in the case of the Crested birds if it be desired to breed Variegated or Marked Crested Cinnamons, because the mating of a Self-coloured Crested Green with a pure Cinnamon would produce Self-coloured Crested Cinnamons, though, from the fact of the Green being full of Crest blood, there might be a few irregular sports. Self-coloured Crested Cinnamons can be more readily obtained in this way than by following up heavy variegation till light feathers be all eliminated and a perfect self-colour result, though the latter process might produce the more brilliant bird. This outline of pairing, though much condensed, will be a useful guide to the breeder in producing the several varieties of the Cinnamon Canary.

CHAPTER XXII

THE CRESTED CANARY

The Name.

THE "Crested" Canary takes its name from the topping, or crest, which adorns its head. It was formerly known as, and is still sometimes called by old breeders, the "Topping" or "Turncrown" Canary. The term was originally used for any crested Canary, and not for the Norwich type in particular; for it is a feature of old date, and common enough among German song-birds. It is most striking, and just one of those points likely to catch the eye of a fancier when even in an imperfect form, and on which he would expend some pains to build it up to his ideal standard; and so furnishes a capital illustration of his work, as distinct from that of the naturalist. The crest, once permanently fixed, would soon attract attention and be grafted into more than one variety. Prominent among such stands the Norwich type, on which the crest has been so carefully cultivated as to have long become an established variety. We say Norwich, though the bird is now far removed from that type; but the fancier's aim is to produce a chubby-built bird, though "Crest" in his Crested birds and massiveness of head with density and length of head feather in his Crestbreds are the first considerations.

We also find the crest existing under its old name of "Coppy" in the Lancashire of to-day, but we do not regard this on that account as the original stock, for both it and the old Norwich Turncrown must have long flourished coincidently in days of difficult travel with the existence of each scarcely known to the other. The crest now is more of a made-up type than the old Norwich Turncrown, which is seldom seen now, though some years ago very beautiful crested birds used to be bred in Norwich, and though they lacked colour, they were essentially true to type in shape and feather. This absence of colour may have led to the supposition that these old Turncrowns were of inferior blood, and, while rejoicing in a good crest, were used to produce crest-formation among higher-class birds. It is more probable that the old crest-breeders were obliged to relinquish colour in following up good strains, and that although there is such a disparity between the colour of the Norwich Plainhead and the Crest, they may, after all, be not so distantly related, and the crest or turncrown may have been a native feature.

For years, great effort has been made to improve the style by importing good crest from every available source, the object being, after having bred *in* the crest, to breed *out* all those points in which the offspring differ from the high-bred Norwich stem upon which the crest is grafted; and in doing this considerable judgment and care are required to ensure success, and a specimen showing the correct properties of a Norwich Plainhead with a large crest is still the exception. For many years now the type has been so altered from that of the original that the word "Norwich" has been almost dropped, and the bird called the "Crest Canary."

From the character of feathering of the Norwich Canary, there is a bound beyond which it cannot pass in crest-development. Breeders have found that to maintain the larger crest it is necessary to depart from that severe type which demands a quality of feathering at variance with the requisites for a full crest. Crest in conjunction only with coarse feather is quite as objectionable as fine feather and poor crest. What is required is a blending of the two in a bird which can still bear the time-honoured name and a resemblance of the family features.

A LARGE CREST WITH GOOD FEATHER, SPREAD, AND DROOP.

How far this is capable of accomplishment is still a problem, but from careful observation of crests of Norwich type we see that the modern bird does, and necessarily must, if it is to retain its magnificent crest, lose many of the characteristics of the Norwich Plainhead. That good work has been done in improving both size and quality of crest we have proof on every hand; for owing to the increased length of head feather, a crest with a large bare patch visible on the back of the head is as rare to-day as it was plentiful thirty years ago. True, many birds bear a strong resemblance to the Coppy in shape of body, owing to the constant use of this cross, but we already have, in addition to an approximation to Norwich carriage in contrast to the erect attitude of the Coppy, dark crests and variegated plumage, both foreign to

A Limit to Norwich Type.

the Coppy, and a steady approach to a quality of feather more in harmony with that of the Norwich than the looser plumage of the Lancashire. Further improvements, however, can yet be made in type of body and compactness of body feather, for it must be borne in mind that all the properties which become the Norwich should be found in the Crest in as great a degree as possible, always remembering that there *must* be good crest, which is a top-knot of feathers radiating from a common centre on the crown, and falling evenly over the head in every direction. In shape it should approach, as nearly as possible, a circular form, though such are comparatively rare, the more general shape being an approximation to an ellipse.

In size a good crest should extend in front to or over the end of the beak, the circumference passing round to the back of the head on the plane of the eyes, which should be almost, if not entirely, hidden, giving the bird an arch expression. Assuming reasonable compactness—by which we mean the absence of coarseness and irregularity—the most important features in a crest are its size, shape, and density; colour is a secondary consideration, though if this be good and the feather of a broad, leafy texture it is a splendid finish.

Size is mainly dependent upon the length of the feather; shape upon its distribution.

Formation of Crest.

The width and general contour of the skull have also something to do with it. A small crest will make any head look mean and spare, but a small head can carry a large crest, and show it to perfection, too, if the feather and form be there. It does *not* require an extra area of skull to hold the foundation of a well-feathered crest; but if the feathers be individually not much larger than the petals of a daisy, as was the case in many of the old Norwich crests, the case is different. The most beautiful forms which have appeared during the last twenty-five years have been of the long, wide sort, and many with a flat, leafy feather, a description of feather entirely different from that we have indicated as characteristic of a Norwich head, in which extreme shortness prevails, or should do. The shape is dependent on two things—a small centre, and the position of that centre, which should be sufficiently remote from the base of the beak to ensure a good frontage of regularly radiating long feathers, known technically as a good "entrance." It will be plain that, in the case of a crest at all elliptical in form, the farther the centre of the ellipse is from the base of the beak so will its value increase. Nothing will compensate for a bad entrance; any defect there is fatal. The centre which gives the neatest and best balance to a large crest is the one immediately behind the eye—in the centre of the top of the head, of course. If it is more forward it detracts greatly from the frontal crest, and if farther back, though it will often increase the frontal crest, it is at the expense of the balance of the crest. Thus it is important to study the position of the centre of the crest as well as other properties, as it assists to either mar or give a good finish.

The back of the crest is also a very important part of it. If a young dark-crested bird be examined in the nest before there are any indications of feathers, there will be observed at the back of the skull a light, crescent-shaped, scar-like mark, the rest of the crown being covered with black skin, indicative of the future colour of the feathers. On this light-coloured spot feathers never grow, and if the head be examined as the young quills present themselves, it will be seen that they sprout from every portion of the surface except this, which remains permanently bare. We have heard breeders remark that such and such a crest was a good one, "only the bird had knocked out a portion of the feathers from the back in putting its head through the water-hole." It is simply a popular fallacy: there never were any feathers to knock out. The larger this pale spot, the greater the probability of an inferior back to the crest, which ought to cover this naked place entirely, and can only do so by a proper disposition of the feathers. Having only a small vacancy constitutes what is known as being well "filled in" behind, and is more frequently the case in Buff birds than in Yellow, in which the feather years ago was so scanty as to show plainly this openness, and in those made up of the daisy-petal type of feather the vacancy behind became a positive eyesore. Of late years, however, so great has been the progress that it is rare now to see even a yellow crest display this bare patch at the back of the head.

A good crest should not stand up in the front, and, if a dark one, should show no light feathers over the beak, or on any other part of the crest. It should not be narrow or pointed in front, but every part of its circumference should be, as far as possible, equidistant from its centre. The idea of an oval-shaped crest is not intended to convey the notion of a narrow front, only that its length exceeds its width; the front must still be circular without any clipping away of corners. Neither should a good crest be "tucked in" at the sides, by which is meant having the outer edges broken or pinched-in behind the eyes, giving the crest the appearance of being formed of two parts. It should not have any split or opening in the front, nor should the "centre" assume the shape of a line dividing one side from the other, called by fanciers a "running centre"; nor should it be a point from which diverge two lines or partings in a backward direction right and left, destroying the appearance of perfect radiation. Nor should it be without *any* centre, and simply a heavy tuft of feathers falling smoothly over from back to front; nor should it be a mop. Neither should it be flat and exhibit no texture or feathery appearance, as if pressed out with an iron, which it will be observed is the exact converse of falling over the head in a drooping form. It should not be wider at the back than in the front; nor should it be tilted up at the back, and carried as if there were a danger of its sliding off; nor should it be shaped like an escutcheon, nor be square at the back, nor have dexter and sinister corners twisted up as if having been put into curl-papers. The edges must not be ragged, as it is often when composed of pointed feathers, giving it a slovenly appearance as if combed out into hair; but the imbrication must be complete and the outline as clearly defined as the small arch of the extremities of the feathers of the outer edge of the circle will permit. It must not be thin and sparse, but dense and full of feather, radiating evenly all round from a well-filled, neat centre. This full description is well aided by the illustrations given of the Crest Canary in our Coloured Plate and other engravings.

Classification. The classification of Crests is similar to that of Norwich Plainheads, but the order is inverted. We have the three main divisions—Dark Self-coloured, Variegated, and Clear, with subdivisions broadly corresponding:

Plainheads	Crests
(*a*) Lightly Variegated	(*a*) Clear Body with Dark Crest.
(*b*) Evenly-marked.	(*b*) Evenly - marked Crested.
(*c*) Unevenly-marked.	(*c*) Unevenly - marked Crested.
(*d*) Heavily Variegated.	(*d*) Variegated Crested.
(*e*) Ticked.	(*e*) Grey Crested.
(*f*) Green.	(*f*) Self-coloured Green Crested.
(*g*) Clear.	(*g*) Clear Crested.

It is a matter of taste as to which of the first two takes precedence, as both are singularly beautiful; but as it is more difficult to produce a clear body with *sound* dark crest than it is to breed a bird with even wing marks and dark crest, the order in which we have placed them is that generally accepted. Groups (*c*), (*d*), and (*f*) are in most schedules combined under the head of "Variegated or Self crested." Also, (*a*), (*e*), and (*g*) are similarly grouped under "Clear body with Green, Grey, or Clear Crest," and rank in value in the order named.

The Dark-crested Clear-bodied birds are the beau ideals of the careful breeder's eye, and rightly so if we take into consideration their difficulty of production. The Evenly-marked Dark Crest is also very difficult to obtain, and some think should therefore stand before the Clear Body Dark; and while on this ground the claims of the Marked bird can be justly urged, yet we are satisfied that it is no more difficult to breed an Evenly-marked Dark Crest than a Clear Body Dark Crest, and this granted, then for beauty, the pure, unbroken colour in the body in contrast with the dark crest, seems to us to be more marked than when the surface is broken by the mosaic-work on the back, beautiful as it is, and we give the palm to the Clear Body. We should be the last, however, on this account to disparage the Evenly-marked bird, for we want to see both colours bred plentifully, for we can spare neither of them.

The Evenly-marked bird must have no mark of any kind whatever on the head or cheeks, eye-marks *not* being recognised as "marks" among the Crests, as they are apt to assume the objectionable character of cheek-marks. The entire crest, of course, is dark, and should stand out clearly defined in bold relief against the golden ground-colour of the body. There are rare instances of marked wings with the remainder of body clear, and *bona-fide* grey or grizzle crest, in which case the birds are admitted in class (*b*) by virtue of their wing-marks, the deficiency of colour in the crest being weighed against their winning points. Any marking on the back of the neck, also, is very objectionable and counts against the bird according to its extent. It is, however, a very common blemish and one very difficult to get rid of, being usually present with Crests having no decided character at the back. It forms no part of the crest, and no argument can elevate it to the dignity of a mark, or show that it is a desirable adjunct, its chief use being to spoil the appearance of a symmetrical crest or deceive the eye as to the demerits of a bad one.

The colour of the crest depends a good deal on the strain of blood in the bird, and this also largely affects its shape and general character. An admixture with a more open-feathered variety will give a darker or blacker green to the crest; in hens so much so, that they can generally be picked out from the cocks by this difference in colour and texture of feather alone. Whatever the particular shade of the crest may be it should be bright and glossy, not dull, and this is dependent on the judicious use of Yellow blood.

The rules for wing and tail marks are the same as for Plainheads, and while we admit that it is quite illogical to attempt to show that an unevenly-marked tail is no blemish in an Evenly-marked class, yet with the leading feature, the crest, exhibited in perfection, and the most striking marking—viz. that on the wings also exact, and the body spotless and free from the suspicion of the smallest tick, it has always seemed to us such a pity to have to hold the bird up above the level of the eye, and turn it this way and that way in search of feathers which, when present, are of so trifling a value.

That others think with us is evident from the fact that to-day less attention is paid to tail marks in breeding Evenly-marked Crests than ever, the object now being to produce the even-marked wings and Dark Crest with clear tail as well as the rest of the body.

Body-colour, as the family is at present constituted, must be good, with feather replete with the pregnant attribute of "quality." The colour of the legs and feet is practically of no value: it inclines to dark, but is never very decided or uniform. Any description of the next two classes, (*c*) and (*d*), is unnecessary, beyond saying that, for reasons which we will presently adduce, their marking and variegation are, under ordinary circumstances, of no value whatever. We pass on to class (*e*), Grey-crested, a most important class in the breeding-room, as will be seen in its place, and a not less important one in the show-room. A good grey crest is very pretty, although it has no recognised value from a colour point of view, as it matters not how grey or how grizzly it may be, and as a variety it is simply a

Clear Yellow Goldfinch Mule Ticked Buff Linnet Mule
Yellow Canary-Bullfinch Mule

warmer hue. This cross will also furnish the breeder with several classes of birds, all of which are valuable for different purposes. There will probably be Self-Cinnamons, at once, which will show the highest and purest form of colour, and which may be mated with the original strain without more ado. It must not be expected that such mating will produce nests entirely free from blemish, because the Clear Norwich blood is very near the surface, and will, in all probability, bubble up; but it is a very safe cross, and one from which very little trouble may be expected. Then there will be others in all degrees of variegation, heavy and light, which will require dealing with according to the extent and quality of the cinnamon marking. Some may be merely ticked, some have nothing more than pied wings or tail, and others may be irregularly splashed. For every one there will be a place. Some may be green or broken green: these also can all be treated as Cinnamons, and worked accordingly. But some will probably show very fair *marking*, either cinnamon or green, and one or two may be clear from cinnamon-coloured feathers entirely, but yet have the *pink eye*, which, we may remark, can be discerned by the merest novice directly the young birds leave the shell, and is the distinguishing mark by which the breeder can determine at once the character of a mixed nest in which he anticipates finding Cinnamons. The existence of this pink eye as the infallible tell-tale of Cinnamon blood does not appear to be so well known as it should be. Many instances have come under our notice of persons having pink-eyed birds without having the slightest idea of their descent, any knowledge of of the fact being further kept out of view owing to many of these birds having been bred for one purpose or another perfectly clear, without as much as a single cinnamon feather being discerned in them. Having thus passed from hand to hand they have come into the possession of persons who were quite unacquainted with their character, and, not suspecting it, have mated them with birds of other breeds, with some of the perplexing results to which we have referred. Young birds of this class, when feathered, it will be well to mark by a distinguishing notch on one of the flight-feathers, or in some similar way, or by placing a numbered Canary marking-ring on one leg, taking note of the number to ensure identification at a future day. The value of those found to have good technical marking, or even a decent approach to it, cannot be over-estimated. We have in them the starting-point of a *marked* strain, and there are many ways of pairing, a few of which only need to be suggested in order to indicate the direction in which the work can be carried out. The Cinnamon-marked birds, *being all hens*, may be mated with Clear-bodied pink-eyed cocks, with the tolerable certainty of having marking of some kind reproduced. The Green-marked cocks might also be similarly mated with these hens, and by that means two like tendencies would be concentrated in one channel, even at the risk of producing a heavy form of marking, or a leaning towards irregular variegation through the infusion of two streams of Cinnamon blood, followed up as explained in the chapter on breeding Evenly-marked Canaries. Or these valuable Green-marked cocks might be paired with Clear hens of a fresh Norwich strain, with a reasonable expectation of throwing lightly-marked Cinnamons or a further supply of pink-eyed Clears, both cocks and hens, if these Norwich hens have any Cinnamon blood in them, to be made use of in the almost endless ways in which the principles of pedigree-breeding can be brought to bear upon this remarkable Canary.

Mr. C. L. Quinton, of Great Yarmouth, one of our most successful Cinnamon breeders, writing to us, says:

A Personal Experience.

"I have been breeding Cinnamons for the past twenty-four years, and have always found the Norwich cross the best with which to increase size and colour in the Cinnamon, when I found it necessary to take a cross. I breed my birds pure so long as they retain good size and colour; but if I find I am losing size, colour, or quality, I select the largest Clear or Ticked Yellow Norwich hen I can, with good shape, colour, head and quality. I pair such a hen to one of my best Cinnamon cocks, and select the best of the young from these to pair back to my pure Cinnamon. I have never used any other cross, and have found such most successful in yielding me the points I crossed for. The young hens from this cross I have sometimes paired back to their father, or birds of the same strain, with good results, fixing the points I required—of course selecting from their young only those possessing the improvements I required for future breeding with. Some of these young ones so bred have given me splendid results in their progeny. My object in in-breeding, when I do resort to it, is to fix points I desire."

Crested Cinnamons.

We do not think it necessary to devote a separate chapter to the subject of breeding Crested Cinnamons in all its detail, because the line of operation can be deduced from our foregoing observations, the chief point for consideration here being how to introduce the crest in the first instance—this, of course, implying the assumption that the breeder has no Crested Cinnamon of any kind at command. The most direct method, it is obvious, will be to import it through the hen, since in that way the object sought is obtained at once. It is not material what class of hen we select, but we should prefer a Grey-crested or a Clear-bodied Dark-crested. Hens of this description, paired with a rich Jonque Cinnamon cock, would produce—what ? In accordance with the law of Cinnamon first-cross we should expect to find Greens, Cinnamons, Variegated birds of either kind, and also Clears with pink eyes, the nests containing, as a natural consequence, both Crests and Plainheads, probably by far the greater number Plainheads ; this, however, could to an extent be checked by using a Crested hen which has been bred from two Crested parents, not Crest and Crest-bred as usually paired. Of these young, bred from the Cinnamon cock and Crested hen, the Cinnamon-marked Crested birds must, at least, be hens, whatever the amount of their variegation, be it merely a few cinnamon feathers mixed in the crest or a more widely-distributed form of variegation. And the Green-marked Crested will be—what ? Cinnamon-bred, of course ; the cocks being a medium through which cinnamon crest can be planted on any variety, just as the corresponding form in the Plainhead can produce cinnamon marking. Similar forms of feather will also be found among the Plainheads, and there will also probably be the pink-eyed Clear body. What are we to do with these varied products ? If we have put up several pairs, or have mated the same Jonque Cinnamon to two or three hens, we shall have material at command to carry out our pedigree-breeding efficiently, without forming a series of alliances too far within the prescribed bounds of consanguinity ; though, in commencing, we should mate irrespective of such laws if any two streams ran in the direction wished, only too glad to unite them in one. Take the Green-marked cocks first, Crested or Plainhead : a Crested bird we would pair with a lightly Cinnamon-marked hen, and expect to find among the produce Variegated Crested Cinnamons of either sex, more or less evenly-marked according to the marking of the parents. If our Crests were very few in our first cross we should not hesitate to pair these Cinnamon Green-marked Crest cocks to lightly cinnamon-marked Crested hens or pink-eyed Clear Crested hens (the same way bred) with a view to increasing the number of Crests in the next generation. A Plainhead from our first year's work we would mate up with a Clear-bodied Cinnamon-crested hen, and expect them to produce the same as the previous pairing, with probably lighter marking; we would also pair a Green-marked Crested bird with a Clear Crest-bred hen, and a Green-marked Plainhead with a Crested hen, and look for similar results, with the addition of more Green-marked and pink-eyed Clears, in all of which we should expect to find increased depth of colour. So far we have worked only with the produce of the pairs put up for crest-breeding, but in any room in which the breeding of colour-Cinnamons has been carried on there will be Plainhead cocks and hens in every stage of develop-

chance result in an endeavour to get other markings. A grey crest is neither dark nor clear, but is composed of a mixture of dark and light feathers, or of feathers having a dark midrib and light edge, which, in a Buff bird, has a very pleasing effect, and we think it could well be systematically bred, both as a show bird and as a valuable asset to the breeding-room. It is rather remarkable that the majority of Grey Crested Canaries are buff—casual ones have a slight grizzle mark on the wing; when such is the case it forbids their admission to a Clear-bodied class. They generally have a clear body quite free from marking, and also generally " blow " clear in the flue, and are thus very nearly allied to the last on our list, the Clear-crested bird, and we see no reason why a Clear-crested strain having good crest properties should not be more cultivated, for several have been produced which in size, shape, and density would compare favourably with the Green-crested. Shape and feather and every requisite could be had as well in the Clear as in any other, but the want of contrast in colour is doubtless the cause of no decided steps having been taken by fanciers in this direction. Yet curiously enough, in the giant Coppy, a clear crest is the highest point of perfection, and no one who has seen the best specimens of this breed can have any doubt as to the air of refinement the clear crest gives, and we submit that there is a fair field open here for the breeder's skill in producing good " Clear Crests."

We have left the Self-coloured Green standing out in the cold, because we have a difficulty in assigning him his true place. Probably it is strictly immediately behind the Heavily Variegated, which is the first remove from the Green, and is the class with which he usually competes at shows. The Self-coloured Green is most valuable in the breeding-room, even if not very attractive on the show-bench, and when properly mated, does much towards the production of the good points of the bird at the head of our list of Crests. Only in the event of superlative merit in crest (for nothing else can serve him to take first position in the class) the Self-coloured Green generally remains at home.

Throughout the whole of these classes the prominent idea is crest, and after connecting it with the two forms with which we first coupled it, the fancier entirely ignores the value of such marking as remains. He groups the classes (*c*) and (*d*) into one, and sees merit in them only in so far as it is connected with crest development. With a fancier's innate love for marking, he cannot but accord to it its value when of the right kind, but would rather combine still further and unite the two Marked and the Variegated than subtract one iota from their crest-worth by recognising any body-marks in them as superior to it. His creed is crest, *and* marking, if possible, but the former at any cost. He does not assign to these minor points the values they carry when separate from crest, but accepts their perfect development, when they fall to his lot, rather as fortunate adjuncts than the results of systematic breeding. Correct as this reasoning may be up to a point, we confess that we should like to see more attention paid to the production of the various markings and colours without, of course, any sacrifice in crest properties, for then better classification could be demanded, and, what is more important, there would then be the birds to fill the classes. Nineteen out of every twenty Crest breeders to-day give no thought to colour or marking, or to breeding a good Yellow Crest, their whole craze is to breed a winner, never mind colour. It is a blind policy to pursue, one class or colour of bird, for it kills classification for the breed, and as the various marked and coloured birds become scarcer, all drift into the one channel of ordinary variegation. Breeding-rooms are over-run with such birds to-day to an alarming extent, and while we know that we cannot afford to risk the loss of one important structural point in an endeavour to fix some other foreign to it, marking should yet have due consideration without sacrifice of crest, if a variety is to flourish. The various markings and colours have been produced, and it is our duty to endeavour to perpetuate and fix them.

The admired colour in Dark Crests is a blackish green margin or fringe and a black midrib, commonly known as a "veined" crest. The body should be of stout build, similar to the Norwich, but larger, short, full neck, and heavily feathered, though close, the bird standing well across the perch on short legs, with a firm command of its body. It is also desirable that the beak be small and neat, which gives a good finish to the front of the head and crest.

In classifying the Crest we give seven distinct classes of colour or marking, but if Yellows were bred in a like number to Buffs the same number of classes could be allotted to them, as we have similar marking in Yellows and Buffs, which would make fourteen classes alone for Crests, and these could be further sub-divided by having separate classes for cocks and hens. Therefore breeders will see what a large field for cultivation is open to them. At the present time the most extended classification given at a few shows is (*a*) Buff, clear body, with clear, grey, or dark crest; (*b*) Buff, any other variety, crested, cock, which includes evenly-marked, unevenly-marked, vareigated, and green; (*c*) Buff-crested hen other than clear body; (*d*) Yellow-crested cock, any colour crest; (*e*) Yellow-crested hen, any colour crest; (*f*) Crests any colour, current year bred.

The washing and dressing of crests will be found dealt with in Chapter XIV.

The Crestbred.

We have next to consider the Crestbred Plainhead of the variety under consideration. This is now just as important an exhibition bird as the Crest, although formerly it was not recognised as such, classes being allotted to it for the first time at the Crystal Palace Show in 1888, prior to which date any of these birds had to compete in the "Any Other Variety of Canary" class. This recognition caused more attention to be paid to the Crestbred in the breeding-room, and resulted in greater development of head and denser and longer head-feather points, which have assisted in the development of our Crests to a marked degree.

The Crestbred, like the Crest, should be of massive build, thick-set body, like the Norwich Plainhead, but larger; feather in abundance lying as close to the body as possible, though it is next to impossible to get it as close as that of the Norwich, owing to its great length. Some feathers which we have taken from the sides and flanks of our own birds measure from 2¼ to 2½ inches long, and we have measured body feathers from other breeders' birds equally as long. Like the Crest, the head of a Crestbred is of more importance than the body, in fact a Crestbred without the right head and head-feather is no Crestbred at all, no matter how densely clothed the body may be with long feather. It is practically impossible to get the necessary head-feather without a corresponding abundance of body-feather. The head should be large and broad, and the entrance to the skull over the base of the beak wide, in a good specimen coming to an abrupt stop, the feather rising suddenly from the very commencement of its growth owing to the denseness and length of feather at the base of the beak. This flow of feather should gradually expand in width as it falls gracefully over the skull to the back of the head, its density causing it to fall over the eyes at the sides, giving the bird a frowning appearance, called by fanciers "lashing" or "browing"; it almost covers the eyes like a crest. This falling of the feather over the sides of the head gives a more expansive appearance to the skull, finishing off gracefully with a wonderful expanse at the back of the poll, a short neat beak intensifying the beauty of the massive shapely skull, a shape peculiarly this bird's own. A glance at the illustration on page 283 will convey to the reader the accuracy of our description of a good Crestbred.

The usual classification of Crestbreds at some of our best exhibitions is (*a*) Yellow cock or hen; (*b*) Buff cock, clear ticked or lightly marked; (*c*) Buff cock, green or heavily variegated, more dark than light; (*d*) Buff hen. This classification, like the Crest, could be further extended if the various colours were bred in sufficient numbers to warrant it, which would be the case if every breeder endeavoured to produce them in the Crested birds, for as a natural consequence we must get similar colour and markings in the Crestbreds. Classification in the Crestbreds might then be extended as follows: (*a*) Yellow cock, (*b*) clear or ticked Buff cock; (*c*) unevenly-marked or variegated Buff cock; (*d*) Buff green cock; (*e*) Yellow hen; (*f*) clear or ticked Buff hen; (*g*) Unevenly marked, variegated or green Buff hen.

Be ore we proceed to deal with their breeding we quote the Crest Canary Club's descriptions of these birds, with which, we may add, we entirely agree:

"The standard of perfection in a Crest shall be as follows:—Size and formation of crest shall be the first consideration. A crest cannot be too large. It should consist of an abundance of broad, long, and veiny feathers, evenly radiated from a small centre well over the eyes, beak and poll. A good crest may be flat if well filled in at back, and without splits, but a drooping or weeping crest shall have the preference. Type and quality are of the next importance. The body shall resemble in shape that of the Bullfinch, possessing substance in proportion to its length, with a broad back nicely arched, full and well circled chest, tail short and narrow, wings not extending beyond root of tail, nor crossed at tips, but fitting close to the body. The neck should be full, and the beak short. The bird should stand well across the perch on short legs, with thighs and hocks well set back."

"The Crest-bred should possess a body as above described. The head should be large and round, broad at every part, with a small beak, with an abundance of long, broad feather, commencing at entrance of beak, continuing over the crown, and flowing well down the poll, and shall be well browed. In a good Crest-bred the feathers on the crown when turned over should reach to end of beak, and the heavy brows should give the bird a sulky appearance without brushing."

BREEDING CRESTS

The first general rule to be observed in pairing birds for crest-breeding is to mate a Crest with a Crestbred, that is the Plainhead bird bred from a Crest and a Plainhead, and this rule is so general as to be almost invariable. The reason for this is somewhat obvious, if we bear in mind that a Canary's crest is not a high spherical tuft, but a flat, fimbriated arrangement of the feathers on the top of the skull, which, radiating from a centre, would have their character entirely altered if any approach to a high tuft were to take place. We have seen indications of this tufted form, and a crest without a centre is not so uncommon an occurrence as to excite much surprise. Tuft-crests, if we may coin the word to describe these occasional departures from the regular form, seem to present no methodical arrangement of the feathers, which themselves are different in character from those found in a radiated crest, being much shorter as a rule and apparently but a slightly enlarged form of the ordinary feathers on the crown, increased in number, and, to use a homely but expressive phrase, "combed the wrong way." Such tuft-crests are generally very dense and more like rough mats than anything else; and it has been found that repeatedly pairing two Crests ultimately leads to the production of similar forms in which *excess* of feather, without any regard to arrangement, takes the place of the radiated type so dear to the fancier's eye, hence the use of the Crestbred to retain radiation and droop. At the same time, this does not always follow as an immediate and direct result; and the general rule is occasionally departed from when it is found desirable to pair with a view to obtaining excess of crest-feather at the risk of sacrifice of form and radiation, which are not always, as a necessary consequence, affected by a *first* double cross. Much depends upon the character of the two crests so paired; if of perfect radiation and good droop, some of the most effective forms which have ever appeared on the show-bench have resulted from a happy hit in this direction. In a general way, however, what is gained in feather is lost in symmetry, which requires to be afterwards developed by systematic mating of Crestbreds with such Crests.

For, besides such direct "hits" and crests of approved type, there will be some objectionable forms which it is not desirable to perpetuate. We have already referred to some of these on page 271, but it may be well to illustrate some of the most objectionable faults. Fig. 89 shows neat front but defective arrangement in the rear, where two ugly partings on either side of the crest, usually called "splits" or "gutters," destroy the uniformity of the radiation—a not uncommon defect. Fig. 90 illustrates the "split" in front of crest, in which the absence of any defined centre affects the character of the front very materially; it will be noticed, in fact, that there is *no* centre. A split seems to be the first attempt at radiation, and its presence appears to indicate a reversion to some form we certainly do not want; moreover, this fault is extremely difficult to breed out. The centre of some of our good crests have an inclination this way, only in a modified form, not interfering with the proper arrangement of the frontal crest, nevertheless the tendency is there, and they are termed running centres, and a sharp eye needs be kept on them when pairing such birds up. Fig. 91 also represents neat front, but broken or tucked in at the sides—a defect sometimes noticeable in the original Coppy. This fault is described by most Crest-breeders as weak or short at sides. It will be observed that up to the present these various faulty crests are all good at back. Fig. 92 is not sufficiently filled in behind, and is also badly carried, being too much tilted up. The largeness of the puckered or scarred-like skin at the back of the head of a crested bird spoken of earlier in this chapter, caused by the formation of the skin in radiating the feather round the head, has much to do with this gap or roughness at the back of the head. To pair a bird with a rough or tilted back crest to a Crestbred with rough feathers or horned at sides of back of head will further intensify the fault, while to pair such a faulty-backed Crest to a Crestbred having perfectly smooth feathers at the back will reduce the tendency, such pairing having the tendency to reduce the size of the puckered or scarred-like patch on the back of the head of the Crest, and the smaller this is the smoother the crest will be. This illustration also shows an open centre and short frontal. Fig. 93 delineates neat feathering, but bad shape, being too narrow in front, and too square behind, with the objectionable corners described in our list of forms to be avoided, and termed by Crest-breeders "shield shape." There are some such crests with the ear-like corners, and both types should be erradicated or improved to the proper shape by judicious pairing. Fig. 94 represents a crest of proper formation and shape spoiled by a dark patch at the back of the neck, in which the crest feathers merge and lose their outline. A clear body is not in any respect improved by such a mark. This illustration shows the centre well placed and of the right shape, being perfectly round, but too open; another defect which tells against an otherwise good bird, and a bird of equal merit with a centre similar to that shown in Fig. 91 will always get in front owing to its better filled centre showing no open space yet of the perfectly round, desired shape. A further detraction of value in Fig. 94 is the smallness of the crest, none of these illustrations in any way represent the size of our modern crest; but are given as an object lesson of the faults to be avoided and got rid of as quickly as possible by judicious pairing. The more perfect specimens are portrayed on the Coloured Plate and other illustrations.

Defects in Crest.

It is sometimes said that the produce of two Crests will be more or less bald on the pate, sometimes even to complete nudity. We never found such a thing happen, nor have we ever seen such a specimen or any person who could vouch for such a thing having occurred. We have bred Plainheads often enough from two Crests—a

Pairing two Crests.

thing easily accounted for on the hypothesis that the recognised form of Crest has much of the Plainhead in it, and we have seen more or less disturbance of the usual type, but never anything remotely approaching baldness—in fact, always the reverse. And further, among the thousands of crests we have seen of all conceivable styles, bred, doubtless, in all sorts of ways from Crest and Plainhead, and, for want of better knowledge, frequently enough from repeated successions of double Crests, we never remember seeing a head *so* bald as to lead us for a moment to infer that it arose from any such method of pairing as we refer to. We therefore unhesitatingly affirm that to pair two Crests is a sure way to obtain, not baldness, but excess of feather, which can afterwards be regulated and brought into shape by pairing back to Crestbreds with a nice smooth flow of feather over the head. One thing we have proved —and we know that many other breeders have experienced the same thing—is that double-cresting, if repeated to any extent, has a tendency to produce running ulcers at the back of the head or over the nostrils; but this defect disappears from the offspring if such birds are paired to Crestbreds.

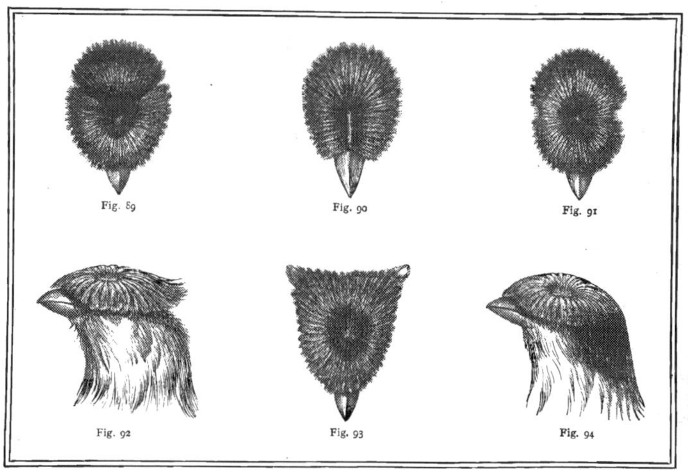
Fig. 89 Fig. 90 Fig. 91
Fig. 92 Fig. 93 Fig. 94

Dealing with general principles, we say, as a second thing to be observed, that whereas in breeding Norwich Plainheads two Yellows are sometimes paired to obtain colour even at a probable sacrifice of feather, so, in breeding for crest, double Buffs are paired to get or thicken the feather at the expense of colour, and the latter practice has been carried on to too great an extent, much to the detriment of the colour and quality of feather of Crests, to say nothing of having rendered Yellow-Crests obsolete, although most useful for show and breeding purposes. Its judicious use improves the colour of the crest and body feather, giving a finish to both which double buffing can never produce. We know it is next to impossible to breed a heavy crest from a thinly feathered bird, and the nature of the work to be accomplished will therefore suggest a reason for frequent departure from the line of procedure usually adopted in breeding Norwich Plainheads. What is wanted is crest, bear in mind; and since we *must* have crest, just as we *must* elsewhere have marking or any other leading feature, we must furnish the elements at all hazards. Once obtained, it then rests with the breeder to restore and maintain a balance of other properties by the exercise of skill in his art. But owing to lack of attention by breeders the majority of our stock now are simply Heavily Variegated birds. When breeders succeeded in obtaining the large modern crests they should then have paid more attention to colour and marking; and even now it is not "too late to mend." For many years we have advocated a cross with Yellow blood every third season, double-buffing the two intermediate seasons. If Yellow blood were used in this manner great benefits would ensue, without any loss in density of feather. Breeding from a Buff bred from Yellow and Buff paired to a bird bred from Double Buffs has most beneficial effects.

These elementary principles of crest-breeding learnt, we must at the outset caution the reader against supposing that he has nothing to do but to go to some big show, open his purse-strings, and at once commence to breed Crests of merit equal, or anything like equal, to those he has purchased, unless he selects suitable partners for them. This is the rock on which so many come to grief, for they think if they pair two first-prize birds together success must follow, and are bitterly disappointed when it does not. They forget that possibly those two first-prize birds were not absolutely perfect, and, though well on that way, may both possess the same faulty tendency in one or more points, and to pair them together because they happen to win first prizes is not "breeding," but happy-go-lucky mating, for each in its partner should have a counterbalancing tendency against its particular failing. Outward development is the guide to all careful breeders in pairing, and though everyone who can afford it wisely purchases the best stock he can, our advice would be not always to buy the specimens most perfect at all points, unless for exhibition purposes, but rather to invest in such as show extreme development of the one point desired in your stock or the bird you want to pair it with, for when a cultivated ideal reaches its zenith it must be maintained, or it will assuredly decline.

We have already alluded to the fact that the modern Crest can hardly be considered as native to the Norwich variety unless the old Norwich "Turncrown" be accepted as the original type, and also hinted that in its progression to its present stage of perfection it owes much of its improvement to the Lancashire Coppy, a mine extensively worked some twenty or twenty-five years ago, but not used so much now as when the large crest was in its manufacturing stage, and also because of the difficulty of procuring a suitable "Coppy," or a Lancashire Plainhead, to cross with the Crest.

We need not describe the Coppy here further than to say that it is a giant, and stands very erect, is inclined to be coarse in feather, carries very little colour, is clear or only ticked, or the coppy slightly grizzled, and thus has many properties with which we wish to have as little to do with as possible in Crest-breeding. Yet crossing this bird occasionally with the Crest, and judiciously fining its progeny down by pairing back to Crests, has the effect of producing a crest in size never dreamt of, and marvellous heads and feather on the Crestbreds. Its use, however, must not be abused, or its benefits are lost. In selecting our Coppy when a cross is necessary, let it be chosen for crest properties entirely; but if the bird shows less roughness of feather, and less Coppy points generally than are cultivated by Lancashire fanciers, we shall have the less foreign matter to eliminate. It is immaterial whether the bird be cock or hen; but the advantage of working from a cock consists in being able to run him with several hens, and so secure at once a greater number of "first crosses" from which to make selections for future operations in pedigree-breeding, according to the principles enunciated in previous chapters. As to whether it be Yellow or Buff, we should prefer the former, as yielding a better quality of feather, but if size of body is wanted as well as crest, then use the Buff, and if it be a hen it will probably show less coarseness, remembering to observe the law of pairing Yellow and Buff as far as possible, as the surplusage of feather will continually require toning down.

The Lancashire Cross.

If you use a Lancashire Plainhead you would naturally pair it with the best Crest you have, or if using a Lancashire Coppy, pair it with a Crestbred, although we have had good results from pairing a Coppy to a good Crest. Remember that Crestbreds are the Plainhead offspring from Crested nests—by which we do not mean the issue of double Crests, but of birds paired for crest-breeding in the ordinary way, which always throw a fair average of Plainheads as well as Crests. Such birds contain a latent tendency towards crest, which is further shown in some by the feathering on top of head and overhanging eyebrows, giving the bird a rather sulky expression altogether, different from that of the highly bred Norwich Plainhead. Whatever be their parentage, it will be advisable to select birds of some size and with broad skulls, and, having these properties, to get combined with them the highest type of Norwich properties, as shown in colour and quality of feather. We already have size on the Lancashire side, but we do not wish to perpetuate it in that form, and therefore select our Crests with size and the distinctive shape of the Norwich, in the hope that these features may play their part in moulding the offspring to the Norwich persuasion, and so leave us less to tone down in after generations of our crosses.

Another important matter remains for consideration. We said that the Coppy is clear in colour, or practically so, and as such we must here treat it. This will not satisfy the breeder, who wants the contrast of clear body and dark green crest, or clear body with dark wings and crest, in quest of which typical forms of ideal beauty he creates variegation *ad infinitum,* for every shade of which there is a place on the show-bench if only good crest accompany it. When once the green is brought into play, a very intractable element is infused, requiring all the skill of the thoughtful breeder to control it, despite which it will occasionally break away just when it is wanted to stand still. So if the breeder does not care to embark on the troubled waters of variegation, there is open to him the breeding of entirely clear-crested birds of Norwich type, which at this day have but few representatives, and to whose charm we have already alluded. To breed Clear Crests and Crestbreds is comparatively easy. All that is necessary is to pair clear birds together, occasionally pairing a Grey Crest with a Clear Crestbred, or a Ticked Crestbred with the Clear Crests, with a view of maintaining brilliancy of colour, pairing the offspring of these back to clears.

Reverting to the thread of our subject, we remark that any amount of variegation can be introduced into Crested stock by pairing a Clear and a Variegated bird together, yet we have frequently been asked: "How can we breed Dark Crests?" We reply that if one of the parents be Variegated there will be a full average of Dark Crests in every nest, on which fact we base our final general rule, that if our Coppy be a Buff cock, he must be paired with Variegated—or, as they are known in the Fancy, broken Green Crestbred hens, or he may be paired to Self-green, Yellow or Buff hens. In either case, if a Buff is used a good plan is to have one that has been bred from Yellow and Buff. If he be a Yellow cock the hens must be similar in character, but Buff; and if we elect to breed with a Coppy hen our Crestbred cock must be a Variegated Yellow or Buff, as the case may demand. There need be no apprehension as to the chances of procuring Dark Crests, for every bird, if it be in the slightest degree marked and have a crest, will have a dark crest, than which there is nothing easier to breed, as regards colour.

We say every bird, because practically it is so; and we do not remember having seen more than a very few indeed which, having dark wings or variegation of any kind, had other than a dark crest. We have known of a few grey-crested birds having a slight grizzly tick on a wing or other part of the body. We have also had and known of wing-marked and variegated birds with dark crests in the first year moulting out the following year with crests composed of light and dark feathers, yet still retaining their variegated body or dark wings. We never knew one to regain its dark crest again entirely, after having once moulted out piebald.

The first cross from the Coppy will present, as regards shape and general conformation, a strong resemblance to the Lancashire, with considerable improvement in feather, but this coarse, notwithstanding something of the Norwich impress. Although this extreme roughness is in itself most undesirable, yet it has its value, because where it exists there is frequently a corresponding growth of crest and a marked enlargement of the individual feathers of which it is composed—a valuable property, which every endeavour should be made to maintain. We might indicate many forms which will probably be found in the first nests, but they may be summed up in two—refined Coppies and Plainheads, and coarse nondescript Crests and Crestbreds. Occasionally we have bred first crosses, both Crests and Crestbreds, which have displayed so much of Crest characteristics that they were exhibited in these classes and got well into the prize list.

Of the two classes produced, we will deal first with what we have called the refined Coppies and Plainheads which have taken largely after the Lancashire, and have neatness of crest rather than size, and which for future operations are not of such value as the coarser Norwich type of birds.

We therefore leave these very neat Crests and "Plainheads" (we do not say Crestbreds on account of their Lancashire tendencies) alone, unless they have more than average size, in which case the Crested cocks will prove valuable mates either for Crested-bred hens of a fresh strain or for some of the coarser-feathered Crestbred hens of your own from nests which show most Norwich type. If hens, they will prove perhaps more valuable still to pair with Crested-bred cocks from another strain, whose Norwich shape is already or nearly fixed, or selected as before. This will in all probability put the breeder well on his journey, for it requires but few crosses back to Crests to produce a fair bird in which the redeeming feature of an extra good crest atones for minor deficiencies. Suitable Plainheads from the first crosses are paired back in like manner to good, shapely Crests of Norwich type.

The real strength of the Lancashire cross will, however, be found in the birds showing a departure from the Coppy shape, for even though connected with coarseness, as good crest can only emanate from plenty of feather we must put up with the surplus, and by careful mating endeavour to get rid of it as best we can. To this end pair the best Crested cocks with good, leafy feathered Crestbred hens, taking strongly to the Norwich in shape with good heads, size, and colour points and general neatness. Handsome Crests are sometimes bred small, but a decrease in size will come quickly enough by the constant infusion of the more refined type, in which the Coppy blood has been well bred out without being courted too soon by breeding with small hens, unless counteracted by a mate with extraordinary size. The modern Crest of Norwich type is larger than the Norwich Plainhead proper, and loses nothing in that respect in natural beauty, and is admitted by all Crest breeders to be superior, particularly in size and crest, to the bird of long ago.

If the breeder prefers to work with material made or partially made, he can do so, and take a shorter cut by "picking up" a good stock bird here and there, and importing fresh strains of Crest blood, in which the Coppy element has been well mixed and assimilated.

In pairing to secure crest, it is manifest that some sacrifice must be made on one side or the other, or on both, and the mode of procedure to be followed is, briefly, in the first place to reject those birds which show no marked character either way, and then to select from the rest those in which crest has been stamped with the least loss of character consistent with the greatest amount of gain in improved condition of body-feather. Systematic pairing of these birds among themselves, or with approved strains, will accomplish all that can be desired. Out of the varied produce will occasionally spring a specimen apparently far in advance of his fellows; but the breeder must not come to the conclusion that the three points—crest, feather, and shape—are fixed until he sees them repeated, not in isolated cases, but with sufficient frequency to warrant him looking in some particular direction for some special feature, and finding it produced. As the distinctive features of each bird become gradually merged in the type, quite as much attention will be required to maintain the ground gained as has been expended in making it, and any tendency towards decline must be met by the introduction of a fresh supply of the failing element. The breeder who has worked with several pairs, and has noted carefully the character of his stock, knows exactly where to lay his hand on what he requires. Here he notices a falling away in crest, and mates with it a rather coarse or extra heavily feathered Crestbred. It scarcely looks like the sort of bird we would like to cross with a fine strain, but he knows it was the only rough one out of a fine nest, and can do wonders in resuscitating crest without affecting body-feather. And here is a rather persistent coarseness, at which he fires a shot by pairing with an exquisitely neat bird, and so on, doing nothing without a reason, adding crest, and reducing coarseness. Even width of the web of the feather has something to do with adding feather, as a wide web must carry more feather substance than a narrow one.

Two wide-headed Crestbreds are sometimes paired together to counteract a tendency to lose width of skull in the Crestbreds, and the young from these are paired back to Crests which have been bred from two Crests, so as to increase the percentage of Crests in the resulting progeny. Some pairs throw good Crests and inferior Crestbreds, and others just the reverse. These results must be carefully noted for the pairing of their descendants, as for breeding and show purposes alike, equal care must be given to the production of both good Crestbreds and good Crests.

Breeding for Markings.

It is much easier to produce marking in the Crested than in the ordinary Plainhead variety, less being demanded, and what is required being more easily controlled. The only two points are a dark crest and even marking on the wings, the dark crest appearing either by itself or in connection with the wing-marking. We have said how the same marking that stamps the wing also stamps the crest, and it only remains to show the best means to adopt to secure one or both. What difficulty there is arises from the previously explained erratic character of variegation generally, which, when once introduced, is apt to turn up in places where its company is not wanted.

We will take the Evenly-marked Crest first, as it is usually considered to occupy the foremost position as the more difficult to breed. To obtain these the Green element is required on one side only, and in selecting the Crested parent we would as soon choose a Grey, or even a Clear Crest, as any other—though good examples of the latter are seldom seen—and pair it with Crestbred hens neatly and exactly marked on the wings. We should not, unless under special circumstances, select birds marked on the eyes, because any such marking on the face of a Crest is fatal to its reputation. This is all that is required, and the produce will most probably consist of (*a*) Grey Crests, which, of course, will be Clear-bodied — with but very few exceptions, and these exceptions will usually be a very small grizzle tick on one wing, the rest of the body clear ; (*b*) Dark Crests also Clear-bodied ; (*c*) Variegated Dark-crested, with perhaps (*d*) a good Evenly-marked Dark Crest among them, and generally (*e*) a few Crestbreds, Clear or otherwise—not all in one nest certainly, but the birds we have described will constitute the average results of such a mode of pairing. Much the same results would follow the pairing of an Evenly-marked Crested and a Clear Crestbred, though there might not be so many Grey Crests, the darker form being likely to repeat itself. In both, however, we should expect to find a full average of *respectable wings,* the point we wish to secure. There also might, and probably would be, if the original marking were light, consisting of, say, not more than about four dark feathers in each wing, one or two birds marked only on one wing —a useful form, but given to be rather obstinate. Analysing these nests, we should take care of all the Grey Crests worthy of the name : they are special favourites of ours and are useful in many ways ; moreover, among any number of crests of all kinds, there will be found a higher average of quality among the Greys than among the darker ones, though the paler colour may not show off the shape to such advantage. These Greys we should pair with the marked Crestbreds, sailing as close to the wind as possible in the matter of selecting the nearest approach to even and exact marking, our object being to put in crest without offering any temptation to run to irregular variegation, perpetuating the desired points as we explained in the chapter on Even-marked breeding.

Suitable mates would probably be found among the Crested-bred young ones, in which case we should prefer pairing the offspring of various hens by the same cock to bringing in any fresh blood at this early stage ; and if the sexes have been reversed in one or two of the original pairs —viz. by pairing a wing-marked Crestbred cock with a Grey-crested hen—there will be material sufficient for any combination. The Clear-bodied Dark-crested we should pair with Clear Crestbreds to reproduce the same class of bird, or with wing-marked birds to procure that form, or Clear-bodied Crestbreds with partial or whole Dark caps. The Variegated Crested and Evenly-marked Crested can be paired with Clear Crestbreds in a similar manner ; but we have such a wholesome dread of variegation breaking loose that we should not venture to couple two wing-marked birds unless the markings had been perpetuated for two or three generations, and were of the lightest possible description and the body perfectly clear, showing little dark underflue. This dark underflue is a capital guide. Wherever it is found lurking, it only waits the first opportunity to come to the surface. The one-wing marked birds may be paired with comparative safety, and, in the case of reverse wings, with advantage.

Some breeders are most particular to pair alternately—that is, pair a Crested cock bred from a Crestbred cock and Crested hen to a Crestbred hen bred from Crested cock and Crestbred hen, or vice versa. The plan is certainly worth carrying out as far as possible ; but never allow alternate pairing to interfere with the first essential of correct mating—viz. putting birds together which are suitable for each other.

The name of Mr. F. W. Barnett, of Fakenham, Norfolk, is familiar to Crestbreeders the world over, and we are indeed indebted to Mr. Barnett for allowing us to be the first to publish his complete experience :

Mr. Barnett's Experiences.

" It is now some thirty years," says Mr. Barnett, " since I started to improve my stock of Crested Norwich by introducing the Lancashire Coppy, also a few cross-bred Lancashire and Norwich. At that time my crests were all a little open at the back, rather square, and some were flat owing to having a broad skull, and not being sufficiently long in feather to give the droop we see now on some show Crests. But they had deep chests and broad, well-filled backs. To obtain the above cross-breds I went to a Norwich dealer (I believe he is still living in the same place on Grapes Hill), and asked him if he would reserve for me the best he met with, which he did, the prices running from about 60s. to 90s. When I called on him he had just got a consignment of Lancashires from the North. Among them was an immense bird with very long, drooping sides, but open frontal coppy, showing the whole of his beak. Nevertheless, I fancied him, as I thought he had the densest, longest, and broadest feather I had ever seen on a bird. His price was 7s. 6d. I paired him to the longest and broadest frontal-crested hen I had, and they turned out some very useful stock, both Crests and Crestbreds.

"A year or two later I claimed at the Norwich Show a Grey-crested Buff cock that was in the money in the Light Crest Champion class. He was a model for shape of body, and had good formation of crest. I also claimed a Dark Crest in the money in the Marked Yellow Amateur class. This bird was considered by many to be too long for a Norwich class, and showing the Lancashire. Fortunately, it turned out to be a hen, and bred two of the largest youngsters I had had. I paired her to a Buff Crestbred cock, a real Bullfinch shape, but who had a broken wing. I also got a Clear Body Buff Dark Crested hen from the late Robert L. Wallace. She had a very large mop. About the same time that I was buying, a gentleman living a few miles from here cleared out his common birds, having caught the Crest fever through visiting a Norwich Show. He purchased from the Mackley Brothers some half-dozen of the best pairs he could get; but after two years' breeding he found he could not make of the youngsters he bred anything like the prices he had paid, therefore was disgusted, and offered me the lot, which I bought, and advertised them in the only Fancy paper I then knew, *The Exchange and Mart*, reserving about half a dozen of the best for myself. It, is therefore, quite clear that I had at least six, probably ten, different strains at the commencement. It was all selection in this case, as I was crossing to make a strain of my own. Pedigree had to

A CRESTBRED WITH TYPICAL HEAD AND FEATHER.

be looked into later on. I did well in breeding each year, getting an average of from six to nine per pair; then, thinking I could do with a little more Yellow blood, I purchased a Yellow Crestbred cock from the late George Wones, of Norwich, he having put down year after year at the Norwich Show some very grand Yellow Crests. I also got another Lancashire from the North, a Buff Plainhead cock, from which I kept two or three of his sons. Of course, I was now getting various-shaped crests; some had fair backs, but frontals ran almost to a point. These I paired with Crestbreds bred from the nicest-backed crests for two or three seasons until I had a few with broad, perfectly finished back crests. At the same time I was pairing those that had long, broad frontal crests, but were open and square at back, with Crestbreds bred from heavy frontal crests. Two or three pairs of these latter I mated cousins. Up to this time I had mated every pair Crest to Crestbred. I now ran a few pairs of double Crests—I prefer a Grey and Green Crest for double Cresting in preference to two of the same colour—those with the heaviest frontal crests with faulty backs to the most perfect back crests that had faulty frontals, reserving for stock from these crosses the best all-round crests and those with the heaviest frontals, also nearly all the Crestbreds. The rest I discarded—that is, all those with faulty fronts.

"The next season those bred from the double Crests were paired Crest to Crestbred. I was now getting some nice Crests and Crestbreds, and a few of the most perfect I paired unrelated to work from for the first twelve or fifteen years and through keeping about fifty pairs this last fifteen years I had a big school to select from, which enabled me to keep going much longer than anyone with a small stock. I have mated together cousins also, uncle and niece, and aunt to nephew, but I have never run anything nearer in relationship. As an experiment I double-crested a pair or two for three or four generations, and being quite satisfied by the result that nothing was gained by such repeated double-cresting, I have never tried it again.

"I have heard several times of Crest men recommending the cross of two Crestbreds. I may be a bit dense, but I could never see where any good could come from such crossing, that is for stock for crest-breeding. I usually get too many Crestbreds without breeding especially for them, and some good ones too, in the same nest as a good show Crest. I have bred a nest of five youngsters, four of which took a first at the Crystal Palace Show, a Crested cock and Crested hen, and a Crestbred cock and Crestbred hen, the fifth bird was, I believe, a Grey Crest, not worth more than 20s. Therefore I never thought it necessary to breed specially for Show Crestbreds. I have bred two or three Show Crests from Double Crests, but as a rule they come rather rough in crest, and some have ulcers on their heads, though they make very useful stock birds.

"The best Crests that I have bred were all bred from a Crest and Crestbred together. My 'King of Crests,' which I refused £70 for at the 1897 Crystal Palace Show, was bred from a wing-marked Buff Dark-crested hen, and a Heavily Variegated Buff Crestbred cock. Two years later I bred a better bird still, a Variegated Buff Dark-crested hen 'Queen of Champions,' and showed her at the Crystal Palace. I then sold her, and she was taken out to Australia. She was bred from a Dark - crested Buff cock, and a Buff Green-crestbred hen. My present best Crest, the largest and densest crest I have ever had, was bred from a wing-marked Dark-crested Buff hen and a Lightly Variegated Buff Crestbred cock. Also the best Crests and Crestbreds staged during the past ten or twelve years I bred from a Crest, and a Crestbred paired together.

"I have done very little double - cresting during the past fifteen years, only a pair or two sometimes—several seasons none at all. If I run a pair now they must be of different shape, crests and colour, as I previously inferred. Some twenty years ago Crest men used to say that all the best Yellow Crests shown had Cinnamon blood in their veins, and that you could not get them good without. Although I never saw a cinnamon feather in my bird room I soon bred what I thought to be the best Yellow Crest I had seen. After getting a nice lot of youngsters from him I sold him to Mr. John Hector, of Aberdeen, and after doing a little work in Scotland he came to Nottingham, where he was called the 'Champion of Nottingham.' I heard that there was a wonderful Yellow Crest coming from the home of the Yellows to the 1894 Crystal Palace Show, and when I was going through the Crest classes I was surprised to find the winner in the Yellow class was none other than the old bird I had sold to Mr. Hector. He was then bought by Mr. George Winter of Norwich, and shown at the next Norwich Show, where he was named the 'World's Wonder.' He then passed into the hands of Messrs. Mackley Brothers, and won again for them at the next Crystal Palace Show. I have bred some grand Yellow Crests since, and have now the largest Yellow Crest I have ever seen, all without Cinnamon blood.

"I have not double - buffed for more than two or three generations, then a Yellow cross is necessary—that is, when the Buffs used each year were bred from double Buffs. But when pairing double Buffs if one of them is bred from a Yellow I have paired double Buffs for five or six generations. I am fond of a *good* Buff bred from a Yellow, and always look (even if I do not get it) for an improvement from this cross.

" It is some fifteen years since I introduced any fresh blood into my stock. The last bird was an old Buff Coppy cock, a Manchester winner, from which I bred a good number of youngsters. During the past ten years I have mated my birds as distant in relationship as I could, in order to hold the strain as long as possible without introducing any fresh blood. It's been a bit of trouble to me lately to know where to get a change of blood from, therefore I have put in this year another Buff Coppy cock, a Rochdale and Manchester winner. I think I ought to have had a change of blood four or five years ago, and I would not recommend anyone to breed so long without introducing fresh blood.

" In selecting my stock I always pick out the best type and quality in preference to a bird simply nothing but a bundle of long loose feathers. I like long and very dense feathers, but I like them as tight and compact as I can get them."

Mr. C. L. Quinton.

We have spoken of the benefits derived from the Lancashire. Mr. Barnett has told us also of the excellent results from its *use, not abuse.* Like testimony is also forthcoming from Mr. C. L. Quinton, of Great Yarmouth, an old breeder and successful exhibitor who has bred many good Crests and Crestbreds in his time, who says :

" I introduce the Lancashire into my Crested strain about every fourth or fifth year, selecting the best of the young first crosses to pair back to the Crest variety, selecting some of my best Crests and Crestbreds in shape and head properties to pair with them to bring up the proper shape of the crest again which takes a season or two. When I have got them back to the proper shape I then inbreed for a season to set the work accomplished, and have even paired father and daughter for one season, when he possessed the head properties desired, then paired the young right out again. I find this method answers well, and I have bred some of my very best Crests and Crestbreds in this way."

Mr. Thos. Taylor, of Gateshead-on-Tyne, a noted breeder and exhibitor, who has achieved great distinction in breeding and exhibiting Crests, thus gives his experience :

Mr. Thos. Taylor on Breeding.

" The breeding of Crests and Crestbreds must be conducted on well-considered lines, as there are certain principles laid down to which every breeder must conform, no matter in what way he sets out to achieve his ideal of perfection. In regard to the right class of bird, the chief centre of attraction is the head, be it Crest or Crestbred, which is apt to somewhat detract our attention from the body of the bird ; but it must not be entirely overlooked. One of the essential points of this variety is size of crest, and to carry a large, heavy crest we must have a large head, and to carry a large head we should have body in proportion. I do not say it is not possible to have a large head on a small body, but my aim is to get the whole frame improved in proportion by paying more attention to the body. This eventually adds to the frame as a whole, without in any way injuring the chief point—viz. the head. In fact, it enhances and improves the birds all round, not only their appearance, but the birds themselves, as this all-round building up helps to strengthen and invigorate them, which is greatly needed in the present day.

" The formation of head is one of the essential points in breeding this variety, for unless birds have well formed heads we can never hope to breed a first rate crest. Many birds have flat skulls. When I use such birds I pair them to birds with nicely arched heads. I have seen some very good results from such pairing. Speaking of flat heads, one year during my early experience I paired up a Variegated Yellow Crestbred cock with grandly arched head and grand length of head feather to a Crested hen a trifle flat in head. From this pair I bred a Crestbred hen, lightly ticked, with grand headpiece, well covered with long feather of rare quality. This bird held her own in many competitions, and also left her mark in the breeding-room. In the same nest was a Yellow Crest cock, heavily variegated, but, unlike the hen, very flat-headed, and although the crest was of good size, it had not the taking appearance of a bird with nicely arched head, as it lacked the droop. I paired this bird up the following year with a Crestbred hen of rare head formation, and had the good fortune not to have a single flat-headed bird amongst the offspring. The following year I paired the first-mentioned Yellow Crestbred up to a rather small Green-crested hen, though very well bred. In the second nest from this pair I reared a lightly marked Crestbred cock and a heavily Variegated Crest (apparently a hen). This latter, which would have been a keen competitor on the show-bench, I had the misfortune to lose when about six weeks old, through some 'idle' young Norwich pulling out most of its tail feathers, causing it to lose a large quantity of blood, but the Crestbred went ahead and grew into one of the finest birds seen on the show-bench at that time.

"Whilst it is a fault for a Crest or Crestbred to have a small head, it is wonderful the amount of feather which can be carried on a small head, and as long as birds have heads of the correct formation, it does not always pay to discard such; in fact, it is often when endeavouring to work an improvement that we breed our champions. Such was the case when I bred my bird 'King Edward.' He was a great sensation at the time, and won many cups, etc. I had all along the line kept in stock a bird or two bred from a Buff Crest cock brother to my old Yellow Crestbred first mentioned, and had been working these in with a very neat Crested strain, and although I bred some nice Crests and neat, they were small from an exhibition point of view. I paired half-aunt and half-uncle together. From this pair I bred a trifle better birds, but still not what I expected. Amongst them was a rather small-bodied but fair size, leafy Crest hen. Although small in head, I paired this up to a large Green Crestbred cock, with fine large head and grand length of feather. The first nest all the eggs got broken but one. This hatched and was reared, being none other than the above-named 'King Edward.' I had adhered to the theory that by breeding-in the desired points (not blood relations) carefully each year I was bound to succeed in the end. These neat Crests appealed to me, and I could never screw myself up to parting with them, although they had been so far 'disappointments'; but this shows the value of a little patience and perseverance. 'King Edward' was as round in the crest as possible, the centre very neat and right in the centre of the crest, and indeed was more than a wonder when one looked at the size of his mother, whose neatness he inherited combined with the size of his father, who also was bred from a large Crest cock. The next nest from this pair also proved grand birds, one Green cock oft-times a winner, and a nearly Green Crestbred hen, splendid head formation and feather, winning many distinctions, including Crystal Palace Show, and also bred me some good winners.

"It is most interesting and instructive to follow up the breeding out of faults in one's stock, and although sometimes one comes across cases more stubborn to remove than others, yet it is these very self-same cases which go to make a thorough fancier, his enthusiasm giving an insight into the breeding of his stock which allows him to grasp and work out successfully and methodically any recurring faults which from time to time appear. It pays one to work up their stock from the beginning—viz. stock birds—as a breeder has a far better hold, and has far more interest in birds of merit that he has bred himself.

"Unlike other varieties, colour is not taken so much into consideration, length of feather and size of crest being the main points; but I find we must have the Yellow blood, as there is a certain quality of feather we must adhere to. I have bred, from Yellows and Buffs paired together, Buffs as long and dense in head-feather as from two Buffs, yet it is not so in general practice. My method of introducing colour is to take a Buff bred from a Yellow bird. This improves the quality without the risk attached to running a Yellow bird direct. Of course, to do this one must needs keep a Yellow strain of the very best. I find a great deal of careful selection must take place to maintain quality of feather without direct contact with Yellow. When any of my birds show a tendency to be what is termed 'fine' in feather, I select partners for them with nice broad, leafy feather, and continue to do this until the tendency has disappeared.

"The most important of all points in breeding Crests is the selection of the Crestbred. In selecting this bird have the proper-shaped head and good feather. This to my mind is one of the main roads to success. The feather of a *good* Crestbred to-day will cover a five shilling piece when turned over with this coin. Combined with this length and spread we should have density and quality, as in the Crest; but unless a Crestbred has a nice equal spread when turned over with finger or coin, it is not of much value in the breeding of good Crests. It is also an advantage if the Crestbred is descended from a first-class crested strain—a strain where the blood of the Crest and Crestbred has been thoroughly intermingled, and which has been carried out on well-thought-out lines. I always endeavour as far as possible to breed my birds together, so that it is just as possible to breed as good a Crest as Crestbred, and in this I have been very successful; but I have found that it is always policy to favour the Crest—as breeders will know, more Crestbreds are bred than Crests, so that it pays to favour the Crested side.

"My ordinary pairing is Crested cock bred from Crestbred cock to Crestbred hen bred from Crested hen, or vice versa. I have in some cases succeeded by in-breeding, but my chief guide has been selection. By this latter means I have been the most successful, and in various talks with other breeders I generally found that to be the case. I always found that in-breeding was only useful when carried out on very moderate lines, and to carry it on season after season is what I term 'suicide.' There is no doubt whatever that it is done, and that it is possible for a certain period to do so; but a very great deal of the most careful selection must take place, and it goes without saying that not a few of the outcasts are the means of disheartening not a few would-be fanciers, as it is assumed from wild bird life that it is a 'survival of the fittest.' It is only when in-breeding is resorted to as a means of stamping the good points into our strain that it is made a legitimate use of."

Mr. G. Colledge, of Kilburn, near Derby, an old and successful breeder and exhibitor of the Crested Canary, says:

Mr. G. Colledge on Crests.

"I have found the best method to give the best results in breeding is not only to have good stock birds with the necessary desirable points, but that they shall have good ancestral force behind them, and be clothed with the right kind of feather for the production of good Crests and Crestbreds, broad, leafy feather, with a nice dark midrib down it. This is well displayed in some of our crested hens. I also like the Crestbred to have that beautiful silver-like cord, or raw hemp yarn-like threads glistening out from amongst the neck feathers. We usually get this texture with a little Yellow blood; the contrast between this feather and excessive double-buffed feather is marked. A pair of such birds run together I have always had good results from. I have also used the Lancashire crossed with my Crests, with a view to getting more size and density of feather. I paired a Buff Lancashire Coppy hen bred from two Coppies to a large Green Crested cock. From these I got three young, all Crests. One of them took entirely to the Coppy in shape, the others were just the birds I wanted in size and density of feather. I kept one of them, a hen, and paired her up to a good Crestbred cock bred from Yellow and Buff—his ancestor had been bred from double Crests for four successive generations. I only got two from this pair, one of them a splendid Crestbred shown successfully by Mr. McLay. I also purchased a first cross Yellow Crestbred bred by Mr. Buckley, the well-known Lancashire breeder, from a ticked Buff Lancashire Coppy, and a Yellow Crestbred hen. I paired this first-cross hen to the best Crested cock I had. From those I bred a Yellow-Green Crested hen, which won the Cup at the Derby Show. This hen I paired to a very large Clear Buff Crestbred cock, from which I bred several real good show and stock birds, and these direct from Yellow blood.

"I also maintain that Yellow blood will neither shorten nor weaken the density of Crests or the feather on the head of Crestbreds if coarse, leafy feathered birds be paired with them. Some of the best birds I have ever bred or possessed have been bred direct from Yellow and Buff, my noted Clear Body Dark Crest, which I bred in 1908, and which won for me the Crest Canary Club's Ten Guinea Silver Challenge Bowl for best Young Crest, was bred from a Yellow Crested cock that had been bred from Yellow and Buff direct for four generations, and a Buff Crestbred hen which was also bred from Yellow blood.

"When using Lancashire blood I always pair back the first, second, and third crosses to thick Norwich-typed birds possessing beautifully concaved skulls, as these add to the shape and droop of the Crest.

"I have tried in-breeding, but I lost size and stamina. Odd ones may become robust and well worth breeding with; but give me 'Pedigree' and 'Judicious Selection.' The quickest way to reach the ideal is to pair the very best birds together with the least faults, and by careful selection and pairing improve any slight fault that may be in your stock each year; also occasionally double-crest a pair. The Crestbreds from these I have found give me excellent results."

Mr. John Tyson, of Chelsea, another well-known breeder and exhibitor of the variety, says:

Mr. John Tyson's Experiences.

"My experience extends over a period of twenty years, during which time it has been my ambition to annually produce exhibition specimens; and for some years I have been fairly successful, although I have not reared by any means the desired number. In Crests, however, we must be satisfied if we breed from any one stud two or three really classic winners yearly, and I know of no variety which requires greater patience and determination to gain success. I prefer the best possible exhibition specimens to breed from, and have for years past made a strong point of retaining quality of feather, ignoring fine or hairy-like feathered specimens, no matter how well bred. I would rather breed with a good feathered Crestbred cock if he had good length of head-feather although with very pinched or narrow entrance to skull, than with a bird of perfectly shaped head but fine in feather.

"I am a firm believer in a plentiful infusion of Green blood as the foundation of good colour, and as an essential for the maintenance of that much-desired dark midrib in the feather. I consider periodical double-cresting advantageous not only in increasing the percentage of Crests in the progeny, but more especially if you are fortunate to breed a Crestbred from the mating, and if you pair this bird to a Crest also bred from Double Crests, you are, to my mind, proceeding the most effectual way to produce winners.

"With regard to Yellows, my experience with these has been too limited to give. I have religiously avoided in-breeding so far as I know, except in 1908, when I experimented with uncle and niece; but although the progeny were good specimens, their powers of reproduction seemed to be so impaired, and their offspring, although reared, so lacking in stamina that I decided to indefinitely postpone any further experiments in in-breeding. The necessity for the introduction of fresh blood must come sooner or later, and in this it has been my practice to secure the best possible Crested or Crestbred male I could for the purpose, preferring one entirely unrelated, a good show bird for preference, and if bred from exhibition specimens so much the better, which, to my mind, is the true value of a pedigree-bred bird. Owing to the fact that almost every fancier of the variety has drawn on one source for the purpose of introducing fresh blood, it is very difficult to secure absolutely unrelated stock, and it may have been that my introductions were remotely related to my own stock, but for the purpose of explaining my practice I feel perfectly justified in saying I have for some years bred exhibition specimens consistently from birds which, so far as I know, were absolutely unrelated. My winner of the London Cage Bird Association's Challenge Cup was bred in this way, also my young Crestbred winner of the Crest Canary Club's Ten Guinea Silver Challenge Bowl, 1910.

"To my mind it is very questionable whether we should seriously consider the advisability of breeding with birds which are backward in asserting their sex, as I am of opinion that they are not constitutionally fit, otherwise Nature would surely assert itself. I think it is a mistake to try to patch up weakly specimens, and I strongly believe in the law of the 'survival of the fittest,' breeding only from the physically fit. One is then not only encouraging stamina, but every other essential for successful propagation. For the purpose of increasing stamina and consequent reproductive powers of the variety I commend my experiments for consideration: I tried, last year, to secure the biggest and roughest Norwich Plainhead or Lancashire-Norwich male bird I could, but, failing miserably, I set to work and paired a Buff Lancashire Coppy cock to a large Yellow Plainhead Norwich hen, and one of the young, a Buff cock, can pass very well for a Crestbred. The feather is both dense and turns back to the end of beak. This year it is my intention to pair this to the best Crested hen I have, which has been bred from two Crested parents, and thereby I hope to make up the ground lost by the introduction of the Norwich Plainhead. One or two of my friends who knew my purpose criticised my action, and suggested that the introduction of a Yellow Norwich Plainhead cock direct to a Crested hen would have been more satisfactory, with the possibility of obtaining a good Yellow from the first cross; but although I am always open to learn I cannot see eye to eye with them. That I must lose some ground and time is sure, but I think I am now on the more certain if not the shortest road. Time will, of course, prove. One thing I have long realised we must have to achieve that which raises us to the highest pinnacle of success, that is 'patience.' Be prepared for some sacrifice, give considerable thought to the work, and be determined to conquer any obstacle that may appear."

SCALE OF POINTS FOR JUDGING CRESTED AND CRESTBRED CANARIES

Crested

(*a*) CLEAR BODY WITH CREST OF ANY COLOUR

Points of Merit

Marking	*Maximum*
Shape of crest, depending on—	
Form of individual feathers: ovate	5
Fall of feathers: radiating and drooping	5
Position of and well filled in neat centre	5
Front of crest: broad and round	5
Sides and back of crest: well filled-in	5
Size of crest: length of feather, quality and area	10
Density of crest: quantity of feather	8
Colour of crest: for purity of its kind, birds of equal merit with Dark Crests to take precedence over Grey or Clear	7
Colour of Bird: depth and purity	20
Feather—Compactness of body-feather and carriage of wings and tail	10
Size and Shape	10
Condition	10
	100

(*b*) EVENLY-MARKED CRESTED

Marking	*Maximum*
Crest (deducting colour-points from foregoing scale)	40
Marking—Exactness of wing-marking	10
Saddle—Width and clear margin	5
Body-Colour—Depth and purity	15
Feather—Compactness of body-feather and carraige of wings and tail	10
Size and Shape	10
Condition	10
	100

It is scarcely necessary to fix any scale for judging the Variegated Crested birds. It will have been gathered from our detailed description of them that in their case the crest is virtually the entire bird if expressed in numerical values. But inasmuch as it may be desirable to set some limit to fineness of feather and other objectionable features which have crept in with the crest, we give the following values to certain necessary points and apportion the balance to the crest :—

(*c*) VARIEGATED CRESTED

	Maximum
Body Colour—Depth and brilliancy	10
Feather—Compactness of body feather and carriage of wings and tail	10
Size and Shape	10
Condition	10
Crest	60
	100

Negative Properties

The Crest should not be small nor of Coppy shape, nor should the centre be too near the front of the head, or too far back, or more to one side than the other, nor should it be in the form of a clear open area, nor as a line or parting in the centre. The Crest should not be deficient in true radiation, nor should the feathers be flat on the head or project without drooping or assume any position other than falling away from the centre. It should not be narrow or short in front, neither should there be any vacancy of any kind at the back, or split at sides or front or roughness at back, or tilting or lack of density and quality of feather, nor should the beak be coarse.

In a Clear Body Dark Crest the colour of crest should not appear pale, or undecided, or sagey, nor should the dark colour of the crest run into the neck beyond the back of poll, nor should there be a single light feather in any part of the crest. The surface colour of the whole body, wings and tail must be free from any dark colour beyond the crest.

An Evenly-marked Dark Crest should not show any light flight feathers mixed with the dark. The outer flights should not be dark, and not more than five or six of the inner ones dark. Nor should there be any marking on the greater or lesser wing coverts or the still smaller coverts fringing the upper margin of the wing, which, when the bird is at rest, is hidden by the scapulars; nor should the feathers of the bastard wing be dark, it should not show any dark feathers on the margin of the saddle where the feathers merge with those of the wing-coverts, nor any discoloration in the upper or lower tail-coverts, nor should there be any mark whatever to interfere with a clean run above and below from the back of the crest above and from the beak below to the tail. The dark feathers of crest should not extend beyond the back of poll. The Dark Crest should not have a single light feather in any part of it.

A Clear Body Grey Crest should not have any marking of any kind on any part of the body, the crest feathers only being speckled with light and dark. A Clear Body Clear Crested bird must not have any dark colouring on any part of the body wings, tail, or crest. All Crested birds should *not* have long thin bodies or unproportionate long wings or tail, neither should they cross wings at the tips, nor be erect in carriage, or carry themselves with a slovenly curved demeanour. The body feather should not be loose and slovenly, or frilled on breast, nor should the bird be long and stilty on legs.

CRESTBREDS

Points of Merit	*Maximum*
Head—Large and round, broad at every point with good rise over centre of skull	25
Length, density and broad leafiness of head feather, commencing at base of beak with a good flow over head and poll	25
Eyebrows—Heavy and overhanging	10
Beak—Small and neat	5
Body Colour—Depth and brilliancy	5
Compactness of body feather and good carriage of wings and tail	10
Size and shape	10
Condition	10
	100

Negative Properties

A Crestbred should not exhibit any feature opposed to the character of a Crest, and especially should not have a small or narrow head ; nor should the head be flat or narrow at the entrance over beak, nor have a narrow contracted back, or be of shield-shape, nor covered with short scanty fine feather or be sagey in colour. Neither should it be rough or tucked up at the sides at back of poll ; nor guttered behind the eye, or have a coarse beak, nor show any disposition to be slim and puny in build of body, nor have unduly long flights and tail, or cross the wings or be erect in carriage. The body feather should not be carried loose or slovenly, or be frilled on breast. Neither should it be long and stilty on legs.

CHAPTER XXIII

THE BORDER FANCY CANARY

THIS is one of the smallest of the Canary family, and is also the most recent addition to its recognised varieties. There is no need to enter into the early history of this bird beyond saying that, like all others, it is a branch of the common stock, but bred to a certain type appealing to the tastes of the people in the Border district from whence it takes its name. The Borders of Scotland and Cumberland have long been —and are to this day—its strongholds, though its cult has spread throughout the United Kingdom. The type is now firmly established by careful selection and the judicious introduction and breeding-in of Cinnamon, Norwich, and Yorkshire blood to assist in perfecting the Border's desired characteristics.

The variety for a brief time towards the end of the eighties of the last century was called the "Cumberland Fancy," but as this created some feeling amongst breeders on the Scottish side of the Border, its present name was agreed upon.

Since 1890 the Border Fancy Canary has made rapid progress, for about that time its breeders agreed upon a standard of perfection which was adopted by the Border Fancy Club, founded on July 5th of that year. This proved the beginning of its success, as there was now a definite type to which to breed, and no longer were individual breeders left to guess at the essential points of a good bird and to give good, natural colour and marking their first consideration. Fixing upon a standard has not resulted in the neglect of good, natural colour and of marking, but type and quality now lead the way, whether it be a Clear, Evenly Marked, Green, or Cinnamon Border. Colour-feeding, it should be noted, is not recognised in this variety.

Points of the Border.

In build the Border is lightly made, compact, and very close in feather. It is not quite so chubby as a German, nor quite so thin as a small Yorkshire, but a happy medium, just showing a little more fullness of chest than a Yorkshire, and having a much shorter body. The head is small, round, and neat, with well-formed cheeks, free from any tendency to meanness. The beak is small and rather finely tapered, eye bold and bright, neck fine and proportionate, forming a harmonising junction between head and body. The back is well filled, with a nice level appearance running in an almost straight line, with just a gentle rise over the shoulders to the tip of the tail. It is important that the tail should be carried out in direct line with the body and have no tendency to drop. The chest is nicely rounded, neither heavy nor prominent, the body cutting or tapering away gradually to the vent. The wings are neatly folded, and must be tight and close fitting to the body, just meeting at the tips. The tail, also, must be neat and closely folded, well filled in at the root, resembling somewhat the stem of a pipe, the whole bird harmonising as if turned out of a mould, so short and compact is the body feather, and this should carry a nice silky sheen over its entire surface. The legs are of medium length, showing little or no thigh, and the feet correspondingly neat, toes and nails perfect in formation. The length of the bird should not exceed 5½ inches. The colour, of whatever shade, should be rich, soft, and pure in tone; the position semi-erect, standing at an angle of about 45 deg., the head being elevated and the line of the back just over the shoulder and the back of head forming a rather acute angle. The carriage is gay and jaunty, with the fine free pose of a bird possessing good manners. This description coincides with that given in the Border Fancy Club Standard, and is well portrayed in our coloured plate and the full-page illustration on page 157.

Breeding Borders.

Good health must at all times have due consideration paid to it in the breeding-room by breeding with sound, robust stock. We have said that the Border was perfected by the assistance of the Cinnamon or "Dun," which in those days was small, as noted in our chapter on Cinnamons. It was also very tight in feather, and from this bird we obtained much of the quality of feather now so firmly established as one of the recognised characteristics of the Border Fancy; it also assisted much towards good marking. From the old-fashioned Norwich we obtained much colour, that bird also then being small and very tight and short in feather, with wonderfully rich colour. From the Yorkshire we obtained smart carriage, and reduced any undue bulkiness of body. Such crosses are not now necessary, for type and general characteristics have been fixed for so many years past that there is plenty of material at hand in the variety itself, without wasting time in resorting to out-crosses. Still, if necessary, we should not hesitate to cross a very small, slim Yorkshire with any Border showing a tendency to get stout in body and full in neck, pairing the offspring back again to pure Borders. In this way we should not be long in producing birds fit for the exhibition bench. But whoever attempts such crossing must have experience, thoroughly know what he wants, and also be a keen observer; otherwise his safest plan is to stick to the ready-made material and leave out-crossing with foreign blood to older hands.

Influence of the Yorkshire.

In the nineties of the last century, Mr. William Armstrong, of Armthwaite, near Carlisle, a Border Fancy breeder, visited Yorkshire and brought back with him some small evenly marked and almost evenly marked Yorkshires. These he paired to some of his Border Fancies, and their young back to Borders, following up the process with the result that by careful selection he produced some of the finest and most successful Even-Marked Borders in Cumberland, and there are descendants of his strain in the district to this day. The perpetuation of such markings we fully dealt with in the chapter on "Even Marks," and as those principles hold equally good as regards Borders, we refer those desirous of breeding them to that chapter.

Like Mr. Armstrong, we, too, have used a small Yorkshire to improve characteristics in our Borders, both clear and marked birds, and with equally good results, pairing the crosses back to generations of suitable Borders until we attained our object. After using such a cross it is years before its repetition is necessary.

A Needless Fear.

Some fanciers seem horrified at getting a bird just a little too stout or full in neck, or one possessing both these faults, whilst they ignore other good points the bird may possess, such as excelling in quality of feather, smart carriage of wings and body, neat head, etc., and they strenuously advise that such birds should on no account be used for breeding purposes. Yet it would be just as reasonable to warn breeders against the use of a bird a little too thin in neck or too slimly built, which no one with practical experience would get rid of provided it possessed other good qualities. We have found birds a little too stout or too full in neck most valuable to pair up to those failing the reverse way, and have succeeded even to the extent of producing show birds from such pairing. Even faulty birds can thus be paired together to produce more perfect specimens, and there is no need to discard such birds so long as they have suitable partners. It is the same in this variety as in all others: what is lacking in one bird must be made up abundantly in the bird with which it is paired. This will apply to all defects.

Other Points for Breeders.

The usual orthodox pairing of Yellow to Buff should be adopted unless there is some specific object for doing otherwise; then sometimes Yellows are paired together, or Buffs, as the case may demand. Occasional double-buffing in this variety assists in getting close, compact feather, just as double-yellowing will intensify colour. If, however, a little Green blood is introduced occasionally by pairing a marked bird to a Clear instead of Clear to Clear, there will be little need to double Yellow, though the process of double-yellowing will tend to reduce stoutness as well as improve colour.

Mr. Thos. Arnot on Borders.

Mr. Thos. Arnot, of Hawick, Scotland, one of the partners of the well-known exhibitors, Messrs. Arnot and Jameson, says:

"When pairing up my birds I give special attention to type and quality, and extra care to see that if one bird has a fault that its mate is quite free from the blemish, as I have found by pairing two birds together having the slightest tendency to the same fault the progeny from them were good for nothing, except that the cocks were useful as songsters. I never despise a bird with a bad fault if the pedigree is good and I have a suitable bird free from that fault to pair with it. The defects I dislike most are flat heads, short, thick necks, too pointed or frilled breasts, slack or open back feathers, too high or long in leg, too long in flights, too strong in beak, and cutting off too short at vent, as this gives a Border too much the appearance of a German. I am most careful if I use any birds having any of these faults to pair them with specimens which are particularly good in these points, and which have come from good stock. I also like type and quality in my hens, as in my opinion much more depends on the hen for the production of these points than the cock.

"I make free use of Cinnamon blood in my pairing, and always pair with a view to producing Even Marks, as plenty of Unevenly Marked are always obtained even in aiming for the more perfect form. In breeding Even Marks I depend more on the hen than on the cock, especially for good eye-marks. Of course, there is always the exception, but I have invariably found this the rule. The hen that I like for Even-Marked breeding is one with good dark marks right round the eyes and well on to the cheek, or else a Self Green bred from Even Marks, pairing these to a Clear or Ticked cock bred from Even-Marked stock. I have also found occasional double-buffing excellent to keep the feather close and solid if at any time there happened to be a tendency to looseness. When double-buffing, I always select birds with good under colour, short feather, nice round heads, and finely drawn necks—birds that stand at the correct angle."

Mr. T. McCredie's Experiences.

Mr. Thomas McCredie, of Dumfries, a breeder and exhibitor of note of the Border Fancy, says:

"During my fifteen years breeding of this variety I have tried double yellow breeding, but do not approve of it, as I have never had any really good results from such pairing, not even colour. The little I might have gained in this direction was more than lost in quality and finish, which is of greater importance. I have always practised a little double-buffing, as I think it is here we get our fixity of compact, close feather, provided the practice is not abused. I bred some of the best birds I ever exhibited from two Buff parents with a little Cinnamon blood in them. Cinnamon blood is good in the stock, and I have always bred splendidly feathered birds from its use, working it in on the one side. I prefer, as far as possible, to pair Yellow cock to Buff hen, or vice versa, getting the best results from such pairing, having a little dark blood on the cock's side with a Clear pink-eyed hen, which, of course, is derived from the Cinnamon. By this pairing I have got splendid colour, quality of feather, and good show specimens. In the case of using a marked hen, I pair her to a Clear cock."

It will be observed that Mr. Arnot pins his faith greatly to the hen for the production of Even Marks, while Mr. McCredie places more reliance on the cock, and says:

"In the breeding of Even Marks we often get one in the ordinary way when least expected; but still we must usually breed for a few seasons to get birds suitable for producing good marking. I like the cocks with good marking on the eyes and wings only, and as free from dark flue as possible, pairing such birds to Clear or Ticked hens bred from evenly marked stock."

It would appear at first that these gentlemen differ widely on breeding evenly marked birds, but in reality their principles are the same; it is simply a matter of the one working through the hen and the other from the cock, and it matters not from which so long as it is followed consistently, as explained in the chapter on Even-marked Breeding.

Clear, Ticked or Unevenly Marked Birds.

The production of Clear, Ticked, or Unevenly marked Borders is regulated, as in other varieties, by the pairing of Clear to Ticked or Marked, as the case requires. If a fancier is breeding a preponderance of Marked birds, this tendency must be checked by pairing Clear Yellow to Clear Buff for a season or two until the desired number of Clears is produced amongst the stock.

By kind permission, we here publish the Border Fancy Canary Club's standard of excellence:

The Club Standard.

The grand essentials of a Border Fancy Canary are type and quality. Without these it is worthless.

The general appearance is that of a clean-cut, lightly made, compact, proportionable, sprightly, close-feathered, smallish-sized Canary, showing no tendency to heaviness, roughness or dullness, but giving the impression of fine quality and symmetry throughout.

Head.—Small, round, and neat looking; bill, fine; eyes, dark and bright; neck, rather fine and proportionate to head and body.

Body.—Back, well filled and nicely rounded, running in almost a straight line from the gentle rise over the shoulders to the point of the tail; chest, also nicely rounded, but neither heavy nor prominent, the line gradually tapering away to vent.

Wings.—Compact, and carried close to the body, just meeting at the tips.

Legs.—Of medium length, showing little or no thigh, fine, and in harmony with the other points; feet, corresponding.

Size.—Not to exceed 5½ inches in length measured in the usual way.

Plumage.—Close, firm, and fine in quality, presenting a smooth, glossy, silky appearance, and free from frill or roughness.

Tail.—Close-packed and narrow, being nicely rounded and filled in at the root.

Colour.—Rich, soft, and pure, as level in tint as possible throughout, but extreme depth or hardness, such as colour-feeding gives, are objectionable in this breed, and should be discouraged. Red-fed birds distinctly debarred.

Position.—Semi-erect, standing at about an angle of 45 deg.

Carriage.—Gay and jaunty, with a fine, free pose of the head.

Health, condition, and cleanliness shall have due weight.

In judging marked birds, "type and quality" should form the first consideration in these as in other classes, and no prize should be awarded for good marking alone where the type does not conform to the Club standard.

Further to enhance the value of the description of the essential points described in the Border Club's standard, we apportion a scale of points to them:

Points of Merit	*Maximum*
Shape	10
Head, neck, and beak	10
Back well filled and level	10
Plumage: body feather close, firm, and good quality	10
Wings: for compactness and good carriage	10
Tail: closely folded and good carriage	5
Colour: depth, brilliancy and purity	10
Position and jaunty carriage	10
Size: not to exceed 5½ inches	10
Legs and Feet: medium length, and free from blemish	5
Condition: health, cleanliness and sound feather	10
Total	100

CHAPTER XXIV

THE LIZARD CANARY

We enter now on a description of the birds included in the second of the two groups in which we have arranged the Canary family—viz. those having a Distinctive Plumage, as opposed to the one simple notion embodied in the idea of colour. To this group belong the Lizard and London Fancy—tribes most probably intimately related. It is by many considered an open question whether the Lizard is an offshoot or a cultivated form of the London Fancy, or whether it is the parent of a bird known to have been in existence more than a century ago, and for which its admirers claim an ancestry exceedingly remote, for far back in the olden time, in the early history of the London Fancy, we believe there is to be found in its unpublished archives a legend that "about this time common Canaries were introduced into England," which is a sad let-down for the Lizard family, who appear to possess neither a written nor a traditionary history. We compromise, and suggest the possibility of each being as old as the other, though, if we have any leaning, it is in favour of the Lizard, which we think, from sundry features in its character, presents indications that seem to point to its being the parent stem rather than an offshoot. We shall pursue this question further in our remarks on the London Fancy.

"Spangling."

Most probably the Lizard was born of a desire to develop to its fullest extent a description of feather-marking more or less common to every dark Self-coloured Canary, which bears the name of spangling—a form of feather not entirely absent even in some Clear birds, in which it may be traced in a rudimentary shape. This fact alone is evidence of its fixity, while the highest examples of its cultivated development show what it is possible to do by careful breeding and selection. This spangled form of feather early attracted attention, and even in its imperfect embryo state seems to have been regarded as a feature worth encouraging. The old volume we have previously quoted from in our notes on the Cinnamon says :—

> "The Fine *Spangled Sort*, commonly called, *French Canary Birds*, and the *Mealy* Ones, are the Best to Breed with, for *Those*, who are very Curious.
> Because, A *Spangled Cock*, with a *Mealy Hen*, will Produce a more *Regular* Spangled Feather, than if Cock, and Hen were *Both Spangled*. For *Then*, They would Breed too *High* upon the Yellow.
> Because, The Young Ones, *Take* mostly after the *Cock Bird* in their Feathers, rather than the *Hen*."

It is quite possible that the term "spangled," as here used, may have a wider and more general significance than in the restricted form in which we apply it; but it is evident that spangling of some sort is referred to, even if the meaning be as obscure as that of "ashen-grey" and other forms of colour mentioned by old chroniclers.

The description of feather-marking to which we have referred as being in all probability rudimentary spangling, and common to most dark Selfs, we may describe as consisting of nothing more than a darkening of the web on each side of the mid-rib, edged by a lighter margin, in some instances more decided than in others, but in all cases essentially the same in character and consisting of the ground-colour, the dark centre and the lighter edge; and we are not surprised that the presence of similar feathers should have set some of the thinking fanciers of the olden time pondering how, on such a foundation, they could rear the structure we are about to describe—a structure so complete and so elaborately finished in every part, as to have become one of the highest, if not the very highest, triumph of the breeder's skill.

Colour and the Lizard.

The Lizard Canary has been named from the striking resemblance its glittering plumage bears to the back of its scaly prototype, the comparison being not at all inapt, especially in the case of some of the old-fashioned sort. In size it is somewhat smaller than the Norwich Canary; but in shape and general conformation it is similar, except that it is scarcely so full in the neck or so large in the head, and though belonging to the chubby school, in no way claims to have any connection with the birds of Shape or Position. Its colour, also, so far as regards the clearly defined line between Yellow and Buff, is as decided as that of any of the colour section; the Yellow form is appropriately known as Golden Spangled, and the Buff as Silver Spangled. But here we may at once remark that the Yellow or Golden bird is not really of a yellow or gold colour, but is rather, as regards what is called its body-colour, a rich, dark, bronzy yellow very difficult to paint in words so as to be recognised, unless we have a familiar acquaintance with the warm tones of some of the rich umbers of the artist's colour-box. The richer, warmer, and purer the tone of this body-colour, the more valuable it is, and in it there should be no admixture of a greenish tinge.

The body-colour, or, as it is frequently called, the ground-colour, can be best gauged by its display on the breast, which is generally a pretty good index of the quality in this respect. It will be obvious to all who have carefully read our remarks on the nature of the colour on the *back* of any dark Self—a Cinnamon, for instance—that that is not the best place to look for an exhibition of ground-colour in a mass, the formation of the feathers of the back and the graduated colouring of each being adverse to such display, though the educated eye soon detects the appearance of the true shade in whatever place it appears. On the breast, where there is less of this graduated shading than anywhere, and where what is present does not in any way affect the display as a whole, there is, however, to be seen, delicately traced and softened down into hazy indistinctness, something like rudimentary spangling, which takes a more definite form as it approaches the sides and stretches away towards the region of the waist, where it not unfrequently seems to gather itself up into dark stripes, all of which indicates possession of that species of feather which produces good spangle.

The Cap.

So far, we have referred to the colour of the Lizard only in general terms, and the bird, as it at present appears on our canvas, must therefore at this stage be understood to be simply roughed out in the warm ground-colour we have indicated, and we will now proceed to finish it in detail.

Beginning with the head, we remark that it is one of the most important features in a good Lizard, and, while having extreme neatness and finish, must also have good width of skull, in order that it may show to the greatest advantage what is held by many fanciers to be the greatest ornament of the bird—viz. the cap covering the crown, which in a Golden Lizard is a patch of pure yellow, and in a Silver pure buff. It will be sufficient to say that just in proportion to the warmth of the ground-colour will be the richness of the pure colour on the crown, which is no doubt only one form of development of the body-colour. In shape the cap should approach an oval, though there are almost as many opinions on this matter as there are slightly varied forms; some like to see it bounded by a straight line at the back, or, as it is called, "cut square," and others perfectly elliptical. Perhaps the best form is what is familiarly termed a "thumb-nail," which may be taken as midway between the two, being, in fact, a "square-cut" cap with the corners rounded off, by which nothing of the width is lost, while there is no harshness of outline.

A perfect cap should be bounded by a line commencing at the top of the beak and passing over the top of the eye round to the back of the head in the same plane, and returning in the same way on the other side. It must not come lower than the top of the eye, and the boundary-line at this part should be a hair-line of clearly defined feathers. The outline must be unbroken, and the entire area clear and unsullied by the presence of a single dark feather. A good type of the desired cap may be seen in the Golden Lizard on our coloured plate, and also the illustrations of Clear Caps on pages 137 and 302. The cap of a nestling, when just beginning to sprout, often presents the appearance of a mere streak, and seems to bear no proportion to the amount of dark feathers on either side; but if it be regular in shape—and at this stage of its existence every feather can be seen, and the slightest defect ascertained—there need be no fear as to its ultimately covering its allotted space, and such apparently too wide margin of dark feathers becomes no defect, but develops into the fine hair-line we have referred to as the cap arrives at maturity.

Any intrusion of the surrounding dark feathers on the clear surface is recognised as, and called, a "broken" cap, and any intrusion of the cap itself on the dark feathers of the neck is called a "run cap," or "over-cap," than which more suggestive terms could scarcely be used. The term "broken," of course, attaches also to ticks or patches of dark colour remote from the margin. There are also non-capped specimens, in which the entire cap is dark instead of light.

We furnish illustrations of the most common forms assumed by defective caps.

Defective Caps.

Fig. *a* represents a decided patch of spangling in the centre, and speaks for itself. It is not always, however, so clearly defined as this, but may assume the character of a minute tick, consisting, in fact, of but a single feather. Fig. *b* also represents a form of broken cap unmistakable in its character, a great portion of the area of the cap being absorbed by the encroachment of the dark neck-feathers in a solid, unbroken mass. We have given this illustration for a twofold purpose—to exemplify this particular form, and to show clearly the difference between it and Fig. *c*, representing a "run cap," in which the clear colour is seen running over and down the back of the neck. If the entire width of clear cap runs over its normal margin into the dark neck feathers, it is described as "over capped."

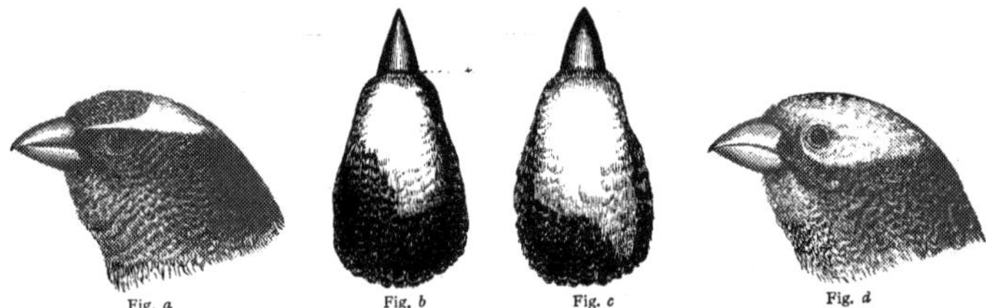

COMMON FORMS OF DEFECTIVE CAPS IN LIZARDS.

The forms we have described—viz., the greater and lesser isolated blemishes, and the clearly defined intrusion of the neck-spangles in a connected mass—constitute the three representative examples of the broken-capped bird, the presence of any of the blemishes entailing the penalty of disqualification in a clear cap class.

There is one other blemished type, in reality one form of the run cap, but run in a direction different from that indicated in Fig. *c*; we refer to what is known as a *bald face,* an example of which is seen in Fig. *d,* in which the cap includes not only the eye but a portion of the cheek. This is a very serious defect, and is frequently accompanied by other departures from soundness of body-colour, of which we shall treat in their proper place. This bad blemish, which seems to brook no control, might perhaps be classed with departures from sound body-feather; but emanating, as it most frequently does, from the cap, we prefer to treat of it now. Figs. *e* and *f* illustrate two forms which, while perfect in their way, are undesirable shapes. The first represents a short or undersized cap, and the latter which droops in the rear, and is, therefore, not on the same plane throughout: of the two, the latter is the least objectionable, provided always that the base be decided in its outline.

We have been thus minute in our detail of every point, good, bad, and indifferent, which belongs to the cap, because it is considered by some of our best breeders to be *the* feature of the bird.

We now pass on to what, with all respect to the cap, we consider to be the feature of a Lizard—viz. its spangling. A Lizard with beautiful spangling always has its value, even if the cap be very defective; but let the cap be ever so good and the spangling bad, and it is held in slight estimation. Of the two we prefer to see a well-spangled Lizard without a cap rather than a good cap without spangle. The one is still a Lizard, but the other nothing. Our idea is that even balance is more difficult to obtain than excess of any one property; but if asked what we consider the essential feature of a Lizard, our answer is "Spangle."

Importance of Spangling.

And what is spangle? We have in our opening remarks briefly referred to what is probably spangling in its rudimentary form. An examination of a feather taken from the middle of the saddle will show what it is in its developed shape. The flue of each feather—that is, the soft, silky portion next the root of the quill—is entirely blue-black, and we may say here that as a standard point the blacker the flue the better; but as the feather finds its way to daylight, and the flue assumes the character of feather proper, the colour changes, and the centre

Fig. *e* Fig. *f*
UNDESIRABLE FORMS OF CAP.

of the feather becomes black-brown, margined with a lighter shade, the central colour increasing in depth till it reaches nearly to the extremity of the feather, where it expands into a circular form corresponding with the outline of the feather, and is then as nearly a true black as possible. The marginal edging also assumes a new tone, becoming of the shade we have described as the body-colour, its extreme edge being fringed with a very narrow bordering of a still lighter shade, which in the Golden-spangled bird is the same as the cap, and in the Silver has, in addition to what coloured edge it may possess, an extreme outer verge of white; it is, in fact, simply the buff or mealy form of the yellow bird, and takes its name from the frosted, silvery appearance this mealy fringe produces. A reference to the illustration given on page 298 will show this formation of the feather and explain how one feather overlapping another produces the appearance we term "Spangling"; and will further show, better than we can describe, how, the wider and blacker the expanse of the central dark colouring, the larger and more distinct will be the dark eye forming the nucleus of each individual spangle. This arrangement of colour is seen in every feather, from the small ones at the back of the head, and *on* the head in a broken-capped bird, down to the larger feathers of the saddle; and when it is borne in mind how gradually these increase in size, and how regularly they overlap each other, a pretty fair idea may be formed as to what the back of a good Lizard should be like. Commencing imme-

THE FEATHER OF THE LIZARD SHOWING SPANGLING.

diately at the back of the cap, it should consist of a series of continuous chains of spangles, gradually increasing in distinctness and size. At first the spangles are not distinct, but have more the appearance of black specks, owing to the disposition of the neck-feathers and the continuous shifting of their position from the motion of the bird; but when the spangling is carried up on the crown, as is seen in a broken cap, it assumes all its regular form, though on a small scale.

We have used the expression "continuous chains." Regular rows of spangling are necessary to form a good back, but they must on no account resolve themselves into mere longitudinal stripes. Each link in the chain must have its clear edging, and each spangle must be as decided as the eyes in a peacock's tail. They must not be thrown on as if indiscriminately and without method, but arranged with the greatest regularity, to which anything approaching open-feathering is directly opposed.

And this leads us to our closing remark on this feature. Excess of spangling, when it assumes the form of diminutive moons and over-development of lacing, produces a hazy indistinctness technically termed "moss," which is perhaps the most dangerous shape in which it can appear, as any disposition to obliterate the dark eyes of the spangles means doing away with the dark centre in the feather which produces them, and thus destroying the very life of the variety. Write down a "mossy" back as being to spangle what a bald face or other tendency to "running" is to the cap.

The Wing. "Black, home to the quill," is one of the oldest laws of a very old code, and indicates, broadly, what should be the general character of the feather in the wing of the Lizard. It is not, however, intended as an exact definition so much as to convey the idea that black, or some form of black, is the standard colour, and that white or any tendency thitherward is forbidden. The web and flue should be "black, home to the quill," but the shaft or quill itself is only black for as much of its length as is exposed, its base being nearly as white as that of any ordinary clear flight-feather. A reference to the illustration below and the coloured plate will show that the inner flights in particular are margined with a paler shade of colour (a feature common to all dark wings of whatever colour), and the beauty of the wing, so far as this arrangement is concerned, consists in the darkness of the web and stalk and the rich character of the marginal edging, which is more or less brilliant as it is found in the Gold or the Silver form of the bird. Notice, further, that the extreme outside

FOUL WING IN LIZARD.

margin of the primary flights, or ten outer feathers, is also fringed with an edging of colour for some small portion of its length, but it should not extend so far as that part of the feather where the narrow portion of the web is so much narrowed as to cause the stalk to become almost the actual margin ; else, when the wing is closed, the effect of these minute edgings of colour placed side by side will be to give the appearance of a transverse band of light colour extending in the direction of the middle of the wing, just so far into it as the close packing of the primaries will produce it, entirely destroying the effect of what should be a uniformly dark wing. This defect is sometimes very patent, and an examination of the individual feathers of such a wing will show an extended margin of distinctly grey edging which is very objectionable. It should be remembered that it is the broader inner flights—technically, the tertiaries, or tertials—those in which the stalk is found in the middle of the web, which have the wide marginal lacing, and that as the stalk nears the outside the light margin should vanish. We strongly recommend a careful examination of a living wing, closed and expanded, when the distribution and effect of the colour will be plainly discerned.

The larger wing-coverts also have much to do with the make-up of a bird in which every feather has its definite value. Each covert must represent a smaller edition of its corresponding flight, the position and the extent of outer edging displayed demanding the most exact lacing: the innermost are hidden by the marginal feathers of the saddle. With these larger coverts, lacing may almost be said to end and spangling to begin, for the second or smaller coverts with their rounded extremities possess something very much resembling the dark terminal eye which determines spangle, albeit the marginal fringe does not assume a silver or a golden colour until we reach the row of feathers next above these, which, however, are not on the wing, but are the outer row of the scapulars overlapping the base of these beautiful second coverts with the most perfect regularity.

It will now readily be seen that our term Distinctive Plumage is not misapplied, since the character of our bird depends, literally, on the distinctive character of each feather.

It sometimes happens that an otherwise beautiful wing is spoiled by the presence of one or two (one is enough to disqualify under the rigid Lizard law) clear feathers, which, when they occur in the smaller coverts, constitute what is known as a "rose shoulder," "rose wing," or "shell wing" (*see* p. 298). This is a most vexatious and fatal blemish. A white flight-feather will also only too frequently intrude where "black, home to the quill," forbids its presence. Such a feather is fatal and entails summary disqualification, though if it be not absolutely white, but show some trace of black in stalk or web, it does not actually disqualify ; but however good the bird may be in other respects, it practically ruins its winning chances.

Any dark flight-feathers lost by accident are usually replaced by dark or grey flights tipped at the outer ends with white, and though they are not an actual disqualification, they tell to their extent against an otherwise good show bird. We need scarcely add that if any feathers ought to be blacker than the rest they are those of the bastard wing.

The Tail, Legs, and Beak.

Travelling to the other end of the bird, we find the tail, the twelve feathers of which must be essentially the same in character as the flights. It must not be spread out like a fan, nor piped, but expanded just enough to show the extreme outer margin of each feather, its base being thatched by the upper coverts, which must not show the slightest approach to coarseness—a defect not for a moment to be tolerated anywhere in a Lizard.

Cap, spangle, wings, and tail: there cannot be much remaining, except the beak, legs, and claws, which ought to be as dark as possible, since the clear beak and flesh-coloured legs and claws are indicative of a tendency towards paling in colour. The general appearance of a Lizard is dark, and he belongs to a dark-flue school: light points are, as a matter of contrast, objectionable ; as a matter of breeding, still more so. Dark beak, dark legs, and ebony claws are the correct thing in a Lizard :

they are his hat, gloves, and boots—things some people don't care about. We do. He should be a perfect gentleman in all the details of dress. There is a fitness in things: sheep-skin kid gloves, sizes too large, and seditious-looking boots spoil the best costume.

Although it is considered difficult to breed a perfect Lizard, it is not more so than to produce any other bird in perfection. Indeed, we think there is every encouragement in commencing to breed this interesting variety, because its leading features may be said to be fixed. The fancier will not find himself pairing Clears and producing Pieds; mating marks, and looking in vain for their reproduction; nor will he find any of the many seemingly unaccountable results which follow ploughing in some of the fields of the Canary fancy. If he pair Lizards he will obtain Lizards, capped and spangled, and from any given quantity of genuine material will obtain a greater proportion of satisfactory results than can, perhaps, be arrived at in any other direction, simply because he will find himself working with elements constant in their action. Indeed, considering the comparatively small number of Lizard breeders and the few birds bred, we think the percentage of high-class specimens exhibited is far in excess of those found in any other variety, a point worth noting by any breeder undecided as to a variety to take up.

Breeding.

The general principles which should guide the breeder in selection of stock and its subsequent management may be gathered from our chapter on "Pedigree Breeding." The importance of beginning right will be manifest. Let the selected parents be the most perfect in all points that can be procured, and obtained from some *reliable strain on both sides.* We have said "perfect in *all* points," but remember that the most important are spangle and sound body-colour. These properties must be maintained whilst at the same time endeavouring to avoid deterioration in the cap, otherwise we shall eventually have no perfectly clear capped birds. Unfortunately, there is a tendency to degeneration in this point even now, and hence the necessity for this caution, for we regard the cap entirely as a cultivated and not a native development. It is the least constant feature, and the most difficult to manage. Sometimes it is present in excess, at others in a very imperfect form, and not unfrequently entirely wanting. Its erratic character is sufficient evidence of its having been originally a chance beauty-spot, captured and made the most of, and its presence is no more astonishing to us than is the white topknot on a black Poland fowl. Any feature may be made constant by selection, though it may be a work of time and difficulty, the development of native features being more easy than the cultivation of sports, which are apt to revert to their original form even under the most careful management.

A few specific directions will now suffice for the breeder's guidance in the mating of approved stock. Pair Gold with Silver always, should be taken as a rule. The advisability of exceptional departures from this law will occasionally suggest itself in this as in any other variety in which quality of feather and colour are properties involved, though here quality of spangle is also concerned. The gain from mating two Golds may be set down as comprising improvement in colour and in brilliancy of spangle; the loss, falling off in size of spangle, want of compactness of feather, and consequent lack of regularity in arrangement of spangle arising from the display of an excess of meal or silvery frosting, causing the bird to be too light, or to have a cloudy, "mossy" back. Birds undecided in the character of their feather should be mated accordingly—*e.g.* a dull Gold having white marginal fringe, pair with a bright Gold, not with a Silver, which would probably only increase the fault, while there would, on the other hand, most likely be found in such an undecided Gold so much colour, in addition to the close feather indicated by the presence of the mealy fringe, as to warrant the expectation of something more than a mere restoration of balance of power from a feather point of view only.

As far as possible, pair dark birds. Do not break up a pet arrangement to do this, but try to work a breeding system with this as one of its bases. Remember that dark feather means dark spangling, and that the Lizard will deteriorate in this respect quickly enough if encouraged. White beak, white legs, and white claws are frequently followed by white something else. Mate with a view to a balance of good properties—a problem not always easy of solution, the practical outcome of the "concentration" theory being that in most good breeding-rooms two strains insensibly grow up, good in most points, but *strong* in *one;* the exceptional bird, the lion of its year, being generally a happy hit in which, by means of two sister strains, good spangle and fair cap have been augmented by union with fair spangle and superlatively good cap. But since experience has shown that the *cap* is the most variable and intractable feature, never hesitate to pair birds, however wanting in this respect, even to the extent of having no cap, if good caps have been bred from the strain. And further, inasmuch as a *bald face,* though connected with the cap, is in reality a defective condition of *body*-feather frequently accompanied by other body blemishes, and is further indicative of a disposition to grow light feathers instead of dark—do not breed from these unless for good reasons.

Points for Breeders.

This leads us to a brief notice of a few things to be avoided or dealt with cautiously, and chief among them is the frequent use of any birds showing white feathers either in the wings or tail. These will occasionally appear even in the best strains, and puzzle the breeder as to their origin. We are disposed to regard them, in such cases, as mere sports rather than decided indications of foul blood, and we would not altogether discard an otherwise superior strain simply on account of its now and then producing a pied wing or tail. But we need not say that it would be contrary to the principles of Pedigree Breeding to pair two pied birds unless we wished to follow a suicidal policy with our stock. Counteract the influence and check the sport by mating with the blackest of black wings. Do not try to stamp out *any* defect in a hurry: it cannot be done any more than good properties can be fixed all at once; and take care that in doing this or anything else some other point is not stamped out which ought to be stamped in, or something added which ought to be subtracted. Attention to or neglect of these matters either means breeding or else mere waste of time.

In a discussion which took place in *The Feathered World* some years ago on the Lizard Canary, Mr. F. W. Baker, of Shaw, Lancashire, a prominent breeder of the variety, pointed out "the advantage of pairing clear capped birds to broken or non-capped partners, the reason being that we were likely to get better ground-colour and spangle, also neater caps; whilst in pairing two clear capped birds together there was a strong tendency to produce over-capped young and to lose ground-colour."

There are, of course, times when it is advantageous to pair two clear capped birds together, for if there is a very large percentage of broken caps among the young birds, the pairing of two clear caps will tend to increase the percentage of clear caps.

Mr. Rukin's Experiences.

Mr. John Rukin, of Rawtenstall, Lancashire, a very successful breeder and exhibitor, in giving his experience of breeding and pairing, says:

"I generally follow the orthodox way of pairing yellow to buff, or, as the Lizard is called, Gold to Silver, and I usually get the best results from such pairing. I have occasionally paired two Golds together or two Silvers, but unless you have some special point you are working for this method is better left alone. When selecting my pairs for breeding the first thing I look for is good spangle and ground-colour, as a Lizard, however good in size and cap, unless well spangled would stand little chance under a good Lizard judge in competition. I like to see a nice clear cap of thumb-nail shape in conjunction with a well-spangled body and good ground-colour. I also like size, but this is no use without the spangle and ground-colour, and that is why I look for the two important points first in pairing. I select a clear capped Gold cock of as good size as possible, with a nice broad back well filled in, not hollow, and legs, feet, and beak as dark as possible, and wings and tail jet black. Of course I am speaking of a bird with its first flights and tail, as after the first year, when they have had their second moult, the flights come grey; but it does not matter if they were black the first season. I pair such a cock to a good Silver hen (broken capped preferred), also good in spangle and colour.

CLEAR-CAPPED LIZARD CANARY.

"When using a Silver cock I go on the same lines of selection, pairing him to a Gold hen. I very seldom pair two clear capped birds together. Birds whose first flights and tails are of a grizzle grey colour I do not use, nor any with bald faces, as if such defects get fixed in one's stock they take a lot of getting out. If the cocks fail in any little point I always pair them with a hen particularly good in *that* point.

"Many grand Lizards fail in head; they are inclined to be puny and snipy-looking. The skull of a Lizard should be broad, rather long, and slightly flat on top. When selecting my breeding pairs I always try to keep these points well in view, as they give a set-off to good birds. Some fanciers I know have a fancy for pairing their Lizards all one way; that is, all Silver cocks and Gold hens, others vice versa. Either way gives good results; for instance, my well known 'King of Golds' was bred from a clear capped Silver cock winner of diploma for best Lizard at the Crystal Palace, and a non-capped Gold hen, this hen not having a single light feather in her cap. Then, again, my non-capped Gold hen 'The Queen,' acknowledged by most breeders to be one of the best Lizards ever bred, and which won against cocks a diploma at the Crystal Palace for best Lizard, was bred from a broken-capped Gold cock, himself a Palace winner, and a broken-capped Silver hen. I have, in fact, always bred good birds from both Gold and Silver cocks.

"I breed in the ordinary sized box breeding cage, and moult all my young birds in single cages 15 inches long, 16 inches high, and 8 inches deep from back to front. This makes certain of no plucking. I cover the front of the cage with a piece of brown paper during the moult with holes cut in it, where the water, seed hopper, and egg drawer are. I also run a white sheet in front of the cages, and I am sure by this that I get my birds through the moult quicker and also a better colour. The covering down helps to prevent their plumage getting damaged. I use the best colour food I can procure, adding 4 oz. of best hot Natal pepper to each 1 lb. of cold, as well as the usual quantity of sugar and almond oil."

Show Plumage of the Lizard.

The Lizard possesses its show-plumage for one year only. In its nest-feathers it shows no spangle whatever, but is just like a common Green Canary with a yellow cap, though some indications of its future character may be discerned by a practised eye. The breast of a good Gold nestling is speckled not unlike that of a Skylark, and sundry other small items are so many grounds of hope on which breeders pin their faith on such and such a bird moulting out a good specimen.

The changes which take place at the first and second moults are these: In common with all others of the family, the bird casts its entire suit at the first moult except the flights and tail-feathers, which retain their original dark hue while the body puts on its spangle, and it is then, as we have said, in its show-dress. At the second moult the whole is renewed with a great alteration in character. The body-feathers become much lighter, the delicate marginal fringe turns paler in the Gold and whiter in the Silver, extends farther into the web and defaces the clearly-defined eye of the spangle, which itself becomes less distinct as the entire feather loses its original brilliancy, and a general fading results, shared by the stalk or quill also, which, from being black, turns to grey, and " black, home to the quill," no longer represents the new state of things. This takes place with all Lizards, but with some more than others. We have seen some year-old and even older birds of high character very little changed, but all are so far changed as to unfit them for show purposes, except in classes given especially for them, while others put on age very rapidly; and this tendency to decline in colour, which increases with each successive moult, is a feature to which we shall have to call attention in our remarks on the London Fancy. A change, equally striking, also takes place in the flight and tail feathers, which become perfectly white at their tips and not unfrequently for a considerable portion of their length. It will be obvious, then, that extreme care should be taken to prevent any misadventure during moult, which may result from its losing any of the feathers and having them replaced by others white-tipped. But whether the feathers be moulted in the due course of nature or abstracted by accident, the damage to the show prospects of a bird which ought to have its eighteen flights and twelve tail-feathers " black, home to the quill," is equally great. Supposing the young Lizard to have left his nest with his full complement of flight and tail feathers, and to have come unscathed out of the nursery-cage—to which he should be transferred as soon as able to leave the nest—there is still the ordeal of the " flight-cage " and the prospect of persecution and mischievous plucking by his fellows to be faced; and he is a lucky and generally a plucky Lizard who in such a cage reaches the mature age of eight weeks in full possession of his entire original wardrobe. Hence the precaution taken by Mr. Rukin and other practical breeders of moulting their young birds in single cages, placing them in such as soon as they can well do for themselves. It is not absolutely necessary, but is a safe plan specially with those birds that possess perfect flights and tails. It is fairly safe to allow two birds to live together if the cage is of good size, and it is rare under such conditions that either will attempt to pluck the other; but if more than two are together there is a great risk.

Risks of Handling.

To reduce the chances of accident to a minimum, in the first place, *never catch or handle a young Lizard* if it can possibly be avoided. In transferring young stock from one cage to another, do it gently and without any fuss. Place the open doors opposite to each other, and, quietly and patiently, coax the birds to hop from one to the other. Do not hold the second cage in such a way as to expose the hand. The first mental act of a bird on entering a new cage is repentance, and actuated by fear and fright he always makes strong efforts to do himself as much injury as possible in endeavouring to get out again. If a bird *must* be handled, as in case of sickness, when it may be necessary to administer medicine, or examine it for other reasons, do not hold him in the orthodox fashion by the tail and tips of the wings, but lightly grasped in the hand, or the consequence of a sudden flutter may be that he will leave his tail-feathers between your finger and thumb.

The same general treatment as regards diet applies to the Lizard as to the Norwich and other varieties.

The classification of Lizards must, it is evident, be restricted in the first place to the two forms, Golden Spangled and Silver Spangled. These again can be sub-divided into classes for Clear caps and Broken caps, and yet further extended by giving classes for cocks and hens. By the kind permission of the Lancashire and Lizard Fanciers' Association; we publish their description of a Lizard, with standard of points :

Classification and Standard.

Lizards, like all other Canaries, are of two varieties —viz. yellow and buff jonque or silver, or gold and silver spangled. They are divided into four classes —viz. Golden Spangled Clear Cap, Silver Spangled Clear Cap, Golden Spangled Broken Cap, Silver Spangled Broken Cap.

The cap of a Lizard should be oval in shape, extending from the beak to the base of the skull. There should be no dark feathers on the top of the beak, and the cap should cut off clean over the eyes, leaving a fine dark line at the sides of the head, called the eyelash. The skull should be wide and proportionately long, rather flat than otherwise on the top.

The ground colour of a Gold Lizard is a golden bronze, of a soft, neutral tint. The Silver Lizard is a warm, silver grey colour. It is customary to colour-feed Lizards for the show bench. This considerably alters the colour of the birds, giving them a much warmer tint, the Golds turning into something of a chestnut colour, the cap a deep orange red. Colour-feeding enriches the Silver Lizard very much, giving the bird a soft, warm shade. This is most distinct on the head; the effect on the body is a soft, velvety grey, the softer and more velvety the shade of ground-colour appears the better the bird is considered. A green tinge in the ground-colour of a Lizard is a serious blemish.

A broken cap or mis-capped Lizard is one that has dark feathers on the head, other than the fine lines over the eye forming the eyelash. A bird whose cap runs down below the base of the skull is called over-capped.

The spangling on a bird should commence well up in the neck, increasing in size to the wing coverts, each row of spangles should be separate and distinct, perfectly linable down the back. On the sides of the bird the rows should commence with the lacing on the butts, increasing in size to the central row down the back. The wings and tail feathers should be black, the outer edges fringed with gold or silver, as the case may be. The wings should meet at the tips. The size and shape are of importance. The breast should be round, full, and wide, the back broad and full, the lacing feathers on wing butts should be of good size, clear and distinct, lying regular, the covert feathers on the wings the same, the outer edges clearly defined. The work on the breast, sometimes called rowing or lacing, should be soft in colour and linable. The beak, legs, and feet should be dark.

STANDARD OF POINTS

Cap, for size and regularity	10
Ground colour	15
Eyelash	5
Spangle, for size, quantity, and regularity .	30
Wings and tail	10
Size	5
Lacing and covert feathers on wings, for size and regularity	5
Breast, for rowing or lacing. . . .	10
Beak, legs and feet, for darkness. . .	5
Condition, health, etc.	5
Total	100

Negative Properties

A Lizard should not be hazy or indistinct in spangling, nor should its spangles be arranged without regard to regularity, nor should they have small eyes, nor should the terminal edges be of a character inconsistent with the true type of feather of the class to which the bird may belong, nor should any Silver trait whatever be mixed with Gold, or the opposite. It should not have a narrow skull or a narrow cap, nor should the cap be sensibly narrower at the back than the front, nor should the back of it be pointed or extend further than the base of the skull. There should not be the slightest indentation in margin of the cap, nor should it include any portion of the eye or face in its area, which should be neither run, broken, nor fouled by a single speck. A Lizard should not have a pale throat or show a clear spot under the beak, nor have a pale breast. It should not exhibit a grey or a white feather in wing or tail in its show-dress. It should not show light flue or white skin anywhere except on the crown. It should not show a dirty green cast in its ground-colour, or any shade that is not brilliant and decided in tone. It should not have white beak, legs, feet, or claws. It should not be shown dirty, nor in such loose condition of feather as may militate against the most effective display of every beauty belonging to Distinctive Plumage.

The same. applies to broken capped birds, except the references to cap.

Disqualifications

A white feather either in the flights or tail; or a clear feather in any other part of the wing or on the body.

The scale for judging broken capped classes is the same as the foregoing, except that the points for cap may be distributed proportionately over spangle and colour.

HYBRIDS

SISKIN-GREENFINCH
GOLDFINCH-BULLFINCH
GREENFINCH-BULLFINCH

REDPOLL-GOLDFINCH
LINNET-BULLFINCH

CHAPTER XXV

THE LONDON FANCY CANARY

In endeavouring to arrive at the origin of this remarkable Canary, we must admit that we have little else than conjecture to guide us in lifting the veil which shrouds its early history. That it is, as already stated, very closely allied to the Lizard there can be little doubt, and we think we shall be able to show how circumstances seem to point to its being an offshoot from, if not really simply nothing more than a modified form of that bird. In so far as regards reliable data, the London Fancy can certainly point to its name in eighteenth century registers, and say to any other Canary, "Here is evidence that considerably more than a hundred years ago *I was*, and that at a time when, in the absence of proof to the contrary, I assume you *were not*." That, however, might arise from the fact that its admirers were better organised and banded together under stringent laws, which have been handed down to us, for the purpose of developing this then *new* fancy from something *older*. It may be, and probably is, quite true that the London Fancy is the oldest "fancy" development and the first Canary which, singled out from many other varieties, made for itself a name among its contemporaries who may not have been known by any special designation or distinguished by other than general terms more or less characteristic of some peculiar feature; e.g. "The Fine *Spangled Sort*, commonly called, *French* Canary Birds."

The historical relation between the Lizard and London Fancy may only be slight, but

LONDON FANCY "OLD GOLD." (See p. 306.)

we think it more than probable that the "fine spangled sort, commonly called French Canary birds," would form part of the *penates* of the Protestant refugees, chiefly silk-weavers and workers of other textile fabrics, who found shelter here from the persecutions in France and the Low Countries over a century before we hear of any form of that "fine spangled sort" being known by the special name identifying it with the locality in which it was cultivated; and it is a fact worthy of note that the "fine spangled sort," now known as the Lizard, is now, as then, the pet bird of the same class of handicraftsman, whether the community be planted in Nottingham, long the centre of the Lizard fancy, or in Lancashire, where certain known strains descend as heirlooms in families.

Origin of the London Fancy.

But whence evolved, is the problem we have to solve, and, Is the London Fancy originally from the loins of the Lizard? the direct question we have to answer. We are of opinion that it is. The general tendency of the whole domesticated Canary family is to struggle out of darkness into light, and we think it more in accordance with this natural law that the dark, spangled body should develop into a clear form than that the clear should grow dark.

This argument of Mr. Blakston is supported by the fact that in the year 1888 Mr. J. Green, of Leigh, Lancashire, bred a perfect London Fancy from a pair of Lizards. So good was this young bird that Mr. Green entered it in the London Fancy class at the Crystal Palace Show, Feb., 1889, and it secured first prize. So fine a representative of this variety was it that London Fancy breeders talked of it for months after.

It may be said that there is no necessity to raise the question. Here is the bird; make the best you can of it, and never mind where it came from. That is all very well; but the two birds are so singularly alike at one period of their lives—viz. in their nest-plumage—and so unlike at another, after their first moult; and again, as age creeps on them and they turn their backs on the show-world and go down the hill together, they once more become so much alike that, forgetting the middle period of their lives, when, inflated with pride, each scouted the idea of the remotest relationship with the other, they seem willing to say, "We were wonderfully alike in our cradles, and are nearly as much so in our last days, and perhaps, after all, may be of the same family-tree."

We shall begin with the London Fancy in its nest-feather, and at this stage it requires exactly similar care and treatment as the Lizard in order to keep its plumage perfect for exhibition purposes. The same general management, therefore, laid down in our previous chapter may be safely adopted.

Changes in Plumage.

The young bird in its nestling stage is so much like a nestling Lizard that the difference between the two can scarcely be distinguished even by the most experienced. It has the clear cap, the same dull greenish brown body-feather, the black wings and tail, with pretty much the same general character of detail, even to the grey margin on the outside of the narrow web of the premier flights, producing the identical effect of the pale transverse band referred to in our notes on the Lizard wing; and this description of the young bird will, apart from its serving to show the resemblance between the two, suffice for our purpose. There are exceptions where the body of the young are not all dark like the young Lizard. Our Yellow hen, "Old Gold" (p. 305), which was acknowledged by all breeders to be one of the best and most perfect London Fancies ever seen, had the whole of her saddle or back feathers perfectly clear when she left the nest, and a sister had this almost clear, the rest of the body being dark.

On its first moult, which consists in the shedding of only the small body-feathers like all other Canaries, the character of the body-feather entirely changes, the dark nondescript green or brown giving place to a brilliant orange; in the most carefully bred specimens, entirely free from ticks or dark feathers of any kind, but in former years more or less ticked or spangled, the really perfect bird is exceptionally rare. The dark flight-feathers, as well as the bastard quills, of course, remain, and with the dark tail form a very beautiful contrast to the rich orange of the body, as shown in the coloured plate of Lizards

and London Fancy. This high state of perfection it retains only until its next moult.

This change we take to be analogous to that supervening on the first moult of the Lizard, though the resulting effects may have become so widely sundered in the lapse of two centuries as to appear, superficially, to have no relation. Here, however, is the foundation of a metamorphosis which we think more likely to have progressed in the direction of from dark to light, the line in which it always drifts, than in the opposite way. The Lizard still has, after who knows how many years of persistent endeavour to fix and enrich its dark plumage, a latent disposition to pale, every avenue of escape requiring careful watching. The *perfect* development of either the dark spangled coat of the Lizard or the light rich dress of the London Fancy is the work of extreme care and systematic breeding, and we do not think that the presence of occasional light ticks in the one or dark ticks in the other proves much for either side, since the argument *pro* and *con* is equally cogent; for if it be urged that the Lizard has a direct disposition to pale, and that there are not wanting instances which could be adduced to show how colour and spangle have vanished very rapidly—and, *ergo*, the London Fancy is the perfect development of this tendency—it might be urged with equal force that since the fault of the London Fancy is a leaning towards ticks and rudimentary spangle, *ergo* the Lizard is the perfected development of this feature. We think that the fountain whence flowed these two streams is more likely to be discovered by following the broader theory that, of two given forms of colour, one dark, but having a tendency to fade, and the other light, with an inclination towards a darker form, the first would descend through a greater space than the second could climb, and would ultimately lose more of its original character and approach more nearly the level of the second than would the second be able to do in an opposite direction by any latent energy.

Following the bird a stage further in its existence, we find that on its second moult it undergoes another change. Its body plumage loses much of its brilliancy, and what ticks or rudimentary spangles may have been present either disappear or become much less distinct. But the great change is in the wings and tail-feathers, which are now replaced by yellow ones in which the shaft alone is dark, giving the bird a grizzly, pencilled appearance. And this is just the case with the Lizard in a corresponding degree. His body does not turn yellow, nor do his strong quills; the bird has been too carefully bred with a view to *maintaining* these in their native strength to suppose this all at once possible, but the *tendency* is there and shows itself in the most decided way. We need not say that the occasional presence of exceptionally strong colour which requires more than one moult materially to affect its tone, proves nothing but the evidence of skill on the part of the breeder to combat a tendency which is known to exist; and which in time always asserts its potency. In the ordinary run of Lizards, however, this decadence sets in steadily on the shedding of the wings for the first time; and we intentionally refrained in our Lizard notes from referring to the *extent* to which this sometimes does take place, in order that we might apply it to our present purpose. Golden Lizards in particular are frequently seen after one or two moults so entirely changed as to be almost unrecognisable as Lizards; the cap is gone altogether, and in its place an irregular patch of colour, including the face and throat, and covering a great portion of the neck; spangle, gone altogether, and resolved into a grizzly form, rendering the back much clearer than we have seen in many a "strong" or heavily ticked London Fancy.

After the Second Moult.

We shall not follow this any further. For the fancier's purpose it is immaterial which was the parent stem, or even whether either is really the foundation of the other, though it is quite within the bounds of probability that in trying to perfect the development of spangle in some ancient type, a form of albinism was detected and encouraged; or that in attempting to found a school which should moult from dark to light, spangle was discovered, and the admirers of each carried out either property to its ultimate issue, fixing and perpetuating it till from one fountain flowed the two streams.

Continuing our description the cap or crown ought to be quite clear and free from ticks or foul feathers of any description. These may disappear in the moult, but occasionally are not so easily disposed of. The flights and tail-feathers, we have said, should be black, or as nearly approaching black as possible. A white feather here is a fatal blemish, and at once cancels all hopes of future greatness; but if there be but the faintest trace of grey in any part of it, shaft or web, it does not disqualify. Here the parallel between the show requisites of the London Fancy and Lizard will be seen, and also how identical are the essentials of either bird.

The Adult Bird.

In the adult bird the body-colour is of the richest hue. It is seen in the greatest profusion on the crown, as is usual with colour-birds; and in all the old standards, some of which, however, are very hazy and unintelligible, considerable weight is attached to "purity and richness" as displayed in this place. Throughout the entire bird, and notably on the breast, deep golden orange should prevail. We make no separate mention of the Buff form, because we take it that its characteristic features are familiar to the reader and thoroughly understood in every point, and it will be unnecessary to say more than that it exists in the London Fancy, as in other varieties, in all its attractive beauty. If it possess any one feature peculiar to itself, it is a mellowness and absence of the harshness sometimes observable in certain schools of overgrown Norwich, though there is little or no difference between Buff in the London Fancy and its development in the purest type of the Norwich bird. In the old days of the plain feeding, this Canary was as deep in colour as anything on the show-stage, and, in a good specimen, was not surpassed by the warmest tones of the best examples of the Norwich variety, with which, indeed, we have known it to be crossed with a view to the improvement of colour, and with the best results. We did not refer to this cross in its place, simply because the bird is so very scarce now as never to be used for the purpose.

Show Plumage.

The show plumage of the adult London Fancy should exhibit no trace of its dusky first-feather garb, though very frequently a decent approximation to this has to suffice. Referring to this propensity to retain something of its dark feathers, the late Mr. Brodrick, of Chudleigh, Devon, wrote to the late Mr. Blakston in the following terms:

"When I first obtained the London Fancy in 1842 there was not a bird to be seen free from ticks or spangles; now [referring to a period some twenty years later] numbers of them are quite spotless. I was, unfortunately, obliged last year to introduce fresh blood into my old strain, and that has thrown them somewhat back. Before this was done I bred as many as ninety young birds with only *two foul* feathers amongst them, and the large majority of them are quite free from ticks."

The wing and tail feathers of the adult obviously require no further comment, unless it be to note that in a show specimen they should be black. Here also the parallel between the London Fancy and Lizard is apparent.

One wing-feature remains to be noticed, in respect to which an amount of licence is granted which would not be tolerated in the Lizard. Black bastard feathers are imperatively demanded in the latter; but in the London Fancy, although they are considered most desirable and are highly esteemed, they are not included in the category of wing-feathers, numbering eighteen, which must be black, and therefore they may be white. Many otherwise perfect specimens exhibiting this shortcoming —for such we consider it—which have come under our notice have been admitted to honour under the *dictum* of professed London Fancy critics of a stern school.

The underflue, a feature of considerable importance, should be black in the Yellow or Jonque, and blue-black or slaty in the Mealy or Buff bird. It has a good deal to do with the body-colour, since it must be remembered it is only the exterior portion of the feather which assumes the golden hue, and the quality of this hue depends much on the quality of that portion of the feather hidden from sight by the imbricated arrangement of the plumage. The more intensely black the flue, the more brilliant will be the marginal edging of gold.

Beak, legs, feet, and claws should all be dark, though light ones are not a disqualification, for it is rare indeed to get dark beak, legs, feet, and claws with a perfectly clear surface to the body. The bird shown on the coloured plate is an ideal specimen after its first moult in full show plumage.

We shall not think we have written a word too much about this interesting bird if only we succeed in exciting fresh interest and bring it into fashion once more. We shall have succeeded in popularising one of the most beautiful of the Canary tribe.

THE IDEAL LONDON FANCY CANARY.

Decline of the Variety.

That the bird is not popular now arises really from no fault of its own, unless it be that "one season" birds are never likely to become *so* popular as those which continue in good plumage year after year —a remark that applies with some force to the Lizard. For this reason, and also on account of the care required to breed it up to the required standard, it will probably ever remain more of a fancier's bird than an every-day production, and always live in somewhat select circles; but that its admirers should be *so* few and its orbit *so* circumscribed can arise from nothing but a misapprehension as to its general character.

Then there is an idea that it is delicate. We say idea, because it is an idea, a mere supposition not endorsed by those who breed the bird, and therefore worthless as an opinion when expressed by those who do not. That the bird has been a good deal in-bred, and has, probably, to some extent deteriorated in consequence, it would be idle to deny, but hearty co-operation on the part of some of the principal breeders could yet do wonders in regard to saving the variety from extinction. Freer breeders and more attentive parents to their young could not well be had, and though London Fancies only retain their show plumage during their first year they are just as good for breeding with after the show plumage has gone, for their power of reproducing young with dark wings and tail remains intact.

In the very early days of the bird "ticking" over the light feathers of the back was permissible, and in fact common, as already noted, and Mr. Brodrick also refers to this; but as time went on this "ticking" lost favour amongst breeders, and the eradication of these ticks was thought desirable and carefully bred out.

Breeding.

In endeavouring to breed up to the modern standard, the clear-bodied bird must be regarded as the perfected development, and the ticked or spangled body as the raw material. To breed the former from the latter would not be a task of very great difficulty if *nothing else* were demanded, especially as the ticked bird is already a long way on its journey to the clear, and we should have nothing else to advise, as a means to this end, than insisting on a persistent selection of the clearest specimens with good dark wings and tail. The consequence of this repeated clear selection, however, would be that the gradual approach to a clear body would be accompanied by gradual loss of colour. And not only this, but inasmuch as brilliant black wings and tail mean rich body-colour, a decline in the latter would mean a falling off in the other most important features. A strain of high-coloured clear-bodied birds might be maintained with a fair degree of excellence for some time by mating the highest-coloured specimens, but the most careful management would not result in much increase of colour, if indeed anything more were effected than simply maintaining it for a while. We mean maintaining it in that rich form which supervenes upon the departure of the last trace of dark feather, for we do not mean to convey the idea that colour in a carefully bred, slowly but surely built up strain would, if unsupported, at once fade away; but remember that the tendency has been encouraged and is progressive; at each step colour has been supported, and if no longer supported must slide.

This is amply borne out by the experience of Mr. A. G. Filby, of Ealing Common, whose limited stock, becoming impaired in colour, has resulted in his breeding nothing but Buffs for several years. In some of these the dark flights and tail have become practically a dark grey, owing to the deterioration of colour not having been checked when it first set in.

Apropos of this reversion Mr. Brodrick said with much point: "There is a top to the ladder, and those near the top are inclined to give you progeny not quite so high up. I would rather breed with a full brother of a first-prize bird, even if not quite perfect, provided only he was not 'foul,' than with the prize bird himself." Or, in other words, prize birds when they reach the stage when deterioration is likely to set in must be paired to good stock birds, particularly strong in the points likely to be lost. Such stock birds are invaluable adjuncts to the breeding-room in conjunction with the show bird.

The position, then, is this: a clear body has to be *ob*tained, and at the same time colour has to be *re*tained, and finally *main*tained. And what is the material at command? All London Fancy stock may be classed under one or other of two heads—viz. "strong-coloured" and "fine-coloured." The strong are those in which there is much grizzled feather and dark flue, and the "fine" or "soft" birds those in which the ticks are pale and indistinct, consisting for the most part of little more than a dark or grey stalk with only an occasional grey tinge on the web. A "fine" bird will also show less dark flue on being blown, and an additional "fine" feature is a white leg. These distinctions, of course, are supposed to be referable to the bird on its first moult only, though the absolute "strength" of any strain is further gauged by the tenacity with which the ticks cling to the feather in subsequent moults. The pairing of Yellow and Buff, with all its relations to a balance of colour and feather properties, obtains here as with any other variety, while the pairing of two "strong" or two "fine" coloured birds, or "strong" with "fine" properties, is based on precisely the same principles as regulate the pairing of analogous forms in the Norwich. Breeding from two "strong" birds will, as a general rule, result in increased colour at the probable expense of increase in ticks and kindred features; while mating two "fine" or clear-bodied birds will produce contrary effects, remembering that these general results may be materially modified by the action of latent tendencies. It would be perfectly needless to wade through all the details of a system of pairing which has its exact parallel in the method to be adopted in developing a Clear Norwich, already fully explained. The natural laws governing the whole are identical, whether it be required to develop a light body or a dark, to remove spangle or to perfect it, the difficulty in every case being the intrusion of *other* features *not wanted*. The plan the London Fancy breeder has to follow is obviously the mating of "strong" with "fine" coloured birds, which, without considering *other* features, is essentially pairing for *colour*.

Points for Breeders.

We have found this method answer well, not only producing good coloured bodies, but also retaining dark flights and tail. My bird, "Old Gold," and several others of my noted winners, were all produced by the pairing of Yellow cock to Buff hen, or vice versa. "London Pride," owned by Mr. W. J. Stokes, Bow, a grand bird, and one of the best Buff London Fancies ever seen, was bred from Yellow and Buff parents. The pairing of two Buffs tends to give a larger appearance to the young, as it thickens the web of the body-feathers, and this thickening of the close-lying feather adds to the bird's apparent size.

In favourable circumstances a breeder has usually in his own cages a supply of "bottled up" material of which he knows the exact strength, or, more plainly, whether it be progressive or retrogressive in its character. Here are one or two ticked cocks: they scarcely look like the sort of stuff one would like to pair with a clear-bodied hen; they might "put back" the work a little. Not they; the direction of that strain has ever been upward. Here is another—a very "strong" bird, apparently a dangerous one. Not at all; it is perfectly safe and a little gold-mine, being an exceptionally strong bird from a well-established clear strain, and may be relied on to do more good than harm. When this is the case, the breeder knows where to look for colour or any other standard property; but when, from misadventure of any kind, he *must* make a dip into another strain, he should be most careful to ascertain that the imported "fresh blood" has been bred for the purpose required, or he may find that the effect of the alien cross will cover a wider field than he anticipated, and afford him work for years to come in pulling up weeds, the growth of unsuspected seeds long buried, but now brought to the surface.

The supply of these stock birds is now very limited, and it will be necessary for breeders to break new ground if they would resuscitate this ancient breed. We have bred some useful stock birds from a Golden Spangled Lizard cock, paired to a small, tight-feathered Clear Yellow Norwich hen, and also from a Golden Lizard cock and a chubby-built, close-feathered Clear Yellow Border Fancy hen. In the progeny of these we selected only those birds which approached the London Fancy by possessing dark wings and tail, or those most perfect in this respect, and showing a tendency to have clear bodies. These we paired back to pure London Fancies—Yellow to Buff—and the best of their young back again to pure London Fancies, selecting the most perfect each time. By this means in a few years we produced some birds fit to show and take prizes. Some such procedure must be again adopted to resuscitate the breed if we would see its numbers increased and become popular. The Lizards we selected for crossing were birds having good dark wings and tail, but as light as possible in body-colour. The spangling of such light-coloured birds is not distinct, being intermixed with a grizzly light shade, a point in the breeder's favour. We found, by using a Clear Norwich or Border Fancy hen from stock Clear bred for a generation or two, we got better results than from hens that possessed Green blood.

The late Mr. Charles Needham, of Hassocks, Sussex, a most successful breeder, greatly improved his stock by an occasional cross with the Lizard. This he found recovered lost colour in the wings and tails of his stock by working the resultant young showing the greatest amount of London Fancy properties back to pure London Fancies.

Every detail with respect to *moulting* as given in our Lizard notes applies strictly to the London Fancy, every precaution that ingenuity can devise being necessary to prevent any accidental shedding, plucking, or knocking out of the flight or tail feathers, the value of which for show purposes is, as with the Lizard, one of its essentials. We conclude our notice of this beautiful bird with a Standard Scale of Points which we think will be acceptable to all admirers of the bird:

Scale of Points for Judging London Fancy Canaries

Points of Merit

	Maximum
Colour.—On the body, including the cap or crown: for depth and purity, absolutely clear cap, and freedom from ticks or spangles on back	20
On the wings: for blackness of web and quill of flight-feathers and bastard-feathers	20
On the tail: for the same	10
Underflue: for blackness	5
Feather.—For fine silky quality and compactness	10
Shape.—Head, broad and neat; back, for width; breast, for fullness	10
Size.—For generally robust appearance	10
Legs and Feet.—For darkness	5
Condition.—Health, cleanness, and sound feather	10
Total	100

Negative Properties

A London Fancy Canary should on no account show the slightest tick on or about the region of the crown or cap; nor, in the perfectly developed form of its show-plumage, should it show any dark feather or any feather ticked or grizzled in web or quill on the neck, back, breast, or other part of the body, or any tendency to a ticked or spangled habit of plumage. It should not on any account have a white feather in the wings or tail, either in its nest-feathers or as the result of accidental shedding; nor should any of these strong quills show a grey or grizzled form, or other than a glossy black colour. It should not have white bastard-quills. Neither should it exhibit white underflue or white skin anywhere except on the crown, nor is it desirable that it should have white legs or feet, or similar features belonging to clear-bodied birds of other varieties. It should not have coarse feather, nor a slovenly carriage of wings or tail. It should not have a narrow, mean head, nor be long and narrow in body, nor upright in position, as opposed to the broad-backed, full-breasted, semi-erect type of Canary, nor should it be small or puny in its build. It should not be shown dirty or with broken feathers, or in a way calculated to hide the brilliancy of its clear body or mar the effect of the contrast furnished by its distinctive plumage.

Disqualifications

The presence of dark feathers on the cap or crown, constituting the bird "foul capped." An *entirely* white feather in wing or tail—i.e. a feather which does not show *some* trace of dark colour either in web or quill.

In this, as in previous scales, we have given only what we consider the leading features of the bird, and have endeavoured to avoid any hair-splitting in our valuations, adopting 5 as our base or unit, and making other values multiples of that number.

CHAPTER XXVI

THE BELGIAN CANARY

We now pass to our third group—the birds of Shape and Position, which include the Belgian, Scotch Fancy, Lancashire, Yorkshire and Dutch Frill Canaries, five most important families, and each possessing strongly marked distinctive features which single them out in an unmistakable way.

We commence with the Belgian Canary, which still retains the name of its birthplace, and where to this day it is an object of the greatest interest. However uncertain some points of its history may be, it can be accepted that over sixty years ago Courtrai ranked first, from a Canary point of view, of all Belgian cities, followed in order by Brussels, Antwerp, Ghent, and Bruges as regards birds of position.

The chief characteristics of the Belgian is, in fact, its peculiar shape and position; length, too, is a valuable adjunct. For a capital definition of these features we reprint, with slight modification where necessary, the late Mr. Blakston's remarks on these properties:

Shape and Position.

These terms require some explanation; hitherto, shape has in every case occupied a place in our lists of properties which the varieties of Canaries already described are supposed to possess, but in no case presenting such marked peculiarity as the Belgian. And the same with the idea of position. Beyond a general statement as to the ordinary posture of any birds such as semi-erect, implying nothing peculiar or out of the ordinary course, no further idea has been attached to this feature, which, with its companion, shape, must now be considered as special cultivated developments before which all other considerations must give way.

We commence our description with shape, as including that peculiar physical conformation on which possible perfection of position depends, although the results of that conformation are not at all times presented to the eye in the form of a constant beauty, the bird being able at will to shut itself up, as it were, destroying all its elegant proportions, which are only exhibited in their highest form during periods of nervous excitement and which are considered by some to be malformations. From this it will be seen how much the one property is dependent on the other, since so much of outward shape is gathered from position, and so much of position must depend on anatomical construction.

Shape.

The head of the Belgian is singularly neat; it is smaller in proportion to the size of the bird than in any other variety—the Scotch Fancy, which is an offshoot from this tribe, only excepted—and is much flatter on the crown, causing the bird to be what is known among fanciers as "snake-headed." The eye, too, is full of softness and intelligence, possibly the result of long-continued effort in the direction of taming or quieting down and subduing native restlessness.

The neck appears to be formed on a telescopic plan, being capable of a remarkable degree of extension or elongation, of which we shall speak when we put our bird into "position." At present we are supposing our bird to be at rest, or standing "at ease," under no excitement whatever, at which time it is sufficient for our present purpose to say its attitude is erect, or nearly so—the body assuming practically the same posture as when "in position," but the head and neck an entirely different one. When "at ease" the head projects from the body at as nearly as possible a right angle, the summit of the crown and the tips of the shoulders being about on the same level, the upper line of the neck being practically concave, though made up of a series of small convexed arcs. The upper line is that which is generally referred to when speaking of length of neck in general terms, because the underneath line has little more of length belonging to it than attaches to the throat, which speedily joins the breast. We refer to this simply as an explanation of what is technically "neck," because parallel lines drawn across the neck at the beginning and end of the throat would easily show how

40

much of the longer upper line really belonged to the outline or domain of shoulder, which extends much farther than that point indicated by the tips of the pinions.

The shoulders themselves are very high and prominent, and in a good specimen should be broad and massive, the pinions not projecting through the scapular feathers or those at the upper part of the back and leaving a vacancy between, but being well covered by them, thus destroying every appearance of angularity by producing a rounded surface of considerable area, and further by filling in the space between the shoulders to a level with the back, which itself should be long and well filled, all of which features are considered strong points in the configuration of a Belgian. A line from the back of the shoulder through to the breast will give the deepest transverse section. The breast itself should be prominent, but not full or broad, and, following a profile line from the bottom of the throat, may be observed to project in a very graceful curve.

The wings are long, and cannot be carried in too compact a form. Their apparent length frequently depends on the style in which the bird stands; but in a good specimen they will frequently reach to a point below the junction of the feet with the legs, and consequently below the upper surface of the perch on which the bird may be standing. Some birds, when in the least excited, have a habit of opening out the extremities of the wings and showing the upper tail-coverts; but this is a most undesirable exhibition.

The body, from the breast downwards, should gradually taper, the feathers of the vent and lower regions merging in those of the under tail-coverts in a regular way, giving a wedge-like appearance to the body from every point of view.

The tail is long and narrow, and should appear like a continuation of the taper arrangement of the body rather than of a fish-tail form. The shape and arrangement of the tail-feathers necessitate the formation of a small fork at the extremity, but the more compact the tail the smaller will be this fork, and the nearer will the tail approach to the standard, which requires it to be piped as opposed to expanded. Thighs and legs should be long and straight, the former well covered and hidden for the greater portion of their length in the feathers of the body. Flexed knee-joints present an unsightly appearance, as if dislocated, and are to be avoided. The feet and claws should be perfect; they do not differ from those of other Canaries.

The feather throughout should be fine in quality and compact, though many otherwise beautiful specimens are inclined to be rough, and some dispose their feathers in such disorderly fashion as to present a really ludicrous appearance. Shape and position, however, cover a multitude of sins in a Belgian. Beauty of plumage we have ever maintained should play a most important part in the show economy of every bird, and an exaggerated display of coarseness we hold to be a serious drawback even in a "position" bird. Colour is seldom displayed to any great extent, but when present adds much to the beauty of a fine-feathered specimen, of which a good example is shown in our Coloured Plate.

Such is the Belgian Canary in his formation, the peculiarities of which are not presented to the eye until, in a state of nervous excitement, he braces himself together and shows what the little frame is capable of doing in the way of "position," much in the same way as the Pouter among pigeons shows himself in his pride, the difference being in our bird that "shoulder" is the elevating point.

Position.

On entering a room in which a number of Belgians may be caged singly, or in numbers in flight-cages, we are not at first struck with the peculiar merit of any one specimen. The very best of them, which when put in position may exhibit the most remarkable conformation, is seen hopping in a slovenly manner from one perch to another, or sitting apparently in meditation. His legs are certainly too long, and set too far back. He cannot, when on the bottom of the cage, keep his tail off the ground, and when pecking at a grain of seed stiffens his legs into two splinters, straightens his tail into the same line with the body, like those artistic conceptions on children's toys, and looks eminently uncomfortable. Wait awhile. He hops on a low perch, and from that to a higher, drops his tail, which was never intended to be dragged about on the ground, pulls himself together a little, stretches an inch or two, and is already not the swan out of water he was a moment ago. You pass him into an open show cage, and possibly one or two others hop in at the same time. Let them remain. Don't hurry or frighten them in any way; a few minutes will set them to rights. Hang the cage a little higher, on that nail just above the level of the eye in the far corner of the room, where the attention of the birds will not be distracted by the bustle and twitter in the other cages. Don't lift the cage by the top, or the birds will perhaps cower and become more frightened at the novelty of the situation: take it by the bottom and keep the hand out of sight. Surely these cannot be the same birds we saw in the flight? They are already standing in an erect attitude with their legs straightened, their wings tucked up closely, tails so nearly in the same line with the back that a plumb-line would not show much deflection. Some may differ from us in this respect, but we hold that the line from the shoulders to the tip of the tail cannot be too straight, any tendency of the tail to deviate from a straight line with the back is a serious fault or blemish in a Belgian Canary. On this question we perhaps hold extreme views, but we have been educated in a severe school, and have for years had opportunities for closely examining some of the grandest Continental specimens, in all of which the line of the back is straight, in contradistinction to anything approaching a decided curve or a tendency towards "circling" as it is sometimes termed; in this point a hard-and-fast line *must* be drawn between the Belgian and Scotch Fancy. These faults are far too much in evidence in some so-called Belgians at the present time, which have no right to the name Belgian, being simply just crosses from the Belgian and Scotch Fancy, and have no right in Belgian classes.

Our birds now being nicely steadied, we approach them quietly, first divesting ourselves of our hats, objects of dislike to a sensible Belgian—an evidence of its superior intelligence and good taste—we gently scratch the underneath part of the cage with the fingers or a little wand. Just a faint tap and a little scratch to attract attention, and they draw themselves up farther and farther till their legs are perfectly straight and rigid, showing a portion of the thigh: a little more and an encouraging chirrup, and the shoulders are raised, higher and higher, and still higher yet, as if the bird were trying to reach a point which, once touched, still cannot be maintained without continued exertion, consisting, not in an undignified straining, but singularly graceful action. In this straining with the shoulders the head is depressed and the neck stretched to its extreme limit, not with any distressing exertion, but with the most consummate ease and grace; and in that posture it will stand, occasionally turning its head on one side and looking up with a soft pensive glance, with nothing defiant about it but just simply an air of thorough-bred gentility and quiet dignity. A bird of very strong nerve will sometimes, when apparently doing its utmost and when at its seeming greatest tension, grasp the perch with renewed energy, and, leaning back till its tail is brought under the perch and one would think it would lose its centre of gravity, literally double itself in a way not unlike the picturesque attitude boys assume in playing at leap-frog, till head, neck, and shoulders form an almost unbroken bend. If in this position the tail should be brought into a curve it is no improvement on the standard idea of perfection of posture, and a bird which can do all that is asked of it while still maintaining a perfectly erect stand is to be preferred.

And now note the *direction* of the head and beak when the bird is thus extended, as contrasted with their position when it is "at ease." When at rest, that is, when standing in a fairly

IDEAL BELGIAN CANARY.
(By kind permission of the United Kingdom Belgian Canary Association.)

erect attitude without being in any way excited, at which time we have said the top of the head and the shoulders are about in the same straight line, then, and *only then*, is the head in a horizontal position. The moment the bird begins to extend its neck or to "reach," as it is technically termed, and the head is correspondingly depressed, its direction is altered, and it begins to point *downwards*, continuing to do so till, at the extreme point of extension and depression, the previously concave or beautifully hollowed upper line of the neck becomes arched, and the head is bent till the beak points *inwards*, every upward movement of the shoulders being accompanied by a further development of the arch and a more determined tucking-in of the head, as seen in the illustration of the Ideal Belgian Canary.

This "position," the credential of a high-class Belgian, is an inborn quality which clings to it as long as life lasts. Some birds possess the tameness or familiarity necessary to a display of their properties from the nest, while others, though good birds, require constant training in the show cage (*see* page 176) before showing off to perfection. Still if there be gentility it will come out; but if it be *not* there, all the training that can be brought to bear will not develop that which does not exist. A high-bred young bird, when sitting on the nest-edge, can be made to show to a surprising degree what promise it has of future greatness, and there can be no "training" here. Still all birds should be steadied and made familiar with the show cage by running them into it and handling the cage gently whenever a few spare moments are available.

Colour.

We have made no mention of colour, beyond that it adds to the beauty of a good specimen, and in the way in which exhibitors understand colour it has no more appreciable value in Belgian than in the Scotch Fancy, for the simple reason that shape and position are *the* essentials of these two birds, and other points are quite subsidiary, and yet, in our opinion, they should not be altogether neglected.

A useful classification to popularise the Belgian amongst fanciers, provided we had a few more breeders, would be as follows :—

(*a*) Clear and Ticked Yellow Cocks.
(*b*) Clear and Ticked Yellow Hens.
(*c*) Clear and Ticked Buff Cocks.
(*d*) Clear and Ticked Buff Hens.
(*e*) Variegated Yellow Cocks.
(*f*) Variegated Yellow Hens.
(*g*) Variegated Buff Cocks.
(*h*) Variegated Buff Hens.

To which might still be added a class each for current year Yellows and Buffs. An idea held strongly in the seventies of the last century that Marked Belgians were much inferior to Clears has long since been exploded, and in fact some of the best show birds of recent years have been saddle marked. For instance Mr. J. Robertson's (High Harrington, Cumberland) saddle-marked Buff had an almost unbeaten record. For shape, shoulder, and position he was indeed a marvel, and we could give many similar instances.

We illustrate a useful travelling cage for Birds of Position. The sliding end door allows them to run in or out as required, and by placing the open door in front of their cage, and gently passing a thin wand between the wires to guide them to this open door, the birds soon learn their lesson, and pass quickly from one cage to another. The perches in the travelling cage are arranged just sufficiently high to keep the bird's tail from touching the bottom.

Breeding.

As regards stock, Belgians can be obtained through an agent on this side or in Belgium, or by being your own agent and going across for it yourself. Good Belgians are, however, not so rare in this country that they cannot be procured; but specimens above the average quality always command long prices in private hands, not only on account of their intrinsic worth, but from their value as show-birds. The age of the birds is not very material, though the custom in Belgium is to pair an over-year cock with a first season, i.e. maiden, hen. The main point is to start with good *breeding* stock, which is not always the best *show* stock. For instance a bird of exceptional size, even though a little coarse in build, so long as it possesses plenty of shoulder and good position (which must never be sacrificed) would be preferable to an all round show bird to pair with a typical specimen lacking in size. The former stock bird is just over the line of fine show properties, but is a valuable asset in building them up.

Certain types of the old Dutch and Dutch Frill Canaries are not far removed from the Belgian, and doubtless beneficial crosses have been taken from these at times.

In selecting our first pairs, if opportunity

occurs, choose massive proportions in the cock coupled with good broad shoulders—the better the position of the bird the more prominent these will be—and look for elegant conformation in the hen. If the cock lacks this massiveness, but is otherwise good, his partner must be strong in this respect, with also other good properties; remembering, when pairing birds, that what is lacking in one must be well developed in its mate.

The laws affecting colour and feather rule as in every other variety, Yellow and Buff being mated according to the established plan, but, if two Buffs are at any time more suitable in shape and position, they can be paired Buff to Buff; but as far as possible pair Yellow to Buff, and a Ticked or Marked bird, too, is usually paired to a Clear.

Belgians as Parents.

The Belgian Canary is popularly supposed to be weakly, and having seen it under nearly every condition we might instance as many examples in support of its robustness as of the reverse; still we think that the careful breeding it has gone through has developed extreme sensitiveness, and for this reason we have usually given its eggs to Yorkshires to hatch and rear. Our friend, Mr. J. Robertson, allows his Belgians to rear their own young, and assured us some years since that he never found any ill effects from so doing. Mr. George Baker, of Barnstaple, does the same, but Mr. G. H. Mackereth, of Ulverston, in a correspondence in *The Feathered World* some years ago, said he had found them anything but good parents. We ourselves have had a Belgian hen so attentive to her brood as to drop exhausted from the side of the nest while feeding them. Breeders must therefore be guided by circumstances, but it is advisable to have a few pairs of another variety available rather than run the risk of losing young birds owing to a parent's neglect.

We illustrate a nest box attached to the breeding cage used in Belgium, but we, however, prefer the ordinary box breeding cage, with the earthenware nest pan hung in the cage in the usual way, as being more sanitary.

From the hour the young leave the nest the rule *must* be laid down that except

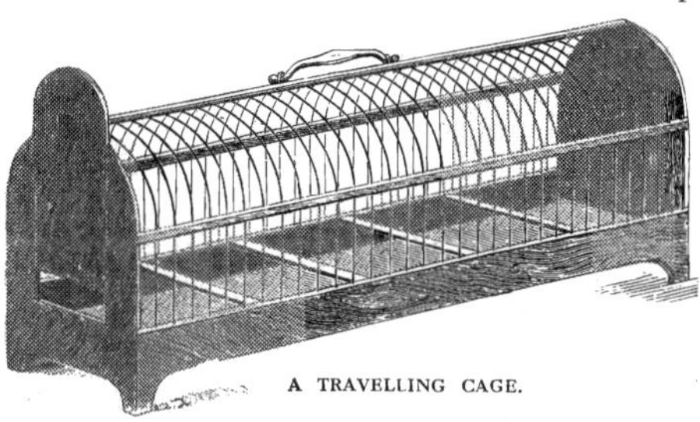

A TRAVELLING CAGE.

in cases of emergency *they must never be handled*, owing to the nervous nature of the breed. Other Canaries require to be tame, but a good show Belgian needs this property more than all. Moveover the Belgian has a strong repugnance to being caught, especially when young. The birds from infancy are easily taught to pass from one cage to another in the way already alluded to when speaking of the travelling cage.

Training the Birds.

Training should be commenced when they are quite young so as to get them familiar with and steady in the show cage. The custom is to hang the show cage on a nail in the wall for a few minutes each time the birds are run into it; but it is also advisable to accustom them to stand on the table as well, as they will then be at ease when on the show bench.

Moulting.

The ordinary routine is necessary in moulting the Belgian, which is not colour-fed. Every care, however should be taken to encourage a quick moult, by keeping the birds free from draughts and in an even temperature. Give just sufficient "tit-bits" with the ordinary moulting diet to maintain the birds' strength up to concert pitch until the moult is completed.

It is also essential, when dispatching Belgians to a show, to see that they have a good supply of Canary seed, and a tit-bit in the cage such as a good pinch of maw seed, or a little egg food, as they show to greater advantage after a good feed.

Scale of Points for Judging Belgian Canaries

	Maximum
Head.—Small and neat, slightly oval in shape	3
Neck.—Long and slender, capable of extension	10

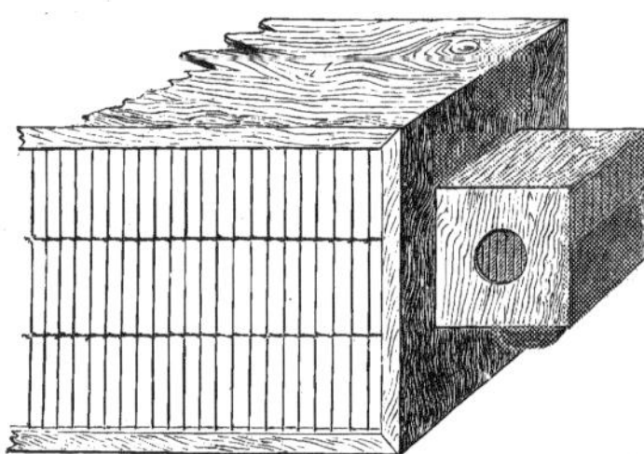

A BELGIAN BREEDING CAGE.

Shoulders.—High, square, broad and massive, well filled in between the pinions . .	10
Back.—Long, broad, straight, and well filled	5
Body.—Long, tapering gradually and evenly toward the waist	5
Breast.—Prominent and deep through from back to front	5
Wings.—Long and compact, carried close to the body, meeting evenly at the tips . .	5
Tail.—Long, narrow, and straight, carried stiff and compact	5
Legs.—Long and straight thighs well clothed.	4
Size.	4
Feather.—For smoothness and condition .	4
Total points of merit	60

Position

Attitude.—Erect stand, easy pose, the line of back and tail as nearly plumb as possible	10
Legs.—Straight and rigid . . .	4
Shoulders.—Elevated	10
Head.—Depressed	6
Neck.—Length of reach and arching . .	10
Total points of position .	40
Grand total .	100

Negative Properties

SHAPE

A Belgian should not have a large, coarse head, nor a short, thick, straight neck, nor narrow shoulders with the points of the pinions raised so as to cause a cavity between them; nor should the point of deflection formed by the meeting of the lines of the neck and back be sharp or angular. Nor should the line of the back be round, nor should it be hollow or have any sign of a "spout" formed by a continuation of a hollow between the shoulders. Neither should it have a broad, full breast, nor should the body generally be short or chubby. It should not droop its wings, neither should it cross them at the tips. The tail should not be thick or fan-shaped, nor deeply forked. It should not have short legs. The body-feathers should not be open or rough to a degree which interferes with the general neatness of the bird, and it should not be diminutive in size.

POSITION

A Belgian should not stand with the line of the back and tail forming other than a right angle with the plane of the perch, neither should the line be curved; nor should it be restless and unsteady. It should not stand with its knee-joints projecting forwards till thighs and legs are thrown into a curve, neither should it be cow-hocked or inclined to squat, nor should it refuse to rise to its full height. It should not refuse to elevate its shoulders, nor to depress its head, nor to reach out and arch its neck; nor should it be sluggish or manifest any want of nervous energy in any of its position movements.

The above standard of points is practically the same as that adopted by the United Kingdom Belgian Canary Association except that we give more points for good carriage of tail and slightly reduce the number for smoothness of feather and condition. Our definition of position also differs slightly. We feel justified in making these alterations, owing to the repeated complaints of many Belgians having a tendency to "hinge" tail, that is, not carrying the tail stiff and straight in line with the body. The way to remedy this is to give more points to birds free from the fault.

CHAPTER XXVII

THE SCOTCH FANCY CANARY

As its name suggests, this remarkable Canary is to Scotland what the Belgian is to Belgium—the national bird. It is doubtless an offshoot of the Belgian, and in its early days was known as the Glasgow Fancy and Glasgow Don, prior to breeders generally adopting the name of Scotch Fancy.

No authentic history of the bird is forthcoming, and, as the late Mr. Blakston wrote :

Origin of the Variety.

"So far as we can gather there is nothing directly connecting the bird with historical events, its development being probably of local interest, but the bird itself is an unwritten narrative of deep interest. We define the Scotch Fancy to be a Belgian built on a curve instead of on the ordinary rectangular scaffolding. The bird repeats itself, with never a reversion to any form not essentially Belgian in type, nor is there anything in its conformation, as fixed by the best standards, which it requires any other than Belgian blood to produce ; neither is any other ever infused on a decline of any of those requisites which, though they may be *modified forms*, are essentially Belgian, and can only be recruited from a Belgian fountain. The bird can be regarded as belonging to a 'mixed' breed only in the sense of mixing fresh Belgian blood with the accepted standard type ; and it certainly does not follow that, because some breeders may make a freer use of the Belgian element than others who possibly may work with such care and skill as not to require it, the bird is therefore to be spoken of as of 'mixed' blood. Gaps must be repaired and missing links supplied ; retrogression must be carefully guarded against and any departure from a fixed standard of beauty at once intercepted by returning to the source whence derived ; but *these* requirements are no evidence of alien blood, and no *other* evidence of alien admixture, however remote, crops up in the best strains. If it be of mixed blood, what are its elements ? Belgian and *what?* We know that some English fanciers are apt to speak disparagingly of the bird, and assert that it can be knocked together out of next to nothing ; but we know of no two varieties we should put together in the expectation of turning out a bird with the many pronounced features of the Scotch Fancy, while on the other hand we find no difficulty in tracing the reflection of every feature, more or less distinctly, in the Belgian bird alone, of which, we repeat, there is external and internal evidence that it is a skilfully modified form, a lineage to be proud of."

Of late years breeders have been carried away too much by "shoulder," and have allowed many faults to creep in, such as straight backs and tails, also too great breadth at shoulder, all Belgian characteristics, and not those of the Scotch Fancy. This departure has caused some heartburning amongst Belgian breeders, many maintaining that such birds win in both Belgian and Scotch Fancy classes.

Characteristics.

We have described the Scotch Fancy as practically a curvilinear Belgian. The head of a good specimen differs from that of the Belgian only in that it is a little more round, how much so would scarcely be imagined unless the two are compared side by side. This may seem but a small point, but we refer to it as illustrating the extreme care which has been exercised in producing a curve which should continue to the extremity of the beak. The under surface from the throat to the breast, thence to the vent and on to the end of the tail, should form a complete concave. Of course there is a little extra dip at the top end, especially if the bird is very long in reach—that is, has good length of neck—a desirable feature which every practical breeder endeavours to obtain as much of as possible, especially when sustained in the desired position. The head should be small and neat, and the beak fine, giving a neat finish to the head. A good head has all that pretty, graceful style of modest carriage and all the delicately soft expression belonging to the Belgian character, with nothing bold or vulgar.

The neck should be long and rather slender, as if drawn out, tapering finely in harmony with the head at that end, gradually expanding to the shoulders and breast, giving a harmonious finish to these particular parts, which are of great importance in the shape of the body. The shoulders should be prominent, like the Belgian, *but narrow*, being well braced together, well filled in and clothed with feather, giving a nicely rounded finish to the top of the shoulders, in direct contrast to the square top of the Belgian. There should be good depth through from the point of breast to the peak of shoulder; the breast should not be broad, but run off somewhat to a point, though the pointed tendency should not in any way break the concave of the breast and body. The junction of the neck expanding at this point when the bird is in position, gives the breast the appearance of being arched out with a spokeshave, yet at the same time leaving plenty of substance.

The back from the shoulder should be narrow and round, or convex, of good length and well filled; the wings should be long and carried closely and compactly in harmony with the body, exposing plenty of side, which assists materially in defining the contour of the bird. Nothing can compensate for slovenly wing carriage, it simply ruins the whole contour. The tail should be long and closely folded, well packed at the base, and gradually curved in towards the perch, coming under the perch at the tip, and forming a continuation of the curve given by the round back. The lower coverts and vent feathers play an important part in the continuance of the unbroken curve of body and tail, and give the required finish, too, where the body ends and the tail begins. The long body should gradually taper away from the breast to the vent, giving a fine, symmetrical finish to the waist without any tendency to break.

The legs should be long and well clothed at the thighs with short close feather, and the thighs lie well into the body, but show no tendency of being cow-hocked or stilty.

The "Hop."

The bird should take a firm grip of the perch with its feet, so as to have full command of its powers ready for the indispensable "hop," which it must perform *ad lib.* without disturbing or ruffling a feather, and without opening its wings to assist it in any way. To "travel" properly the bird must be possessed of two requisites, "nerve" and "action." If the cage be taken in the hands gently and quietly without alarming or in any way disturbing the bird, which we will suppose to be in the attitude of "attention," as seen in the cut on page 145, and if the thumb of the hand, which we will suppose to be elevated against the wires at the end of the cage next the bird, be suddenly depressed, the bird will hop to the other perch and instantly face about and assume its position, continuing to do this almost any number of times at command, showing in its action its true shape and never once attempting to flurry itself. The promptness with which it acts, the liveliness of its motion, and the sharp way in which it whisks itself round into position, determine the merit of the performance.

This free action is not insisted upon now to the extent it was in the days of the old Glasgow Don, or we should see less of the Belgian stiffness displayed in modern Scotch Fancies.

Close-fitting body feather is not strictly enforced, but it certainly displays the shape of the body to greater advantage than when loose.

The Ideal Position.

Such is the description of an ideal Scotch Fancy, and to realise it the reader must see a good specimen in form in its show cage. To obtain this the cage is held, and a gentle scratch given to the bottom with the finger-nail; the bird then grips his perch as if trying to pull it over, elevates his shoulders, and brings his head down below their level, extends his neck, and moves his head about as if trying to sight some particular spot, finally bringing his tail right up against the perch, the tip extending beyond it—the whole forming a picture of grace and action to its admirers, and well portrayed in our Coloured Plate and the illustration on page 201.

Classification.

The Classification at some Scotch Shows where the Scotch Fancy is largely catered for is as follows:

Cocks	*Hens*
(*a*) Clean Yellow.	(*b*) Clean Yellow.
(*c*) Clean Buff	(*d*) Clean Buff
(*e*) Foul-feathered Yellow.	(*f*) Foul-feathered Yellow.
(*g*) Foul-feathered Buff	(*h*) Foul-feathered Buff
(*i*) Piebald Yellow	(*j*) Piebald Yellow
(*k*) Piebald Buff	(*l*) Piebald Buff
(*m*) Yellow Green	(*n*) Yellow Green
(*o*) Buff Green	(*p*) Buff Green

In all, sixteen separate and distinct classes.

The word "Clean," used in some schedules to this day, is the equivalent of our expression "Clear," but applies to the external feather only, while the English term refers to every part of the feather, whether stalk, flue, or web.

The "foul-feathered" birds correspond with our bona fide "Ticked" examples, but a tick however small, will qualify, and very lightly variegated specimens are also admissible, e.g. such as are slightly marked on the wing or head, but are clear of body-marks. These and Piebalds compete together now at many shows. The "Piebald" section answers to our Heavily Variegated, and we remark, further, with reference to the Variegated groups—that is, the Piebald proper and the Foul-feathered—*any* ground-colour is admissible, by which we mean either Green or Cinnamon, A Green bird in Scotland is one which has no break in the green on the back—head, neck, and back must be all green: that is sufficient. Few Scotch show-specimens would pass muster in our Green classes, where even a slightly run waist would disqualify. The body-colour of these birds—i.e. the green —is, however, of the most brilliant description.

The hen, as a rule, is more lightly built and less sprightly than the cock.

Breeding.

In breeding use can be made of a non-show specimen, if it has shape combined with size, by counteracting the tendency to be flat in back or too stiff in tail by pairing it up to a more refined specimen good in these properties. Such a pair will often turn out young of the highest merit.

Colour is not much esteemed, though in close competition it might turn the scale between a Yellow and Buff. As far as possible Yellow is paired to Buff and Clear to Ticked (or, as it is called in Scotland, "Foul marked"), or else to Piebald or Green, not so much to regulate colour, but rather just as the birds are found suitable to each other in the essential points. Some breeders pair systematically for the production of Piebalds, and others for Clears, by pairing a "Foul" and "Piebald" together, or two Clears. But the general principles observed in pairing Clear to Marked in other varieties are equally applicable, provided that essential properties are not sacrificed.

A Warning.

A word of warning here will not be out of place, and that is that the Scotch Fancy must not be carried farther in the direction of the Belgian, for if we cross the line farther, then the Scotch must either be lost in the Belgian or the Belgian in the Scotch Fancy. Already many Scotch Fancies have gone too far, and should never have appeared on the show bench. Breeders must be in earnest about this, for the welfare of both varieties. Without wishing to dictate, we say the Belgian has for some years been too freely used. We have got size in our Scotch Fancy, we have length, shape, and all other properties, and we should only resort to the Belgian to maintain shoulder and reachiness of neck and depression of head when we are unable to obtain suitable material among Scotch Fancies. It is the pairing up of birds not far removed from the Belgian to the Belgian direct that has produced so many broad shoulders, straight backs, and stiff tails on the show bench to-day. Had such birds been paired to third or fourth crosses from the Belgian, better results would have been attained—young with shoulders good, but much narrower, the back well rounded, and the tail more curved into the perch—properties the very essence of a good Scotch Fancy.

Of course, a bird that has been worked back for several generations, and has become very much refined, and is beginning to lose "top" or shoulder and reach, may be safely paired back direct to the Belgian with the best of results, and the young from them will supply breeding material for several years without further recourse to the Belgian. The point is not to run beyond your object; "short cuts" are often dangerous: feel your way at every turn you take, follow the results closely, and remember that nervous energy and sensitiveness are traits of character not necessarily allied to form, and should never be overlooked in conjunction with other essentials in our bird. As far as possible get the coat to fit the birds neatly by pairing a loose-feathered bird to a close-feathered one suitable in other points. "Oh!" some breeder may say, "I am not going to trouble about loose feathers"; but a careful breeder whose ambition is to produce the highest state of perfection should do so.

Practical Management.

Of the practical management of this variety during the breeding season there is also nothing fresh to say. Our large stacks of breeding-cages are not in vogue, at any rate in the Scotch circuit. Open wire cages, such as we should at first sight regard as "general purposes" or "flight" cages, each a separate establishment by itself, are in common use The nesting-place is a wooden shelf fixed across the one end of the cage resting on the middle cross-bars; a round hole is cut in the centre of this shelf sufficiently large to allow the nest to drop in level by the rim which keeps the nest secure. This shelf is removed at the close of the season, when the cages —which, in a well-ordered room, are of uniform pattern—are placed side by side, and being generally of superior design and workmanship, look well, and in their light, airy structure harmonise with the character of the bird. For many years we bred Scotch Fancies in the ordinary English box breeding-cage with every success, and many other breeders on both sides the Border follow the same system.

As with the Belgian, it is well to keep two or three pairs of common feeders to take the eggs of any hen that may turn out a poor mother. Feeding is just the same for this variety as others of the Canary tribe. It is a usual custom with many breeders to shorten the tails of their breeding stock fully half the length when the show season is over and the birds are relegated to domestic duties.

No more "training" is required for the Scotch Fancy than that already described for the Belgian. It appears to be born with a full consciousness that the chief business of its life is to hop the regulation seven inches between the two perches of its show-cage, of which an illustration is given on page 178.

Judging.

These birds are judged by couples in Scotland; there may be more than two judges, but two judges take a class. The mode of judging is for each man to take a cage, and then, facing each other, each trots his bird out, indulging, the while, in little soliloquies. Then they exchange cages, and the better bird is kept for comparison with the next, every specimen being most critically examined, the best being set aside for a final sifting.

In attempting to frame a scale of points for judging the Scotch Fancy, we are conscious that we are doing something of which, to the best of our knowledge, Scotch breeders themselves have seen no necessity; at all events, we have not met with any such scale having an authoritative impress. Our intention is simply to give our readers in the usual tabulated form some idea of the relative worth of the parts which make up this interesting whole, attaching to each a value which will leave sufficient margin for a subtractive process, and not rendering complications more complicated in an attempt to draw too nice distinctions. To feather and colour we have apportioned just the value they appear to have in Scotland—viz. *nil;* but in taking leave of this most beautiful creation we commend feather to the consideration of breeders, at least, as a feature which seems to us to play an important part in assisting to make or break the fine curves which determine outline. Capital representations of the Scotch Fancy will be found in our Coloured Plate and on page 201.

Scale of Points for Judging Scotch Fancies

Shape	*Maximum*
Head.—Small, neat and slightly oval on the crown	5
Neck.—Long, thin, and tapering . . .	10
Shoulders.—High, narrow, rounded, and well filled in between the pinions . . .	10
Back.—Long, narrow, round, and well filled .	10
Breast.—Good depth through from shoulder without any prominence, being nicely arched out as the bird stands to position.	10
Side.—Long and well exposed . . .	5
Wings.—Long, carried very closely . .	5
Tail.—Long and supple, with good inward curve well covered at base	10
Legs.—Long, without being rigid, thighs well covered and set into the body, shins set well back	5
Total	70
CONTOUR, OR MODEL	
Attitude.—Erect. Head carried well forward and brought low down, with neck extended and forming with back and tail—which must be curved under the perch—one continuous arc. Throat, breast, and under surface of the body forming the concave sweep of the crescent	15
Nerve.—Sprightly regulation hop and smart recovery	5
Condition.—Health and sound feather . .	5
Size	5
Total	100

Negative Properties

SHAPE

A Scotch Fancy should not have a large, coarse head, nor a high skull, nor should it have a short, thick neck; neither should it have broad, angular shoulders, nor show any hollow between the pinions. It should not have a short, broad, or hollow back, neither should it have a prominent, chubby breast, nor should the breast be frilled, nor show any development of feather or similar obstruction to the clear concave sweep from the throat downwards. It should not be short in the side, nor carry its wings so as to hide the side, nor should its wings be short or in any way slovenly in carriage. It should not have a short tail, neither should the tail be straight and inflexible, broad, fan-shaped, or deeply serrated. It should not have short legs.

CONTOUR, OR MODEL

A Scotch Fancy should not stand " over the perch," nor should it stand rigidly erect, neither should it destroy the curve-line of the body by depressing its head and elevating its shoulders like a Belgian in position. It should not expose its thighs, nor stand with its legs forward, nor with its tail tucked-in under the perch as if attached to a hinge, nor disport itself in a way so as to break the continuity of the convexed outline of the back. It should not be small.

ACTION

A Scotch Fancy should not be sluggish or listless, nor should it be slovenly or shuffling in its gait, neither should it be fussy or wanting in precision in any of its movements. In its hop it should not make any use of its wings, nor land on the opposite perch as if from a flight; nor should it appear nervous or timid or cling to its perch, leaning back and thrusting its tail underneath as if for a counterpoise. Neither should it hesitate nor steady itself before or after its hop by holding-on to the side of the cage with one foot, nor should it delay a moment in whisking round into position, nor in any of its motions destroy the general outline of its shape.

CHAPTER XXVIII

THE YORKSHIRE CANARY

THE Yorkshire of to-day is not precisely the same bird as the Yorkshire of fifty years ago; but while other varieties have been bred, some locally, and others over a wider area, there has always been a bird of eminently distinctive character—a long, slim, straight, erect Canary, identified with Yorkshire fanciers to such an extent as to be known by the name of the county. Regarded thus, the Yorkshire has as much right to be considered a pure breed as any other, and no doubt the original strain of birds of which we still hear old fanciers speak was as free from alien admixture as any other variety of the Canary. Yet, looking at the Yorkshire of to-day, we find evidence of not one cross but many rather than of a carefully worked-out modification or adaptation of one particular form. It is, however, in a qualified sense that we use the expression "mixed breed," and do not mean to imply that the Yorkshire Canary can be compounded out of raw material in a year. Rather will it be found that those who have turned out the best specimens are men who carefully selected their material, building, shoring and propping up the edifice, leaving nothing wanting and no one point exaggerated.

This bird probably owes its origin to the fact that in both Lancashire and Yorkshire there have long been two varieties of Canaries of the erect school, Crested and Plainhead, in some respects resembling each other, and in others very dissimilar; and while one set of breeders adopted the one form, a second with equal care followed up the other channel; in the one case the majestic Lancashire Coppy and Plainhead proper resulted, and in the other the refined Yorkshire.

We now give a detailed description of a typical Yorkshire:—

Description. Shape is its essence! The head should be round, of medium size, and narrow in the skull. The neck, moderately long and straight, and between it and the shoulders there must be no indentation or break of any kind beyond the natural subtle curves of the leading lines. From these beautifully rounded, well-filled-in narrow shoulders depend long, taper wings, the long flights tucked in closely and stowed away, tip to tip, at the end of a long, narrow back, without any suspicion of a spout. A well-filled-in back is a natural consequence of level shoulders, and any hollow or spout indicates faulty construction in the shoulder. Continuing the line of the back, the tail must be long, perfectly straight, narrow, flat, and shut up so closely as only to show the mere edge of the outer feathers. From the back of the head to the tip of the tail should present, practically, a straight line, which is the line of beauty in a Yorkshire.

The breast must be narrow and perfectly round, which, taken in conjunction with the narrow shoulders, means small girth, another important point. Broad shoulders mean broad back and large girth, which detract from the apparent length of the bird by throwing it out of drawing. A bulky Yorkshire usually has near relations somewhere in Lancashire. From the breast downwards the bird must taper away gradually till it ends in a fine waist, where there must be no loose or fluffy feather, neither must there be on the breast any trace of a frill, the entire feather throughout being of the closest and most compact description possible, in which respect we think no Canary can compare with a first-class Yorkshire, of which "feather like wax" is no inapt expression. The legs must be straight and long without being stilty, and should support the bird in an attitude as nearly erect as possible, and the thighs well clothed with short, close feather.

Attitude is one of the vital points, and a bird with the slightest disposition to stand across the perch is of little use in a show cage. Size also

—or perhaps it will be better to say length—is an important feature; for it will be evident that length without bulk is what is required.

Such is the description of a typical Yorkshire, and a nice bit of "swagger," or, as the Yorkshiremen call it, "breed," sets off the ideal to even greater perfection, providing, of course, that it is steady in the show cage, and is in good, hard, proud condition. A good idea of the breed's beauty can be obtained from our coloured plate and the capital engraving on page 103. As many as twenty-four competitive classes are given at some Yorkshire shows, the classification being as follows:—

(*a*) Clear Yellow	(*b*) Clear Buff
(*c*) Ticked Yellow	(*d*) Ticked Buff
(*e*) Unflighted Yellow	(*f*) Unflighted Buff
(*g*) Clear or Ticked Yellow Hen	(*h*) Clear or Ticked Buff Hen
(*i*) Even, Uneven, or Heavily Variegated Yellow	(*j*) Even, Uneven, or Heavily Variegated Buff
(*k*) Even, Uneven, or Heavily Variegated Yellow Hen	(*l*) Even, Uneven, or Heavily Variegated Buff Hen
(*m*) Cinnamon Ticked or Variegated Yellow	(*n*) Cinnamon Ticked or Variegated Buff
(*o*) Cinnamon Ticked or Variegated Yellow Hen	(*p*) Cinnamon Ticked or Variegated Buff Hen

NOVICE CLASSES

(*a*) Clear or Ticked Yellow	(*b*) Clear or Ticked Buff
(*c*) Even, Uneven, or Heavily Variegated Yellow or Buff	(*d*) Even, Uneven, or Heavily Variegated Yellow or Buff Hen
(*e*) Unflighted Yellow	(*f*) Unflighted Buff
(*g*) Clear or Ticked Yellow Hen	(*h*) Clear or Ticked Buff Hen

Influence of Other Varieties.

Years ago there were two schools of fanciers of the variety—those who adhered closely to the original type, and who allowed a manifest deterioration in length and size generally to creep in; and those who, to recover these features, imported such a lot of foreign element that there was at one time imminent danger of the massive Lancashire Plainhead supplanting the genuine Yorkshire. Decisive action in the show-room, based on strict adherence to the standard, eventually settled the question, and the variety was established on a sounder basis than had existed for years, the importation of the Lancashire and other elements, in which Belgian, Norwich, and Cinnamon also played no inconsiderable part, not having been without some advantage. The bird, in those days, was really declining, and required vigorous treatment, though the work of restoration was rather hastily performed. The features even now requiring the most careful watching are chiefly the imprints of the Belgian and Lancashire blood. From the latter came bulkiness and a certain coarseness of feather and width of skull, and a tendency, common to the Lancashire, and even, to an extent, the Belgian, to grow a breast frill. The first of these bad points, undue size, was to some extent toned down by the Belgian cross, which in its turn left the curved lines, prominent shoulder, hollow neck, and too fine head, not wanted in the Yorkshire. The Norwich was also called into requisition, and to this may be attributed the improvement in colour and breast frills. The Cinnamon added another shade of colour, and further enhanced the existing excellent quality of feather.

The Yorkshire variety formerly was always to the fore in producing Even Marks, and a good class of Yellows and another of Buffs was common enough, but to-day Border Fancies take the lead as regards "Marked Classes," a fact which should make Yorkshire Breeders bestir themselves to recover their old position, and a perusal of Chapter XIX. on Breeding Even Marks may assist them.

The National Green-marked Yorkshire Canary Club is doing a good work in the interests of the marked bird, and already has the word "Even" included in the marked classes, as will be seen in the classification already given. Even-marked Yorkshires of the Cinnamon shade—also referred to in the chapter on Even Marks—are singularly beautiful, and many perfect specimens were exhibited by that astute Yorkshire breeder, the late Mr. Thackery.

Mr. R. L. Crisp, of Chelsea, London, a well-known breeder, in relating his experience to us accredits his success to following the principle when selecting breeding stock of securing length, shape, and style without coarseness.

Mr. R. L. Crisp's Experiences.

He never troubles about pedigree, his first concern being, does the bird possess the desired characteristics? If so, he has no fear of the results. To illustrate his statement, we may mention that at the Crystal Palace Show in 1900 Mr. Crisp claimed Mr. W. Mundell's second prize Yellow Cinnamon-marked cock and Mr. G. Wilcock's second prize Buff black-eyed hen. This pair bred successfully for five or six years, and with their young played an important part in the building up of Mr. Crisp's stud. From them the first year he bred three large Cinnamon-ticked Yellow hens, all good birds, one of which won in a cock class at the show held at the Aquarium, Westminster. In 1903 Mr. Crisp claimed Messrs. Mallinson's second prize Buff Cinnamon-marked stock cock at the Crystal Palace, and also a hen from Mr. J. Thornton, and from an admixture of these and a hen bred down from one of the first-mentioned Cinnamon-ticked hens he produced his well-known Buff Cinnamon-ticked cock, which won first at the Palace in 1907, in a strong class of nineteen. This same bird stood third in 1908 and second in 1909 at the same show, as well as winning many other firsts at other events. Mr. Crisp jokingly remarks of this bird that it was "a regular plum pudding of good ingredients."

In 1908 Mr. Crisp also showed a Yellow Cinnamon-ticked hen which stood second at the Palace; another outcross accomplished purely by selection.

"I purchased," says he, "a black-eyed Yellow hen from Mr. John Broadley, and paired her to the 'Mallinson' Cinnamon-marked cock already referred to. From these I had four show birds in one nest, three of which I sold at good prices, the fourth being the above second prize Palace hen. This 'Mallinson' cock rendered me splendid service. I bred something like twenty young from him the first season, one an excellent reproduction of himself. Subsequently I showed two Clear Buffs (a son and grandson) second and first respectively at Battersea Show, and the latter did a fair amount of winning for me. I afterwards sold him for about £8 at the L.C.B.A. Show, and I believe he did very well for his new owner, being grandsire to a Buff that won at the Crystal Palace and elsewhere. He was also paternal grandfather to the Yellow unflighted that won the Dulwich and Peckham Challenge Bowl and Silver Shield for best bird. He was bred from a Yellow cock on the small side and a large Buff hen. I have bred some of my best birds from this kind of mating, and although it is unorthodox it has satisfied me on two points, viz. that size can be influenced by hens and style by cocks. I purchased a Buff cock from Mr. P. Mason which bred with me successfully for eight years. He was related on the maternal side to the Dulwich Shield winner, and also with the winner in the unflighted class at the same show, which subsequently won for me in a class of about thirty-three at Cardiff in the same season. This bird afterwards captured the L.C.B.A. Cup. I could name many other winners, but think I have given sufficient proof that selection of stock having the desired characteristics irrespective of pedigree is a success in breeding Yorkshires, and that close in-breeding is not essential. In so expressing myself I do not belittle pedigree, for pedigree should not be confused with in-breeding. But my remarks and facts on produce are given to show that selection is the leading factor if we wish to progress. I have always endeavoured to pair my purchases up to some of my best and most suitable birds, and always endeavoured to purchase a bird strong in the points in which my stud showed weakness."

As a rule we get a greater percentage of neatly moulded and smart birds among the medium and smaller

Mating Small Birds.

Yorkshires than in their larger brethren. Such birds, if not too small, are useful to pair up with very large Yorkshires, a little coarse or open in feather, for generally the small bird's feather excels in closeness of fit. Where ample material is at hand we prefer that the cock should excel in size rather than the hen, for it is generally found that the male exerts a marked influence in determining the size of the offspring.

Mr. H. W. Battye in *The Feathered World* some years ago said he preferred a cock of good length both in body and leg, and a hen as perfect as possible in shape with close feather, but at the same time stated he had bred good birds from a small cock and large hen.

Mr. Crisp, we also know, favours a cock of good length, with shoulder and style, and a typical hen. His citing breeding with a small cock and large hen was to show that good birds are bred from them when paired to a suitable hen.

Some Other Opinions.

Mr. W. Mundell, when lecturing in London some few years ago, said: "We in Yorkshire want size in our cock birds, and typical, breedy hens. From such pairing we usually get the best results." Mr. P. Mason says: "I like a bit of size in my cock birds, and a nice close-feathered breedy hen." Mr. John Broadley, one of Yorkshire's oldest breeders, does not favour very large stock birds of either sex. He says in his excellent book published by *The Feathered World*:

"I never go in for very large stock birds; there are very few birds in my room above 6¾ inches in length. Better type and nicer feather can be got from birds of this description, and I want style and quality to breed from. If birds do not get long enough the first year, I keep them another year—that is if I think there is anything in them. I always find that when we use large stock birds we breed young birds up to about 6¾ inches in length, and, say at seven or eight weeks old, they nearly always get too thick and coarse in feather, and every year they are kept become worse.

"Young birds bred by the former method, on the contrary, nearly always grow better, and they last a great deal longer on the show table. I like to see them as tight as wax in feather, and of racy-like appearance; this stamp of bird nearly always catches the fancier's eye."

We believe we are right in saying that Mr. Matthew Broadley follows a similar principle.

Mr. J. Bailey likes the cock about 6¾ inches long, and a hen 6½ inches, as such medium-balanced pairs in his opinion are likely to breed birds with fewer faults, if there is type and quality in them, than from the excessively long birds. Mr. W. H. Shackleton, in his interesting articles in *Canary and Cage-Bird Life,* says "he always endeavours so to pair that he has the combined essentials of good points in the two birds." Mr. R. Halliday believes in pairing as far as possible two long typical show specimens, of course suitable also in other points, but at the same time says "if he had a little typical, smartly made hen which he did not want to part with he would pair her up to an extra long cock of opposite colour."

Such opinions command respect, and practically bear out what we have already said that anything lacking in one bird must be counteracted by mating it to a bird exceptionally good in these points, and if it comes from pedigree stock noted for freedom from the faults which it is desired to overcome, so much the better for the prospects of improvement in the offspring. The usual pairing of Yellow to Buff is followed, and also Ticked or Marked paired to Clears, unless, as explained before, the general rule is departed from, to gain some advantage, such as pairing two poor-coloured Yellows to improve colour, or two extra slim Buffs with a view to getting a better filled-in back or improving the tendency to be too thin in neck, or of getting closer feather.

The breeder must not be surprised if, from some of his Green-marked birds, he obtains a sprinkling of Cinnamon-marked young ones. These he will understand how to manage if he has carefully read our remarks on Cinnamons in Chapter XXI. He may or may not get these Cinnamon-marked birds, according as Cinnamon blood is present in the strain or otherwise; but in any circumstances its presence will soon declare itself, and, when so declared, is easily controlled, adding much to the value of a strain at the same time that it increases the field of operation and renders the work even more interesting and to a great extent more certain. And we may observe here, as a corollary to the foregoing, that if it be desired to breed the Cinnamon form of the Marked Yorkshire, Green-marked birds bred from the Cinnamons will produce them in obedience to the physiological peculiarities we have explained, precisely in the same way as the Green-marked birds are obtained from some of the Cinnamons.

Mr. R. L. Crisp, whom we have previously

quoted, had a rather strange experience in the mixing of Cinnamon and Green blood.

A Strange Experience.

"It is pretty generally known," he says, "that the young with Cinnamon feather from the mating of a Cinnamon-marked cock and a Black-eyed hen will be hens, and the Green-marked birds usually cocks. Some years ago, however, I mated a Cinnamon-marked cock to a Black-eyed hen and a Cinnamon-ticked hen bred from this pair, I mated to a Black eyed cock. From these I got a Green-wing-marked hen which I mated back to her grandfather (the Cinnamon-marked cock), and at least expected to breed Cinnamon-marked hens; but to my surprise both cocks and hens came Green-marked. Had I been using a Green-marked cock bred from Cinnamon and a Pink-eyed or Cinnamon-marked hen it would have been different. I should have expected either Cinnamon-marked cocks or hens or Green-marked cocks and hens. I must even now confess I cannot reconcile the result with my experience of the variety, unless, of course, the two crosses of Black-eyed blood gave a greater influence; but why should it be so, when one frequently gets Cinnamon-marked hens from a Black-eyed hen and Cinnamon-marked cock? In fact, I have bred my best Cinnamon-marked hens from such mating."

Mr. Crisp's strange experience was no doubt due to the repeated introduction of birds of a Green-marked strain. The grandfather himself was most probably bred from a Cinnamon-marked cock and Dark-eyed hen, and if so it made three generations in which Dark-eyed birds had been introduced to the Cinnamon strain in rapid succession, and either variety will reproduce itself with certainty if there has been no admixture.

The Best Results.

In claiming birds at a show there will always be uncertainty as to connection with the Cinnamon, but in purchasing from a breeder pedigree should be ascertained and the birds paired accordingly. As a rule the best results and markings of an Uneven character are obtained by pairing a Clear Pink-eyed to a Cinnamon-marked, or a Cinnamon-marked bred from such pairing to a Cinnamon-ticked. If two Cinnamon-Marks are paired together, the young are liable to be much too heavily marked—some, indeed, almost self Cinnamon.

Opinions of the Cinnamon-marked.

The Cinnamon-marked Yorkshire is a most handsome bird. Mr. Crisp says of it: "A really nicely marked specimen is, to my mind, the most beautiful bird of the variety, and the production of nicely marked cocks has always presented greater difficulties than hens." Mr. H. W. Battye says: "The Cinnamon-marked Yorkshire has always been a favourite of mine; some say it is not so robust as the Dark-eyed bird, but my experience is that it is quite as robust as its Dark-eyed brother." In breeding Cinnamon-Marks we have found them just as robust as the Green-marked and Clear Dark-eyed Yorkshire.

Influence of the Lancashire and Belgian.

We spoke of the Lancashire and Belgian having played an important part in the production of the present-day Yorkshire, and, of course, wherever resort is made to either source now the results have to be refined down for two or three generations by selecting the most suitable birds to pair back to the Yorkshire. A Belgian, the cross usually selected now, should for this purpose have as little shoulder as possible, providing he possesses other good points of the breed, and the Yorkshire most suitable as a mate should have good length, nice round head, but a shade larger than that of a typical show Yorkshire; the neck, also, should be a shade full, but not short or "bull-necked." The body should be long and proportionate, feather close, and breast nicely rounded. Such birds, as a rule, do not possess much "swagger," but the Belgian puts that right as well as the other properties.

Mr. John Broadley says:

"You will find it beneficial sometimes to introduce a nice long quarter-bred Belgian and Yorkshire, one that is very straight and smooth in feather. A cross of this sort gets your bird's more stylish and racy in appearance."

Mr. R. L. Crisp, who has used the Belgian cross with success, says of it:

Song Thrush Blackbird

Waxwing

" From observation, I have come to the conclusion that when using the Belgian hen length and the desired Belgian traits are better maintained than when introducing it from the cock's side. The only advantage to be gained by adopting the latter course is that quality of feather is probably more quickly regained ; but a cross with Cinnamon blood I have found very useful for this purpose. In all matings with birds closely allied to the Belgian it is necessary to use a bird rather large in head with a good rise and full neck. The snaky, small head of the Belgian is entirely unsuited to the Yorkshire. The latter should have a nice round head in proportion to its body, not too large or too small, and a neck of fair length and nice delineation, not bull-necked or too thin."

The Lancashire Plainhead is resorted to for length of body and leg, and the bird selected should not only be a long but very slim bird, well up on leg and in carriage, and a Yellow for preference. The most suitable youngster from this cross should be paired back to the Yorkshire, and the result again, until all undesired points have been bred out. No one, however, should resort to such crossing until they have *good* experience and a *thorough* control of their stock, and *understand* the work they are undertaking. It will be noted that Mr. John Broadley recommends a quarter-bred Belgian and Yorkshire as a valuable bird in the breeding-room, and from experience we quite agree with him, but at the same time we must not overlook the fact that someone must take the first cross, or the quarter-cross would not be obtainable.

Management.

The Yorkshire in the bird-room is kept in the ordinary box-shape single or flight cage, but this should be not less than 16 inches high, so as to allow plenty of head room above the bird as it stands on the perch, and so prevents it acquiring a crouching attitude, altogether contrary to proper carriage.

To exhibit a Yorkshire to the best advantage it should be shown in the recognised cage for the variety as illustrated on page 177. They should also be taught from the time they leave the nest to run from their living cage into the show cage, so as to become steady and familiar with it.

The feeding, management, and colour-feeding of the Yorkshire is precisely the same as for other varieties. Free use of the bath is a fine conditioner and burnisher of the feather.

By kind permission of the Council of the Yorkshire Union of Cage Bird Societies we herewith publish their standard of Points of the Yorkshire Canary :

SCALE OF POINTS

In giving a number of points to the various items, it is not intended that the judging shall be by points, but as showing the relative value under the various heads.

CLEAR BIRDS

Shape	*Maximum*
Head.—Small and round, skull narrow	5
Neck.—Moderately long, straight	5
Shoulders.—Narrow, rounded, and well filled	5
Back.—Long, straight, well filled ; wings long and evenly carried	5
Breast.—Round and smooth; the body long, gradually tapering to a neat waist	5
Legs.—Long, without being stilty, thighs well clothed	5
Tail.—Long, straight, and closely folded	5
	35
Size.—For length 6¾ in., with corresponding symmetrical proportions	10
Position.—Attitude erect, with fearless carriage; head, neck, back, and tail in straight line	20
Feather.—Short, close and tight for compact body feather, and close carriage of wings and tail	20
Colour.—Pure body colour, beak, legs and feet clear (*see note*)	5
Condition.—Health, cleanness, and sound feather	10
Total	100

EVENLY MARKED

That an evenly marked bird must be four-pointed (both eyes, both wings) or six pointed (both eyes, both wings, both sides of tail) ; these are called *technical* marks (*see note*).

Markings	*Maximum*
Eyes.—For neatness and regularity of outline, and for distinctness	25
Wings.—For exactness, decreasing in value as the marking extends beyond the secondary flights	15
Tail.—For exactness	5
	45
Shape and Position.—For symmetrical proportions, fair size and erect carriage	30
Feather.—For short, compact body feather and close carriage of wings and tail	15
Colour.—Pure body colour and brilliance of marking	5
Condition.—Specially for sound feather	5
Total	100

That a Ticked Bird is one with dark feather on thighs, rump, or any part of an otherwise clear body; it may also have a mark on one eye, wing or on tail, but not more than one such *technical* mark, separately, or in addition to any other variegation on its body (*see note*).

That an Unevenly-marked bird may have two, three or five *technical* marks on eyes, wings or tail, separately or in addition to any other variegation on its body. A bird with four or six marks, if variegated on head or body, is also considered an Unevenly-marked Bird (*see note*).

Ticked and Unevenly-marked Yorkshire Cinnamon.

In drawing up a standard for this variety it is necessary to note that what is usually recognised as *Ticked*, namely, the presence of dark feathers on thighs, and of dark underflue, cannot well be admitted; and seeing that variegation in some form or other is the object aimed at, therefore it is necessary that a well-defined *Cinnamon* mark or tick must be clearly discernible. And as an Evenly-marked Bird is the highe t form of variegation, it is desirable the object of breeders should be directed to try for the nearest approach to evenness of markings, whilst still retaining all the essential Yorkshire qualities, so that while form and approximate excellence in marking will count above equally good form and merely irregular variegation, still *superior form* will count above *anything* in this class.

(The Evenly-marked Birds of this variety will have to be shown and judged as Evenly-marked Yorkshires.)

Type and length as for other Yorkshire varieties.

Shape	*Maximum*
Head.—Small and round, skull narrow . .	5
Neck.—Moderately long, straight . . .	5
Shoulders.—Narrow, rounded and well filled .	5
Back.—Long, straight and well filled, wings long and evenly carried . . .	5
Breast.—Round and smooth, the body long and gradually tapering to a neat waist .	5
Legs.—Long, without being stilty, thighs well clothed	5
Tail.—Long, straight and closely folded . .	5
	35
Feather.—Short, close and tight for compactness of body feather, and close carriage of wings and tail	15
Position.—Attitude erect, with fearless carriage, head, neck, back and tail in a straight line	20
Markings.—For approximate excellence in marking, and nearest approach to evenness .	15
Colour.—Pure body and brilliance of markings	5
Condition.—Health, cleanness and sound feather	10
Total . . .	100

Note.—*Clear Birds.* Discoloured beak, legs or feet on an otherwise Clear Bird are not a "disqualifition," but count against the bird according to their extent.

Note.—*Evenly-marked.* The presence of dark feather on the thighs or rump are not a "disqualification," but count against the bird according to their extent.

Note.—*Ticked and Unevenly-marked* are to be judged by the same scale as Clear Birds (except where special classes are provided for Unevenly-marked), when such classes shall be judged by the same scale as the Yorkshire Cinnamons.

Negative Properties

A Yorkshire Canary should not have a large, flat, coarse head, nor any overhanging brow indicative of Plainhead extraction; neither should it have a short, thick neck, nor should the neck project after the manner of a Belgian or appear to be set on in any other way than in the line of the body. It should not have broad, square shoulders, neither should the shoulders show undue prominence or have any hollow between them. It should not be short in the back or body, neither must the back be hollow, nor curved in the direction of its length. It must not show a prominent breast, nor have any frill or similar arrangement of feathers thereon. It should not have short legs, neither should they be rigid or stilty. It should not have short flights, nor should the wings be carried in a slovenly way or cross each other at the tips, neither should the tail be short or fan-shaped. A good bird should neither be short and squatty nor large and bulky. It should not stand across the perch; nor, in whatever position it stands, should the line from the back of the head to the tip of the tail be a curve. It should not have loose, fluffy feather, nor should the colour, however pale, be undecided. A clear bird should not have dark underflue, nor should beak, legs, or feet be discoloured, nor should it be shown except in perfect feather and scrupulously clean.

For further Standard and remarks on Evenly-marked Yorkshires, we would refer our readers to Chapter XIX.

CHAPTER XXIX

THE LANCASHIRE COPPY

THE word "Coppy," which signifies a crest or topping, requires no further explanation, its connection with the bird being plain. The prefix "Lancashire" seemed at one time as if it were on the point of being superseded by "Manchester," but when the latter began to come into general use, the breeders in other Lancashire towns, where the bird is extensively and almost exclusively cultivated, protested against even the great Cottonopolis itself (where they maintained the bird was *not* bred in any numbers) assuming the title, and so secured for the bird its county name.

In Lancashire the Coppy reigns conjointly with the Plainhead, and, though one of the most interesting Canaries, it is also one of the most local varieties, seldom travelling beyond the bounds of its county, to which fact can be attributed its comparative want of popularity. It is a bird which formerly was generally exhibited under the auspices of some local society at the "house" where its meetings were held. These shows were common in Lancashire some thirty-five years ago; but open exhibitions have now practically supplanted them. The home shows, however, in those early days had their good side; they were meetings of breeders as distinguished fron mere exhibitors, and they were also the strongholds of the Fancy as then constituted.

Size.

In stature the Lancashire is the giant of the family, standing almost a full head and shoulders above any of its fellows, though we doubt if the very large good specimens can be found to-day in such numbers as they were twenty-five or thirty years ago, the time when the great demand was at its height for good specimens to cross with Crests. Lancashire breeders then thoughtlessly sold many of their best specimens for tempting prices, and the effects have not yet been recovered.

With the modifications necessary we quote the late Mr. Blakston's description of a Lancashire, which is well illustrated by our Coloured Plate:

Characteristics.

Length and massive proportions, a large crest or coppy, and a bold, defiant, erect stand are the breed's characteristic traits. The Plainhead is the non-crested form of bird, and in no way differs from the Coppy in contour, its head only requiring special description, which we will give, as it is the base on which good crested formation is developed. A Plainhead skull, then, should be large, very broad and rather long, having a flattish tendency on top, though not actually flat; it cannot have these features too largely developed. Not content with mere width of skull, it should also have heavy overhanging eyebrows; and a redundant crop of soft, long feather, as if with very little encouragement it would grow into crest. The expression under its drooping brows is stolid and sulky.

The Crest.

Such a skull is, in the Coppy, thatched with a large crest somewhat differing from that of the Crested Canary. It is not in all cases so large as might be expected from the great size of the bird, but is invariably neat, with well-placed centre, good circular frontage, and regularly radiating feather. The difference in shape consists in what fanciers call all front and no back, that is, with a perfect frontage, but showing little or no true crest formation or radiation from the centre in a backward direction, the crest extending no further on each side than serves to form a horse-shoe frontage.

The hinder portion is destitute of true radiation, or falls over the back of the skull in such a smooth way as to make it difficult to say whether it consists of true crest-feather or not.

Such a crest contains an exaggerated form of a feature shown in Chapter XXII. to be most valuable—the well-filled nape—so valuable a feature in its place that the Coppy cross is frequently resorted to for no other purpose than to obtain it.

The large, full coppy, with just a slight tendency to droop, especially towards the tips of the feathers, owing to the flat tendency of the skull, is as rare as is the perfect development of any other cultivated feature. There is the average in respect of size and good form, but nothing further; the rest is made up by the

LANCASHIRE PLAINHEAD AND COPPY.

size and majestic carriage of the bird, and the modern crest of Norwich type is undoubtedly indebted to the Lancashire for its large dimensions. The monster crests of either the Lancashire or Norwich Crest are not simply enlarged editions of its ordinary type. Only very few crests would, if indefinitely increased in size, assume the form which common assent has declared to be perfection; it requires a certain description of feather to produce this, and only when it is present, be it in Coppy or Norwich type, is this exceptional standard of excellence obtained.

One feature in connection with the Coppy Crest and Plainhead is worthy of note, and in this respect it takes the lead of all others—viz. in the average and exceptional superiority of its yellows, while the difficulty of obtaining a good yellow crest in the Norwich type is well known.

The highest standard of beauty in a Lancashire Coppy in respect to colour is the Clear form, though this is not so marked as of yore, and the Clears do not usually contain the largest or best coppies. These are generally found among the Grey or Ticked Coppies, beyond which slight departure from clear feather the Lancashire bird knows no variegation whatever.

Shape.

In shape the Lancashire Coppy is throughout massive in its proportions. The neck is moderately long, also straight, but loses something of its apparent length in its stoutness, as the head and crest must not appear as if attached to a mushroom stalk. The shoulders are broad and well filled, but not in any way prominent. The back is broad and long, and should be well filled in, the straighter the better, though being of such gigantic size, as the bird stands in its show cage there is a slight tendency to a curve which only extraordinary size can be weighed against. The tendency of all *very* long Canaries is in the direction of a curve.

Average birds, however, and birds *above* the average, especially among the Yellows, are to be found rigidly straight, but some of the huge Buffs really set all rule at defiance.

The Wings and Tail.

The breast is very full and prominent; the body long and tapering, though not finely, and showing plenty of side. The wings are long, and not infrequently, especially in Buffs, crossed at the tips; this is a defect, though difficult to overcome when a certain point with respect to size has been passed. The tail should be long, and though somewhat thick, nicely folded. The legs are long and strong, with the thighs well feathered and not too much exposed, or what we have elsewhere described as stilty, i.e. straight and rigid. The body-feather ought to be long without being coarse, and there should be plenty of it, with a profusion of white, flossy underflue. The commonest fault in feather is a ruffle on the breast, and a general fluffiness about the waist and larger upper tail-coverts. These tell in close competition, but unusual size and a superior style of coppy will somewhat compensate, for the Coppy is no exception to the rule which assigns high values to ultra-excellence in a cultivated feature, even if accompanied by others not in themselves desirable.

Colour.

In colour there are but four forms recognised in the Lancashire: Clear Yellow, Clear Buff, Ticked Yellow, and Ticked Buff. Breeders are very particular as to the purity of their birds' colour, and that it be kept strictly within the limit of "Clear" or "Ticked." Breeding from Clears for generations is not the best way to produce colour, and though not much can be expected Yellows must be Yellows, and Buffs must be Buffs; there must be no indecision in either form, no nondescript, mealy admixture to destroy the tone of the Yellow, nor any trait, peculiar to yellow feather alone, present in the Buff to cheat the eye into a belief that it is better than it really is. It may be that the Ticked birds play a not unimportant part in keeping up some brightness in the Yellows, as their colour is frequently not to be despised, and is a feature to be maintained and credited with a reasonable value.

The classification of Lancashires is the same for Coppies and Plainheads alike: (*a*) Clear Yellow Coppy, (*b*) Clear Buff Coppy, (*c*) Clear Yellow Plainhead, (*d*) Clear Buff Plainhead, (*e*) Ticked Yellow Coppy, (*f*) Ticked Buff Coppy, (*g*) Ticked Yellow Plainheads, (*h*) Ticked Buff Plainhead. This was the classification given at Rochdale twenty-three years ago. To-day four additional classes are given—viz. Coppy hens, Plainhead hens, current year Coppies, and current year Plainheads—twelve classes in all, and they could be further subdivided by separating Yellow and Buff Coppy hens and Yellow and Buff Plainhead hens, also current year Yellow and Buff Coppy and the Plainheads in like manner if entries warrant it.

Breeding Lancashires.

Breeding is similar to that of the Norwich type crest, that is Coppy cock to Plainhead hen, or vice versa, and as a rule the pair consists of yellow and buff; and a ticked bird, be it Coppy or Plainhead, is usually paired to a Clear. These principles are, of course, at times departed from to obtain some special point. For instance two Coppies are paired together to obtain a greater percentage of coppies in the offspring, but the breeder when thus pairing should be careful to select two of the neatest and most perfect Coppies, yellow and buff, of course, and if one is a Ticked bird so much the better colour and quality. A glance at the chapter on Norwich will explain the reason. Two Coppies, which run narrow at the back of the poll, and whip up at the sides behind the eye, should never be paired together, or the breeder will so emphasise the faults as to take two or three breeding seasons to get them under control again.

Two Buff Coppies are also paired to get the Coppies denser in feather, as it tends to thicken the web. Some breeders also pair two Coppies together to breed larger Coppies. This system we have never been able to follow, because it is rare for a Coppy to have the width of skull of a Plainhead, and as the narrower the skull the smaller the coppy and vice versa, it is reasonable to anticipate larger coppies from a Coppy and Plainhead than from two Coppies. Wide - skulled Plainheads are paired together to develop width of skull, two Buffs by preference, and their young paired back to the Coppy, Yellow and Buff, and if the Coppies have been double-Coppy bred so much the better in this case, as it will tend to secure a fair percentage of Coppies in the progeny.

It is also an advantage to pair a Ticked Coppy with a Ticked Plainhead if losing colour, or a Buff Coppy with a Buff Plainhead if losing size, or wanting to increase density of feather, or gain stronger bone. Size must at all times be kept in view, length and massive proportions being leading characteristics. Remember that the body is not only bulky, but must be long too, and if length and bulk are to be maintained one, if not both, of the birds paired must possess it. As in other varieties birds faulty in any respect must be paired to partners particularly good in these points.

What to Avoid.

In starting to breed the beginner should avoid what are known as "Bumble-fronts" in the Coppy, that is a strong heavy undergrowth of short, bristly feather growing upwards at the base of the beak just over the nostrils, and causing the Coppy to lift and appear untidy in front. These bristly feathers are present in all birds, but their proper position is to lie down in the direction of the beak close to its base. It is the upward growth that divides the front of the Coppy, and causes it to be termed "split fronted."

This same fault also causes great trouble in the Norwich type Crest, and it is well to guard against it at the commencement.

We believe those well-known breeders of the Lancashire, Messrs. Robert Barriss, of Rochdale, and John Garner, of Hazelgrove, both follow similar principles in breeding to those that we advocate. Our experience is that the Lancashire, whilst a free breeder if the stock is healthy, includes some indifferent feeders, even though we have had some hens turn out splendid mothers. Still it is well to have a few pairs of feeders, such as Yorkshires, Norwich, or common Germans to transfer the Lancashire's eggs to, to sit, hatch and rear where you find they will not do so.

Dutch Influence.

For some years past occasional crosses have been taken from the Crest to improve the Lancashire, pairing the best of the young inclining most to the Lancashire back to the Lancashire. If only two or three descendants of the original Dutch stock with their massive build, unfortunately now almost extinct, could be imported and crossed into the Lancashire it would put new life into the variety for many years to come.

Cages.

The size of the birds will suggest the use of commodious cages and roomy nest pans; and with all these erect and comparatively loose-feathered Canaries it is advisable to shorten the feathers a little immediately round the vent with a pair of small scissors. Some breeders also cut about an inch off the end of the tail to prevent their getting very dirty while breeding.

We conclude our remarks on this remarkable bird by publishing, with their kind permission, the description and standard of the Lancashire and Lizard Fanciers' Association.

Description of a Lancashire

The Lancashire should be a large bird, of good length and stoutness, and when in the show-cage should have a bold look. The Coppy should be of a horse-shoe shape commencing behind the eye-line, and lay close behind the skull, forming a frontal three-quarters of a circle without any break in its shape or formation, and should radiate from its centre with a slight droop. There should be no roughness at the back of the skull. The neck should be long and thick, and the feathers soft and lying close to the neck, the shoulders broad, the back long and full, the chest bold and wide. The wings of a Lancashire should be long, giving to the bird what is called a long-sided appearance. The tail should also be long. When placed in a show-cage the bird should stand erect, easy and graceful, being bold in its appearance, not timid and crouching. It should not be dull or slothful-looking, and should move about with ease and elegance. Its legs should be long, and in strength match the appearance of the body. When standing upright in the cage the tail should droop slightly, giving the bird the appearance of having a slight curve from the beak to the end of the tail. A Lancashire should not stand across the perch, nor show a hollow back. It should have plenty of feather, but lying closely to the body, and the feather should be fine and soft. The properties of the Plainhead are the same as the Coppy, with the exception of the head. The head should be broad and rather long, the eyebrows clearly defined and overhanging, or what is often called lashed. The feather on the head should be soft and plentiful, and not tucked or whipped up from behind the eye into the neck.

Standard for Lancashires

	Maximum
Head.—Coppy	30
Neck.—For fullness and thickness	10
Back.—Round, full and long	10
Length of bird and substance	25
Upstanding position and type	15
Condition and cleanliness	10
Total	100

In judging the Plainhead the standard is the same, the 30 Points given for Coppy being given for head properties in the Plainhead,

Negative Properties

The crest of a Lancashire Coppy should not be formed of small daisy-petal feathers, nor of such as are fringy in texture. The "centre" should not be too near the front of the head, nor should it be in the form of a clear, open area, nor as a line or parting in the middle. The crest should not be deficient in true radiation at the front, nor should the feathers lie flat on the head or project without drooping, or assume any position other than falling away from the centre. It should not be narrow or short in front, nor should there be a vacancy of any kind at the back. It must not be small or wanting in quantity of feather.

The bird itself must not be other than large and massive in its proportions, and should not have a thin neck, prominent or open shoulders, narrow, hollow back, or narrow, ruffled breast; neither should it be short in the body, nor carry its wings crossed at the tips nor its tail like an open fan. The body-feather should not be loose or disorderly, nor deficient in quantity. The bird should not stand in other than an erect attitude. It should not be undecided in colour, nor should a Clear bird exhibit a single ticked feather in crest or body; neither should it have dark or discoloured beak, legs, or feet, nor be shown other than with perfect feather and in clean condition.

A Plainhead should not exhibit any feature opposed to the character of a Coppy, and, specially, should not have a small, round, narrow, or contracted style of head, or show any disposition to be slim or puny in its build or curved in the line of its stand.

CHAPTER XXX

THE OLD DUTCH CANARY AND DUTCH FRILL

ALTHOUGH the Canary of Holland by name, this variety is perhaps as much a native of France and Belgium, but its original stock was the old "Dutch," a bird extensively bred in Holland and the north of Belgium as far back as 1700. They were often inaptly termed Dutch-Belgian, and a good specimen was a large handsome bird, the giant of the Canary family. Type beyond erect carriage did not appear much valued, and length and massiveness were the objects of the breeder. These old Dutch played some part in establishing our present-day Belgian; and our English giant, the Lancashire, as well as the present "Dutch Frill," are also offshoots. A good specimen of the old Dutch was eight or more inches in length, with a large, shapely head, a neck of good length and thickness, broad, massive shoulders, not elevated, broad, full chest, long, stout body with long wings and tail, a massive frame, somewhat coarse in finish owing to the feather, though of a fine, soft, silky texture, being a little open and rough through its extreme length. Such was the original "Dutch" as imported in our early days to this country, and some, it is said, still exist in outlying parts of South Holland and Northern Belgium.

The frilled variety known as the "Dutch Frill" has now become prominent on the Continent, while the old-fashioned bird is almost extinct. The greatest care in selection is required to retain these frills, and we have found by experiments that one out-cross is sufficient to destroy the proper formation of the frills, and in many instances produce a bird perfectly smooth in plumage. Of course, if such birds were paired back to the "Frill," it would in time revive the frill; but it shows the care required to maintain this peculiar form of feather, which is not roughness.

Points of the Dutch Frills.

In shape, Dutch Frills are not unlike the Belgian, with this difference, they carry their head erect like the Lancashire, which takes off the hump-like appearance of the shoulders, though these are broad and massive. The bird is heavily built, of almost erect carriage, immense length, its heavy mantle and lengthy breast frills greatly adding to its massive appearance. The legs are very long and inclined to be stilty, showing much of the

A DUTCH FRILL.

thigh. Wings and tail are of great length, and the tail is inclined to drop or curve a little, giving position and carriage a slightly curved appearance. The head is inclined to be somewhat coarse, narrow, and long, and the feathers in some birds turn up a little in a shell-like form at the back of the head, like a nun pigeon. The beak is rather long and tapering; the neck long and thin for the build of the bird. The feathers over the entire body should be long, fine, and silky in texture, and part down the centre of the back, forming up into curled-like clusters on either side. This is called the "mantle," and the heavier this mantle and the more even the long curls on either side, the greater its perfection. On either side of the breast the feathers are wavy, converging to the centre in the shape of a shell, the larger the clusters the better; these are called the "craw." Those to the right and left forming two large bunches of loose feathers in the region of the thigh-bone, well formed and frilled up, are called "fins." It is on the parts named where the frills form up to their greatest perfection, and it is surprising how even they are in a good specimen.

There are Clear, Yellow, Buff and Variegated birds, as in other varieties. The roughness of the old Dutch Canary was taken advantage of by Continental breeders with a taste for properly formed frills, and it only wanted careful selection of the most suitable birds for fixing and perfecting the desired points.

Views of Dutch Breeders.

Mr. John L. J. Quarles von Ufford, The Hague, when writing in *The Feathered World* of the Dutch Canary and the "Frill" in particular, says:

"Long ago Holland was known all over Europe for the beautiful and splendid variety of Canary there cultivated; that must have been about 1700; and soon after, in the stormy times that followed in our country, most of our birds were sold; some went to England others to Belgium, and even farther south to Roubaix, a town in the north of France. There can be little doubt that the splendid varieties of the Canary now in England must largely owe their origin to the old Dutch Canary. Of them all the Lancashire is now the nearest to it in appearance. When did the Dutch Canary change into yours? Impossible to tell; changes of which there are no record took place, and slowly, by being crossed and re-crossed, the varying types evolved. When we got a nice bird from an ordinary pair we put it apart and tried to get a similar one to match it, and so we improved the breed."

Mr. C. L. W. Noorduyn, Holland, says in the same journal:

"Years ago we had much larger birds in the south of Holland, and doubtless such are still to be found there, and also probably in North Belgium. It is quite within the probabilities that the *Frises* (Frills) have come from these birds in the following manner. When the curly feathers were first noticed on certain birds, an effort was made to improve and increase them by constantly pairing those birds together which were most frilled, so at last appeared the *Frises* which are bred so much in the north of France (Roubaix and surrounding country). From there the breed was taken to Paris, where it was steadily improved, till we have the noble examples which we have had the pleasure of seeing at English exhibitions for the past few years, some of the best of which have been imported."

Baron du Theil, Dordogne, France, says:

"There is some slight difference in the type of some of the Dutch Frills, some being very much smaller and not so stilty on leg, though well frilled, taking more to the Yorkshire type."

Breeding Dutch Frills.

It may be necessary at times to take an out-cross to keep up stamina or some other property, but a rough and not a smooth-feathered bird should be selected. We have produced perfectly smooth-feathered birds from the first out-cross of a good Dutch Frill hen and a Yorkshire cock. Not a youngster from these showed the slightest signs of frill, the back, too, being perfectly smooth. We produced similar results from a good Dutch Frill cock and a Yorkshire hen, some of the young after the moult showing the slightest tendency to a frill on the point of the breast, such as would be produced from a Belgian and Yorkshire cross. The wisdom will thus be seen of using only birds with rough, open plumage, looking as if the feathers had been stroked the wrong way and causing the tips to slightly curl.

In pairing pure-bred Frills, as a rule Yellow cock is paired to Buff hen, or vice versa. Some Continental breeders make a rule of pairing Clear cock to Clear hen and Marked cock to Marked hen ; but much the better plan is to pair a Clear and Marked together—buff and yellow, of course. You can then produce both Clear and Marked birds from the same pair. It is also an advantage occasionally to pair two Buffs together, as by this method you keep the web of the feather thick, and this tends to better curls. The birds, however, must have the tendency to long, curly feathers or mere double-buffing will not produce it. If it did, how is it the frequently double-buffed German Canary is so small and tight in feather ?

The management and feeding is practically the same as for other Canaries, except that many Continental breeders give no green food and add a little millet seed to their seed mixture. We have found them as well without this seed, and they enjoy a little green food without ill effects, and we have never withheld it. The hens not being over-attentive mothers, many Continental breeders use German hens as foster-parents. English breeders will also do well to give their eggs to German, Norwich, or Yorkshires to sit, hatch, and rear, letting the Dutch Frill hens sit on dummy eggs for the period of incubation fourteen days before encouraging them to go on breeding again. At good exhibitions on the Continent these birds have eight classes allotted to them, as follows :—(*a*) Clear Yellow Cock, (*b*) Clear Buff Cock, (*c*) Clear Yellow Hen, (*d*) Clear Buff Hen, (*e*) Yellow Variegated Cock, (*f*) Buff Variegated Cock, (*g*) Yellow Variegated Hen, (*h*) Buff Variegated Hen.

Management.

By kind permission of the Editor of *Canary and Cage Bird Life* we give Baron du Theil's standard for this bird printed in that paper :—

STANDARD FOR JUDGING DUTCH FRILL CANARIES

	Maximum
Size.—As large as possible	10
Attitude.—Elegant, slightly curved (above all without a humpy appearance), firmly set and well elevated on the legs	10
Feathers.—Long, fine, and silky	
1st.—These should be parted down the back, falling symmetrically down the back, called le manteau (the mantle)	8
2nd.—Those on the chest undulating or wavy-like, converging to the centre in the shape of a shell, called the " craw " —le jabot	10
3rd.—Those to the right and left forming two very fine branches of feathers in the region of the thigh-bone, well formed and frilled up. These are called " fins " or " nageoires " or " oriflammes "	12
If these last frills exist on one side only, or if the feathers are flowing down and not, as it were, affording a support for the wings, the bird is not a show bird.	
Tail.—The tail should be long, with a few fine feathers drooping each side of the rump, accompanying the large feathers of the tail ; these are called cock feathers (plumes de coq)	5
Wings.—Only to cross slightly. Some clubs prefer them to meet like those of a Yorkshire Canary	5
Head.—Size in proportion to the body without any crest, but if the back of head is slightly hooded, as in the case of a Jacobin Pigeon, additional points are allowed, but this is not essential	10
Legs.—Long and supple without stiffness	5
Colour.—Usual Canary colours—yellow, buff, or variegated, with bright plumage, not patchy in colour	10
Condition.—Vigorous, showing nerve and action	10
Cleanliness	5
Total	100

CHAPTER XXXI

THE GERMAN OR ROLLER CANARY

To thousands the Canary is chiefly known as a *singing* bird; but there is one variety, the German or Roller Canary, the sweetness and perpetual melody of whose song cannot be equalled by the uncultivated notes of ordinary Canaries, although it is one of the poorest-coloured and most insignificant of the whole Canary family—the Wild Canary excepted.

Its Development.

As we have had to go to the Continent already for three of the most remarkable varieties of the Exhibition Canary, it is not surprising to find that the Song Canary was "made in Germany." It has been developed by generations of careful training and breeding, and so popular has this trained songster become in England that to-day there are several Roller Clubs established. The first of these was formed in London in 1901, and the result is that there are numbers of breeders here now, but Germany still remains by far the largest Roller breeding centre. In fact, it is a valuable commercial asset to that country, as the birds are exported by thousands during the months succeeding the breeding season. The first consignments are usually hens or a very large proportion of them, the cocks being exported later. It was estimated years ago that not fewer than a quarter of a million Canaries were exported from Germany annually, and the number continues to increase.

The main object of the German breeders is either to produce great numbers of the ordinary song birds regardless of the quality of their notes, for sale and export, or else fewer numbers of superior stock for exhibition contest singing.

The Song.

For this purpose the birds are trained to sing whenever called upon by the vendor or the judge, which they will do provided the room is kept at a genial temperature, and the birds are in good form. Rollers in this country are, as a rule, judged separately in a room adjoining the exhibition hall of the other varieties of Canary.

In Germany, team, as well as individual prizes, are given. A raised staging or table is arranged in the room with chairs round it for the judges, and an exhibitor's team is placed on the table, and the doors of the song boxes opened, or the coverings removed from the front of the cages. The birds' vocal performance is keenly scrutinised, a harsh note, a too rapid deliverance of the various tours or an inclination to "Japp," or a halt in the middle of the performance, are all noted down on the judge's sheet against that particular bird or team of birds, if necessity demands. To obtain a first prize a performer must come up to the desired standard, he must have the necessary quality and variety of song, and go through it with the regularity and precision of the swing of a clock's pendulum, neither too long nor too short, with the even rise and fall of a perfect musician, and finish off well. Such a bird is awarded a first prize as the best of that breeder's team. Others if merit warrants, will be awarded prizes of varying grades.

After the team has been thus carefully gone over it is removed to the hall, and another breeder's team is brought into the room to undergo the same test. Possibly not a bird from this team will be selected, or they may be put back for later hearing, to see if there are any improvements. Thus all the teams are gone through, and awards given to the individual performers, according to merit, as well as team prizes for the excellence of a team.

During a conversation with that well-known authority, the late Mr. Albert Rettich, he pointed out to us that there is a difference between the awarding of prizes in Germany and England. Here teams are not entered, and first, second, and third prizes mark the comparative merits of particular birds at individual shows, but the same awards in Germany would indicate respective degrees of proficiency in song. At one of their competitions there may be several first, second, and third prize birds in the same class, owing to their method of analysing the merits of the different tours; but otherwise the judging is the same. It is not noise that a competent judge desires, but depth, purity, sweetness, and variation, with good deliverance. An expert judge can tell the song of a bird by the movements of its bill.

About forty years ago in the best Rollers not only were good tours, deep sonorous rolls, and liquid bubbles, expected, but a wide variety of song and quality, delivered with the greatest sweetness, precision, and modulation of voice. There can be little doubt but that the German breeders' indifference to colour and other properties natural in fancy Canaries has assisted them immensely in the development of their birds' vocal organs, and in their capacity for marvellous endurance in song. These are the points cultivated by careful breeding; but the song is taught, and to retain it each generation must in turn be taught, and hence it is next to impossible to import the finest songsters from Germany except at fabulous prices. They are kept as schoolmasters for the young cocks of each season's breeding.

A few years ago there was great lack of variety in the song of even the best birds imported into England; for, although sweet, it was simply a repetition of three or four rolls, with no variation whatever, possibly owing to the birds being exported before their training was complete. A marked improvement in many of the birds is, however, now noticeable, there being much more variety and quality in the song.

This bird is called by various titles, such

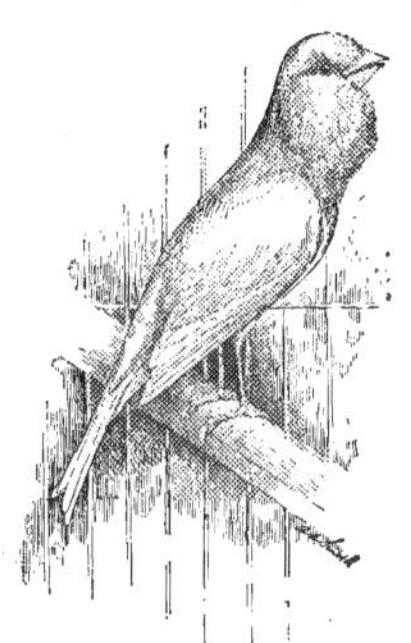

ROLLER CANARY
In the act of executing a long soft roll.

as "St. Andreasberg," "Hartz Mountain," "Trute," or "Seifert" Rollers, etc.; the names being used to indicate the district or strain from which the birds come.

Points in Breeding.

In breeding Rollers we have heard of good results with birds turned loose into a room as if in an aviary; letting there be a cock to, say, every four hens. The Germans, too, use a large wire flight cage with six, eight, or ten nest boxes arranged round it, and six, eight, or ten hens, and three cocks are turned into it; but we have not heard of much success following this arrangement in this country. The majority of British Roller breeders use the ordinary box-breeding cage, and breed the birds in pairs or run one cock with two hens, letting him put one to nest and then the other, as is the custom with other varieties. The breeder, in selecting his pairs or groups for breeding high-class songsters, devotes his attention to selecting birds with good voice, perfect song, and robust health. While breeding they are fed pretty much as other Canaries, with egg food, green food, seed, etc., except that they have a more abundant supply of German rape seed, which is one of the staple foods of this variety at all times. The young birds too, when they leave the parents, are fed in much the same way as other young Canaries, with egg food and seed, gradually weaning them on to the German rape as a staple food at the age of about six weeks; egg food and other seeds can be given in small quantities as tit-bits.

By way of variation in diet a few split groats may be given or a pinch of maw seed; but at all times, except during the breeding season, let good mellow German rape, with a little Canary seed, form the staple diet, the other being given at intervals in small quantities.

Training the Songsters.

We now come to the most important period of the Roller's life when, removed from its parents, it has to take its singing lessons, and its future as a great vocalist or the reverse is decided. Few people, except those who have some knowledge of their breeding and teaching, have any idea of the amount of education a trained Roller Canary has gone through before its song is perfected. We are now speaking of a properly trained bird, not a young bird which has been under the tuition of a "schoolmaster" for a few weeks, and then drafted off under the name "Roller." As soon as the young birds are able to leave the parents and do for themselves, they are transferred to another room and turned into flights in groups. The breeder at the same time places one or two of his most proficient adult songsters in the room. These schoolmasters may have been allowed to put one or two hens to nest, but beyond this they have not been permitted to exert their strength at all, so that they are in splendid condition and full song with clear and distinct notes, yet soft and sweet. These birds repeat their various tours. Hollow-roll, Hollow-flute, Arched-roll, Bass-roll, Water-roll, Scoller-roll, Bell-roll, Schoekel, etc., etc., day after day, week after week, and thus the young birds are kept isolated under this tuition until they have completed their moult, and are themselves in full song. The breeder, however, does not trust solely to these "schoolmasters," though they are his "right-hand men" and exercise marked influence over the youngsters' song, but also devotes his leisure to playing to them with various bird flutes, and also utilises mechanical organs which play a certain number of tours.

When the moult is complete the young cocks are each given a separate cage, and are placed in a darkened position, which keeps them quiet, and thus they sing in a steady, subdued and well-regulated voice. Of course any birds that utter faulty notes are removed as soon as detected, so that they shall not contaminate the others. The partial darkening of the cages is done to prevent the birds exhausting themselves under the excitement of their song, and full light is admitted two or three times a day. By November or December the young scholars will, if in full song, have completed their training.

The aim of the breeder is to turn out birds that will sing softly from fifteen to twenty or twenty-five good tours without an offensive note, and the percentage of such specimens is not large even in Germany. However, English breeders are making good headway.

A bird when ready for contest singing is in good condition and full song, but must not be in too high or breeding condition, or he is apt to race too quickly over his song and so spoil his chance of success. The cages in which Rollers are sent to singing contests are all wood, with a wire front and two wooden shutters in front of this which can be opened or closed at will. These are called "Song-Boxes" (see p. 338), and are about nine inches square. Some are made separately with a wire cage to fit inside. Our earlier chapters hold good as regards the management of the Roller, which, as the sweetest songster of them all, may fitly ring down the curtain on the Canary section of this work.

HYBRIDS

CHAPTER XXXII

BRITISH FINCH AND CANARY HYBRIDS

Hybrid Classification.

THE highest standard of perfection in all Hybrids in which the Canary is one of the parents is a *Clear*; that is, a bird as free from dark colour in its plumage as a Clear Canary. Very few such Hybrids, however, occur, and a Clear Yellow is indeed a *rara avis,* though such have been produced and reared in at least three crosses—the Goldfinch and Canary, Linnet and Canary, and Siskin and Canary. In Clear Buffs at least three crosses have also been reared—Goldfinch and Canary, Linnet and Canary, and Greenfinch and Canary. There may have been others, but these are authentic, and there are more clear buffs produced than yellow.

GOLDFINCH-CANARY.

The next highest standard of the Canary Cross is the "Evenly Marked." These as yet have only been produced in the Goldfinch and Canary Cross, except in one instance on record, where a Linnet and Canary Hybrid became with age a legitimate Even-Marked bird. This bird was originally marked on eyes and wings, with slight grizzle marks on the head and neck; these latter in time moulted out clear, and the bird retaining the eye and wing marks qualified as an "Even-Marked." A few of this cross have been also produced with eye marks only, and others with wing marks alone.

Next in order of exhibition merit is the "Dark" or "Self" Hybrid. While endeavouring to produce these three standard specimens we get the intermediate stages, amongst them such as "Ticked," "Lightly Marked," and "Heavily Variegated." A clearly defined, distinctive character of feather runs through the whole, separating the two divisions of Yellow and Buff in the most unmistakable manner. Plumage of a nondescript character occasionally appears, and is dealt with just as is a similar undecided shade among Canaries, according to its approach to one or other of the recognised fixed forms.

Hybrids of which the Canary is one of the parents are commonly called "Mules" to distinguish them from Hybirds bred from two

British birds. But as the term "Hybrid" is obviously applicable to all, we prefer to adopt the one heading defining the crosses by their parents, remembering that with Hybrids the sire is always mentioned first.

We lead off with the Goldfinch and Canary Hybrid because we believe it to be *one* of the if not *the* actual first true Hybrid bred from parents belonging to two distinct species, and also because it is the most popular and beautiful of crosses. In shape a good Goldfinch and Canary Hybrid should resemble the Norwich type Canary as much as possible, with the exception of the head only, which ought to be long and "snaky," like that of the Finch. There is a great difference in shape even in the heads of Goldfinches, and the practised eye soon learns to single out the long beak and peculiar form of head which give the character to the bird so much prized by fanciers, and it is this formation which should be shared by the Hybrid. We will not stay to describe the exact difference between the head of the Canary and that of the Goldfinch, but a glance at the coloured illustrations will show that the former is furnished with a short, strong beak, while the beak of the latter has a larger base and much greater length—more length, indeed, than many would suppose until made aware of the fact by critical examination. The Goldfinch's beak also is very tapering, ending in a very fine, needle-like point. We have never yet seen a genuine Hybrid of this cross which did not markedly possess the head and beak of the Goldfinch persuasion. The body shape and style of the bird will largely depend upon that of the hen from which it has been bred.

Goldfinch-Canary.

The points of a Clear Goldfinch-Canary, apart from the indispensable spotless plumage, are the richness of the bloom on the wings, and the intensity and area of the Goldfinch blaze or flush on the face, great weight being attached to the continuity of the latter feature, and its freedom from such defects as are indicated in our notes on the general characteristics of a good face. These, with *good* size, and perfectly clear body colour of a rich shade throughout, be it yellow or buff, without the slightest suspicion of a dark tick anywhere, form the perfect Goldfinch and Canary Hybrid. A Clear Yellow, such as shown on our Coloured Plate and on p. 77, will always take precedence over a Buff of equal merit.

We now come to the Ticked Goldfinch-Canary, a bird with but one small patch of dark, grey, or grizzle coloured feathers on an otherwise clear body. Such a Hybrid, owing to its being only this one step from *perfection*, usually competes in the class with Clear Hybrids, in which case, if otherwise equal in merit, the "tick" would turn the scale in favour of the Clear. The Ticked bird is often a shade richer in body colour. Not infrequently a Hybrid with two eye marks, the rest of the body clear, or two wing marks, if only two or three feathers in each wing are dark and the rest of the body clear, also competes with the Clear and Ticked birds. They are termed two-pointed, and technically are just as much an Even-marked as a bird marked both eyes and wings (see p. 341), but owing to a two-marked bird being vastly inferior—as an evenly marked bird—to a four or six-pointed one—that is, marked eyes and wings, or eyes, wings, and a dark feather or two on either side of tail, they are allowed by licence to compete with the Unevenly-marked birds, if not classified with the Clear or Ticked.

Next, though second in order of merit, are the Evenly-marked birds, of which the different points of excellence in marking have been minutely detailed in Chapters XVII. and XIX., for there are two, four and six-pointed birds amongst Hybrids, just as in Canaries. We may, however, observe that good eye-marks (that is, clearly defined and neatly pencilled marks encompassing the whole of the eye without a break) are not common among the Jonques (Yellow).

Among the Buffs, however, this feature is frequently of most singular beauty, being not only accurate in outline, but astonishing in colour, sometimes being found literally as black as jet. Negative properties, such as dark flue in the region of the vent or smoky tail-coverts, tell, every feather of them, against high-class Hybrids in close competition.

Apart from this severe standard as applied to marking, the leading points in an Evenly-marked Goldfinch and Canary Hybrid are purity and richness of the body-feather. Jonque plumage must be glittering and transparent, without a trace of the opacity induced by the presence of meal. Want of character here tells with fatal effect, and is a failing more frequently seen among Jonques than Buffs, where the colour is generally so decided as to leave no room for doubt, a questionable Buff being a rarity. The texture of the feather, too, is a thing by itself. In the finest-feathered Norwich Canary ever fledged there is always perceptible in the body-feather more or less of what we may call grain, but the clear plumage of a Goldfinch Hybrid is, in comparison, as glossy satin is to the finest ribbed silk: it has no grain, but simply a polished surface, a singularly fine texture which, as we explained, is attributable to the hybrid character of the bird, and which, in its highest form, is the tangible expression of the idea of quality. The wings of both Jonques and Mealies (Buffs) are margined by the pure natural yellow of the Goldfinch wing. This "bloom," as it is termed, adds much to the beauty of the otherwise almost colourless flights of the Buff bird, and is a strong point in setting off other good qualities. The ground-colour of a Buff Hybrid is a pure dead white, delicately shaded by creamy tones which, under the effects of colour-feeding, become richer and warmer, particularly on the breast, where the colour scintillates with great beauty. Both forms of the bird should show as much Goldfinch " blaze " as possible, which should be ruddy and full of " fire." In the Jonque it is generally evenly distributed and delicately shaded off towards the margin, but in the Buff is sometimes found less so, and occasionally in small disconnected patches, possibly more discernible than in the Jonque from the nature of the ground-colour, a ticked form of face having its counterpart in some examples of the Goldfinch itself. These disconnected ruddy feathers must not be confounded with the darker specks occasionally present near the margin of the face, which are in reality bona fide dark feathers connected with the cheeks, which, whilst not fatal blemishes to a Marked bird, are altogether inadmissible in a Clear. When endeavouring to obtain good marking, size must not be overlooked.

Thirdly we list the Dark self-coloured Goldfinch-Canary of which a Yellow figures on our coloured plate of Dark Canary Mules. This is the form in which ninety-nine out of every hundred appear, except that many have either one light feather in the tail or wing, or perhaps two at the back of the head, or perhaps a light throat. Such feathers at once classify the bird as variegated. Forty years ago Dark Selfs were of no value except the cocks, for song purposes, for which they still are in great demand. The dark hens are worthless, though a few are used as foster mothers. Variegated hens are of more or less value according to the beauty of their markings, but they seldom find their way into exhibitions unless of extraordinary merit, and even then are of comparatively little value, owing to the absence of brilliancy of colour and the dash and commanding deportment characteristic of the male bird. But with regard to the Dark Selfs, these are now bred for from carefully selected large hens, and a perfect specimen is of more value than an irregularly variegated one, and a good Dark self-coloured bird is a bird of singular beauty. The Jonques are the most taking in appearance, though a high class Buff is a grand bird, especially if carrying a good face. A good Dark Jonque should be of a rich, warm bronzy-yellow, deepening into a dark shade of rich brown-like colour on the top of the head and back, the distribution of this ground-colour being not unlike that of the Cinnamon in its varying tones, but darker. The colour cannot be too glossy or too brilliant, and, under colour-feeding, it can be wonderfully intensified in birds bred from hens capable of assimilating the stimulating diet. But whatever its character, it is imperative that it shall not be broken by the presence of a single clear feather, however small. The underflue is black, and is generally considered as a test of the character of doubtful feathers, in which, if really clear, the flue will probably be clear also. The richest display of warm colour is on the breast, and is continued underneath right through to the waist, where, in the highest-coloured examples, it has a tendency to merge itself into yellow. Still, if this yellow shade be compared with the yellow of a Variegated bird, it will scarcely be found to be the same colour, and does not detract from the value of the bird as a Self, being, in fact, a guarantee of high excellence in other respects. It is probably nothing more than an exhibition of the tendency all Canaries, and the Goldfinch also, have to run lighter in colours in the region of the vent, and bears the same relation to the bird, as a whole, as the corresponding paling of colour does in a Self-coloured Green or Cinnamon Canary, and the distinction between this and bona fide breaking will be easily recognised by those who know the difference between the paling of the waist of a pure Green Canary, and the breaking into a yellow which is *not* green. Having due regard for the prevailing character of vent-feather, some licence is here allowable, and, we think, on substantial grounds. The most dangerous place for a break is at the back of the head, where, not unfrequently, a few unmistakable ticks spoil the winning chances of a gem if honestly shown. Some Dark Hybrids will show more of the decided character of the Goldfinch wing than others, but the yellow bars and edging should be as full of colour as the bloom on a whin-bush. The greatest beauty of the bird consists in the blaze or flush on the face. This, in the Finch, is of a carmine tint bounded by a cleanly cut line, and covers just so much area that its limits can be seen on a front view. In the Hybrid, however, its character is entirely altered, the blaze spreading over a larger surface, sometimes far down the throat and over a considerable portion of the breast, where the colour, a fiery red, loses itself among the rich tones with all the delicacy of a carefully-shaded vignette. This effect is much increased by colour-feeding. The colour of the face, and of the bird generally, becomes more brilliant in the spring, as is the case with some of our wild Finches when assuming their nuptial plumage.

These are the leading points of a Dark Jonque, and are, as might be presupposed, mainly colour-features. To them we may add commanding size; and it is worthy of note that though large size is not common among *Variegated* Jonques, yet among the Selfs it is the rule rather than the exception, arising from the fact that in breeding Selfs there is no restriction in the selection of muling hens, because *any* hen, from a Lancashire giantess downwards, will throw a Dark Hybrid, and size is so far under some control; but any hen will *not* throw a Variegated Hybrid, as we shall presently explain. The most compact form of feather imaginable is also a property, to lack which is to put any otherwise good Hybrid almost entirely out of court; it is, however, generally ensured by the admixture of the naturally close plumage of the Finch. The same features may be accepted as indicative of the general character of the Dark Buff or Mealy bird, the distinction between the two consisting in the colour, which in the Buff is less brilliant, and if we say *greyer* we shall perhaps include the whole in one word. The face is also more Goldfinch-like in type, the blaze not extending so far nor changing so much in character, though even in this there are exceptions.

We now come to what are called by many the "Nondescripts," the first departure from the Dark form the "Variegated," in which more or less clear feather is present, the slightest break—as we have already inferred in describing the Dark Self—rendering the bird eligible for the class. Among these Variegated birds are to be found splendid examples of form, colour, and feather—birds in which every valuable property short of technical marking is displayed in excess. Where separate classes are given for them they are judged entirely for their colour, its purity, brilliancy, and extent, and every good quality *except* marking. Natural beauty, as distinct from technical display, is the actual standard, and implies some degree of regularity pleasing to the eye, though amenable to no rule. A combination of Goldfinch and Canary traits, sometimes singular in their beauty, of clear and dark colour and disposition to approach something resembling the recognised forms of standard technical marking. These observations apply principally to the heavier types of variegation, for when it comes to a case in which a Hybrid is almost, but not quite, up to the form demanded by the rules binding on Evenly-marked birds, an average display of colour and general good quality will give it a prominent place in this class, so valuable is approximate excellence in marking when once it passes the line separating it from mere variegation. In this category, also, are placed Unevenly-marked Hybrids, though free from the blemishes in body-feather which determine variegation as distinct from marking. There is nothing inconsistent in their being so placed, since they meet on a common footing, and are judged, not for their peculiar property, but for the general good qualities shared alike by all belonging to the Colour school. There is yet a third shape in which the bona fide Variegated bird appears, which belongs to neither of the above forms, and that is when the entire body, wings, and tail are clear, but the bird is disfigured by, not a simple tick, but by one or more distinct patches or blotches of dark colour on the head or neck. Such are difficult to place; but assuming the body-colour and texture of feather to be unimpeachable, the fact of such a display of colour and approximation to the highest type of all, viz. the Clear form, classifies them usually with the Clear, Evenly-marked, and Ticked birds. Such birds might well have a class to themselves, styled "Lightly-marked" which might also include two-pointed birds, which are at a disadvantage when competing against Clear, Ticked, and Evenly-marked specimens. Such a class would also remove them from competing against the heavily variegated and Unevenly-marked, to the disadvantage of these two forms.

Linnet-Canary

In shape and carriage this Hybrid follows largely after its sire, the Common Brown Linnet, and if bred from a large Canary of Norwich type shows fine bold attitude and lively movement, and the cocks are free songsters. Like the Goldfinch-Canary, they are very hardy and long lived under proper care and feeding. In colour they are much more sombre than the Goldfinch-Canary, and, like it, range from the self-coloured Dark through the phrases of technical variegation up to the Clear, which, to breed, means lasting fame, especially if a Yellow, the Clear Buff ranking next. The same rules apply, as regard colour and marking, as for the Goldfinch Hybrid, except that blaze is non-existent. Specimens are improved in colour by colour feeding, and a "fed" Dark Self, if bred from a large good coloured hen, is very beautiful, developing in the Yellow form a rich ruddy umber, its glistening breast showing up the Linnet pencillings in beautiful relief. The usual Pied form is of the irregularly variegated type, the blotches being patches of Linnet-coloured feather. Anything like technical marking is exceedingly rare, especially found in the shape of decided eye-marks. Indeed, we do not remember having met with more than about two or three "four-marked" Linnet Hybrids. Several two-pointed birds have to our knowledge been bred—that is, marked both eyes or both wings; but there appears much more difficulty in transmitting good marking to the Linnet Hybrid than to its Goldfinch confrère.

We may add that most of the Variegated Linnet Mules are Buffs; a few Yellows have appeared, but the colour is not sufficiently striking to render it valuable except on account of its rarity. Improvements will probably be made in the colour of the Clear and Marked Hybrids of this cross. The feather of both Yellow and Buff is very soft and silky, and, like that of most Finch Hybrids, very compact. Good examples of a Ticked Buff and a Yellow Dark Linnet-Canary are shown on our Coloured Plates, of a two-pointed on this page, and a Dark on p. 351.

Greenfinch-Canary.

This Hybrid has now become very popular. The type of bird recognised is of chubby build, like its sire, but a little longer, and is such as we should expect to produce from a Greenfinch cock and Norwich type hen. The cocks are free songsters, though their notes are rather harsher than those of the Goldfinch or Linnet Hybrids. Size, combined with good colour and shape, are required; and close-fitting feather, with a nice silky-like sheen over its surface, adds greatly to the merit of an exhibition specimen. Highest in this cross ranks a Clear Yellow, of which we are not aware that one has as yet been produced, although at least three Clear Buffs, and possibly more, have been reared, as well as several Lightly-marked, some of which have been especially good Yellows. It is quite possible that a Clear Yellow may soon be produced, for remarkable progress has recently been made in breeding Lightly-marked and Clear birds of this cross. The colour of the Dark Self is a brilliant edition of the Finch, in which its dusky green plumage is wonderfully brightened and made very transparent, especially in the natural development of the yellow on the wings, which maintains a character so distinctive, even in the Clear birds of the cross, as to indicate the parentage at a glance, though there are always other characteristics, such as formation of beak, head, tail, etc. The yellow on the wings, and colour generally, is intensified by colour feeding.

Of late years important shows have given a separate class for Dark Greenfinch-Canaries (see illustration on p. 351), leaving Lightly-marked and Clear specimens to compete with other crosses.

The Siskin being much smaller than the Finches already dealt with, the hybrid resulting

LINNET-CANARY.

from its cross with the Canary, whilst losing in size, is still a perky, bright little bird, whose

The Siskin-Canary.

confiding ways are very attractive. In appearance it generally resembles an enlarged and brilliantly feathered example of its sire. We have seen a few pied to the extent of light feathers in the wings and tail, and in rare instances, the pied form of plumage has extended in an irregular way to the body, and about twenty years ago we bred one half clear, a Yellow.

During the last few years marked strides have been made in the production of almost Clear birds of this cross. There is no reason why a more regular form of marking, and also Clear birds, should not occur with this and the last-mentioned Hybrid if sufficient numbers were bred to increase the possible chances. The highest standard of perfection in this Hybrid, as in those already described, is a Clear Yellow, and this has been attained in a specimen owned by Dr. Galloway, illustrated on p. 35—would that we could have a few more to compete with it. Next in order comes a good Dark Self, either Yellow or Buff, which, from the exhibition stand-point, is preferred to a Heavily Variegated bird, which latter in some exhibitions, competes in a separate class for "Heavily Variegated" Hybrids of other crosses as well.

The Canary-Bullfinch.

In this cross we have the order of pairing reversed, the sire being the Canary, as up to the present all authentic specimens have without exception been produced from the cock Canary and hen Bullfinch. To our knowledge occasional specimens of this Hybrid have appeared during the past twenty-six years at exhibitions; though always looked upon with some suspicion, and by the majority of fanciers believed to be Greenfinch-Bullfinch Hybrids exhibited as Canary-Bullfinch. This mistaken identity by those who were not careful observers was excusable to an extent, owing to a certain amount of similarity in the Canary-Bullfinch and Greenfinch-Bullfinch Hybrids. There is, however, a distinct difference in the colour of the backs of these two hybrids; both are of a slatey grey (following the Bullfinch), with the faintest suspicion of cinnamon tint in it. But in every instance the slatey grey back of the Canary-Bullfinch is striped with dark stripes, lighter, but similar to those on the back of a Green Canary. The back of the Greenfinch-Bullfinch on the other hand has the plain slatey grey perfectly free from dark stripes. We have, we think, seen every specimen of this cross exhibited during the last twenty-six years, and without exception have found the difference described present in the two hybrids.

The Canary-Bullfinch's beak, as a rule, is not so large or stout as that of the Greenfinch-Bullfinch, and there is also a difference in the shape of the two birds, marked in some more than others. Again, the tail of the Canary-Bullfinch is longer than that of the Greenfinch-Bullfinch. Doubts as to the genuineness of the Canary-Bullfinch Hybrid reached a climax when a protest was lodged against a specimen at a show held by the National British Bird and Mule Club at the Crystal Palace in October, 1898. This action followed upon a lengthy correspondence in *The Feathered World*, for and against this bird, which had won at another show at the Crystal Palace a few months earlier, but the National British Bird and Mule Club upheld the Judge's decision that the exhibit was genuine. The controversy brought the Canary-Bullfinch into such prominence as to stimulate breeders' efforts to produce the cross, with the result that as many as eleven genuine specimens have of late years competed in one class. Some of these have been pied in tail, with patches of light canary colour on their body, evident proof of their being genuine, and of the achievement of the ambition of hybrid breeders.

A Yellow Dark cock is a noble bird, generally larger than the ordinary Bullfinch, and stout in build, except where the Canary sire has been of the Yorkshire type. These hybrids are of genial disposition without bluster or flurry, and so look well in the show cage. The back of a Yellow Dark Canary-Bullfinch is a dark slatey grey, slightly striped, the grey running up into the nape of the neck. The top of the head deepens into a blackish cap, but not so dark as that of the Bullfinch. The wings and tail are black or blackish grey, with a lighter bar across the wings, similar to the Bullfinch. With colour feeding this lighter colour not infrequently becomes slightly tinted with rufous-orange, and the light band round the forehead, cheeks, throat, breast, and under body, being a rich rufous-orange, is intensified to almost vermilion on the breast, and not infrequently a dark streak or two appears on the flanks intermingled with a rufous shade, the vent running off to a whitish grey—a striking blending, which appeals to the most fastidious taste, and is well depicted on our Coloured Plate. The shade of a Buff Dark Canary-Bullfinch is naturally paler, the breast colour verging into a vinous chocolate, not unlike that of the hen Bullfinch, though of a richer and lighter shade.

Up to the present most of these Hybrids have been Dark specimens; those that have been "marked" have only had a few light feathers in the tail or wing or a small patch of light on the flank. One we have seen had a light patch at the back of the head. Whether Lightly-marked and Clear birds of this cross will be produced is problematical, but the accomplishment of such a feat will indeed be noteworthy.

The Redpoll-Canary.

This is about the smallest of our Hybrids, and owing to this and the sombre colour and lack of song of the specimens yet produced, it is less popular and attractive than other of the Finch crosses. We do not remember seeing a Pied or Marked bird of this cross, all have been Dark specimens, and of these only two were Jonque, the rest buff. One of these Jonques was owned by ourselves, and it won prizes at various exhibitions, including third in a mixed class at the Crystal Palace in 1897, competing against Clears of other crosses. This scarcity of Jonques is no doubt owing to so few specimens having been bred of this Hybrid, which is illustrated on p. 351.

The Redpoll itself in its way is quite the "Dandy of the Town," so perky, active, and happy is it, and the Hybrid from it and the Canary takes largely after its sire in size, shape, manner, colour, and marking, except that the Jonques display a rich ruddy umber on the breast, and the pencilling is darker and deeper than that of the Buff. If the Redpoll-Canary Hybrid had more attention paid it in regard to breeding, and was produced in greater numbers, we should undoubtedly have more handsome specimens produced and possibly a "clear" yellow or buff which would be the highest stage of excellence.

The Twite-Canary.

This Hybrid compares in popularity with the Redpoll-Canary. It is larger, being about the size of and not unlike a small Linnet-Canary in shape; but the Dark specimens are a darker brown, much more heavily pencilled, and with the throat and breast a more reddish brown. They are usually longer in tail, with a more slender bill, and a small and neat head. A buff Twite-Canary figures on our Coloured Plate of Dark Mules. Twite-Canaries are of sombre colour, and having little or no song, and not being very attractive on the Show bench, there is not much encouragement to the fancier to produce them. Both the Redpoll-Canary and the Twite-Canary would, however, become more popular if a class for dark specimens of these two crosses could be given at exhibitions. Clear specimens could, of course, compete with Clears of other crosses. An almost clear specimen was shown by Dr. Galloway in 1909, so that the feat of producing a Clear Twite and Canary Hybrid does not seem impracticable.

THE CAPE CANARY (*Serimis Canicollis*) and THE DOMESTICATED OF ENGLISH CANARY HYBRID.

Although this Hybrid scarcely comes within the scope of this chapter, we may be pardoned for introducing such an interesting Cross. The few specimens we have seen have all been Dark, about the size of a small Greenfinch, and of similar shape, except that the bill is not quite so strong or long. Birds of this cross might indeed be easily mistaken for a Dark Greenfinch-Canary Hybrid if not looked carefully into, then you find the Green body colour has a yellow reflect on its surface, and is of a darker and more even shade throughout than we have ever seen on the richest coloured Greenfinch Hybrid, and this attractive feathering fits the body closely. Birds of this cross are of lively disposition, and the cocks are fine songsters. About 1909 Mr. George Davidson, Stanwix, Carlisle, bred one of these Hybrids answering to our description, and we see no reason why light-coloured specimens should not also be bred, and the Hybrid become popular.

Classification.

We have referred to classification of these various Canary Hybrids, and suggested fresh classes for some, such as the Redpoll and Twite Hybrids, but the matter really rests with breeders and exhibitors themselves, by breeding a good supply of the various hybrids to fill the classes when given. There is no difficulty in obtaining a separate class for Dark Goldfinch-Canary, Linnet-Canary, or Greenfinch-Canary Hybrids, and some exhibitions even give one for Dark Siskin-Canary Hybrids. Why? Because all these Hybrids are bred in good numbers, and the classes usually fill well. The same holds good throughout the Hybrid section; only popularise them, and there will be no difficulty in getting classes for them. The following classification we think covers present needs at our largest shows for Canary crosses, and could be extended as occasion arose by giving separate classes for Yellow and Buff, and for other crosses as they became numerous enough to deserve special classes:—

(*a*) Clear, Ticked, and Evenly-marked Canary Hybrid; (*b*) Lightly Variegated, more light than dark, including two pointed Canary Hybrids; (*c*) Heavily Variegated, more dark than light, Goldfinch-Canary Hybrid; (*d*) Heavily Variegated, more dark than light, any other variety Canary Hybrid (Canary-Bullfinch excepted); (*e*) Yellow Dark Goldfinch-Canary Hybrid; (*f*) Buff Dark Goldfinch-Canary Hybrid; (*g*) Dark Linnet-Canary Hybrid; (*h*) Dark Greenfinch-Canary Hybrid; (*i*) Dark Siskin, Redpoll, or Twite-Canary Hybrid; (*j*) any other variety of Canary Hybrid.

As to what constitutes a Clear, the word speaks for itself, and of Ticked,

Evenly-marked, Variegated, and Self-Colours, we have dealt at length in the early chapters on the Canary, and a reference to these will fully explain the definitions to the Hybrid breeder.

Points for Judging.

In attempting to frame a scale of points for judging Hybrids we are doing something which to the best of our knowledge has not seriously been attempted before, at all events we have not met with such a scale. Our intentions are to give in the usual tabulated form some idea of the relative worth of the parts which go to make up an interesting whole, attaching to each a value which will leave sufficient margin for a subtractive process, and not rendering complications more complicated in an attempt to draw too nice distinctions. It will be seen that in our scale of points we have given not only what we think to be the leading features of the various Hybrids, but in the negative properties described, the most common forms in which inferior breeding asserts itself. Size we have relegated to its proper place, as, though a most important feature in an Exhibition Hybrid, it is useless without colour and other characteristics. In the case of a Clear Yellow and Buff of equal merit it is usual for the Yellow to take precedence, owing to the great difficulty experienced in producing this colour of equal merit to buff.

CLEAR, TICKED, AND LIGHTLY-MARKED GOLDFINCH AND CANARY HYBRIDS

Points of Merit

	Maximum
Colour.—Flush on face large and rich	10
Body Colour.—For depth and brilliancy	10
Wings.—For good display of Goldfinch Yellow	5
Feather.—For smooth compactness and fine silky texture	15
Marking.—If any, for neatness	5
Shape.—Head bold and neat	5
Body, chubby build, good broad chest, neck harmonising with head and body; body tapering nicely to a fine waist	10
Wings and tail harmonising with body closely folded and smartly carried	5
Size.—Good size with general robust appearance	10
Position.—Semi-erect, standing at an angle of about 45 degrees with a bold defiant air	10
Condition.—Health, cleanliness, sound feather, and steadiness	15
Total	100

CLEAR, TICKED, AND LIGHTLY-MARKED CANARY HYBRIDS OTHER THAN GOLDFINCH

Points of Merit

	Maximum
Colour.—For depth and brilliancy	20
Feather.—Smooth compactness and fine silky quality	20
Marking.—If any, for neatness	5
Shape.—For chubbiness of build in harmony with parentage	15
Wings and Tail closely folded and smartly carried	5
Size.—Good size in accord with the variety	15
Condition.—Health, cleanliness, sound feather, and steadiness	20
Total	100

Negative Properties

A Hybrid should not be small or puny-looking, but have good size in accordance with its parentage. It should not cross its wings or spread its tail like a fan. It should not be unsteady in its cage or in any way deformed; neither should a Goldfinch-Canary Hybrid be lacking in flush on face nor should the plumage of any Hybrid be rough and untidy.

EVENLY-MARKED CANARY HYBRIDS

Points of Merit

	Maximum
Marking.—Eyes for neatness and regularity of outline, anterior mark, 10, posterior, 10, entire	20
Wings.—For exactness, decreasing in value as the marking extends beyond the secondary flights or encroaches on the wing coverts	15
Tail.—If not accompanied by discolored tail coverts, for exactness	5
Colour.—For richness and brilliancy of body colour and denseness of marking	15
Feather.—For smooth compactness and fine silky quality	10
Shape.—For chubbiness of build in harmony with parentage	10
Wings and Tail closely folded and smartly carried	5
Size.—Good size in accordance with the variety	10
Condition.—Health, cleanliness, sound feather, and steadiness	10
Total	100

Negative Properties

An Evenly-marked Hybrid should not have broken or ragged eye-marks, nor badly balanced, irregular patches on the side of the head, nor marks running towards the top or front of the head over the beak; nor should it have a cap, however symmetrical. It should not show any light flight feathers mixed with the dark nor any marking on the greater or lesser wing coverts, nor on the still smaller wing coverts fringing the upper margin of the wing; nor should the feathers of the bastard wing be dark. It should not show any dark feathers on the margin of the saddle where the feathers merge with those of the wing-coverts, nor any discoloration in the upper or lower tail-coverts, nor should there be any mark whatever to interfere with a clear run above and below from the beak to the tail; nor should it cross its wings at the tips or the plumage be rough and untidy, nor should it be unsteady in its cage or deformed in any way—a Goldfinch-Canary Hybrid should not be lacking flush on face.

Heavily Variegated Canary Hybrids

Points of Merit

	Maximum
Colour.—For richness and brilliancy . .	25
Feather.—For smooth compactness and fine silky quality	25
Shape.—For chubbiness of build in harmony with parentage	15
Size.—For good size in accordance with variety	15
Condition.—Health, cleanliness, sound feather, and steadiness	20
Total	100

Negative Properties

A Heavily Variegated Hybrid should not be small or puny in appearance, according to its parentage, nor should it be dull in colour, neither should it carry its wings badly, nor should its plumage be coarse, rough, and untidy, nor should it be unsteady in its cage or deformed in any way—a Goldfinch-Canary Hybrid should not lack flush on face.

Dark Goldfinch-Canary Hybrids

Points of Merit

	Maximum
Colour.—For largeness and richness of flush on face	10
Body Colour.—For depth and brilliancy. .	10
Marking.—For good display of wing bars and other Goldfinch characteristics . .	10
Feather.—For smooth compactness and fine silky quality.	15
Shape.—Head bold and neat . . .	5
Body, chubby, with good broad chest, neck harmonising with head and body. Body tapering nicely to a fine waist . . .	10
Wings and Tail closely folded and smartly carried	5
Size.—Good size, with generally robust appearance	10
Position.—Semi-erect, standing at an angle of about 45 degrees with a bold defiant command	10
Condition.—Health, cleanliness, sound feather, and steadiness	15
Total	100

Dark Canary Hybrids other than Goldfinch

Points of Merit

	Maximum
Colour.—For richness and brilliancy with good blending of parentage	25
Feather.—For smooth compactness and fine silky quality.	25
Shape.—For chubbiness of build in harmony with parentage	15
Size.—For good size in accordance with variety	15
Condition.—Health, cleanliness, sound feather, and steadiness	20
Total	100

Negative Properties

A Dark Hybrid should not be small or puny in appearance, according to its parentage, nor should it be dull in colour according to its kind, nor should it carry its wings untidily, nor should its plumage be coarse, rough and untidy in appearance. It should not be unsteady in its cage or deformed in any way. A Goldfinch-Canary Hybrid should not be lacking flush on face.

CHAPTER XXXIII

BREEDING FINCH-CANARY HYBRIDS

Hybrids, that is, true hybrids bred from parents belonging to two different species, are one of those perversions—we use the word for want of a better—of Nature's arrangements which remind us, after taking one step, how futile are our efforts in the direction of new creations; and well it is, no doubt, that they cannot reproduce themselves. Touching this latter point, there is some contradictory evidence to be obtained, but in the face of the most trustworthy of it (and the most trustworthy generally has a broken link in the chain) there exists the fact that nowhere do we see living proof of the reproductive power of any true hybrid of those enumerated in Chapter XXXII.; and in the absence of this evidence we dismiss this portion of our subject in as summary a way as possible, simply adding our own testimony, the result of extensive experiments and observation, to the mass of proof demonstrating its general if not absolute impracticability —most certainly in the case of the birds we are describing; for although they will manifest the most ardent natural desire, the cocks pairing up readily and going through the routine of successful breeding even to copulation with any hen put to them, and the hen Hybrids will build, lay, and sit with commendable perseverance on their tiny eggs, sometimes not much larger than peas, here the matter always ends in unfertility. The great charm of Hybrid-breeding is its uncertainty, and, apart from the natural difficulties to be overcome, there is always the excitement attendant upon the chance of producing a Clear Hybrid, be it Yellow or Buff, and so drawing a rich harvest of prizes, besides being the sensation of the next show season.

The Start. Before commencing Hybrid-breeding a man should be sure he has the right sort of stuff to work with. And first, his own pedigree must be as certain as that of his hens. If he cannot go back in a direct line to the patriarch whose patience has passed into a proverb, or satisfy himself that that virtue has been a fixed trait in the strain from which he *is* descended, he had better not vex his soul with Hybrid-breeding. The next indispensable—and it is *the* indispensable of indispensables—is to procure the right class of hens, that is, hens which will throw Pied or Clear Hybrids. If it be wished to breed only Dark birds, *any* description of hen will answer; but the larger, more stylish, and richer in colour the hen, the more likely is it that corresponding good points will be found in the Hybrids; and note also that yellow hens are to be preferred before buff, whether breeding for Clear, Marked, or Dark Hybrids. If breeding for Dark, and your object is to produce exhibition specimens, it is much better to use Yellow Green hens or Heavily Variegated Yellow hens, large and stoutly built, of the Norwich persuasion, for though many Clear hens breed Dark hybrids, there is always a tendency to throw a light feather in the tail or wings, or a patch of light the size of a pea on the back of the head or to have clear throats, which at once designates the bird as Variegated, as already explained in the previous chapter. About the best class of hen we have used in the production of Dark Hybrids is a large Yellow Green Norwich

DARK HYBRIDS.

1.—GREENFINCH-CANARY. 2.—LINNET-CANARY. 3.—REDPOLL-CANARY.

type, bred from Cinnamons, a first or second cross from the Cinnamon. We have always had excellent colour from such hens, and, in the case of Goldfinch Hybrids, secured a fine rich Goldfinch flush on the face, an important feature in a good Goldie Hybrid. We do not advise the use of Buff, Green or Marked hens, for the simple reason that we then get a very large percentage of Buff Hybrids, and by using only Yellow hens there is a possibility of producing more Yellow hybrids, and the Buff Dark hybrids bred from Yellow hens are, as a rule, a much richer colour than those bred from Buff hens.

Muling Hens.

We have read recipes for compounding hens for muling purposes, elaborated with extreme care, in which each ingredient is weighed out as carefully as if for making pills ; but we regard them as utter nonsense. How muling hens, as they are called, that is, a hen Canary which has proved herself to be a producer of light Hybrids, originated we cannot undertake to explain. Starting with the knowledge that ninety-nine out of a hundred hens will throw only Dark self-coloured Hybrids, it is likely that the singular phenomenon of one throwing Variegated birds may have attracted attention, and, by careful breeding in the same family, a strain may have been established, having a tendency to throw Variegated rather than Dark birds. But excessive inbreeding is not borne out in Dr. Galloway's experience, given later, as being beneficial in Light Hybrid breeding. Neither is it justified by our own experience, and the few Clear Hybrids that have been bred prove conclusively that inbreeding is not the solution, or else to-day Clear Hybrids would have been almost as plentiful as Clear Canaries. Some few Canaries, it is true, exist which *do* produce Light Hybrids, but we have never met a breeder who ventured to say that he had built up his strain by simply inbreeding. *The tendency must be there to begin with, and their judicious* inbreeding may assist to fix and perpetuate that tendency.

Breeding Light Hybrids.

During a conversation with Mr. John Dixon, of Wigton, a well-known Hybrid-breeder, we learnt that he is convinced by experience that the British bird plays quite as important a part in the production of Light Hybrids as the Canary, and that it is when a British bird, with a tendency to throw light offspring, is paired to a Canary with like tendency, that the Clear Hybrid is produced. We have the greatest respect for Mr. Dixon's opinion, but feel that if this is the real solution we should expect, when two such birds were paired together, far more Clear hybrids would be produced than at present; still, we agree that some British birds assist more than others in the production of Light Hybrids, and we have produced half-Clear Hybrids from Yellow Heavily Variegated Cinnamon hens. Some twenty years ago we bred a Siskin-Canary Hybrid half Clear from a Yellow Cinnamon Ticked hen, but we obtained the best results in Light Hybrid breeding from Clear Yellow Lancashire hens and Clear Yellow Pink-eyed Norwich type hens, not necessarily inbred with blood relations, but Clear bred for many generations. It is quite possible to do this with little or no inbreeding, selecting out-crosses each year from your own stock, so that you know how they are bred. Start with Clear Pink-eyed birds, or even Variegated Cinnamons of Norwich type, pairing them to Clear Norwich, and continue to pair up Clear with Clear generation after generation, without inbreeding, until the blood is so free from dark pigment that no dark feather is reproduced. By avoiding inbreeding you retain good size and robust health in the stock, and, although it takes time, so favourable have the results been from hens thus bred for a few years, especially if the tendency to throw light feathers in Hybrids was present at the commencement, that we are convinced its general adoption would produce a much larger percentage of Light Hybrids.

We do not recommend Yorkshire hens for Hybrid breeding, as the offspring run too slim in body and too upright in

BRAMBLEFINCH
GREENFINCH
CHAFFINCH
GOLDFINCH

position. If the Lancashire be used, select a short, stout-bodied bird, tight in feather; but clear bred hens of this class are difficult to procure, and it is best to breed your own muling hens on the lines indicated, occasional inbreeding being permissible to fix work accomplished, but its use must *never be abused.*

As Even-marked Canaries have grown fewer, so have Even-marked Hybrids. For many years a separate class was given at the Crystal Palace Show for Even-marked Goldfinch-Canary Hybrids, and over twenty such hybrids have competed in that class at a time; but, interest declining, the numbers dwindled, until in 1903 the class was struck out, and they now compete with the "Clear or Lightly Marked." This points very definitely to one fact, that as soon as fixity of marking was neglected in the Canary we lost the source from which we bred those marks into our Hybrids, and that ground must be regained ere we can produce Even-marked Hybrids in numbers again. It is a charming branch, the neglect of which is to be deplored, and we refer our readers to Chapter XIX. for the method of establishing "marks" in Canaries, using only Cinnamon blood to perpetuate Even Marks for Even-marked Hybrid breeding.

Even-marked Hybrids.

We have advised the use of Yellow hens in Hybrid breeding, and explained our reason; but we should not hesitate to use a Buff which had proved herself a Light Hybrid producer, or an Even-marked or two- or three-pointed or a Ticked Buff hen with a tendency to produce well-marked Hybrids. We have also advised the use of large Norwich type hens to get good size in the Hybrids; but it is not advisable to pair too large a hen to such small birds as the Siskin and Redpoll, owing to difficulty of copulation and fear of unfertile eggs. Hens not quite large enough for pairing with the larger finches such as the Goldfinch, Linnet, Greenfinch, etc., can be utilised for the smaller birds.

Most of the Hybrids dealt with in the previous chapter can be bred either by pairing the cock British bird to the hen Canary, or vice versa. Several have been bred in the latter way, but, as a rule, captive hen British birds are not such free breeders in a cage as the cocks. And thus the almost universal use of the cock Finch and hen Canary. Greenfinch and Siskin hens, however, pair up quite freely with either a cock Canary or other British Finch, and will rear their own young, and, as we pointed out, the Canary-Bullfinch Hybrid has only as yet been produced from the cock Canary and hen Bullfinch. The latter not being a reliable mother, her eggs are always transferred to a hen Canary to hatch and rear.

Bullfinch Hybrids.

The question is often asked as to which is the more likely Bullfinch hen to breed in cage or aviary—one reared by a Canary, hand reared, or wild caught. Our own experience is that there is no difference, provided that the wild-caught hen is good-tempered; and remember, you are just as liable to get faults of temper in hand and Canary-reared birds. We have had both hand-reared and wild-caught hens pair up with the cock Canary, and succeeded in getting fertile eggs from both; unfortunately, none of them hatched out. Where these Hybrids are successfully hatched the difficulty is to get the hen Canaries to continue feeding them; they will go on all right for a few days, then they appear to lose confidence, and become frightened by the appearance of the large gape which is common to these Hybrids—being double that of a young Canary. The hen will go up to the nest to feed them, and as the young hybrids open their large mouths, will rush away as if terrified at the yawning chasm. This is applicable to all Bullfinch Hybrids and may account for the difficulty that Mrs. C. J. Skey, of Plymouth, experienced with these Hybrids. This lady had to resort to partial hand-feeding in the specimens she successfully reared. On the other hand, Mr. Ernest Stevens, of Sidmouth, Devon, in 1908, reared one of these Hybrids and a young Canary in the same nest together, simply supplying the hen with the ordinary food for rearing young Canaries. The incident occurred in this way. Mr. Stevens procured two wild-caught hen Bullfinches in October, 1907, and partitioned off half of a large flight which he had for young Canaries, 2 feet high, 2 feet wide, and 18 inches deep. In February, 1908, he put one of the hen Bullfinches into this compartment with a young cock Canary, bred by himself during 1907. They appeared to agree all right, and in April he noticed the cock Canary feeding the hen Bullfinch. Mr. Stevens then hung one of the small German wicker cages up in the compartment, removing all the wickers from one end, for them to build in if they would, at the same time supplying them with some hay cut into short lengths, rootlets and a piece of cocoanut matting a few inches long. The cock Canary and hen Bullfinch both set to work and pulled the matting to pieces, and built a nice nest, the hen Bullfinch laying on June 7th, though on the bottom of the cage, not in the nest they had built; she laid two more eggs, both in the nest. Mr. Stevens had a hen Canary which had just laid, and commenced to sit, so he removed all her eggs but one, and gave her the Bullfinch's three eggs, with the one of her own. In due course the young Canary hatched out, and one of the Canary-Bullfinches; one of the other eggs was unfertile, the other fertile, but dead in shell. Both the Hybrid and young Canary were successfully reared by this hen Canary on egg food, canary, hemp, and rape seed, with watercress as green food. The hen Bullfinch had two more nests that season, of four eggs each, laid in the nest. Two of the eggs in each of the clutches were fertile, but did not hatch; the hen Bullfinch would not sit on the two first clutches, but sat closely on dummy eggs in the third nest, her own each time being given to Canaries to sit and hatch for safety.

This young Canary-Bullfinch, which was successfully reared, though bred from an English hen Bullfinch, was one of the largest Hybrids of the cross we have seen, as large, in fact, as some of the Siberian Bullfinches. Success in breeding this Hybrid greatly depends upon getting the cock Canary and hen Bullfinch on good terms with each other, and both in high breeding condition, which is largely achieved by judicious feeding and healthy suitable surroundings, factors which apply equally to all Hybrid breeding.

Some hen Canaries are a little fastidious about pairing up with the various British Finches, some are downright obstinate, and will not go to nest with them, doing nothing but pace about the breeding cage calling to the cock Canaries they may hear singing. We have usually been successful in reconciling such hens by hanging a cock Canary in a small wire cage, such as a Yorkshire show cage, in front of the breeding cage containing the Finch and hen Canary, hanging it close to the wires. The cock Canary so placed sings to the hen through the wires, and attempts to feed her as best he can, while she builds quite happily, and on calling to the Canary for mating, the Finch immediately copulates with her.

Hen Canaries and Finches.

Many Canary hens pair up quite freely with a British bird without showing any displeasure at their strange partner, except perhaps for the first day or so; and if the British bird is in high breeding condition he will, as a rule, be quite anxious to make friends, but if he is not in breeding condition there will be a display of spite on his part, and the confidence of the hen Canary is thus often broken. Most experienced Hybrid breeders, since the majority of British birds do not come into breeding condition quite so early as Canaries, take a nest of young Canaries from each of their muling hens first, and then pair them up with the British birds for the second and third nests at the end of April or during May. Taking a nest of Canaries first answers a twofold purpose, it prevents waste of the hens' strength in having unfertile eggs to the Finch, and enables the breeder to maintain his supply of muling Canaries, the young produced each year from the first round supplying any wants in that direction for the next year, and filling up any gaps made by sales or loss. Incidentally, we may mention that the Cinnamon-coloured Hybrids exhibited of some Canary crosses are produced by pairing a Cinnamon cock canary to a hen British bird.

The selection of the British bird is the next important step. Any British bird will not do, for although good Hybrids are sometimes produced from indifferent finches, such results are exceptional, and our selection must be birds of good size and shape, rich colour, and the other good properties incidental to the bird. In the case of the Goldfinch, we not only like birds with a large blaze, but those which also show a distinct yellow tint blended with the breast colour. As far as possible birds should be chosen which take kindly to cage life, as these pair up readily, and make good hybrid breeders. If possible the British birds should be procured early in the year, so as to become tamed and thoroughly domesticated by breeding time. Some fresh caught birds captured late, just on the verge of the breeding season, will breed readily in captivity, but are frequently short-lived, and go off after the first nest. Sound over-year birds which have been moulted in captivity, and have proved their ability, are much prized ; and a breeder who wishes to have more than one string to his bow will generally manage to secure a few reliable cage moulted birds in the course of a season or two, and very old-fashioned little fellows they become. Some breeders house moult a few "grey-pates," that is, Goldfinches in their nestling plumage, against which we have nothing to say, as the experienced breeder knows exactly how to supply all their wants and get them safely through their first moult. The inexperienced fancier will, however, act wisely to secure mature birds that have moulted at liberty, and are such a plentiful commodity in the market that a good selection can be made ; an extra finch or two being very necessary, as they have a little way of their own of making up their minds very quickly when they think of departing for the happy hunting grounds, and often at a time of year when it is next to impossible to procure suitable birds.

Selecting the Finch.

The Goldfinch, when in breeding condition, becomes very proud and consequential, and as he alights on his perch with a light airy spring, he spreads his tail like a fan, whisking it from one side to the other, and rings out his "Metallic" call sweetly and clearly, rattling off his song in rapid succession with his wings slightly drooped at the tips. These signs, together with the disappearance of the black streak on the tip of the upper mandible—the beak putting on a rich pinky flesh colour—are sure indications of breeding condition, coupled with his incessant song.

Signs of Breeding Condition.

The Linnet on coming into breeding condition, becomes very active, almost dancing on his perches when not hopping from one to the other, and showing himself markedly sleek in appearance owing to the compact condition of his plumage. His beak too puts on a rich bluish-black tinge as if polished, and his song is full and continuous, his "Tolloe-ejup-i-weet-weet-weet-cher," repeated in wild excitement, and at times as if he had lost all self-control. We have had Goldfinches and Linnets in such high condition as to drop their wings to their sides the moment they were introduced to the hen Canary, and to sing her round the cage, similarly to a cock Canary.

A Greenfinch's coming into breeding condition is apparent by his coat looking as if it had just been well brushed, his plumage showing a nice rich sheen. His song becomes more incessant and louder, being chiefly composed of "Yek-yek-churr-yek-yek-churr-churr," the latter "churr" swelling in volume. The fleshy pink colour of the beak also becomes very rich, and the bird moves about his cage with marked grace and precision.

The Siskin, like the Goldfinch, is a very active bird, and full of life, especially when in breeding condition, and then his peculiar song, consisting of a few sharp musical notes not unlike those of the Goldfinch, and finishing up with a long "cher," is incessant, and even when pecking at the wires or some other part of the cage the chattering song still continues. The beak also puts on a rich fleshy tint which shows up vividly through the dusky surface colour.

The Redpoll in manner is much like the Siskin, and when in breeding condition is either performing his chattering song—which can only be called a chatter—or is "feeding" his feet or the end of the perch the whole day through. These are fairly sure signs as to his readiness for pairing up.

The body colour of the Twite is a wonderful rich tint of reddish brown at all times; but as this bird comes into breeding condition the brown assumes a much richer lustre than at other periods, and the yellow of the beak becomes intensified. The plumage also fits the body exceptionally closely, giving the bird a more sprightly appearance. He is also very active and sings what little song he has more fluently than at other times, all being indications of his being ready for pairing.

The Cape Canary in breeding condition displays a richer hue than usual over his plumage, and sings his sweet musical song louder and more incessantly. The Hybrid mentioned in the previous chapter as bred from this bird was paired in 1910 to a hen Canary—it being a cock bird—by my special request to ascertain results. Both birds were in the very best condition, the Hybrid singing lustily, and going through all the performance of pairing, etc.; the hen Canary built nests, and laid, but all the eggs were unfertile, and the results were thus similar to those from our British Hybrids.

The cock Canary's breeding condition has been fully explained in our Canary chapters. Where convenient the hen Canaries and their British partners may be allowed to fly together in groups, in flight cages, all the winter, so that they may get familiar with each other. This is not, however, absolutely necessary, for we have had birds of the various crosses pair up quite freely which have never seen each other until we paired them.

Breeding.

If there be several approved Finches at command, they may be mated up with hens precisely as Canaries, but if not, a good bird in high condition may be "run" through almost any number of cages, where he will not fail to leave his mark. He need not, of necessity, be allowed to remain long with his hens. A more tractable bird than a Goldfinch does not exist, if allowed to settle down with his hen he will make the most attentive mate, and nurse and feed in the most exemplary manner. It is well, however, not to tax him in this way, as a hen is well able to attend to the duties demanded by her offspring, and he is more likely to remain in robust health and vigour if not overworked. There is some risk in leaving an untried bird with a hen till she lays, as he may take it into his head to examine into the contents of the eggs, for which purpose his pointed beak is well adapted; but this mischievous propensity is happily rather the exception than the rule. The Siskin is really a greater sinner in this respect, and when such a bad habit has been acquired there is one simple preventive—*don't allow them a second opportunity.*

The most inexperienced can soon learn when a hen is on the eve of laying, for she becomes very heavy behind, and usually less sprightly in her movements the day previous to laying; and by removing her partner each night just before dusk, returning him to the hen again in the morning when you have secured the egg, is safer and more effective than trusting to being in the room in time in the morning to secure the egg before it is interfered with. A dummy egg should be placed in the nest each morning instead of that removed, until the hen has completed her clutch. Then remove the dummies, and put the Finch in a cage to himself, and return the hen her own eggs, leaving her to sit, hatch and rear the brood by herself.

When she is ready to go to nest again, run the Finch with her again as before. It is rare that any British bird, other than the Goldfinch or Siskin, attempts to touch the eggs or nest. Birds that are likely to interfere with eggs frequently have a habit of pulling the nest to pieces as fast as the hen builds it, and such birds should always have a close eye kept on their movements. It is always well to remove the first three eggs laid, for reasons which are explained in the chapter on Canary breeding.

As to cages, the ordinary Canary box breeding-cage answers well, though most Hybrid breeders prefer a double one, with one compartment a little larger than the other for the convenience of shutting off the British bird each night, where it is found necessary to do so, with a movable partition, hanging the nest pan in the larger compartment. These double cages are made in just the same way as those described for Canaries, but see that the water holes are not too large, or the smaller young Hybrids may get out through them when they first leave the nest, for, as a rule, all Hybrids fledge more quickly, and leave the nest earlier than Canaries. The usual time is at about fourteen days, and they may then leave the nest any day. The ordinary earthenware nest pans used for Canary breeding answer equally well for Hybrid breeding. If preferred, and space admits, the little German wicker cages can be used for the hen Bullfinches, such as described in Mr. Stevens' experience.

Food. As a diet for the respective pairs, the following will be found a very good seed mixture for Goldfinch, Greenfinch and Canary-Bullfinch pairs. Canary seed two parts, with one part German rape, a like quantity of teazle, hemp, niger, linseed, groats, and white sunflower seed, all mixed together; the husk of the sunflower seed should be first cracked before giving.

For the Linnet, Siskin, Redpoll, and Twite pairs the same mixture in like proportions answers well, omitting the hemp and sunflower seeds as too fattening if given regularly. When the hens are rearing young a little hemp should be added to their mixture, the same as for the others. They should also all have a supply of a good wild seed mixture composed of charlock, thistle, knapweed, dock, plantain, shepherd's purse, etc., etc., to which may be added, when procurable, a supply of the sweepings from the threshing-room floor, which is obtainable from most farmers who thresh their corn for the mere carrying away. Various wild seed heads should also be given as they come into season, scarcely any of them come amiss to the birds, even to the seed of the common stinging nettle. The only trouble is that the majority of the birds do not get sufficient of them, as a rule, in their half-ripe succulent form. A supply of egg food in moderation must also be given, as in the case of canaries, and a little maw seed with it. Other green foods can also be given, such as watercress or seeding chickweed, but see to it that it is fresh and sweet. The hens, while sitting, are better without egg food, but while rearing young they must have a fresh supply two or three times a day, in addition to the seed and green food, just the same as if rearing young canaries.

When the young Hybrids first commence to feed themselves—which they can do by the time they are four weeks old, most of them a few days before—they must have egg food and their seed cracked, as explained in the chapter on feeding young canaries, weaning them off on to the hard seed in a similar manner. The seed mixture recommended for the parents answers well for the various Hybrids as soon as they can crack the hard seed, except omit the hemp seed for each of the crosses except the Goldfinch cross, and even for this cross this seed should be given very sparingly, a little just as a tit-bit. The various wild seeds in their succulent form and the wild seed mixture will also be much enjoyed by the Hybrids as tit-bits. A small meal worm occasionally will please Master Greenie while breeding, and the hen bullies also, after they have once tasted them, and some of the Bullfinch Hybrids will not say no to one. Moderation in all feeding must be the order of the day, free use of the bath, with roomy cages for exercise if good robust health and condition are to be enjoyed by the birds. Hen Bullfinches are also very fond of young buds of fruit-bushes and trees.

The Nestling.

The hatching of a nest of Hybrids is an event of importance, and beginners are often deceived by appearances. All Dark Hybrids are not born equally dark in skin and down, though they usually are veritable little "niggers," nor are all Variegated Hybrids born with such decided indications of variegation as are seen in the discoloured skin of young Canaries; but an experienced eye soon detects the unwelcome signs. When one bird is whiter than the rest, paler in the flesh, or shows no visible signs of discoloration, hope runs high; but alas! all light skinned and light downy looking youngsters do not develop into "Clears" by any means. It is when the real feathers begin to grow that the dark patches put in their appearance, and the supposed "Clear" turns out a "Variegated." It often happens though that a young bird with only a few slight ticks on it will moult out clear. These feathers are often plucked two or three times in one moulting season to get them to come clear, if they have not done so with the first ordinary moult. It is a *most cruel* practice, and one to be discouraged, as it does the bird no good, and another season would in many instances put matters right without recourse to such plucking. It is at the interesting stage of the first few days of a young Hybrid's life that most Clear (?) Hybrids die, and well it is they do, for by their decease is kept alive a hope in the breast of their breeders which would be cruelly crushed out of most men if the young birds survived to disappoint anticipations.

The following notes by Dr. A. Rudolf Galloway, of Aberdeen, on "Light Hybrid Breeding" will be read with interest:—

Light Hybrid Breeding.

The laws which govern the production of Light Hybrids cannot be very different from those concerned in the evolution of our light and variegated Canary varieties, or from those which direct the occurrence of sports in our wild birds.

I have entered into this question at some length, at pp. 15–26 of this work, and I am sure that further experiment and study on the lines there indicated will soon result in the appearance of a larger number of Light Hybrids. In this connection I may add that, as *two* parents are always concerned in the process of reproduction, there is no special reason why we should confine our attention to *one* side of the parentage in working towards Light Hybrid production. It is, of course, possible to get fairly light, occasionally clear, Hybrids by devoting attention solely to the Canary side of the parentage, but by giving attention also to the wild bird side, the chances of producing very light and clear birds, will be greatly increased.

The result of depending mainly on the Canary parent is seen in the table I give at p. 4 of my "Canary-Breeding." Shortly described, the table gives the following result:—Of 526 Hybrids bred, 293 were completely dark, 110 slightly variegated, 101 variegated, 21 lightly variegated, and 1 clear.

At the same time this table proves that inbreeding alone, or combined with breeding out the dark colour, has no great effect on the production of Light Hybrids, for the Canary strain concerned was very much inbred, and mostly clear or ticked.

Those fanciers who are interested in this fascinating problem of light-muling would do well to study carefully Chapters II. and III. of this work.

There is nothing fresh to offer in the way of general management of young or old Hybrids, which in no respect differs from that necessary for Canaries. During the moult, colour-feeding and every other "move" being applied with telling effect on Hybrids, the colour food must be given with precisely the same regularity as given to Canaries, mixed with a little egg food or other substitute. Do not forget an extra liberal supply of linseed in the seed mixture until the moult is complete. Cleanliness, roomy cages of the box pattern, and free use of the bath are the only further requisites necessary to ensure a successful moult.

CHAPTER XXXIV

HYBRIDS BETWEEN TWO BRITISH BIRDS

In addition to the more common hybrids of which the Canary is one parent dealt with in our two previous chapters, there are the rarer hybrids produced by pairing different species of British birds together.

Goldfinch-Bullfinch.

Chief among these stands the Goldfinch-Bullfinch hybrid, beyond all comparison the most beautiful example of the whole class, and though one of our oldest crosses a good specimen still ranks high as an exhibition bird. It is almost needless to describe this lovely hybrid, for our coloured illustration is a singularly happy and life-like delineation, and shows how remarkably the plumage and shape of the parent finches are blended in their progeny. The bird illustrated is a cock, a good specimen of this cross, and its beauty is not exaggerated, for in some very exceptional specimens the under portion of the crimson blaze extends even farther than shown, being finally lost in the blending with the brown on the breast. We had such a specimen in 1894, and exhibited it with great success during 1895 and 1896. The hens of this cross are clad in sober attire, and more closely resemble the female Bullfinch in colour. In size this hybrid should be as large as a good-sized English Bullfinch, and some are a little larger. It resembles the Bullfinch in its quiet demeanour and generally "old-fashioned" deportment, showing but little of the restlessness native to most Goldfinches. Its song is low, very sweet, and continuous, as distinct from a jerky, snatchy style of vocalisation.

The Linnet-Bullfinch.

This is another of our oldest hybrids, and so handsome that we are surprised that more are not bred. A glance at the specimen portrayed on our coloured plate will give the reader an excellent idea of what a good specimen is like. The rich vermilion tint of the breast, throat, cheeks, and forehead is marvellous, taking strongly after the Bullfinch, while the back colour is the rich brown of the Linnet, though without its stripes or spangles. The illustration depicts a male, the hen being much more sober in colour and lacking the vermilion tint on breast and throat. These hybrids are of a most kindly, free disposition, full of life, but rarely wild, and the cocks are excellent songsters. Their shape, like their colour, is a happy blending of both parents, and for exhibition purposes the larger they are the better combined with good colour.

REDPOLL-BULLFINCH.

The Greenfinch-Bullfinch.

This is another familiar hybrid at exhibitions. It is a noble-looking bird, and of very chubby build, as we should naturally expect from its parentage. The colour is a charming display of rich reddish orange on the breast, throat, and cheeks, a faint tinge running round the eye. The back is slatey grey, with a faint tinge of the Greenfinch-green covering the surface, becoming richer towards the neck. The top of the head is dark, while the rump displays a rich tint of reddish orange. The wings are a curious mixture of the Greenfinch and Bullfinch colouring —barred like the Bullfinch, the bar being slightly tinted with the reddish orange, but the outer flight feathers having a slight edging of Greenfinch-yellow to the outer web. The tail is dark, and there are other little tints here and there which it is quite unnecessary to describe in detail, for by reference to our coloured plate the cross will be easily recognised. This cross can also be numbered amongst the hybrids with attractive plumage. They vary in size according to that of their parents; but the larger and richer the blending of colours the more valuable they are as exhibition specimens. Our description is of the cock, the hen being duller and without the rich breast colour. In movement the birds have much in common with others of the Bullfinch cross, but the cocks are not generally quite such fluent or sweet songsters as the Canary-Bullfinch.

The Redpoll-Bullfinch.

This hybrid is much rarer than the three just dealt with, and is also smaller. All those we have seen, have, in shape, followed that of the Redpoll, and this graceful form, combined with a blending of the Bullfinch colour, makes this a most attractive hybrid. The breast, throat, and cheek colour is similar to that of the Linnet-Bullfinch; but the head is smaller, taking decidedly to the Redpoll in shape, with much of its marking, though we have seen one of these hybrids (of which there was no question as to its parentage) with the dark cap of the Bullfinch, though smaller, and a large dark bib, points we should anticipate seeing more frequently if there were more of these hybrids bred. The bill is finer than that of the Linnet-Bullfinch, though stouter than the Redpoll, and though dark, there is just the suspicion of the yellow tint on the sides abutting the gape—similar to the Redpoll. The colour on the back and sides is largely that of the Redpoll, though not so heavily striped. The flight feathers of the wings are dark, with a bar of light brown across them. Birds of this cross are most cheerful and lively, with many of the Redpoll's habits. We have not heard them give vent to any song worth mentioning, but from an exhibition point of view they are a most valuable asset amongst a team of hybrids. The hens are minus the vermilion tint on breast and throat.

The Goldfinch-Greenfinch.

This hybrid is much less valued than those of the Bullfinch cross. It is not a very pretty bird, being built more on the lines of the Greenfinch than of the Goldfinch, and partaking to a considerable extent of the former's dull colour. Occasionally, however, a more brilliant example than usual, with a good deal of the Goldfinch character, appears on the stage to keep alive an interest in a hybrid easy to produce, but at no time a very popular favourite or often seen at exhibitions. We have seen a few specimens of singular beauty, with large Goldfinch blaze and lustrous plumage—different in texture to either parent, the rich green body colour merging into a deep turmeric yellow on the lower parts of the body and breast. If they were bred in sufficient numbers to have a class to themselves at our exhibitions they would no doubt become more popular, as their chance against rarer crosses in mixed classes is not great. The cock's song is full of melody without being noisy. The hen is altogether much duller in colour, lacking the rich yellow tint, and with little Goldfinch blaze —sometimes, indeed, but the merest impression.

The Goldfinch-Linnet.

This is another of the more sober-coloured hybrids, which may account for so few of the cross being bred and exhibited. In shape and size it takes after the Goldfinch, and is inclined to be snakey in head, like that bird, which it resembles also in bill. In its "little ways" it is a Goldfinch all over, and will fight with one's finger, and in other respects deport himself like that bird. The body colour is that of the Linnet, with just a shade richer tint of brown, and not so much lacing. The outer white edging to the flignt feathers of the Linnet give way to the yellow of the Goldfinch, and the cross has a distinct patch of the Goldfinch blaze on the forehead, though none on cheek or throat. The birds are lively in disposition, and the cock's song is somewhat sharp, the notes being short but musical, and not at all unpleasant. The red cap is usually absent in hens of this cross, and they are duller in general body colour.

The Goldfinch-Siskin.

This hybrid is somewhat smaller than those already dealt with, owing to one of its parents being very small. It is really an enlarged type of the Siskin, but of more brilliant colour, its body colour partaking largely of the yellowish green and dark markings of the Siskin. It also has the dark cap of the Siskin, with the flush or blaze of the Goldfinch on the face, giving a very pretty effect. The head and bill in shape are practically those of the Goldfinch, both parents being similar in these respects. As we should naturally expect from such lively parents, it is a charming bird in manner, full of life and vivacity, "the cock of the walk," as it were, and it insists upon making itself heard with its chattering, lively song, and is a happy cage and excellent exhibition bird. The hens of the cross lack the rich, yellow tone of body colour, and have little or no Goldfinch blaze, often merely an impression, with a few pale red straggling feathers distributed over the face.

The Siskin-Greenfinch. This Hybrid is a little larger than the Goldfinch-Siskin and of somewhat stouter build, following the Greenfinch largely in shape of body. The head, however, is smaller and the beak longer—points acquired from the Siskin. An excellent example appears in our coloured plate depicting the happy blending in colour of both parents, the green of the Greenfinch being intensified, while the marking of the Siskin is subdued. The cap is of the Siskin persuasion, though not so black, having a greenish tint. The breast and under surface are a rich, bold bright green-tinted yellow running off at the vent to a buffish shade.

In manner and movements the Hybrid takes much after the Greenfinch. Its song, too, resembles that of the Greenfinch intermingled with a few of the Siskin's lively notes. The hens of this cross are paler and duller in colour, an ashen-grey covering the surface.

The Redpoll-Goldfinch. This, one of the smallest of our Hybrids, can be bred either from a Goldfinch cock and Redpoll hen, or Redpoll cock and Goldfinch hen. The finest specimen that we ever saw was bred in the latter way, and hence our preference for the Redpoll cock as the sire, and reference to our coloured plate will convey a capital impression of this Hybrid's shape and colour. The specimen to which we have just alluded had the largest Goldfinch blaze we ever saw on one of these Hybrids; it was bred by Mr. Alexander, near Annan, Scotland, and was successfully exhibited for several years by Mr. E. J. Lamb, of New Malden, Surrey, who once told us that it was one of the most easily kept birds of his collection. These Hybrids are of lively disposition, ever on the move like the Redpoll, tripping about with a most consequential air, and though not gorgeous in colour except for the blaze on the face, are most attractive birds. The cocks have a short but pretty song, combining the Goldfinch and Redpoll notes. The hens have a much smaller blaze than the cocks and of a pale hazel tint, some, indeed, having but the faintest impression of blaze at all.

The Redpoll-Siskin. This is, perhaps, the smallest of our Hybrids, and is a graceful, proportionately built bird. It is not quite the rich colour of the Siskin-Greenfinch, but its happy blending of the Redpoll brown and yellowish green of the Siskin gives a very pleasing effect. The head in shape and colour is similar to the hen Siskin, with just a tint of brown in the marking, and the bill, too, follows the same parent. The Redpoll-Siskin is a cheerful little bird, full of life and activity. The cocks have a continual chattering song, and the hens' notes are very similar, but in colour and marking the hens are altogether paler and more sober in appearance. We had a couple of these Hybrids in 1896, and found them not at all difficult to keep in good health and condition. The cross, however, has not been a great success on the show bench, and we think that a separate class should be given in which the various smaller Hybrids could compete together, instead of, as now, being outclassed in competition against the larger crosses. If a separate class were provided fanciers would find some inducement to breed these smaller hybrids in larger numbers.

The Redpoll-Greenfinch. We now come to some even more sombre coloured Hybrids, and amongst these is the Redpoll-Greenfinch, a small but chubbily built bird. This cross is not an easy one to secure, and when obtained it has little to recommend it as an exhibition bird except its rarity. In colour it is a dingy green, slightly streaked with dark brown, and the outer web of the flight feathers of the wing are lightly tinged with yellow, and though not striking in colour the plumage carries a beautiful sheen on its surface. The hens are more dingy in colour, with a decided ashy-grey shade over the surface of the body colour, and lack the yellow in the wing. The cock's song is a continued chatter, with a good deal of " churr " about it. The bird is fairly active in its movements, and has a graceful carriage and close and compact feathers. This and other sober-coloured Hybrids are much handicapped at shows by having to compete with more attractively coloured birds, and in common with the smaller Hybrids, which suffer from lack of size, should have separate classification.

The Siskin-Linnet. The Siskin-Linnet is a trifle smaller than the Linnet, but a little larger than the Siskin. Its general colour is that of the Linnet, a reddish-brown with darker stripes, tinted here and there with the yellowish green of the Siskin, especially on the cheeks, breast, and flanks. It is of lively disposition, and the cocks have a cheerful song, chiefly that of the Linnet intermingled with a few of the sharp notes of the Siskin. The hens are buffer on the cheeks, breast, and flanks than the cocks, with but the faintest impression of the greenish tint.

The Linnet-Greenfinch. This Hybrid is about the size of a Linnet, but a little stouter in build and fuller in neck, with a larger head, and it also has a stouter bill, characteristics obtained from the Greenfinch. Its colour is a blending of the two parents, though the brown of the Linnet predominates. The bright yellow of the Greenfinch wings and tail show up in a striking manner on the outer web of the flight feathers of the wing, and on the edge of the tail feathers towards the base. Linnet-Greenfinches are, as a rule, inclined to be more lively than either of their parents, and do not show themselves off with the graceful "hop" from perch to perch characteristic of the Linnet and Greenfinch. In song some take after the Linnet, while others follow the Greenfinch. All that we have heard have, however, had a slight blending of the notes of each. The hens are a more dingy colour than the cocks and have no yellow in the wings.

The Twite-Greenfinch.

This is one of the most sober-coloured of Hybrids, and we say this with no intention of disparagement, but rather to emphasise our suggestion that a separate class should be given at shows for these quiet-coloured crosses, for here we have a most rare Hybrid, yet it has little or no chance at an exhibition against more gorgeous-coloured specimens. Birds of this cross follow the Twite in size, shape and colour, except that the flight feathers of the wings and tail are shorter, and there is just the faintest tint of the Greenfinch green on the breast and flanks, and of the Greenfinch yellow on the outer web of the flight feathers of the wing. Our description is from a specimen exhibited by Mr. W. H. Vale, of Clapham, London.

The Linnet-Redpoll.

The Linnet-Redpoll is another very sober-coloured bird, the degree of reddish brown and darker striping largely depending upon the parents. For instance, a Hybrid bred from a Linnet and Lesser Redpoll has a much more rufous brown body colour than one that is bred from a Linnet and mealy Redpoll. The Hybrid from this latter pairing has lighter and more buffish tone covering the surface of the brown, and it is as a rule larger than the Hybrid from the former pairing. In either case, however, they are of the Linnet shape, with just a little fuller breast and smaller head, having the sweet round head of the Redpoll. They are cheerful, active birds; the cocks have much of the Linnet's song, though not quite its fluency, intermingled with a little of the Redpoll chatter. The hens are duller in colour and more heavily striped on the breast than the cocks.

The Bramblefinch-Chaffinch is not only a rare cross, but the blending of the colours of the parents is very pretty. They have been produced from the Bramblefinch cock and Chaffinch hen, and vice versa. Some of the finest specimens that have graced our show benches were bred by that enthusiastic lady Hybrid breeder, Miss Janet Reeves, of Wateringbury, Kent.

Bramble-finch-Chaffinch.

As their parentage would indicate, they are of nice size, being similar in shape and movements to their parents. The song of the cocks that we have heard was largely that of the Chaffinch, and they had the same peculiar manner of raising the feathers on the top of the head upon our approaching their cage, as if pleased to see a visitor. These Hybrids are hardy and not at all difficult to keep, and meet with a fair amount of success on the show bench, even in a mixed class. The hens are not so rich in colour as the cocks and display none of the orange rufous body colour.

Other Crosses.

A Hybrid has been produced from the Tree Sparrow and House Sparrow. There are also other crosses said to have been produced, but as we have no authentic proof of such, we shall refer to them in our chapter on breeding Hybrids from two British birds.

Classification.

We have already referred to the scanty classification of Hybrids bred from two British birds, and may, perhaps, be allowed to suggest the following classes for large exhibitions:—(*a*) Any variety Bullfinch Hybrid except Canary-Bullfinch; (*b*) Goldfinch-Siskin, Goldfinch-Redpoll, Siskin-Greenfinch, Redpoll-Siskin; (*c*) Goldfinch-Greenfinch, Bramblefinch-Chaffinch, Goldfinch-Linnet, and Siskin-Linnet; (*d*) Any other variety of Hybrid between two British birds.

This would allow of all Hybrids, whatever their colour or size, of competing much more equally than at present, and as numbers increased the classes could be further extended by subdivision, or even giving some Hybrids a class to themselves. This would also encourage the production of the more common crosses in goodly numbers.

Scale of Points.

In attempting to frame a scale of points for judging Hybrids, we believe that we are doing something which has not been attempted before. Practical men, as a rule, however, give due consideration when judging to the correct blending in the Hybrid of the essential points of their respective parents. For instance, a good Goldfinch-Bullfinch must have a large, rich, brilliant coloured blaze after that of the Goldfinch, with a tint of the Bullfinch's vermilion. The further the rich flush runs down on to the breast the better, as it thus shows the blending of the two parents to greater perfection. Size without blaze is useless.

Then, again, a Linnet-Bullfinch *must* have the rich vermilion tint of the cock Bullfinch on the breast; the more brilliant this colour, in conjunction with other marking, the better. The Goldfinch-Redpoll must have a large, rich blaze akin to that of the Goldfinch, just as the Siskin-Greenfinch and the Redpoll-Siskin Hybrids must display the colour of both parents to a marked degree on various parts of their body. The same thing applies through the whole race of Hybrids; we must have the leading features of the parents shown in happy contrast; get size *with them*, but size without them is useless. Our intention is simply to give our readers in the usual tabulated form some idea of the relative worth of the parts which go to make up an interesting whole, attaching to each a value which will leave sufficient margin for a subtractive process, so that the scale of points can be equally applied to all Hybrids bred from two British birds.

Scale of Points for Judging Hybrids Bred from two British Birds

Points of Merit

	Maximum
Colour.—For richness, good marking, and brilliancy with the prominent colours of both parents well developed . .	30
Feather.—For smooth compactness and fine silky quality.	20
Shape.—Well developed, proportionate with parentage	15
Size.—For good size in accordance with parentage	15
Condition.—Health, cleanliness, sound feather, and steadiness	20
Total	100

Negative Properties

A Hybrid should not be small in accordance with its kind, nor crouch on its perch, or be unsteady in its show-cage. Nor should its blending of colour be blurred or indistinct to raise doubts as to its parentage. It should not have any deformity or broken or otherwise damaged feathers. Hybrids of the Goldfinch cross must not be poor in blaze, or those of the Bullfinch lack the rich breast tint of the cock bullfinch or orange red; or those of the Siskin cross be lacking in the breast colour of that bird.

As regards getting Hybrids steady and accustomed to the show cage, and washing and exhibiting them, be they bred from two British birds, or a British bird and Canary, our instructions on these points for Canaries are equally applicable to Hybrids, and will be found in Chapter XIV. The show cages for Hybrids are of similar shape to the Norwich show cage illustrated on page 175. For the Goldfinch-Bullfinch and Hybrids of similar size, the show cage should be the same size as that used for the Norwich Canary.

For the Goldfinch-Redpoll, Siskin-Redpoll, and Hybrids of similar size, the cage should be a size smaller, and a little more closely wired, the wires being half-inch apart, the water holes, too, may be made round if preferred. For those Hybrids of which the Goldfinch or Bullfinch is one of the parents Brunswick green enamel answers well for the inside of the show cage and black outside, but for other Hybrids mid-green enamel answers well for the insides and black outside.

CHAPTER XXXV

THE BREEDING OF HYBRIDS FROM TWO BRITISH BIRDS

Selections.

To produce good colour and marking in Hybrids, we must see that these properties are present in the parents, or our chance of producing an exhibition Hybrid will be poor indeed. Good specimens are occasionally bred from mediocre parents, but they are the exception rather than the rule, and we do not believe in trusting to such chance work. No matter what the cross may be, we advise the selection of the largest, richest - coloured, best - marked specimens of British birds of the kind you require that you can lay your hands on to pair together. If it be a cock Goldfinch, see that he has a large, rich-coloured blaze, good body colour, large, rich-coloured yellow wing bars and moons; and if it is a Bullfinch hen you are intending to pair him to, see that she is of good size and rich colour, with a large, shapely cap. If you have these good characteristics in the parents, there will be every possibility of their being implanted in their progeny. In support of our advocating such, we may say that the largest and best-coloured Goldfinch-Bullfinch Hybrid we have ever seen, and which was pronounced a wonder by all who saw it at our exhibitions a few years ago, was bred from a large, rich-coloured Siberian Goldfinch cock and a Siberian Bullfinch hen. The Siberian Goldfinch is a much larger bird than the British, and as it carries the same plumage, but on a larger scale, we get a better display of colour on the Hybrids bred from it combined with size. Some very fine Hybrids, too, are bred from our English birds. German Goldfinches and Bullfinches are also useful for breeding purposes, being a little larger than ours. But as we said before, whatever their kind, be they Goldfinches, Bullfinches, Siskins, Linnets, Redpolls, Greenfinches, Twites, Bramblefinches, Chaffinches, or any other, select the finest cocks and hens you possibly can to go together. It is immaterial whether they be birds that have been reared under Canaries from the British bird's eggs, or hand reared, or caught wild in the usual way. If caught birds, then it is well to secure them early in the autumn, so that they get accustomed to cage life and their surroundings.

The birds which are intended to be bred together can be allowed to fly in pairs in the same cage throughout the winter; they then get on good terms with each other. Some British birds do not breed the first year, but do so successfully the next and succeeding years. It is also very important that the pairs intended to breed together agree well after a reasonable acquaintance, for if continual quarrelling goes on results are seldom good, as cocks that have been severely hen-pecked, or hens that have been ill-treated by a tyrant male, rarely gain sufficient mutual confidence to breed successfully. There are exceptions, but it is best where such battles continue for any length of time to separate the birds and give each a fresh mate, if, as it is advisable, you have a surplus to select from, until they find an eligible partner. It is surprising how birds recognise an old mate. Mr. G. Munday, of Bermondsey, had a Bullfinch hen paired up to a clear yellow Norwich cock, from which he obtained fertile eggs. He tried to pair that Bullie hen with every other clear yellow cock Canary in his room, even to the brother of the one she had taken to, but she would have none of them, and went for each newcomer open-mouthed. Yet when her old partner was put back she was as fussy and loving with him as possible. Of course, a little scrimmage at first need not be noticed, and in many cases there is no quarrel at all, and as a rule these are the successful breeding pairs.

Most of our hen Finches will sit, hatch and rear their own broods, the Bullfinch perhaps excepted, and even she will do so in an aviary. In *The Feathered World* some years ago, Mr. John Hector, of Aberdeen, wrote that Mr. William Ramsay, of Maryton, Forfarshire, had a hen Bullfinch who, with a cock Goldfinch, reared three young Hybrids, and doubtless some kindly disposed pairs would do the same if given the opportunity, but these Hybrids are so valuable that breeders will not risk the eggs, but transfer them to a hen Canary, or a hen Siskin, or Greenfinch as more reliable foster-parents.

Breeding Cages.

Roomy breeding cages, about 3 ft. long, are advantageous, especially if fitted up like a miniature aviary, with a nest pan in or behind a bushy branch of broom, heather, privet, or other shrub in one corner. Seclusion of this kind is a great inducement to the hen to take to the nest and lay in it. Failing this, see that the breeding cage and its door are sufficiently large to admit a small German wicker cage being hung up as a nesting place. Most British hens nest readily in these little wicker cages, with the wickers at one end removed, so that the birds can pass in and out. A liberal supply of short lengths of hay, fine rootlets, moss, lichen, doe-hair, small, soft feathers and, when procurable, even cobwebs and thistledown, should be provided for building material.

Some may say, why take all this trouble ? To which we reply, the difficulty in breeding with many wild Finches is not in inducing them to lay, but in securing the eggs when they are laid ; and hence the importance of doing everything to lead them to construct their own nests—a thing they frequently do not seem to care about in captivity. To prevent any mishap to eggs laid in the cage, or even dropped from the perch, which is of common occurrence, it is well to cover the bottom of the cage with bran to the depth of an inch, and, if persistently dropped from the perch, to lower it to a height from which no danger from fracture can be anticipated—say, about three inches from the floor of the cage. The number of eggs is uncertain, the natural order of things being occasionally disarranged in a strange way ; two or three only being sometimes deposited, while at others a " clutch " of five will be laid in the nest with regularity, or a considerable number—a dozen or more—at uncertain intervals. These should all be placed under Canaries which have just commenced to sit, to be hatched, literally not putting too many in one nest—say, two or three in each—both on account of the ordinary risks and the extraordinary demands the young birds will make on the feeding capabilities of their foster-parents. The rest is only a question of ordinary management.

Mr. Ernest Stevens, of Sidmouth, Devon, built a large flight along one side of his bird room to turn young Canaries into. He partitioned a portion of this flight off 2 ft. by 2 ft. and 18 ins. deep, and in October, 1907, he caught two Bullfinch hens ; one of these, in February, 1908, he put into this portion of the flight with a cock Linnet. They were quite amiable to each other, and as the spring advanced he noticed the birds feeding one another, so he hung a German wicker cage, as advised above, in their compartment, supplying them with some hay, rootlets, and a strip of coconut matting about 4 ins. long. They were soon busy pulling the matting to pieces, and built a nest nearly as large as a Rook's with this and hay and branches of shepherd's purse, but on the top of the wicker cage. In due course the hen laid four eggs in the nest. Mr. Stevens put these under a hen Canary to incubate, three proved fertile—one hatched out, the other two, though fully developed, were " dead in shell." The survivor was a fine chick, but only lived three days. The Bullfinch hen had two more clutches of eggs, three in each fertile, but did not hatch out.

Many rare Hybrids, on the other hand, have been bred in ordinary sized Canary breeding cages, and some hen British birds take to the nest quite freely; but the breeder of Hybrids must study the temperament of individual birds to be successsful. In many cases progress is very slow, the birds taking little notice of each other before April or even May; then, as the hens come into breeding condition, the cocks will become more attentive and follow the hen closely, even superintending the building of the nest, and also feeding the hen freely. These are sure signs of progress, and if the hens look a little heavy behind, but do not frequent the nest, cover the cage bottom with bran, as already advised, although usually when the birds build a good nest they lay in it. Still, it is well to take every precaution, and if Master Goldie or Master Siskin appear very inquisitive about the eggs and nest, shut them off each night, admitting them to their hens again in the morning. Many of our rarest Hybrids have been bred from groups of British birds flying together in an out-door aviary fitted up with growing shrubs and dead gorse bushes, broom, thorn, willow, etc.

To ensure success, cocks and hens of the same species must not be introduced into the aviary.

Breeding Hybrids in Aviaries.

Given sufficient accommodation for six hen Chaffinches and the same number each of Greenfinch and Bullfinch hens, no cocks of these species should be placed in the aviary, but instead introduce three cock Goldfinches and the same number each of Redpolls, Bramblefinches, Siskins, Linnets and Twites, then any offspring obtained must necessarily be Hybrids. If a pair of birds can have a small aviary to themselves, so much the better.

Miss Janet Reeves, of Wateringbury, Kent, has bred many rare Hybrids in her out-door aviaries from birds grouped as described above, amongst them being the Bramblefinch-Chaffinch and the Redpoll-Bullfinch. This lady has bred quite a number of the former Hybrids, both from the Bramblefinch cock and Chaffinch hen and Chaffinch cock and Bramblefinch hen, but not, of course, in the same aviary.

As regards food, we have at all times to give as a "stop-gap" to British birds

Food.

what is usually called a stock or Finch mixture, so that they have always a supply of one kind of food or another. But as far as possible the birds should be fed on the wild seeds and berries upon which they feed when at liberty. The more attention the would-be Hybrid breeder pays to these items the greater his chances of success; for no food has the conditioning properties of the succulent wild foods. The regular seed mixture will need to be regulated a little to suit the individual pairs. For the Goldfinch and Bullfinch pair, a good staple mixture is equal parts of Canary and teazle seed with one-third niger, rape, linseed, white sunflower, and a little hemp. If it is found that the birds do not crack the husk of the sunflower seed, then crack it for them fresh each day, and a few split groats may be added. A good wild seed mixture should also be given during the winter and early spring, in its dry state, in which thistle, knapweed, dandelion, plantain, dock, and similar seeds should abound. To this a little maw-seed can be added, and privet, hawthorn, and other berries are much liked by Bullfinches.

As soon as the various wild seeds are procurable during the spring, summer and autumn in their green, succulent, almost ripe state, give them liberally every day, fresh gathered; in fact, let the birds live on them if you can procure a sufficient supply. Flowering heads of groundsel and dandelion seed heads are about the first obtainable, then come shepherd's purse, seedy chickweed, the various docks, the common nettle, various thistles, knapweed, commonly called hard-heads or horse knops, burdock, plantain, etc., none of which comes amiss. When the supply of these is short, green food in the shape of water-cress or young dandelion, or lettuce leaves when about 4 ins. high, should be given. In addition to the regular seed mixture, give a little egg food every other day when the time for breeding arrives; and if the birds are allowed to rear their own young, whilst doing so a supply of fresh made egg food must be given twice daily.

A similar bill of fare answers well for Greenfinch-Bullfinch, Goldfinch-Greenfinch and Goldfinch-Linnet pairs; also for all the other pairs for producing the various crosses mentioned in the previous chapter, with the omission of the hemp seed, and in addition to the wild seed heads above quoted wild convolvulus might be given for the Linnet, Greenfinch and Chaffinch. Branches infested with green fly, blight of wild rose trees, and other bushes will also be much enjoyed. Live ants' cocoons, and gentles—the latter being allowed to clean themselves well in silver or fresh river sand before being given—will not come amiss to Chaffinches and Bramblefinches, and, in fact, many of the other Finches will not say them nay. During the breeding season additional luxuries are smooth green caterpillars, fruit and seed maggots, and other grubs, as well as flies, when procurable, for the partial insect-eating birds. The same bill of fare will answer equally well for the birds when flying together in groups in an aviary. Two or three fresh clover sods placed on the floor weekly will be much enjoyed, and any uprooted plants from the garden will be diligently overhauled in search of insects or grubs if thrown in as soon as taken from the ground.

The same method of feeding answers well for the various Hybrids when they can feed themselves, gradually weaning them off the egg food until it is given in a very sparing way when five or six weeks old. Occasionally a little bread soaked in scalding milk, if they will partake of it, is good, and wards off many little troubles. Of course, the husk of the hemp and sunflower seed must be cracked for the young Hybrids until they are able to crack it themselves, just as for young Canaries. Young Hybrids leave the nest earlier than Canaries, usually when only about fourteen days old. It has been necessary to give this detailed management as it differs so much from the management of Canaries, and the breeder must not mind the little extra trouble entailed in procuring the fresh wild seeds and berries, for by paying attention to these items those who have hitherto written "Failure" may yet be able to write "Success" in their Hybrid breeding record.

During the moult, if it is decided to colour feed the Hybrids, colour and egg food should be given in addition to their seed diet, as explained for the Canary Hybrids in Chapter XXXIII. Free access to the bath is indispensable for both the British birds when breeding and their Hybrid offspring.

Crosses yet to be secured.

Doubtless as time goes on many new crosses will be added to the existing list, such as the Siskin-Bullfinch, Twite-Bullfinch, Hawfinch-Bullfinch, Hawfinch-Greenfinch, Crossbill-Hawfinch, Goldfinch-Twite, Twite-Siskin, Twite-Linnet, Redpoll-Twite, etc. Already the Tree Sparrow-House Sparrow cross has been produced, and who knows whether we may not yet see the much-talked-of Canary-Chaffinch, and Canary-Bramblefinch, to say nothing of various Hybrids of the Bunting cross, as well as a host of Hybrids from various insectivorous birds. Owing to limitation of space, we have had necessarily to be brief in many of our remarks; but sufficient has been said to give the keynote, as to how to proceed to be successful in the breeding, keeping, feeding and exhibiting of the various Hybrids. Hybrid breeding is a most fascinating pursuit, and those who do not feel interested in Canary breeding will find ample scope therein to test their talents and patience in securing some of the rare crosses that we have cited.

BRITISH BIRDS AMENABLE TO CAPTIVITY IN CAGE OR AVIARY

CHAPTER XXXVI

FAMILY TURDIDÆ

THRUSHES AND THRUSH-LIKE BIRDS

The Missel Thrush.

Turdus viscivorus (*Linn.*)—A well-matured specimen of this species is the largest of the Thrush family, being ten to twelve inches in length, and of more massive build than the Song and other Thrushes. The general colour of its plumage is ashy-brown above, lores and eyelids white; feathers below the eye and ear-coverts ochreous-buff, the feathers tipped with black and forming a line on the upper ear-coverts; cheeks, throat, and under surface of body clear ochreous-buff, spotted with triangular tips to the feathers, forming a line above and below the cheeks; the spots on the throat are very small and faint, those on the breast are bold and increase in density towards the flanks. The abdomen is buffy-white. This happy blending of colour and its commanding size make the Missel Thrush an attractive bird for exhibition purposes. The larger the better, if combined with richness of colour and well-defined marking. Perfect plumage, toes, and feet, with steadiness, are all of vital importance. When free it is rather a shy bird, but when breeding does not scruple to approach the outskirts of towns. It usually builds in the fork of a tree at varying heights, an orchard frequently being selected. We have had a pair build in the fork of a pear tree in our garden at Peckham, close to the house, and successfully rear their brood, not displaying the slightest fear when we stood close by watching them feeding their young. Mr. H. J. Wilson, of West Dulwich, even succeeded in getting these birds to breed in captivity, in a large shed in which was inserted some fine mesh wire netting, to allow of plenty of light. They built their own nest in a shallow box in which fertile eggs were laid, but did not hatch. Mr. Wilson also had fertile eggs from this bird mated to a Song Thrush, but they did not hatch, though the hen Missel Thrush sat closely throughout the whole period of incubation; but when wild Thrushes' and Blackbirds' eggs were taken and placed under the hen Missel Thrushes they hatched and successfully reared the broods.

The song of the Missel Thrush consists of a few notes only, which are uttered in a loud and wild tone, mixed with a certain strain of melancholy. From its habit of singing during or preceding a storm from the topmost branches of a tree it has obtained in some districts the name of the Storm Cock. The bird is also known as the "Holm" Thrush, and "Screech" Thrush, the latter name no doubt being derived from the harsh "screech"-like note which it utters both when flying and perched.

From its pugnacious habits and large size, the Missel Thrush is not a desirable companion in an aviary for smaller birds. It will, however, thrive and keep in good plumage in a box-shaped cage of 3 feet long, 18 inches or more in depth, with not fewer than two perches, made of soft pine wood. If the cage is lofty enough, say 2 ft. high, a third perch is an advantage arranged thus .˙. The bird then gets a series of nice hops. The cage requires constant cleaning, and plenty of gritty sand on the bottom. The food and water vessels should be arranged on the outside of the cage. Hand-reared, or young Missel Thrushes captured soon after they can do for themselves, are best for pets, and for exhibition purposes. A nest of young taken when the feathers are almost covering the body are easily reared by hand, on almost any insectivorous food mixture, supplemented by a little finely minced hard boiled egg, and the whole made crumbly moist with new milk. Sufficient may be made moist at a time to last half a day, but it is much better prepared fresh twice or even three times a day, so that it is perfectly sweet and good. The young birds must be fed with this once every hour from early morning until dusk, giving them just as much as they will eat from the end of a blunt-pointed narrow piece of wood pared down very thin at the end. A drop or two of milk or water should also be dropped into their beaks from the tip of the finger or the blunt stick, after each feed. When they cease to gape they have had sufficient for that feed. They can also be successfully reared on barley meal and hard-boiled egg. The latter must be minced fine by being passed through a wire sieve or egg mill, and a little plain biscuit pounded up fine should be added in the proportion of equal parts of barley meal and egg, and half part biscuit, and the whole made crumbly moist with new milk. Occasionally a little bread made into a pulp with scalded milk may be given by way of a change with beneficial results. During the intervals between feeding, two or three gentles—which have been well cleaned by allowing them to wriggle themselves through silver or river sand—or any other grubs or insects, will be welcome morsels, and all assist to build up a good frame and constitution. As the young birds get older, just before they are able to do for themselves, a little finely granulated meat meal may be added to the food, reducing the quantity of hard-boiled egg by one-half. The hand feeding must be stopped by degrees, and when the birds are seen picking up for themselves give only an occasional feed, gradually lengthening the intervals.

When taking a brood of Missel Thrushes, remove the nest with the young in it, and place it in a basin or flower-pot just large enough to hold the nest firmly, then place the pot in a box of about 18 inches square, or 18 inches by 15 inches, with a piece of fine mesh wire netting tacked over it so that it can be unhooked to feed the birds. By taking this precaution, if one of the youngsters should scramble out of the nest it will not be overlooked or perhaps trodden upon. The nest must be kept perfectly clean and free from droppings. Each young bird passes its excreta immediately after being fed, so that there is no difficulty in keeping the nest and young birds clean if the droppings are cleared away after each feeding time. This is most important, as young birds will not thrive unless they are kept scrupulously clean. After their last meal at night, until the feathers cover the body properly, a piece of old flannel should be laid lightly over the top of the nest, leaving the sides open; this keeps the youngsters cosy and can be removed in the morning.

When the birds can feed themselves continue the same food for a week or two and give each a separate cage, then gradually wean them on to a diet consisting of a good poultry meal, free from grit, with a little meat meal, made crumbly moist with hot water, and afterwards add a few clean ants' cocoons. Mix only the quantity required for each day's consumption, and this will be found to answer well as a staple food. A little hard-boiled egg minced fine may occasionally be added instead of the meat meal, after the poultry meal has been made moist, as may also a little grated carrot or boiled potato or tender lettuce chopped fine. A varied diet is beneficial to all birds. A meal-

BLACKBIRD, THRUSH, MISSEL THRUSH, OR STARLING SHOW CAGE.

worm or two or other grubs will also be welcome morsels, for the Missel Thrush's food in its wild state consists of slugs, worms, insects, and the very small species of snails found in the marshes and meadows. In the autumn the Missel Thrush feeds also on various berries, especially the mistletoe and juniper, and is called "Mistle Thrush" by some from its fondness for the mistletoe berries. A supply of any of these foods should be given in small quantities as a change whenever procurable, as well as ripe fruit in season. If giving a snail a stone should be placed on the bottom of the cage in a corner for the bird to break off the shell, which it does by holding the snail in its bill and beating it against the stone.

Free access to the bath is essential to good plumage and health. A little colour food added to the bird's daily food supply—just sufficient to tint it—during the moult enriches the colour of this bird with pleasing effect. A box cage similar to that illustrated on this page is the most suitable in which to exhibit a Missel Thrush. It may either have the small portion of the top at the front wire as shown in the illustration, or the wooden top may come right to the front. This is a matter of taste. As regards size, a very good dimension is 18 inches or 20 inches long, 16 inches high, and 10 inches or 11 inches deep from back to front, painted or enamelled pale blue inside, and black outside.

The Song Thrush.

The Song Thrush, *Turdus musicus* (*Linn.*), known as the "Throstle" in the North and many districts, is deservedly one of the greatest favourites among British songsters, and, from its singing so cheerily long before the trees have burst into leaf, has generally been called the "herald of spring." It frequents the whole of Europe, but is found more generally towards the north, and breeds throughout the British Isles. During the autumn a considerable migration of our home-bred Thrushes takes place for more southern climes, while many visitors from the continent considerably augment the numbers of our home-bred birds which winter with us. There is a blithe, bluff heartiness about the song of the Thrush that carries with it a certain feeling of rusticity, and which makes it peculiarly attractive in a town, bringing as it does so forcibly remembrances of those green fields and shady hedgerows where we loved to roam in our boyhood days.

One of its favourite habits is to repair in the early morning and cool eventide to the topmost branch of a tree, selecting some withered twig for its perch, and from thence pour forth its flood of melody. Two or three of them will make a whole district echo with melody indescribable. One strange feature in connection with this bird is that while attending to a brood of young the cock bird rarely sings during the day; but towards the dusk of evening, when his day's work is over, then he pours forth his song well into the darkness, and has doubtless often been mistaken for the Nightingale by those not conversant with the song of the two birds. Thus the Nightingale may have been accredited with visiting districts in which it is never seen, and in reality has never been heard. The Song Thrush commences singing as early as January, if the season be mild, continuing through the spring and summer. The Thrush, being slightly endowed with imitative powers, in captivity has been known to "catch a tune" when whistled or played upon a wind-instrument.

The size of the bird varies considerably, the average length from the tip of the beak to the end of the tail being about eight inches, though at times reaching nine inches. It is a fine bird, neatly shaped, and its plumage is pretty. The whole of the upper part is an olive-brown, deepening somewhat in colour on the head and neck. The fore-neck and breast, which are a golden buff, have a darker tinge on either side, and are thickly marked with triangular oval spots of a very dark almost black brown, reaching from each side of the throat over the chest, and down to the thighs; the throat, however, is a yellowish-white, and nearly free from spots, which are more thickly spread at the sides, gathering in clusters on the breast of some birds; the abdomen and under parts at the base of tail are buffish-white. The wing-coverts are brown, tipped with a reddish-yellow, whilst the rest of the wing is of a dark olive-brown, the under wing-coverts being bright tawny-brown; the tail is also of dark olive-brown, rather slender and rounded at the tip. The beak is dark-brown, except the half of the lower mandible nearest the base, which is yellow. The difference between the sexes is scarcely distinguishable, except, of course, by the song, the hen being mute. Most authorities maintain that the cock is more slender and has a finer beak than the hen, and undoubtedly hens that we have known have without exception all displayed a stouter-built body and quieter demeanour than cocks. As a rule, also, the dark spots on the breast are denser and more evenly distributed than those of a cock, and thus the hen usually makes the best exhibition specimen. The standard properties of an exhibition Song Thrush are—a thick-set well-rounded body, standing well across the perch, the various shades of colour rich and distinct; throat and breast marking distinct, the spots on the breast dense and evenly distributed, running well down the flanks; plumage, feet and toes perfect; steadiness being essential, with nice jaunty confiding movements.

Hand-reared birds or young ones captured soon after they commence to do for themselves are usually the best for exhibition purposes; they can be hand-reared on the same bill of fare as the Missel Thrush and with equal success. When they can feed themselves, they will do well on a staple food of equal parts chicken meal, powdered plain biscuit, and half part finely granulated meat meal, made crumbly moist with water. A few ants' cocoons or dried flies can be added alternately. Occasionally a little finely minced hard-boiled egg should be given instead of the meat meal. Also scraped raw carrot, boiled potato, or finely minced lettuce should be given alternately as recommended for the Missel Thrush. The bird's food, when at liberty, consists of snails, worms and insects, and, in the summer, fruit and whatever berries there are in addition, and so a supply of these should be given as well as the ordinary bill of fare. A meal worm or two occasionally, or two or three grocer's currants soaked and squeezed dry, will not come amiss, and when giving snails do not forget to provide the stone whereon the bird may crack the shell.

A little colour food, just sufficient to tint it, added daily to the food, during the moult, gives lustre and richness to the bird's plumage.

A good roomy cage fitted with perches, etc., as for the Missel Thrush, free access to a roomy bath, and scrupulous cleanliness are all that is necessary to complete good management. A show-cage similar to that for the Missel Thrush is suitable, except that the measurements need not exceed 18 inches long, 16 inches high, and 10 inches deep.

When wild, Thrushes will have as many as three broods during their breeding season, which extends oftentimes from April until July, and though they have as yet not been known to breed in cages, will do so freely in an aviary, if supplied with the necessary nesting materials. They seldom, however, rear more than one brood a year when in confinement. The eggs are generally hatched in fourteen days, and within a fortnight of that time the young will probably leave the nest. While they are rearing young a plentiful supply of live insect food, grubs, etc., should be supplied in addition to the ordinary soft food. If strong healthy birds the young cocks may be expected to make an attempt at singing in a low tone when about six or eight weeks old.

The Redwing.

The Redwing, *Turdus iliacus* (*Linn.*), is the smallest of the six British representatives of the genus *turdus*, and is a most handsome bird. The general colour above is olive-brown, head a darker shade than back, the lesser wing-coverts like the back, the medium and greater coverts darker brown, edged with lighter brown tipped with buffy-white. The inner greater coverts margined with reddish-brown, tail feathers light olive-brown, with an ashy shading. Over each eye there is a streak of yellowish white, and a streak of buff below the eye, the fore-neck, breast and under parts a much whiter shade than the Song Thrush, the markings on the breast being more oblong and as a rule not so evenly distributed as the Thrush, while the sides of the body are washed over as it were with a rich chestnut hue. This brief description will suffice to distinguish this bird from the Song Thrush. The Redwing breeds in Norway and the greater part of the Northern Palæarctic region, and visits these shores in the middle of October or beginning of November, staying with us until the following April or beginning of May. When it arrives it is somewhat shy, keeping to the open country, unless pressed by hunger, when it will approach human habitations in search of food. As it is rather smaller in size than a Thrush, the same kind of cage is well adapted for its keeping. Its food should also be similar, The remark as to the kind of snail eaten by the Missel Thrush applies equally to this bird, as their food when wild is very similar, though a more liberal supply of live food in the shape of snails, meal worms, and other grubs, should be given. Considering that we have no opportunity to procure nestlings, owing to the Redwing not breeding with us, the adult birds become fairly steady in a cage with care and patience, and with its happy contrasts in plumage the Redwing makes a pleasing cage-bird, and also takes kindly to an aviary. It possesses a fine song, though somewhat broken and irregular. Linnæus met with the bird in Lapland, and says, "Its amorous warblings from the top of the spruce-fir were delightful. Its high and varied notes rival those of the Nightingale herself." In length it is about 8 inches. The female is smaller than the male, and her colours are not so bright. The exhfbition properties of the Redwing are good colour, and well-defined markings, combined with size, steadiness, perfect plumage, feet and toes. The show-cage recommended for the Thrush answers well for this bird.

The Fieldfare.

Like the Redwing the Fieldfare, *Turdus pilaris* (*Linn.*), is a visitor to these islands during the winter, and is also gregarious. On their arrival the flocks often betake themselves to the vicinity of berry-bearing trees, where they remain until the crop has been stripped. The fruit of the Mountain Ash, being in season at the time of their arrival, is eagerly sought after. In Norway the Fieldfare is the most common bird, and nests in the spruce-firs.

It is about 10 inches in length. Its plumage is somewhat different to that of the rest of the Thrush tribe. The tip of the bill is darker; and from the base, which is brown, to the eye, the feathers are black; the upper part of the head ash-grey, laced with brown; the neck, ear-coverts, rump, and upper tail-coverts are also ash-grey; the back wings and wing-coverts are a rich chestnut-brown, towards the end of the wing slightly shaded with bluish-grey, which shows more perceptibly during flight; the throat is ochreous-buff, merging on the breast into pale orange-rufous intensified in richness at the sides, the lower throat streaked and breast mottled with dark tippings to the feathers similar to the Thrush, but much denser at the sides of breast, running down on to the flanks. The abdomen and under tail-coverts are greyish-white. The female differs slightly from the male, being rather smaller and slighter; the upper part of the bill is darker, the back less clear in colour, the breast paler and the marking less defined.

The Fieldfare is a charming bird either in cage or aviary, and though somewhat restless, it is not quarrelsome. The exhibition properties are good size, rich colour, well-defined markings, perfect plumage, feet, toes, and steadiness. Its living- and show-cages should be quite as large as those of the Missel Thrush, and with a similar arrangement of vessels, etc. As with others of the Thrush family the caged Fieldfare should not be kept in an overheated room. The Thrush bill of fare is most suitable, but a liberal supply of berries whenever procurable should not be forgotten, and free access to the bath should be secured.

The Blackbird.

A cock Blackbird, *Turdus merula* (*Linn.*), as its name denotes, is jet-black over the whole of its body, wings and tail. The bill, which is an inch long, is of a brilliant orange, showing markedly against its sable plumage; the eyelids or cere are also of the same brilliant yellow, surrounding a bright full dark brown eye. The feet and claws are a very dark brown or black. In length this bird is about 10 inches. The tail is long and slightly rounded. Birds in their wild state lose some of the brilliancy of bill and eye-ceres in winter. The female differs considerably from the male. She is darkish brown on the head, neck and back, having the throat and breast a light rust-colour, the abdomen a paler brown. The bill is brownish-yellow, sometimes with age becoming quite yellow. Cock birds in captivity improve in appearance each year with age so long as they keep in good health. The young are quite easily hand-reared, in the same manner and on the same food as the young Song Thrushes. When fledged they are blackish-brown on the upper parts, each feather being streaked with reddish-brown in the centre; the under parts are a light reddish-brown, tipped with dark spots, which are clearer in the males. When in the nest the sexes of the young may be distinguished by the males having blackish-brown wings and tails, the female's being a lighter brown. When at liberty in its wild state this bird is of a shy and restless disposition, and quickly detects the approach of strangers. It frequents hedgerows, furze, and copses, and may be found in thick shrubberies. It has a peculiar habit, when disturbed, of lying close until the interruption is past, when it will suddenly rise with a frightened screaming cackling noise, darting off to take refuge in the nearest available thicket. The food of the Blackbird at liberty consists chiefly of worms, slugs, caterpillars, beetles, and similar insects; it is also fond of fruit and berries, according to the season of the year. It is particularly destructive amongst cherries, strawberries, currants, gooseberries, apples, and pears; the blackberry, too, furnishes the Blackbird with many a meal.

Blackbirds pair and breed early in the spring. Their nest is composed of coarse roots and grasses with the mud still adhering, which form a strong fabric, moss and dead leaves being interwoven with it at times. Over the mud is an inner lining of fine grasses, forming a smooth bed for the eggs. It may be found in a variety of situations, as the builders are very erratic in their choice; a hedgerow bordering a copse or wood appears to be a favourite position, but they will sometimes build on the stump of a tree, or in a slender fork against the trunk, or even on the ground. The eggs are also very erratic in their colouring, there being seldom two nests alike. The ordinary colour is a light greenish-blue, speckled and streaked with pale reddish-brown, sometimes gathered in a ring towards the larger end, the rest of the egg being faintly covered, or else distributed in an irregular manner over the whole. They are generally four or five in number, though we have found many containing six eggs. Though such a shy bird when at liberty he adapts himself quickly to cage life, and when reared by hand from the nest, the Blackbird is capable of forming strong attachments, and, from his wonderful imitative powers, will make himself a great favourite. He will, if trained when young, learn to whistle almost any tune that may be taught him, if played over to him daily until he is proficient. The melody of his wild song is not surpassed by any of the Thrush tribe. He also makes a charming exhibition bird, hand-reared specimens being preferable. This bird requires quite as large a cage to live in as the Fieldfare, and of the box pattern if you wish to keep his plumage perfect. The same food as recommended for the Song Thrush, with a more liberal supply of fruit, of which Blackbirds are particularly fond, not forgetting insects, snails, worms, and other grubs, and the bath. The Blackbird's exhibition properties are good size and shape, rich jet-black body, colour carrying a nice lustre, beak and eye-cere a rich orange, perfect plumage, feet and toes, also perfect steadiness. A show-cage similar to the Missel Thrush answers well, letting the colour

LESSER REDPOLL
SISKIN LINNET
BULLFINCH

the wings being slightly brighter, except the primary quills, which are dusky-brown; the tail-coverts chestnut, the tail feathers brown, tinted with chestnut, rather long and rounded; the cheeks ashy shading into the sides of the neck; the breast is a dull whitish-grey, slightly tinged with brown, the throat and abdomen pale whitish-grey, the under tail-coverts pale tawny-yellow; the legs (which are rather long) and claws a greyish-brown. The female is somewhat smaller than the male, but the difference between the sexes is very difficult to distinguish, and we would recommend any purchaser to choose a large bird with a bold eye. It has also been held by some authorities that the throat of the male is lighter than that of the female; it may therefore be advisable to keep that point in view.

The stay of the Nightingale in this country is but short. In the early part of April the birds begin to arrive, the males preceding the females sometimes by as many as ten days or even a fortnight, leaving us again towards the end of July and during August for North-eastern Africa. A feature in these birds, worthy of particular notice, is that they invariably, by some inscrutable instinct, fly direct to their last year's nesting-place; only the young of the preceding year straying from the old familiar spot, since they necessarily must choose a fresh situation wherein to build their nest.

The Southern and Eastern districts are most favoured by this welcome visitor, and they are quite plentiful in Surrey, Middlesex, and Essex. The Nightingale's chief charm is its wonderful power of song, almost as loud as that of the Song Thrush in some of its parts, though proceeding from a much smaller bird. The Thrush's song has frequently been mistaken for it, though the notes of the Nightingale are quite distinct from those of the Thrush to any ornithologist. The Nightingale sings not only during the day, but long after darkness has set in, and we have listened to his deep flute-like notes at midnight in a small village in Surrey. His melodious deep "jug, tiuu, tzu, zqua," notes uttered one after the other, are indescribable, though much has been written round them by poets, and to hear the Nightingale at his best is to hear him (for the cocks alone sing) in the stillness of a summer's night, or on a dull warm day, when, answering the song of a rival in a neighbouring coppice, each reply seems to swell in volume, and be given with greater vigour. London is favoured by the Nightingale's presence in some of its well-wooded parks, Epping Forest, in particular, being well patronised, but it must be remembered that the bird sings but little on cold blustery days.

The nest is built principally of dead leaves, usually those of the oak, and grass, the outside being rough, but the inside nicely shaped and rather deep and generally lined with fine grasses and horsehair. It is sometimes built in a hollow in the ground, in the roots or stumps of trees, with a clump of nettles growing round, the nest generally being well down amongst these. It is also found towards the bottom of a hedgerow. The eggs are generally five in number, and of an olive-brown colour, some slightly tinted with green. As soon as the young are hatched, generally in June, the song of the male bird practically ceases, unless the first nest has been taken or destroyed, in which case they immediately commence another, and the singing is continued until the eggs are hatched. The whole time of the parents is then employed in providing their young with food, which is principally composed of small green caterpillars. The food of the adult bird consists of insects, such as caterpillars, small worms, beetles, moths, and flies, and it is particularly fond of fresh or live ants' cocoons.

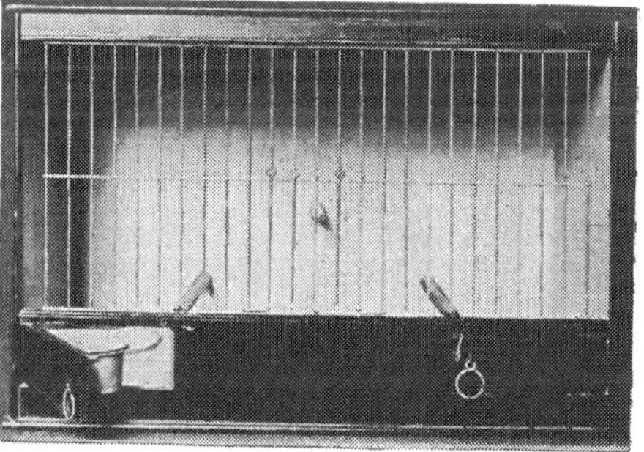

STOCK CAGE FOR INSECTIVOROUS BIRDS.

Young Nightingales can be successfully hand-reared from the age of ten days on a mixture of equal parts hard-boiled egg, minced fine by passing it through a fine sieve, and powdered plain sweet biscuit, and good ants' cocoons, steamed until they have filled out to the size of live cocoons. These three ingredients should be mixed together, moistening only sufficient to a pulp with fresh new milk to last several feeds so that a fresh supply is made up about three times a day, as it is most important that the food should be fresh and sweet. Feed the nestlings with a blunt piece of wood pared down as for feeding Thrushes (or a tooth-pick answers the purpose), and as soon as they cease to gape they have had sufficient for that meal. If two or three well-cleaned gentles cut in half, or a small green caterpillar or two are given in addition several times a day, so much the better, and the birds will thrive and grow apace. In fact we have hand-reared young Nightingales from the age of five days on hard-boiled white of egg alone, cut up into fine shreds about the size of a gentle, feeding every half hour from early dawn until dusk, occasionally dipping some of the shreds of egg into new milk before giving them to the birds. We never lost a youngster, reared in this way, and they grew up as fine and robust as any specimen ever seen in its wild state. Of course their nest (their own by preference) must be kept perfectly clean, clearing away the droppings at each feeding time. The nest should not only be placed in a box (as in the case of Thrushes), but it should also be well surrounded by fine-cut meadow hay, as so frail and brittle are the legs of these birds until they leave the nest, that a fall over its side on to any hard substance is sufficient to fracture a limb (which, by the way, if the accident should happen, quickly re-unites at this early age if properly treated).

SHOW CAGE FOR INSECTIVOROUS BIRDS.

As the young Nightingales get older and commence to feed themselves, a little boiled carrot may be mixed with the food mixture, and the quantity of biscuit gradually increased until it constitutes one half, the remainder being egg, ants' cocoons, and fine granulated meat meal in equal parts, made crumbly moist with milk or water. This diet may be varied by adding a little hard-boiled bullock's liver or heart grated up fine instead of the meat meal or egg occasionally. A further change may be made by adding a little silk-worm pupæ instead of the egg or meat meal occasionally. A little finely grated raw carrot or swede turnip or a little finely minced tender lettuce should be added to the mixture daily before moistening it, as there is a certain amount of moisture in these. A supply of insects, grubs, etc., such as the birds live on in their wild state will be welcomed, and when there is a shortage of these, gentles may be given in their stead, or even a meal worm or two, but the wild food is preferable.

Adult birds are best captured just on their arrival in April, as they then as a rule take more kindly to cage life and food. Young birds captured when they can do for themselves are not difficult to get on to food either; but whether adults or young birds, let them have a box cage about 18 inches long, 12 inches high, and 10 inches deep, with a piece of baize or stout calico stretched tightly across the top for a roof instead of wood. This prevents the birds injuring their heads should they bang up to the top of the cage when first caught, and for the same reason a piece of fine muslin should be hung inside the wire front for a few days. The muslin must be white and very thin so as not to exclude any light. The newly caught Nightingale should be placed so that there is ample light in all parts of its cage, in a quiet room to itself, and be given the food mixture just recommended for young birds past the nesting stage, in a shallow dish inside the cage, with a good supply of live gentles over it to induce the birds to eat. When once they have had a pick or two they will soon be quite safe; but a close watch must be kept that they *do* eat. Those that do not must be taken in the hand several times daily for a day or two, and their beaks opened with the fingers, and two or three live gentles or small green caterpillars slipped in, afterwards passing a finger lightly over the bird's chin and throat, so as to cause the bird to gulp them down. A few feeds in this way generally lead to the food being taken properly, provided a plentiful supply of live gentles be added until they eat the ordinary mixture freely. Close attention in this way for a few days prevents many losses. When the birds have steadied down, they can be kept in the stock cage for small insectivorous birds illustrated on p. 375 (20 inches long, 13 inches high, and 10 inches deep). Some wild caught specimens, though to all appearances males, never break out into song in captivity, while others sing quite freely soon after being caught.

The exhibition properties of a Nightingale are good size and colour, with a nice sheen over its surface; steadiness and perfect plumage, feet and toes. For many years a class has been given for Nightingales and Blackcaps at the Crystal Palace, and when so classified it is an excellent exhibition bird; but when competing in a mixed class against rarer birds in equally good condition its chance of success is not so good. The show-cage illustrated on p. 376, answers well for the Nightingale; but should not be less than 18 inches long, 14 inches high, and 9 inches deep. If preferred, the top portion of the wire front may be made bow shape, and form the front portion of the top of cage for about an inch and a half, as shown in the illustration of a Wagtail or Pipit show-cage. It should be enamelled light holly green inside, and black outside, a piece of blotting-paper should cover the bottom of the cage to absorb the droppings, which should be renewed daily. The rule holds good particularly with this bird, that the nearer the food assimilates to that it would obtain when wild the more healthy the bird will be, and the better its song. In such circumstances a Nightingale will live as long as fifteen years, and in rare cases even longer.

The Red-Spotted Blue Throat.

The general colour of the Red-Spotted Blue Throat, *Cyanecula suecica* (*Dresser*), is dark brown above with olive tint, the basal half of tail feathers orange-chestnut, terminal half blackish-brown, except the two centre ones, which with the tail-coverts are all dark brown. Wing-coverts dark brown and scapulars paler; crown of head verging into umber-brown; lores black with an eye streak of buffy white; feathers below the eye and ear-coverts light brown. Throat rich azure-blue extending down the sides of the neck, and crossing the fore-neck so as to enclose a large chestnut spot on the lower throat; the blue band on the fore-neck is succeeded by a black collar which is again succeeded by a white one, then a broad chestnut one which covers the breast. This blending of colours has a very pleasing effect; the lower breast and abdomen is a dirty white or what might be called smoky-grey; sides of body olive-brown; thighs and under tail-coverts whitish. The throat and chin of the female is white, not blue as the male, surrounded by deep brownish-black, each feather having a pale margin.

This charming little songster, though listed as a British bird is not recognised by the National British Bird and Mule Club as a British bird. At their competitions it must therefore compete in a Continental class. Its occurrences in England have usually been in the southern and eastern counties, generally on the autumn migration, though we remember a very fine specimen being caught near Shields a few years ago on some waste land. It breeds in the high north of Europe, and loves swampy situations. It is a fluent little songster with good variety of song. It takes kindly to cage life, and does well on the diet and in the cage recommended for the Wheatear.

The Wheatear.

To the ornithologist the Wheatear, *Saxicola œnanthe* (*Macg.*), is an interesting bird; it is one of our first spring migrants, arriving early in March, often before the last snow showers of spring have left us. It frequents waste land, pastures, and rocky places, where it may be observed perched on a stump, wall, mound, or stone, on alighting on which the bird has a peculiar bobbing movement of the tail. On approach the bird drops down behind the wall or hedge, flies low, and again appears on the top a few yards in front, only to disappear once more, to rise behind the intruder, and alighting on another of its favourite perches. The young birds never go far from the spot where they were bred during their sojourn here, and though it breeds throughout the British Isles, the Wheatear is more common in the north than the south. The nest is built in holes, disused rabbit burrows, old quarry walls, beneath a ledge of rock, and amongst heaps of rough stones. The eggs are four, five, six, and sometimes even seven in a clutch, and are a delicate greenish-blue of exquisite tint.

The Wheatear's adult plumage harmonises beautifully, though giving plenty of contrast. The adult male is about 6 inches in length; the bill is black; from its base to the eyes, and thence to the ear-coverts, runs a band of black, over which is a similarly shaped streak of white; the forehead is also white; the head, neck, and back are a delicate light slaty-blue grey; the wings are blackish-brown; the upper tail-coverts white; the tail-feathers blackish-brown, those on the outside edge being white towards the roots; the chin, breast, abdomen, and under tail-coverts are very pale greyish-white, delicately tinted with tawny-buff, which colour increases in depth towards the breast and sides. The female has the head, neck, and back brown, tinged with grey; the wings are dark brown, each feather being deeply fringed with light brown; the band on the cheek is brown, and the stripe over the eye tawny; the whole of the under part is pale rufous brown, paler towards the chin and abdomen; the tail is dark brown, tipped with light brown; all except the two centre feathers are white towards the roots; rump white. After the autumn moult the males greatly resemble the females in plumage; they resume their full colour again in the spring. These birds vary very considerably in colour, according to their age and the season of year. In the old birds the grey on the back becomes more decided, the breast whiter, and the brown tints deeper in colour. Hand-reared specimens improve in colour each year as they get older.

The Wheatear is a very difficult bird to thoroughly tame if captured when mature; but kind attention and offering tit-bits from the finger will in most cases overcome its fear and establish confidence; and some of the most perfect specimens seen on the show-bench have been wild-caught specimens. They can, however, be hand-reared from the nest without difficulty, and should be taken when about nine or ten days old. We have reared them on hard-boiled white of egg alone, cut up into fine pieces the size of a gentle (maggot), feeding every half-hour by dropping the shredded egg into their open mouths, giving one drop of milk from the tip of the finger after every second or third mouthful. The nest must be kept perfectly clean from droppings, as explained in the section that dealt with Thrushes. They can also be successfully reared on a mixture of equal parts of hard-boiled egg (minced fine by passing through a fine sieve), powdered sweet biscuit, and good ants' cocoons previously soaked in hot water and mopped dry with a cloth. These ingredients must be mixed together two or three times a day, and then moistened to a pulp with new milk and given to the young birds from a narrow, blunt-pointed piece of wood. The birds should be fed every half-hour from dawn until dusk, and when they cease to gape they have had enough for that meal. It is best to plunge the egg, when sufficiently hard-boiled, into cold water, leaving it there until cold without breaking the shell. By treating the egg thus it remains a better colour, and also retains more moisture than when cooled in a gradual way. Wasp grubs, spiders, small smooth caterpillars, gentles cleaned in sand, and other grubs should be given in moderation between whiles or as one of the meals. As the young birds get older a little boiled carrot may be pulped up with the egg, biscuit, and ants' cocoons. When able to do for themselves the youngsters should be gradually weaned on to a diet of one half powdered plain sweet biscuit, the other half of equal parts of hard-boiled egg, ants' cocoons, and fine granulated meat meal, the whole made crumbly moist with water. Variations can be made by rubbing a little well-boiled cold bullock's heart or liver through a fine grater into a meal and adding to the mixture; and on another day a little silkworm pupæ or a few dried flies, instead of one of the other ingredients. A little finely grated raw carrot, swede turnip, or finely minced heart of a tender lettuce can also be added; but when these moist ingredients are given less water will be necessary, and it is better to add these first. A little finely minced cream cheese or curd added to the food is another variation. A supply of live insects of one kind or another should be given daily, such as gentles which have been well cleaned in sand, beetles, small snails, and other grubs. Crickets, too, are a choice dainty; these and beetles are easily obtained from the neighbouring baker, who will be delighted to know that his greatest nuisances are of some use at last. A meal worm will not come amiss if other live food is scarce. In the summer wasp grubs, flies, and live ants' cocoons are procurable, all of which afford a wide and varied diet, ensuring this bird's good health and condition. The Wheatear in its wild state lives chiefly on insects, small worms, and small snails; therefore if adults or young birds after they can do for themselves are captured, feed thus, and keep them at first in a light but quiet room by themselves, with the cage so placed that they cannot see anyone, but with ample light thrown upon their food. Care must be taken to see that they partake of the food, as some at first sulk and refuse artificial food. In that case they must be fed a few times each day. To do this, catch the bird, open its bill, and slip in two or three well-cleaned gentles, one after the other. As you observe it swallow one down, give another. A few such feeds are usually sufficient to cause an appetite for more, and the bird begins to partake of the food offered it in its cage.

"Meating Off."

Some fanciers have a peculiar recipe for inducing freshly caught birds to take food, which is called "Meating off." It is managed in the following ingenious manner. Some insectivorous food mixture is moistened in the usual way, and for the first day or two a few meal worms, or beetles cut up, are placed amongst it. This mixture is placed in a shallow food vessel. In the middle of this food is placed a large, deep watch-glass, or if that is not obtainable a very small inverted liqueur glass, with the stem broken off. Under the glass are put three or four lively meal worms, whose oft-repeated endeavours to break out of prison attract the attention of the bird. Not understanding how these worms are placed beyond its reach, it continues to peck at them, until by degrees it tastes the food which is artfully rubbed over the sides of the glass. This being palatable, the bird satiates its appetite, and soon feels a zest for more, particularly as his attempts to get at the meal worms always prove abortive. This arrangement is more likely to succeed if a few live gentles are placed in the food as well. The bird will soon eat regularly, and is then termed " meated off." But until it does start eating of its own free will it must be hand-fed as explained. This close attention is only necessary for a very brief period.

A suitable cage for keeping Wheatears in is of the box pattern, 18 inches or 20 inches long, 13 inches high, and 9 inches or 10 inches deep, with three perches, one higher and two lower. Glass or earthenware food and water vessels are hung in a wire frame on the inside of a little wooden door, one of which is arranged at each end of the bottom front bar of cage. Such a cage is illustrated on page 375. Free access to the bath will benefit the bird's health and plumage.

The essential points of an exhibition specimen are: Size, combined with good colour; markings well defined—in which a steady old bird has the advantage of a younger one; plumage, feet, and toes perfect. A suitable show-cage is shown on page 376, and should be 17 inches or 18 inches long, 13 inches high, and 7 inches or 8 inches deep; the colour inside mid green, outside black. Enamel of the same colour can be applied to the stock cage inside, or, if preferred, white.

The Greater Wheatear.

The Greater Wheatear is larger than the Wheatear, and arrives in England about the middle of April. It may be called the Bush Wheatear, for, unlike the Wheatear, it invariably settles on a bush or tree. Many naturalists devote but a passing word to this bird, but it has often come under our notice, although it is of a much wilder nature and not so docile in confinement as its smaller relative, from which its chief distinctions (which it otherwise greatly resembles) are its size; the band which runs from the base of bill to the ear has the feathers edged with brown; the head, neck, and back are shaded with brown; the wings are dark brown, each feather being edged with lighter brown; and the legs and bill are larger even in comparison with the increased size. It can be kept in captivity as successfully as the preceding bird under the same conditions, food, and treatment.

The Isabelline, the Black-Throated, and Desert Wheatears could all be successfully kept in captivity; but though counted as British birds, owing to their rarity in Great Britain (their presence even then being thought accidental) the National British Bird and Mule Club does not include them in its list as being eligible to compete in British bird classes.

The Whinchat, *Pratincola rubetra* (*Dresser*).

The genus *Pratincola* forms an intermediate link between the Chats and Flycatchers. Though difficult to keep, the Whinchat repays all trouble by its handsome appearance and sweet song. The general brown colour above, with darker centres to the feathers, the fringe forming a beautiful lacing of lighter shade; the broad, white eyebrow, commencing at the base of the bill, running well behind the eye; the dark wings, with their contrasting white patch in the greater wing-coverts; the white chin streaks, which run down the side of the light, rufous-coloured throat; the light cinnamon-rufous breast colour, intensified at the sides, toning down to a lighter shade again towards the abdomen; the tail white at the base, except the two centre feathers, which, together with the rest of the tail, are brown, edged with lighter brown, bill and feet black—all go to make up an attractive bird, which is about 5 inches in length. The hen differs from the cock in that the streaks over the eyes are buff instead of white, the sides of the breast and throat much paler, and the back browner. It is a summer migrant, not arriving until late in April, leaving us again early in October—even before this if the weather is unfavourable—for a warmer clime in North-East Africa.

It is lively and cheerful when at liberty, living on heaths, commons, railway embankments, or amongst furze, retiring from these haunts in the autumn, and visiting arable lands and cornfields, where it may be seen sitting on the sheaves or hanging to the ears of corn, from which habit it is known in some districts by the name of " Barleyear." It may often be found at that time of year in the fields of mangel-wurzel or between cabbage rows, searching for insects; and quickly attracts attention by its well-known call-note, *U-tack, U-tack*.

It can be successfully kept in captivity on the food recommended for the Wheatear, and a similar cage answers well. It should be kept in a genial temperature during the winter months, but at all times have plenty of fresh air. When first placed in confinement, it is very difficult to induce this bird to partake of the ordinary food, and it therefore requires special care and attention. It should first be enticed with gentles mixed with its food, or small beetles and flies, and kept in a light, quiet room. If it does not take food at first, it must be caught and given two or three clean gentles in the same manner as the Wheatear, three or four times a day, and in time it will take to the food mixture quite freely. At all times a liberal supply of live insect food should be given. Live gentles are excellent for this bird, and the young may be successfully hand-reared from ten days old on these and white of hard-boiled egg alone, shredded up fine as for the Wheatear, and fed at similar intervals, giving the gentles for one meal and the egg the next and so on. As they get older gradually wean them on to the adult food mixture. Flies are an especial luxury, and should be given whenever procurable. The birds should be allowed free access to the bath.

The exhibition points of a Whinchat are: Good colour; well-defined markings, combined with perfect plumage, feet, and toes. Steadiness is most essential, and a well-matured specimen with these merits would naturally take precedence over an immature specimen, even though it possessed these points of merit. The show-cage is the same as that for the Wheatear.

The Stonechat.

The ways and habits of the Stonechat, *Pratincola rubicola* (*Dresser*), are very like those of the Whinchat. It is a frequenter of dry heaths and commons, where it may be seen perched on a topmost spray of furze or brushwood, uttering its peculiar call, *U-tack*. From thence it will suddenly dart to the ground in pursuit of some insect, and just as suddenly return to the spray it had quitted. It also flutters in the air at a slight elevation, and there sings its pretty little song. It is generally resident in the British Isles, though many migrate. Its length is about 5¼ inches. The head, cheeks, and throat of the male bird are black, slightly shaded with brown; the back is black, the feathers of which are edged with brown; the upper tail-coverts white, speckled with blackish-brown and margined with a light rufous colour; the tail feathers blackish-brown; the wings also blackish-brown, with sandy-brown margins; the tertials white; the sides of the neck white; the breast rich chestnut-brown, shading lighter until it becomes almost yellowish-white on the abdomen, vent, and under tail-coverts. The female has the whole of her upper part dusky brown, feathers edged with buff; the upper tail-coverts rufous, with black centre (not white, like the male); tail feathers dark brown, with whitish edging; eyelid whitish; chin and throat blackish-brown, spotted with white; the breast very light chestnut-brown, and the white space on the neck and wings of smaller extent than in the male.

In the wild state the Stonechat's food consists of insects and their larvæ, and worms; the former are taken on the wing, after the manner of the Flycatchers. It is a delicate bird if captured as an adult, and will seldom live through the moult, even if kept till then. It may, however, be reared from the nest quite as successfully as the Whinchat and on the same food. A young bird of the season, captured soon after it is doing for itself, may sometimes be "meated off," and turn out well if great care and attention are bestowed on it. They must be treated and fed like the Wheatear, and the same cages answer well. A cock in adult plumage is a handsome fellow, and makes a good exhibition bird if steady, as the beautiful blending of colours can then be seen to full advantage. The richer the colour, combined with well-defined markings, perfect plumage, feet, toes, and steadiness, the greater the chance of success on the show bench. The more live insects, grubs, etc., this bird has, with free use of the bath, the better will be its condition.

The Redstart.

The Redstart, *Ruticilla phœnicurus* (*Macg.*), arrives in the British Isles early in April, and departs during September or early in October, according to the season. It is a handsome bird, in length about 5¼ inches; the bill is black, except for its yellow corners and inside; the forehead is white, this colour extending in a line over the ear-coverts; the neck and back are slaty-grey, slightly tinged with red; the rump and upper tail-coverts orange-chestnut; greater coverts and primary quills dusky-brown, with the narrow outer fringe rather lighter; ear-coverts, sides of face, chin, throat, and fore-neck black, the feathers being generally slightly edged with grey; the breast, sides, and upper part of the abdomen are rich orange-chestnut; the lower portion of the abdomen below the tail-coverts orange-buff, being clouded with white; the tail feathers a rich orange chestnut, the outer webs darker, with the two centre feathers dark brown.

The female, unlike most birds of this class, differs materially from her mate. She is a trifle smaller; the upper part of the body is a uniform greyish-brown, the chin and throat dusky white, the breast a dull sandy-brown, the wings lighter than those of the male, and the tail not so bright. The adult males in winter, as also the young males of the year after their autumn moult, lack the white forehead, the feathers being edged with brown ; the chin, throat, and breast are variegated with whitish-grey ; the upper part of the body pale reddish-brown tinged with grey. The pale margins, which cover much of the richer colour, disappearing in the spring, when the full beauty of the summer plumage is visible. Birds in captivity, if kept in nice, cosy quarters, not infrequently display their summer plumage through the greater part of the winter.

This clean, handsomely coloured bird frequents the outskirts of woods and plantations (particularly those of considerable age), old gardens, orchards, parks, and grazing land where there are sheds for cattle and boundary walls in rather a state of neglect, and where the trees have been allowed to decay. In the holes of these and chinks of the old walls and sheds will its nest be found, but always with its pretty blue eggs well concealed. It is rare that we have visited such spots without finding a nest and seeing a pair of these birds. By their quick, yet silent motion, they give rise to an impression of solitariness ; and during the period of incubation the cock generally perches on some old stump or branch, shaking its tail with a peculiar trembling motion, and, when disturbed, flits downwards, keeping low along the cover or hedge to another favourite perching place, then as quickly back to the old one. It sometimes chooses the most sequestered spots for nesting, and at other times even building in a hole in the wall of an old inhabited house. The Redstart has a very pretty song, although composed of but few notes. It becomes very tame in captivity, although when free a very timid bird. When alighting on a perching place the tail is given a peculiar short, sharp vibration, not up and down like that of the Wheatear or Whinchat.

We kept and successfully exhibited this bird twenty-five years ago, and have a particular leaning to hand-reared specimens for exhibition purposes. Where a good classification is given and they have not to compete against rarer birds, a good specimen will usually make its mark.

Redstarts are easily hand-reared and kept afterwards on the food recommended for the Chats, with the addition of a small green caterpillar or two. The same stock and show cages answer equally well for the Redstart. In its wild state the bird feeds principally on ants and their larvæ, flies, and moths, worms, spiders, caterpillars, and beetles. It will catch flies and moths on the wing as well as when on the ground, and a supply of insect food should therefore always form part of their diet ; they are also fond of ripe pear and small, soft fruits. They should be kept during the winter months in a genial temperature.

As soon as the young birds are fledged and the tail feathers appear, the youngsters hop on to any branch adjoining their nest, and the parent birds feed them there until able to forage for themselves. They are not difficult to " meat off " if captured when able to do for themselves, if given the same care and attention as the Wheatear.

The exhibition points of a Redstart are : Good size ; the various shades of colour, rich and well defined ; steadiness ; and perfect plumage, feet, and toes.

The Black Redstart.

The Black Redstart, *Ruticilla titys* (*Newton*), is not black, as its name would indicate. Its general colour above is a bluish-grey ; rump and upper tail-coverts orange-chestnut ; head the same colour as the back, running a little lighter in shade towards the forehead ; forehead, face, throat, fore-neck, and breast black, the latter with grey margins, giving the black the appearance of being lightly frosted ; sides of the body and flanks bluish-grey ; abdomen light greyish-white ; under tail-coverts cinnamon ; wing-coverts blackish, edged with bluish-grey ; primary quills blackish-grey ; tail orange-chestnut, except the two centre feathers, which are amber-brown.

The hen differs from the male in that her general colour is slaty-brown, with a slight olive tint on the back ; rump and tail-coverts chestnut ; tail the same colour, with brown tips. The male Black Redstart is distinguished from the Redstart by its black forehead and breast, but resembles that bird much in size and habits, except that it prefers stony ground or chalk cliffs. It also frequents gardens, farmyards, and manure heaps in the fields. It is a rare, but regular visitor to this country, chiefly along the southern coast ; and, unlike the Redstart, arrives in the autumn, spends the winter here, and returns in the spring to its breeding quarters in Central and Southern Europe, and is a common bird in Germany and France.

It is not at all difficult to keep, and may be fed and treated precisely as the Redstart, the same care being taken in " meating off " freshly caught specimens, as explained for the Wheatear.

The exhibition points of a Black Redstart are : Good size ; well-defined colours, brilliant in their respective shades ; perfect plumage, feet, and toes ; combined with steadiness. Good specimens, as a rule, succeed at exhibitions.

CHAPTER XXXVII

WARBLERS, ACCENTORS, ETC.

SUB-FAMILY SYLVIIDÆ

The Whitethroat.

THE Whitethroat, *Sylvia cinerea* (*Macg.*), arrives in April, and usually leaves towards the end of September, to winter in Africa. It is the most common of all the Warblers in England. It generally frequents hedgerows, gardens, the edges of woods, thickets, or any brushwood, where it may be seen sitting on a spray of the bramble, through which a clump of nettles is growing. This is a favourite nesting-place, though any low thick herbage or hedge-bank is also chosen. Owing to its nest often being suspended in the nettles the Whitethroat has gained in many country districts the name of " Nettle Creeper." The bird has a habit of raising the feathers on the top of its head like a crest when perched, whence it will rise fluttering in the air to a height of sometimes about 30 feet, singing its merry little song, and then suddenly and silently drop to the bush. When disturbed, though keeping out of sight, the Whitethroat gives a continual alarm call.

The bird is very sprightly, rather slightly built, and about 5½ inches in length. The beak is horn-brown, the head and neck slaty-grey ; the back grey, deeply tinged with brown ; the tail, dark greyish-brown, slightly edged with pale umber-brown, the two outer feathers being greyish-white, which are distinctly perceptible in flight. The wings are dark brown, each feather being edged with a light umber-brown. The throat and abdomen are white ; the breast, sides and vent very pale grey, delicately tinted with a beautiful rosy-pink.

In captivity the colour brightens with age, and we presume the same is the case with birds at liberty. The colours of the female are more subdued, particularly the edging to the quills, and the pinkish tint on the breast is sometimes entirely absent. During the winter months the slaty-colour of the head and pinkish tint on the breast of the male birds disappear, the colour resembling then that of a hen, the summer plumage being regained the following spring.

The Whitethroat takes readily to cage life, and does well on the food recommended for the Redstart, and may also be kept and shown in similar cages to that bird. It can also be hand-reared in the same way as described for a Wheatear. In its wild state the Whitethroat feeds entirely on insects, small green caterpillars and small fruits. A supply of these should therefore be given with ripe fruit in season during the winter, fruit being very beneficial to all such birds in captivity.

The exhibition points of the Whitethroat are good size and colour, perfect plumage, and superb condition. With these essentials, where a class is given for the more common small insectivorous birds, it is not at all a bad exhibition bird, and is an interesting pet.

The Lesser Whitethroat.

The Lesser Whitethroat, *Sylvia curruca* (*Newton*), is another summer visitor, but is not so widely distributed as the Whitethroat. It is most numerous in the Southern and Midland counties, and is of a more retiring nature, though nesting in similar situations, and low thick hedgerows. As its name indicates, it is a smaller bird, though not to any remarkable extent, being just over 5 inches in length. The Lesser Whitethroat has the bastard-primaries longer than the primary-coverts, in which it differs from the Common Whitethroat. In colour, the head, nape, and rump, are light bluish-grey ; back, mouse-grey ; wings and tail, brocali-brown ; coverts edged with yellowish-brown ; the outer web and tips of the three exterior tail feathers white ; throat and centre of abdomen pure white, with a reddish tint on the breast and sides, and a shade of pink over the whole ; flanks, yellowish-brown, shaded with pink. The female differs from the male by having the brown on the back extended to the crown, and is more subdued in tone throughout, and smaller.

This elegant little bird is well worth keeping, as it will become very tame and attached to the person who attends it. Its song also, though rather weak, is full of variety and very pleasing. The same food and cages as for the preceding bird are suitable, and the fruit and ripe berries when procurable must not be forgotten. The Lesser Whitethroat is equally interesting, either for exhibition or as a pet, though in competition, like the greater Whitethroat, it has not much chance against rarer and more gorgeously coloured Warblers, and hence our citing its proper place as in a class for the more common small insectivorous birds.

The Blackcap.

The Blackcap, *Sylvia atricapilla* (*Macg.*), like the Nightingale, sometimes arrives in England from early in April up to the middle or even end of that month. It is pretty generally distributed over England and Wales, becoming rarer in Scotland, though well distributed on the Borders and in Cumberland. It leaves us in August or September, although some few stragglers apparently spend the winter with us at times. The male Blackcaps usually precede the females in arrival, and also, like the Nightingale, they can be found in the same local spots year after year. The beak is shaped similarly to the Nightingale's, its colour dark horn-brown, paler beneath, the edges yellowish-grey, the inside of the mouth bluish-grey. Its distinguishing characteristic is a jet-black cap or hood on the crown of its head, which has earned for it in Germany the name of the "Monk." The cheeks and nape of the neck are slatish-grey ; the back and wing-coverts are ash-grey, shaded with olive-brown ; the pinions and tail are dark brown, edged with the same colour as the back ; the breast is light slatish-grey, paler towards the throat and abdomen. The female differs from her mate, inasmuch as she is a trifle *larger*, while the cap on the head is a chocolate-brown, the other parts of the body being slightly tinged with brown.

The song of the Blackcap is so agreeable, first a few notes sounding as if at a distance, then bursting into beautiful sustained melody, that it is called the "Mock Nightingale." Its tones are loud, yet sweet, and especially flute-like, the fullness of the song being remarkable in a bird smaller even than the Nightingale. The average length of the bird is about 5¾ inches. The Blackcap nests in some secluded copse, undergrowth, or orchard ; it is shy and rather restless ; a slight noise or the intrusion of a stranger will silence its song in a moment, and it will take itself off to a more secluded spot so quietly that its flight is quite unobserved. While breeding, when wild, it is also somewhat pugnacious, and will hardly ever breed very near to another pair. Its nest is found amongst honeysuckle, nettles, overgrowing brambles, low hedges, or small bushes, generally near the ground, but never on it ; the bird has been known to build in gooseberry and currant bushes. The nest is lightly built of thin bents of dry grass and fibrous roots, with sometimes a little moss and scantily lined with horse-hair. The eggs are usually five in number, and there is great variation in their colour and markings, but they are generally of a dull-white, lightly tinged with green, mottled with grey and light brown, mingled with a few spots of darker brown. We have sets of eggs in our collection with a decided grey-brown ground colour, faintly clouded here and there with a darker patch ; others of a rich salmon pink ground colour, spotted and streaked with rich red, faintly tinged with brown, and also have various other shades, showing the variation that exists. The male Blackcap assists the hen in the duties of incubation, and they sit very closely. The plumage of the young is very similar to that of the adult female, the distinctive features of the males not showing until after the first moult.

The young can be successfully hand-reared on the same food as young Nightingales, and the adult bird can be fed and treated in the same way as that bird, but let a liberal supply of ripe fruit at all seasons be included in the bill of fare for the Blackcap. In its wild state it is very partial to elderberries, currants, raspberries, and green figs. In the early part of the season caterpillars, spiders, flies, and other insects form its chief food, so that these, when procurable, should be added to the menu. The Blackcap is very fond of bathing. It should have a cage similar to that of a Nightingale, and is not a difficult bird to keep. It is a charming pet, being a lusty songster in captivity without any harshness. At large exhibitions this bird and the Nightingale usually have a class allotted to them, so that they compete together on common ground.

The exhibition properties of a Blackcap are good size and colour, cap large jet black, with a nice gloss ; steadiness ; perfect plumage, feet, and toes. The show cage recommended for the Nightingale, but one size smaller, answers well for Blackcaps. They are also quite sociable inmates of a group aviary of small insectivorous birds ; but the males do not appear to sing so freely under such conditions as they do in a cage.

The Garden Warbler

The Garden Warbler, *Sylvia hortensis* (*Bech.*), is another summer visitor, though it does not arrive until the beginning of May and departs again in August or September. In colour, the whole of the upper part of the body is olive-brown ; the wings and tail darker brown, slightly edged with lighter brown ; above the eye is a faint streak of buff ; the under parts are grey, much paler on the abdomen, and tinged with pale reddish-grey on the breast and flanks deepening in colour towards the vent; the feet, toes and claws, lead-colour. The female is scarcely distinguishable from the male; a little lighter colour on the back, and a more uniformly brownish-grey on the under part being the only difference.

Although rather a common bird, the Garden Warbler is not very generally known on account of its retiring disposition; and perhaps, also, from the fact that its plumage is not very striking it has often escaped notice. Though a visitor to most parts, it is more locally distributed than the Blackcap, though it extends farther north than that bird. Its exceedingly fine song, however, places it next the Blackcap as a songster, the notes being especially deep and flute-like, and usually delivered from some elevated position such as the top of a tree. The song will last almost uninterruptedly for nearly half an hour; it is somewhat irregular in time and tone, but it is certainly very sweet. If disturbed or alarmed the bird will immediately cease singing, and drop stone-like from its perch to the thicket, whence it makes its way, by hopping or flitting, out of reach.

THE DARTFORD WARBLER.

The Garden Warbler is a small bird rather more stoutly built than a Blackcap, but not quite so long. It frequents gardens, orchards, and woods; the nest is built near the ground in a secluded spot, amongst nettles, in bramble bushes or traveller's-joy when densely matted, or in shrubberies with plenty of overhanging foliage. The eggs are four or five in number, very similar to those of the Blackcap, except that the markings are coarser in appearance. The Garden Warbler's main food consists of caterpillars and insects, as well as their larvæ. In the summer it will be found in the gardens feeling upon currants, raspberries, and other soft-skinned fruit; it is also very fond of elderberries.

Though generally avoiding observation the Garden Warbler is not a wild bird, and will take kindly to a cage, which should be such as described for the Nightingale. It will agree well with other birds, especially those of its class. It is not at all difficult to meat off, the only fear being that it will get over-fat, having a tendency to that when in captivity, and it is then, though apparently in the best of condition, likely to go off in a fit without any warning. It does well on the Blackcap diet; but quite one-half the menu should consist of ripe fruit all the year round, which will avert this over-fat tendency. Thus fed, the bird will live for years in the best of condition and cheer all with its song.

As with all the Warblers, variety of food is a great feature in the treatment, and attention to this alone may add several years to their life. All the longest-lived birds we have known received very frequent changes of diet, and with such care bestowed on it the Garden Warbler will not unfrequently sing, with a very slight interval, during the whole of the year.

It is a useful bird for exhibition, though not often shown, and, as usual, good size, colour, and perfect plumage with steadiness are essentials. A show cage similar to that for the Blackcap answers well. Garden Warblers, it is needless to say, like those already treated of, require to be kept in a cosy room during the winter, though it should not be hot or stuffy.

The Dartford Warbler.

The Dartford Warbler, *Sylvia undata* (*Saunders*), is resident with us throughout the year in the Southern counties, stretching westward as far as Cornwall, and is probably the rarest of our British Warblers. It derives its name from the fact that it was first discovered by Dr. Latham in 1773 near Dartford, in Kent, as a separate species, though, owing to its skulking habits, keeping well under cover in its wild state away from habitation on the furze- and heather-clad commons, its numbers may not be quite so limited as is asserted by most naturalists. The bird is rather difficult to obtain, but could this difficulty be surmounted, no doubt many aviculturists would be delighted to keep specimens in order thoroughly to investigate their nature and habits. We had the pleasure of closely inspecting two living specimens in captivity in 1910, one exhibited by Mr. J. Frostick, and the other by the Hon. Mrs. Bourke. Mr. Frostick's bird was then in mature plumage. The general colour above is blackish with a covering of brownish purple-red; the wings and tail assume a rich clove-brown, and the tail a darker shade than the wings; the cheeks and auriculars are grey; the throat, upper breast, and flanks are like the back, but the throat-feathers are faintly tipped with tiny white spots, forming a faint streak; the brownish purple-red becomes paler at the vent, shading to greyish clove-brown on the upper tail-coverts; the centre of the abdomen is white. The tail is of extraordinary length for so small a bird, and is cuneated, having the outer feather tipped with greyish-white, and about half an inch shorter; the others graduate from this; the iris and eyelid are orange-yellow; the feet and claws sienna-yellow. The female is similar to the male, but paler and more ashy brown. The total length is 5 inches.

A more active, sprightly, cheerful little bird it would be impossible to find; it is quite at home in a cage and a most rare exhibition bird. It is always on the go, elevating its crest the while, and in its hop from perch to perch it is inclined to take the wires as an intermediate perch, but this does not appear to injure the plumage, which in the birds we saw was superb, not a feather disarranged or damaged. These birds were hand-reared by a Mrs. Smith, in Hampshire. Mr. Frostick wrote of them in *Canary and Cage Bird Life*, Oct. 1st, 1909, as follows: "The three Dartford Warblers in my possession were taken from the nest on July 15th last, and successfully reared on live ants'-eggs (or cocoons), and then gradually accustomed to my insectivorous birds' food, which is now their principal diet. Like all other birds they are fond of meal-worms, but I am afraid to supply these except in the most frugal manner, as my experience teaches me that they are most dangerous food when given *ad lib.* for any of the tiny Warblers or Tits; live ants'-eggs, caterpillars, garden insects, and house flies are the best and safest tit-bits to supply. I have tried them with fruit, and I find they readily take to banana, which must be beneficial to them. As the opportunity occurs I shall offer various other fruits and wild berries in season."

A letter from Mr. Smith, husband of the lady who reared the three birds, published by Mr. Frostick in the same journal, reads: "The Dartford Warbler is one of the earliest birds to pair up. It nests early in April, and again about the end of June or the early part of July—two nests a year. This year (1908) they were later than usual. I found three young ones on August 21st last, the latest I have ever seen any. They feed their young on a little smooth green caterpillar, and spiders that they find on the gorse-bushes, but what they live on in winter is a mystery to me, unless it is some sort of insect life underneath the heather or gorse. They are very Wren-like in their habits; in winter they pop up in the heather when you disturb them, and down in the heather again and creep away for yards. The breeding season is the best time to see them; they are not shy then. The cock bird is especially saucy, with his pretty little song and funny habit of flying in the air, spreading out his long tail. The song is not unlike that of the White-throat. I believe they are very hardy birds. Their greatest enemy is the frequent common fires, which destroy a great many."

Mr. Frostick in the same journal described a visit he paid to Mr. Smith to see the birds in their wild haunts—clumps of gorse or furze dotted amongst great stretches of heather and bracken. "Writers of bird books," says Mr. Frostick, "all state that the Dartford Warbler's nest is placed in the centre of a furze-bush, but Mr. Smith assures me that all that he has found, and those he showed me, were in the heather about a foot from the ground and about ten paces from the gorse, which seems to be used as a playground. The nest is composed of the long stalks of goose-grass, entwined with the young and tender branches of the furze. The outside is ornamented with what at first sight looks like little balls of wool, but on closer inspection they are found to be the silken bags that spiders make for the reception of their eggs. Probably these self-same eggs, together with their producers, form no small part of the bird's larder. The eggs are greenish white, with olive or reddish-brown markings. As a cage bird the Dartford Warbler appears to me to be everything one could desire—beautiful in form and colouring, graceful and active in movement, and with a pleasing little song. From the fact that they are resident birds they ought to be fairly hardy, at least quite as much so as the various Tits and Wrens which we have kept and moulted for years past with little difficulty. As exhibition birds they will doubtless render a good account of themselves."

On October 15th, 1909, Miss Florence Burn wrote to *Canary and Cage Bird Life* giving her experience in rearing and keeping the Dartford Warbler, which was as follows: "I hand-reared two in June, 1905. One drowned itself in an attempt to wash a little more than a week after it could feed itself. The other I kept until the August of 1906, when it was killed by a girl shutting the cage door on its leg and breaking it. This bird was very tame. I used to have nearly every boy in the Church Sunday-school up to see it. It used to come out and jump up their fingers like going up a ladder. Lots of men came to see it, too, and wanted me to show it. Although I have kept birds almost all my life I never exhibit. Though tame and friendly my bird was very nervous, and dropped off its perch in a faint when 'Poole's Diorama,' in a hall opposite our house, was firing salutes, but when I held him in my hand he was all right. How I came by the birds was in this wise: A boy who delivered bread at our house brought me an egg he had found on the outskirts of his garden (a lodge about a mile distant). The nest was built amongst nettles, though there was a lot of furze about; it was built of grasses and very soft furze. It was so thin one could scarcely expect it to last while the young were reared. I at once recognised the egg—and it is still in my possession—something like a White-throat's, only smaller and more elongated and the markings much finer, forming a darker ring round the large end. I asked the boy to get me the young, which in due time he did. Two young birds and an addled egg. This one I could not blow, as the outside shell had already began to peel off. As they were the very first small Soft-bills I had attempted to rear I had nothing in the house to feed them on, and no shops open, as it was six in the morning. However, I chopped some raw beef finely and made some sops. For the first half-hour they would not gape. I, however, opened their beaks and dropped in a tiny morsel of beef; after that it was all plain sailing. They were the easiest Soft-bills to rear I have ever tried, and I have reared many Soft-bills since, including a perfectly White Thrush."

From these experiences it is plain that the Dartford Warbler can be kept successfully in captivity to a good age on practically any good insectivorous food and a supply of ripe fruit, such as bananas, pears, and raspberries, ants' cocoons, live insects, small green caterpillars, or a few well-cleaned live gentles in addition, thereby varying the diet and at the same time making it nearly the natural food. A box-pattern cage suits this bird well, such as that for the Nightingale; but it must be a little closer wired. A similar show-cage to that shown on page 376 is required. Good-coloured, well-matured birds, perfect plumage, and steadiness are the essential features for exhibition specimens.

The Chiffchaff.

The Chiffchaff, *Phylloscopus rufus* (*Bechst*), though one of our most diminutive songsters, is one of the first of the summer warblers to reach this country; it is only preceded by the Wheatear, and arrives often by the middle of March. It may be seen early in the spring flitting about in shady woods, bushes and hedgerows, uttering its fussy *chiff-chaff*, which is practically the sum and substance of its song, though as the breeding season advances it at times sharpens the note into *chivvy-chavvy.* It is from these notes that it derives its name, and they are so plainly uttered as never to be mistaken if once heard. The notes are sweet and musical, and may be heard for some time before the songster is located, for the bird's motionless attitude when perched on the slender bough of a tall tree, and the similarity of its plumage to some of the tints of the surrounding foliage often delude the eye for a considerable time. The nest is generally placed on the ground or on a tuft or low, stunted bush, or amongst straggling branches, half covered with dead grass. The nest is as a rule half dome-shape, and it is a pretty sight to watch the industrious little parents flitting backwards and forwards attending to the needs of a young brood. We have stood quietly within a couple of yards of the nest, and the birds have continued to feed the little mites as if no one were near.

The colour of the male bird is—upper parts dull olive-green, shading to oil-green tint on the rump. Wings and tail dusky- or hair-brown, edged with olive-green, the eyebrow streaked with yellowish white, but faint and undefined; the underparts pale primrose-yellow, shading into olive-green on the side of neck and breast; under wing-coverts rich sulphur-yellow; feet and claws blackish-brown. The colour of both sexes are similar, except that the males are a little brighter colour, and the hen has the shorter bill of the two.

The Chiffchaff is not at all a difficult bird to adapt to cage-life, and will do well on similar food to the Dartford Warbler. It may also be kept and shown in similar cages, and as it is seldom seen at exhibitions it would have a good chance of success if steady and in perfect plumage.

The Willow Warbler.

The Willow Warbler, *Phylloscopus trochilus* (*Newton*), also known as the Willow Wren, is a summer visitor to nearly every part of the British Isles and Europe, arriving a few days later than the Chiffchaff, usually by the end of March, and leaving again for Africa about the end of September or beginning of October. It is not unlike the Chiffchaff in appearance, though the wing of that bird is much rounder, but it is best distinguished by the colour of its feet and claws, which are light brown. There is very little difference between male and female, the latter being a shade smaller and a little more tinged with brown above and having the yellow of the under parts less clear, but even when side by side this difference is very slight.

The Willow Warbler inhabits woods, copses, plantations, shrubberies, thick hedgerows, and bushes or furze on commons and hills, building its nest upon the ground. It is a pretty and lively bird, quite amusing in its actions, flying or hopping from branch to branch, capturing any small insect that comes in its way. It has a very soft and pleasing song, not unlike the Robin's, though not so powerful; it does not possess much variety, yet has the advantage in its favour of being commenced in the early morning and continuing with slight intermissions until the fall of evening.

Like the preceding bird, it is capable of being easily tamed, and will then feed from the hand, or if allowed to range the room will pursue and capture the flies, or peck them off the walls and ceiling. It should be kept in winter in a moderately warm room, and should be fed and kept in a similar cage to that for the Chiffchaff; it may also be shown in a similar show-cage and is an equally useful bird for exhibition purposes.

The Yellow-browed Warbler.

The Yellow-browed Warbler, *Phylloscopus superciliosus* (*Newton*), is a charming little bird. It has olive-green plumage running into yellowish-green on the rump; the medium and greater wing-coverts are tipped with yellow, forming into bands, with a distinct eye-stripe of pale yellow; the under parts are ashy-whitish, with streaks of yellow on the breast. It could be kept in captivity equally as successfully as the Willow Warbler, and on a similar diet. Were it a more regular visitor to our isles (only casual specimens have visited us up to the present) it would not have to compete with Continental birds. It is a smaller bird than the preceding one.

The Wood Warbler.

The Wood Warbler, *Phylloscopus sibilatrix* (*Newton*), is also kown as the Wood Wren. It arrives in this country towards the end of April or the beginning of May, and is found in most parts of England, Wales and Scotland. It frequents plantations and woods, giving a decided preference to beech. It lives almost entirely among the trees, being seldom seen at any great distance from them, and hardly ever on the ground. Its presence is soon made known by its well-known *chit-chit, chit-chit-chitee*, followed by a long run similar to *tr-tr-tr-tr-tr-tre*, the latter swelling in force and making the woodland echo. When not singing the bird is usually examining the leaves above and below with minute scrutiny for insects, which it catches on the wing. It is a very handsome bird, and though somewhat similar in plumage to the Chiffchaff and Willow Warbler, is decidedly brighter in colour with more contrast. The whole of the upper part is olive-green, tinged with sulphur-yellow; this latter is more pronounced on the rump; from the base of the bill, over the eye to the ear-coverts, runs a narrow streak of yellow, underneath which is a brownish line; the chin, throat and breast are yellow, inclining to a silvery-white on the abdomen; the wings and tail are brown, each feather being edged with greenish yellow.

It can be successfully kept in captivity on the same food and in similar cages to those recommended for the preceding birds. The more live food is supplied in the shape of insects, live ants' cocoons, grubs, small caterpillars, gentles and such-like the more perfect will be the diet, with consequent longevity of the bird and high condition of colour and plumage.

The nest is spherical, and built upon the ground, sometimes under a tuft of grass or amongst beech leaves, of which the external portion of the nest is often composed; it is lined with horsehair. The eggs are very pretty, with a white ground colour thickly dotted with dark, purplish brown and underlying spots of violet-grey.

The Wood Warbler becomes exceedingly tame, and may be induced to perch on the hand and take flies or other dainty morsels. The show-cage recommended for the Willow Warbler answers well for this bird, which is also a welcome addition to an aviary of the smaller Warblers, but in winter it must be kept in genial, cosy quarters.

The Reed Warbler.

The Reed Warbler, *Acrocephalus streperus* (*Newton*), arrives about the same time as the Wood Warbler, and is quite common in the southern and midland counties as well as Wales, in localities favoured with reed and willow beds. From its retiring habits amongst the reeds and willows, which are its breeding haunts, it is not often seen, but its song may be heard through the greater part of a light summer's night, when warm and calm. The bird is just over 5 inches in length, and in general colour above is not unlike the Nightingale, though much smaller, as will be noted by the length; it has a white streak over the eye, whilst the breast is lighter, and the back and tail not so rich a brown. The nest, composed of dried grasses and wool, is built suspended between three or four reeds or woven to the stalks of aquatic plants over a ditch or stream, and is frequently so fragile as to almost touch the surface of the water as the reeds or plants are swayed by a gust of wind. This bird will thrive well in captivity on a bill of fare such as that given for the Wood Warbler, and may also be exhibited in a similar cage. Though sober in colour, it is a pleasing acquisition to an aviary of small insectivorous birds.

The Marsh Warbler.

The Marsh Warbler, *Acrocephalus palustris* (*Dresser*), is one of our latest summer visitors, not arriving until the middle of May and leaving again about the end of August. It is very rare, and appears to be largely confined to Somersetshire and the surrounding districts. Possibly far more of these birds visit us than we think, owing to its similarity in colour and appearance to the Reed Warbler. It may, however, be distinguished from this bird by its more olive-tinted plumage and the absence of the russet-brown rump colour, which is always more or less in evidence on the Reed Warbler. It is a more fluent songster than that bird, and, like it, a great mimic of other birds' songs. It certainly would be a most successful exhibition bird owing to its rarity, and may in every way be treated in captivity as its predecessor in these pages, and shown in a similar cage. Steadiness and perfect plumage are essential to success on the show-bench. It would also make a welcome addition to the aviary with other small insectivorous birds.

The Sedge Warbler.

The Sedge Warbler, *Acrocephalus phragmitis* (*Seebohm*), stays much longer with us than the Marsh Warbler, arriving towards the end of April and remaining to the end of September, when it leaves to winter in South Africa. It apparently breeds everywhere, and is not confined to the sedges, as its name might indicate; it frequents reed-brakes and willow-holts, moist meadows surrounded with underwood, the margins of rivers fringed with brush or tall aquatic plants, and young woods planted in low, damp lands. When passing near these spots, this little bird may be heard rattling off such song as it possesses well into the clear summer nights as well as by day. When disturbed, it gives vent to a harsh "*churr*"-like note, as if resenting intrusion on its domains.

In colour its head and neck are russet-brown, each feather being tipped with dusky-brown so as to form stripes; the back is russet-brown, and from the base of the bill to the ear-coverts is a distinct band of brown, darkening in shade towards the crown; over this, running from the bill over the eye, is a narrow streak of white. The whole of the under part is a delicate yellowish-white, deepening into a rich tawny-buff on the sides of breasts and flanks and the under tail-coverts; the wings are brown, each feather being edged with lighter brown; and the tail is also brown, the feathers edged with a lighter shade. The female only differs from the male in its duller colour: it is less reddish on the rump, and the eye-strip is less pronounced.

The Sedge Warbler is a rather difficult bird to "meat off" if full grown when caught; and though this is not an impossible task, it is preferable to rear this bird from the nest, when it should be hand-fed upon the same food as young Nightingales. When able to feed itself it should be gradually weaned on to the food recommended for the Wood Warbler. It should be given plenty of water for bathing, but must not be allowed to indulge too much in this luxury during winter. Though rather difficult to keep, the Sedge Warbler is lively, and adds to the attractiveness of an aviary of small insectivorous birds; it can also be kept and exhibited in a similar cage to that recommended for the Reed Warbler.

The Grasshopper Warbler.

The Grasshopper Warbler, *Locustella nævia* (*Sharpe*), though somewhat similar in its manner to the last-mentioned bird, differs very widely, though of the same skulking disposition. It is a true walker, and runs through the thick herbage with great rapidity, uttering its call-note or song, which has a ventriloquial sound, being heard in one direction at one moment and in quite a different one the next. Mr. Sydney L. Cocks, of Peterborough, hand-reared quite a number of these birds a few years ago, and, writing about one of them, said: "In captivity, if placed upon the floor of the room, it would run across it like a partridge."

WHITETHROAT GOLDCREST REDSTART
BLACKCAP NIGHTINGALE

Although not very generally known, the Grasshopper Warbler is not at all uncommon in some parts of England, and would seem to be pretty generally dispersed throughout the country. It arrives about the middle of April and leaves again in September. It is so very retiring that it manages to elude any but the most patient observer. From the colour of its plumage, and a habit of running along the bottoms of hedgerows or amongst the grass and sedge, it has often puzzled those who have heard its cricket-like song, seemingly close at hand, yet provokingly deceptive as to its real position. It may be heard singing in the evenings as well as during the day, though, as a songster, it cannot claim much attention, the song being very peculiar, resembling the call of the cricket, from which it derives the name, "Green Grasshopper."

It is a valuable species for exhibition purposes and is about 5¾ in. in length. The bill is brown and thin; the head, neck, back and wings are olive-brown, all the feathers centred with darker brown, producing a spotted appearance; the tail is dark greenish-brown, shaded with cross-bars of dusky-brown and wedge-shaped; the chin and throat are yellowish-white, the latter being sprinkled with small brown spots; the breast is yellowish-green, shading to greenish-brown on the sides, running to whitish on the abdomen; feet pale brown or flesh-colour.

In a cage it has much in common with the Pipit in its movements, and a similar cage to that used for keeping and exhibiting that bird answers well for this Warbler. It will also do well on the food recommended for the other Warblers, and should be allowed free use of the bath. In hand-rearing these birds, Mr. Cocks says, "nothing equals live gentles for them. I never lost a bird taken. I use the gentles from the bright blue-green-bodied fly; it is about half the size of the meat fly (blue-bottle) gentle, and is yellow when cleaned and scoured. I use pine sawdust for cleaning the gentles, sifting the sawdust through a $\frac{1}{16}$-inch mesh sieve, then sifting the gentles out of it when clean; they are then ready for use, and are given to the birds impaled on a sack- or packing-needle; I use one slightly bent and about 7 inches long. If the gentles are given whole, without the skin being pierced, I believe the smaller insectivorous birds pass them entire, and starve to death; but by giving them impaled from the packing-needle they obtain the nutriment from them through the pierced parts. I took one nest of six at four days old, and fed them every half-hour from 5 a.m. until 8.30 p.m. for the first three days, giving each one one or two gentles each time, if they would take the second. After the third day they were fed every hour, and given as many gentles each time as they would take. Another nest of five was taken at eight days old, and successfully reared in the same way. In each case all the birds were doing for themselves before they were three weeks old, and were fed on gentles only until they were about eight weeks old. They were then gradually weaned on to the ordinary insectivorous food, with a liberal supply of gentles." All who remember Mr. Cocks exhibiting these birds will recall their splendid condition.

The Hedge Sparrow.

The Hedge Sparrow, sub family *Accentoridæ Accentor modularis* (*Macg.*), is one of our resident birds, though some migration is said to take place. It is known by the various names of Dyke, Dunnock, Hedge Warbler, and Shufflewing. and is a frequenter, as its name denotes, of hawthorn hedges, where it may be heard uttering its plaintive little song, which, though not of any great variety, is very pretty and may be heard almost all the year round. It builds very early in the year, and the first nests are therefore quite exposed in the leafless hedgerows or other sites with their delicately tinted light blue eggs. It seems peculiarly liable to the depredations of the Cuckoo, it being notorious that as many young Cuckoos are reared by this little bird as by any other victim of that houseless robber. The manner in which the young Cuckoo obtains sole possession of the nest is peculiar. The egg is deposited in the nest by the shiftless Cuckoo, and is hatched by the Hedge Sparrow in blissful ignorance of the enemy that has been insinuated into her otherwise happy family. The young Cuckoo soon shows its superior strength, and having a peculiar hollow in its back, heaves the unfortunate nestlings one by one out of their warm abode, they of course perishing, whilst the unsuspicious parents continue their attentions to the murderer of their unfortunate offspring.

Though so common and sober in colour, the Hedge Sparrow is a most interesting and desirable pet for cage or aviary. In length it is about 5½ inches. Its plumage is rather unpretending, the whole of the upper part, including the wings and tail, are chestnut-brown, the back being speckled with blackish-brown, whilst the head and neck are shaded with bluish-grey; the under part is slaty-grey, slightly tinged with brown, and speckled on the breast and sides with chestnut-brown. The food of this bird when at liberty consists of insects in their various stages of development, worms and seeds such as grasses and grains. In hard weather it will visit the towns and farmyards, frequenting gutters and sinks, where it picks up crumbs and other morsels from amongst the sweepings; but in the milder weather it depends principally upon the larvæ of insects and worms. It may be kept in a cage such as that recommended for the Wheatear, and will do well on a similar diet.

The Bearded Reedling.

The Bearded Reedling, *Panurus biarmicus* (*Newton*), Family *Panuridæ*, is commonly called the Bearded Tit. It is a resident and a native of marshes and reed-growing localities, feeding on aquatic insects and tiny mollusca; in the winter it subsists largely on the seeds of the reeds, a mode of sustenance unlike that of Tits. It has, we regret to say, become very rare in this country, which may be partly owing to the scarcity of food in unduly hard winters, though we think the chief cause is the draining and tilling of the fen and marsh-lands in many counties which were once the happy breeding and living quarters of this interesting bird. It is now said to be only found in the two counties of Norfolk and Devon. We trust every assistance will be given for its preservation in these districts, so as to increase its number. It is a very handsome bird, having the whole of the upper part fawn-colour, the face and ear-coverts grey, and from the bill across the eye down each side of the throat of the male bird runs a jet-black band, forming a moustache, which the bird has the power of puffing out at pleasure. It is from this feature that it derives its name. The chin, throat and breast are greyish white, with a rosy tint over it, shading to cinnamon on the flanks; the tail is long and wedge-shaped, of a light, veinous-chestnut colour, with the outer feathers striped with white; the wings are dark brown, the feathers edged with fawn-colour and the primaries edged with light grey. This bird has built a nest and laid in confinement, but we have not heard of any young being reared. Doubtless this could be accomplished if a sufficient supply of natural food could be given while the young were being reared. It is an interesting pet, both in cage and aviary, handsome in appearance, and usually does well as an exhibition bird. Size, of course, with good colour and markings, combined with perfect plumage and steadiness, go a long way to assist its success. It should be fed as recommended for the Reed and other Warblers, giving a supply of its natural food whenever procurable. Care should also be taken not to let it get too fat, as if so it is very liable to go off in a fit. Cages such as are used for keeping and exhibiting the smaller Warblers are suitable for this bird, but the living cage should not be less than 2 ft. long.

CHAPTER XXXVIII

TITS, WRENS, WAGTAILS, SHRIKES, ETC.

The Tits (family *Paridæ*) are most interesting in manners and ways, and also remarkable for their small but powerful sub-conical-shaped bills, which are so densely set with setaceous feathers at the base as entirely to hide the nostrils. In captivity they all, without exception, prefer a small box or nest-like receptacle, such as a cocoanut-husk, to sleep in, to perching on a perch.

The Long-tailed Tit.

The Long-tailed Tit, *Acredula rosea* (*Sharpe*), also known by the name of Bottle-Tit, is resident and generally distributed over the British Isles. It is remarkable for its very small body and very long tail, the feathers of which vary in length and are arranged not unlike those of the Magpie. Its body feathers have a downy-like appearance, especially on the head, and more particularly on the forehead. The general colour above is black, with a rose tint, a heavy black stripe running on either side of the head from the gape over the eyebrow into a glossy black mantle, and a stripe of white running from the forehead over the centre of the crown of the head. The feathers round the eye are white; the ear-coverts, cheeks, and throat ashy-white; there are blackish streaks on the forehead; the under-surface of body is lightish, with rosy tint; the wings black, with secondaries deeply edged with white; the tail black, with the three outer feathers tipped at the ends, and the outer web edged with white. The black stripe over the eyes is said to be broader in the female than the male.

This bird is of somewhat restless disposition, like its congenitors, though from experience we consider this bird the most quiet of all the Tits in a cage. Although said by some to be difficult to keep in captivity, we have experienced no more trouble in keeping this bird than any others of the Tit family;

and Mr. J. Dewhurst, of North Kensington, London, and other fanciers whom we know, have had a like experience. Certainly it is the most valuable of the family as an exhibition bird, and is usually successful.

The Long-tailed Tit has little or no song beyond its well-known notes, "*ui-ui*" and a hoarse, croaking, churring-like note peculiar to itself. The nest is not built in a hole like those of the other Tits, and besides being large in proportion to the size of its builder, is a most wonderful piece of architecture. It is a domed structure of moss, heavily lined with soft feathers, and the tiny entrance to it is arranged at the side near the top. A variety of places are selected for the nest—sometimes a thorn hedge —or else it it is woven among the branches of an evergreen. We have one in our possession built on the thick bough of an apple tree, the sides of which are securely interwoven with the little shoots on the bough, and the similarity in the colour of the moss and silver lichen with its covering of spider web, is so perfect that the nest appears like a clump grown out on the bough.

At liberty, the Long-tailed Tit's food consists chiefly of insects, which are searched for diligently on trees, hedgerows, and shrubberies. In captivity, the staple food recommended for the Wood Warbler answers well for these birds; but at all seasons a little live food in some form or other is most beneficial. During the summer months live ants' cocoons and even a few of the insects themselves, disabled before being put into the cage, are welcome tit-bits. In the winter a few live gentles will act as a substitute, and dried ants' cocoons by way of a change may be given, swollen to the normal size by steaming over boiling water. These birds are best kept in a roomy, box-shaped cage, all wood, with a wire front, for if placed in one with a wire roof they run along the wires like mice and are liable to damage their plumage. Show cages similar to those recommended for the smaller Warblers answer well to exhibit this Tit in; but instead of the usual perches, a small branch of a fir or other tree, with numerous little off-shoots, should be arranged in a slanting position towards the roof. This is much better than the ordinary perches. The cage should be a little more lofty than for the Warblers, say 15 inches high. Good health, perfect plumage, full of life, yet perfectly steady, are all conducive to success with this bird at exhibitions.

The Great Tit.

The Great Tit, *Parus major* (*Linn.*), is widely distributed, and is a regular visitor to town gardens in winter, when it usually associates in small groups. These groups appear to have regular beats, for day after day we have observed them busy in the trees in the garden, moving off in the morning in a westerly direction from garden to garden, examining every tree, and returning by the same route in the evening just before dark, attracting us by their well-known shrill but sweetly musical call, which is repeated several times.

The largest of its tribe, the Great Tit, is a very striking bird, owing to its distinct colours and the marked contrast which they display. The forehead, crown, throat, and a narrow band encircling the auriculars are deep, glossy, steel-bluish black; the black of the throat extends in a mesial line upon the breast and abdomen, expanding on the centre of the abdomen and there forming a broad patch. The steel-blue lustre of the head does not appear on these parts; the cheeks and auricular feathers are pure white, forming a triangular spot, which is very conspicuous from its contrast with the surrounding colours. The back of the neck and back are olive-green, of a paler and clearer tint on the nape, and becoming nearly white where it joins the black hood; on the rump and tail coverts it spreads into bluish-grey. The breast, abdomen, and flanks, with the exception of the black mesial line, are sulphur-yellow; the vent white; the shoulders, outer edges of lesser coverts and quills, bluish-grey, giving that tint to the wing, when closed, which is relieved by a yellowish-white band formed by the tips of the lesser coverts, which are tinted with that colour. The secondaries are black, the outer web broadly edged with yellowish-green; the tail is black, and the outer web edged with bluish-grey; the tips and exterior web of the outer feathers are pure white. The female is similar to the male, except that the black streak down the centre of the abdomen is narrower and duller in colour.

Like the rest of its tribe, the Great Tit has great activity and vivacity; when wild, it hops from branch to branch and clings to the trees which it examines most minutely in search of any insects or larvæ that may be secreted in the leaves or bark. It has, however, a reputation for being extremely dangerous if placed in an aviary with other small birds, being credited with having killed its neighbours by repeated blows of its hard bill on the head of the victim, whose brains are thereupon picked out and eaten. If reared as recommended for young Wheatears, from the nest by hand, however, these birds may be turned into the aviary with comparative safety. An aviary of Titmice is one of the most interesting of any, because of the beauty, diminutive size, and unflagging vivacity of the birds; and if given plenty of perches, or, better still, the branch of a fir or other tree with many boughs and twigs, they will be continually flitting from perch to perch, uttering their short note the while. All of the tribe are fond of water and bathing. Their aviary must be very finely wired, for they can escape through very small holes. A good staple food is composed of equal parts of ants' cocoons, dried flies, fine meat meal and powdered biscuit, all mixed well together. Just sufficient for the day's consumption should be prepared, and made crumbly moist with cold water each morning. Any good insectivorous food will also do, and occasionally a little boiled potato, scraped swede turnip, or finely minced tender heart of lettuce, may be mixed with the food, giving, of course, in addition live insects whenever procurable. Live ants' cocoons, wasp grubs, or a few gentles that have been well cleaned all make a welcome change. Sunflower seeds and a few shelled nuts of any description afford the birds especial pleasure, as will also picking a meat bone. They are capable of being easily tamed, and will in time eat out of the hand of their feeder. The same cages and perch arrangement recommended for the Long-tailed Tit answer well for this bird.

The Cole Tit.

The Cole Tit, *Parus britannicus* (*Sharpe and Dresser*), is resident throughout the British Isles, although less plentiful than the other British Tits, except in the south of Scotland. It is much smaller than the Great Tit, and is not quite 4 inches in length. The general colour above is olive-brown, and, like the Great Tit, it has a black head, a white patch on the nape, white cheeks, and a black throat, the black spreading on to the sides of the upper breast. It differs, however, from the Great Tit in under colour, the breast and abdomen being greyish-white, the flanks rich buff, the wings and tail grey, the inner web of the feathers being dusky brown. The Cole Tit is found principally in woods, pine woods being especially favoured spots, where it may be seen clinging in acrobatic style to a cone, extracting its food. It also visits small plantations, and is particularly active and indefatigable in its search for insects, whose larvæ form its chief food. The Cole Tit is a pretty little aviary pet, and may be made exceedingly tame. It does well on the same bill of fare as that for the Great Tit, and requires the same cage accommodation.

The Marsh Tit.

The Marsh Tit, *Parus palustris* (*Linn.*), is another resident, and though not so generally distributed as the preceding species, is still to be found plentifully in some localities, which are not actually marsh and low lands, with brushwood and old willow trees. The bird is equally fond of woodlands, and may be seen consorting with other Tits in these parts. It is a lively, active little creature, continually chirping its one solitary note; but from the amount of dusky brown in its general plumage it is not so striking or attractive as the Tits previously mentioned. The crown of the head is glossy blue-black, forming a cap, which extends backwards down the nape, joining the dusky brown mantle; it has no white patch like the preceding bird. The side of the face and ear coverts are ashy white; the chin and upper throat black; the under surface of body ashy-white; sides and flanks pale brownish buff; wings light brown, with the outer web edged with brownish-white; the tail is ashy brown with olive-brown margins. Yet withal the Marsh Tit is a pretty little bird, and enlivens the aviary with its continuous twittering and restless activity. In its wild state it lives chiefly on insect life. In captivity it will thrive and do well in the same cages and on the diet recommended for the Great Tit.

The Blue Tit.

The Blue Tit, *Parus cœruleus* (*Linn.*), is another well-known resident, found practically everywhere, even to the far north of Scotland, and is very common in Ireland, though it is of a much more migratory nature than others of the Tit family. Wherever a moderate proportion of woody plantation or hedgerow timber exists we are almost sure to find this little bird at one time or another within the limit of its range, and it is a frequent and welcome visitor to suburban gardens. It is a very diminutive bird, being only 4½ inches in length, but so common as to be little appreciated, or no doubt its beautifully marked blue head and back, combined with its grace and activity, would cause it to be found in aviaries much oftener than is now the case. In colour it is one of the most beautiful of the family. The general colour above is light green; the crown of the head is a rich blue surrounded by a band of greyish-white with another band of very dark blue-black, forming from behind the eyes and running round the nape, where it expands, narrowing down again as it proceeds round the cheeks on to the chin and throat. The whole of the cheeks and face, including the ear-coverts, are greyish-white; the wings and tail are blue, beautifully tinted with lighter shades; the breast and under-body are pale yellow, shading almost to white on the abdomen, and a green tint on the flanks, with a faint wash of blue on the breast; even the feet and toes are of a leaden blue tint. It is a striking bird for colour from beginning to finish, and in many districts it is called the Blue-cap. The female is not such a bright colour as the male.

When in search of food, which consists principally of insects, this bird is most amusing in its actions, often assuming the most grotesque positions, hanging beneath the branches upside down and in various other attitudes, searching with most critical eye every possible hiding place that could shelter its prey.

This bird is perfectly safe if placed in the aviary, as it is not dangerous to the other birds. When first caught it should be placed in a cage for a few days, and fed upon live insects and gentles, and gradually meated off on to the diet recommended for the other Tits, when it may be turned into the aviary. Care must be taken that it does not get too fat through too much indulgence, or it is apt to go off in a fit. The Blue Tit, when once steadied, is a most attractive bird for exhibition purposes ; but it must be allowed no hiding place in the show cage, or all that will be seen of it most of the time will be its head bobbing in and out. A cage such as advised for the Long-tailed Tit answers well for this bird.

The Crested Tit.

The Crested Tit, *Parus cristatus* (*Linn.*), is a very scarce bird in England, though often found in the pine forests in Scotland. The general colour is olive-brown, with wings and tail of ashy brown. As the name indicates, it has a crest or tuft of extra long feathers on the head, the longest of which are inclined to curve forward in an upward direction. The crest is black, edged with white ; the throat, under part of breast, and a narrow collar to the occiput are black, enclosing a white space in the region of the eyes and on the side of the neck. The under-parts are light, tinged with yellowish-brown. As it is a very pretty bird, it is a desirable addition to an aviary of Tits, and it will feed upon the general food recommended for them. Several specimens have been exhibited from time to time ; but all were said to have been imported from the Continent, where it is fairly common. The same cages as for other Tits answer for this bird.

The Golden-crested Wren.

The Golden-crested Wren, *Regulus cristatus* (*Newton*), is the smallest of all British birds, and is resident throughout the British Isles, chiefly frequenting the districts planted with pines. These trees afford it not only shelter but an abundance of food in the great varieties of insects which frequent their shoots and cones. It is particularly fond of the insect pest *eriosoma*, which infests the silver firs, and it is owing to this bird's energy that the pest is kept in check. Golden-crested Wrens breed as early as April, and their nest is usually suspended hammock fashion from a branch of a fir, pine, or other tree. It is a beautiful structure of green moss interwoven with horse-hair. the nest being laced to the branch and foliage with the hair and a few fine grasses. The inside is warmly lined with soft feathers ; the entrance is at the side, the top being domed over.

The number of Gold Crests is sometimes largely augmented by migrants from the Continent during the autumn. The Golden-crested Wren is only 3½ inches in length, and is exceedingly beautiful. The neck and back have a greenish tint shading to a yellowish-green on the rump ; the crown of the head is a patch of reddish-orange shading to gamboge yellow at the front and sides ; on each side of this runs a deep band of black setting off as it were a beautiful ornament ; around the eye is a pale dusky ring, encircled by another of dull white. The wing coverts are like the back ; the remainder of the wing running to a blackish-brown, double-barred with white, and edged with greenish-yellow on the pinion feathers ; the tail is brownish-black with the outer web of feathers edged with wax yellow ; the under parts are whitish-grey, darkened on the breast and tinged with brown and yellow, running to greenish-olive on the flanks. The patch on the crown of the head is paler in the female—it has not the rich orange tint—and the body a duller green. Very fine illustrations of these birds are given in our coloured plate, and on page 168. In their movements and ways they have much in common with the Tits, in fact they unite with them in small social parties during the winter months, travelling from tree to tree in search of food together. The song, though weak, is decidedly superior to that of the Tits. As a cage pet or for exhibition purposes the Golden-crested Wren seems to be sadly neglected, perhaps under the impression that it will not repay the trouble the nature of their food necessitates. Its habits are extremely interesting in captivity, and especially as a cage pet. It is inclined to feel the cold largely owing to the limited space for exercise, and, therefore, cosy, though not necessarily warm quarters are required for the bird's general comfort. With ordinary care and proper food it is not so difficult to keep as is generally supposed.

Mr. S. H. Mays, of Wansford, Northants, a well-known exhibitor and judge, has one of these birds, and writes : " This bird I have now had for over five years ; it was not hand-reared, but caught late in the autumn, a fully matured adult, and must then have been at least three years old. The full colour and size of crest are not acquired until that age, and these were fully developed, so my bird must now be at least eight years old. I have never experienced the least trouble to keep it in health, it has not had a day's illness, and is nearly always in song, even during the moult." Some might say this bird is an exception rather than the rule, but Mr. Mays goes on to say, "Personally I do not consider Gold Crests at all difficult to keep; they are difficult to get on to food when first caught; but once over that I have never had any trouble. I have only lost two all the years I have kept them; one through the neglect of an official at a show to give the bird water. They are most merry and active pets. I like to give them a roomy cage, and as a staple diet 1 part ants' eggs, 1 part dried flies, 1 part powdered plain biscuit, and ¼ part Brand's meat meal, mixed together. Occasionally I add a little preserved yolk of egg (not hard boiled), also a little ground silkworm pupæ. I also often sprinkle a few ants' eggs on top of the water in the bath; they appear to enjoy taking them from the surface of the water. As live food I give a few meal-worms cut up into several pieces, also gentles, when in season, especially in the chrysalis state. Gold Crests are also very fond of house flies, and of bathing, and I give them a bath all the year round. I keep a slender branch of fir in the cage, which they appreciate as a perch." A similar cage to that recommended for the Tits answers well for this bird; but it must be very closely wired. The food and water are best given inside; if the arrangements are as for the Warblers, feeding and drinking holes in the wire through which the bird might escape are thereby avoided.

The Fire-crest Wren.

The Fire-Crest Wren, *Regulus ignicapillus* (*Macg.*), is a much rarer bird than the preceding, and differs from it in that it is only a winter visitant to our Isles. It is seen chiefly in the southern and eastern counties, arriving in September, and leaving again in April. Its habits are similar to those of the Gold Crest, and greater numbers may visit us than are supposed, owing to its similarity to the Gold Crest, and its consorting with that bird. The chief difference between the birds is that the crest of the Fire-Crest Wren is, as its name indicates, of a richer orange or fire-like tint. It is further distinguishable by the yellow patch on each side of the neck. It has a decided white eyebrow, and a black streak between the gape and the eye extending beyond the eye, and another black stripe running from the gape below the eye on to the lower portion of the cheek. The crest of the female is similar in colour to that of the Gold Crest; but the three black bands on each side of the head and face always serve to distinguish it from that bird. It is a little larger in size, but this difference is chiefly accounted for by its length of tail. The directions for the management of the Gold Crest are equally applicable to this bird.

The Nuthatch.

The Nuthatch, *sitta cœsia* (*Meyer*), Family *Sittidæ*, holds an intermediate position between the Creepers and Tits, and is a resident of Britain. It is very beautiful; the general colour above is light slaty-blue shading to grey on parts; a black streak extends from the eyes on to the neck, expanding as it travels to the neck. The primary feathers of the wing are dusky brown, the secondaries and coverts slaty-blue; the tail blue, except the centre feathers, which are dark brown and all tipped with white, and increasing in size towards the outer sides; the under tail coverts are white; the cheeks and throat ashy white; the remainder of the under surface is umber-brown running to a rich chestnut on the flanks. The bird is scarcely 6 inches in length, the male bird being the larger of the two. The female's bill is longer and more slender than her consort's. The Nuthatch is a rather shy bird, and its habit of climbing like the Woodpecker on the trunks of trees in search of insects, enables it to keep well concealed from view if there are any hiding spots at hand. Indeed if virginia cork is so arranged in the Nuthatch's cage or aviary that the bird can get behind it you will see little of it except its head, or when it comes out to feed. With its incessant activity it is the most interesting of birds in an aviary. If given a nut it is very amusing to notice with what adroitness the nut is fastened into a crack of the cork or some cranny, in order that it may break the shell more readily. When wild the Nuthatch feeds not only on insect life but upon almost every variety of nut—especially beechmast—berries, and seeds. In confinement it should be fed upon the kernels of nuts, and beechmast whenever obtainable should be given; a few hemp seeds will also afford the bird amusement by husking the kernels. A good insectivorous food, such as that recommended for the Wrens, should be given as a staple food, made crumbly moist with cold water sufficient for each day's consumption; a little boiled potato or finely minced heart of lettuce may also be mixed with it by way of a change, and live insects and grubs of any kind, including gentles, will all help to make a perfect diet, and thereby keep the bird in good health and plumage. A show-cage of a similar pattern to that used for Woodpeckers, but not quite so lofty, answers well.

The Wren, *Troglodytes parvulus* (*Newton*), Family *Troglodytidæ*, familiarly called Jenny or Kitty Wren, holds almost as popular a position as Robin himself. Associated as both are in many a nursery tale, and in being residents and winter visitors to our gardens and houses during inclement weather, their familiarity justifies the affection with which they are regarded. The Wren is lively in its habits, hopping cheerily from place to place, seldom flying far, but keeping principally to the hedgerows or gardens, though oftentimes climbing trees, running round and round them in search of the insects or larvæ that may be secreted in the bark. It has an exceedingly pretty song, loud and of great strength considering the size of the bird, and very nearly resembling some of the notes of the Canary.

The Wren.

The Wren is one of the smallest of British birds, being only about 4 inches in length, and until closely inspected of apparently unpretending plumage. Then in the various shadings of its sober-coloured feathers beauty is to be discerned. The head and neck are bright rusty brown, barred with darker brown; the back reddish-brown, also marked transversely with bars of darker brown; the cheeks, chin, throat, and breast are dusky grey, tinged with brown towards the abdomen; from the base of the bill, over the eye to the back of the ear, runs a narrow streak of dusky grey; the wings are reddish-brown, each feather barred with darker brown, the outside feathers being lighter. The tail, which is carried in a tilted-in-the-air fashion, the wings dropping below it on either side at the tips, is also reddish-brown, barred in the same manner with darker brown.

The nest of the Wren is extremely interesting; it is built of a variety of materials, the selection of which is generally determined by the nature of its surroundings. In shape it is spherical, with a dome, and a small aperture at the side. It is built in a variety of situations; in fact, no place seems to come amiss when necessity occasions. A favourite spot is against the trunk of an old ivy-clad tree or old wall overgrown with moss, bramble, and honeysuckle. Plenty also are built in the hedgerow, ivy-covered banks, and under the eaves of haystacks; and they have even been found between the leaves of a cabbage and in disused garments hanging in outhouses, and other curious spots.

From their merry and lively habits, Wrens are exceedingly pretty additions to the aviary. They should be provided with some small covered boxes, or the outside husk of a coco-nut, having a hole cut in them, and lined with moss, as these birds, although staying in England when wild during the winter, are very subject to cold when in confinement, and always huddle up closely together for warmth when roosting. They are also fairly successful at our exhibitions if exhibited in good condition of plumage and health. A cage similar to that for a Gold Crest answers well for the Wren, and also a similar diet, occasionally adding a little boiled bullock's liver, grated, and giving a supply of live insects or grubs; failing these, a mealworm or two cut into pieces. A bath should always be given.

The Tree Creeper, *Certhia familiaris* (*Linn.*), Family *Certhidæ*, is resident and widely distributed over the British Isles. It frequents old-established woods and parks, and is remarkable for its extremely long, slender, curved bill; its pointed tail, with stiff shafts; and its long hind claws. Owing to its retiring habits and its trick of suddenly retreating behind the tree or branch upon which it is resting, the Tree Creeper is not easy to discover. It flies only on necessity, more usually progressing in short, jumpy flights from one part of a tree to another, running and clinging to the trunk and branches like a miniature Woodpecker, and with the dexterity of a mouse. Herein lies the use for its long claws and the stiffened shaft feathers of its tail. In favourable spots its weak, sibilous note, *Wheist*, will be heard repeated at short intervals, and, locating it, the bird will be seen scaling a tree trunk or branch; the least sound causes it to jerk round to the opposite side with lightning-like rapidity, where it pursues its way with an occasional peep to ascertain whether the cause of alarm is still present. The tree's summit or end of a branch gained, the bird swiftly falls as it were or "jumps" to the base of some other tree, and again commences its spiral course upwards, searching the bark for insects and their larvæ.

The Tree Creeper.

It is a small bird, about 5½ inches long. The general colour above is light tawny-brown, shading to a darker tint on the rump and tail, with light buff centres to the feathers on the head and back, which give these parts a very pretty bespangled appearance. The primary feathers of the wings are dusky-brown, with a diagonal band of yellowish-white crossing them and the secondaries about the middle, forming practically three bars; nearer the tips there is another pale band on the outer webs. Over each eye is a streak of silky-white running in a downward direction to the throat and encircling a patch of tawny below the eye; the lower portions of the face, throat, and under parts are silky-white. All these colours are beautifully shown in our coloured plate.

The Tree Creeper is not a difficult bird to keep in captivity, and is quite a popular exhibition bird. A show cage similar to that for the Golden-crested Wren is suitable, but instead of the branch for a perch, stretch tightly over the back and sides of the cage a piece of green or red baize. On this the bird will run playfully up and down with ease, never leaving it except to feed. It can be successfully hand-reared on the food recommended for the various Warblers. Mr. Sidney L. Cocks, of Peterborough, hand-reared seven of these birds from eight days old on live gentles only. They were fed every half-hour from 5 a.m. to 8.30 p.m., the first three days receiving one or two gentles each feed, and after the third day as many as they would take each time. The gentles, after being pierced, were given from the end of a sack needle, as with the Grasshopper Warblers already mentioned. At the age of three weeks the young birds fed themselves and were given gentles entirely until eight weeks old, when they were gradually got on to the usual insectivorous food, composed of ants' cocoons, dried flies, and powdered biscuit in equal parts, with a little meat meal and a few live gentles in addition. The living-cage should be 20 or 24 inches long, 18 inches high, and 10 or 12 inches deep. A branch can be placed in this, and it may be lined with Virginia cork. Tree Creepers should be kept in cosy quarters during winter.

The Wagtails.

We now come to one of the most graceful groups of British birds—the Wagtails. These are true ground-walkers, and to the dainty bobbing movement of their tails when so progressing they owe their name. In this family, *Motacillidæ*, are included the Pipits, another graceful group of birds, the family being really intermediate in character between the Warblers and Larks. The Wagtails have little or no song; but their double-note, *Chiz-zit*, is very musical, and their docility in a cage quickly endears them as pets. As a rule, they make good exhibition birds; but the Yellow and Grey, as a rule, stand a better chance in competition than their common relative, the Pied Wagtail.

The Pied Wagtail.

The Pied Wagtail, *Motacilla lugubris* (*Temm.*), is a resident, and though a certain amount of migration takes place, it breeds over the greater portion of our isles, but does not winter in the more northern parts.

The plumage of the male bird in summer is black in the upper parts of the body and tail—except the two outer feathers on each side—and the throat and breast are also black; towards the rump there is a fringe of grey; the outer feathers of the tail are white; the ear-coverts, lower breast, abdomen, and under tail-coverts are white. In the winter the black throat is lost, and that colour on the breast is restricted to the form of a crescent; the black throat gives way to a white patch at this period; the forehead, too, is white, and the centre of the back becomes deep blackish-grey. Specimens frequently occur in which the black of the former state continues intermixed. The secondaries, greater and lesser coverts become more broadly edged with white, and the feathers of the rump assume narrow edgings of the same hue. This change of plumage in summer and winter is a most interesting feature. The bird is often found near water, either wading in the shallows or, sylph-like, alighting on the lily leaves whilst in search of aquatic insects or larvæ, although not disdaining flies, gnats, and similar insects. They also frequent lawns on which they look extremely handsome, especially when the male bird makes love to his mate in very similar fashion to a dove or pigeon. In the cage or aviary there should always be plenty of water provided, both for drinking and bathing.

The White Wagtail.

While the Pied Wagtail, which the White so much resembles that the one is often mistaken for the other, is resident with us all the year round, the White Wagtail, *Motacilla alba* (*Linn.*), is only a summer visitor. Its nesting and general habits are similar to the Pied Wagtail, but it is slightly smaller. In its breeding plumage it is distinguishable from the Pied by its general colour above being a blackish-grey, except the crown, throat, and breast, which are black; the forehead and ear-coverts are white, and besides the two outer feathers on each side of the tail being white, the two centre feathers are also edged with white. In their winter plumage the two species are very similar, but the White Wagtail always carries a greater amount of white on the wing-coverts and is a lighter shade of grey on the back. As an exhibition bird, an equally good White would beat a Pied on account of its rarity.

The Grey Wagtail.

The Grey Wagtail, *Motacilla melanope* (*Pall.*), is resident, though somewhat locally distributed, and is largely an autumn migrant to the southern counties. It, however, breeds in some parts of the South, but more generally in Scotland, Cumberland, and the North. In summer it frequents the margins of rocky streams in the hilly parts of the British Isles, and during the breeding season is plentiful in the North. Its nest resembles that of the Pied Wagtail, and is generally found near a stream on the ledge or in a chink of a rock behind or below some rough herbage. Though possessing but little song, the Grey Wagtail's plumage places it high amongst cage and aviary favourites or as an exhibition bird; but not more than one pair should be kept in an aviary with other insectivorous birds.

In winter the bird is plainly and chastely

REDSTART AND GREY WAGTAIL.

dressed. The upper part, as far as the rump, is a very light bluish-grey faintly tinged on the back with yellow; the rump and upper tail-coverts are yellowish-olive; a white streak runs over and down the nape from behind each eye; the throat is white, shading into pale lemon-orange on the breast, which again shades into a pale gamboge-yellow on the abdomen and under tail-coverts; the wings are dusky-brown with the long scapulars edged with yellowish-white; the tail is the same colour as the wings, the centre feathers being edged with olive, the outer feathers pure white, and the second and third edged with dark brown on the outer web. In summer and during the breeding season the Grey is the most handsome of our Wagtails, all the colours becoming much more vivid and brilliant; the uniformity of the lower parts is then broken by the gorget of deep jet-black which covers the throat and fore part of the neck, running off to a point on the breast, and giving a most pleasing effect to the surrounding brilliant yellow of the breast. From the gape a white streak runs on each side of the throat between the bluish-grey on the sides of neck and black throat; the streak behind the eye is also more pronounced.

The Grey Wagtail's food consists largely of insects, but the smaller aquatic mollusca form a portion, and its ways of capturing its prey are similar to those of the other Wagtails. Through the winter the bird frequents springs, ditches, ponds, and streams, and often visits the farmyard to secure any insects that may be found in the gutters and puddles. The female is duller in colour, more brownly tinged above, and is paler in yellow on the under parts.

The Blue-headed Wagtail.

The Blue-headed Wagtail, *Motacilla flava* (*Linn.*)—also known by earlier writers as the Grey-headed Wagtail—is an accidental summer migrant to England and Scotland; but it has a wide range in Europe and Asia. It frequents the same localities, but is not quite so large as the Grey Wagtail, and it has the same slender, graceful build. Colour: the crown of head, nape, and auriculars are bluish-grey, streaked with a darker shade from the nostrils to the eyes, and passing over these and above the auriculars is a streak of white; the back is olive-yellow, running to a lighter shade on the rump; the wings are light brownish-black—secondaries, scapulars, and coverts—with the outer web edged with yellowish-white; the tail—except the outer feathers, which are white, streaked with brown on inner web—is dusky-black, the feathers being faintly edged with brown; the throat is white, and the remainder of under parts brilliant yellow. It is a handsome bird in a cage or aviary, and also for exhibition, but should be kept in genial, but not stuffy quarters during the winter.

The Yellow Wagtail.

The Yellow Wagtail, *Motacilla raii* (*Dresser*)—also known as Ray's Wagtail—is amongst the earliest of our summer migrants, arriving in March. It breeds in most parts of England, the South of Scotland, and parts of Ireland, and leaves us again in September. It is one of the most handsome of our insectivorous birds, and has the same graceful build and light, airy carriage as the four preceding species, but, like the Blue-headed, has not quite so great a length of tail. The general colour above is olive-yellow, with a faint tinge of green; the forehead is bright yellow, with a rich brilliant streak of the same colour over each eyebrow; the under parts are yellow, deepening in tint to richness on the breast; the wings are a yellowish-brown, deepening almost to black on the primaries; the coverts are tipped and edged with yellowish-white; the tail, deep brown, shading to a blackish tint, except the two outer feathers on each side which are white, the second one of which has the outer web pale brown, and both a streak of pale brown on the inner web.

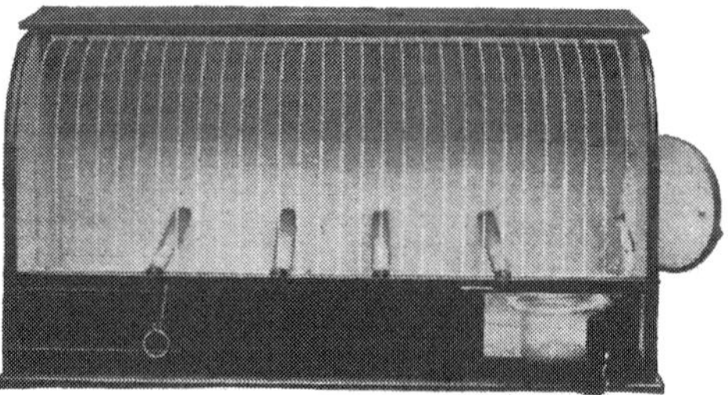

WAGTAIL OR PIPIT SHOW CAGE.

From a habit which the Yellow Wagtail has of frequenting meadows where cows are feeding, and of running around and between the legs of those animals to catch the insects aroused by their trampling, it has obtained the name of "Cowbird" in many country districts. It is a most attractive bird for either cage, aviary or exhibition purposes, and a well-matured, rich-coloured specimen, steady and in perfect plumage, is, indeed, a keen competitor for the highest possible honours. Though an artificially-heated room is not necessary during the winter, it is well to let this bird, like its predecessor, have cosy living quarters. A suitable cage in which to exhibit Wagtails is illustrated on page 397. This should be 18 or 20 inches long, 10 inches high, and 10 inches deep. We like mid-green enamel as well as any colour for the inside, and black outside. The close arrangement of the low perches in the middle of the cage for the birds to walk over should be noted, as it enables them to display their beauty. The food and water vessels should be arranged one at each end in the front of the cage and hung by a wire frame on the inside of a small door. To keep Wagtails in good health and plumage in a cage, plenty of floor space must be allowed in the regular living cage, which need not necessarily be lofty, but what one might term a "runner" adapted to the movements of these birds. In shape it should be similar to the show cage, and have a floor space of from 30 to 36 inches, 12 inches deep and 14 inches high ; half a dozen perches should be arranged close together in the centre of the cage, as shown in the show cage, and placed at a height that will allow the bird to pass beneath as well as over them. The doors at each end should be large enough to admit of a shallow bath, about 9 inches by 12 inches and 1½ inches deep. This should be half filled with clean water daily, or more often if it becomes soiled, and especially in warm weather. A few ants' cocoons thrown on the water will afford the bird much pleasure in picking them off. A fresh green clover sod should also be supplied weekly or more often, if procurable, and the bottom of the cage strewn with clean river sand.

As to food, that recommended for the Golden Crested Wren answers well as a staple diet for the Wagtails. A little boiled potato, finely minced heart of lettuce, or mustard and cress can be mixed with the supply daily, and give variation, besides being beneficial to the birds. Ants' cocoons swollen to normal size by steaming can be given when live cocoons are not procurable, and live insects and grubs are always acceptable. Kept thus, the Wagtail will enjoy good health, and be a source of pleasure for years.

The Pipits (*genus Anthus*) differ from the Wagtails in having brown, heavily-streaked plumage, shorter tails and more Lark-like appearance.

The Tree Pipit.

The Tree Pipit, *Anthus trivialis* (*Newton*), is a fairly common summer migrant which arrives in April and leaves in September. It breeds in most well-cultivated and wooded parts of England, is rarer in Wales and the northern parts of Scotland, and almost unknown in Ireland. The bird is very graceful, though its plumage is not striking. The general colour above is sandy-brown, paler on the nape ; the centres of the feathers on the crown and back are dark umber-brown forming into lines ; the wings are umber-brown, with primaries faintly edged with greyish-white, and the greater and lesser coverts tipped and edged with the same colour, the latter of a clear tint, forming a double bar across the wings. The tail is umber-brown, outer feathers on each side white with an oblique mark of dusky-brown on the inner web ; the under parts are yellowish-white, shading into buff-orange on the breast and flanks ; the lower throat, fore-neck, breast, sides and flanks are beautifully streaked with dark umber-brown. The female is duller in colour, browner above, paler below, whiter at throat, and the breast marking is not so pronounced as in the male.

The Tree Pipit's song is very pleasing, and the bird, being very tameable as well as sociable, will thrive in an aviary, where its graceful carriage will be well displayed. It is fond of water, and often found near a pond or stream. It bathes, not dusting itself so much as the Skylark. Its food, when wild, consists of insects and their larvæ, especially flies, caterpillars and worms ; and it therefore does well for years in a cage on the diet recommended for the Wagtails, with a supply of caterpillars, wasp-grubs, and other live food in moderation, and even two or three gentles by way of a change. Young Tree Pipits are easily hand-reared in the way recommended for Nightingales, but if caught wild just before they migrate they are so easily reconciled to a cage that it is quite unnecessary to hand-rear them. They are excellent for exhibition, and should be shown in the cage recommended for Wagtails, but a size smaller, say 16 inches long, 9 inches high, and 9 inches deep. The Wagtails' stock cage is also suitable for these birds if made 2 feet long, with the other measurements as for the Wagtails.

The Meadow Pipit.

The Meadow Pipit, *Anthus pratensis* (*Macg.*), is a resident, although many migrate south for the winter, and it is asserted that those which return to our shores in the spring are much brighter in plumage than those which winter here. It occurs throughout Central and Northern Europe, and is common throughout the British Isles, especially in low-lying marshy pastures and seaside commons, besides frequenting uplands in the summer. It was formerly included with the Larks, and in many districts it is still known by the name of Titlark. It is much more common than the Tree Pipit, which it somewhat resembles, though smaller, and of a more decided olive-green colour on the back. The eyebrow, too, is a paler sandy-buff, whilst the breast is not so bright a buff, and the dark streaks on these parts and the flanks are not so beautifully outlined as in the Tree Pipit. This bird is well portrayed on our coloured plate. As it is docile and easily tamed, it does well in an aviary of insect-eating birds, and also on the same food and in the cages recommended for the Tree Pipit.

The Rock Pipit.

The Rock Pipit, *Anthus obscurus* (*Newton*), is a resident, and has much in common with the Meadow and Tree Pipits in its flight. Its song is inferior to that of the Tree Pipit, and while somewhat similar in colour it is larger. Its plumage above is olive-brown with the dark centres somewhat broader and heavier. It is also lighter on the throat and breast, the throat being a dull white and a very conspicuous light streak passes above the eyes. Though called the Rock Pipit, from its favourite haunts being the rocky solitary seacoast, the bird also frequents low flat seashores, feeding on the insects and small mollusca left by the receding tide. The bird thrives in both cage and aviary on the diet recommended for the Tree and Meadow Pipit, and the same show and stock cages answer well. The Pipits may occasionally be given, as a tit-bit, a little canary seed which has been soaked in cold water for two days, changing the water two or three times, straining the seeds as dry as possible, and drying with a cloth before use.

The Red-throated, Richard, Tawny and Water Pipits being only accidental visitors we shall not treat of, beyond saying that they can be kept in good health on the same food and in the same cages as the other Pipits.

The Shrike family, *Laniidæ*, includes many insectivorous birds, usually possessing a hooked bill with a notch near the end of the upper mandible. They are sometimes called " Butcher " birds from their habit of impaling small animals and insects on thorns ; but we need only allude to two of the family, viz. :

The Great Grey Shrike.

The Great Grey Shrike, *Lanius excubitor* (*Linn.*), is a winter and rather uncommon migrant, and being very handsome, is a favourite and successful exhibition bird. It is about 9 inches in length, the plumage is a pretty ashen-grey throughout the upper part, shading to white on the shoulders and under part, and light grey on the breast and sides of body. The greater wing-coverts are black, the lesser ashen grey ; the primaries are the same colour as the greater coverts, but the inner have white spots at the ends and the outer are edged with a whitish grey. Two white patches are formed on the wings from the white base of the primaries and outer secondaries. The tail is wedge-shaped, and the outer web of the outer feathers is white ; the others are black, and all tipped with white on the centre feathers, gradually increasing in extent to the outer feathers. From the bill across the face runs a broad black stripe, a fine stripe of white running round the forehead, along the top and round the end of this black band, losing itself in the white streak. The female is not so bright in colour as the male ; the white patches on the wings not so bold, and the breast has a slight indication of greyish-brown bars.

This Shrike's food when at liberty consists of small mammalia, reptiles, small birds and their young, the larger insects, such as beetles, bees, moths, etc., which it first impales on the strong thorns of a bush before proceeding to devour them. In captivity, the nearer its food resembles that obtained when at liberty, the better the bird's health and the longer its life. It should have a good insectivorous food made crumbly moist, and be given in addition small live, but disabled mice, or a sparrow whenever procurable. Failing these for variety, give a few live gentles, next day a few beetles, and on another a few meal-worms or wasp-grubs, and occasionally a little minced raw lean beef. Shrikes must be kept in a cage or in a small aviary by themselves and not with other birds. They should have an all-wood cage, except for the wire front, 3 to 4 feet long, 2 feet high, and 18 inches deep, with three perches arranged thus .·. A nail can be driven through one of the perches close to the front of the cage, projecting sufficiently to enable the bird to impale its larger tit-bits thereon. Although a bit unruly when first caged, patience and a tit-bit whenever the bird is approached usually gains their confidence. A well-matured, steady bird with good colour and markings, perfect plumage, rarely misses the prize list. The show cage should be of the box pattern, 18, or 20 inches long, 16 inches high, and 10 or 11 inches deep, enamelled inside hedge-sparrow egg blue and black outside. It should have two perches and food and water vessels as for other insectivorous birds.

The Red-backed Shrike.

The Red-backed Shrike, *Lanius collurio* (*Linn.*), is a summer visitor, most numerous in the south-eastern counties, extending as far west as Cornwall, and north as Yorkshire, becoming rare beyond these boundaries. It is, like its predecessor, known as the Butcher Bird, and has the same habit of impaling upon the thorns of a bush the remains of its victims, such as beetles, bees, wasps, and other insects, and sometimes even small birds, mice and frogs. It possesses a most voracious appetite considering its size, and is very serviceable in destroying many garden pests. In habits it has much in common with the Flycatcher. It is a handsome bird; the head, back of neck and rump are ashen-grey, and the other parts above vinous-chestnut; the upper tail coverts are reddish-brown; the four centre feathers of the tail are black, those at the sides white, that colour forming a bar across the base, where the shafts are blackish; the web of the outer feather at each side is white and the black assumes the form of an irregular spot at the tip; the wings are dusky-brown, with coverts of vinous-chestnut. A black line commences at the base of the forehead and surrounds the eyes and auriculars with a faint white streak running along the top of the black. The cheeks and under parts are vinous-pink, shading to whitish on the throat and abdomen. There is a great difference between the colour of the male and female, the latter being reddish-brown above, while the head is duller grey, and has no black band, but a pale buff eyebrow stripe instead; the underparts are buffish, barred with brown; the tail feathers are brown with a tint of whitish-red on the outer ones and small white tippings.

This Shrike is about 7 inches in length, and is possessed of some song, which is pleasant and unintermittent, though occasionally mixed with some harsh notes. If taken young, it may be easily hand-reared like the Nightingale. It should never be placed with other birds, owing to its fierceness. It can be fed as advised for the preceding species, and similar cages answer well, though they need not be quite so long.

The Waxwing.

Of the family *Ampelidæ*, the Waxwing, *Ampelis garrulus* (*Linn.*), is a winter visitor to these islands, sometimes appearing singly, and at others in flocks. The name is derived from the wax-like appearance of the white ends of the secondary wing-feathers, and a small tip or appendage to the shafts of some of those feathers, which has been likened to red coral or sealing-wax. It is a very handsome bird, about the size of a Redwing; the feathers on the crown are elongated and form a beautiful crest, which can be raised or lowered at pleasure. It is drab-brown in colour, shading into dull chestnut; round the eyes a narrow black stripe stretches above the nostrils, and is continued behind the eyes, separating the crest from the nape; the throat and forepart of the neck are black. The general body colour is drab-brown, shading to various tints; on the face and ear-coverts to rufous and chestnut; on the rump and under-parts to grey. The wings are black, barred with white and yellow, with coverts like the back; the tail is black tinged with grey and tipped with yellow. On the older birds a tiny oval shaft-tip of wax-like red is appended. The Waxwing takes readily to cage or aviary life, and is a charming exhibition bird, besides being docile with other birds. It does well on a not too rich insectivorous food, such as recommended for the Thrush, but the egg food should be omitted, and a few grocer's currants scalded or a few raisins or sultanas cut up fine should be added. Live grubs, a few gentles or a meal-worm, and insects are much relished tit-bits. A supply of privet, juniper and hawthorn berries should be given during the autumn when procurable. To avoid over-fatness, and consequent fits, a liberal supply of ripe juicy fruit should be given the whole year round. Its cage should be of box pattern, and at least 3 feet long, 2 feet high and 12 or 14 inches deep with two perches, allowing a nice wide hop between, or three may be arranged with the centre one higher. The show cage and food and water vessel recommended for the Thrush family will answer well for the Waxwing. The cage-bottom can be covered with blotting-paper or peat moss, but in either case the tray, except its front bar, should be made of zinc, and frequently cleaned.

The Flycatchers.

Of the family *Muscicapidæ*, the Flycatchers show their affinity with the Thrushes by the mottled character of the young birds. They are generally small, of not very attractive colouring, and of solitary habit. They seize their prey on the wing, for which purpose they are in every way beautifully formed. Two of the family concern us:

The Pied Flycatcher.

The Pied Flycatcher, *Muscicapa atricapilla* (*Linn.*), is a regular summer visitor, but much less common and more local than the Spotted Flycatcher. It reaches our shores towards the end of April, and breeds chiefly in Wales, the Lake district, northern counties of England, and eastern and midland counties of Scotland, the nest being usually placed in a hole in a decayed tree. Though not easy to keep in a cage, this bird is much more amenable to confinement than the "spotted," and may be caged or placed in an aviary with Warblers. It is a very striking bird; the forehead, under parts, and greater wing coverts are pure white, contrasting against the other more or less black parts; the primary coverts and quills are dark-brown with a fawn-coloured spot on the secondaries. It is about 5½ inches in length. The female differs from the male in being brown instead of black on the upper parts of the body, and the white portions have a buffish tint. At liberty it feeds almost entirely on insects, grubs, worms and berries. Its cage should be of box pattern, 2 feet or even longer, 16 inches high, and 10 inches deep, and food the same as the

TREE CREEPER
RAY'S WAGTAIL
SKYLARK
MEADOW PIPIT

Gold-crested Wren, with a liberal supply of live insects or grubs. It is, if steady and in good plumage, a successful exhibition bird, and may be shown either in the show cage recommended for Warblers or Gold-crests.

The Spotted Flycatcher.

The Spotted Flycatcher, *Muscicapa grisola* (*Linn.*), is an abundant summer migrant to England, but rarer and more local in Scotland and Ireland. It generally reaches our shores in May, and is one of the most familiar of British birds, often choosing some briar, vine, or other tree that may be trained against a house or wall, in which to build its nest. It is also known as the Beam-bird, from a habit of sometimes building on the end of a projecting beam. The general colour is brown, shading to lighter and darker tints, with dull white on cheeks and underbody. It is a little larger than the Pied species. The song, as with the Pied, is very limited. From the nature of their food and habits, the Flycatchers are very difficult to keep in confinement, and young birds are, therefore, best. These can be successfully hand-reared, as recommended for the Warblers, and when able to feed themselves, weaned on to the food given for the Pied Flycatcher, using similar cages.

CHAPTER XXXIX

THE FINCHES—FAMILY FRINGILLIDÆ

THE Finch family is large and widely and plentifully distributed, and many of its members are special favourites as pets and exhibition birds.

The Greenfinch.

SUB-FAMILY COCCOTHRAUSTINÆ.—The Greenfinch, *Ligurinus chloris* (*Dresser*), is resident and common throughout our cultivated districts, nesting in hedges, forks of trees, and other situations. In winter this species congregates in large flocks, searching the stubbles and fields for small seeds. The Greenfinch is a short-bodied bird, 6 inches in length, somewhat heavily built, with a thick, powerful bill. Its plumage is rather handsome, the general colour being olive-yellow shaded to an ashen tint on the ear-coverts and sides of neck, the forehead, and running over the eyebrows bright yellow; the outer web of the wing and tail primary feathers are brilliant yellow; the breast and underbody bright yellow, shading to white on the abdomen. The shades of colour are much richer on some specimens, and these are classified "yellow" by British bird keepers; the others with a general colour of a more ashy hue are termed "buffs." The female differs from the male in being much duller in colour—browner above and paler below—and the primaries have simply a bare margin of pale yellow on the outer web. Greenfinches have a slight but incessant song, the notes sounding like *cher-cher*-CHER, the last note swelling in volume as drawled out. The Greenfinch is hardy, and becomes very tame in captivity; and there is no need to resort to hand-feeding for nestlings. Of late years it has become very popular for exhibition purposes and for hybrid breeding. It does well on a diet of canary seed with half part German rape, linseed, and white sunflower, with a very little hemp twice a week. If hemp is given more often the bird has a tendency to get too fat. A supply of wild seeds should also be given in their dry state in winter, and fresh gathered during the spring and summer. A mealworm, gentle, small smooth green caterpillar, or spray with green-fly blight, given in moderation, assists the bird's condition and improves the bloom on the plumage. A cage, similar to that illustrated on page 48, 18 inches long, 13 inches high, and 10 inches deep, answers well. A suitable show cage is illustrated on this page; size, 12 inches long, 10 inches high, and 5 inches deep; colour inside hedge-sparrow-egg blue and black out-

SHOW CAGE FOR FINCHES.

side. If preferred, the whole of the top of the cage may be wood instead of about an inch being bow wired, as in the illustration. Good shape and size, combined with rich colour, perfect plumage, and steadiness, are required for success in competition.

The Hawfinch.

The Hawfinch, *Coccothraustes vulgaris* (*Dresser*), the largest of the British Finches, is resident but rather locally distributed, although it has probably bred—nesting usually in scrubby whitethorn bushes—in all counties south of and including Cumberland. A friend of ours, Mr. T. W. Sharpe, of Carlisle, found a nest and eggs in Netherby Orchard, Longtown, on June 21st, 1907, which is believed to be the first authentic record of its breeding in Cumberland. It is only an accidental visitor to Scotland and Ireland. The Hawfinch has become most popular as a cage bird, and though at liberty of a shy disposition, in captivity it becomes bold and most confiding, taking tit-bits from one's fingers, albeit a nip from its most powerful bill is best avoided. It is a handsome bird, having a line of black round the forehead and in front of the eyes, with a beautifully defined black bib on the throat. The general colour above is chocolate-brown, running to pale cinnamon on the forehead, a bluish grey colour dividing the brown on the hind neck just below the nape; the under-parts are pale red tinted with brown, shading to white on the abdomen; the wings are black, glossed with purple-blue, the first four primaries having a narrow bar of white on the inner webs, which is more broadly continued upon the same parts of the secondaries. One of the striking features of the wings are the peculiarly shaped blue feathers that overlap the primaries of the wings. The tail is short for the size of the bird, in colour blackish-brown, tipped with white. The female is a much paler shade all over, has a smaller bib, and the breast and under-parts of a very pale brown. These birds do well on a diet of canary and white sunflower seeds with a little English rape, dari, or hemp added on alternate days so as to vary the diet. A few oats may occasionally be given, and when green peas are in season these can form half their food. The various small berries should be given as they ripen, especially those of the hawthorn and kernels of various stone fruits. A meal-worm or two can also be given sparingly when other tit-bits are plentiful. Free access should be given to the bath.

The Hawfinch is most hardy, and not at all difficult to keep; the young, taken at about ten days old, can be reared on any good insectivorous food, or upon equal parts of finely minced hard-boiled egg and powdered plain biscuit, mixed to a creamy substance with new milk or warm water. To this should be added a little German rape, prepared by soaking in cold water for forty-eight hours (changing the water two or three times), and finally well rinsing under the tap. It should then be dried through a strainer, and pulped up with the back of a spoon before mixing with the other food. Two or three green peas may be minced up fine and added if procurable. Little and often is the secret of success; do not cram the bird at one time and give no more for hours; a little food should be given from the end of a blunt-pointed piece of wood every half-hour from early morn till late at night. Two or three clean gentles, with the skins pierced, a meal-worm cut into two or three pieces, or a small, smooth, green caterpillar or two may be given two or three times a day in addition. Keep the nest clean and in a box as recommended for insectivorous birds, and when the youngsters can do for themselves, gradually wean them on to adult diet.

The Goldfinch.

SUB-FAMILY FRINGILLINÆ.—The Goldfinch, *Carduelis elegans* (*Macg.*), is one of if not *the* most popular and general favourites of our British resident Finches. It is pretty generally distributed, but owing to the cultivation of waste land formerly abounding with thistle and other weeds, this bird has become much more local and rare in Scotland, but is fairly plentiful in parts of Ireland and some districts of England, and reports indicate that they are on the increase. There is no necessity to describe this bird minutely; a reference to the coloured plate will show that it is of particularly striking plumage. The difference between the sexes is very difficult to distinguish; the female, as a rule, is smaller, the feathers immediately over the beak are lighter, the black feathers on the back of the head are edged with brownish-grey, as are also the black feathers on the shoulder, whilst the head is invariably smaller; the red on the face, or the "blaze," as it is called by fanciers, cuts off immediately with the eye, whereas that of the cock runs right past the eye, especially that portion over the forehead. Though the Goldfinch frequents wild waste-lands for its food, for nesting it favours orchards, evergreens, the branches of the horse-chestnut, birch, and oak, and other situations. The nest is most ingenious and pretty; it is cup-shaped and composed principally of moss, lined with wool and the down from the thistle, groundsel and dandelion seeds, with sometimes a few soft feathers or a little horsehair. The outside is covered with lichen, and the eggs are generally from four to five in number. There is no need to hand-rear the Goldfinch, as it takes readily to cage life, and though at first restless, continually hopping about, clinging to the wires, and rattling its bill against them as if wanting to escape, this apparent discontent very soon passes off, and the bird becomes most confiding and steady. In an aviary the Goldfinch sometimes is a bit of a tyrant, and although it seldom fights, will drive the other birds from the food until it has had its tit-bit. Goldfinches will breed in an aviary and even in a breeding cage, and we have known several lots so reared. The illustration on page 173 shows an adult bird and one in its nest feathers.

The Goldfinch possesses a sharp but exceedingly sweet song, combining a clear metallic ring with modulated power, much softer and sweeter than the Canary's, and linked together by a continual twittering, making the song last for a long time without intermission. In common with all Finches, it shows a very varied taste in regard to seeds, but the best food is composed of a selection of the following seeds : Canary and teazle in equal parts, with a little niger and flax (also known as linseed), oat-grits, rape, hemp and maw-seed. Some birds will not eat all these seeds ; therefore it is advisable to watch the general choice, and give those only, as otherwise it will scatter and waste the rest in order to obtain the favourites. Should the bird show a decided preference for hemp, it is not advisable to let it have too much, as this seed is very fattening. In order to break it of scattering when in search of the hemp, give a few—say twelve—seeds upon the top of the rest, and the bird will soon understand the arrangement, and give up its endeavours. A supply of wild seed should also be given, of which dandelion, thistle, and knapweed will form a large portion. Give these dry during the winter, and fresh gathered in their succulent form during the spring and summer. When wild the Goldfinch is of very great service to the gardener and farmer, as in spring it feeds almost entirely upon the seeds of groundsel and dandelion. In the summer, when the thistles have run to seed, Goldie may be seen hanging to the thistle-heads, and with its long, sharp-pointed bill extracting the seeds. The red feathers on its head are particularly short and strong to form a protection against the prickly thistles. In the autumn and winter the seeds of the thistle and button-weed form its staple food. It also greatly enjoys a piece of watercress or lettuce. One very important item in its treatment consists in providing plenty of sharp, gritty sand over the bottom of the cage. This assists digestion, and is also a source of great pleasure to the bird. A free use of the bath will complete the arrangements for good management. As in all British birds, partial albinism is fairly frequent in this species, the most common form being what is known as the Cheveril Goldfinch, which has the distinction of a white streak dividing the red on the chin and throat. In some specimens this band is very narrow, but in others the white extends to the shafts on either side of the throat.

The points of an exhibition Goldfinch are a large, rich, brilliant-coloured, clean-cut face, free from any intermixture of black in the red ; good body colour with well-defined markings ; large moons—that is, the white tippings to the wings ; the yellow wing bars brilliant and bold ; good size and shape. Perfect plumage and steadiness are also essential. The cages recommended for the Greenfinch answer, but the inside colour of the show cage should be dark green, and black outside.

The Siskin.

The Siskin, *Chrysomitris spinus* (*Dresser*), although a resident, breeding in some of the pine woods of Scotland, parts of Ireland, and also, it is said, in many English counties, is also a not very abundant winter migrant to England. It is a very beautiful, prettily marked little bird, as a glance at our coloured plate will show. Its black crown, usually called by fanciers the " cap," and black bib contrast with pleasing effect against the yellowish-green body striped with black. The cheeks and upper portion of the breast are primrose-yellow ; the lower portion of the breast light grey, shading to white on the abdomen. The Siskin's beauty is especially displayed when seen flitting amongst the branches of the alder trees, feeding upon the seeds and keeping up a continual twitter the while. The female differs from the male in having no black cap, paler body colour, and white under-parts with just a tint of yellow. The Siskin has not much song, and that little is occasionally interspersed with harsh, jarring notes, yet the bird is a very pretty addition to an aviary, breeds in captivity, and is largely kept for exhibition purposes. The Siskin should be fed upon canary and niger seed in equal parts with a little linseed and teazle. Wild seeds as advised for the Goldfinch should be added, and a supply of birch and alder seeds whenever procurable. Maw-seed and oat-grits may also be given in small quantities occasionally as tit-bits. Some fanciers give hemp-seed, but this is far too fattening, and as the Siskin is inclined to be somewhat of a glutton, a few hemp-seeds should only be given very occasionally. Siskins are fond of bathing, and should always have free access to a bath. The living and show cages recommended for the Goldfinch answer well for this bird, but they can be one size smaller, and the colour of the show cage be dark blue inside and black outside. A Siskin for exhibition must be of nice size and shape ; the blacker the cap the better ; the bib large and shapely, rich body colour ; wing bars and other markings distinct; the dark stripes running well down on to the sides of breast and flanks; perfect plumage, a good lustre on the surface, and steadiness.

The House Sparrow, *Passer domesticus* (*Macg.*), the commonest of all resident British birds in town and country, is really handsome, but the smoke and dirt of towns completely hide its beauty. In a country specimen its general colour is rich chestnut-brown streaked with black, with a crown or cap of dark slate-grey; the ear-coverts and sides of face are ashy-white, with a white patch behind each eye; the throat is black, shading to a blackish-grey, and forming up on the breast in crescent shape; the under-parts are ashy-grey. The female differs from the male in not having the black throat and being a lighter brown.

The House Sparrow.

The Sparrow is so well known that it is unnecessary to dilate upon its habits; and though not a desirable cage-bird owing to its having no song beyond a continual chirping or harsh chatter, if it is reared from the nest when quite young it will become a very interesting pet, and show great attachment to its keeper. Any ordinary roomy box pattern cage will do to keep it in. It should be fed on canary seed with a few oats added and a little bread soaked in cold water and squeezed dry as a tit-bit, though nothing seems to come amiss to its voracious appetite. Spiders and moths will be equally enjoyed, and seeding lettuce as green food is greatly appreciated. The House Sparrow has been exhibited from time to time in beautiful condition in a Finch show cage, but without success.

The Tree Sparrow, *Passer montanus* (*Macg.*), is both a resident and migrant, though very local and nowhere abundant in this country, appearing partial to low-lying country. It breeds locally in many parts of England, in the eastern portion of Scotland, and very sparingly in two or three districts of Ireland. In habits the species closely resembles the House Sparrow; it assembles in small flocks, feeds in a similar manner, and builds its nest in like situations, except that it favours holes in pollard and other trees. If closely inspected it is much more handsome than suspected by a cursory glance, the markings upon its head and throat being especially noticeable, but the sexes are not distinguishable. It differs from the House Sparrow by being smaller, and it has not the dark crescent mark on the breast; the ear-coverts are lighter, with a black patch on the lower parts; the sides of the neck are creamy white and the shade of chestnut is more uniform. It is also a much more active bird. When caught it should be kept in a cage until tame, and not be placed immediately in an aviary, or it will invariably sulk, behave wildly, and frighten the other birds. It does well on the same diet as its relative, and is a desirable addition to a mixed aviary of small birds. For an illustration of the Sparrows *see* page 125.

The Tree Sparrow.

The Chaffinch, *Fringilla cœlebs* (*Linn.*), is resident and common in almost every moderately wooded locality. It is a winter visitor only to the Shetlands, and a common winter migrant on all our eastern shores. During the summer, Chaffinches, like nearly all our smaller birds, continue in pairs, and as the broods become able to associate with their parents they may be found in small parties. As winter approaches these small parties join up into flocks, frequenting woodland districts, and feeding on seeds in the stubble fields and farmyards in company with Greenfinches and even Sparrows. During the summer and the breeding season their food and that of their young is largely insectivorous, the caterpillar of the *Lepidoptera* forming no small part. The nest is one of the prettiest of structures; it is cup-shaped and generally built in the forks of smaller branches of bushes, in hedges, apple and other fruit trees, gorse bushes, and in the ivy which clothes the trunks of trees. It is often placed high up and then requires a sharp eye to detect it, being built into a notch or amidst small branches, and so carefully covered with lichen matching that on the tree as to appear almost part of it, and often on our rambles, but for the end of a tail poking over such an excrescence, we might have passed it. As can be seen from our coloured plate, it is one of the most handsome of the Finches. The bird depicted is in full summer plumage, and in winter the colours are scarcely so bright. The female has similar markings to the male, but is altogether paler in colour and ashy-brown above instead of chestnut. The breast and under-body too are a pale ashy-brown, not vinous-red, as in the male.

The Chaffinch.

From its compact and elegant shape, combined with lively habits and short but pretty song, the Chaffinch is deservedly held in high estimation. It is a bold bird, and approaches the bars of the cage or aviary with extreme confidence, chirping the while or uttering its lively call-note of *pink*. In Germany, where the Chaffinch is much admired, singing matches are held to test their comparative merits, and similar contests take place in England. The song is composed of several distinct notes, each of which is successively repeated, forming a short phrase or song, which, to be perfect, should consist of so many syllables. This bird's song appears to differ slightly in different counties; for instance, the Essex bird's song is said to be *Toll-loll-loll-chickwedo*, while that of the Kentish birds is *Toll-loll-loll-kiss-me-dear*, or at any rate these are the sounds conveyed by the notes. When the former song is sung each repeat must finish with a distinct *wee do*, the latter with a distinct *me-dear* uttered in a rather higher pitch. Some birds give different terminations, and a good songster will repeat its phrases with extreme pertinacity, which may be stimulated by placing the young bird with an older one of acknowledged singing powers. Amongst a certain class this fact has been made the basis of matches that are managed in a business-like manner. A judge, referee, and scorers are appointed; and the rival birds, confined in small cages, are brought into the room covered and are hung up, but so that they cannot see each other. The signal is given, they are uncovered, and the match commences. Every *perfect* "song" is scored down to the respective singer until time is up, when the singer of the highest number of songs wins. The judge notifies each song to the scorer, and, in case of dispute as to the imperfections of any song, the assistance of the referee is called in. No song counts, however often rendered, unless it finishes in the manner already described.

The Chaffinch is also a popular bird for exhibitions, and generally competes successfully in mixed classes, and at some shows a class is given for this species alone. Size, combined with good shape, colours rich and brilliant, well-defined markings, perfect plumage with a good surface lustre and steadiness are the necessary exhibition points. The cages recommended for the Goldfinch are suitable for this bird, with the inside of the show cage painted light green and the outside black. The diet should be canary seed with a little German rape, linseed and white sunflower seed, and a supply of various wild seeds as recommended for the Green and other Finches. As the Chaffinch is a partial insectivorous feeder, a little good insectivorous food should also be given, as well as a meal worm or two or three gentles. During the summer, caterpillars, wasp grubs, green fly blight, and similar live food can be supplied, and free access to the bath always allowed. Chaffinches need not be hand-reared, as wild caught adults soon settle down to cage-life, and many become remarkably tame.

The Brambling.

The Brambling, *Fringilla montifringilla* (*Linn.*), also known as the Bramble or Mountain Finch, is a winter visitor to our isles, arriving between September and November, sometimes in very large flocks, and leaving us again early in the spring for its breeding haunts on the Continent and Siberia. While with us the Bramblings frequent beech woods, partly wooded districts, or localities interspersed with old hedgerows, feeding largely on beechmast and seeds of the alder. They consort with Chaffinches, which they somewhat resemble in manners, visiting farmyards in their company, and feeding on loose grain or seeds. The Brambling has practically no song, but its handsome plumage and lively movements make it an attractive bird. Many raise the feathers on the crown of the head in crest form when looked at as if to denote pleasure. In size and shape the Brambling is similar to the Chaffinch, and a good idea of its handsome plumage is given in the male bird depicted on our coloured plate. The female differs from the male in being paler and browner in colour. The colours of the winter plumage are not so brilliant, the black feathers having sandy-coloured margins, which gradually become black again as the birds come into breeding condition. Many Bramblings are shown at our exhibitions during the autumn and winter months in summer plumage as the result of good feeding. An exhibition bird should possess good colour with the various tints rich and brilliant; marking and spangling distinct; good size and shape; perfect plumage and steadiness. Food should be as for the Chaffinch, but add to the bill of fare a supply of beechmast and alder seeds whenever procurable, and allow free use of the bath.

The Linnet.

The Linnet, *Linota cannabina* (*Newton*) is a plentiful resident distributed over the British islands, frequenting commons, furze-coverts, and the borders of moorland districts in summer to breed, and then migrating to the coasts, stubble-lands, and fallows in large flocks during the autumn and winter. It is rare in some parts of Scotland. Its range extends throughout Europe, and there are large migrations of Linnets from the Continent to our shores in the spring and autumn. Its favourite nesting situation is in furze, white-thorn and black-thorn bushes, but it also resorts to broom, heather and other undergrowth. Generally the nest is placed low, but we have found it 8 or 10 feet up in a tall white-thorn. Its food in its wild state consists chiefly of seeds, the young being largely reared on soft, succulent seeds, charlock and knotgrass being especially sought after; it also feeds on speedwell, flax (linseed), hemp, dandelion and other weeds. Linnets are named Brown, Grey or Rose Linnet, according to the colour of their plumage, which varies greatly with the age of the bird and the season of the year. When young—that is, birds of the year with their first moult—Linnets are lighter in colour than the bird depicted on our coloured plate, have no crimson on the forehead, and but little on the breast, and this is largely concealed by the light amber-coloured fringe to each of the feathers; they are by some then called Grey Linnets. When wild, after the second moult, the male obtains the crimson hue faintly on the forehead, but much more pronounced on the breast than in the first year; the sandy-brown colour of the breast sides and flanks also puts on a richer hue, and it is then known as a Brown Linnet. With the third moult the forehead and breast assume a bright carmine tint, and the bird is then known as a Rose Linnet. This carmine or crimson tint on the forehead and breast is brightest and richest on all male birds of whatever age during the spring and breeding season, the amber-tipped margins of the feathers which cloud it at other periods having then faded off, leaving the crimson fully exposed; the whole of the body colour assumes a much brighter hue during the breeding season. The coloured plate depicts a male bird in breeding plumage, and it must be noted these remarks as to changes of colour only apply to birds in their wild state. With the first moult in captivity the crimson colour on the breast and head disappears, and does not return; but the brown body colour is a richer hue when the bird is in breeding condition than at any other period, even in captivity.

The Linnet has a pleasing song of great variety, beautifully modulated and flute-like, and so sweet that it heads the list of British Finch songsters, and its talents have made it an especial favourite as a cage-bird. It is also, like the Chaffinch, in great demand as a contest singer and as an exhibition bird. The coloured plate shows an average coloured Linnet in its wild plumage, but many birds display more sandy-brown on the breast, this being quite covered with but just the faintest shade of light in the centre. For exhibition birds the less the display of this whitish-buff on the upper portion of the chest, and the brighter and richer the brown above and below, with plenty of dark brown stripes on the breast and sides running well down the flanks, the better. A good margin of white to the outer web of the primaries of the wing and the throat nicely pencilled, gives a further set-off to a bird. These points all well pronounced, coupled with good size and shape, perfect plumage and condition, with steadiness, constitute an exhibition bird. The female differs from the male in that it has no crimson on the breast or head in its wild state, and the sandy-brown on the breast is much paler. The stripes are of a dull, dusky tint, and the hen does not carry so much white on the outer web of the primaries.

The Linnet becomes exceedingly attached to those who feed and tend it, and, as with the other Finches, is extremely erratic in its choice of food, except that all show a preference for hemp and rape. The former seed, however, is much too fattening, and should be given very sparingly, just a few seeds as a tit-bit, especially as the Linnet is rather a greedy bird and apt to overfeed itself. The majority do well on a diet of equal parts of teazle, German and English rape, with a little linseed, canary, and golden pleasure, together with a supply of the various wild seeds. The Linnet is particularly fond of shepherd's purse, dandelion, charlock, knotgrass and knapweed, and a supply of these should be given in their succulent state whenever procurable, as well as dry during the winter. They should have free use of the bath, and the cages advised for the Goldfinch. There is no necessity to hand-rear this bird.

The Mealy Redpoll.

The Mealy Redpoll, *Linota linaria* (*Newton*), is a winter migrant, but somewhat erratic in numbers. In the autumn and winter of 1910–11 they appeared in quite large flocks, whilst in some other years few were seen here, though general throughout Northern Europe. Its habits and food are similar to those of the Lesser Redpoll, with which it frequents the birch and alder trees, which provide their chief food. In shape it is similar to the Lesser species, but considerably larger, and its general colour much lighter. The back and general colour above are a light brown-grey; the under-parts are whitish-buff, the male bird having a rich rose-pink tint on the breast, forehead and rump in its wild state. It also has the light wing-bars and black bib of the Lesser Redpoll. The female differs from the male in not having the rosy tint on the forehead, breast, or rump, is smaller, darker above, and the breast and flanks are more heavily striped. It, therefore, makes the better exhibition bird, as good markings and a large shapely bib are important features in this respect, combined with perfect plumage, prim, smart appearance and steadiness. The Mealy Redpoll has a little chattering song, but lively, engaging ways. It does well on the diet recommended for the Linnet, with a little niger seed added twice a week, and requires similar cages to those advised for the Siskin. The Mealy Redpoll can be safely placed in an aviary with other birds.

The Lesser Redpoll.

The Lesser Redpoll, *Linota rufescens* (*Newton*), is a resident, but its numbers are reinforced by large autumn and spring migrations from Europe. It is local during the breeding season, usually selecting retired spots; we have seen quite a number breeding in a small triangular coppice in Surrey. It nests in the alders, willows on the fringe of streams, sometimes in low bushes and scrub-wood. Our coloured plate represents a male in wild plumage; the female does not possess the red breast and similar tint on rump, though the male also loses these in captivity. It is a small but very pretty bird, and its lively, confiding ways make it quite a desirable pet in a cage, and is a great attraction to the aviary. Its song is a mere simple twittering note, but, continually uttered, as it is, acts as an incentive to the rest of the birds, and will often cause them to sing. The Redpoll is a very affectionate bird, which is easily tamed and taught many tricks. Of late years it has become a popular exhibition bird, and is also much in request for hybrid breeding. The desired points of a show specimen are the rufous-brown colour coming well down on to the sides of the breast and flanks, the richer the better; the breast and flanks also richly streaked with darker brown; the colours generally rich, bright, clear and well defined; wing bars distinct; the black bib on throat of good size and well defined, not zig-zag; body shapely and well matured; perfect plumage, and steady. The bird does well on the diet recommended for the Mealy Redpoll, and should be kept and shown in similar cages. It is quite hardy, and should be allowed free use of the bath.

The Twite.

The Twite, *Linota flavirostris (Dresser)*, is a resident and migrant, regularly breeding in the northern parts of Britain, assembling in large flocks during the winter and migrating southwards. Many become permanent residents in the North, and it has bred in wild, hilly parts of Yorkshire, Derbyshire, Staffordshire, and Ireland. It is not unlike the Linnet, though slightly smaller and more slender-looking; the bill is smaller and is yellow, not brown. The whole plumage, too, is darker, the throat, sides of breast, and flanks being a reddish-brown and the dark streaks on those parts are of a blacker tint than those of the Linnet. It also resembles the latter in its habits, except that of nesting. In its wild state the male is distinguishable by the red rump, which, however, disappears when cage-moulted. Like the Redpoll, it has little or no song, and its name is derived from its peculiar call-note. It is a popular cage bird, and for exhibition purposes the essential points are good size and shape, rich colour; head well laced; good profusion of rich brown all over the breast, and plenty of dark streaking, perfect plumage and steadiness. The cages and diet recommended for the Linnet are suitable, and we may add that the bird is very hardy, and quite safe for the aviary.

The Bullfinch.

The Bullfinch, *Pyrrhula europœa (Vieill.)*, is a fairly plentiful resident throughout the British Isles except in the extreme north, and is found in Western Europe, eastwards to Germany, south to the Mediterranean. A larger species, *Pyrrhula pyrrhula*, is found in Eastern Europe and is known as the Russian or Siberian Bullfinch. Our beautiful English bird is of retiring habits, and frequents woods and plantations in pairs, its piping call-note imparting a touch of life and melody to the surroundings. It is a stout-built, compact bird of very striking plumage, as may be seen from our coloured plate, its bright red breast contrasting most forcibly with the black hood on the head and the beautiful bluish-grey back. A white band runs across the rump, and another of bluish-grey across the black wings. The tail is black and a faint tint of vermilion adjoins the lower abdomen, with the under-tail coverts white. The female differs from the male in having the breast chocolate-brown and the grey on the back tinged with brown.

Although the Bullfinch has but a moderate song, it is possessed of imitative powers in the highest degree, and it may be taught to pipe a tune more readily than any other British bird. This may be done in a somewhat similar manner to that recommended for the Blackbird, but the tedious task is much more often successful, and the Bullfinch then attains a great value. In Germany regular piping schools are established, where the birds are taught when quite young. It takes kindly to captivity, and is an attractive pet and exhibition bird. It can be hand-reared, as recommended for the Hawfinch, though the trouble is not necessary, for adults readily take to cage or aviary life.

The Bullfinch is a somewhat slovenly bird, and very apt to scatter its food. It should be kept clean, and be given plenty of sharp sea or fresh river sand. It breeds very freely in the aviary if provided with proper materials for building. We find that it prefers small pieces of heather and fine roots, and is also partial to the fibres of coco-nut matting. When rearing young they should be given a plentiful supply of buds of fruit trees and bushes, dock, ragweed, and thistle seed heads in their half-ripe, succulent form. In addition give also a little good insectivorous food made crumbly-moist each day, with a little hard-boiled egg added. The regular diet should consist of canary seed, German rape, groats, and white sunflower seed in equal portions. They are fond of rape seed soaked, as advised for the Hawfinch, but unpulped. Sunflower seeds may be given in all stages of growth towards the end of summer and autumn;

blackberries, mountain ash, hawthorn, privet, dew, and other berries also assist to a good moult, and aid in getting the good colour so important in an exhibition bird. Bullfinches are also fond of seeding chickweed and other green stuff. A good exhibition specimen should be well matured, have a wide skull, a large black cap of good shape with a glistening lustre or polish over it. The various body colours and their terminal points should be well defined and have a nice bloom or finished appearance, called "condition" by fanciers, and also be perfectly steady. A bath assists to keep them in good health and plumage. Similar cages to those recommended for the Greenfinch answer well.

The Crossbill.

The Crossbill, *Loxia curvirostra* (*Linn.*), a resident and winter migrant, is a handsome bird, especially noticeable for the peculiar formation of its bill, from which feature it derives its name; the mandibles cross each other and are also curved towards the end, the top one down and the bottom one up. The general colour of the male is pale vermilion; the wings and tail are dark umber-brown tinted with vermilion. The general colour of the female is yellowish-green tinted with olive. There appears to be some variation in colour according to age, the adult male putting on much of the female colour after a moult in captivity. The Crossbill is not a common bird in England, generally frequenting fir plantations and breeding in the pine districts of Scotland, Ireland, and Wales. It feeds chiefly on the seeds of pines, cleverly extracting the seeds from the cones with the hook-like points of its bill; it also eats berries and other seeds, and is fond of the pips of an apple, which it will skilfully extract from the core. The Crossbill's cage must be all wire, like those for Cockateels and Budgerigars, for it would soon destroy a wooden one. It should be fed upon canary, rape, sunflower seeds, a little hemp and fir cones. A piece of apple or its pips can be given occasionally, and a few juniper berries when in season, of which it is very fond. The Crossbill's song is somewhat harsh, and not at all pretty.

SUB-FAMILY EMBERIZINÆ.—In this species the form of the bill is the leading characteristic, and separates the Buntings from the other Finches; in many the internal roof of the mandible projects in a hard knob, with the maxilla strong, forming an angle at the gape.

The Corn Bunting.

The Corn Bunting, *Emberiza miliaria* (*Linn.*), is a resident and migrant throughout the British Isles; though occurring very locally, its range extends to the Shetlands and throughout Europe, where it is most numerous in the south and centre parts. It is a thick-set bird of plain plumage, rather larger than the rest of the true Buntings. The general colour is sandy-brown, with blackish centres to the feathers, giving a streaked appearance; the wing-coverts are edged with sandy-buff, the brown shading to dull white on the abdomen. It is a noble-looking bird, but has little song, and this is harsh and unmusical. The female is smaller and paler in colour. The Corn Bunting feeds principally on grains and other seeds, for breaking or shelling which the hard knob or tooth in the upper mandible is admirably adapted. While seeking its food on the ground it doubtless picks up insects as well, especially during the breeding season, as most Buntings are fond of a meal-worm or a small smooth, green caterpillar. It is a good exhibition bird, the essential points being size, good shape, rich colour, the darker stripes on the breast and flanks plentiful and well defined, and the bird steady in its cage. Its cage should be similar to those for the other Finches, the living cage not less than 20 or 24 inches long, and the show cage 14 inches long, 12 inches high, and 6 inches deep; colour inside mid-green, outside black. For diet, give canary seed with a few whole oats and a little grass seed. Occasionally add a few grains of hemp or sunflower seeds, and once or twice a week a half teaspoonful of good insectivorous food made crumbly moist. A meal worm or two per day and the various succulent wild seeds may be offered whenever procurable. Free access to the bath should be given at all times.

Yellow Bunting.

The Yellow Bunting, *Emberiza citrinella* (*Linn.*), commonly called the Yellow-hammer, is a handsome resident and breeds almost everywhere in the British Isles except the extreme north of Scotland. It is known to almost every country dweller by its continuous little song uttered from the top of the hedge, which sounds as if it were calling for "a little-bit-of-bread-no-cheese." The head, throat, and breast are rich yellow, the head being marked on each side of the crown with dark green in the form of a V, meeting on the forehead at the base of the bill. Between these two stripes some specimens are much dappled with small specks of dark green; but the more free from these the more valuable is the bird for exhibition purposes. Another streak passes before and behind the eye, and there is also a patch on the ear-coverts. The upper portion of the body is brown streaked with blackish-brown; the rump is vinous-chestnut; the lower portions of the breast, sides, and flanks are rich chestnut, but the flanks are heavily striped with blackish-brown; the wings and tail are blackish-brown, edged with brownish-orange. The female differs somewhat from the male in her colours being less brilliant, and the crown a brownish tint heavily striped, with just a faint tint of yellow appearing between the stripes.

The Yellow Bunting frequents small thickets and hedgerows, generally building its nest under shelter of some small bush in a hedge-bottom or amongst the grass of a ditch. It feeds principally upon seeds, small grains, and insects, and in the summer-time is one of the most attractive of British birds, flitting from bush to bush, and displaying to marked advantage the bright yellow on its breast and head. It is a good exhibition bird, and a desirable addition to an aviary, and will breed therein. It does well on the diet recommended for the preceding species, and is equally fond of the bath. It should be kept and exhibited in the cages recommended for the Goldfinch, with the inside of the show cage dark blue and the outside black. The essential points of an exhibition specimen are good colour and marking, the crown of the head as clear as possible except for the V mark, which, with the ear-coverts, should be of a good dark, dense shade; good size and shape; plumage perfect, with a satin-like gloss over the surface, and perfect steadiness.

The Cirl Bunting.

The Cirl Bunting, *Emberiza cirlus* (*Linn.*), is a resident and migrant, very local and rather scarce in our islands. In England, except to ornithologists, it is little known, for when wild it closely resembles the Yellow Bunting. Its chief distinctions from the latter are its black throat; the head and hind part of the neck are olive-green streaked with black, shaded with bluish-grey, and the lower part of the back and upper tail-coverts are olive-green. The female differs from the male in not having the black throat, owing to which it has often been mistaken for the Yellow Bunting, but the latter has a chestnut-brown rump, whilst the hen of the Cirl Bunting has olive-green, and the lesser wing-coverts are greenish-grey. These features always serve to distinguish them. It breeds in most of the Southern counties. Outside these islands its habitation is chiefly the western portion of the Continent. As with the Yellow Bunting, its song is not very elaborate, consisting also of one note rather more rapidly delivered and without the prolonged finishing note. The Cirl Bunting is somewhat shy, being rather a woodland species, although it often approaches habitations to build its nest. It is kept chiefly for exhibition purposes, or to add variety to an aviary of mixed birds. Diet as for the Yellow Bunting, with a more liberal supply of fresh, succulent grass seed during the spring and summer as long as procurable. Free use of the bath should also be allowed, and similar cages to those for the preceding bird. The essential points of an exhibition specimen are good size, rich colour, markings well defined; steadiness and perfection of plumage.

The Reed Bunting.

The Reed Bunting, *Emberiza schæniclus* (*Linn.*), is another resident and migrant found everywhere in marshy situations throughout Britain, except the Shetlands, where it is only an occasional visitor. It is generally distributed over Europe. This species differs considerably in its habits from those already mentioned, breeding near its marshy haunts, and feeding largely on the insects with which those places abound in the summer. In winter it feeds on the seeds of reeds, aquatic plants and other weeds, only approaching houses when driven by the severity of the weather for grains and other food. It is rather a handsome bird, having in the summer-time a jet-black head and throat, with a band or collar of white running round the neck and down to the breast. The general colour above is brownish-black, the centres of the feathers being black with a broad fringe of chestnut; on the lower part of the back and rump the centres of the feathers are of the same dark tint edged with grey; the wings are brownish-black with a narrow edge to the outer webs of the primaries of pale reddish-brown; the secondaries and coverts are of a darker tint, broadly fringed with chestnut; the centre tail feathers are greyish-brown, paler at the edges, others are black; the two exterior feathers have white running diagonally from the base to the tip of the inner web; the sides of the breast and flanks are streaked with blackish-brown; the abdomen, vent, and under tail-coverts are white. In winter the plumage is less brilliant, and the hen has not the striking characteristics of the black head and throat; shades of brown and chestnut predominate over the black. The Reed Bunting is a very attractive addition to an aviary, where it should be given plenty of water, for it is remarkably fond of bathing. It is also an attractive cage-bird, and is frequently seen at exhibitions. It should be fed as the preceding bird, and similar cages used. Its essential exhibition points are a well matured body, colour rich and lustrous, markings well defined, steadiness and perfect plumage.

The Snow Bunting.

The Snow Bunting, *Plectrophenax nivalis* (*Sharpe*), is a regular winter visitor, sometimes arriving in large flocks on the eastern coast. They appear in the south of Scotland towards the end of October or early in November, visiting the sub-alpine districts and descending to the borders of cultivation as winter advances, and in very severe weather retiring even to the Lowlands. It is probable that a few scattered pairs breed on some of the higher mountain ranges of Scotland, but such instances are so rare that we can only look upon the bird as a winter visitor. In the breeding season its general colour above is black; the wings are black, with the primaries at the base and coverts white; the tail is black except the outer feathers, which are white, tipped with black; the head, neck and under-body are white. The female is similar to the male, but the black is not so dense, the feathers being fringed with greyish-white. In their winter plumage the dark parts and even a portion of the white are fringed with pale chestnut, and it is chiefly while clothed in this colour that we see it. It is rather restless in a cage, and not so easily tamed as some of the other species, though when once confidence is gained some specimens become fairly steady, and then make useful birds for exhibition. The cages and diet recommended for the other Buntings answer well.

The Lapland Bunting.

The Lapland Bunting, *Calcarius lapponicus* (*Sharpe*), is almost entirely a Northern species of both hemispheres, but an occasional visitor to our islands has given it a place in the British list. The general colour above is blackish-brown tinged with yellowish-grey, with the greater wing-coverts and secondary quills blackish-brown, deeply margined with chestnut, the tips being white; the primaries are dusky with pale edges; the tail is dusky, the exterior feathers having the outer web and half the inner one sullied-white; the next feathers are marked with a small, wedge-shaped white spot near the tip. The head, throat, and upper portion of the breast are black, relieved by a margin of white running into the creamy-white of the under parts. The female has not the black head and rufous collar on the neck. In winter these birds are of a sandy rufous colour. They are quite safe for either cage or aviary, and soon become very tame. They should be kept in similar cages and fed as the other Buntings.

CHAPTER XL

STARLINGS, CROWS, LARKS, WOODPECKERS, ETC.

FAMILY STURNIDÆ.—The Starlings, like the Crows, are "ground walkers," using a walking step instead of "hops," like most passerine birds, but only one of this family concerns us.

The Common Starling.

The Common Starling, *Sturnus vulgaris* (*Linn.*), is a common resident throughout the British Isles, and is rapidly becoming more so. Enormous flocks from abroad also arrive in the autumn, sometimes pouring into our eastern coasts for days together. This bird is found throughout Europe in the summer, and is a winter visitor to the Mediterranean countries. There is no need to describe this bird minutely, for its black body with a predominance of purple reflections intermingled with green and violet, and the light fringes to the body feathers causing a spangled appearance, are quite sufficient for its identification. The gloss on the female is never so brilliant as on the male, and also shows more of the sandy-buff tips which give the spangled appearance to these birds. It is very handsome, and is seen to advantage as it runs upon the lawn searching for worms or insects. An intermediate species, more heavily spangled and having green ear-coverts, is said to visit us, and we have certainly observed these differences of colour. Starlings build in hollow trees, holes in walls, under the eaves of houses, and often in dove-cotes, and we have even found the nest in a corner on the floor of a hay-loft.

Though its chattering kind of scream is not much of a recommendation, the Starling is a very nice pet, and, like most of this class, from the breadth of its tongue, may be taught to whistle and talk with tolerably clear articulation. It is a wonderful mimic, and will often form curious attachments, especially if allowed to roam the house. The Starling should be fed and treated as the Thrush, giving fruit as a variation, and garden worms are an especial treat. A meal worm, wasp, or other grubs, spiders, a few flies, or any insects occasionally will greatly add to the bird's health and enjoyment. The bath should be given daily. They are easily hand-reared on the same food as Thrushes, and the same cage answers well; they can also be kept in an aviary. Starlings are frequently seen at exhibitions, the Thrush show cage answering well, but coloured white inside and black out. Essential points are even, abundant spangling, rich colours and gloss, perfect plumage, and steadiness.

FAMILY ORIOLIDÆ.—This family differs from the Crows not only in gaudy coloration, but in having a notch in the upper mandible.

The Golden Oriole.

The Golden Oriole, *Oriolus galbula* (*Linn.*), is the only species of this family which has any claim to a place in the British list, and that only as a rare summer migrant to England and Ireland, occasionally crossing from the Continent. It is one of the handsomest birds that visit us, being of a bright lemon-yellow with black wings, as are also the two middle feathers and the base of its tail. Though it has not much natural song, its very handsome plumage accords it a very prominent position in the aviary, or it may be kept in a cage of box pattern not less than 4 feet long, 2 feet high, and 12 or 14 inches deep, with two perches wide apart so that the bird can take a good hop from one to the other. It should have free access to the bath and be fed and treated in the manner recommended for the Blackcap, always providing a supply of juicy fruits, such as orange, grapes, ripe pear, or banana.

FAMILY CORVIDÆ.—In this family, and especially in its sub-section, the Perching birds, *Conirostres*, we find such great variety and high development as to rank them first in typical form among the "Birds." We can, however, only refer to those which concern the scope of this work.

The Chough.

The Chough, *Pyrrhocorax graculus* (*Dresser*), is commonly called the Cornish Chough owing to it at one time largely favouring the cliffs of Cornwall. It is resident, breeding on the rocky coasts of the British Isles, and more rarely than formerly in some few inland situations. It is also a migrant and a cliff and mountain dweller on both sides of the Mediterranean. It is a large, handsome bird, 15 inches in length, with a wing measurement of 12 inches. In colour it is jet black with the exception of its bright-red legs and bill, which latter is long and thin. The plumage is covered with a beautiful gloss, and the sexes are alike. The Chough is kept as a pet and for exhibition purposes, and becomes very tame. It requires a very large living-cage of the box pattern, 4 to 5 feet in length, 3 feet high, and 2 feet deep, with two perches similar in thickness to those used for Parrot cages. The show-cage should be of the same pattern and at least 2 feet long, 20 inches high, and 18 inches deep, with two perches similar to those in the living-cage ; the inside should be creamy white, and the outside black. The essential points for exhibition are size, rich lustrous colour, and perfect condition, to which free use of the bath with good feeding conduces. Choughs should be fed on an insectivorous food, similar to that recommended for the Missel Thrush, with boiled bullock's liver and heart minced up fine ; also a little finely minced raw beef added two or three times a week, and especially a few days before going to an exhibition. Shellfish chopped up fine should occasionally be given with the food.

The Jay.

The Jay, *Garrulus glandarius* (*Macg.*), is a resident and migrant in all well-wooded districts of the British Isles, rarer in Scotland and the North of Ireland, and occurring throughout the greater part of Europe. It is a remarkably handsome bird, the delicate light fawn-colour of its vinaceous-tinted general plumage contrasting most effectively with the bright blue-black and white bars on the dark wings ; the forehead is whitish, and it and the crown are streaked with black ; the head-feathers are long and capable of being elevated as a crest ; the throat is white, and the under-body of the same colour as the back, but paler, shading to pure white on the under tail-coverts ; the rump and upper tail-coverts are also of the same pure tint, and the tail black. This bird is about 13 inches long, and the sexes are alike. It builds in the thickest parts of woods, in the fork of a tree, or on the top of a bush, and after the young have left the nest they generally accompany the parent birds, living in bands, and then the eggs and young of other birds often fall victims to their voracious appetite. On account of this the Jay usually gets short shrift from gamekeepers, while its beautiful blue feathers are also much sought after as artificial flies for anglers. Owing to this continued destruction, Jays are decreasing in number. Apart from its predatory food, the Jay's diet consists of acorns, fruits, beech-mast, worms, cockchafers, and other insects, as well as mice, frogs, and small reptiles.

It is of an inquisitive and garrulous disposition, and its true note is decidedly harsh ; but it has great powers of mimicry, and may be taught to imitate a variety of sounds, and even learn to talk slightly. Jays are easily hand-reared on the same food as Thrushes, but should be given a more liberal supply of grubs and meal and earthworms. The cages for living and exhibition should be similar to those advised for the Chough, and the adult Jay does well on the same food with the addition of tit-bits from its bill of fare when wild. It is very fond of a bath. Rich colours, perfect plumage, and steadiness are essential exhibition points.

The Magpie.

The Magpie, *Pica rustica* (*Dresser*), is generally resident throughout the British Isles, though more plentiful in some parts than others. It is also found throughout Europe, Asia to China, and in North America. It is a woodland species, building in the topmost branches of trees, and often in tall, rough, neglected hedges. The Magpie is so well known as to make description superfluous, though perhaps many casual observers have little idea that the black in its plumage (which contrasts so markedly with the large patches on the wings and body of very pure white) is shaded, especially upon the lower part of the back and the tail, with varied rays of glistening sheen. Its very long black tail, shading to green and purple, adds to its beauty; the sexes are alike in this respect. Its thieving propensities in captivity have occasioned many a tale, and one naturally associates the bird with silver spoons and the "Maid and the Magpie." These pilfering habits have often relegated the Magpie to a cage, though when reared from the nest it is exceedingly tame, and, apart from its immoral notions of property, becomes a very nice pet; it is easily taught to talk, and but for the mess it makes can be allowed to range the house, when it invariably contracts either great friendship or antipathy for the dog, cat, or any other rival.

When wild the Magpie is the terror of all small birds, preying upon their young, and they often band together in order to drive off the intruder. Its appetite is not at all dainty, carrion, insects, fruit, and grain all serve to meet its requirements. Young Magpies are just as easily hand-reared as the Jay, and on the same food. The cage should be similar to that recommended for the Chough, and if 5 feet long and 3 feet deep so much the better, as this will help to preserve the bird's long tail. The Magpie should be fed like the Jay, and exhibited in a similar show-cage. Bright colours, the patches of white well defined, good shape, perfect plumage, and steadiness are essentials for success at exhibitions.

The Jackdaw.

The Jackdaw, *Corvus monedula* (*Linn.*), is an abundant species, resident and pretty generally distributed, though it favours certain localities, and lives as freely in the midst of a populous city as amongst wild woodland and rocks. It is also migratory, large numbers reaching us every autumn from Northern Europe. The Jackdaw is a wise-looking bird, and from its droll antics is a special favourite with boys. Young Jackdaws can be easily reared on the same food as the Magpie, and we have even reared them on barley meal alone, made crumbly moist with cold water; they matured well, and turned out fine, healthy, strong birds. They may be taught to speak a little. Its comical cry of "Jack," accompanied by its mock-serious look, will always make the Jackdaw a cheery companion; though, like the Raven, it is, unfortunately, very fond of stealing (which circumstance has given us the laughable legend of the "Jackdaw of Rheims"), and all bright articles should therefore be placed beyond its reach. It will become very affectionate, and may be allowed its freedom, so far as the clipping of a few wing-feathers will permit, and will then sometimes form friendship with a dog or cat.

There is a peculiarly reverend appearance about the Jackdaw, with its general black plumage, save for the glossy blue-black cap on its head, shining grey collar, and the purple sheen of its wings and tail. The sexes are alike. The Jackdaw nests in church towers, old ruins, holes in trees and in cliffs, and sometimes even in a deserted rabbit warren. It does well on the same diet as the Chough, and may be kept and exhibited in the same cages as that bird, and allowed free use of a bath. Though usually more of a pet than an exhibition bird, some very fine specimens have been shown. High condition, with glossy sheen to the feather, perfect plumage, and steadiness are essentials in exhibition specimens.

FAMILY ALAUDIDÆ.—True Larks are easily distinguished from any of the preceding birds by their less conical bill and peculiar form of feet. By far the greater number live almost entirely on the ground, run swiftly, bask in the sun and amongst the dust. Their flight is powerful and capable of being long sustained. Three of this family concern us here.

The Skylark.

The Skylark, *Alauda arvensis* (*Linn.*), is a well-known resident throughout Great Britain, though it migrates from the more northern parts during the winter. It is also common in Europe, whence a large migration takes place into England during the autumn. The Skylark is entitled to a prominent position among our songsters, whether soaring high amid the clouds or as the pet of some family cramped in between the walls of narrow streets, enlivening a whole neighbourhood by the clear and lively tones of its inspiring song. Even in a cage the Lark seems constrained to combine some muscular exercise with singing, for it then flutters its wings and tramples its little patch of turf. It rivals the Nightingale in its attraction for poets, and yet, as with most of our sweetest songsters, its plumage is most unpretending.

The bill is dark brown above, pale yellow-brown at the base; the feathers on the top of the head are dark brown, edged with paler brown, and rather long so as to form a crest, which the bird can elevate at pleasure; the cheeks are pale brown. The whole of the upper part is varied with three shades of brown, and as the centre of every feather is dark, the bird has a spangled or spotted appearance; these spots become very minute on the head. The tail is brown except the outside feathers, which are white; the throat and upper part of the breast are pale brown, streaked with darker brown; the abdomen is pale yellowish-white; the legs are strong, and the feet especially formed for walking, the hind toe being long and straighter than with the perching birds. All these points are well depicted in our coloured plate. Though it is very difficult to distinguish the sexes, the female is slightly smaller than the male, and its plumage usually rather darker. Song or no song is the best guide as to sex, for we have had some of these small dark birds undoubted cocks and the finest songsters we ever possessed. In fallow lands, or meadows, in a slight indentation of the ground, the Skylark builds its nest; it is very simply constructed of dry bents of grass, and the eggs are from three to six in number. The young are easily reared, if properly attended to, on the food recommended for young Warblers, though they are inexorable in their demands to be fed early. This should be about four or five o'clock, and by no means later than six o'clock, when a few mouthfuls must be given, and so on at short intervals during the day. A little given often is far better than overcramming. Birds thus reared make good specimens for exhibition purposes, and, as a rule, are very tame; though some wild caught birds equal them in this respect. The Lark is strong and hardy, long lived, and will stand much cold weather. Unfortunately, fowlers sadly decimate them during the winter months, as they are considered a table dainty. Larks are very fond of dusting, and when caged should always be provided with plenty of road sand (such as may be found in gutters after a heavy shower), or sea or river sand, such a dust bath getting rid of parasites in the plumage. No perches are required, but a piece of turf should be placed in the circular front of the cage. An illustration of a suitable cage in which to exhibit these birds is given on this page. It should be 16 or 18 inches long, 9 inches high, and 8 inches deep, and in colour creamy white inside and rosewood outside. The living-cage should be similar, but not less than 2 feet long, 10 inches high, and 10 inches deep, and need not have the circular front, the turf being placed in a corner. The top of the cage may be made of wood or canvas stretched tightly over and tacked securely. Many prefer the latter method, so that if the bird is startled and jumps upwards, it does not injure its head; but wood is safer for the show cages. As regards diet, adult Larks do well on any good insectivorous food with a few live insects added, such as gentles, live ants' cocoons, wasp grubs when procurable, and a meal-worm or two as a variation. A little tender lettuce minced up fine, grated raw carrot, or even cucumber grated fine, can be mixed with the food occasionally, which should be made crumbly moist by adding a little water. A little canary seed or crushed hemp seed may also be given occasionally as a further tit-bit. The essential points of an exhibition bird are size, steadiness, perfect plumage, rich colour, and good marking above on the face, throat, and breast, as shown on our plate.

LARK SHOW CAGE.

The Woodlark. The Woodlark, *Alauda arborea* (*Linn.*), is a very local resident, nowhere abundant, but most frequent in the southern and western counties, breeding there and becoming rarer towards the north and restricted to a few places in Ireland. It is also partially migrant, and is found generally distributed throughout Europe and Persia, migrating southward in the winter. This species, as the name indicates, is more woodland in its habits than the Skylark, or, indeed, any British Lark. In its ways it resembles the Tree Pipit, and, while not an arboreal bird, clings to woodland country or places interspersed with old hedges and copses of brushwood. It loves to sit on some tree or bush, taking flights therefrom, singing the while, and ascending in spiral gyrations. Its notes are considered superior to those of the Skylark, and are certainly softer and more melodious, but of much shorter duration. It rarely sings so fluently in a cage, whereas captivity makes no difference to the Skylark. Both these birds also sing when on the ground, and both build their nests thereon, usually well concealed under a tuft of grass or herbage, the Woodlark sometimes below a small bush. The latter's bill is dark brown above, pale yellow-brown beneath; over the eye and ear-coverts runs a pale yellowish-brown streak; the feathers on the top of the head are of a light brown colour, streaked with dark brown, and are long, forming a crest, which can be elevated at pleasure; the whole of the upper part is rufous brown, streaked on the neck and patched on the back with dark brownish-black; the tail has a very light brown feather on either side, and two of pale brown in the middle, the rest being brownish-black, triangularly tipped with white; the whole of the under-part is pale yellowish-brown, speckled with elongated flecks of dark brown, smaller and more thinly scattered on the throat, and gathering in size and number on the breast, and none at all on the abdomen, which shades to white, faintly tinged with yellow. The Woodlark is smaller than the Skylark, and its tail and hind claws are shorter. The sexes are alike. It is a good bird for cage or aviary, and the cages recommended for keeping and exhibiting Pipits answer well. The diet should be as for the Skylark, except for the canary seed. Essential exhibition points are good colour, distinct markings, perfect plumage, well-matured body, and steadiness.

The Shorelark.

The Shorelark, *Otocorys alpestris* (*Newton*), is a winter migrant to our shores, and of much more regular occurrence than formerly. Its breeding quarters are Northern Europe and Asia, and it is also found in the northern parts of America. It is a very handsome bird, uncommonly marked. The general colour above is ashy, slightly tinged with vinous; the tail is black, except the centre feathers, which are edged with ash-brown; the outer edge of the outer feathers and the half of the next are white; the forehead is pale yellow bounded behind by a black band, terminating at each side with some narrow black feathers elongated, which can be raised at will; the lores, cheeks, and throat in the form of a crescent band are deep black; the chin, sides of neck, and a streak above each eye are sulphur yellow; beneath the black gular band the breast is hyacinth-red varied with blackish-brown, and the sides of the breast are the same colour; the flanks are vinous with darker centres to the feathers; the under-body shades to white at the abdomen. The female is yellower on the forehead, and the black band on the crown is not so pronounced. The song is somewhat eccentric but sweet, though comparatively short and uttered generally when on the wing at a slight elevation. The Shorelark is a somewhat difficult bird to steady, but patience is soon rewarded by its confidence. It is often exhibited, and the essential points for this purpose are maturity, rich colour, markings well defined, perfect plumage, and steadiness. The cages for keeping and exhibiting the Skylark and the same diet answer well.

FAMILY PICIDÆ.—This family includes in its sub-sections *Iynginæ* and *Picinæ*, and is represented in Great Britain by the Wryneck and three Woodpeckers.

The Wryneck.

The Wryneck, *Iynx torquilla* (*Dresser*), is a summer visitor to south-eastern England, is much rarer and more local in the north and west, and only twice recorded in Ireland. It arrives early in April, and, owing to the Cuckoo arriving at about the same time, it is widely known by the name of "Cuckoo's Mate." It leaves again in September to winter in Africa. It is very shy, and its soft musical call-note *pee-pee* first attracts attention. The Wryneck favours wooded districts, and though a true member of the family *Picidæ* by reason of the structure of its feet and its extensile tongue it is not adapted for climbing trees like the Woodpecker, the soft plumage of its tail not furnishing much support. At times, however, it will run up a tree smartly, but may more often be seen sitting on a branch like an ordinary Passerine bird. The name "Wryneck" is due to a peculiar snake-like movement of the head and neck, giving the neck a wry-like appearance. It deposits its eggs in existing holes in decayed trees, on the bare wood, and builds no nest.

The Wryneck is a beautiful example of the effect of blending a few simple colours. Grey and brown, with shades of yellowish-white, form practically the only tints; but these are charmingly distributed, the colours forming into stripes and bars of varying shades, ticked and mottled between with lighter and darker spots over the brown-grey ground colour; the dark stripes on the back and the irregular bars of light and dark across the tail feathers are very prominent, as are also the marks on the head and ear-coverts. The sexes are alike, and the bird is of medium size, about 6¼ inches long. Its food at liberty consists entirely of insects and their larvæ, ants and their cocoons being the favourite diet. These it takes by darting out its long tongue and touching its prey, which then adheres to the glutinous secretion with which the bird's tongue is abundantly supplied. In confinement it does well on the diet recommended for the smaller Warblers by just adding a little extra supply of ants' cocoons.

Whenever procurable, give ants also, first disabling them before placing them in the food vessel. The young, if taken at about ten days old, can be hand-reared on the same food as the smaller Warblers, or on live gentles, as explained by Mr. Cocks in his notes on rearing Grasshopper Warblers, gradually weaning them on to the adult food. They require a box pattern cage, 2 feet or $2\frac{1}{2}$ feet long, 16 inches high, and 10 inches deep, with the usual two perches arranged to rest on the middle cross-bar. For exhibition, specimens should be well matured with the colours rich, and markings well defined, and in good condition and steady. The Nightingale show-cage answers well, but the higher centre perch should be omitted ; the colour inside should be creamy-white, with the outside black.

The Great Spotted Woodpecker.

The Great Spotted Woodpecker, *Dendrocopus major* (*Newton*), is a not uncommon resident in thickly wooded districts, breeding probably throughout England, but more rarely in Wales and Scotland. In the North it appears to be partly migratory, our residents being reinforced by visitors during the autumn migration. This bird is also generally distributed in suitable localities throughout Europe, and parts of Asia, but, owing to its shy nature, it is very difficult to observe. It builds no nest, but lays its eggs on the dust in a hole of some decaying tree. A natural hole is made use of sometimes, but more often this is very cleverly excavated by the birds themselves, beautifully rounded and frequently 12 inches or 18 inches deep. The dominant colours in the plumage of this bird are black and white, the wings are spotted or barred with white ; the forehead yellowish-white ; the crown and nape blue-black, with a red patch on the back of the head, and on the under tail-coverts. The female is not possessed of the red patch upon the head. In its wild state it feeds principally upon spiders and caterpillars, or ants and their cocoons, which latter it digs out of the ant-hills ; failing these or other insects, it will feed upon soft-skinned fruits, nuts, and even acorns and berries. In captivity it does well on a diet of 2 parts good chicken meal, 1 part finely granulated meat-meal, and 1 part ants' cocoons, mixed together until crumbly moist with warm water. Make sufficient only for each day's consumption. Give also live ants' cocoons, meal-worms, gentles, beetles, or other insects, either separately or mixed with the food in moderation, as well as fruits and berries. If reared from the nest, the bird will become quite tame. Mr. J. Dewhurst, of West Kensington, London, has hand-reared young specimens from seven days old on Spratt's Lark food, 2 parts ; Brand's Meat-meal, 2 parts, ground up fine in a mill, and mixed with boiling water until crumbly moist. The young birds were fed on this every two hours from 7 A.M. to 8 P.M., being given as much each time as they would take from the smooth point of a thin piece of wood. In about nine days the youngsters could feed themselves, and the food was then changed to Spratt's Chicken Meal, 2 parts ; and Brand's Meat-meal, 1 part, mixed as before. This formed the staple diet, with occasionally fruit or a few sunflower seeds, or a bone, and on rare occasions a few meal-worms. " I kept one Great Spotted Woodpecker," says Mr. Dewhurst, " for eleven years

WOODPECKER'S SHOW CAGE.

in the best of condition on this diet." They make interesting pets, and are also very successful at exhibitions, for which full maturity, good colour, distinct markings, perfect plumage and steadiness are necessary essentials. A suitable show cage is illustrated on page 415; it is 18 inches long, 20 inches high, and 12 inches deep; no perch is required, but it will be observed that the back and sides of the cage are lined with Virginia cork firmly secured. This takes the place of perches, and the birds prefer to climb about on this. A similarly constructed but larger cage does for general use, but it should be not less than 2 feet long, 2 feet high, and 1 foot deep. Both show and living cages must be strongly made and wired, and the corners inside tinned over to prevent their occupant making a hole through with its powerful beak.

The Lesser Spotted Woodpecker.

The Lesser Spotted Woodpeeker, *Dendrocopus minor* (*Newton*), is resident south of Yorkshire, and whilst more numerous in many districts than the preceding species, is nowhere abundant. In Scotland it is very scarce and in Ireland even rarer. It is generally distributed throughout Europe, but less frequently in the south, and also inhabits Southern Asia. It differs somewhat from the Great Spotted Woodpecker in flight and call note, but breeds in the same situations, drilling holes like it in trees. Though considerably smaller, this species is rather similar in plumage to the larger, except that the whole of the top of the head of the male is crimson, and the female buffy-white. Its food is the same, and in captivity it should be treated similarly. It is even more successful at exhibitions than the Great Spotted, and should be shown in a similar show cage, 16 inches long, 14 inches high, and 12 inches deep. It can also be hand-reared on the same food. Mr. Sydney L. Cocks, of Peterborough, hand-reared three of these (taken when about three weeks old) on live gentles from the bright blue-green bodied fly, which is about half the size of the meat fly (bluebottle). These gentles were first well cleaned in pine sawdust, and one given every half hour, from 5 a.m. to 8.30 p.m., impaled on a bent sack needle, 7 inches long. This task lasted until they were ten weeks old, but Mr. Cocks remarks, "they were too old when taken, for, undoubtedly, with all British birds, eight to ten days old is the best age to take birds for hand-rearing." When able to feed themselves they were gradually weaned on to the usual insectivorous food with a supply of live gentles. This nest of young were taken from an ash tree at a height of 30 feet, and another from an oak at a height of 60 feet.

The Green Woodpecker.

The Green Woodpecker, *Gecinus viridis* (*Dresser*), is a fairly common resident in most well-wooded districts of England, south of Northumberland; breeding occasionally in the Border Counties, and a very rare accidental visitor to Scotland and Ireland. It occurs throughout Europe, but not beyond the Mediterranean. Its nesting habits are similar to those of the preceding species, but it is more gaudy in colour. In the adult male the space round the eyes, nasal plumes, and fore part of face are black, with a red lengthened patch over the lower part running along the sides of the chin on to the sides of throat; the top of the head is bright red, running down in a narrow point upon the nape; the general colour above is yellowish-olive tinted with green, shading on the rump to gamboge-yellow; the hinder sides of the face, throat, breast, and under-part are yellowish-grey; the primaries of the wings are greenish-black, marked on the outer webs with square spots of yellowish-white, and at the base of the inner webs with round spots of the same colour. The tail inclines to black tinted with pale green indistinctly bordered with a deeper shade. The female is similar to the male, save that it is without the red on the lower sides of the face, and is not so brilliant in colour. The screaming or laughing-like call of this bird has long earned for it the name of "Yaffle." It has the habit characteristic of its species of clinging to a tree in search of insects, which its long bill and peculiar tongue are particularly adapted to extract from the crevices of the bark. The tail is short, strong, and pointed, being used as a support in climbing. The same kinds of cages and diet as recommended for the other Woodpeckers answer well, but in exhibiting the larger show cage should be used. Essential points for show are rich colour, the shades distinct, bright and lustrous, combined with good size, perfect plumage, and steadiness.

The Dipper, Hoopoe, Kingfisher, and Nightjar, the various Doves, Raven and other Crows, Hawks, Owls, Plovers, and many other birds, are amenable to captivity under certain conditions, and where space is not at a premium, many of these make delightful pets. The scope of this work does not, however, permit of our dealing with them here, and for the same reason we have had reluctantly to omit many interesting birds which occasionally visit these islands. We are deeply indebted and grateful to those who have so willingly given their experiences with various birds, and thus helped us in our endeavour to make our text instructive and interesting to the experienced and inexperienced alike.

HAWFINCH CORN BUNTING LESSER SPOTTED WOODPECKER YELLOW BUNTING

Propagating Meal-worms.

As meal-worms are always in great demand where insectivorous or partially insectivorous birds are kept, the following method of propagating meal-worms may be carried out with great advantage. Fill a half-gallon jar with wheat bran, barley, or oatmeal, and a few pieces of sugar-paper or old shoe-leather. In this half a pint of meal-worms may be placed, and if allowed to remain for three months, occasionally placing the rough canvas cover from two or three beer-barrel bungs in with them, or failing this a piece of canvas moistened with beer, they will become beetles, which again lay eggs and propagate their species with great rapidity. Another method of securing a supply of meal-worms is to stock a cheese barrel or other box with about two quarts of meal-worms, and add the wheat, bran, etc., as previously directed, making sure that the case is secure so that the worms cannot get out.

CHAPTER XLI

THE DISEASES OF CAGE BIRDS

THE ailments to which cage birds are subject are happily few, provided proper attention is given to them. The most common causes of disease are (1) exposure to draughts, (2) lack of fresh air, either from badly ventilated rooms, or from being placed high up above the gas or lamps of sitting-rooms, (3) an abuse of dainties in feeding, and (4) sour or unwholesome food or bad water.

In case of illness, first and foremost, find out how the ailing bird has been fed, whether green food was given, and whether this was fresh or stale. Then see what state the bird's bowels are in—whether loose or constipated; and next turn your attention to the bird itself, and before you attempt to handle it, observe the position in which it sits or perches—that alone often gives a clue to internal troubles. Listen to any chest-sounds it may emit, such as coughing, panting, or wheezing. You may next handle the bird, for the purpose of examining the vent and abdomen. A small bird ought to be handled as gently as possible. Do not, if possible, alarm it, or cause it to flutter all round the cage; approach the hand gently, then seize it with one quick pounce, and hold it with the necessary degree of firmness, but not so as to injure it.

The medicines administered ought to be of the best quality procurable. There are two kinds of castor oil, for example; and while the better is one of the safest and most effectual aperients we possess, though it has been accredited with killing many birds, the coarser kind may set up irritation of the bowels, which it will be difficult to subdue.

We recommend that ordinary catarrh, colds and coughs should be treated as if they really were—as they often are—symptomatic of the first stage of other internal troubles, the result generally of exposure to cold, draughts, or excessive damp. Improper feeding will likewise produce them as well as overfeeding. They are also sometimes associated with a deranged state of the bowels or indigestion.

Diseases of the Respiratory Organs.

Birds so affected should be kept free from draughts and damp, the food should be nutritious, and easy of digestion. The seed vessel should always contain a supply of good, sound, sweet canary seed, for the bird to go to when it feels so disposed; and if a British bird a supply of its natural wild food should be given, or the best substitute other than that it has been having. A piece of bread soaked in scalded milk, and given when cold, is a capital remedy, but it should be frequently changed. Hemp-seed ought to be avoided, it is too stimulating. After three days with the bread-and-milk, a very small quantity of egg food made fresh each day, with 2 drops of glycerine and 1 drop of paregoric mixed in it, may be substituted for the next three days, and a due allowance of fresh green food given each day. Our aim is to improve the general health of the bird, and its bowels should be regulated by the occasional addition to the water of a little carbonate of magnesia, and from 10 to 15 drops of tincture of conium. At the commencement of the attack give 10 drops of the etheral tincture of lobelia to a wineglassful of water, changing the water and adding the drugs fresh daily. The addition too of a little glycerine can do nothing but good. Tonics should be given after the attack has abated; iron in some form we specially recommend, and to it may be added a few drops of the compound tincture of gentian, 5 drops to a wineglass of water. This treatment is sure to do good;

fresh cases it is pretty certain to cure, and chronic ones to ameliorate.

Loss of Voice.

Loss of voice is a common complaint, especially with Canaries, and in our opinion nine-tenths of the cases are caused by exposure to currents of cold air. If birds are allowed to moult in a draughty place, even if nothing worse happens, their song is affected, and attacks are not confined to the moulting season. Such cases, however, are not difficult to treat; at first give a drop or two of castor oil direct into the beak, and fill the drinker with a mixture composed of 10 drops of glycerine in a wineglassful of water, with a bit of gum-arabic the size of a large pea, and 5 drops of paregoric. A little piece of fat raw bacon with the rind adhering to it, fixed between the wires of the cage for the bird to peck at, is also most beneficial. Let the diet be a little more generous, but not overdone with dainties. There is nothing else required, unless it be a small spray of fresh watercress or a little seeding chickweed.

Diseases of the Digestive Organs.

Diarrhœa or looseness is usually brought about by errors in diet, which cause irritation of the digestive canal. Green food if given in too large quantities, too wet, or stale, will produce diarrhœa. Stale or unwholesome water is another frequent cause, and so are stale egg, and bread-and-milk that has turned sour. Exposure to cold, by sending the blood to the internal organs, is one more source of diarrhœa; while, again, the disease is often induced from an overflow of bile, which is a laxative naturally.

The stools are generally watery, and contain shreds of half-digested food. If there is much irritation of the alimentary canal, the fæces will have an unpleasant, sour odour. This disorder is very weakening, and cannot prevail long without causing emaciation, and probably death. When a bird is attacked by diarrhœa, if the cage has not been washed for some time it is advisable to put the bird at once into a clean dry cage, and hang in a well-ventilated room, where it may obtain warmth without being deprived of fresh, wholesome air. Its food ought to be changed; if a Canary, plain canary seed should be given; if a Britisher, a supply of its natural wild food if possible, or the nearest substitute other than it has been having; luncheon or arrowroot biscuits soaked in new milk should be given fresh daily for a day or two, and the purity of the birds' drinking water seen to.

As diarrhœa is so often caused by the lurking in the system of some offending matter, which the looseness is merely an effort of nature to expel, a couple of drops of pure warm castor oil should begin the treatment. When the oil has had time to operate, we must try by healing remedies gently to check the diarrhœa. To this end a teaspoonful of lime water should be added to the wineglassful of drinking water. Should this fail to check the purging after a reasonable time, say forty-eight hours, about 15 drops of elixir of vitriol and 5 drops of tincture of opium may be added to the water instead. If the stools are very watery and offensive, and an inflammatory or congested state of the mucous membrane suspected, ipecacuanha and opium in conjunction will do good—say of the tincture of laudanum 5 drops, of the wine of ipecacuanha 15 drops, with 3 or 4 grains of nitrate of potash, to a wineglassful of drinking-water. Extra care will be required after the bird is cured of diarrhœa. Plain canary seed, and a little maw seed daily, a very small portion of egg food every other day and half a teaspoonful of split groats on alternate days will be the most suitable diet for a while, and a bitter tonic should be given for about a week. (Gentian is extolled by some; it is an excellent bird tonic, but it should be remembered that it has a tendency to relax the bowels, and should therefore be avoided in treating *this* complaint.) We find cascarilla bark do well. The infusion is made by steeping half an ounce of it in 5 ounces of boiling water for an hour, and afterwards straining. The dose is a teaspoonful to the drinking-water. Other tonics which we have used are the dilute nitro-hydrochloric acid, 10 drops to the bitter water, and Schacht's liquor of bismuth; and we should not forget calumba infusion. It is made like the infusion of cascarilla, only with cold water instead of boiling. It is a capital tonic.

Constipation.

This is an ailment from which cage birds sometimes suffer, resulting in loss of appetite and general dullness of the bird. It is usually caused by some error in the diet, and although in bad cases a little oil should be given to effect relief, permanent cure of the complaint should be effected through the medium of the food. Watercress and other green foods may be given in the summer-time; and the tender leaves of young dandelion to the Canaries, and a liberal supply of the various wild seeds in their green succulent state to the seed-eating British, while a spider or two is excellent for insectivorous birds. In winter give a slice of ripe apple or a slice or two of well-boiled carrot. The water ought to be sweetened with glycerine which is an excellent tonic and laxative; and a teaspoonful of the infusion of gentian also added.

Termed by the medical practitioner enteritis, inflammation of the bowels is one of the most serious ailments to which birds are subject.

The causes most likely to produce it are over-eating, especially of too stimulating food, or partaking of green food which is in a state of decomposition. Again, if the water for drinking, which ought to be *fresh every morning*, is left for days, or if it has not been very fresh when placed in the drinking-glass, and afterwards receives the addition of particles of green food, etc., it becomes next thing to an irritant poison, and is very likely to cause inflammation. A chill will also produce the disease. The symptoms are those of much suffering and acute pain in the regions affected. The bird is dull and drooping, cares little to move about, has no note, and often lies on the belly on his perch ; there is loss of appetite and urgent thirst, the bowels are usually very costive ; but at times this may be the reverse, and diarrhœa, with frequent straining at stool is present. An additional occasional symptom is frequent vomiting of the offensive products of inflammation, or of bile and mucus. Manual examination, which must be conducted very gently, will reveal a swollen and distended condition of the lower part of the abdomen, with some change of colour, varying, according to the stage of the disorder, from pale to dark red, amounting in very dangerous cases to an almost black hue.

Inflammation of the Bowels.

If taken at once, inflammation of the bowels may be cured, but the treatment must be decided. As we advised in diarrhœa, let the bird be put in a clean dry cage and hung in a warm, well-ventilated room, and the food changed. The latter must be entirely non-stimulating, but at the same time nourishing; bread soaked in scalding new milk to which may be added a little moist sugar should be the sole food for a day or two. The bread should be placed in the milk in a solid piece, and lifted out when cold. The bowels—if constipation be present, and if the case has been seen at the commencement—should be opened with two drops of best castor oil ; but if much inflammation has taken place, purgatives should not be employed. The bread-and-milk has slight laxative properties. Counter-irritation will do much good, and it cannot be applied by a better plan than that of painting the lower part of the abdomen, by means of a camel's-hair pencil, with warm turpentine ; the pencil must be merely damped, and the bird's skin barely touched. The process makes the part tingle for a moment, but it soon passes off, and gives relief.

Opium is of great service in the treatment of this complaint. Place therefore every morning, in a wineglassful of fresh water, 20 drops of ipecacuanha wine, and 5 of laudanum, along with a bit of gum-arabic, and 2 or 3 grains of nitrate of potash. Continue the milk diet, and a little plain canary seed ; a quarter of a teaspoonful of maw seed will also be beneficial.

If the bird exhibits a tendency to sink or collapse, there will be little chance of saving him, but a little brandy may be added to the other mixture as a last resource. If it gets better, tonics are required, and one small dose of castor oil (2 drops) ; this latter often acts like a charm, after the inflammation has been subdued. The best tonic is the infusion of calumba, a teaspoonful to the water, with a few drops of tincture of iron. Give at the same time a little egg with the food, and before the ordinary diet is resumed scald a little German rape for a time or two.

We have reason to believe that many more birds die of inflammation of the liver (hepatitis) than people are aware of. It is a very dangerous illness, and often proves speedily fatal. Prevention is far more easy than its cure when established. It is caused by keeping the bird in too hot a room or position, by giving him too little fresh air, and feeding on too nutritious and stimulating a diet, such as hemp-seed, dainties, etc. The symptoms of the chronic form are somewhat obscure, but after death dissection reveals an abnormally large liver. In the acute form of the disease there are the usual signs of inflammation. The bird is in evident distress and pain, nervous, thirsty, hot, and restless ; while there is the absence of cough on the one hand that would indicate lung mischief, and the absence on the other of the dark redness always present more or less in inflammation of the bowels. This, with a knowledge of previous feeding and treatment, and a complete history of the case, makes diagnosis comparatively easy.

Inflammation of the Liver.

We believe in supporting the little patient from the beginning, giving aperients to relieve the circulation through the liver, and opium to remove the pain and restlessness. Half a teaspoonful of fluid magnesia may be placed in the water, but we recommend a dose of 2 drops of castor oil to commence with. When the bowels have been well acted on put in the water daily 5 drops of tincture of opium, and half a teaspoonful of dandelion juice. When the pain has subsided, the laudanum may be omitted, and the juice continued for some little time. The diet during the illness should be light and nourishing, such as the bread and milk prepared as previously explained, with plain canary seed only in the hopper. Towards convalescence a little egg food occasionally, on other days a little sponge cake slightly moistened with a few drops of good sherry, may be given.

Tonics—gentian and iron—5 of the former and 10 of the latter, or a small half teaspoonful of quinine wine in the drinking water, will probably be needed to complete the cure. In chronic cases the plainest food only should be allowed, the bath not being omitted; a small quantity of dandelion juice in the water, and about twice a week a senna-leaf or two as well, and a little glycerine.

MISCELLANEOUS AILMENTS, AND ACCIDENTS

These are of several kinds, and depend upon different causes. Birds that are either constitutionally weak or weakened by injudicious treatment are most subject to them. Gluttony and the use of over-stimulating food predisposes to fits; so, by weakening the heart, does injudicious pairing, as by keeping a male bird with too many hens during the breeding season. As the treatment we adopt is nearly the same in all cases, we need do no more here than give the symptoms of two kinds. The first is syncope, or fainting, during which the heart's action is all but suspended. It is nearly always caused by fright, as by attempting to catch the bird, or letting anything strike the cage, or bringing the cage and bird suddenly from a dark position to a very bright one. The cage should be placed in a dull cool place, and the bird's head gently sprayed with a little cold water from the mouth. Should a bird faint when in the hand, immediately lay it down on the floor in a shaded place, and it will soon revive. On no account retain it in the hand.

Fits.

Another kind of fit is apoplectic in its nature. and, in addition to the usual causes, is often brought on by the thoughtless habit of hanging the cage in a hot, blistering sun. This is more dangerous and deadly, and probably a drop or two of brandy will be needed, as well as the application of cold water, to revive the bird. But whatever the nature of the fit, the bird will require the most carefully regulated diet and the plainest of food, with now and then a drop or two of castor oil. For the fainting-fit, give bark and iron tonic; for the apoplectic, bark alone, adding sufficient to make the water taste fairly strong.

Surfeit.

Surfeit is a name given to a kind of exanthematous disorder. There is irritation of the skin, with a slight eruption, and the bird gets gradually bald. The cause, so far as we yet can tell, is an error in the feeding; and a return to the natural diet, with some opening medicine (Epsom salts is best—a few grains in the water), a small but regular supply of green food (a little lemon juice and 3 or 4 grains of chlorate of potash should also be placed in the drinking-water), and will not fail to remove it. The head should be anointed with the purest, simplest ointment to be obtained, just sufficient to moisten the skin. The process should be repeated every third day for three times.

Cramp.

Cramp is a common complaint among birds, especially among such as are kept in a filthy state, and in small "poky" cages. It may proceed, too, from indigestion; but, from whatever cause it arises, it should be looked upon as merely symptomatic. The bird should be given 3 drops of castor oil, and 5 drops of laudanum in the drinking water for a day or two. If the limbs are attacked, it may be removed by immersing them in warm water, and afterwards hanging the cage in a comfortable place quite away from all draughts; if the cage is a small one, replace it with one that is more roomy, with good perches.

Claws.

The claws of Canaries often require attention, and at times even the beak gets elongated, and causes discomfort in feeding. The remedy is to shorten the claws or beak with a pair of sharp nail scissors; but it should be done carefully, and too much should not be taken off, to avoid cutting into the quick.

Sore Feet.

The treatment for sore feet is to clean the feet, and get rid of all sources of irritation, such as dirty cages, perches that are too small or made of hard wood. After being carefully soaked in lukewarm water the feet should be washed and gently dried, and afterwards anointed with a touch of boracic ointment. The bird should then be placed in a well cleaned cage, and seen to every day until the feet are well. This is a very painful and distressing complaint.

Fractured Limb.

In a case of a fractured limb all perches should be taken out of the cage, and the bottom filled with soft meadow hay. A very tiny thin splint should then be laid against the fractured parts, and gently bound to the limb. Care must be taken not to stop the circulation by binding too tightly Food and water should be placed so that the bird can easily get at them. Nature will do the rest.

Accidents to the Joints.

Accidents sometimes occur to the joints, and are followed by painful inflammation which must be subdued by frequently bathing the parts in hot water, and afterwards applying a little tincture of opium. At the same time a little Epsom salts put in the drinking water will help to reduce the swelling.

Wounds are the result of accident, and are most common about the feet. The bird must be caught, and the feet carefully washed in warm water; the wound should then be touched with some astringent to favour healing. The sore or wound must be seen to twice a day, until it is perfectly healed. A weak solution of sulphate of zinc is a good astringent—say about 5 grains to the ounce of water, care being taken that the bird does not get any of this in its bill—or the wound may be touched with wetted alum, or Friar's balsam, or with tincture of myrrh. But whichever is used, perfect cleanliness must be maintained both as regards the bird and the cage.

Wounds.

Wounds in other parts of the body are best treated on somewhat similar principles, but for these we recommend for antiseptic purposes a wash of carbolic acid lotion and water. A couple of teaspoonfuls of the strong lotion which chemists make should be thrown into a cupful of cold spring water, and the surface of the wound washed daily therewith. If the wound looks unhealthy, stimulation is necessary, and for this purpose the sulphate of zinc lotion already recommended will do, or the sulpho-carbolate of zinc may be used, in the proportion of 3 grains to the ounce of water.

Ulceration may be checked by a weak solution of chloride of zinc, or by this lotion: 2 ounces of water, 20 drops of the dilute nitric acid, and 10 grains of extract of opium; this relieves the pain while it cools the surface.

While birds are suffering from wounds or any suppurating sore, they should be liberally fed and kept warm, but at the same time have plenty of pure fresh air.

Pest.

Pest is a term applied, in lieu of a better, to a kind of fever, or plague almost, that sometimes breaks out in bird rooms where a large number of Canaries are crowded together. Death often takes place very rapidly in such cases, and the feathered ranks are thinned by the dozen. Its cause we attribute to the neglect of sanitation and the common laws of hygiene, the lack of pure air and cleanliness, the use of poor quality cheap food-stuffs, or the importing of unhealthy birds or old contaminated cages into the bird room.

When such an outbreak takes place, no time should be lost; the cages should be at once thoroughly cleaned and disinfected, and the birds removed into another room where they can get fresh air and a moderate amount of sunshine. Some mild aperient should be given, and a teaspoonful of good brandy placed in the drinking water, with a few drops of paregoric. The food should be light and nutritious, but no hemp or rape should be given. A bowl or two of sawdust soddened with carbolic should be placed in the room and replenished when the strength has gone off. Afterwards every cage should be thoroughly prepared with the same care as a breeding cage, and the bird room itself completely cleaned and disinfected.

In all our dealings with cage birds we should be as gentle as possible, and in their more severe illnesses regularity in giving the medicines, and sticking unflinchingly to the plan of treatment that seems necessary, will generally pull the worst cases through.

Everyone who has a bird room should possess a small box or cabinet, containing the following drugs:—Castor oil, gum arabic, glycerine, fluid magnesia, cod-liver oil, vegetable charcoal, nitrate of potash, gentian root, cascarilla and calumba barks, dandelion juice, Epsom salts, vinum ipecacuanhæ, elixir of vitriol, Hoffman's anodyne; and the following tinctures—Tinctura ferri, tinctura camph. co. (paregoric), tinct. catechu, tinct. opii (laudanum), tinct. conii, tinct. gentianæ, and tinct. lobeliæ. A pestle and mortar, a minim measure, and small camel's hair brush will also be found useful.

THE END

INDEX

Printed in Great Britain
by Amazon